Hyperconverged Infrastructure Data Centers

Demystifying HCI

m Halabi

T0342186

Cisco Press

Hyperconverged Infrastructure Data Centers

Sam Halabi

Copyright© 2019 Bassam Halabi

Published by:
Cisco Press

01   18

Library of Congress Control Number: 2018959195

ISBN-13: 978-1-58714-510-0
ISBN-10: 1-58714-510-3

Warning and Disclaimer

This book is designed to provide information about hyperconverged infrastructure data centers. Every effort has been made to make this book as complete and as accurate as possible, but no warranty or fitness is implied.

The information is provided on an "as is" basis. The author, Cisco Press, and Cisco Systems, Inc. shall have neither liability nor responsibility to any person or entity with respect to any loss or damages arising from the information contained in this book or from the use of the discs or programs that may accompany it.

The opinions expressed in this book belong to the author and are not necessarily those of Cisco Systems, Inc.

Trademark Acknowledgments

All terms mentioned in this book that are known to be trademarks or service marks have been appropriately capitalized. Cisco Press or Cisco Systems, Inc., cannot attest to the accuracy of this information. Use of a term in this book should not be regarded as affecting the validity of any trademark or service mark.

Special Sales

For information about buying this title in bulk quantities, or for special sales opportunities (which may include electronic versions; custom cover designs; and content particular to your business, training goals, marketing focus, or branding interests), please contact our corporate sales department at corpsales@pearsoned.com or (800) 382-3419.

For government sales inquiries, please contact governmentsales@pearsoned.com.

For questions about sales outside the U.S., please contact intlcs@pearson.com.

Feedback Information

At Cisco Press, our goal is to create in-depth technical books of the highest quality and value. Each book is crafted with care and precision, undergoing rigorous development that involves the unique expertise of members from the professional technical community.

Readers' feedback is a natural continuation of this process. If you have any comments regarding how we could improve the quality of this book, or otherwise alter it to better suit your needs, you can contact us through email at feedback@ciscopress.com. Please make sure to include the book title and ISBN in your message.

We greatly appreciate your assistance.

Editor-in-Chief: Mark Taub

Alliances Manager, Cisco Press: Arezou Gol

Product Line Manager: Brett Bartow

Managing Editor: Sandra Schroeder

Development Editor: Marianne Bartow

Senior Project Editor: Lori Lyons

Copy Editor: Gill Editorial Services

Technical Editors: Mallik Mahalingam, Aaron Kapacinskas

Editorial Assistant: Cindy J. Teeters

Cover Designer: Chuti Prasertsith

Composition: codemantra

Indexer: Erika Millen

Proofreader: Lori Eby

Reader Services

Register your copy at www.ciscopress.com/title/9781587145100 for convenient access to downloads, updates, and corrections as they become available. To start the registration process, go to www.ciscopress.com/register and log in or create an account* Enter the product ISBN 9781587145100 and click Submit. When the process is complete, you will find any available bonus content under Registered Products.

*Be sure to check the box that you would like to hear from us to receive exclusive discounts on future editions of this product.

Americas Headquarters
Cisco Systems, Inc.
San Jose, CA

Asia Pacific Headquarters
Cisco Systems (USA) Pte. Ltd.
Singapore

Europe Headquarters
Cisco Systems International BV Amsterdam,
The Netherlands

Cisco has more than 200 offices worldwide. Addresses, phone numbers, and fax numbers are listed on the Cisco Website at **www.cisco.com/go/offices**.

About the Author

Sam Halabi is a well-known industry figure with many years of experience in the field of information technology, multicloud, hyperconvergence, enterprise software, and data networking. Sam is a trusted advisor, capable of establishing close relationships with customers at the executive level, linking complex technologies with business benefits. Sam has worked at major companies in the United States and international markets, where he led sales, presales, consulting, marketing, and business development efforts targeting enterprises building scalable data centers. Sam is the founder of VirtuService (www.virtuservice.com), a provider of customer service, and IT consulting in private, hybrid, public cloud, and multicloud.

Sam has authored many Cisco Press books, including the bestsellers *Internet Routing Architectures* and *Metro Ethernet*.

Follow Sam Halabi on Twitter @VirtuService.

About the Technical Reviewers

Aaron Kapacinskas attended the University of California at San Diego for his undergraduate education in Mechanical Engineering. He subsequently attended Stanford University where he obtained his master's degree.

He is currently a Senior Technical Marketing Engineer at Cisco Systems, Inc., focusing on hyperconverged infrastructure as it relates to stretched deployments in synchronous replication, as well as security-related items for complex HCI deployments. He has written the *Cisco HyperFlex Hardening Guide* along with numerous white papers covering topics from encryption, native replication, and metro-level DR deployments, and is currently under patent review related to Cisco's HX replication technology.

Mallik Mahalingam is a Distinguished Engineer and CTO of HyperFlex product at Cisco, where he leads the technological and production direction for HyperFlex product-line.

Prior to Cisco, Mallik co-founded Springpath Inc., in 2012. Springpath built the software that was branded as Cisco HyperFlex, and he ran the company as its CEO and CTO until its acquisition by Cisco in 2017.

Prior to founding Springpath, Mallik led the core vSphere networking team at VMware, and built several features including VXLAN. As an early member of the VMware R&D team, which he joined in 2002, he built several networking and storage products during his decade of stay at VMware.

Mallik has developed several server technologies and products for enterprise markets over his 28 years of industry experience. He holds close to 80 US Patents and six published papers in leading academic conferences and journals.

Dedication

I would like to dedicate this book to my wonderful family, who continues to endure the agonizing process of book writing.

To my beautiful wife Roula: Thank you for your support and constant encouragement and for taking on double chores so I could finish this book.

To my wonderful sons, Joe and Jason: I am very proud of your academic accomplishments in the field of computer engineering, and I thank you for keeping me plugged into the latest technologies.

Last but not least, to my loving mother Josephine: Thank you for your persistence in asking me every day whether the book was done—that by itself was a huge incentive to finish writing it.

Acknowledgments

Special thanks to Mallik Mahalingam, CTO of the HyperFlex product and formerly cofounder and CEO of Springpath. Mallik's deep knowledge of hyperconvergence was insightful, especially in the architecture of software-defined storage and distributed file systems. I would like to thank Aaron Kapacinskas from the Cisco HyperFlex Product Management team for taking the time to thoroughly review the book and keep me up to speed on the latest in the HyperFlex development. Many thanks to Michel Khouderchah from the Cisco security business group for his input on hyperconvergence and for encouraging me to write the book. Also, special thanks to my brother Mitri Halabi for his support in the areas of data networking, hyperconvergence, and multicloud; your deep knowledge and guidance were very instrumental. Much research for this book was done by sifting through heaps of design guides, specifications, and videos, so many thanks go to all of the technology professionals out there. I do reference their work where appropriate.

This book couldn't have been possible without the support of many people on the Cisco Press team. Brett Bartow, product-line manager Pearson IT Professional Group, was instrumental in sponsoring the book and driving it to execution. Sandra Schroeder, managing editor and design manager, was masterful with book graphics. Marianne Bartow, development editor, did a wonderful job in the technical review cycle; it was a pleasure working with you. Lori Lyons, senior project editor, thank you for leading the book to success through the production cycle. Finally, many thanks to the numerous Cisco Press unknown soldiers working behind the scenes to make this book happen.

Contents at a Glance

Introduction   xxiv

PART I   Basics of Data Center Networking and Storage   1

Chapter 1   Data Networks: Existing Designs   3

Chapter 2   Storage Networks: Existing Designs   19

PART II   Evolution in Host Hardware and Software   63

Chapter 3   Host Hardware Evolution   65

Chapter 4   Server Virtualization   77

Chapter 5   Software-Defined Storage   95

PART III   Hyperconverged Infrastructure   105

Chapter 6   Converged Infrastructure   107

Chapter 7   HCI Functionality   117

Chapter 8   HCI Business Benefits and Use Cases   135

PART IV   Cisco HyperFlex   151

Chapter 9   Cisco HyperFlex   153

Chapter 10   Deploying, Provisioning, and Managing HyperFlex   197

Chapter 11   HyperFlex Workload Optimization and Efficiency   211

PART V   Alternative HCI Implementations   221

Chapter 12   VMware vSAN   223

Chapter 13   Nutanix Enterprise Cloud Platform   255

Chapter 14   Open Source—Compute and Storage   289

PART VI   Hyperconverged Networking   305

Chapter 15   Software-Defined Networking and Open Source   307

Chapter 16   VMware NSX   335

Chapter 17   Application-Centric Infrastructure   351

PART VII   Public, Private, Hybrid, and Multicloud   393

Chapter 18   The Public Cloud   395

Chapter 19   The Private Cloud   423

Chapter 20   Hybrid Cloud and Multicloud   439

Glossary   451

Index   475

Contents

Introduction   xxiv

PART I   Basics of Data Center Networking and Storage   1

Chapter 1   Data Networks: Existing Designs   3

Information Technology Equipment of a Data Center   4

Network Equipment   4

Networking Services   4

Traffic Redirection and Optimization   5

Security   5

Multitier Data Networking Architecture   6

Logical Server Grouping   8

Challenges of Existing Designs   9

Oversubscription Between the Tiers   9

Large Flat L2 Networks with Stretched VLANs   10

Traffic Hopping Between Tiers, Inducing Latency   11

Inter-VLAN Routing via SVI   12

Complexity of Mechanisms Used for IPv4 Address Scarcity   12

Private VLANs   13

Flooding of Broadcast, Unknown Unicast, and Multicast (BUM) Traffic   15

Loop Prevention Via Spanning Tree   16

Firewall Overload   17

Looking Ahead   18

Chapter 2   Storage Networks: Existing Designs   19

The Storage View of Multitier Designs   20

Types of Disk Drives   21

Hard Disk Drives   22

SATA Drives   22

SAS Drives   23

SAS Self-Encrypting Drives   23

FC Drives   23

Solid-State Drives   23

Disk Performance   23

Throughput or Transfer Speed   24

Access Time   24

Latency and IOPS   24

RAID　26

    RAID 0　26

    RAID 1　26

    RAID 1+0　26

    RAID 0+1　27

    RAID 5　28

    RAID 6　29

Storage Controllers　30

Logical Unit Numbers　31

Logical Volume Manager　33

Block-, File-, and Object-Level Storage　35

    Block-Level Storage　35

    File-Level Storage　35

    Object-Based Storage　36

Storage-to-Server Connectivity　37

    Direct-Attached Storage (DAS)　38

    Network-Attached Storage　39

    Storage Area Networks　40

    Fibre Channel SANs　41

    Fibre Channel Addressing　42

    Fibre Channel Zoning　43

    LUN Masking　43

    Fibre Channel Switching　44

    Multipathing　44

    iSCSI SANs　46

    iSCSI Addressing　47

    iSCSI Network Segmentation　48

    iSCSI LUN Masking　48

    iSCSI Multipathing　48

    Fibre Channel over Ethernet SANs　49

Storage Efficiency Technologies　50

    Thin Provisioning　50

    Snapshots　51

    Traditional or Physical Snapshots　52

    Copy on Write Versus Redirect on Write Logical Snapshots　52

    Cloning　55

Replication   55

Deduplication   55

File-Level or Object-Level Deduplication   56

Deduplication at the Block Level   56

Target- Versus Source-Based Deduplication   57

Inline- Versus Post-Process Deduplication   58

Local Versus Global Deduplication   58

Data Compression   58

Disk Encryption   59

Storage Tiering   59

Caching Storage Arrays   60

Looking Ahead   61

PART II   **Evolution in Host Hardware and Software   63**

Chapter 3   **Host Hardware Evolution   65**

Advancements in Compute   65

x86 Standard Architecture   66

Single-, Multi-, and Many-Cores CPUs   66

Physical Cores Versus Virtual Cores Versus Logical Cores   67

Virtual CPU   68

Evolution in Host Bus Interconnect   70

Non-Volatile Memory Express   71

Emergence of Flash-Based Products   72

Enhancement in Flash Technology   73

New Breed of Storage Arrays Falls Short   73

All-Flash Arrays   73

Hybrid Arrays   74

Host-Based Caching   75

Looking Ahead   75

Chapter 4   **Server Virtualization   77**

The Virtualization Layer   78

Type 1 Hypervisor   79

Type 2 Hypervisor   80

Docker Containers   80

Datastores   82

Virtual Machine Creation   84

LUN Configuration   84

Datastore Configuration   84

New VM Creation   84

Guest OS Assignment   85

vCPU Assignment   85

Memory Allocation   85

Adding the Network Interface Card and SCSI Controller   85

Assigning a Virtual Disk   85

Power On and OS Installation   86

Virtualization Services   86

Clusters of Servers or Nodes   86

VM Migration   87

High Availability   88

Fault Tolerance   89

Compute Load Balancing   89

Storage Migration   90

Storage Load Balancing   90

Provisioning and Management   90

Virtual Switching   90

Looking Ahead   93

References   93

Chapter 5   Software-Defined Storage   95

SDS Objectives   96

Preserving the Legacy and Offering New Features   97

vSphere APIs for Storage Awareness (VASA) and VVols   99

Creating More Granular Volumes with VVols   100

Learning Storage Array Capabilities Through VASA   102

Integration with Storage Policy–Based Management   103

Looking Ahead   104

PART III   Hyperconverged Infrastructure   105

Chapter 6   Converged Infrastructure   107

Cisco UCS—The First Step in Convergence   108

The Converged Systems   112

Pros of Converged Systems   114

       Converged Systems Cons   114

   Looking Ahead   116

Chapter 7   **HCI Functionality   117**

   Distributed DAS Architecture   118

       Distributed Controllers   119

       Scale-Out Architecture   120

       HCI Performance   120

       Resiliency Against Hardware Failures via Replication   121

       File Systems   122

       Change in the Provisioning Model   124

       Hardware Acceleration   125

       Networking Integration   125

       Networking Policies   126

       Networking Automation   126

   Advanced Data Storage Functionality   127

       Deduplication and Compression   128

       Erasure Coding   128

       Replication and Backup for Disaster Recovery   129

       HCI Security   130

       HCI Provisioning, Management, and Monitoring   131

   Looking Ahead   133

Chapter 8   **HCI Business Benefits and Use Cases   135**

   HCI Business Benefits   136

       Fast Deployment   136

       Easier-to-Scale Infrastructure   136

       Enhanced IT Operational Model   137

       Easier System Management   138

       Public Cloud Agility in a Private Cloud   138

       Higher Availability at Lower Costs   139

       Low-Entry Cost Structure   139

       Reduced Total Cost of Ownership   140

   HCI Use Cases   140

       Server Virtualization   140

       DevOps   141

       Virtual Desktop Infrastructure   141

       Problems of VDI with Legacy Storage   143

How HCI Helps VDI   144

Remote Office Business Office (ROBO)   144

Edge Computing   146

Tier-1 Enterprise Class Applications   146

Data Protection and Disaster Recovery   148

Looking Ahead   149

PART IV   **Cisco HyperFlex   151**

Chapter 9   **Cisco HyperFlex   153**

HyperFlex Physical Components   154

Cisco HyperFlex Hybrid Nodes   156

Cisco HyperFlex All-Flash Nodes   156

Cisco HyperFlex Edge Nodes   157

Cisco HyperFlex Compute-Only Nodes   157

Cisco USC Fabric Interconnect   157

Cisco UCS 6200 and 6300 Fabric Interconnect   158

Cisco UCS 6248UP 48-Port FI   158

Cisco UCS 6296UP 96-Port FI   158

Cisco UCS 6332 32-Port FI   158

Cisco UCS 6332-16UP 40-Port FI   158

Cisco C220/C240 M4/M5 Rack Servers   158

Cisco VIC MLOM Interface Card   159

Cisco UCS 5108 Blade Chassis   159

Cisco UCS B200 Blade Server   159

Cisco UCS XP Fabric Extender   159

HyperFlex Performance Benchmarks   160

Integration with UCS   162

Logical Network Design   162

Service Templates and Profiles   164

vNIC Templates   166

HyperFlex Integration with External Storage   167

Cisco's HX Data Platform   168

HX Data Platform Controller   169

HyperFlex in VMware ESXi Environment   170

HyperFlex in Hyper-V Environment   171

Docker Containers Support and Volume Driver   172

HyperFlex Data Distribution   174

HyperFlex Data Striping   176

Data Protection with Replication Factor   178

Cluster Resiliency   179

Logical Availability Zones   181

Details of Read and Write Operations   181

Log-Structured File System   181

Data Virtualization   182

The Lifecycle of a Write Operation   183

Destaging and Data Optimization   185

The Lifecycle of a Read Operation   186

Advanced Data Services   187

Deduplication and Compression   187

Snapshots   188

Cloning   189

Asynchronous Native Replication for DR with Remote Clusters   189

Synchronous Native Replication for DR with Stretched Clusters   190

Integration with Third-Party Backup Tools   191

HyperFlex Security   192

Securing Data-at-Rest   192

Operational Security   193

Complying with Security Regulations and Certifications   194

Management Security   194

Looking Ahead   195

References   195

Chapter 10   Deploying, Provisioning, and Managing HyperFlex   197

Installation Phase   197

HyperFlex Workload Profiler   199

HyperFlex Sizer   199

Management Provisioning and Monitoring   199

Cisco HyperFlex Connect HTML5 Management   200

Dashboard   200

Monitor   200

Analyze   200

Protect   201

Manage   202

VMware vSphere Management Plug-In   203

Summary Tab   203

Monitor Tab   203

Manage Tab   204

Cisco Intersight   204

Claiming the Nodes   205

Looking Ahead   209

References   210

Chapter 11   HyperFlex Workload Optimization and Efficiency   211

Enterprise Workload Issues   211

HyperFlex with Cisco Tetration   212

Data Collection   214

Tetration Analytics Cluster   214

Open Access   215

Using the Data   215

Cisco Workload Optimizer   216

Cisco AppDynamics   217

Looking Ahead   219

References   219

PART V   Alternative HCI Implementations   221

Chapter 12   VMware vSAN   223

vSAN Physical Components   224

vSAN Hyperconvergence Software   225

The Object File System   226

vSAN Datastore   228

vSAN Storage Policies   228

Caching   232

I/O Operation Details   232

vSAN Advanced Functionality   233

Data Integrity   234

Data Encryption   234

Deduplication and Compression   235

Erasure Coding   236

Snapshots   236

Cloning   236

vSAN Replication for Disaster Recovery via Stretched
Clusters   238

vSAN Backup for Disaster Recovery   241

Integration with Legacy SAN and NAS   243

vSAN iSCSI Target   243

vSAN and VVols   243

SMB and NFS Support   244

Persistent Storage for Containers   244

vSAN Management   244

Graphical Interfaces   244

Ease of Installation   245

Cloud-Connected Health Checks   245

Performance Diagnostics   245

VMware Update Manager   245

vSAN vRealize Operations and Log Insight   245

Thoughts on vSAN Versus HyperFlex   246

Hardware Comparison   247

Scaling Up   247

vSAN In-Kernel Versus Controller-Based Solutions   248

Distributed Versus Not-So-Distributed File System   249

One-to-One Versus Many-to-Many Rebuild   250

Implementations of Compute-Only Nodes   250

Advanced Data Services   251

Management Software   252

Networking   252

Looking Ahead   253

References   253

Chapter 13   Nutanix Enterprise Cloud Platform   255

Nutanix Enterprise Cloud Platform   256

ECP Hyperconvergence Software   257

Distributed Storage Fabric   257

Nutanix Cluster Components   258

Physical Drive Breakdown   260

I/O Path   261

Write I/O   261

Read I/O   262

Data Protection   262

   Metadata   263

   Availability Domains   263

   Data Path Resiliency   264

Nutanix Advanced Functionality   264

   Deduplication   264

   Data Compression   265

   Erasure Coding   266

   Disk Balancing   266

   Storage Tiering   267

Snapshots and Clones   268

   Shadow Clones   269

   Era Database Services   269

   Backup and Restore, Replication, and Disaster Recovery   270

Metro Availability: Stretch Clustering   271

Data At Rest Encryption   272

Nutanix Acropolis Block Services   272

Nutanix Acropolis File Services   273

Support for Hyper-V   274

Docker Containers   275

Provisioning, Managing, and Monitoring   275

   Infrastructure Management   276

   Operational Insight   277

   Nutanix Tools   278

   Calm Orchestration Tool   278

The Nutanix Competitive Landscape   279

   Hardware Comparison   280

   Distributed Architecture   281

   Log-Structured Versus Write-in-Place File System   282

   Data Tiering   282

   Deduplication   283

   Arguments Against Post-Process Deduplication   283

   Arguments Against Inline Deduplication   284

   Data Locality   285

   Pros of Data Locality   285

   Cons of Data Locality   286

Looking Ahead   287

Reference   287

Chapter 14   Open Source—Compute and Storage   289

OpenStack   290

Nova   294

Cinder Block Storage   296

Swift   297

   Proxy Server   298

Ceph   300

Looking Ahead   303

References   303

PART VI   Hyperconverged Networking   305

Chapter 15   Software-Defined Networking and Open Source   307

The SDN Background   308

The Overlay and Microsegmentation Edge   309

   Host-Based Networking   310

   Switch-Based Networking   312

The Switching Fabric   313

The Underlay Network   315

The Overlay Network   315

Microsegmentation in the Data Center   319

Networking Open Source Initiatives   320

   Neutron   320

   Neutron Server   320

   Neutron-APIs   321

   Neutron Plug-Ins   321

   Agents   321

   OVS Architecture   322

OVN—The Open Source SDN   324

   Open vSwitch   325

   OVN   326

   OVN Functionality   326

   OVN High-Level Architecture   327

   Improvements over OVS and Neutron Integration   328

State of Vendors with Open Source   331

Looking Ahead   332

References   333

Chapter 16   VMware NSX   335

Setting and Enforcing Policies in NSX   336

Security Groups   336

Security Policy   337

Policy Enforcement   338

The NSX Manager and Controller Cluster   339

NSX Manager   339

The NSX Controller Cluster   340

Enhancements for vDS   341

Flooding Avoidance   342

NSX L2 Switching and L3 Routing   343

NSX L2 Switching   343

NSX IP Routing   343

Distributed Logical Router   343

Handling of Multidestination Traffic   346

Basic Multicast Model with No Optimization   347

Unicast Method of Replication   348

Looking Ahead   350

Reference   350

Chapter 17   Application-Centric Infrastructure   351

Cisco Application-Centric Infrastructure   352

ACI Microsegmentation Constructs   353

The Endpoint Groups   353

Application Network Profile   355

Service Graphs   358

ACI Tetration Model   360

Cisco Application Policy Infrastructure Controller   360

ACI Domains   362

Virtual Machine Manager Domain   362

Physical and External Domains   364

Physical Domains   365

External Domains   365

The ACI Fabric Switching and Routing Constructs   365

Tenant   366

VRF   366

Bridge Domain   366

EPG   366

Virtual and Physical Connectivity to the ACI Fabric   367

   Virtual Connectivity to the Fabric   367

   Physical Connectivity to the Fabric   368

The ACI Switching and Routing Terminology   369

The ACI Underlay Network   371

   Handling External Routes   372

   ACI Fabric Load Balancing   373

The ACI Overlay and VXLAN   373

   The VXLAN Instance ID   376

   L2 Switching in the Overlay   378

   L3 Switching/Routing in the Overlay   380

Multicast in the Overlay Versus Multicast in the Underlay   383

ACI Multi-PoD   383

ACI Multi-Site   384

ACI Anywhere   386

High-Level Comparison Between ACI and NSX   386

   Policy Setting   387

   Policy Enforcement   388

   Performance Requirement for VXLAN   388

   Control Plane   389

   Performance of Data Forwarding   390

   Automation and Visibility in the Fabric   390

   Networking Learning Curve   391

Looking Ahead   392

References   392

PART VII   **Public, Private, Hybrid, and Multicloud   393**

Chapter 18   **The Public Cloud   395**

The Cloud Services   395

   Infrastructure as a Service   396

   Platform as a Service   397

   Software as a Service   397

Amazon Web Services   398

   AWS Global Infrastructure with Regions and Availability Zones   399

   Networking   401

   Storage   404

   AWS S3 Storage   405

   Amazon Elastic Block Storage   406

Launching Multitier Applications in AWS   409

 Compute Instances   409

 Amazon Machine Images   410

 Security Groups   410

 Identity and Access Management   411

 Launching an EC2 Instance   412

 Adding Volumes   414

 Auto Scaling   414

 Cloud Monitoring   416

Cloud Automation   416

 Infrastructure as a Code   417

 Software Development Kits   420

Looking Ahead   421

References   421

Chapter 19 **The Private Cloud   423**

What Is a Private Cloud?   423

 Convergence and Hyperconvergence   425

 Automation and Orchestration   425

Cisco UCS Director   427

 UCS Director Policies   427

 Virtual Data Center   429

 Orchestration Concepts   430

 Catalogs   431

Integration Between UCSD and HyperFlex   431

 UCSD Interfaces   433

 APIs and Infrastructure as a Code   434

Looking Ahead   437

References   437

Chapter 20 **Hybrid Cloud and Multicloud   439**

Why Hybrid Cloud?   440

Why Multicloud?   442

Cisco CloudCenter   446

Looking Ahead   450

References   450

Glossary   451

Index   475

Icons Used in This Book

Cloud

Data Center
Switch

Networking
Services

Fibre Channel
Fabric Switch

ToR L2
Switches

Load
Balancer

Router

File
Server

Campus

Data Center
Aggregation

Command Syntax Conventions

The conventions used to present command syntax in this book are the same conventions used in Cisco's Command Reference. The Command Reference describes these conventions as follows:

- **Boldface** indicates commands and keywords that are entered literally as shown. In actual configuration examples and output (not general command syntax), boldface indicates commands that are manually input by the user (such as a **show** command).

- *Italics* indicate arguments for which you supply actual values.

- Vertical bars (|) separate alternative, mutually exclusive elements.

- Square brackets [ ] indicate optional elements.

- Braces { } indicate a required choice.

- Braces within brackets [{ }] indicate a required choice within an optional element.

> **Note** This book covers multiple operating systems, and a differentiation of icons and router names indicates the appropriate OS that is being referenced. IOS and IOS XE use router names like **R1** and **R2** and are referenced by the IOS router icon. IOS XR routers will use router names like **XR1** and **XR2** and are referenced by the IOS XR router icon.

Introduction

Hyperconverged infrastructure (HCI) is the integration of different technologies such as compute, storage and storage networking, virtualization, data networking, and automation, all under the umbrella of software-defined storage (SDS) and software-defined networking (SDN). Legacy data centers are normally built by system administrators, networking engineers, storage administrators, software virtualization engineers, and network management engineers, all working within their own area of expertise. This creates different silo groups within the same IT organization trying to optimize their own set of tasks without much visibility into the other groups. In essence, the IT professionals are segmented and find pride in being the experts in their own tasks. So here comes HCI with a paradigm shift that integrates all the different technology fields into one product—hence, the need for cross-technology knowledge.

This book approaches the HCI topic from the point of view that any individual working this field needs to have enough knowledge in all the different areas, including storage, storage networking, compute, virtualization, switching and routing, and automation. The book explains each area in the context of a legacy data center design, detailing the problem statement for the particular technology and how HCI solves the problem and to what extent. The *Hyperconverged Infrastructure Data Centers* book will be the bible for IT professionals, technical folk, and management in all technology areas. It will guide them through the decision process to move in the HCI direction.

Despite this being a Cisco Press book, this book tries to be vendor neutral by objectively comparing and contrasting the Cisco HyperFlex approach with other vendor implementations. The SDS and the distributed storage file systems that the Cisco HyperFlex HX Data platform has adopted, VMware vSAN and Nutanix Enterprise Cloud software, are described. A compare and contrast between the different SDN solutions—such as Cisco application-centric infrastructure (ACI), VMware network virtualization and security platform (NSX), and the open source Open vSwitch (OVS)/Open Virtual Network (OVN) and OpenStack are also described. This gives you enough ammunition to ask the right questions when choosing an HCI solution.

Aside from describing HCI in detail, a key aspect of this book is a comparison between HCI and public cloud services from Amazon Web Services (AWS). This book helps IT professionals, chief information officers (CIOs), and information technology (IT) managers in their decision to move into an on-premise HCI deployment versus a public cloud deployment. It describes in detail and from a technical and business aspect the pros and cons for building on-premise versus outsourcing. This book also covers products such as the Cisco CloudCenter, which facilitate the migration into a multicloud environment.

Last but not least, this book goes into detail about automation and software management by gathering information from different HCI vendors and approaching the topic from a vendor-neutral angle, allowing the reader to make a decision on existing and needed automation functionality.

Goals and Methods

CIOs and IT professionals who want to simplify their IT and networking environment are now challenged with the decision of whether to move fully into the cloud, build their own HCI data centers, or both. Making such decisions depends on factors that include the scale and complexity of the CIO's and IT professionals' existing setup, the level of control over their own resources, security, availability of IT and networking resources, level of expertise, and overall fixed and recurring costs.

Because many new vendors are introducing products that offer HCI and are challenging the existing network design, the new technologies are becoming confusing to IT professionals who are trying to move into next-generation architectures while maintaining a current setup that is generating revenue. This book walks the reader step by step through the existing data center setups and the issues faced in scaling current designs. The book explains all HCI elements in detail and how to achieve high availability (HA) and scale in dealing with compute, storage, networking, and virtualization requirements. As automation becomes a key benefit of HCI, this book compares the automation functions and tools of HCI with cloud offerings from the likes of AWS and others. The objective is to provide IT administrators with a solid knowledge base across all technology areas and compare and contrast HCI offerings from different vendors. This gives you the tools to ask the right questions when you embark on the transformation of your data center into private and hybrid clouds.

Who Should Read This Book?

HCI is the integration of compute, storage, networking, virtualization, and automation that is driven by software. In general, IT professionals are divided in their areas of expertise. Individuals are spread into focus areas that overlap:

- Servers and virtualization
- Storage
- Backup and disaster recovery (DR)
- Storage networking
- Switching and routing
- Security
- Software applications
- Automation
- DevOps

Because HCI offers a unified platform that combines all these areas in one system, the coverage between the areas will blur. Although HCI will simplify the implementation of each area, cross-knowledge between these areas is essential. This means that the audience of this book is the sum of all system administrators, storage administrators, networking engineers, software virtualization engineers, and network management engineers. Also, because the book touches on the business aspects of HCI and the pros and cons of moving from private clouds to public clouds, IT managers and CIOs will benefit from understanding the impact that HCI has on the transformation of their data centers and the speed of deploying highly available applications.

How This Book Is Organized

For those readers who are familiar with the author's writing style from his previous bestseller books, including *Internet Routing Architectures*, Sam Halabi emphasizes easy reading and making the difficult look easy. This book goes through a smooth progression of the topics in a storytelling style. Many of the basic concepts are laid out in advance, so you do not miss a beat and feel comfortable progressing through the chapters. It is recommended that you read the chapters in order so that you get the full benefit of this book.

Networking, storage, compute, virtualization, and automation are not easy topics and are getting more complex every day. Not only are system administrators, networking engineers, storage engineers, and virtualization engineers asked to become multifunctional, they also need to become programmers. The learning curve is huge, and many people aren't sure where to start.

Sam Halabi has put a lot of effort into putting you on the right track and giving you the launch pad into tackling HCI. His many years of experience in both vendor and system integration tracking across different technology areas make a difficult topic such as HCI sound simple. The advantages you see from this book follow:

- An easy reading style with no marketing fluff or heavy technical jargon

- Progression through the chapters from easy to advanced topics

- Comprehensive coverage of the topic at both technical and business levels

- First book to address storage, compute, virtualization, networking, and automation in detail under one umbrella to bridge the technology gap between the different IT departments

- Benefit to IT professionals trying to evaluate whether to move in the HCI direction

- Benefit to IT management, CIO, and chief technology officer (CTO) in evaluating HCI versus the public cloud

- Coverage of the latest HCI functionality

- Discussion of automation as it compares to cloud offerings such as AWS

- Comparing and contrasting of different implementations objectively and with vendor neutrality

Book Structure

The book is organized into seven parts.

PART I: Basics of Data Center Networking and Storage

Chapter 1, "Data Networks: Existing Designs": This chapter describes the different networking equipment that constitutes the data center and discusses the challenges of the existing designs in meeting the needs of application-aware data centers. It covers challenges with the three-tier architecture, including oversubscription between the tiers, stretching VLANs over large L2 networks, latency of traffic crossing tiers, flooding of broadcast traffic, complexity in dealing with IPv4 address scarcity, loop prevention, and firewall overload.

Chapter 2, "Storage Networks: Existing Designs": This chapter presents an essential background of the different storage technologies and terminology. It describes the three-tier storage network and discusses fundamental topics such as disk drives, disk speed throughput and latency, and input/output operations per second (IOPS). The chapter familiarizes you with redundant array of independent disks (RAID) systems, storage controllers, and logical unit numbers (LUNs). Block-, file-, and object-level storage are discussed, as are the different storage architectures of storage area network (SAN) with iSCSI and fibre channel, network-attached storage (NAS), and direct-attached storage (DAS). You will see an overview of storage efficiency technologies, such as thin and thick provisioning, deduplication and compression, snapshots replication and cloning, caching, disk encryption, and storage tiering.

PART II: Evolution in Host Hardware and Software

Chapter 3, "Host Hardware Evolution": Advances in processing power make an individual server more powerful than the traditional storage controllers. This chapter covers the terminology of central processing unit (CPU), virtual cores, logical cores, and virtual CPUs. It discusses the latest advancement in host bus interconnect with technologies such as Peripheral Component Interconnect express (PCIe) and Non-Volatile Memory express (NVMe). The evolution in flash memory and cache and the emergence of a new generation of flash-based storage products are covered as well.

Chapter 4, "Server Virtualization": This chapter gives an overview of software virtualization, hypervisors, and the difference between virtual machines (VMs) and containers. It discusses the concepts of datastores and logical volumes and shows the steps in the creation of a VM. Different virtualization services such as VM migration are explored to provide HA and fault tolerance and to provide load distribution. The chapter also explores the concepts of standard and distributed virtual switches in providing VMs with all the networking attributes of a physical switch. The definition of networking and storage policies at the VM level puts the application at the center of attention.

Chapter 5, "Software-Defined Storage": This chapter introduces SDS and its objectives in decoupling storage software from hardware. Some early implementations of SDS are discussed, but they do not meet the goals of hyperconvergence. You will also learn about some important topics such as vSphere APIs for storage awareness (VASA) and Virtual

Volumes (VVols). Such architectures, although fit in a legacy converged model with storage arrays, pave the way for giving the application better visibility into the storage capabilities and putting the application in the driver seat.

PART III: Hyperconverged Infrastructure

Chapter 6, "Converged Infrastructure": This chapter introduces the Cisco Unified Computing System (UCS) and how it changed the server, compute, and networking landscape. It led to the emergence of what is called converged infrastructure (CI). The objective of CI is to simplify data center rollouts and management with better integration between the different products that make up the converged solution. The pros and cons of deploying CI are presented to give you a feel for why the data center transformation into hyperconvergence is a must.

Chapter 7, "HCI Functionality": This chapter defines HCI and delves into its functionality. A detailed description of the HCI physical and logical distributed architecture is covered. Distributed data controllers create a scale-out architecture that moves away from the legacy centralized storage architecture. Data replication provides hardware resiliency and data protection. The chapter introduces the log-structured file system (LFS) and its benefits for HCI. Advanced HCI functionalities are introduced, and you learn how services such as backup and disaster recovery are native to the architecture. You also get a feel for the new provisioning, deployment, and management model that simplifies the deployment of applications and setting of policies.

Chapter 8, "HCI Business Benefits and Use Cases": This chapter discusses HCI business benefits as seen by CIOs and IT managers who want justification for moving from a legacy SAN and converged environment to hyperconverged. The chapter discusses the multitude of HCI use cases ranging from simple server virtualization to more complex environments. It includes details about sample applications such as DevOps, virtual desktops, remote office business office (ROBO), edge computing, tier-1 enterprise-class applications, backup, and disaster recovery.

PART IV: Cisco HyperFlex

Chapter 9, "Cisco HyperFlex": The chapter gives an overview of the Cisco HyperFlex platform and its physical components. It discusses the integration between HyperFlex and UCS through the use of service profiles and templates. A detailed description of the HX Data Platform is presented, which covers the data platform controller, support for VMware ESXi, Microsoft Hyper-V, and Docker containers. The chapter also covers data distribution in the cache and capacity layers, and the life of read and write input/output (I/O). HyperFlex Advanced Data Services including deduplication and compression, snapshots, clones, synchronous replication for backup and disaster recovery, and integration with third-party backup software vendors are described. Also discussed is HyperFlex security with the use of self-encrypting drives and the adoption of industry security standards.

Chapter 10, "Deploying, Provisioning, and Managing HyperFlex": This chapter covers the deployment provisioning and management of the HyperFlex platform. It includes reference tools to help with sizing the platform depending on the workload. Different software products are used to help in managing all aspects of deploying and monitoring the data services from inside the private data center as well as from the public cloud.

Chapter 11, "HyperFlex Workload Optimization and Efficiency": This chapter describes the different issues that face enterprise workloads, including reactive mode to growth, lack of visibility into their applications, overprovisioning, and cloud creep. Better visibility into the traffic flows and the service chain between the applications is done using the Cisco Tetration platform. The Cisco Workload Optimizer (CWOM) automation tool monitors the performance consumption of applications and matches the resources with the needs of the application. Cisco AppDynamics is an application and business monitoring platform that allows enterprises to monitor their business applications and transactions and make sure they are delivering the best performance. The platform gives root cause analysis of performance issues at the code level.

PART V: Alternative HCI Implementations

Chapter 12, "VMware vSAN": vSAN is VMware's hyperconverged software product. This chapter describes vSAN's hardware implementation, including ready nodes and integrated systems. It also introduces the vSAN hyperconvergence software, including the object file system and the input/output (I/O) operation within the cache and capacity layers. The vSAN advanced data services, such as deduplication, compression, erasure coding (EC), snapshots and clones, disaster recovery, and backup are discussed as well. In addition, the chapter covers the integration of vSAN with legacy SAN and NAS. You will also see a high-level comparison between HyperFlex and vSAN, pointing out architectural differences and giving you enough ammunition to ask the right questions from your vendors.

Chapter 13, "Nutanix Enterprise Cloud Platform": This chapter describes the Nutanix Enterprise Cloud Platform software components. The distributed storage fabric, read/write I/O path, and data protection techniques are discussed. Similar to HyperFlex and vSAN, you will see a detailed description of the advanced data services, including deduplication, compression, EC, and support for backup and disaster recovery. The chapter also covers a competitive landscape, comparing the Nutanix architecture with HyperFlex, highlighting pros and cons in different areas.

Chapter 14, "Open Source—Compute and Storage": This chapter gives an overview of the open source approaches to hyperconvergence. It presents a description of OpenStack and the different components that are relevant to HCI, including Nova for Compute, Cinder for block storage, and Swift for object storage. Also, a description of important open source initiatives such as Ceph for combined block, file, and object services is presented.

PART VI: Hyperconverged Networking

Chapter 15, "Software-Defined Networking and Open Source": This chapter discusses SDN and its background and adoption in today's networking implementations. Host-based and switch-based networking options are presented, with a discussion of how they compete for the networking landscape. The chapter covers the benefits of the new leaf/spine 2-tier networking architecture. The Overlay/Virtual Extensible LAN (VXLAN), and Underlay networking models are covered, as is the important topic of microsegmentation. Open source networking via implementations from OpenStack Neutron, open source OVS, and Open Virtual Network (OVN) are also discussed.

Chapter 16, "VMware NSX": This chapter introduces VMware Network Virtualization and Security platform (NSX). This is VMware's solution for bringing automation, policy, and security into the networking environment. You will see a description of the NSX components, including the NSX manager and controllers cluster. In addition, you will read about the vSphere distributed switch (vDS) enhancements in support of VXLAN. Alternatively, VMware introduced a host-based networking solution by implementing IP routing using the concept of a distributed logical router (DLR) and an edge services gateway (ESG).

Chapter 17, "Application-Centric Infrastructure": The Cisco ACI is a measure to introduce a level of automation into setting and enforcing policies at the application level as well as configuring the switch fabric to support the connectivity requirements of the applications in the data center. This chapter describes how ACI works and presents the microsegmentation constructs, including endpoint groups (EPGs), application network profiles (ANPs), and bridge domains (BDs). The chapter covers the Application Virtual Switch (AVS) and the ACI switching and routing constructs, including overlay/VXLAN and underlay. ACI Multi-Point of Delivery (Multi-PoD), ACI Multi-Site, and ACI Anywhere concepts are also discussed. The chapter ends with a comprehensive comparison between Cisco ACI and VMware NSX, highlighting similarities and differences.

PART VII: Public, Private, Hybrid, and Multicloud

Chapter 18, "The Public Cloud": This chapter defines the different cloud models, such as infrastructure as a service (IaaS), platform as a service (PaaS), and software as a service (SaaS). It introduces services from AWS and highlights the AWS networking, storage, and compute capabilities. A description of how to launch a multitier application in AWS is presented, including initiating compute instances, identity and access management (IAM), security groups, storage, and monitoring. The chapter also covers the topic of cloud automation and the notion of infrastructure as a code.

Chapter 19, "The Private Cloud": This chapter describes, through the use of automation and orchestration, how to transform hyperconverged data centers into private clouds. It covers the characteristics and different models of a private cloud, distinguishing between automation and orchestration. Examples are drawn from the Cisco UCS Director (UCSD) and how it defines storage, compute, and networking policies to create service catalogs. Also discussed are the interaction between UCSD and HyperFlex and the creation of infrastructure as a code.

Chapter 20, "Hybrid Cloud and Multicloud": This chapter concludes the book with a definition of the hybrid cloud and multicloud and a description of the use cases and benefits. It draws on products from Cisco Systems to allow the ease of migration of applications and services between the different clouds. The chapter briefly presents the Cisco CloudCenter and its ability to decouple the application from the underlying cloud and orchestrating applications over private as well as public clouds. Finally, this chapter summarizes the HyperFlex hyperconvergence ecosystem and how it integrates with CloudCenter.

Figure Credits

Figures 9-3 and 9-4 "Hyperconverged Infrastructure with Consistent High Performance for Virtual Machines." Tony Palmer and Kerry Dolan, March 2017, The Enterprise Strategy Group, Inc.

Figures 9-5, 9-9 © Cisco Systems, Inc.

Figures 10-1 to 10 3 © Cisco Systems, Inc.

Figure 10-4 VSphere Web Client © 2018 VMware, Inc.

Figures 10-5 to 10-8 © Cisco Systems, Inc.

Figure 11-1 © Cisco Systems, Inc.

Figures 17-4, 17-5, 17-10, 17-14 to 17-16, © Cisco Systems, Inc.

Figures 18-1 to 18-8 Amazon Web Services, Inc.

Figure 19-3 © Cisco Systems, Inc.

PART I

Basics of Data Center Networking and Storage

Chapter 1   Data Networks: Existing Designs

Chapter 2   Storage Networks: Existing Designs

Data Center Networking and Storage went through many evolutions. However, when discussing the latest and greatest technologies, many assume that enterprises already went through major overhauls and that the network is on par with the latest on the market. The fact is that marketing always superseded engineering by leaps. While it is easy to draw the most efficient architectures in PowerPoint, it takes months of planning before network, compute, and storage professionals can attempt a network change. And when the decision is made, it takes many more months, or maybe years, before a network goes through a major overhaul. Add to this the many justifications to management on why new equipment is needed and why tweaking the current network does not do the job.

The point is that many networks are still built with older technologies and are not to the point of adopting newer technologies. So before getting into hyperconvergence, it helps to go back to the basics of data center designs—from both a networking and storage perspectives—to understand some of the existing challenges and why you need to move to newer architectures.

Chapter 1 discusses the data networks, existing designs, starting by listing the networking components, discussing multitier architectures, and exploring the existing networking challenges. While this might be basic for a networking engineer, virtualization and storage engineers will appreciate some of the networking intricacies.

Chapter 2 covers the storage multitier architecture and storage basics from types of disks, storage networking alternatives, the different storage file systems, and the data services deployed by enterprises. While this chapter might be familiar to storage engineers, some of the basics are not so obvious to virtualization and networking engineers.

Chapter 1

Data Networks: Existing Designs

This chapter covers the following key topics:

- **Information Technology Equipment of a Data Center:** A highlight of networking equipment that constitutes the data center. This includes network equipment such as switches and routers, network services equipment including traffic optimization with load balancers, wide area network (WAN) optimizers, and security equipment such as firewalls.

- **Multitier Data Networking Architecture:** Describes the three-tier data networking architecture from access to aggregation and core. It discusses the placement of networking services and the logical server grouping for multitier applications.

- **Challenges of Existing Designs:** Discusses challenges with the three-tier architecture, such as oversubscription between the tiers, stretching virtual local area networks (VLANs) over large L2 networks, latency of traffic crossing tiers, flooding of broadcast traffic, complexity in dealing with IPv4 address scarcity, loop prevention, and firewall overload.

The existing networking designs in today's data centers, with all their flaws, served their purpose providing robust infrastructures. Some of the largest data centers were built based on networking architectures that are now called *legacy*. However, the shift in traffic patterns, the introduction of server virtualization, and the introduction of multitier applications challenge the existing designs. This chapter discusses the existing network equipment and services and how they are deployed. It also goes into detail about the challenges of the current designs in scaling to meet the needs of application-aware data centers.

Information Technology Equipment of a Data Center

There are different types of data centers depending on their particular usage. Enterprise data centers normally house customer-facing applications such as web servers as well as the applications and services needed for the day-to-day operation of the enterprise. Such applications include email servers, enterprise resource planning (ERP), customer relationship management (CRM), and relational databases. Other larger data centers operated by cloud service providers (CSPs) house many software applications that are sold as a service to enterprises and consumers that connect to the data center over the Internet or private lines. Although data centers differ in size and functionality, the basic blocks for compute, storage, networking, and software applications remain the same. Although data centers contain many elements, such as facility management, physical security, power, cooling, and so on, this book covers only the information technology (IT) equipment of the data center in the context of data center convergence and hyperconvergence, which is defined later. The basic IT equipment of a data center falls under the categories of network equipment and networking services.

Network Equipment

Network equipment encompasses the basic switching and routing equipment of two layers:

- **Layer 2 (L2):** Switches that work at the Media Access Control (MAC) and VLAN levels
- **Layer 3 (L3):** Switches and routers that work at the Internet Protocol (IP) level

This chapter does not go into the details of switching and routing, but Chapter 15, "Software-Defined Networking and Open Source," discusses underlay and overlay networks that essentially combine L2 and L3 networking to allow the mobility of applications between different servers and virtual machines.

It is worth noting that the word *networking* normally describes both data networking and storage networking. The difference between data networking and storage networking becomes clearer in the next sections.

In the context of data networking, switches and routers have different types of interfaces—ranging from Fast Ethernet to 1 Gigabit Ethernet (GE), 10 GE, 25 GE, 40 GE, 50 GE, and 100 GE—that connect the local area network (LAN). In the context of storage networking, switches also have 2 Gbps, 4 Gbps, and 8 Gbps fibre channel (FC) interfaces that connect the storage area network (SAN).

Networking Services

Networking services in the data center are standalone appliances, software running on hardware modules inside network equipment, or software running inside servers. Because data centers are moving toward a hyperconverged space, most of these services will eventually move from standalone appliances and become more integrated into the hyperconverged equipment. Networking services are grouped as either traffic redirection and optimization or security.

Traffic Redirection and Optimization

Traffic redirection involves redirecting the traffic to a certain target based on certain criteria, such as port numbers inside the Transmission Control Protocol (TCP) / Internet Protocol (IP) packets, or based on actual traffic content, or other. There are a lot of products in this space that offer different functionality such as load balancing, WAN optimization, content switching and caching, TCP optimization, Secure Sockets Layer (SSL) offload, data compression, and so on. A sample of such products includes load balancers and WAN optimizers.

Load Balancers

Server load balancing (SLB) distributes traffic across multiple servers to get better server utilization and higher availability for applications. Applications are normally spread over multiple servers in the same data center or multiple data centers for higher fault tolerance. The client trying to reach an application points only to one target—such as a URL or an IP address that is directed to the load balancer. Once the traffic reaches the LB, it distributes the traffic to different servers according to the rules or criteria. LBs work at layer 4 (L4) to balance traffic based on information in transport and session layer protocols, such as IP, TCP, File Transfer Protocol (FTP), and User Datagram Protocol (UDP), or they work at layer 7 (L7) based on information in application layer protocols, such as on Hypertext Transfer Protocol (HTTP) headers and cookies. LBs balance traffic based on various algorithms, such as round robin, response time, and sending traffic to healthy servers only.

WAN Optimizers

WAN optimizers efficiently carry traffic over WAN links. Because most data centers are connected through the WAN to service providers or to other data centers in the case of large enterprises or CSPs, it becomes crucial to make the most of the WAN link bandwidth. The WAN optimizers make sure that traffic is prioritized and bandwidth is adequately allocated. They also perform data compression, traffic shaping, and data deduplication.

Security

Securing the data and transactions between clients and a data center is extremely important, whether the access to the data center is done from the Internet toward an enterprise or from within the enterprise itself. The security terminology and functionality in the industry are overwhelming. Security is done via standalone appliances or software that covers these different areas:

- Packet firewalls

- Proxy firewalls

- Stateful inspection firewalls

- Next-generation firewalls that work at the application level

- VPN with encryption and decryption

- Network address translation (NAT)

- Intrusion detection systems (IDSs)

- Intrusion prevention systems (IPSs)

- Access key and token management

- Protection against denial of service (DoS) attacks

The term *unified threat management (UTM)* combines some of the functionality just mentioned into one product. For the purposes of this book, let's refer to the security functions as firewall (FW), which can encompass one or many of the functionalities. Now let's examine a sample description of the main FW functionality.

Firewall

FWs constitute the first entry point from the Internet into the data center, and they allow only authorized users to enter the data center while blocking unauthorized users. They are applied within the enterprise campus to secure traffic between the different departments of the same enterprise. They are also applied at the server level to allow appropriate access between clients, applications, and databases.

There are different types of firewalls. The most basic ones are packet-based firewalls that allow or deny traffic based on source and destination IP address, TCP port numbers, and direction of traffic. These are comparable with the access control lists (ACLs) on routers that basically deny or allow inbound or outbound traffic from an IP address and port. With the sophistication of attacks based on IP addresses and port numbers, more advanced firewalls do stateful inspection and track the progress of the full TCP session, not just the port number. Also, next-generation firewalls (NGFWs) work at the application level and track traffic based on the application itself. For example, an FW can track a Structured Query Language (SQL) session toward a database and allow or deny access based on an IP address and application type being SQL. Other applications of such firewalls are filtering traffic based on HTTP headers and the content itself.

As you move toward a hyperconverged data center where servers, storage, and network equipment are collapsed into one product, the layer where you apply networking services becomes important because it makes or breaks the network. Things can get complicated with virtualized environments where applications move around between different servers and security policies have to follow. As you'll see later, networking services are moving toward being applied at the application level.

Multitier Data Networking Architecture

When networking (switching and routing) vendors talk about three-tier and two-tier designs, they are referring to how switches and routers are deployed in a data center. The traditional switching and routing layers in the legacy data center are as shown in Figure 1-1.

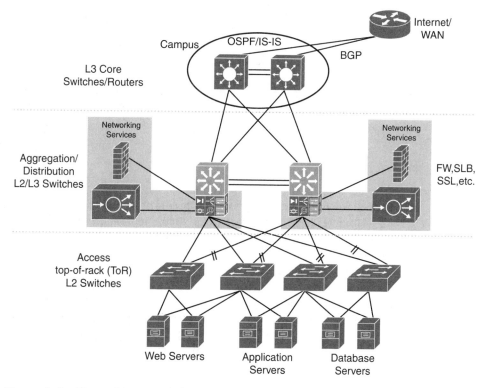

Figure 1-1 *Networking View of Three-Tier Data Center*

Access switches normally connect to the server network interface cards (NICs) and form the first level of data multiplexing. These are also called top-of-rack (ToR) switches because they sit on top of the rack connecting all Ethernet NICs coming from the servers within the same rack. Access switches are usually L2 switches, but they can also be L2/L3. The choice depends on cost and particular designs. L2 switches are a lot cheaper than L2/L3 switches because they deliver less functionality.

Aggregation switches, also called distribution switches, aggregate toward the core all Ethernet interfaces coming from the access switches. The aggregation switches normally work at L2. Traditionally, this layer existed because it reduced the number of "expensive" interfaces at the core router, it created a certain level of redundancy by having dual connections between the access switch and the aggregation layer (keeping in mind that aggregation switches are cheaper than core routers), and it shielded the core layer from L2 functionality. As shown later in this book, the newest designs can skip this layer and go directly from the access (now called leaf), to the core (now called spine). In this case, L3 functionality must start at access switches. The aggregation layer also offers connectivity to the networking services such as firewalls, load balancers, and others, as seen in Figure 1-1. The networking services are either standalone appliances or embedded inside the aggregation switches.

Core switches/routers collect all interfaces coming from the aggregation layer and multiplex them toward the WAN or the campus LAN. Most layer 3 functionality—such as routing between subnets, running routing protocols such as Open Shortest Path First (OSPF), Intermediate System to Intermediate System (IS-IS), and Border Gateway Protocol (BGP)—is done at this layer. As discussed earlier, in the newest leaf and spine designs where there is no aggregation, the core switches connect directly to the access layer and support L2 and L3 functionality. The access switches have to do some L3 functionality as well.

Logical Server Grouping

Servers are connected to access switches and grouped logically into multiple tiers, such as a web tier, an application tier, and a database tier. This distributes functionality over multiple servers, which gives higher availability to the application. Failure in one of the tiers does not affect the others. Also, a more distributed approach spreads each tier over multiple servers; for example, the web server actually runs on multiple servers located in the same data center or multiple data centers. If a web server is down, other servers absorb the load. The same distributed approach applies to application servers and database servers. As discussed earlier in this chapter, load balancers distribute the traffic between different servers based on L4 or L7 and different criteria. Figure 1-1 shows a web server, an application server, and a database server design, with load balancers distributing traffic between different servers and firewalls protecting traffic at the entry point to the data center and between the different application components.

Multitier designs require the existence of multiple servers within the same tier talking to each other and to the other tiers. This communication is normally done at L2 using a logical separation via VLANs. In the simplest form, an IP subnet is associated with a VLAN, and servers within the same subnet share the same VLAN ID and talk to each other via their MAC addresses. The VLAN is considered a broadcast domain and is isolated from other broadcast domains. This means that broadcast packets generated within a certain VLAN are contained within that VLAN. This is important in scaling the network as the number of servers and applications increase. In Figure 1-2, web servers, application servers, and database servers are grouped in different subnets, and each subnet is associated with a VLAN. There could be many web/app/database servers in the same subnet, but for simplicity, only one of each is illustrated here.

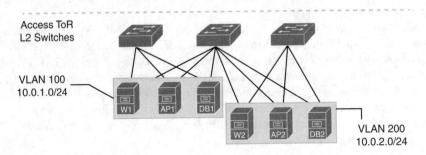

Figure 1-2 *Logical Server Grouping*

Servers house one or many NICs, and the NICs contain one or more Ethernet, 1 GE, 10 GE, or higher speed interfaces. The NICs are dual homed to the access switches for better redundancy and fault tolerance, and NIC ports work in active-active or active-passive modes. Servers within the same VLAN do not need to be connected to the same access switch or in the same rack; they can be connected to different access switches as long as the VLANs are extended across the network. Note that VLANs 100 and 200 stretch across the access and distribution switches.

As a simple example, subnet 10.0.1.0/24 is associated with VLAN 100 and contains web server 1 (W1), application server 1 (AP1), and database server 1 (DB1). Subnet 10.0.2.0/24 is associated with VLAN 200 and contains web servers, application servers, and database servers W2, AP2, and DB2, respectively.

Challenges of Existing Designs

There are many challenges for the three-tier designs in scaling to meet the demands of today's web applications. Today's traffic patterns in the data center have changed. Traditionally, the bulk of the traffic was north-south, meaning from the Internet to the data center and from the data center to the Internet. This affects where the firewalls are placed and how VLANs are designed. With the continued growth in data and storage and with the introduction of virtualization and three-tier web/app/database architectures, traffic is shifting toward an east-west pattern that challenges the three-tier design. This presents the following challenges:

- Oversubscription between the tiers

- Large flat L2 networks with stretched VLANs

- Traffic hopping between tiers, inducing latency

- Complexity of mechanisms used for IP subnet scarcity

- Flooding of broadcast, unknown unicast, and multicast (BUM) traffic

- Loop prevention via spanning tree

- Firewall overload

These issues are described next.

Oversubscription Between the Tiers

One of the challenges of the three-tier architecture is due to oversubscription between the tiers. For example, 20 servers can be connected to an access switch via 1 GE interface, while the access switch is connected to the aggregation switch via a 10 GE interface. This constitutes a 2:1 oversubscription between the access and the aggregation layer. Traditionally, this created no problems because most of the traffic is north-south toward the Internet. Therefore, it was assumed that traffic is limited by the Internet WAN link, and oversubscription does not matter because there is ample bandwidth in the LAN.

With the shift to east-west traffic, the bulk of traffic is now between the servers within the data center, so oversubscription between the access layer and the distribution layer becomes a problem. Access layer switches are normally dual homed into two aggregation layer switches. With the addition of servers, more access switches need to be deployed to accommodate the servers. In turn, more aggregation switches must be added to accommodate the access switches. Usually this is done in pods, where you duplicate the setup repeatedly. This is seen in Figure 1-3.

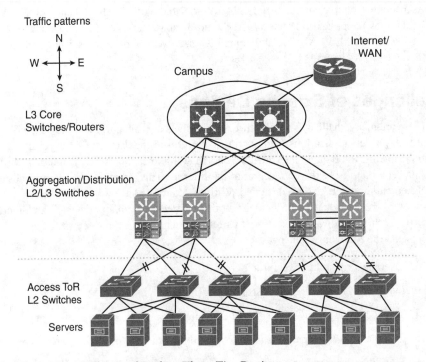

Figure 1-3   *The Challenge of Scaling Three-Tier Designs*

As you see, the addition of aggregation switches shifts the problem of oversubscription from access and aggregation to aggregation and core.

Large Flat L2 Networks with Stretched VLANs

With multitier applications, traffic moves around between web servers, application servers, and databases. Also, with the introduction of server virtualization, virtual machines move around between different servers. When virtual machines move around, they have to maintain their IP addresses to maintain connectivity with their clients, so this movement happens within the same IP subnet. Because the virtual machines could land anywhere in the data center, and because the IP subnet is tied to the VLAN, VLANs must be stretched across the whole data center. Every access and distribution switch must be configured with all VLANs, and every server NIC must see traffic of all VLANs. This increases the L2 flat domain and causes inefficiencies as broadcast packets end up touching every server and virtual machine in the data center. Mechanisms to limit L2 domains and flooding must be implemented to scale today's data centers.

Traffic Hopping Between Tiers, Inducing Latency

Latency is introduced every time traffic crosses a switch or a router before it reaches the destination. The traffic path between nodes in the data center depends on whether the traffic is exchanged within the same VLAN (L2 switched) or exchanged between VLANs (L3 switched/routed).

Traffic exchanged within the same VLAN or subnet is normally switched at L2, whereas traffic exchanged between VLANs must cross an L3 boundary. Notice the following in Figure 1-4:

■ Intra-VLAN east-west traffic between W1, AP1, and DB1 in VLAN 100 is L2 switched at the access layer. All are connected to switch 1 (SW1), and switch 2 (SW2) traffic is switched within those switches depending on what ports are blocked or unblocked by spanning tree.

■ Intra-VLAN east-west traffic between W2, AP2, and DB2 in VLAN 200 is L2 switched at the access layer. All are connected to switch 2 (SW2), and switch 3 (SW3) traffic is switched within those switches depending on what ports are blocked or unblocked by spanning tree.

■ Inter-VLAN east-west traffic between W1, AP1, and DB1 and W2, AP2, and DB2 goes to the aggregation layer to be L3 switched because traffic is crossing VLAN boundaries.

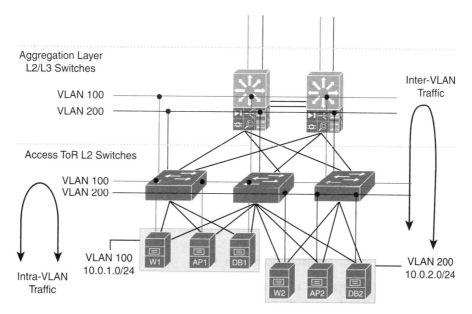

Figure 1-4 *Traffic Hopping Between Tiers*

Every time the traffic crosses a tier, latency is introduced, especially if the network is heavily oversubscribed. That's why it is beneficial to minimize the number of tiers and have traffic switched/routed without crossing many tiers. Legacy aggregation switches used to work at layer 2 and offload layer 3 to the L3 core; however, the latest aggregation switches support L2/L3 functions and route traffic between VLANs via mechanisms such as a switch virtual interface (SVI), which is described next.

Inter-VLAN Routing via SVI

An SVI is a logical interface within an L3 switch that doesn't belong to any physical port. An SVI interface is associated with a specific VLAN. L3 switches have IP L3 switching/ routing between VLANs. Think of them as logical routers that live within the switch and that have their connected SVI interfaces associated with the VLAN. This allows inter-VLAN routing on an L3 switch (see Figure 1-5).

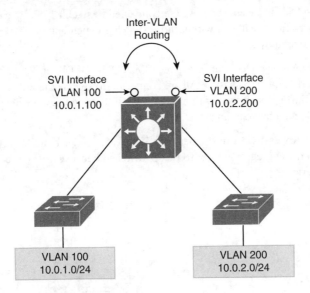

Figure 1-5   *Inter-VLAN Routing via SVI*

As shown earlier, traffic between VLAN 100, subnet 10.0.1.0/24, and VLAN 200 10.0.2.0/24 was L3 switched at the aggregation layer. To do so, two SVI interfaces must be defined: SVI interface for VLAN 100 with an IP address 10.0.1.100, and SVI interface for VLAN 200 with an IP address 10.0.2.200. When routing is turned on the L3 switch, traffic between the two subnets is routed. Servers within VLAN 100 use SVI 10.0.1.100 as their default gateway, and servers within VLAN 200 use SVI 10.0.2.200 as their default gateway.

Complexity of Mechanisms Used for IPv4 Address Scarcity

Defining many subnets in a data center easily consumes the IP space that is allocated to an enterprise. IPv4 subnetting is a complex topic, and this chapter does not go into detail, but if you are starting to get lost with what 10.0.1.0/24 represents, here is a quick review.

A 10.0.1.0/24 indicates classless interdomain routing (CIDR). An IP address is 32 bits, such as a.b.c.d., where a, b, c, and d are 8 bits each. The /24 indicates that you are splitting the IP address, left to right, into a 24-bit network address and an 8-bit host address. A /24 means a subnet mask of 255.255.255.0. Therefore, 10.0.1.0/24 means that the network is 10.0.1 (24 bits) and the hosts take the last 8 bits. With 8 bits, you can have 2 to the power of 8 ($2^8 = 255$) hosts, but you lose hosts 0 and 255, which have special meaning for local loopback and broadcast, respectively, and you end up with 253 hosts. 10.0.1.1 inside subnet 10.0.1.0/24 indicates host 1 inside subnet 10.0.1. You can try on your own what 10.0.1.0/27 results in.

IPv4 addresses are becoming scarce. There is a shift toward adopting IPv6 addressing, which provides a much bigger IP address space. However, so far not everyone is courageous enough to dabble into IPv6, and many enterprises still use IPv4 and mechanisms such as NAT. NAT allows the enterprise to use private IP addresses inside the enterprise and map to whatever public IP addresses they are allocated from a provider.

If a provider allocates the enterprise 128.0.1.0/27 (subnet mask 255.255.255.224), for example, the enterprise has practically one subnet 128.0.1.224 with 32 (2^5) hosts, but you lose 0 and 255, so the address range is from 128.0.1.225 to 128.0.1.254. Therefore, the maximum public IP addresses the enterprise has are 30 addresses inside one subnet.

If the enterprise chooses to divide the network into more subnets, it can use /29 to split the /27 range into 4 subnets (29–27 = 2, and $2^2=4$) with 8 (32–29 = 3, and $2^3=8$) hosts each. The subnets are 128.0.0.224, 128.0.0.232, 128.0.0.240, and 128.0.0.248. Each subnet has 8 hosts, but for every subnet, you lose 0 and 255, so you practically lose 4×2 = 8 IP addresses in the process.

As mentioned, most implementations today use private IP addresses internally and map these IP addresses to public IPs using NAT. The Internet Assigned Numbers Authority (IANA) reserved the following three CIDR blocks for private IP addresses: 10.0.0.0/8, 172.16.0.0/12, and 192.168.0.0/16. With the 128.0.1.0/27 allocation, an enterprise saves the 30 public addresses for accessing their servers publicly and uses as many private IP addresses and subnets internally.

However, early designs used what is called private VLANs to save on the IP space. Although this method is not straightforward and needs a lot of maintenance, it is still out there. This topic is covered briefly because it is revisited later in the book when discussing endpoint groups (EPGs) in Chapter 17, "Application-Centric Infrastructure."

Private VLANs

This is a mechanism that allows one VLAN, called a primary VLAN (PVLAN), to be split into multiple sub-VLANs, called secondary community VLANs. The IP address space within the PVLAN can now be spread over multiple secondary VLANs, which can be isolated from each other. In a way, this removes the restriction of having one subnet per VLAN, which gives more flexibility in IP address assignment. In the traditional north-south type of traffic, this allows the same subnet to be segmented into sub-VLANs, where each sub-VLAN is its own broadcast domain, and flooding is limited. The secondary community VLANs allow hosts to talk to one another within the community. Any host from one secondary community VLAN that needs to talk to another secondary community VLAN must go through an L3 router for inter-VLAN routing. This is illustrated in Figure 1-6.

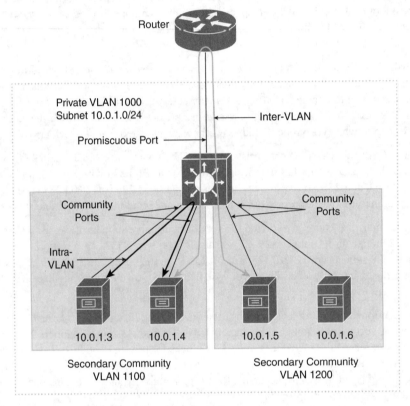

Figure 1-6 *Primary and Secondary VLANs*

The switch ports that connect to the hosts are community *switch ports*, whereas switch ports that connect to the router are called *promiscuous ports*. Ports within the same community talk to each other and to the promiscuous port. Ports between communities must go through the router. Note that hosts 10.0.1.3 and 10.0.1.4 belong to secondary community VLAN 1100, and hosts 10.0.1.5 and 10.0.1.6 belong to secondary community VLAN 1200. All of these hosts belong to the same IP subnet, but they are segmented by the secondary VLANs. So, although 10.0.1.4 talks directly to 10.0.1.3 through intra-VLAN switching, it needs to go through an L3 router to reach 10.0.1.5 or 10.0.1.6 through inter-VLAN routing.

The discussed example is simplistic. As you add multiple access switches and aggregation switches, you need to decide whether L3 routing is done in the aggregation layer or in the core layer. Also, as more and more sub-VLANs are created, such VLANs need to be carried across the network and maintained on every switch. Although these methods give flexibility in decoupling subnets from VLANs, they also add extra overhead. When Cisco's implementation of EPGs is discussed, the decoupling of IP subnets from VLANs will become much clearer, and the whole deployment model will become automated as complexities are hidden from the end user.

Flooding of Broadcast, Unknown Unicast, and Multicast (BUM) Traffic

A main issue of L2 networks is flooding of BUM traffic. Each station needs to have an IP address–to–MAC address mapping to send traffic to a certain IP address on a LAN. If a source station is trying to reach another destination station and it does not know its IP-to-MAC address mapping, an address resolution protocol (ARP) packet is sent to a broadcast address. If a VLAN is configured, then the broadcast address is flooded by a switch to all switch ports that belong to that VLAN. Whenever a device sees the ARP request for its own IP address, it responds to the source station with its MAC address. The source station that sent the original ARP request stores the IP-to-MAC address mapping in its ARP table, and from then on it uses the MAC address it learned to send traffic to the destination station. This is seen in Figure 1-7.

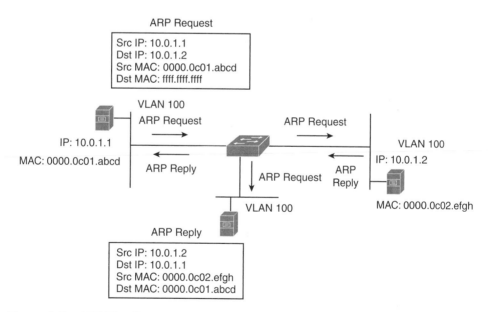

Figure 1-7 *ARP Flooding*

As seen in Figure 1-7, server 1 (S1) with IP 10.0.1.1 must send traffic to server 2 (S2) with IP 10.0.1.2, which is in the same subnet. The switch is configured to have subnet 10.0.1.0/24 mapped to VLAN 100. If S1 does not know the MAC address of S2, it sends an ARP request with a broadcast MAC address of ffff.ffff.ffff. If the switch does not have the IP/MAC address mapping in its ARP table, it floods the ARP to all the ports that belong to VLAN 100. Once S2 sees the ARP, it responds with its MAC address 0000.0c02.efgh directly to S1 (0000.0c01.abcd). After that, S1, S2, and the switch update their own ARP tables.

ARP broadcast is one type of packet that is flooded. Other types could be unknown unicast or multicast. Say, for example, that S1 knows the MAC address of S2 and sends a packet to 0000.0c02.efgh; however, the switch flushed his ARP table and does not know the mapping. In that case, the switch floods that packet to all of its ports on VLAN 100 until a station replies; after that, the switch updates its ARP.

The problem of flooding consumes bandwidth, and many measures are taken to limit it. A side effect of flooding is broadcast storms that are created by loops, as discussed next.

Loop Prevention Via Spanning Tree

The problem with L2 networks is in the potential of broadcast storms occurring in case of loops. Say that an ARP packet is flooded over all switch ports, and that packet finds its way back to the switch that flooded it because of a loop in the network. That broadcast packet circulates in the network forever. Spanning trees ensure that loops do not occur by blocking ports that contribute to the loop. This means that although some ports are active and passing traffic, others are blocked and not used. This is seen in Figure 1-8. Note that an ARP packet that is flooded by SW1 and then flooded by SW4 could return to SW1 and create a loop. To avoid this situation, spanning tree blocks the redundant paths to prevent loops from occurring and hence prevent potential broadcast storms.

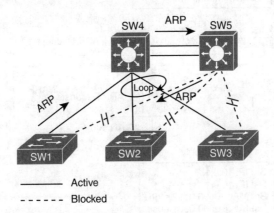

Figure 1-8 *Loop Prevention Via Spanning Tree*

The drawback is that expensive resources such as high-speed interfaces remain idle and unused. More efficient designs use every link and resource in the network.

Firewall Overload

Another issue with the existing three-tier design is that the firewalls that are traditionally connected to the aggregation layer become a catch for all traffic. These firewalls were originally meant to enforce policies on north-south traffic between the Internet and the data center. Because the traffic in the data center dramatically increased as east-west between the multiple application tiers, securing the data center from the inside is now essential. As such, policy enforcement for east-west traffic now must go through the same firewalls. This is seen in Figure 1-9. With practically all traffic going to the firewall, the firewall rules are enormous. Normally, administrators define such policies for a specific service, and when the service disappears, the policies remain in the firewall. For anyone who has worked with ACLs and setting firewall rules, it is well known that nobody dares to touch or delete a rule from the firewall for fear of breaking traffic or affecting an application. Moving into hyperconverged infrastructures and a two-tier design, you see how policy enforcement for applications shifts from being VLAN centric to application centric. Cisco's ACI and VMware's networking and security software product (NSX), covered later in this book, describe how policies are enforced in a hyperconverged environment.

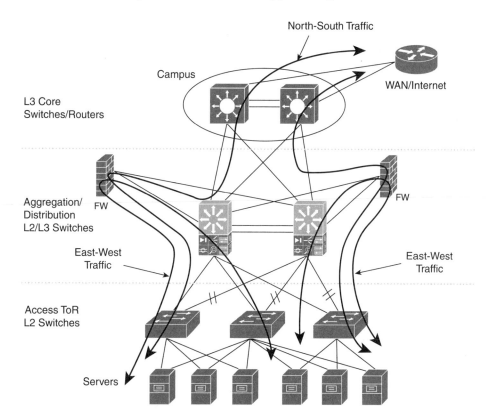

Figure 1-9 *Firewall Overload*

With so many issues in legacy data centers, newer data center designs are making modifications, including these:

- Moving away from the three-tier architecture to a two-tier leaf and spine architecture

- Moving L3 into the access layer and adopting L2 tunneling over L3 networks

- Implementing link aggregation technologies such as virtual port channel (vPC) and multichassis link aggregation (MLAG) to offer greater efficiency by making all links in the network active; traffic is load-balanced between different switches

- Moving firewall policies for east-west traffic from the aggregation layer to the access layer or directly attaching them to the application

The preceding enhancements and more are discussed in detail in Part VI of this book, "Hyperconverged Networking."

Looking Ahead

If you look at the combined picture of data networking and storage networks, it is obvious that something must change. Storage traffic constitutes different protocols, such as Internet Small Computer System Interface (iSCSI), Network File System (NFS), Server Message Block (SMB), and others. Merging such protocols with data traffic over an oversubscribed infrastructure can have huge implications on the stability of storage access and the performance of applications. Also, networking in general needs to move from complex manual configuration to a more automated and dynamic way of network deployment. The advances in switching and routing hardware and software allow you to dramatically simplify the network and minimize the tiers. Advances in server virtualization have changed the way servers and compute are deployed in the data center, which challenges the existing storage networking designs. Hyperconvergence collapses the compute, networking, and storage tiers, offering a pay-as-you-grow approach to storage.

However, the basic needs of the enterprises do not change. Simplifying network deployments should not come at the expense of having highly available and robust networks. To understand the benefits of hyperconvergence, it helps to understand the current storage deployments and their challenges. You cannot solve a problem if you do not understand what the problem is.

Chapter 2, "Storage Networks: Existing Designs," discusses some storage basics that might be familiar to a storage administrator but challenging for a virtualization or a networking engineer. It covers the storage multitier architecture; block, file, and object file systems; storage connectivity; storage protocols and protection methods; and advanced storage functionality. Part II of this book, "Evolution in Host Hardware and Software," discusses the evolution in compute, storage, and networking that allows you to build next-generation hyperconverged data centers.

Chapter 2

Storage Networks: Existing Designs

This chapter covers the following key topics:

- **The Storage View of Multitier Designs:** Offers a high-level description of the three-tier storage network from the point of view of a storage administrator.

- **Types of Disk Drives:** Discusses types of disk drives commonly used in enterprise networks, such as HDD SAS, HDD SATA, SAS SED, fibre channel, and SSDs.

- **Disk Performance:** Covers disk performance, which is affected by the type of drive and the server interconnect. Performance metrics such as transfer speed, throughput, latency, access times, and IOPS are described.

- **RAID:** Highlights different RAID systems, which offer a variety of data protection and faster I/O access.

- **Storage Controllers:** Describes the functions of storage controllers, such as fibre channel and iSCSI, inside hosts and storage arrays.

- **Logical Unit Numbers:** Explains how RAID systems are partitioned into logical unit numbers and volumes to hide the physical disk from the operating system.

- **Logical Volume Manager:** Describes how RAID systems are partitioned into volumes to hide the physical disk from the operating system.

- **Block, File, and Object-Level Storage:** Covers the different types of storage technologies and how various applications use them.

- **Storage-to-ServerConnectivity:** Discusses how storage connects to servers via direct-attached storage (DAS) or via the network using network-attached storage (NAS) and storage area networks (SANs). Describes SAN fibre channel and iSCSI addressing and switching and network security such as zoning and masking.

■ **Storage Efficiency Technologies:** Distinguishes between storage efficiency technologies such as thin provisioning, types of snapshots, cloning, source- and target-based deduplication, inline and post-process deduplication, compression, storage encryption, storage tiering, and so on.

Although some of the information in this chapter might be familiar to information technology (IT) storage professionals, it might not be too obvious to those with a system software or data networking background. Evolution in the storage space is moving quickly, and storage professionals must keep up with the advances in technology. This chapter discusses some storage basics, such as the different types of drives, storage protocols, and storage functionality, which set the stage for more advanced topics in future chapters. Next, it examines the different types of drives and storage protocols.

The Storage View of Multitier Designs

When speaking with storage vendors, the whole data networking piece of the puzzle disappears and turns into a simple black box. As you saw in Chapter 1, "Data Networks: Existing Designs," the black box has many knobs, and it can get complex, so do not take it lightly. With storage vendors, the focus turns to servers, storage controllers, file systems, disks, and backup. Convergence and hyperconvergence emerged to solve the complexities of storage performance and management. However, in doing so the traditional storage networking technologies are heading in the direction of data networking technologies with the adoption of Internet Protocol (IP) and Gigabit Ethernet (GE) networks. From a storage network view, the three tiers are the servers, the storage network, and the disks. Each tier has its share of interoperability and compatibility issues. This is mainly because server vendors had to deal with operating system compatibility issues with network interfaces and disk controllers, disk vendors went through many iterations to improve disk capacity and speeds, and storage networking vendors had to figure out how to deal with the multiple storage protocols like Fibre Channel, Network File System (NFS), and Internet Small Computer System Interface (iSCSI).

The server tier is composed of the servers that provide the processing and compute to run the different applications. The storage network tier is made up of storage switches such as fibre channel (FC) switches—or GE switches in the case of iSCSI or NFS. The storage disks tier contains the actual disks. Hyperconvergence attempts to combine all these tiers into one product that unites the compute, storage network, and disks, and integrates with the data network. Figure 2-1 shows the storage view of a multitier storage architecture and how it relates to the data networking view that was previously discussed. This is one type of storage application. Several others are discussed later in this chapter.

Notice that in the storage view of this example, servers are connected to the storage network via FC switches, and the switches are connected to storage arrays. Storage arrays contain storage controllers to handle the storage transactions and house the actual disks where the data exists. In the cases of iSCSI and NFS, the storage network tier is normally built with GE and 10 GE switches. Regardless of which technology is used for the storage protocols and storage networks, this adds extra layers of complexity to deal with. This is an area that hyperconvergence solves by collapsing the layers and by addressing the performance and management issues of converging data and storage traffic over a unified fabric.

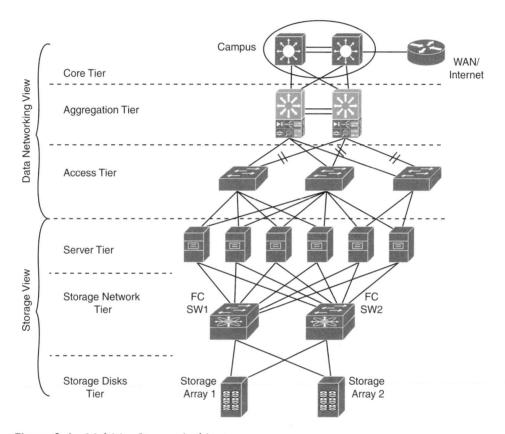

Figure 2-1   *Multitier Storage Architecture*

To fully understand the issues with storage networks, you must start with the different types of disks and the challenges they have in access speeds and durability.

Types of Disk Drives

There are different types of disk drives: hard drives, solid-state drives, optical drives, tape drives, flash drives, and so on. Let's examine a sample of the most typical drives that you encounter in data centers. Optical drives and tape drives are not discussed here.

Hard Disk Drives

Hard disk drives (HDDs) are the lowest cost drives on the market (ignoring tape drives). They are formed of platters that spin around a spindle, with information being read or written by changing the magnetic fields on the spinning platters. A read/write head hovering above the platter seeks the information from the platter. The platter is formed of tracks and sectors, as illustrated in Figure 2-2. The hard disk access time is one of the factors that affects the performance of the application. The access time is the total of the seek time, which is the time it takes the read/write head to move from one track to another, and the time it takes the head to reach the correct sector on the rotating platters. HDDs are cost effective, but they contribute to high access times, they consume a lot of power, and they are prone to failure just because they are mechanical devices.

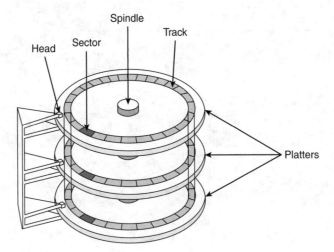

Figure 2-2 *Hard Disk Drive Tracks and Sectors*

HDDs connect to other peripherals via different types of interfaces, including Serial Advanced Technology Attachment (SATA) and Serial Attached Small Computer System Interface (SAS). It is worth noting that although SATA and SAS are interfaces that connect different types of drives to the computer or server, the drives themselves are usually named SATA drives and SAS drives. Other types of drives are the FC drives. The decision to use SATA, SAS, or FC drives depends on price and performance.

SATA Drives

SATA drives are suited for applications that require less disk performance and less workload. The SATA platter speed is 7200 revolutions per minute (RPMs) as used on servers; older, lower platter speeds such as 5400 RPM drives are normally used on computers. A combination of high-performance SATA drives and controllers is used as a cost-effective solution in building server disk arrays. SATA drives use the Advanced Technology Attachment (ATA) command for data transfer.

SAS Drives

SAS drives are suited for applications that require higher disk performance and higher workload. The SAS platter speed is a maximum 15,000 RPM; 10,000 RPM disks are available as well. SAS capacity is much smaller and more expensive per gigabyte than SATA drives. SAS drives are better suited for servers, especially at lower capacity requirements; however, for high-capacity requirements, the steep price of SAS might outweigh the performance benefits. Other networked storage solutions might be more suited. SAS drives use the SCSI command set. Both SAS drives and SATA drives can plug in a SAS backplane; SAS cannot plug in a SATA backplane.

SAS Self-Encrypting Drives

SAS self-encryption drives (SEDs) allow the automatic encryption and decryption of data by the disk controller. SED protects the data from theft and does not affect the performance of the application because the encryption and decryption are done in hardware. SAS SED drives are more expensive than regular SAS drives. SAS SED drives come as SAS SED HDDs or SAS SED SSDs.

FC Drives

Fibre channel (FC) drives are suited for enterprise server applications. They have similar performance to SAS drives but are more expensive. FC connectivity is via multimode fibre. Although FC drives have similar performance to SAS, most of the hard drives in the market continue to be SAS or a combination of SAS and SATA. FC leads as a connectivity method for storage area networks (SANs), and it carries the SCSI command set over the network. SAN connectivity is dominated by fibre channel, but the actual hard disks in SAN arrays are SASs.

Solid-State Drives

Unlike HDDs, solid-state drives (SSDs) have no motors, reading heads, or spinning platters; they are basically built with no moving parts. Early SSDs were built based on random access memory (RAM); however, the latest SSDs are based on flash memory. SSDs are a lot more expensive than HDDs and offer much higher performance because, unlike HDDs that rely on a moving head and spinning platter to read/write the information, SSDs rely on an embedded processor to store, retrieve, and erase data. SSDs have fewer capacities than HDDs, but next-generation SSDs keep increasing in capacity to compete with HDD capacity. SSDs like HDDs connect to peripherals via interfaces. SSDs connect to servers via a SATA interface, or SAS.

Disk Performance

Disk performance for reads and writes depends on factors such as the disk media itself—whether it is an HDD or an SSD—disk queue depth, and other factors such as the interconnect between the disk and the server. This section discusses factors that affect disk performance and the terminology used in the industry. Next, let's examine transfer speeds in terms of throughput, latency, and input/output operations per second (IOPS).

Throughput or Transfer Speed

The transfer speed is essentially the rate at which data is transferred to and from the disk media in a certain period of time. Transfer speed is measured in megabytes per second (MBps) or gigabits per second (Gbps), keeping in mind that 1 Gigabit = 1000 Megabits, so 1 Gbps = 1000 / 8 = 125 MBps. Transfer speed is affected by the actual bus connecting the disk. There are different bus interconnects:

- **SATA:** SATA 1 has a 1.5 Gbps transfer speed, SATA 2 is at 3 Gbps, and SATA 3 is at 6 Gbps. So, for example, a 3 Gbps SATA 2 connection has a 3 × 1000 / 8 = 375 MBps transfer speed, and with overhead it decreases to 300 MBps. In contrast, a SATA 3 connection works at 6 Gbps or 6 × 1000 / 8 = 750 MBps transfer speed, and with overhead it decreases to 600 MBps.

- **SAS:** SAS 1 has a transfer speed of 3 Gbps, SAS 2 is 6 Gbps, SAS 3 is 12 Gbps, and SAS 4 is 22.5 Gbps.

Other interfaces are Peripheral Component Interconnect express (PCIe) and Non-Volatile Memory express (NVMe), which are described in Chapter 3, "Host Hardware Evolution."

Access Time

Access time, discussed earlier, is the overall measure, normally in milliseconds, of the time it takes to start the data transfer operation. Because SSDs have no moving parts, they have much lower access times than HDDs. The access times depend on the vendors' implementations. Typical access times for HDDs are in the 10-millisecond range or less, whereas access times of SSDs are in the 100 microsecond range or less, which is magnitudes faster. The SSD access times continue to decrease.

Latency and IOPS

Other performance indicators that enterprises and data centers designers rely on when looking at disk performance are latency and IOPS.

Latency is defined as the time it takes to complete an I/O operation. This differs whether you are looking at latency from a disk perspective or from a host/application perspective. If, for example, a disk can perform a single I/O operation in 10 ms, the latency from the disk perspective is 10 ms. But if two I/O operations arrive at the same time, the second operation must wait for the first to finish, and the total time for both I/Os to finish becomes 20 ms. Therefore, from an application perspective, the latency is 20 ms.

IOPS is the maximum number of I/O operations per second; an input operation is a write, and an output operation is a read. IOPS is measured as an integer number, such as 210 IOPS or 10,000 IOPS. IOPS are important in applications such as databases that handle a lot of I/O requests in small block sizes in a short time. So even though two disks might have the same capacity, the disk with the highest IOPS handles a lot more operations in a short amount of time. Different factors affect IOPS, including the access time for the disk to perform the operation and the queue depth. The *queue depth* refers to the outstanding I/O operations that a disk attempts to perform in parallel. This can offer a multiplying effect for increasing the IOPS. A host bus adapter (HBA) that supports a queue depth of 4 will have almost four times the IOPS as an HBA with a queue depth of 1. This, of course, depends on whether you are considering SSDs or HDDs. SSDs, for example, have multiple channels, where a larger queue depth translates in more I/O being done in parallel. With HDDs, the effect of queue depth is limited by the fact that spinning disks and moving heads constrain which operations can be done in parallel.

Another factor to consider when looking at IOPS is the I/O transfer size. Many operating systems and applications perform I/O operations in different block sizes. Some will do I/O with 4 KB block size; others will do it with 64 KB, and so on. A disk that can achieve 10,000 IOPS at 64 KB block size is more powerful than one that achieves the same IOPS at 4 KB block size.

IOPS in general has an inverse relationship with latency from an application perspective. Therefore, if an application calculates overall latency of 0.01 ms, the disk IOPS should be in the range of 1/0.01 = 100,000 IOPS.

SSD drives deliver far more IOPS than HDD SATA or SAS drives—normally in the tens and hundreds of thousands and even reaching a million IOPS, and especially in randomized data patterns and smaller block sizes. Other factors affecting performance for local disks are interface speeds, data being sequential or randomized, whether you are doing a read or a write operation, and the number of disks and the fault tolerance level in disk arrays.

Another factor that affects performance is how data is read or written on the disk. If you are reading or writing large files in large block sizes in a sequential fashion, there isn't much movement of the disk head, so the access times are smaller. However, on the other extreme, if data is stored on the disk in small blocks and in a random fashion, the access times to read and write are much larger, which reduces performance. In random patterns, there are a lot of disk seeks with HDDs that reduce performance.

The performance of disks also depends on the disk interface, such as SATA and SAS. It is important that the I/O bandwidth resulting from the IOPS operations does not exceed the disk throughput or transfer speed; otherwise, the interface speed becomes the bottleneck. For example, an SSD disk handling 200,000 IOPS for 4 K (as in 4 KB) data blocks is actually transferring 200,000 × 4KB = 800,000 KBps, or 800 MBps. As you'll recall, you calculated the theoretical transfer speed of a SATA 3 interface at 6 Gbps, or 750 MBps. So, at 200,000 IOPS, the I/O bandwidth that a disk can handle exceeds the interface's theoretical limit, and the interface becomes a bottleneck. As such, it is important that faster IOPS be matched with faster interface speeds. On the other hand, IOPS are related to the number of disks in a redundant array of independent (or inexpensive) disks (RAID) system, as discussed next.

RAID

The RAID (Redundant Array of Independent Disks) system was created under the notion that multiple smaller and inexpensive disks have better performance than one large and expensive disk. This is because if multiple disks are doing read/write operations in parallel, data is accessed faster than with a single disk. This assumes *data striping*, which is equally dividing the data between the multiple disks. So, for example, if there are five blocks of data to be read on one large disk, the access time (time to move between tracks and reach a sector) is multiplied by 5. If five disks are doing the operation in parallel, there is one access time to read all data.

Other than performance, RAID systems offer a more reliable and available storage system to withstand failures of individual disks. As such, different RAID levels were created depending on the required balance between performance, reliability, and availability. Let's look at some of the most popular RAID systems: RAID 0, 1, 1+0, and 0+1, 5, and 6.

RAID 0

RAID 0 combines all drives into one giant drive—mainly like a JBOD (just a bunch of disks)—however, it stripes (equally divides) the data across all disks. This striping improves the performance because all disks seek portions of the data at the same time. RAID 0 has no fault tolerance; if one disk fails, the whole data is lost. Notice in Figure 2-3a how equal-sized blocks B1, B2, B3 are equally striped on three disks.

RAID 1

RAID 1 offers disk mirroring. Say that a disk array has eight disks. Four of these disks are an exact duplicate of the others. From a performance level, read/write speeds are very good, and from a fault-tolerance level, if one disk fails, there is a ready mirror copy of that disk, so data is not lost. The disadvantage of RAID 1 is that half of the capacity is lost; therefore, 8 × 1 Terabyte (TB) drives actually give 4 TB of capacity. Notice in Figure 2-3b how data blocks B1, B2, and B3 are mirrored across two disks.

RAID 1+0

RAID 1+0 is a combination of a RAID 0 and a RAID 1 and requires a minimum of four disks. It is a stripe of mirrored set (stripe + mirror). RAID 0 stripes the data between different arrays, but RAID 1 mirrors the drives within the array. This is seen in Figure 2-4a. The advantage of RAID 1+0 is good read/write performance and the ability to protect against disk failure. Its disadvantage is that if a set of mirrored disks fails—for example, if both disk 1 and its mirror disk 2 fail in the same array—then the whole data ends up being lost. Add to this the fact that half of the capacity of the array is lost because of mirroring.

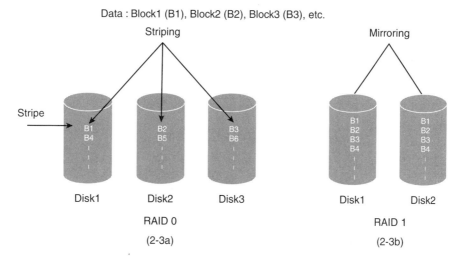

Figure 2-3   *RAID 0, RAID 1 Example*

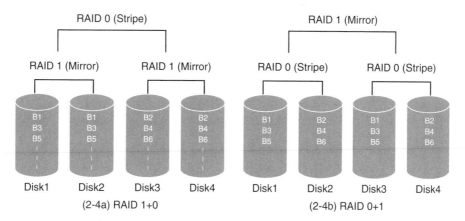

Figure 2-4   *RAID 1+0 (left) and RAID 0+1 (right) Examples*

RAID 0+1

RAID 0+1 is a combination of RAID 1 and RAID 0. It is a mirror of a striped set (mirror + stripe). RAID 1 mirrors the data between arrays, whereas RAID 0 stripes the data between the drives of the same array. This is seen on the right side of Figure 2-4. The advantage of RAID 0+1 is good read/write performance and the ability to protect against disk failure. RAID 0+1 has better protection than RAID 1+0. If disk 1 and disk 2 in the same array fail, the data is still available on the other array. However, if disks with similar data fail, such as disk 1 and disk 3, the data is lost.

RAID 5

RAID 5, which works with block-level striping and distributed parity, requires at least three disks to operate. Blocks of data are striped across all disks at the same layer, except for the last disk, where instead of a data block, parity data is stored. The parity data allows the data to be reconstructed at that layer if one of the disks fails. For example, let's say that you have disk 1, disk 2, disk 3, and disk 4, as seen in Figure 2-5a (top).

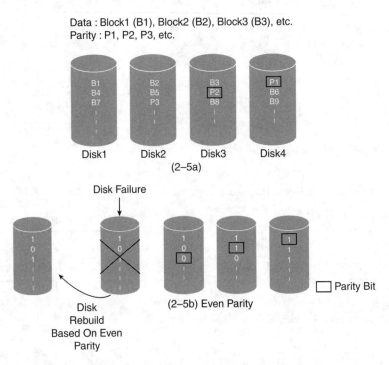

Figure 2-5   *RAID 5 and Parity Example*

Assume that you have data blocks B1, B2, B3, B4, and more. At the first layer you have B1, B2, B3, and P1, where P1 is the parity data at the first layer. On the second layer you have B4, B5, P2, and B6, and at the third layer B7, P3, B8, B9, and so forth. Notice how the parity data is moving positions between layers. If any of the disks fails, the other disks can be used to construct the full data.

It helps to understand what parity is. A parity is like a checksum that reconstructs the data. Let's use the concept of a parity bit as an example. A parity bit is a bit added to a string of binary code that indicates whether the number of 1s in the string should be even or odd. An even parity means that the total number of 1s in the string should be even, as in 1,1 or 1,1,1,1. An odd parity means that the total number of 1s should be odd, as in 1 or 1,1,1 or 1,1,1,1,1. So, in this example of four disks as seen in Figure 2-5b (bottom image), and assuming you are using even parity, if at the first layer you have B1 = 1, B2 = 1, and B3 = 1, P1 should be 1 because between B1, B2, and B3 you have an odd number of 1s. If disk 1 fails, B1 is lost, but you still have B2 = 1, B3 = 1, and P1 = 1. Because you are using even parity, B1 must be a 1 to make the number of 1s even. This is basically how data is reconstructed.

RAID 5 has a good read performance because the data exists on all disks, but it suffers in write performance. Calculating the parity at each layer takes a performance hit, so the write performance suffers. The advantage of RAID 5 is good fault tolerance because data can be reconstructed; the disadvantage is that it takes a long time to reconstruct the data. To solve performance issues with write and with data reconstruction, you can use a RAID controller to offload the host CPU and accelerate performance. Also, because you have parity information that uses capacity at each layer on each disk, the capacity of one full disk in the array is lost to ensure data can be reconstructed. So, if you have four disks at 1 TB each, the capacity of the array becomes 3 TB. That is still better than RAID 1, where the capacity is 2 TB because of mirroring.

RAID 6

RAID 6 works exactly like RAID 5, with the same advantages and disadvantages, but with the added value that it sustains two disk failures instead of one disk failure as in RAID 5. This is because parity information is written on two disks in the array at each layer, as seen in Figure 2-6. This, of course, makes write performance even worse because of the parity calculation, and it makes disk reconstruction upon failure slower. Also, the use of a RAID controller alleviates performance issues. Capacity on RAID 6 is also affected because you lose the full capacity of two disks in the array due to the parity information. If you have five disks with 1 TB each, the actual capacity is 3 TB because you lose the capacity of two disks on parity.

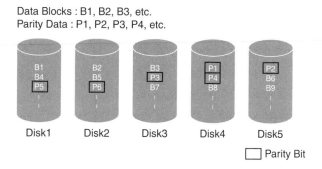

Figure 2-6 *RAID 6, Double Parity Example*

For the purpose of completeness, let's discuss how IOPS is affected when dealing with multiple disks, as in RAID arrays. So far, this chapter has examined how parity affects the write performance in RAID 5 and 6 as an example. RAID systems incur a "RAID penalty" every time parity is read or written. For example, in RAID 5, where data and parity are striped and distributed over all disks, every time there is a change in data, you have to read the data and read the parity and then write the data and write the parity, so consider the penalty as 4. While in RAID 6, for every change in data you have to read the data, read the parity twice, and then write the data and write the parity twice, so consider the penalty as 6. The formula for calculating IOPS in a RAID system is as follows:

Raw IOPS = Disk Speed IOPS * Number of Disks

Functional IOPS = (RAW IOPS * Write % / RAID Penalty) + (RAW IOPS * Read %)

Let's say that you have an SSD drive with RAW IOPS of 100,000. Assume that you have four such drives in a RAID 5 array. Now assume that 40% of the I/O operations are a read and 60% are a write. Knowing that RAID 5 incurs a RAID penalty of 4, the calculations are as follows:

Raw IOPS = 100,000 * 5 = 500,000 IOPS

Functional IOPS = (500,000 * 0.6/4) + (500,000 * 0.4) = 275,000 IOPS

Notice that the IOPS of the RAID system is almost half of the expected RAW IOPS. Therefore, if the application requires 500,000 IOPS from the RAID array, you need at least five disks at 200,000 IOPS each or more to end up with functional IOPS of 550,000.

The RAID functionality runs in what is called RAID controllers, or a combination of RAID controllers and host bus adapters. The next section gives a brief overview on controllers to familiarize you with the terminology.

Storage Controllers

Storage controllers are essential to perform storage functions such as disk volume management and presenting the disks as different levels of RAID arrays. The storage controllers take a set of physical disks and configure them as physical partitions called logical disks or virtual disks. The controller then takes the virtual disks and creates logical unit numbers (LUNs) that are presented to the operating system (OS) as volumes. LUNs are discussed in the next section.

To eliminate any confusion, let's distinguish the terminology:

- The host bus adapter (HBA)
- Software-based host RAID controller
- Hardware-based host RAID controller
- Storage processor or standalone RAID controllers

An HBA is a hardware adapter that connects to the server Peripheral Component Interconnect (PCI) bus or PCI express (PCIe) on the front end and to the storage devices on the back end. The HBA houses the storage ports such as SATA or SAS or FC for disk connectivity. The software-based host RAID controller is part of the server motherboard and performs the RAID functions in the server central processing unit (CPU). In its higher performance form, the RAID controller is a hardware adapter that connects to the server motherboard and offloads the storage functions from the main host CPU. When disks are connected to the controller or added and removed, the controller detects the disks, performs the RAID-level function on its onboard processor, and presents to the OS the multiple disks as logical units. HBAs and hardware RAID can be combined in one adapter. Because traditionally the host CPUs were lower speed and had performance issues, the RAID controllers were essential to increase the storage performance. As CPU power increases on the main host CPUs, most of the controller functionality is absorbed by the main CPU at the expense of burning valuable CPU cycles.

Last, let's discuss the storage processors, also referred to as external RAID controllers. The storage processors are standalone RAID controllers that usually come with dual processors and are packaged with the disk arrays in the same unit. The SAN architecture is mainly based on having one or multiple storage processors connected to the SAN fabric in a redundant manner. The storage processor is a souped-up version of the host RAID controller. It offloads the hosts from all RAID functionality as well as other storage efficiency technology such as thin provisioning, snapshots, cloning, deduplication, compression, and auto tiering. For the rest of this book, storage processors are referred to as *storage controllers*.

Now that you have used RAID levels to group multiple disks into a larger disk with a certain level of performance and protection, consider LUNs as a first level of logical abstraction of the storage system.

Logical Unit Numbers

LUNs are a logical representation or a logical reference point to a physical disk, or partitions of a disk in RAID arrays. LUNs allow easier control of the storage resources in a SAN by hiding the physical aspect of the disk and presenting portions of the disk as mountable volumes to the operating system. LUNs work differently with FC and iSCSI.

In the case of FC, the initiator is normally a server with an FC HBA that initiates the connection to one or more ports on the storage system. The targets are the ports on the storage system where you access the volumes. These volumes are none other than the LUNs.

In the case of iSCSI, the initiator is the server with the iSCSI host adapter or iSCSI software running on the server that initiates the connection. However, the target is not the port that presents the LUN but rather an iSCSI target such as the IP address of a network-connected storage system. The iSCSI target must manage the connection between the initiator and the LUN.

By assigning LUNs, the physical disks are hidden, and the operating system sees only the logical portions of the disks presented as mountable volumes mapped to LUN 0, LUN 1, LUN 2, and so on. A LUN is identified by a 16-bit hexadecimal number. Figure 2-7 shows how LUNs are used to represent partitions or volumes of physical disks.

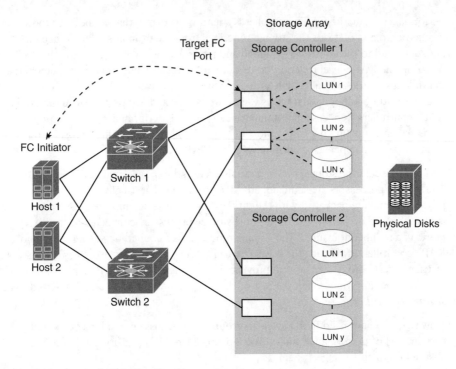

Figure 2-7 *Logical Unit Number Representation*

At one point in time, LUNs were considered a good level of virtualization because they hid the hardware and presented a logical view of the storage. However, as both storage and compute scaled and moved from physical to virtual machines, LUN management became problematic. LUNs created big issues in storage mainly due to the rigid LUN characteristics of storage arrays. Such issues include the following:

- **LUN Maximum Sizes:** LUNs have maximum sizes depending on the vendor. The sizes are large enough, but the downside is that there is a limit. If the limit is exceeded, a different LUN must be created, which poses a problem with virtual machine-to-LUN mapping because virtual machines are tied to LUNs.

- **Number of LUNs:** LUNs also have a maximum number, which depends on the specific vendors and the specific products. If the total number of LUNs is exceeded, data must be rearranged to fit the existing LUNs.

- **Virtual Machines (VMs):** VMs are tied to datastores, which are tied to LUNs. You must track which VM is tied to which LUN; whenever a VM moves, you have to follow the VM to LUN PATH through the fabric.

- **LUN Dimensioning:** Creating the LUN size is critical. Be sure to make initial good sizing estimates for storage needs. If, down the line, you find that the storage is over-allocated, disk space is wasted. On the other hand, if storage is underallocated, there is a need to extend the LUNs or create a new and bigger LUN and then move the data to the new LUN. Extending LUNs might cause performance issues if the data ends up fragmented over multiple storage arrays. Furthermore, creating new LUNs and moving the data in operational environments require careful planning.

- **LUN Security Especially in SAN Environments:** Because multiple hosts connect to the SAN and each host potentially has access to any LUN in the storage arrays, possible conflicts occur. Some HBAs, for example, support 8 buses per HBA, 128 targets per bus, and 255 LUNs per target. The SAN fabric handles a large number of nodes, so conflicts arise. Conflicts occur when multiple applications running on the same host see the same LUNs. Conflicts also occur on the network itself when different hosts access the same LUNs. Security measures to ensure a host has access to specific sets of LUNs are taken via functionality such as LUN masking and zoning. Such measures are implemented in different places such as the host software, the host HBA, the storage controller on the storage system, or via the network switches.

LUN management is not easy. Headaches are introduced in sizing, securing, and accessing LUNs. Remember that the administrators creating the LUNs and configuring access to the LUNs—that is, the storage engineers—are different from the administrators using the LUNs—that is, the system software or virtualization engineers. Going back and forth between the different functional groups is extremely tedious and inefficient. Imagine a virtualization administrator who requested a certain LUN size and IOPS coming back to the storage administrator asking for more storage and higher performance because the application he is using is not performing well under the current disk space and IOPS. The storage administrator must decide whether to extend the LUN or create a completely new one. Depending on how masking and zoning were done for the particular host, the administrator would have to reconfigure the zones or the masks depending on the new LUN location. Also, if the storage administrator decides to extend the LUN and the storage ends up in a different array, the host might have performance issues, making the situation much worse. Depending on what is decided, the storage engineer must decide how to move the data to a different LUN, back up the existing data, and make sure no data loss or outages occur in the process. Note that the issues in LUN sizing and accessibility apply whether you are talking about FC or iSCSI. The issue is not in the network itself, although things can be harder or easier depending on whether you are dealing with an FC fabric or a TCP/IP fabric. The issue is in the concept of having LUNs in the first place and having to do LUN addressing on a shared network. Hyperconvergence will eventually solve this problem.

Logical Volume Manager

This chapter has already discussed how different RAID levels group multiple disks and enhance the performance, redundancy, and fault tolerance of disk arrays. RAID groups the disks at the physical level, and the end result is a bigger physical disk or disks that have certain levels of performance and protection. LUNs, on the other hand, take the resulting RAID array as the starting point and offer a logical view of the disks, segmenting the RAID array into logical disks. From a storage point view, the LUNs are still another set of disks with different capacities and that have a logical unit number. However, from a host operating system point of view, the LUNs still look like a bunch of disks with block-level storage. Operating systems work with volumes—hence, the need

for another level of abstraction to be created using a logical volume manager (LVM).
The LVM takes the LUN as a starting point and performs all kinds of operations. The
LVM manipulates and creates different types of LUNs, including the following:

- Simple LUNs that represent a single physical disk

- Concatenated LUNs that treat multiple disks as a single disk

- Spanned LUNs, in which portions of the LUN exist on multiple disks

- Striped LUNs, in which data is spread equally and accessed at the same time on
  multiple disks

- Striped LUNs with parity for protection

- Mirrored LUNs

The LVM presents the LUNs to the OS as volumes. It takes portions of LUNs and
presents them to the OS as smaller volumes, or it combines multiple LUNs in a larger
volume. The volume is then formatted with the appropriate file system. So in the case
of Windows, the volume file system is the New Technology File System (NTFS), and in
UNIX/Linux machines, the volume file system is the extended file system (ext4 as an
example). Figure 2-8 shows the physical, logical, and volume levels of storage.

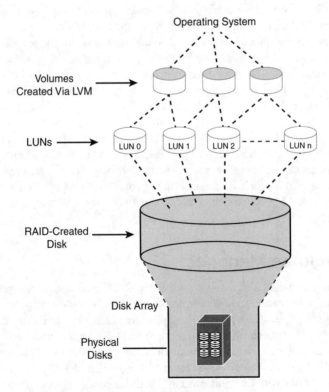

Figure 2-8   *Difference Between Volumes and LUNs*

As shown, the disk arrays are partitioned using different RAID levels. After that, LUNs are created to offer a logical view of the disks. The LVM starts with the LUNs and presents them as volumes to the host operating system. The volumes are then formatted with the appropriate file systems.

Block-, File-, and Object-Level Storage

Storage is used by applications that have different requirements. An engineering firm has a requirement to gather all files in a central location and allows all engineers to access these files either from Linux clients or Windows clients. A content distribution provider needs mass storage of videos to stream to its clients. Database servers need central storage to keep the data updated and replicated into different locations for disaster recovery. The type of the application and how the data is used dictates the type of storage technology: block-level storage, file-level storage, or object-based storage.

Block-Level Storage

Block-level storage is what all end users employ on laptops and personal computers. You start with an empty disk and add an OS such as Windows; then the OS lets you create a drive that you map into. The reads/writes from disk are done via SCSI commands that access the data in blocks. A block can be different sizes depending on the application. Block-level storage does not have information about the blocks it is storing; it mainly treats data as just blocks. In the context of data centers, block storage is used in SANs where hard drives are connected to servers via a storage network. The block storage creates raw volumes, and the OS of the servers uses these volumes as individual hard drives and transmits the SCSI commands over the network. Block-level storage is flexible and scales to large capacities as massive amounts of block storage are segmented into individual drives. Transactional databases and virtual machines use block-level storage. The drives are used as boot drives for different operating systems. The individual drives are used by any file system, such as NFS or SMB. Although block-level storage is flexible, it is harder to manage than file-level storage because individual servers are dealing with their own volumes and management tools and must track which volume belongs to which server over the network.

File-Level Storage

File-level storage is simpler, and it was created for dumping raw files into a central location and sharing them between different clients. The files are put in a structured hierarchy with file naming and file extensions, directories, and paths to reach the files. The files are normally grouped in 4 KB blocks. File-level storage is associated with network-attached storage (NAS), where storage is accessed over the TCP/IP network. Unlike the block-level storage where the blocks are grouped into drives and accessed as C:\ or D:\ drives, with file-level storage, you actually access the storage as a share such as \\RemoteStorage\ sharename. The file system handles permissions and access rights to prevent users from writing over each other's data. Unlike block storage that does not have information on the blocks, file-level storage has information about filenames and paths to reach the files as well as other metadata attributes. The file-level storage supports different file-sharing protocols:

- **Network File System (NFS):** NFS, a file-sharing protocol developed by Sun Microsystems (now Oracle), is mainly associated with the UNIX/Linux operating systems. NFS allows clients to access files and folders in a server over the network.

- **Server Message Block (SMB):** The SMB is a file-sharing protocol developed by Microsoft for its Windows-based operating systems. SMB is a client server protocol that allows clients to share files on servers over the network. The Common Internet File System (CIFS) protocol is a set of message packets that define a particular version of the SMB protocol.

File-level storage is easier to manage than block-level storage. It handles access control and integrates with different corporate directories. However, file-level storage might be harder to back up and replicate because each NAS system is closely tied to its own operating system flavor. As more and more hyperconverged products are emerging, you will start to see consolidation where the best of both worlds—block-level and file-level storage—is implemented on the same storage product.

Object-Based Storage

So far you have seen that data is organized either as block-level or as file-level storage. Object-based storage refers to data being represented as objects. If, for example, most data are unstructured, such as digital pictures, videos, social media, audio files, and so on, instead of looking at the data as a chunk of fixed size blocks, you would look at it as variable-sized objects. There are three components for the object: the data, the metadata, and the ID.

The data is the actual object, such as a photo or a photo album, a song, or a video. The metadata gives all sorts of information about the object, such as a caption in a picture or the name of the artist for a song, and other security data, such as access and deletion permissions. The ID is a globally unique identifier that gives information on how to locate the object in a distributed storage system regardless of the actual physical location of the object. Object storage works well for unstructured data that does not change frequently, such as static web pages, and digital media that is read but not modified. Amazon Web Services (AWS) uses the Simple Storage Service (S3) to store massive amounts of data in the cloud. Applications use Representational State Transfer (RESTful) application programming interface (API) as the standard interface to reach the object storage platform. A comparison between block, file, and object storage is seen in Figure 2-9.

Object storage is not a replacement for either block storage or file storage because it does not have the attributes of either. For example, object storage does not work for transactional databases because they require the data to be constantly modified and updated to access the most updated information. Object storage does not work for structuring files under folders and directories with access permissions as with NAS. Unlike block storage and file storage, where data within a file can be modified, object storage does not allow specific information to be modified; rather, the whole object must be replaced. Object storage has many advantages, such as a simpler and flat addressing space, and it has a rich and customizable metadata. Object storage scales better in a distributed storage system where data is replicated in different data centers and geography for better durability. Scaling block-level- or file-level storage over large distances is more challenging because the farther the data is from the application, which constantly needs the data, the more performance is hindered due to increased network latency.

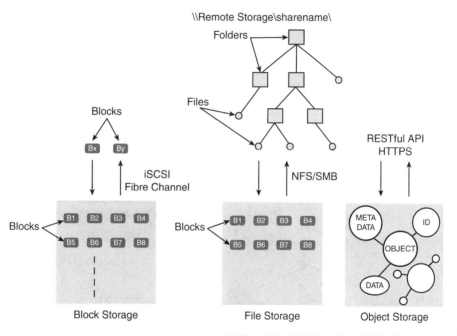

Figure 2-9   *Block, File, and Object Storage*

Having had an overview of the types of storage, let's look closely at how servers actually connect to storage. The next section discusses the three methods that were used in existing data centers. It examines the drawbacks of each method as a precursor to discussing later in the book how hyperconvergence solves these issues. Block, file, and object storage independent of NAS and SAN were examined so you could see the evolution of the data center. Combination products are being developed that are incorporating the storage types into unified products.

Storage-to-Server Connectivity

Servers connect to storage in different ways, such as local storage via direct-attached storage (DAS), or over the network as NAS or SAN. The preference of what type of connectivity to choose from depends on many criteria:

■ The type of the application

■ Capacity requirements

- Increasing storage utilization

- Resiliency and redundancy of the storage system

- The ability to easily move applications between different servers

Now let's look at the three connectivity types.

Direct-Attached Storage (DAS)

DAS refers to the storage device, such as an HDD or SSD, being directly attached to the server. The disk drives are either internal to the server or external for added flexibility. This is shown in Figure 2-10.

The disks between the servers are independent of each other. Different connectivity types are SAS, SATA, and PCIe/NVMe. Notice also that the file system that controls the data is local to the server.

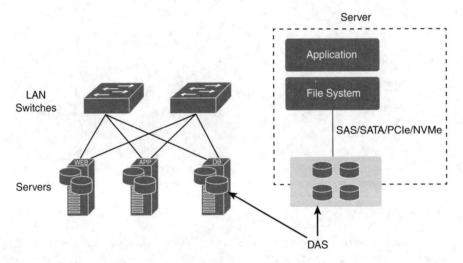

Figure 2-10 *Typical DAS Deployment*

The advantage of DAS is that it is simple and fast and does not rely on a network for connectivity. DAS was traditionally used for small enterprise, non-networked implementations, with the drawback that the system capacity is limited by the number of connected drives, and I/O transfer speeds are limited by the local disk interface of each system. DAS implementations have the tendency to create storage silos with low storage utilization. For example, a typical DAS storage usage could be 20% because some servers have more storage than they need, whereas others have much less than they need. In centralized and networked storage, capacity is more efficiently allocated between the servers and could reach 80% of available storage. Larger storage implementations moved to a NAS or SAN setup. However, as you will see, hyperconvergence DAS plays a major role in building distributed storage architectures with the introduction of software-defined storage (SDS).

DAS uses block-level storage to transfer I/O blocks, similar to SAN, with the difference being that storage is transferred over a local disk. Some of the interfaces used for DAS were briefly covered, such as SATA, SAS, and the respective hard drives. The various interfaces allow multiple disks to connect to the server in a disk array. For example, SAS 1 supports 3 Gbps transfer speed, SAS 2 supports 6 Gbps, SAS 3 supports 12 Gbps, and SAS 4 supports 22.5 Gbps. SAS supports multiple ports, allowing multiple disks to be connected to the server, each receiving the full transfer speed. As an example, a SAS 3, four-port implementation allows four SAS disks to be connected to the same server, each having a 12 Gbps transfer rate. SAS RAID controllers are also used to allow a larger number of drives to be connected to the server.

Network-Attached Storage

NAS is a file-level storage system allowing clients to share and store files over the network. NAS is a massive file server that contains the files, index tables that contain information such as the location of the files, and the paths to reach the files. NAS also contains system metadata that is separate from the files and contains attributes about the files themselves, such as name and creation date. NAS uses the TCP/IP protocol to exchange data and uses NFS and SMB as file-sharing protocols. The NAS server contains multiple drives, including SAS and SATA, and they are often arranged in RAID arrays. The NAS server connects to the rest of the network via 1 GE, 10 GE, or higher speeds and consolidates massive amounts of files for all servers to share. NAS systems do not need a full-blown operating system to function but use stripped-down operating systems. The advantages of NAS include easy file management and operation because it is custom built for file sharing and storage. Figure 2-11 shows a NAS deployment over a local area network (LAN). Notice that the file system is now inside the NAS and is accessed remotely by the servers via NFS or SMB over a TCP/IP Gigabit Ethernet network.

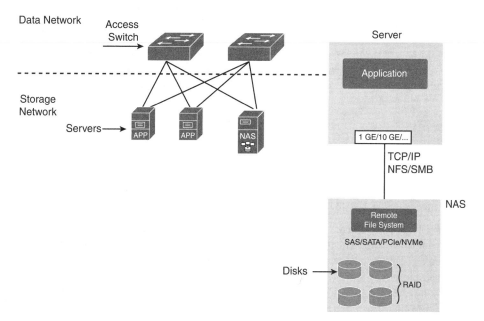

Figure 2-11   *Typical NAS Deployment*

Because NAS is accessing storage over a network, it is crucial that the network itself does not become the bottleneck. This happens if, for example, the NAS does not have enough GE interfaces to carry the data, or the switched network itself is congested because of too much data. High-performance NAS systems provide multiple 1 GE or 10 GE interfaces to the network, allowing enough bandwidth to the I/O operation.

Data growth is challenging to NAS. As the capacity of a NAS system in the data center reaches its limit, more NAS systems must be added—hence, the debate between scaling up or scaling out. Scaling up means acquiring single-box NAS systems with huge capacities to handle present and future file storage needs, whereas scaling out means adding more NAS. The main issue with NAS is with its performance in dealing not only with the files but with the metadata attributes. Because NAS originated as a centralized file storage system, it has its challenges in becoming a distributed storage system such as SAN. For example, to resolve scaling issues, additional NAS systems are added to the network, creating clusters of NAS. Communication between the different nodes in a cluster becomes problematic, and a global file system (GFS) is needed to have a unified system; otherwise, managing independent systems becomes a nightmare. Also, as NAS systems become clustered and the file system is distributed between nodes, it becomes harder to pinpoint where the performance issues are. Performance issues could be in the IOPS capabilities of the RAID arrays or in the network connectivity, creating big latency between the servers and the remote file system. Other performance issues are due to certain clients or servers misbehaving and locking certain resources, preventing other servers from reaching those resources. Performance degradation might also arise in accessing large amounts of metadata and files that are distributed between nodes. As data analytics and machine-to-machine transactions create more and more files and metadata, NAS systems must scale up and out to accommodate the explosion in file storage.

Storage Area Networks

Storage area networks were supposed to solve NAS performance issues by distributing storage on multiple storage arrays connected via a high-speed interconnect. Unlike NAS, which is based on file-level storage, SAN is a block-level storage where data is accessed in blocks and appears as volumes to servers and can be formatted to support any file system.

SAN uses different types of network connections and protocols, such as FC, iSCSI, Fibre Channel over Ethernet (FCoE), Advanced Technology Attachment over Ethernet (AoE), iSCSI extensions for Remote Direct Memory Access (iSER), and InfiniBand (IB). Let's discuss in detail the addressing, switching, and host-to-storage connectivity for some of the most deployed SAN types in enterprise networks.

The "simple complexity" of fibre channel has kept storage engineers the masters of their domain for so long. The technology is usually familiar and considered simple only to the storage engineers who work on it 24/7. For others, fibre channel is a mystery. In any case, if the objective is to move to simple hyperconverged environments, virtualization and networking engineers need to have some level of knowledge of the existing storage network to have familiarity with the technology and to work hand in hand with storage engineers to migrate the applications and data to the new hyperconverged network.

Fibre Channel SANs

Fibre channel (FC) is the most deployed storage interconnect in existing enterprise data centers. It is a high-speed network technology that runs at speeds of 1 Gbps, 2 Gbps, 4 Gbps, 8 Gbps, 16 Gbps, 32 Gbps, and 128 Gbps. FC competes with Gigabit Ethernet as a network interconnect, but FC has struggled in keeping up with the Ethernet technology that grew from 1 GE, to 10 GE, 25 GE, 40 GE, 50 GE, and 100 GE. FC provides block-level access to storage devices. It uses the Fibre Channel Protocol (FCP) to carry the SCSI commands over FC packets, and it uses a set of FC switches to switch the traffic between the end nodes. FC servers use an HBA, the "initiator," to connect to a storage system, the "target." The HBA adapter offloads the CPU from processing many functionalities such as encapsulation and decapsulation of SCSI over FC, that are better done on the hardware level. The HBA connects predominantly over fibre and supports different port count and port speeds. Unlike Ethernet or TCP/IP, FC is a lossless protocol, meaning it is designed not to drop packets or lose data.

Figure 2-12 shows how servers and RAID disk arrays are connected to the SAN fabric. If you recall in Chapter 1, this is what is referred to as the *three-tier storage architecture* that constitutes the servers, the SAN switches, and the disk arrays.

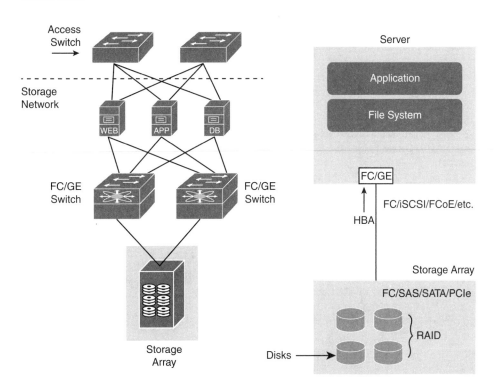

Figure 2-12 *Typical SAN Deployment*

Notice that SAN creates a different storage network in addition to the data network. The storage network is formed with FC switches if the servers have FC HBAs, or GE switches if the servers have iSCSI HBAs. Also notice that in SAN (and similar to DAS), the file system is inside the servers because SAN uses block storage to access the disks.

Fibre Channel Addressing

Fibre channel uses World Wide Names (WWN) to address nodes and ports on the network. World Wide Node Name (WWNN) is the global address of the node, whereas World Wide Port Name (WWPN) is the address of the different individual ports on the FC node. Ports on the nodes are referred to as N-ports (as in Node), whereas ports on switches are referred to as F-ports (as in Fabric), and ports between switches are referred to as E-ports (as in Expansion). For example, an HBA with two FC N-ports has two different WWPNs. These are similar to Ethernet MAC addresses. The WWN is an 8-byte address with 16 hexadecimal characters that contain the vendor company identifier and vendor-specific info. The WWN is either burned into the hardware or assigned dynamically via software. Note in Figure 2-13 that the WWPNs of the host Server 1, HBA1 port 1 is 20:00:00:1b:32:ff:ab:01, and port 2 is 20:00:00:1b:32:ff:ab:02. The WWPN of the storage array storage controller 1 (SC1), port 1, is 20:00:00:1b:32:b1:ee:01 and port 2 is 20:00:00:1b:32:b1:ee:02.

Fibre channel allows the use of aliases to represent the nodes, so an alias to WWPN 20:00:00:1b:32:ff:ab:01 could be "Server 1-HBA11" and for port 2, it could be "Server 1-HBA12." The same is true for the storage array SC1 port 1; the alias for 20:00:00:1b:32:b1:ee:01 could be "SC1-1," and so on.

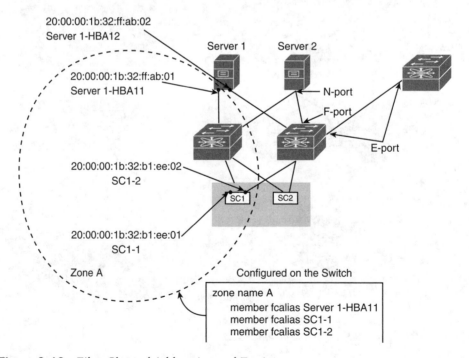

Figure 2-13 *Fibre Channel Addressing and Zoning*

Fibre Channel Zoning

Security is applied in fibre channel to restrict which nodes can talk to each other via zoning. A zone is similar to a VLAN in an Ethernet switch. Zoning is done using WWNs or port IDs or combinations. Zoning is performed on the fibre channel switches and is configured on one switch. It is automatically shared with all other connected switches. First you must define zones, such as Zone A and Zone B. Then include WWPNs in the zones. Finally, group zones into zone sets to activate the zones. For example, if Zone A is defined and WWPNs are added to the zone, only initiators and targets whose WWNs are part of Zone A can talk to each other. As an example, in Figure 2-13, Server 1, HBA1, port 1 (Server 1-HBA11) is in the same Zone A as storage controllers SC1 port 1 (SC1-1) and SC1 port 2 (SC1-2); therefore, if Server 1-HBA11 initiates a connection to targets SC1-1 or SC1-2, the connection goes through.

There are two types of zoning: hard and soft. Hard zoning is applied on the "physical" port level at the switch level. Soft zoning is applied on the WWN level. Vendors have different implementations for zoning on ports or WWN or a combination.

LUN Masking

Hosts see all LUNs on a target port. If, however, you wanted a server to see certain LUNs while hiding other LUNs, masking prevents the server from seeing specific LUNs. Masking is done in host software or in the HBAs or, in the case of SAN, on the storage controllers of the storage system. The decision depends on who you trust to make the configuration, because the person configuring the server is different from the person configuring the storage. LUN masking works on the WWN. Figure 2-14 shows how Server 1 has access only to LUNs 1 and 3 on a RAID 5 disk array. The storage controller was configured to allow initiator 20:00:00:1b:32:ff:ab:01 (which is Server 1-HBA11) to communicate to LUNs 1 and 3 and masked LUN 2 and LUN 4 from Server 1. In the same way, the storage controller is configured to allow only the HBAs of Server 2 to initiate connections to LUN 2 and LUN 4.

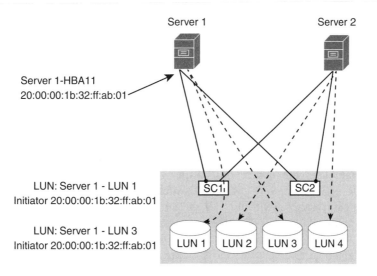

Figure 2-14 *LUN Masking*

Fibre Channel Switching

Switching in a fibre channel network is much different from switching in Ethernet and IP networks. The combination of switches and cables is called *fabric*. Normally, multiple SAN fabrics are configured to ensure redundancy. In FC, each switch is recognized by a unique identifier, called a *domain identifier*, or domain ID. The domain ID is an 8-bit identifier with values that range from 0 to 255, with some numbers reserved. One of the switches is elected as a principal switch and assigns domain IDs for the rest of the switches.

Start with a Fabric Login process (FLOGI), where the FC switch acts as a LOGIN server to assign fibre channel IDs (FCIDs) to each WWPN. This is similar to IP networks, where a client requests its IP address from a Dynamic Host Configuration Protocol (DHCP) server. The FCID is a 24-bit address that contains the switch domain ID, the switch F_port the FC node is attached to, and the N_port of the end node. The switches maintain a table of WWPN-to-FCID mapping and exchange the tables between switches using the fibre channel network service (FCNS) protocol. As such, each switch has information about every WWPN in the network, including to which switch and switch port it is attached. It uses such information to deliver FC frames. During the FLOGI process, buffer credit information is exchanged between N_port and F_port to be used for flow control because FC is a lossless protocol.

After an FC node finishes the FLOGI process and receives its FCID, it must know the other WWPNs on the network. The initiator node performs a port login (PLOGI) process through a Simple Name Server (SNS) function running in the switch. During the process, each node sends to the switch its mapping between its FCID and its WWPN. The switch collects this information and checks its zones to decide which WWPN (soft zoning) can talk to which other WWPNs. As a result, the nodes receive the WWPNs that reside only in their zones.

After the nodes finish the FLOGI and PLOGI processes, they have visibility into other target WWPNs they can connect to on the network. As such, a host initiator does a process login (PRLI) toward the target storage device it wants to connect to. At that time, the storage controller on the target sends the initiator the LUNs that the host can connect to and masks all other LUNs. This is illustrated in Figure 2-15.

Multipathing

Multipathing provides added redundancy in case of network component failures. Also, multipathing is leveraged for higher performance by having the host use the bandwidth available on multiple paths when reaching the storage. The different paths are formed by using multiple HBAs on the servers, different SAN fabric (switches, cables), and multiple storage controllers with multiple ports. Figure 2-16 shows a fibre channel network where redundancy is added at every level, node, switch, and controller. Notice that there are two different fabrics via switches: SW1 and SW2. The fabrics do not interconnect at the switch level for added security and to limit propagation of misconfigured information between the fabrics. If you remember, in fibre channel switches, one switch propagates the configurations to other switches. Notice that Server 1 is connected to the switches via two different port adapters: S11 and S12. Server 2 is connected to the switches via two port adapters: S21 and S22.

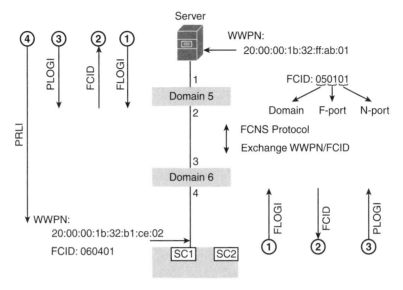

Figure 2-15   *Fibre Channel Routing*

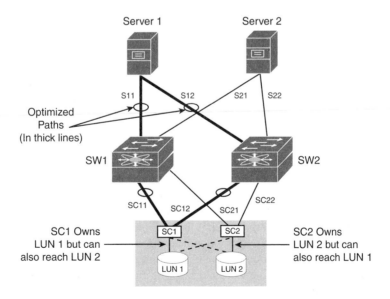

Figure 2-16   *Multipathing in a SAN*

S11 connects to switch SW1, and S12 connects to SW2. Similarly, S21 connects to SW1, and S22 connects to SW2. The switches connect to a storage array and are dual-homed to two storage controllers: SC1 (SC11, SC12) and SC2 (SC21, SC22), which in turn have dual ports 1 and 2. With any failure in the network, the system will find an alternate path to reach the target storage LUNs. To limit the number of paths between a host and its LUNs, zoning is applied.

In the diagram, you find four different paths to reach LUN 1 from server 1. The first two paths are via SW1 and are (S11, SW1, SC11) and (S11, SW1, SC21), and the second two paths are via SW2 and are (S12, SW2, SC12) and (S12, SW2, SC22). The controller ports SC11, SC12, SC21, and SC22 form what is called a Target Portal Group (TPG). Information about this portal group is known to Servers 1 and 2, which use this portal group to reach LUN 1 and LUN 2, respectively. Although both storage controllers can reach all LUNs in a disk array, a storage controller can "own" a LUN and is considered the most direct path to that LUN. So, in this case, SC1 owns LUN 1 and SC2 owns LUN 2.

Another protocol used in multipathing is the Asymmetrical Logical Unit Access (ALUA). ALUA allows the storage system to tell the clients which paths are optimized and which are not. In this case, SC1 tells Server 1 that path (S11, SW1, SC11) is optimized to reach LUN 1 because it owns LUN 1. Also, SC1 tells Server 1 that path (S12, SW2, SC12) is another optimized path. The other two paths are nonoptimized because they go through controller SC2.

Given that the hosts have the ALUA information, load balancing is supported through the host multipath (MPIO) software. Traffic destined to a particular LUN in the storage system can actually be sent over two available paths in an active-active mode, thereby doubling the available I/O bandwidth. The decision to choose one path or multiple is left to the OS at the host, which has all different paths to reach a LUN. Server 1 can utilize both S11 and S12 to send traffic to reach LUN 1. In case of a path failure, connectivity remains, but I/O bandwidth is cut in half.

Also note that the storage array itself can participate in the failover. For example, a storage array experiencing a target failure could indicate to the host to reinitiate the connection to connect to the available working ports.

iSCSI SANs

iSCSI provides block-level access to storage devices by carrying the SCSI commands over a TCP/IP network. iSCSI functions are done in software and rely on a traditional Ethernet network interface card (NIC) for connectivity; however, the system performance greatly suffers as the CPU becomes overloaded. A better choice is to use an iSCSI HBA/NIC with a TCP Offload Engine (TOE) function that offloads the CPU from functions such as encapsulation and decapsulation that are better done in hardware. The iSCSI HBA connects to the Gigabit Ethernet network and supports multiple ports and interface speeds such as 1 GE, 10 GE, 40 GE, 25 GE, 50 GE, and 100 GE. Because iSCSI runs over TCP/IP, the packets run on an L2-switched network or IP routed over an L3 network. iSCSI uses IP, so it runs over LANs or WANs. Figure 2-17 shows a typical iSCSI network. Note that both hosts and storage systems connect to a regular Ethernet/IP network. Depending on IT budgets, the storage Ethernet network could be separate from the existing TCP/IP data network; this gives storage transactions the most performance.

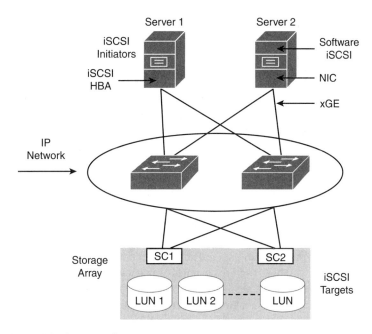

Figure 2-17   *iSCSI SAN Deployments*

iSCSI Addressing

Unlike fibre channel, which works on WWNs, iSCSI addressing is done via the iSCSI qualified name (IQN) or the extended unique identifier (EUI).

The iSCSI IQN can be up to 255 characters and has the following format:

iqn.yyyy-mm.naming-authority:unique name, where:

- yyyy-mm = the year and month the naming authority was established.

- The naming-authority = normally the "reverse" of the authority domain name.

- The unique name = any chosen name, such as a host name.

For example, iqn.2000-01.com.domain.iSCSI:Server1H11 indicates the following:

- yyyy-mm = 2000-01 indicates the year and month the authority "domain" was established.

- Domain name = domain.com, subdomain = iSCSI. So, the reverse is naming-authority = com.domain.iSCSI

- unique name = Server1H11; indicates Server 1, host bus adapter 1 port 1.

The EUI is formed with the prefix eui. and a 16-character name, which includes 24 bits of a company name assigned by the IEEE and a 40-bit unique identifier. An example is eui.1A2B3C4D5E6F7G8H.

Also, like fibre channel, the iSCSI names can be written as aliases for easier representation. For example, an alias of the IQN listed above, iqn.2000-01.com.domain.iSCSI:Server 1H11, could be iSCSI-Server1-H11.

Finally, each iSCSI initiator or target is represented by its own TCP/IP address used to exchange traffic over the IP/Ethernet network. Server1-H11 could be assigned an IP of 10.0.1.1, for example. iSCSI does not support the login processes (LOGI, FLOGI, PRLI), but it does support the concept of a TPG. A set of storage controller IP addresses is grouped in TPG; the initiator must specifically reference its target by pointing to the target IP address within the TPG.

iSCSI Network Segmentation

Similar to FC, where segmentation is done via zones, segmentation in an iSCSI network is done via virtual LANs (VLANs). However, segmentation in VLANs is enforced at the switch level, where the switches pass traffic between ports depending on the port VLAN configuration. This is similar to fibre channel hard zones. Filtering is also done on the MAC addresses; however, because this occurs at the switch level as well, it is a more tedious task to maintain. Also, a level of secure authentication and encryption is accomplished between the initiators and targets to ensure that an authorized initiator accesses a target.

iSCSI LUN Masking

iSCSI LUN masking is supported. As the initiator points to a target via an IP address and a connection process takes place, the target allocates the proper LUNs based on the IQNs and assigns them to a group of initiators. There are many ways of doing LUN masking in iSCSI depending on vendor implementations. Normally this is done on storage controllers, but some implementations put access lists (ACLs) on the initiator side to mask the LUNs. The battle between storage folks and system folks continues, as the storage people want LUN masking on the storage system to prevent unauthorized host access, and system folks want to put the LUN masking on the host just to make sure the storage folks did not misconfigure and expose their data to many hosts. Transitioning into hyperconvergence will hopefully create unified storage/system expertise, where one group is to blame if (or obviously when) a misconfiguration occurs.

iSCSI Multipathing

In an iSCSI environment, multipathing is supported via ALUA and MPIO, as well as by other load-balancing techniques inherited from IP/Ethernet networks. Multipathing is done at the host level using MPIO, with the software having visibility into the different iSCSI ports that connect the host to the network. For example, a host learns through discovery the IP addresses of the targets within a TPG. If the host is connected via redundant iSCSI HBAs, H1 and H2 and the storage arrays are connected via interfaces SC11, SC12, SC21, and so on. Then the host is able to reach such storage via multiple paths, and if one fails, it uses the other. Furthermore, if both host adapters are active, the MPIO software decides to use both adapters for load balancing. Also, because this is an IP/Ethernet network, load balancing and path protection are performed at L2 or L3 through the switches, so traffic is balanced via different methods such as virtual port channels (vPCs), multichassis link aggregation (MLAG), equal cost multipath (ECMP), or other, depending on whether this is an L2 or an L3 network. More on these concepts can be found in Part VI of this book.

Fibre Channel over Ethernet SANs

FCoE works by encapsulating the FC protocol (FCP) over an Ethernet header. Unlike iSCSI, which carries SCSI commands over TCP/IP, FCoE still uses the FCP protocol to carry the SCSI commands, but it extends a traditional FC network over an L2 Ethernet network. Therefore, FCoE is L2 switched but not routed. Unlike TCP/IP, which has many congestion control mechanisms that handle packet loss and flow control, Ethernet on its own needs added functionality in this area. FCoE needed some enhancements to Ethernet to make it lossless. This is done in two standards: Data Center Bridging (DCB) and Converged Enhanced Ethernet (CEE). These two standards define mechanisms such as the Institute of Electrical and Electronics Engineers (IEEE) 802.1Qbb priority flow control to pause the traffic in case of congestion, IEEE 802.1Qau congestion notification to notify the sender of congestion, and IEEE 802.1Qaz enhanced transmission selection for minimum guaranteed bandwidth allocation. Because L2 Ethernet networks do switching at the media access control (MAC) layer while FC does switching based on FCID, mapping must be done between FCID and MAC addresses. The FCoE HBAs now have to deal with both FCP and connecting to an Ethernet network, which is done via NICs. The combined adapter to perform such functions is called a converged network adapter (CNA). The CNA has virtual adapters—one that acts as an Ethernet NIC and the other that acts as an FC HBA. Storage traffic and regular data traffic are separated in different VLANs.

Because FCoE still uses FCP, all that was discussed about FC addressing with WWNN and WWPN still applies. The initiators and targets use the different login protocols, such as FLOGI, PLOGI, and PRLI. And the same FC concepts for zoning and LUN masking still apply.

Although FC remains the most used technology for storage, future data center architectures will move gradually toward Ethernet networks. It is becoming overwhelming and inefficient to maintain two switched networks: Ethernet and FC. Hard-core FC professionals do not appreciate such statements and are comfortable with FC, but the fact is that Ethernet and TCP/IP are more mainstream and better understood than FC. Convergence between the networking layer and the storage layer will happen sooner or later, and technologies like 10 GE, 40 GE, and 100 GE will be at the forefront in enterprise data centers.

Other SAN deployments exist, such as the Advanced Technology Attachment (ATA) over Ethernet (AoE) which is a block-level storage protocol, based on SATA, to exchange commands with disk drives. Like FCoE, the ATA command set is encapsulated directly over an Ethernet frame and switched over an L2 network. Although the ATA command set is exchanged, AoE presents the operating system with the same SCSI commands as FC, iSCSI, and FCoE. AoE is a lightweight protocol that has seen some limited adoption. There are many debates in the industry on the security risks in AoE deployments in shared environments. AoE is open to many attacks, such as unauthenticated disk attacks, denial of service (DoS), replay attacks, and so on.

Kudos to you if you reached the end of this section. Because legacy SAN networks will not disappear overnight, and the storage engineers will not be out of a job soon, it is important that IT administrators have familiarity in all areas to have a better understanding of hyperconvergence.

Storage Efficiency Technologies

Storage controllers in SANs and their roles in creating LUNs and LUN masking were previously discussed. The storage controllers have many other functionalities to improve the fault tolerance and efficiency of the storage system. This functionality is listed because hyperconverged systems must deliver similar and even better functionality to meet the enterprise needs. Some of the main functionality is explored in this section.

Thin Provisioning

Thin provisioning is important in providing an on-demand capacity provisioning. This means that physical storage is purchased when needed and not in advance, thereby minimizing the costs of storage over provisioning. The way this works is by giving the applications the appearance of having enough storage, while in reality a lesser amount of physical storage is available. When the application needs more storage, physical storage is purchased and added to the network.

System administrators tend to overprovision storage for their applications just in case more storage is needed and to avoid storage upgrades and downtimes in operational networks. An application that normally consumes, say, 100 GB in the first year, 200 GB in the second year, 300 GB in the third year, and so on, might get provisioned with 500 GB on day one, leaving a lot of unused capacity that is already paid for. Perhaps you have 10 such servers, so 5 TB of storage is purchased on day one and 20% of it is used the first year, 40% the second year, and so on.

If thin provisioning is used, the application is allocated 500 GB of "thin storage." This gives the application the appearance of having enough storage, while in reality physical storage is much less at 200 GB. This results in major savings. When applying thin provisioning to storage arrays, the storage array presents LUNs that appear much larger than what the host needs, while actually giving the host just enough physical capacity needed at the time. These LUNs are called "Thin LUNs" in contrast to "Thick LUNs" that are normally provisioned. Furthermore, advanced controllers allow the storage to "reclaim" capacity. If the host releases some of its capacity, the storage controller releases the blocks on the physical disks, hence reclaiming the storage. Figure 2-18 shows thick and thin provisioning of disk arrays.

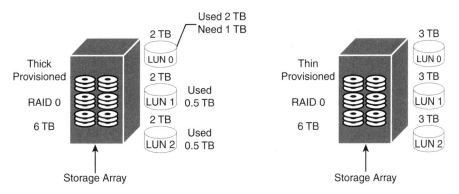

Figure 2-18   *Thick Versus Thin Provisioning*

Disk array 1 has six disks at 1 TB each and is thick provisioned as a RAID 0. This means that when presenting the LUNs, you can at a maximum provision 6 TB worth of LUNs, as shown in LUN 0, LUN 1, and LUN 2, each having 2 TB. In this case if, for example, the capacity needed by LUN 0 becomes 3 TB, you are stuck as you run out of disk space, while LUNs 1 and 2 might still have 3 TB left between the two. On the other hand, disk array 2 is thin provisioned as RAID 0. This means that, when presenting the LUNs, you can actually provision, say, 9 TB of total capacity, where LUN 0 gets 3 TB, LUN 1 gets 3 TB, and LUN 2 gets 3 TB. If in this case LUN 0 needs 3 TB or more, you can reallocate the capacity between LUNs and give LUN 0 extra terabytes. It is important to have management tools constantly monitor the storage because the applications think they have enough storage and could use it and will not report a shortage. Constant monitoring must be applied to ensure that the storage used does not exceed the total physical capacity of disks.

Snapshots

Snapshots is a mechanism that allows data to be captured at any given point in time so it can be restored if there is corruption or damage to the data. The system administrator specifies, based on how and how often the snapshots are taken, a recovery point objective (RPO) and a recovery time objective (RTO). RPO represents the maximum data loss that can be tolerated when a failure occurs. RTO represents the maximum time that can be tolerated for a recovery process after failure occurs.

The use of snapshots varies between simple data restoration at a point in time to creation of full backups. This depends on the vendor implementation of snapshots and the level of comfort of system administrators in the vendor's implementation. The topic of using snapshots for backups is a bit controversial and will be left for a further discussion of primary versus secondary storage. There are many types of snapshots depending on the vendor implementation. Let's examine just a few to give you a feel for the technology.

Traditional or Physical Snapshots

In this case, when a snapshot is taken, the data is actually duplicated somewhere else in the disk in the same disk array. The duplication is done either within the same volume or in a separate volume. The data creates a separate backup on a different disk array or restores the information if there is an issue with the original volume. The main takeaway is that this type of snapshot consumes disk space because it is an actual mirror copy of the data. For 1 TB of data, you lose 1 TB for every snapshot, and so on. Also, the snapshot takes time to perform because you cannot use the snapshot until the full data is copied into the snapshot volume. During the copy, the original data must be kept as read-only, so the data itself does not change during the snapshot. Figure 2-19 shows how the original volume is physically copied on a snapshot volume. Once data is fully synched, the snapshot is created.

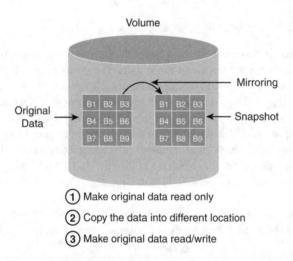

Figure 2-19   *Traditional Physical Snapshots*

Copy on Write Versus Redirect on Write Logical Snapshots

In contrast with physical snapshots, where actual data blocks are mirrored, logical snapshots are done differently. A logical snapshot is done by copying the index to the blocks (block map) rather than the blocks themselves. The snapshot is mainly a set of pointers to the original blocks. This constitutes major savings in storage capacity and better performance as instant snapshots are created. There are different implementations for logical snapshots, including copy on write (COW) and redirect on write (ROW).

In the COW, when a snapshot is taken, the original block map is copied into a separate snapshot area. Whenever an original block is updated, it is first "copied" to the snapshot area, and then the original block is modified (written). This ensures that if data corruption occurs in the write operation, the original data is restored from the snapshot. Let's see how this works.

Figure 2-20 shows the original blocks B1, B2, B3 and the original block map that points to these blocks. If there is no data modification, a snapshot (snapshot 1) would just constitute a set of pointers to the original blocks. If, however, after snapshot 1 is taken a write operation occurs on B3, then B3 would be first copied into the snapshot area, and the pointer in the new snapshot (snapshot 2) would be modified to point to the copy. After that, the write operation takes place and the original block B3 becomes B3'.

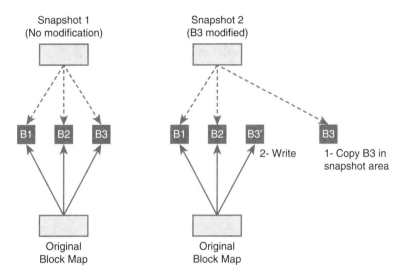

Figure 2-20 *Copy on Write Snapshots*

The drawback of COW is that it consumes three I/O operations when a block is modified: read the original block B3, write the block to the snapshot area, and write the modification B3' to the original area. The more the original data is updated and the more frequent snapshots are taken, the more performance hits are incurred. Also, to get an actual physical snapshot, you need to collect information from all the gathered snapshots. With more snapshots left undeleted, more disk space is consumed.

A more powerful way of taking snapshots is called redirect on write (ROW). Whenever a snapshot is taken, a copy of the original block map is taken, too, and the pointers to the original data are marked as read-only to represent the snapshot. When the original data is modified, the new data is redirected and written to a different area. The original block map is then modified to reflect the new data, while the snapshot still points to the older data. Let's look at this using an example. Figure 2-21 shows an original volume with blocks B1, B2, and B3. When snapshot 1 is taken, the block map is copied and the pointers of snapshot 1 to B1, B2, and B3 become read-only. When B3 is modified, the modified data B3' is redirected and written to a new area, and the file system original block map is modified to reflect the new blocks. If a second snapshot 2 is taken, then the snapshot 2 pointers to B1, B2, and the modified block B3' become read-only, and the file system block map advances upon any new data modification. As such, you minimized the I/O operation from 3 (read, write, write) in copy on write, down to 1 (write) in redirect on write.

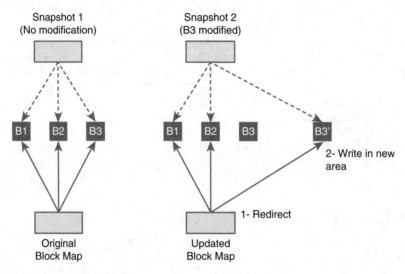

Figure 2-21 *Redirect on Write Snapshots*

The frequency of taking the snapshots could be a lot higher. Snapshots can be taken every few minutes or every few hours or so, and they can be kept for a longer period. Issues might arise with ROW snapshots based on vendor implementations. One issue, for example, is that snapshots can be deleted by simply removing the pointers to the snapshot blocks. This results in many empty blocks scattered randomly on the disk, degrading the performance of I/O operations. To solve this issue, vendors have to do some sort of garbage collection to rearrange the blocks. Another issue with ROW arises from implementations that create a snapshot parent-child relationship. This is called a *snapshot chain*. In this case, the original data is the parent, and snapshot 1 (the child) points to the parent. Snapshot 1 becomes the parent of snapshot 2, and so on and so forth. So, the block map of any snapshot is linked to the block map of its parent, and that could create performance issues upon reads while traversing the chain. The longer the chain, the more negative the impact on system performance. Implementations can avoid this issue by creating different block maps for every snapshot.

Other variations of snapshots use incremental snapshots, with new ones updating older ones. Other implementations use continuous data protection (CDP), where snapshots are taken whenever there is a data update. Vendor implementations should be careful not to create too much snapshot information at the expense of other factors, such as performance, disk space, and reconciliation of snapshots to restore the original data.

Cloning

In early implementations, cloning was basically used for creating a mirrored copy of different entities, such as a database, virtual machine, storage data, and more. As such, clones consumed storage due to full-copy penalty. In most modern file systems, cloning and snapshots are similar. Clones that are based on ROW snapshots do not incur full-copy penalty. The difference between snapshots and clones is that clones are writable, whereas snapshots are read-only.

As already explained, snapshots are a point-in-time representation of the data and are used for achieving a certain RPO and RTO when restoring data. If, however, the data from the snapshots needs to be modified (writeable), a clone is created from the snapshot, so the delta changes to the data do not affect the snapshots. Clones can be used, for example, to launch the same virtual machine/application over multiple servers. And if you take that clone and put it on different storage systems in different locations, you are actually backing up the data.

Replication

If you think snapshots and cloning are close enough to cause confusion, here comes replication to add more confusion. *Replication* is the act of making copies to the data for reproducing information or sharing information between systems. For example, database replication in a distributed database system allows users to work on different databases while keeping the information consistent. Some other uses are merging information between two databases to create a large database. Other applications are read replicas to offload a database of heavy operations that are done offline. Imagine that you have a heavily used database that clients are accessing. You want to perform some analytics on the data without affecting the original system. So you do a read replica of the system somewhere else, and you allow information to be read and accessed without affecting the original system read and write operation. Replication is done synchronously or asynchronously. Synchronous means instantaneous and continuous replication, whereas asynchronous is done offline or at time intervals, but not in real time. The difference between cloning and replication is that cloning is done once to create other systems, whereas replication can be continuous and used for synchronizing data in real time. Also, the difference between snapshots and replication is that snapshots are not copies, and they are used for restore. In the context of hyperconvergence, this book discusses how replication addresses host or disk failures as well as achieves disaster recovery (DR) by replicating data between different sites.

Deduplication

Deduplication refers to the technique of removing duplicate data in a data set. Duplication occurs anytime certain files are modified or similar files are sent to multiple people or environments like virtual desktop infrastructure (VDI), where similar information is repeated for every user. If such information is left as is, it not only impacts local storage but impacts backup storage. Deduplication removes the duplicated data, tremendously improves disk space, and minimizes the bandwidth needed for backup storage, especially when done over WAN. Deduplication is performed at the file level, the object level, or the block level. Different vendors justify the pros and cons of each. Now let's discuss the different types.

File-Level or Object-Level Deduplication

Assume that a 20 MB presentation was sent to five employees and these employees backed up the presentations on their storage system. The storage has 100 MB of the same data lying around. If deduplication is applied, only one file is saved on the main storage system, and 20 MB is consumed rather than 100 MB. This is seen in Figure 2-22.

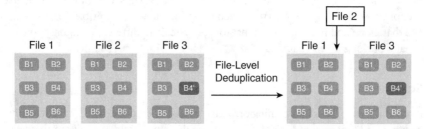

Figure 2-22   *Deduplication at the File Level or Object Level*

However, if the five employees update one slide of the presentation and save it again, you end up with five different versions of the same file that all need to be kept. This is one of the drawbacks of deduplication at the file or object level because it does not produce savings whenever different versions of the same file or object exist. Notice in Figure 2-22 that files 1 and 2 are the same, but file 3 has block B4 modified. When deduplication is applied at the file level, one copy of file 1 is kept, and file 2 becomes metadata or pointers that point to file 1. File 3 must remain as is even though most of its data is the same as files 1 and 2.

Deduplication at the Block Level

Deduplication at the block level is much more granular. Deduplication looks at the individual blocks and removes duplicated blocks, keeping only one copy. If a certain block in a file changed, only that block is copied. This is illustrated in Figure 2-23. Notice that you are applying deduplication at the block level for the same files: 1, 2, and 3. The result is that after deduplication, only one copy of B1 to B6 is kept, as well as the modified block B4'. File 3 points to all the unchanged blocks and to newly changed block B4'. As you see, the savings from block-level deduplication are enormous because of the fine granularity.

Deduplication algorithms take a chunk of data and apply hashing on it to find a unique key, which is a bit string. That key identifies whether any other data hashes to the same key. If it does, the data is considered identical and is not saved. If the key does not match, the data is considered different and is saved, but a pointer is kept to point to the data.

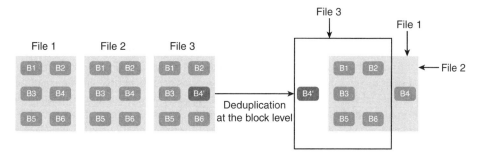

Figure 2-23   *Deduplication at the Block Level*

Various hashing algorithms identify the unique key that describes the data. The Secure Hash Algorithm 1 (SHA-1), for example, produces a 160-bit string hash, and the Message Digest 5 (MD5) algorithm produces a 120-bit hash.

Deduplication at the block level is done with fixed-sized blocks or with variable-sized blocks.

With fixed-sized blocks, hashing is applied on the fixed-sized block and a key is generated. After that, another block of the same size is taken, and so on and so forth. One of the advantages of hashing on fixed-sized blocks is that it reduces CPU processing because the block boundary is known in advance. The disadvantage of fixed-sized blocks is that if the information added or removed causes many blocks to shift, deduplication becomes inefficient. For example, hashing on the blocks of file 1: [paid][-the][-mon][ey--] versus file 2: [I-pa][id-t][he-m][oney], generates a new set of keys for blocks 1, 2, 3, and 4 and saves the data twice, although the information is practically the same. Of course, this is an extreme case. In practical scenarios, when data is modified, inefficiency occurs only on the affected changed blocks that need to be saved.

With variable-sized blocks, the algorithm does hashing on a different sized block, such as 4 KB, 8 KB, or 16 KB, and tries to optimize to find common data. If variable block sizes are used, hashing on the blocks of file 1: [paid-][the-][mone][y---] versus file 2: [I-paid-][the-] [mone][y---], you see that only block 1 changed, and blocks 2, 3, and 4 are saved once. The advantage of hashing on variable-sized blocks is better data matching, but the CPU cycles are much higher. As shown next, deduplication is done inline or at the destination. Inline deduplication could become a CPU hog, which reduces the performance of the system and interferes with the processing of the applications. Vendors differentiate in their architectures by minimizing the performance impacts of deduplication.

Target- Versus Source-Based Deduplication

Target-based deduplication is done at the destination storage system *after* the data is stored. Deduplication at the target usually comes in the form of appliances that perform the deduplication, are integrated with backup tools, or are integrated with the storage array systems. The benefit of target deduplication is that it offloads the host from the added processing and does not require changes to the host software. The drawback of target deduplication is that the target appliance becomes a central bottleneck getting data from all hosts and must have enough processing power to be able to scale.

Source-based deduplication is done at the host, which deduplicates the data before sending it to the target backup system. This is more of a distributed function because each host does its own share of deduplication. This has great benefits in minimizing the bandwidth needed when transferring data, especially over WAN or remote office environments connected via slow WAN links. The drawback of source deduplication is that it affects the performance of the hosts as it competes for processing power with the actual application. It also requires special software on the source in addition to the traditional backup software. Some implementations enhance the deduplication function by offloading this function to hardware adapters on the host. Other implementations minimize the performance hit by performing deduplication after the data is written to cache and acknowledged.

Inline- Versus Post-Process Deduplication

With inline deduplication, the deduplication function occurs in real time as the data is being stored to the target disk. This means that if it is not done correctly, the process of deduplication might interfere with the application performance. Normally, inline deduplication is done at the source host before it is sent to the target storage. Post-process deduplication tries to offload the host from performing the deduplication in real time by storing the data first in a write cache and sending a write acknowledgment to the host operating system so that it continues doing other tasks. After that, the post-process deduplication takes effect. Post-process deduplication occurs when moving the data from the cache to the target storage or after the data is stored in the target storage. This is open to vendor implementation. Semantically, this is how inline and post-process deduplication are defined. However, many vendors deduplicate on writes when they move the data from the cache into the capacity tier, and they still call it inline deduplication.

Local Versus Global Deduplication

Local deduplication is done at the level of an individual storage system. Each system deduplicates the data it receives. Global deduplication is done on a multisystem level, such as multiple hosts talking to each other, or multiple target storage arrays talking to each other. Global deduplication is more costly in terms of processing and more complex. However, with global deduplication, a wider backup and deduplication strategy are achieved because the data visibility is at a cluster of nodes level rather than a single node.

Data Compression

Data compression makes better use of disk space by eliminating redundant information. This sounds like deduplication, but it isn't. Whereas deduplication works on the whole storage system to eliminate redundant files or similar blocks, compression works at the file level or at the block level to eliminate repeating patterns or unnecessary data. Compression is considered lossy if the compressed file loses information when returned

to the original state. An example is the compression of images that results in lower resolution. Lossless compression does not lose information in the compression and decompression processes. Examples of data compression include the elimination of spaces in a
file or the elimination and then restoration of a repeating pattern. The compression factors depend on the original file. Some files achieve 2:1 compression; others may achieve
more or may achieve less depending on how many of the patterns can be eliminated.
A combination of compression and deduplication achieves enormous storage savings.
Different compression algorithms exist. An example of a lossless algorithm that has wider
acceptance due to its near line speeds when using multicore processors is LZ4.

Disk Encryption

Disk encryption is performed by using self-encrypting drives (SEDs), which automatically
encrypt and decrypt the data before it goes to the media. The SED uses a user-provided
password called key encryption key (KEK), which allows the encryption and decryption
of another key called the media encryption key (MEK). The MEK, in turn, encrypts
or decrypts the data to and from the physical media. Storage implementations that use
encryption are more costly because SEDs are more expensive than regular HDDs. Disk
encryption should not hinder the performance of the system because encryption is done
at the hardware level in the disk controller.

Storage Tiering

Storage tiering is the ability to store data on different types of media, including HDD
and SSD, depending on parameters such as application performance needs and frequency
of data access. For example, some applications that require high performance are better
served by having their data stored on SSD drives or SAS drives, whereas lower performance applications do okay if their data is stored on lower speed 5400 rpm SATA drives.
Another aspect is whether the data access is hot or cold. Hot data that is accessed more
frequently is better served with SSDs, whereas cold data that is not accessed that often is
better served with HDDs. The concept of tiering is to divide the storage array in tiers—
tier 0, 1, 2, until n—where tier 0 is the fastest with the highest performance and tier n
is the slowest. The main driver, of course, is to reduce the cost per I/O and the cost per
gigabyte of storage. SSD flash disks are much more expensive than HDDs, and even within HDDs, there are levels of cost performance. Therefore, tiering tries to get the most performance with the least cost. Figure 2-24 shows a storage array that offers three tiers of
storage, with SSD flash being the fastest tier, then a SAS HDD tier, and a SATA HDD tier.

The storage array is configured to do automatic tiering, where it monitors the data access
for a certain application and decides when and if it needs to move the data from one tier
to another. Hot data, as in frequently accessed data, moves to the SSD tier. Warm data,
as in accessed but not so frequently, moves to the SAS tier. And cold data, which has not
been accessed for a while, moves into the SATA tier. Tiering is also configured to lock an
application to a certain tier if the application cannot handle tiering.

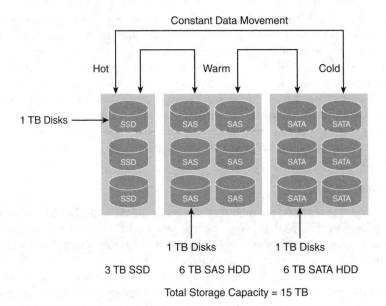

Figure 2-24   *Tiered Storage Array*

The drawback of tiering is that data is being constantly moved between different drives, which introduces added latency that can be avoided by having the data on a single tier. Because tiering architectures introduce fast SSD flash storage, tiering is sometimes confused with caching, which is described next.

Caching Storage Arrays

Caching storage arrays use fast SSDs to temporarily store the data for applications that need high performance and lower I/O access time and for the data that is most frequently used. Although on the surface this sounds like tiering, caching is completely different. In caching, the cache itself is not used as part of the permanent storage, and data is not moved around between fast and slow storage. In caching, the data is copied into cache for faster access, and when finished, it is deleted from the cache, allowing other pieces of data to be copied. So, the cache is not really part of the storage capacity but rather a placeholder for data that needs to be accessed faster. This is seen in Figure 2-25.

Looking back at what was discussed in this chapter, building and scaling storage networks is an art more than a science. There are so many twists and turns that only the experienced storage administrator can handle it, and all of it is shielded from the software virtualization and network engineers. Besides, only those who make a living building fibre channel vouch for its simplicity, while everybody else is in the dark. For the past few years, administrators have realized that designing virtualized networks on top of SANs while meeting the changing demands of applications is not easy. Next-generation data centers will see improvements in the following areas:

■ Moving away from centralized storage controllers to a more distributed storage approach that can scale processing

- Designing networks that anticipate failure rather than networks that react to failures

- Moving away from client server–type file systems to a distributed type–file systems

- Better logical volume management where the concept of LUNs becomes obsolete

- Moving away from fibre channel networking altogether because fibre channel switching and protocols are lagging behind the growth curve in Ethernet

- Moving functionality from closed hardware systems into software-defined functionality that leverages x86 processing

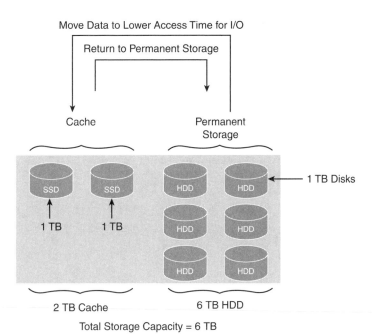

Figure 2-25   *Caching Storage Arrays*

Looking Ahead

This chapter covered most of the basics in storage and storage networking. This is essential in understanding hyperconvergence because most of the discussed principles apply. Hyperconvergence is an evolution of the existing data center designs that still relies on many of the discussed concepts.

However, hyperconvergence is possible because of the evolution of hardware and software that makes host computers faster and storage interconnects faster. And the most important parts are the concepts of software-defined storage (SDS) and software-defined networking (SDN) that form the stepping-stones for hyperconvergence.

Part II of this book discusses the evolution of host hardware and software and how it affects the designs of next-generation data centers. The faster computer processing, coupled with high-speed server-to-storage interconnect and next-generation NICs, makes host computers more powerful than traditional storage arrays. The adoption of software virtualization changed the deployment model and emphasized the application rather than the storage. SDS paves the way for decoupling software from the underlying hardware to allow the move from closed hardware systems to open systems based on x86 processing.

Evolution in Host Hardware and Software

Chapter 3   Host Hardware Evolution

Chapter 4   Server Virtualization

Chapter 5   Software-Defined Storage

Part II shifts the focus to the evolution of hardware and software inside the host itself. Most of the hardware and software principles discussed will be used in hyperconverged systems. However, many of these principles will be used to enhance the traditional storage array networks as well. Hyperconvergence does not mean that traditional storage will disappear; you will continue to see enhancements in all areas.

Chapter 3 discusses the evolution of host hardware such as enhancements in compute power and how central processing units (CPUs) are allocated to virtual machines. It also covers the high-speed server to storage interconnects and the emergence of flash-based storage products.

Chapter 4 covers software virtualization and the mechanisms used to protect virtual machines and balance traffic. Virtualization is a big part of hyperconvergence, and it is important to understand the concepts of virtual machines and containers and how they move around in the network. This chapter also covers the VMware file system used in existing converged network deployments as it evolves into the vSAN hyperconvergence software.

Chapter 5 covers the principles of Software-Defined Storage (SDS) as a basis for decoupling storage software functionality from the storage arrays so that storage software can be adapted to standardized x86 processing. The chapter also covers the principles of presenting storage as a large logical pool to be leveraged by any host, moving away from the rigid concept of logical unit numbers (LUNs). You are encouraged to cover all these principles in order to understand the distributed file systems that are offered by hyperconvergence.

Host Hardware Evolution

This chapter covers the following key topics:

- **Advancements in Compute:** Explains how the dramatic increase in processing power and the introduction of multicore CPUs make the server more powerful than the traditional storage controllers. Different terminology is covered, such as physical CPUs, virtual core, logical core, and virtual CPUs.

- **Evolution in Host Bus Interconnect:** Covers the introduction of fast speed buses such as the PCIe bus and the adoption of protocols such as NVMe that are well suited for handling much higher I/O bandwidth.

- **Emergence of Flash-Based Products:** Covers how the evolution in flash memory is getting cache speeds closer to traditional random access memory (RAM). A new generation of flash-based products is emerging on the host side and storage array side.

A major evolution in hardware has affected the data center. To start with, in compute alone, the latest CPUs for servers have more compute power than the legacy storage arrays that used to handle the input/output (I/O) load of all servers in an enterprise. Server interconnection to disks via Peripheral Component Interconnect express (PCIe) buses and the Non-Volatile Memory express (NVMe) protocol is dramatically increasing I/O bandwidth. The evolution of caching technology has created a new breed of all-flash arrays and high-performance servers. This chapter discusses this hardware evolution and how it affects the data center.

Advancements in Compute

You have heard of Moore's Law, in which transistors per square inch on integrated circuits double year over year and will continue to do so for the foreseeable future. Central processing units (CPUs) are a perfect example. You have seen the quick CPU evolution on your PCs and laptops over the years. Listing the Intel processors alone could fill this page. The technology has evolved from a single-core CPU doing all the work, to multi-core CPUs with clusters of CPUs sharing the load, to many-core CPUs offering larger and larger numbers of cores. The CPU performance, power savings, and scale have dramatically influenced the data center designs. Architectures that used to offload the CPUs with outside software controllers soon realized that the host CPU power exceeded the power of the controllers they were using. What used to be designed as an offload has fast become the bottleneck. A redesign is needed.

This chapter introduces you to some of the terms you hear when dealing with servers and compute to give you a better understanding of virtualization technology and how it uses such processing power.

x86 Standard Architecture

It is impossible to mention virtualization, convergence, hyperconvergence, and storage-defined storage without hearing the term *x86 standard–based architecture*. In fact, the whole movement behind software-based anything is to move away from "closed" hardware systems to standard-based x86. The irony is that many of the closed-based systems are also based on x86. The fact that the software in these systems is tied to the hardware makes them closed.

In any case, the term *x86 standard architecture* is mentioned a lot and deserves a brief definition. The x86 architecture is based on the Intel 8086 CPUs that were introduced in 1978. x86 is a family of instruction set architectures that has evolved over the years from 8-bit to 16-bit and then 32-bit processors. Many of the CPU architectures today from Intel and the other vendors are still based on this architecture. The x86 is the base for many hardware systems that will emerge in the years ahead.

Single-, Multi-, and Many-Cores CPUs

A *core* is the processing unit that receives instructions and performs mathematical and logical operations. The CPU, or the processor chip, has one core or multiple cores on it. Single-core CPUs were mainly used in the 1970s. The single-core CPU kept increasing in performance as companies such as Intel and AMD battled for the highest clock speeds. In the 2000s, the companies broke the 1 GHz clock speed barrier, and now they are breaking the 5 GHz barrier. Gaming had a lot to do with this because the complexity and speed in video games kept increasing. Long gone are the days of kids being happy with playing Atari Pong video games (1972).

As the single-core processor speed increased, heat and power consumption increased, challenging the physics of single core. Then followed the creation of dual-core processors, which began emerging in the 2004–2005 timeframe. A dual-core CPU had two cores on the same die. (A *die* is the circuitry that sits on a little square in a *wafer*, which is a thin slice of semiconductor material.) From the single core, the number of cores increased to 2, 4, 6, 8, and so on. Figure 3-1 shows the difference between a single CPU, single core and a dual CPU multicore. Just to be clear about the terminology, the CPU is the central processing unit chip that contains the bus interfaces and the L2 cache, whereas the core contains the register file and the L1/L2 cache and the arithmetic logic unit (ALU). The cache in the CPU and core allows for faster access to data than getting it from the RAM. Notice in this book that the RAM and solid-state drives (SSDs) are also used as L1/L2 caches for faster access to the data. The *socket* is the connector on the motherboard that forms the contact between the motherboard and the CPU.

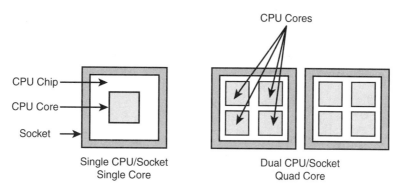

Figure 3-1 *Multicore CPUs*

Note that dual core is different from dual CPU or dual socket. Every socket has one CPU, so dual socket and dual CPU mean the same thing. A dual core or a quad core means that the CPU has in it two cores or four cores. This might seem basic to many people, but confusion arises when physical cores and virtual cores are discussed.

Physical Cores Versus Virtual Cores Versus Logical Cores

You might hear the terms *physical*, *virtual*, and *logical cores*. A physical core is actually what it says: a physical core on a die that sits on the CPU chip. A technology called *hyperthreading* (HT) began emerging, in which the same core processes multiple threads at the same time. Hyperthreading helps in applications that support multiple threads. A core that supports hyperthreading, say two threads, is thought to have performance similar to two cores. This is not actually true. Hyperthreading allows a single core to work better by taking advantage of any idle time to run the second thread. So this, of course, gives performance improvements, but nothing close to having physical cores. A single-core CPU with two threads does not perform as well as a two-core CPU. In essence, when a manufacturer advertises an eight-core CPU with multithreading, it could mean four physical cores and four virtual ones. The virtual core is the extra thread that you get from hyperthreading.

The number of logical cores is the total number of physical cores and virtual cores. Here's an example. A six-core CPU with hyperthreading results in twelve logical cores: six physical cores plus six virtual cores. In a VMware vSphere environment, a physical CPU (pCPU) refers to a single physical CPU core with no hyperthreading or (just for added confusion) to a single logical CPU core when hyperthreading is turned on.

Be sure that the application actually can use hyperthreading to leverage the virtual cores. If an application is designed to run multiple threads, then turning on virtual cores results in improved performance; if not, then virtual cores do not add value.

In addition to the number of cores in the CPU, vendors are incrementing the number of memory channels that connect the CPU to the RAM and are increasing the number of I/O buses that connect to storage. Some implementations have reached 32 cores per CPU and dual CPUs per server, reaching 64 physical cores or 128 logical cores with hyper-threading. Also, the number of memory channels has reached 16 per dual CPU, and the number of I/O lanes has reached 128. These numbers keep increasing, making the servers more powerful than ever.

Virtual CPU

A virtual CPU, not to be confused with a virtual core, is an actual slice of a core. Let's rewind a bit. The physical processor may have one or more cores, and each core can be considered many smaller processing units called virtual CPU (vCPU). The concept of vCPU is used with virtualization, in which the hypervisor allocates a certain number of vCPUs to a virtual machine (VM). The question that is asked the most is how many vCPUs you can have per VM and how many VMs you can run per host. The answer to the first question is easy, mainly because the virtualization software itself, like VMware, does not allow you to exceed certain limits. So in VMware, if you have eight logical cores (four physical and four virtual via hyperthreading), the maximum you can have is eight vCPUs (one vCPU per logical core). What is recommended normally is to have one vCPU per physical core because HT cores give a performance boost for the same core, but they are not actually separate cores.

The bottom line is that you have so many physical cores to work with, you have hyper-threading to make sure these cores do not sit idle, and you have cache and RAM, where you swap information to and from. Starting from these limits, you have to give your applications what they need, not more and not less. So, if an application recommends using two vCPUs and you give it four vCPUs, there is a good chance that the application will have worse performance. This is due to CPU scheduling and fair allocation of tasks. The following is an oversimplification of CPU allocation and memory allocation but should give you an idea of why sometimes more is less.

Assume that there are three applications—let's call them VM1, VM2, and VM3—that need to run on a server that has one CPU with four cores. The CPU allocation is shown in Table 3-1. The CPU has four cores: core 1, core 2, core 3, and core 4. Assume no hyperthreading so that one vCPU is allocated per core. In the rows, notice the differ-ent allocation over time. Allocation 1 is the CPU scheduling at time 1, allocation 2 is the CPU scheduling at time 2, and so on. The specification of the different applications recommends using one vCPU for VM1, one vCPU for VM2, and two vCPUs for VM3. However, because VM1 and VM2 are lower performance applications than VM3, the sys-tem administrator wanted to boost VM3's performance by giving it four vCPUs. Table 3-1 shows the core allocations at different timestamps.

Table 3-1 *CPU Allocation*

	Timestamp	Core 1	Core 2	Core 3	Core 4
CPU Allocation 1	T1	VM3	VM3	VM3	VM3
CPU Allocation 2	T2	VM1	VM2	IDLE	IDLE
CPU Allocation 3	T3	VM3	VM3	VM3	VM3
CPU Allocation 4	T4	VM1	VM2	IDLE	IDLE

At time T1, VM3 occupies all core slots. VM1 and VM2 cannot use that slot, so they must wait until T2, and they are allocated a slice of the CPU in core 1 and core 2. At T2, two more slots are available in cores 3 and 4 that VM3 could have used. But because you allocated four vCPUs to VM3, it has to wait until the third timeslot. The result is that the performance of the CPU is hindered by leaving idle timeslots, while VM3 waits for VM1 and VM2, and vice versa. This shows that overallocating vCPUs to VM3 slowed its performance.

People also wonder how many VMs can be run per host. That depends on the application, how heavily it is loaded, and so on. It is a CPU allocation game and a memory/cache access game. In this example, where the host has 4 cores, you can run 4 VMs (1 VM per vCPU), run 12 VMs (3 VMs per vCPU), or allocate even more. The rule of thumb says not to exceed 3 VMs per core (some use physical core; some use logical core). If you take this example and allocate 12 VMs, you have 12 VMs fight for the 4 cores. At some point, contention for the cores starts causing performance problems. If all 12 VMs, for example, are allocated 1 vCPU each, and their load is not heavy, then the vCPUs free up fast so you have more VMs scheduled. If, on the other hand, the VMs are running a heavy load, then contention for the cores causes VMs to perform poorly.

Another factor that influences the performance in CPU allocation is cache/memory access. Each core has access to L1, L2, L3 cache. These caches are small memories embedded in the core or in the CPU that give the processor faster access to the data it needs. The alternative is for the processor to get its data from RAM, which is also used as cache with slower access to data but with much larger data than CPU cache. The CPU L1 cache is the fastest, L2 is slower and bigger than L1, and L3 is slower and bigger than L2. L3 is called a shared cache because in multicore CPU designs, the L3 cache is shared by all the cores, whereas L1 and L2 are dedicated to each core. It's called a "hit" when the core finds the data in its cache. If the core does not find the cache in L1, it tries to get it from L2 and then L3, and if all fails it reaches to the RAM. The problem with allocating many VMs and vCPUs to the cores is that, aside from CPU scheduling, there is also contention for cache. Every VM can have different data needs that might or might not exist in the cache. If all VMs are using the same L3 cache, for example, there is a high likelihood of "misses," and the cores keep accessing the main memory, slowing the system down.

Most software vendors try to optimize their systems with CPU allocation algorithms and memory access algorithms. However, they do give the users enough rope to hang themselves. Although virtualization is a great tool to scale software applications on shared pools of hardware, bad designs can dramatically hinder the system performance.

Evolution in Host Bus Interconnect

Other than the fast growth in processor performance, there is an evolution in the interconnect technology allowing servers faster access to the network and to storage. This was discussed earlier in Chapter 2, "Storage Networks: Existing Designs." As solid-state drive (SSD) storage grows in capacity and lowers in price, you will see more adoption of SSDs. However, the interface speeds of serial advanced technology attachment (SATA) and serial attached SCSI (SAS), although good enough for hard disk drives (HDDs), are not adequate to handle the demand for faster drives. Also, as storage is connected via high-speed 40 Gbps and 100 Gbps, traditional bus architecture cannot cope.

PCIe is a high-speed serial computer bus standard that offers a high-speed interconnect between the server motherboard and other peripherals such as Ethernet or storage devices. PCIe supersedes older parallel bus interconnect technologies such as PCI or PCI eXtended (PCIX). It is based on a point-to-point interconnect that consists of connecting multiple endpoints directly to a root complex. PCIe is based on lanes, each having two pairs of wires—one pair for transmit and another for receive—allowing full duplex "byte" communication. PCIe supports x1, x2, x4, x8, x16, and x32 lanes, with the biggest physical PCIe slot supporting currently 16 lanes. The "x," as in "by," indicates the total number of lanes. So "x4" indicates four lanes. Added lanes allow more bandwidth on the point-to-point connections. Figure 3-2 shows the point-to-point PCIe interconnects between endpoints. Note that two endpoints can have multiple lanes, offering added bandwidth.

Notice that the "root complex" allows connectivity to PCIe endpoints or a PCIe switch to provide connectivity to many more PCIe endpoints, such as storage devices or high-speed Ethernet network interface cards (NICs). Also, the root complex can connect to bridges for connectivity to legacy PCI/PCIX interfaces.

As data centers increase in scale and capacity, PCIe is needed to allow the adoption of higher capacity interconnects, such as the 100 GE NIC cards, or Infiniband (56 Gbps, 40 Gbps, 20 Gbps, 10 Gbps) and high-bandwidth I/O to storage peripherals.

The PCIe standard has gone through many revisions. The revisions that have enhanced the bandwidth are as follows:

■ PCIe 1.a at 250 MBps data transfer rates per lane, or a transfer rate of 2.5 gigatransfers per second (GTps). The gigatransfer, or megatransfer, terminology refers to the raw data rate that the bus can move. The actual data rate is less because of the 8b/10b encoding where you need to send 10 bits of raw data for every 8 bits of actual data.

■ PCIe 2.0 doubled the data transfer rate to 500 MBps or 5 GTps.

- PCIe 3.0 offers 1 GBps or 8 GTps.

- PCIe 4.0 doubled the data transfer to 2 GBps or 16 GTps.

- PCIe 5.0 at 4 GBps or 32 GTps per lane. This means that a 32-lane PCIe 5.0 interconnect can reach a full duplex data rate of 32 × 4 = 128 GBps.

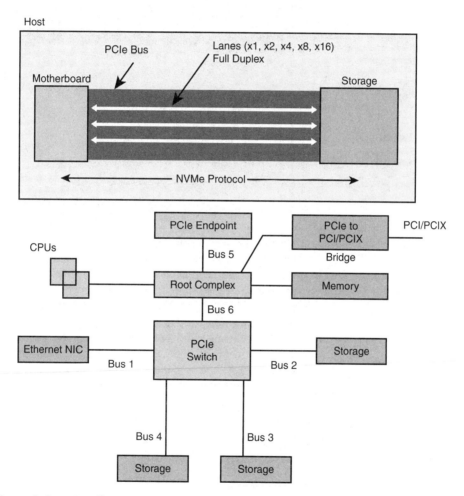

Figure 3-2 *PCIe Illustration*

Non-Volatile Memory Express

Non-Volatile Memory Express (NVMe) is a high-performance storage "protocol" that supports the PCIe technology. It was developed by the manufacturers of SSD drives to overcome the limitation of older protocols used with SATA drives, such as the Advanced Host Controller Interface (AHCI). AHCI is a hardware mechanism that allows the software to talk to SATA devices. It specifies how to transfer data between system memory and the device, such as a host bus adapter. AHCI offers, among other things, native command queuing (NCQ), which optimizes how read/write commands are executed to reduce the head movement of an HDD. Although AHCI was good for HDDs, it was not adequate for SSDs and PCIe interconnects.

It is important to note that NVMe is not an interface but rather a "specification" for the PCIe interface, and it replaces the AHCI protocol. NVMe is a protocol for accessing non-volatile memory, such as SSDs connected with PCIe buses. NVMe standardizes the register set, feature set, and command set for non-volatile memory. NVMe offers many attributes, such as these:

- High performance

- Low latency

- Better efficiency

- Lower CPU utilization

- Lower power

NVMe has driver support to a variety of operating systems, such as Windows Server, Free BSD, Ubuntu, Red Hat, and VMware. NVMe supports deep queues, such as 64,000 queues, where each queue supports 64,000 commands. This is in contrast to AHCI's one command queue, which supports a total of 32 commands. Other specifications, such as better register access, interrupt handling, shorter command set, and others make NVMe a superior protocol for SSDs. Therefore, SSDs have the option of being connected via SAS or SATA interfaces, via PCIe, and via PCIe with an NVMe specification. With the NVMe interface, you now can take full advantage of the PCIe bus reaching performance of 128 GBps and beyond. Moving forward, specifications for NVMe over fabrics (NVMe-oF) transport the NVMe protocol over Ethernet to allow SSDs to be removed from inside the hosts and concentrated as centralized storage over an Ethernet network. Coupling NVMe-oF with Remote Direct Memory Access (RDMA) technology over Converged Ethernet (RoCE), which allows NIC cards to bypass the CPU in processing memory requests, allows much lower latencies in accessing SSD drives.

The combination of high-performance multicore processors, SSDs, PCIe, and advancement in NVMe paves the way for enormous bandwidth and performance in accessing storage devices.

Emergence of Flash-Based Products

In the same way that CPU and interconnects have evolved, storage hardware has continued to evolve with the enhancement in caching technology and the way storage arrays leverage cache for performance and slower HDD drives for capacity. Enhancement in flash technology paves the way for higher performance. However, early storage array products could not take full advantage of flash SSD because their products were designed for slower HDDs and slower bus interconnects.

Enhancement in Flash Technology

Flash memory has evolved dramatically over the years, and it is used in SSDs that are slowly replacing HDDs with spinning disks. Flash memory itself comes in several flavors, and there is a cost versus performance decision to be made in choosing the right flavor. Flash memory based on single-level cells (SLC) NAND (as in a NOT-AND gate) is very expensive, has high endurance, is reliable, and is used in high-performance storage arrays. Multilevel cell (MLC) NAND flash is less expensive, has lower endurance, is less reliable and has lower write performance. Traditional flash is called Planar NAND and is built on a single layer of memory cells. This introduced challenges in creating higher densities to lower the cost. A new type of flash called 3D is being introduced to produce higher densities by building multiple layers of memory cells. A new type of memory called 3D Xpoint was introduced to the market in 2017 by Intel and Micron, which promises to bridge the gap between NAND flash and RAM when considering speed versus cost per gigabyte.

All NAND flash memory suffers from what is called *flash wear*, in which the cells tend to deteriorate as writes are performed more frequently. Software needs to be aware of destroyed cells. The more cells are destroyed, the lower are the performances. An endurance measure for flash SSDs is in Total Bytes Written (TBW), which specifies the total terabytes that can be written per day on an SSD, during its warranty period, before the SSD starts failing. SLC flash with high TBW is normally used for caching, whereas MLC flash with lower TBW is used for lower cost flash capacity devices. Because every vendor's objective is to extend the life of flash devices, mechanisms are adopted, such as wear-leveling, to spread the data across many blocks to avoid repetitive writing to the same block resulting in cell failure.

New Breed of Storage Arrays Falls Short

Chapter 2 discussed storage tiering and caching as enhancements to the traditional SAN arrays. The fact that storage arrays were becoming a bottleneck as many servers and virtual machines were accessing them prompted the emergence of new architecture. One such architecture is a redesign of storage arrays to handle all-flash SSDs or hybrid arrays with cache and HDD. It is worth discussing the new types of storage arrays because they will compete with hyperconvergence for market share.

All-Flash Arrays

Flash is now a strong contender for storage arrays because it offers many benefits, not only in speed and performance but in savings in power and cooling. A new breed of flash arrays started emerging, competing with HDD-based storage arrays on input/output operations per second (IOPS) and footprint. SSDs are used for capacity, and racks of HDD storage are now easily replaced with 2U or 4U chassis of SSDs, thereby saving on power consumption, cooling, and footprint.

Early products of flash arrays produced by the existing storage vendors were actually a variation of the same old storage array architectures. HDDs were changed to SSDs, which gave footprint savings; however, these systems were not designed for flash.

For instance, older storage arrays designed for HDDs used caching to handle both reads and writes in the storage controller to enhance the I/O performance while data is being written and read from spinning disk. These same architectures were adopted for all-flash arrays, where both reads and writes were handled in the cache, and not making use of the fast reads of SSDs. Also, write-in-place file systems were used, writing the same flash cells many times and causing flash wear. So, while early all-flash arrays had some performance improvements, they did not take full advantage of the expensive SSDs they used.

Other attributes that all-flash storage most overcome were the older architectures with SATA and SAS bus interconnects. Although SSDs offer a large number of IOPS, the bus interconnects were becoming the bottleneck. So, in summary, legacy storage vendors tried to jump on the all-flash bandwagon too fast and failed to deliver.

A new breed of flash arrays had to consider the characteristics of flash and high-speed interconnects to design systems from the ground up for better performance. While such newly designed systems are currently available on the market, they are still very expensive and cannot keep up with the huge growth in I/O processing in the data center. Although the flash drives gave much higher performance, the "centralized" dual storage controller architecture remains a bottleneck.

Hybrid Arrays

Hybrid refers to storage arrays that provide different tiers of storage with a combination of flash SSDs for cache and HDD disks for capacity. This, of course, generates a lot of confusion because any vendor who mixes HDD and SSD in their product can claim hybrid, including legacy products that support storage tiering. However, a savvy information technology (IT) professional needs to distinguish between older architectures designed for HDD and newer architectures designed for a combination of flash and HDDs. Many of the differentiations that were discussed in all-flash arrays apply here. Here are some things to look for:

- Is the storage array adopting the latest, faster, and denser HDDs, such as SAS?

- Can the storage array support PCIe and NVMe for flash cache drives?

- How does the controller deal with reads and writes?

- What is the power consumption of the system? Is it in the 1000 W range or the 10,000 W range?

- Where is compression and deduplication done: inline or post process?

- How does functionality such as compression and deduplication affect the performance of the application?

- Is the system doing storage tiering or storage caching?

Some or all of the above give an IT professional a clear idea of whether he is dealing with an older SAN storage array adapted to support flash, it is a new design that supports flash and has been adapted to support HDDs, or it is a system designed from day one to give the best performance to both.

Host-Based Caching

While all-flash storage arrays were evolving, a different architecture that focuses on the host side was evolving in parallel. Host-based caching moves some of the cache into the host for better performance than accessing the cache across the network. Instead of reaching across a SAN fibre channel or Ethernet network to access the storage array, caches were used on the host itself, which gives lower latency. This fast cache was used as the fast tier to do the read operations while the write operations were still done on traditional storage arrays. The drawback of this architecture is that some sort of tuning on the host caching software is needed on a per-application or a virtual machine basis. This adds a lot of overhead versus having all storage operations being taken care of by the storage array. Also, depending on the caching implementation, other drawbacks of the host-based caching architecture occur. In the case of a write-back cache, as an example, data is written to cache and acknowledged and then is sent in the background to the storage array. This results in data being trapped in the cache that does not participate with data management, such as taking snapshots from the storage array. As such, you are not getting consistent data management capabilities between the host cache and the storage array on the back end.

As the number of hosts increases, so does the cost of installing expensive cache cards inside the hosts, to the point where the costs become more than installing a centralized cache array. Although host-based caching is on the right path to hyperconvergence, by itself, it stands short of a complete solution. Evolution in storage software and the adoption of fully distributed storage file systems need to take place to achieve hyperconvergence.

Looking Ahead

This chapter covered the evolution in host hardware from compute to storage. This forms the basis of hyperconverged products that will use faster CPUs, high-speed interconnects, and high-performance flash drives.

Chapter 4, "Server Virtualization," discusses the software evolution in the data center, starting from the advantages of virtualization in providing applications with high availability and reducing the footprint in data centers. Chapter 5, "Software-Defined Storage," discusses the advantages of storage-defined networking in helping the industry move away from closed hardware-based storage arrays to a software-based architecture.

Chapter 4

Server Virtualization

This chapter covers the following key topics:

- **The Virtualization Layer:** This introduces server virtualization and how physical resources are virtualized and presented to the application. The difference between virtual machines and containers is explored.

- **Datastores:** Virtualization necessitates the introduction of datastores and logical volumes that focus on virtual machine disks rather than physical disks.

- **Virtual Machine (VM) Creation:** This section offers an example of VM creation, showing the different steps in the process.

- **Virtualization Services:** Virtual environments require high availability and fault tolerance to protect the application. Virtual machines are protected against different types of failures by using VM migration. This takes into account an even distribution of processing and storage load across multiple hosts.

- **Virtual Switching:** Virtual switching provides the virtual machines with all the networking attributes that exist in physical switches. The concept of standard and distributed virtual switches is explained with the different terminology.

Ample time has been spent so far talking about hardware and evolution in disk, compute, and interconnect. Software plays a huge role in the transformation of the data center, from server hardware, central processing unit (CPU), memory, disks, and so on, to a pool of resources that applications can use on demand. Virtualization is the concept of taking physical elements and presenting them as virtual or logical elements. The concept of virtualization is powerful because it extends to all aspects of hardware and even software. Server CPUs, memory, storage, interface cards, operating systems, applications, and so on, can all be virtualized.

Server virtualization and how it became a main factor in transforming the data center is described in detail. Because VMware was one of the early pioneers in the area of virtualization, many enterprises adopted VMware's vSphere and vCenter virtualization software and management. As such, this chapter explains virtualization, drawing on terminology from VMware's ESXi and vCenter due to their wide adoption.

The Virtualization Layer

This refers to software that runs on physical servers and provides an abstraction layer to processor, memory, storage, video, and networking. An example is VMware ESXi. This layer can create virtual machines and assign different resources from the shared pool.

In the traditional data center designs, servers and applications have a one-to-one relationship. Each application runs on its server and consumes the resources that the hardware offers. You have a separate email server, separate application servers, and separate database servers. These are called *bare-metal servers*.

The traditional design created inefficiencies in many areas. The number of servers in the data centers kept increasing, consuming space, power, and cooling. Also, where some applications consumed little CPU, memory, and storage, others did not have enough. This created problems in sizing the hardware resources to fit the software needs. Too much CPU and memory is great, but not when it sits idle. Too little is not good because it means agonizing upgrade cycles and downtime. That sounds like the same problem statement that was discussed with storage and which prompted the use of storage area networks (SANs) to consolidate disk space for better efficiency. The industry took a turn toward virtualizing the compute resources, which created the concept of a virtual machine (VM). With virtualization, the server is turned into a bunch of mini-servers or VMs, where each VM has access to its own slice of the hardware resources such as CPU and memory and storage and network interconnect. On these mini-servers, you can now run a separate operating system and application independent of the other virtual VMs.

Figure 4-1 shows a bare-metal server versus a virtualized server, where the hypervisor allows the creation of many VM that share the same hardware resources.

Notice that the VMs are running their own operating systems. Call such an operating system the "Guest OS" because it refers to the VM's operating system running on the host. This is in contrast to the "Host OS," which refers to the original operating system running on the server.

Be careful that vendors of some applications such as specialized databases still recommend using bare-metal servers due to the huge CPU and memory requirements of the databases. For other database applications, virtualized environments work perfectly well. As such, it is important that both virtualized and bare-metal servers coexist and share pools of storage.

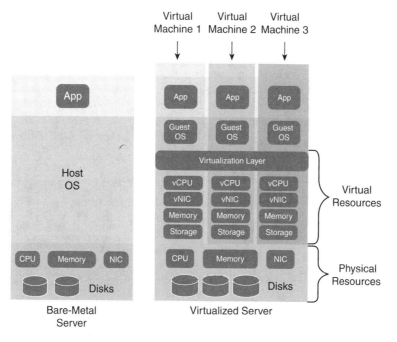

Figure 4-1 *Bare-Metal Versus Virtualized Servers*

A *hypervisor* is the software that makes virtualization happen. It is the piece of software that takes the hardware resources in a server and makes them look like a shared pool of resources. It then allocates a share of this pool to the guest applications as if they were running on their own hardware. Hypervisors come in Type 1 or Type 2 depending on the use case.

Type 1 Hypervisor

A type 1 hypervisor, also known as a bare-metal hypervisor, replaces the host OS and has direct interaction with the hardware. The type 1 hypervisor then creates the different VMs. Each of the VMs runs its own guest OS. The guest OS inside the VM does not see the actual server hardware or other guest OS. It only sees what virtual resources the hypervisor allocates. An example of a type 1 hypervisor is VMware ESXi.

The guest OS operates as if it is running on its own hardware that has a specific processing power, memory, storage, network interfaces, host bus adapters, and so on. Inside the VM, let's refer to all resources as virtual. The slice of the processor allocated to the VM, for example, is called a vCPU, as in virtual CPU. In the same way, the VM receives its virtual network interface card (vNIC), storage, and memory.

Type 2 Hypervisor

A type 2 hypervisor, also known as a hosted hypervisor, does not replace the host OS, but rather sits on top of the existing OS. An example of a type 2 hypervisor is VMware Workstation. Assume, for example, a server that is running Linux OS. A type 2 hypervisor installed on top of Linux can create multiple VMs. Inside a VM, you can run Windows as a guest OS. The VM has no direct interconnection with the hardware but sees the world as presented to it by the hypervisor. Also, the hypervisor itself sees the world as presented to it by the host Linux OS. Figure 4-2 shows the difference between a type 1 and a type 2 hypervisor.

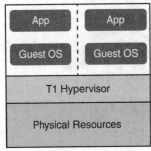 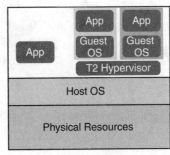

Type 1 Hypervisor　　　　　　Type 2 Hypervisor

Figure 4-2　*Type 1 Versus Type 2 Hypervisors*

There are different hypervisors on the market pioneered by companies like VMware, Microsoft, Citrix, Nutanix, and others. By far, VMware ESXi is the most adopted because VMware was the first to release an enterprise-class type 1 hypervisor to the market. Other type 1 hypervisors gaining ground in the marketplace are Hyper-V from Microsoft and KVM, which is open source. Differentiation between hypervisors in this layer includes what guest operating systems can run inside the VM, whether dynamic memory allocation can be done to all types of guest operating systems, fault tolerance, and so on.

Hypervisors addressed first the virtualization of compute resources. This is when it moved from a one-to-one relationship between application and server hardware to a many to one where VMs use a shared pool of compute resources. Virtualization also addressed the storage layer by moving from a relationship between a host server and a storage to a relationship between a VM and virtual disks.

Docker Containers

A container image is a lightweight, standalone, executable package of a piece of software that includes everything needed to run it: code, runtime, system tools, system libraries, and settings [1]. The container architecture started in the early 2000s when many companies were working part of open-source projects such as Open Virtuozzo containers

(OpenVZ) and Linux container (LXC) to create the container architecture. The idea was to create a software container that had in it everything an application would need to run and isolate it from other applications running on the same server. The concept grew in popularity after the company Docker launched its Docker 1.0 release in 2014. The popularity of Docker increased after many enterprises began adopting the concept to virtualize their applications. In June 2015, some leading companies such as AWS, Cisco, Microsoft, Google, VMware, Docker, and others announced the creation of the Open Container Project (OCP) to establish common standards for software containers [2]. At the same time, Docker announced that it would donate container format, runtime code, and specifications to OCP. Since then, the adoption of containers has continued to grow, leveraging contributions from vendors to OCP contributions. There are different types of container technologies, including Docker and CoreOS rkt [3]. Containers are known today as the Docker containers.

The concept behind containers is similar to the concept behind VMs, but with major differences. This is seen in Figure 4-3.

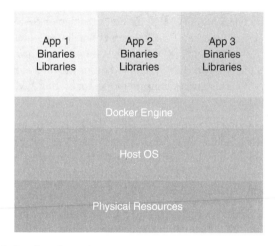

Figure 4-3   *Sample Docker Containers*

Hypervisors virtualize the hardware itself and allow different applications with guest operating systems running on top of the hardware; the container engine virtualizes the host operating system. The advantage of containers is that they are lightweight, which allows many more applications to run on the same server as compared to hypervisors and VMs. This is because containers share the same OS and do not require as much system resources as VMs. The applications are packaged with their own libraries, binaries, configuration files, and all they need to run and are presented as a portable capsule. The drawback is that, with containers, all applications must share the same host OS, so you cannot have applications with different guest OSs running on the same server.

Although containers play a major role in the data center, most hyperconvergence implementations started with virtualization through hypervisors and VMs and have containers on the road map. Therefore, most of the architecture discussions in this book focus on VMs, as the support for containers in hyperconverged networks has not yet reached maturity.

Datastores

Virtualization software stores data in logical volumes or datastores that have a specific file system. This section gives an example of VMware's datastores and how they tie into the storage array logical unit number (LUN). Chapter 5, "Software-Defined Storage" discusses how VMware augmented this model to offer a more recent implementation via Virtual Volumes (VVols), which moves away from the LUN concept.

VMware uses *datastores*, which are logical containers (not to be confused with Docker containers) for VM disk files that hide the physical disk from the virtual machines. LUNs are allocated to datastores, where one or multiple LUNs map into a single datastore. The datastore houses the virtual machine files that are associated with a particular virtual machine. The datastores are then formatted with a particular file system. VMware uses the Virtual Machine File System (VMFS) for block storage on SAN for Fibre Channel (FC), Fibre Channel over Ethernet (FCoE), Internet Small Computer System Interface (iSCSI), and Raw Device Mapping (RDM) for getting access to raw devices through VMFS. It also uses the Network File System (NFS) for file-level storage on network-attached storage (NAS), This gives a uniform model for storing VMs and their data for block, file, and raw devices.

Datastores are used to hold VM files, templates, and ISOs. A template is called a golden image, which is a VM machine image that creates other VMs via cloning. ISO files are a sector-by-sector copy of a disk stored in binary. In the context of VMware, as an example, the ISO files are typically used to store installation disks for Windows or Linux so a full operating system can be installed on a VM.

To make use of the datastore, the virtual machines are allocated many different virtual files that make up the VM. Examples of these files are the .vmx file that contains the configuration of the VM and the .log file that contains log information. The bulk of the VM data is actually inside .vmdk files, which are virtual machine disks (VMDKs) whose capacity is taken from the datastore. The VMDKs are thick or thin provisioned. As discussed earlier, thick provisioning does actual allocation of the blocks, while thin provisioning is a type of overcommitment, where the blocks are assigned only when the data is written to. Multiple VMs share a datastore. Multiple hosts sharing the datastore are needed for functionality such as VM mobility, distributed resource scheduling (DRS), and high availability (HA) for consolidation purposes.

In the case of VMware, datastores are assigned storage capabilities, which classify storage under different tiers. For example, solid-state drive (SSD) storage could be classified as a gold tier, hard disk drive (HDD) SAS storage as silver, and HDD SATA as bronze. Virtual machines are assigned storage profiles that identify the placement of a VM under a specific storage capability. This way, critical VMs that need high performance are

assigned to gold tiers so their VM files are stored in SSD, while VMs with lower performance needs have their files stored in slower HDDs. Figure 4-4 shows a description of
the VMware VMFS file system and the association between VMs, datastores, and LUNs.

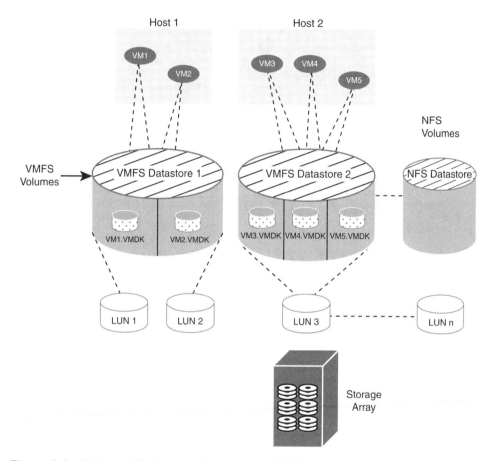

Figure 4-4   *VMware File System: Datastores and LUNs*

Note in Figure 4-4 that both LUNs 1 and 2 were allocated to Datastore 1, whereas
LUN 3 was allocated to Datastore 2. Note also how VM1 and VM2 share the same
Datastore 1 and that VMs 3, 4, and 5 share Datastore 2.

One of the main issues with datastores and LUNs is that their granularity is coarse, and it
affects many VMs at the same time. So, the VM inherits the capabilities of the LUN and
the datastore and not what the VM/application actually requires. To have finer granularity, you must configure one VM per datastore, but then it is limited to the number of
datastores/LUNs supported, which is 256. As you will see in the next chapter, VMware
added additional support to what is called Virtual Volumes (VVols), which offer finer
granularity and tie nicely with the concept of software-defined storage.

Virtual Machine Creation

It is worth taking a pause here to show an example of provisioning a VM in a VMware vSphere environment just to put together most of the concepts that have been discussed. A word of caution: this is by no means an exact step-by-step configuration with actual commands, as it is not meant as a VMware configuration tutorial. The example is just an overview that shows the high-level concepts that were discussed.

We'll look at the case of an IT professional who wants to provision multiple VMs on a physical server that is connected to a traditional SAN array via an iSCSI host bus adapter/10 GE.

Let's start with the hardware functionality at hand.

Server CPU: Two physical CPUs (two sockets) with dual core per CPU

Memory: 4 GB RAM

Storage: Dual controller array, five physical disks that are 1 TB each

NIC: iSCSI 10 GE converged adapter

The following provides an example of provisioning a VM. You need to make a LUN on the storage array to create virtual disk storage. Take a chunk of that storage, allocate it to a VM, and install Windows Server 2012 OS inside the VM.

LUN Configuration

The storage specialist configures the storage array of five disks as RAID 5, which creates a 4 TB logical disk (because 1 TB is consumed by the parity data). The logical disk is then configured as four LUNs—1, 2, 3, and 4—with each LUN presenting a 1 TB volume. Note that the storage team creates the LUNs because this is what happens in normal operation, where storage people are responsible for storage, and virtualization people are responsible for compute.

Datastore Configuration

From the VMware vSphere client, the IT virtualization people configure a VMFS datastore by going to the Hosts and Clusters and then the Storage Configuration menus. From there, they see all the LUNs on the iSCSI target and choose LUN 1 to create a datastore, named Datastore 1, and LUN 2 to create Datastore 2. The datastores can be allocated the full capacity of the LUNs or portions of the LUNs. Assume that Datastore 1 gets the full LUN 1 capacity of 1 TB; the same goes for Datastore 2.

New VM Creation

Now go to the host you are configuring and start a new VM configuration. Name the new VM as VM1, and choose Datastore 1 to give capacity to VM1.

Guest OS Assignment

Assign a guest operating system to VM1, such as Windows Server 2012 (64 bit). Note here the difference between a guest operating system and a host operating system. The guest operating system is what runs inside the VM, whereas the host operating system running on the server is in this case the VMware ESXi OS.

vCPU Assignment

Now you have the option to assign one or multiple vCPUs to the VM. VMware gives the option to configure multiple variables, such as the number of virtual sockets or the number of cores per virtual socket. VMware allows a maximum of 64 vCPUs per VM; however, when assigning vCPUs, you cannot exceed the total number of logical cores. In this case here, you have two CPUs, dual core, so the total number of cores is 4. If hyperthreading is turned on, you have a total of 8 logical CPUs, or, as you recall from Chapter 3, they were called pCPUs. So, in this example, VMware allows the user to allocate a maximum of 8 vCPUs to VM1. This is done with multiple combinations of virtual sockets and core. For example, if you wanted to give VM1 2 vCPUs, choose 1 socket and 2 cores, or 2 sockets and 1 core.

Memory Allocation

Because the physical hardware has a maximum of 4 GB of RAM, VMware allows you to assign the full memory or portion of the memory to the VM. However, because you do not want to have a single VM consume the full memory, VMware guides you on what minimum and maximum recommended memory to assign for maximum performance. In this case, assign 1 GB of RAM to VM1. Memory is allocated from the actual total host memory—in this case, 4 GB. Too much memory will starve the other VMs, and too little memory will cause "paging" by using portions of the physical disk as memory, which slows down the system because of longer access times to the data.

Adding the Network Interface Card and SCSI Controller

After the memory allocation, configure the network interface card (NIC) that is appropriate for the VM and its guest operating system, and then assign a SCSI controller to the virtual machine.

Assigning a Virtual Disk

This is where you create a virtual disk out of the datastore you assigned to the VM. In this case, Datastore 1 has 1 TB, so you can create a virtual disk up to 1 TB of storage. The virtual disk is provisioned as thick or thin. In this case, you assign a 1 TB thin disk, which means the virtual disk is allocated disk space on demand whenever it needs it up to the full 1 TB. Note that other virtual disks can still be created in Datastore 1, and be careful that the total storage space allocated between thin and thick disks does not actually exceed the physical limitation of Datastore 1, which is 1 TB.

Power On and OS Installation

The last step in the VM configuration is to indicate where the guest OS is located, such as on a CD drive inside the host server, and then power on the VM. Now the guest OS loads on the virtual disk you created and is allocated all the resources you gave the VM, including the CPU, memory, storage, and network.

Voilà! You created a VM that acts now as a mini server on top of the actual physical host. The VM acts as any physical server, but it only sees the share of resources that are allocated to it. You can create many more VMs on the same server, and with proper configuration, you can make sure that the VMs do not eventually starve each other, causing major degradation in system performance.

Now that you can create many virtual machines on the same hardware, it becomes important to protect these VMs from system failure and ensure performance. This is where functionality such as vMotion, HA, and DRS comes into play. Let's discuss some of these concepts in detail, starting with server clustering, provisioning models, datastores, and the file system. Again, for the reader who is eager to get to hyperconvergence, everything discussed so far, while still applicable on the same old SAN deployments, leads to hyperconvergence or eventually morphs to hyperconvergence, so stay tuned. We're getting there!

Virtualization Services

With virtualization comes a set of services needed to protect the application and distribute the compute and storage loads across the cluster. This section first defines the concept of clusters and discusses some of the different virtualization services that are applied on the cluster, such as these:

- VM migration

- High availability

- Fault tolerance

- Compute load balancing

- Storage migration and balancing

- Provisioning

- Management

Clusters of Servers or Nodes

A *cluster* is a grouping of servers (most of the time called *nodes*) that work together as a single unit to perform a set of functionalities to clients. The virtualization speaks of server clusters as a block of servers that perform a set of virtualization functionality, such as HA, load balancing, sharing computing resources, and so on. The number of servers in a cluster depends on vendor implementation and how much their software scales. Some define a cluster as 8 nodes, others as 64 nodes, and others as unlimited. Basically, vendors offer a cluster as a bundle when they know their software will work and they try to differentiate in numbers. Many vendors started with VMware's ESXi software implementation, so cluster sizes scaled up to VMware's scaling number. What matters in building small or large clusters is how well the vendor software performs when communicating between nodes and how it handles problematic nodes. For example, a node that is misbehaving can affect the communication between all other nodes and bring down the performance of the system. This happens if the cluster is 8 nodes or 64 nodes or 300 nodes. Differentiation in this area is key in picking the right vendors.

VM Migration

VM migration allows VMs to be moved from one physical server to another for different purposes. Migrating VMs could occur in the case of a server failure, where VMs must be restarted somewhere else. Other cases involve moving VMs to spread the load between overutilized and underutilized servers.

VM migration occurs on cold VMs that are already shut down, suspended VMs, or fully running VMs. In all cases, the originating host and the destination host share storage, so the destination has access to the VM files. Also, when migrating VMs, all the networking policies and networking configuration that are attached to the VM need to move with it. Say that a VM has a certain IP address and a firewall or load balancer that points to it. When the VM migrates, the same IP needs to move with it, as do the firewall and load balancer policies.

Migrating VMs that are already shut down is much simpler than migrating running machines. When migrating a running machine, for example, the existing VM is verified to be in a stable state on the current host. After that, the VM state information, such as memory, registers, and network connections, are copied to the target host. Following that, the VM resumes its activities on the target host. If any errors occur during the migration, the VM reverts to its original state and location. Moving suspended or running machines in VMware is called *vMotion*.

Migrating machines are manual or automatic. With manual migration, the end user is given a set of recommendations on which hosts the VM should be moved to. This is based on the host CPU and memory utilization. The end user then manually instructs the system to perform the migration. With automatic migration, the system does the migration on its own, taking into consideration the same host utilization metrics.

Vendors have different restrictions for VM migration. VMware, for example, prefers that the migration be done between similar hosts, or at least to have compatible CPUs. Another area of differentiation is the boundary of the mobility of the active VM, meaning whether it can be moved between servers in the same cluster, between servers in different clusters in the same data center, between different data centers, or between a private data center and a public cloud.

High Availability

High availability (HA) ensures that if a server failure occurs, the VMs on the source host restart on different servers that are healthy. In the case of VMware, for example, the VMs and the hosts they reside on are pooled into an HA cluster. The hosts in the cluster are monitored and share the network resources. In the case of failure, the VMs on a failed host are moved to other hosts in the cluster.

HA does not ensure zero downtime; the VM has to restart, including its operating system and application. Failures occur for different reasons; perhaps the host where the VM is running fails, the guest operating system inside the VM fails, or the application inside the VM fails. Failures are detected via different mechanisms, such as network management monitoring response times of an application, monitoring the level of responsiveness of an operating system, or simply having hosts within a cluster with a heartbeat, checking on whether the other hosts are operational.

Implementations between vendors vary a lot in this area on how they deal with high availability. An example of dealing with OS or application failure could be simply restarting the VM where the OS or the application exists. Other implementations could choose to totally shut down the host if many applications on the same host are experiencing problems. When the whole host needs to be shut down, be careful to ensure the load can be processed on other hosts. For example, you might decide that a cluster could have a one-node failure or a multinode failure. You must decide whether the failed VMs are launched by spreading the load equally on all other hosts in the cluster or some dedicated hosts designated to support such failures. You also need to decide how much of the compute and storage resources are left as spare, in case there is a failure. If multiple VMs fail and there is no capacity in the network to absorb these failures, you did not configure high availability properly. An example is given in Figure 4-5. This example shows a cluster of three nodes, which you are trying to protect against host failure. Host A is running VMs VM1 and VM2, Host B is running VMs 3 and 4, Host C runs VMs 5 and 6. All hosts share the same pool of storage on a SAN array.

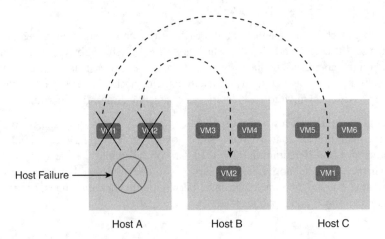

Figure 4-5 *High Availability Within an HA Cluster*

Assume that you configured high availability in such a way that if any host fails, the other hosts run the two failed VMs. To do so, you need to make sure that each host can actually support its VMs and at least one of the other VMs from the failed host. (Load balancing is discussed in the next section.) Protecting for multiple failures is more expensive because you must make sure that running hosts will support the load from all failed hosts. The decision of whether a cluster sustains one node failure or multiple node failures depends on the CPU, memory, and storage services attached to the VMs. If the VM requirements cannot be met if they're initiated on other systems, high availability cannot take place, and the VM is not protected.

Fault Tolerance

Fault tolerance provides continuous availability for VMs by giving VMs zero downtime. This comes at the expense of creating and maintaining a secondary VM that is identical to the source VM. The secondary VM is ready to replace the source VM if failure occurs. The secondary VM is in virtual lockstep with the primary VM and is always updated with inputs and events that occur on the primary VM. If a VM failure occurs, the secondary VM immediately takes over without impact or downtime.

Fault tolerance is not an easy task if it promises zero downtime. This means that the state of the virtual machine must be kept in shared storage so the secondary VM has access to it instantaneously. Also, the active memory and execution state must be transferred across the network so the new VM picks up where the failed VM left off. Any networking attributes such as IP addresses, firewalls, and load balancers that are associated with the failed VM must be transferred to the new VM.

Vendors differ on how many guest operating systems they support, what CPUs they support, whether multiprocessing is supported during fault tolerance (as in how many vCPUs per VM), and so on.

Compute Load Balancing

This functionality monitors the server's utilization inside the cluster to evaluate where a VM should run. This takes better advantage of the existing resources and balances the load between nodes. An example is VMware's vSphere DRS. This function is manual or automatic. If configured in manual mode, whenever a VM must be loaded, it advises the user on the best location to run the VM, and it is up to the user to take the recommendation or not. In automatic mode, DRS initiates a migration of a VM to the location that gives the most balanced resource utilization in the cluster. When high availability was discussed in the previous section, it mentioned that if Host A fails, then VM1 and VM2 are protected by the other hosts. If VM1 and VM2 were to restart on Host B, for example, it creates an imbalance in which Host B is overloaded and Host C is underloaded. Load balancing dynamically checks the utilization of all nodes in the DRS cluster and distributes the VMs for better utilization of the resources.

Storage Migration

This allows the mobility of the VM files and virtual disks from one datastore to another without disruption to the operation of the VM. The files are placed in the same datastore as the VM or in a separate datastore. An example is VMware's vSphere Storage vMotion. This functionality is useful for the user to balance VM files between datastores, move the VM files from thick to thin provisioned virtual disks, or move VM files between SAN arrays.

Storage Load Balancing

In the same way that compute load balancing makes better use of the compute resources such as CPU and memory in evaluating where to place a VM, storage load balancing does the same for storage. Storage load balancing evaluates where to place the VM "files" in the different available datastores. It makes decisions based on available capacity in the datastore and the input/output (I/O) latency in accessing files. This ensures that you do not end up with datastores that are overloaded and with huge I/O latency, while others are underloaded. An example of such functionality is VMware's vSphere Storage DRS. As with compute, this function is either manual, where the user receives recommendations on which datastore to use, or automated, where the load balancing function dynamically places the VM files in an appropriate datastore, taking into consideration datastore capacity and I/O latency.

Provisioning and Management

This is an essential part in provisioning and managing the virtualized environment as you move from few physical servers to hundreds and thousands of virtual machines. Hosts can be provisioned individually via PC clients or web clients or managed in bulk via central management stations. In the VMware environment, as an example, the vSphere client software or web client is used to access the ESXi host and delivers functionality such as provisioning VMs and datastores and other functions on a host-by-host basis. On the other hand, vCenter is a central management station that runs as a standalone or as a VM on top of ESXi and delivers a holistic view of the network—including all hosts and VMs—and allows the configuration of advanced functionality such as VM and storage migration, high availability, fault tolerance, and more. While moving toward simplification of provisioning data centers, such tools are essential in delivering automation of tasks and policies. Automation is discussed in detail as part of the hyperconverged data center.

Virtual Switching

Networking plays a big part in virtualization. Even though you are dealing with VM, the networking requirements do not change. You just swapped physical NICs with virtual NICs, physical media access control (MAC) addresses with virtual MAC addresses, and physical ports on a switch with virtual ports.

Virtual switching is the networking function of the virtualization layer, and it delivers the basic functionality of a physical Ethernet switch; however, it is done in software. The virtual switch delivers all networking functions to the VMs. Configuring VM segmentation occurs at this layer and segments the VMs on the same physical server or across all servers that span the virtualization layer. Virtual switching allows VMs to move around between the hosts while maintaining their network configuration profiles. The area of differentiation between vendors lies in the supported functionality of the virtual switch, such as link aggregation, simple network management protocol, port analyzers, and so on. There are two types of virtual switches: standard/local virtual switches and distributed virtual switches.

A standard virtual switch allows segmentation and switching between VMs in a single physical host. One or more standard switches are defined inside a physical host. A distributed virtual switch is one that spans multiple servers in a cluster and switches between VMs residing on different physical hosts. The distributed switch is an extension of the standard switch; it creates a higher layer via centralized management that overlooks the configuration of all the local switches, making it look like the distributed switch spans across servers. This is illustrated in Figure 4-6.

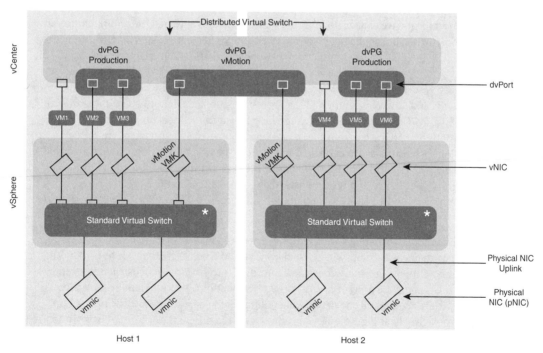

Figure 4-6 *Virtual Switching Terminology*

As you see in Figure 4-6, the standard virtual switch is local to one host, whereas the distributed switch works at a higher layer and is created by management platforms like a vCenter. Most virtualized configurations today have moved away from local switches to distributed switches because of the ease of configuration that distributed switches offer. Distributed virtual switches still rely on local switches, but the local switches work in the background and are hidden from the end user.

When you do a configuration on the distributed switch, it is propagated by vCenter to all the individual hosts via the hidden local switches. The VMware terminology was used In Figure 4-6 due to its widespread usage in the industry. When working with virtual switches, the concept of vmnics, virtual NICs (vNICs), virtual MAC addresses (vMACs), distributed virtual port (dvPort), distributed virtual port groups (dvPG), distributed virtual uplinks (dvUplink), and dvUplink Port Group comes up. It is worth discussing these concepts briefly because they are the basis of networking in a virtualized environment.

Basically, a VM attaches to a virtual switch via a port. In a distributed virtual switch environment, the terminology became dvPort. So, virtual machines are now identified in the network by the dvPort they connect to. So far, this is simple enough. Now each port is associated with network configuration and policies. An example is an IP address that the VM has, a virtual MAC address, whether it is attached to a firewall, as well as quality of service (QoS) or security policies. Because many VMs in the network could have similar policies, the concept of a dvPort Group (dvPG) was created. The port group is a grouping of ports that have similar policies and a mechanism to automate the configuration of many ports with similar characteristics in one shot. So in a data center, a dvPG-production indicates all the VMs in the production network that have similar characteristics, and dvPG-dev groups VMs in the development environment. Another key benefit is that as you apply vMotion to move a VM from one host to another, the VM moves within the same dvPG and, as such, acquires all the networking policies that it had on the previous host. Most dvPGs are created by vCenter and pushed to the local hosts; however, some port groups that are essential to the operation of the virtual environment are created locally on each host and are dedicated to specific functions. Such port groups are called "vmkernel" (VMK) port groups. An example is dvPG-vMotion to allow the vMotion of virtual machines between physical hosts, dvPG-HA for HA, dvPG-Mgmt to carry management traffic, and so on. Note in Figure 4-6 that these VMK dvPorts are created inside vSphere.

As many vendors, including Cisco, adopt vCenter as a management platform for a virtualized environment, virtual switches such as Cisco AVS or others that opt to work with vCenter have to map any new constructs into dvPGs to have these constructs applied to VMs. Upon the creation of a VM or the placement of a VM into a dvPG, the VM automatically acquires all the networking configuration and policies of the port group. If you look closely at Figure 4-6, you can identify the different port groups as vMotion, Production, and so on.

Another terminology that is confusing is vmnics or physical NICs (pNICs) and vNICs. In essence, hosts connect to the physical environment via top-of-rack (ToR) switches. To do so, each host has one or more pNICs. In today's data centers, most of the connectivity is via 10 GE interfaces or higher, and each host has, at the minimum 2 × 10 GE interfaces. The vmnic terminology usually refers to the actual pNIC inside the host. So, a host that has two NICs each with 10 GE interfaces has two vmnics. When a VM connects to the virtual switch (via software), you reference a (vNIC) that has multiple virtual MAC (vMAC) addresses that are configured by the end user. So, the VM connects to the virtual switch via a vNIC, and the virtual switch connects to the physical NICs via a vmnic. This is seen also in Figure 4-6. A dvUplink is the connection between the virtual switch and the vmnic (via the hidden local switch). A virtual switch could have one or multiple dvUplinks that are grouped in dvUplink groups. The physical uplink is the connection between the pNIC card (vmnic) and external ToR switches. The traffic from the VMs that is leaving the host toward the network is multiplexed inside the virtual switches and sent on the dvUplinks toward the vmincs and then to the physical switches.

The virtual switch offers functionality such as Layer 2 switching, VLAN, Virtual Extended LAN (VXLAN), network management capabilities, and so on. Implementations in the industry include Cisco's Nexus 1000v and Cisco's Application Virtual Switch (AVS), VMware's vNetwork Standard Switch (VSS) and virtual Distributed Switch (vDS), and the open source Open vSwitch (OVS). Cisco's AVS integrates with Cisco's application-centric infrastructure (ACI) for applying policies to the VMs from an Application Policy Infrastructure Controller (APIC), while VMware's vDS is tied into the VMware's virtual networking and security software product (NSX). Open source software-defined networks use OVSDB to control OVS. ACI, NSX, and OVSDB in the context of hyperconvergence are discussed in Part VI, "Hyperconverged Networking."

Looking Ahead

Server virtualization took data centers into a direction that challenged both data networking and storage. The networking and storage constructs used to scale physical networks are inadequate for virtual networks.

Chapter 5 discusses the concept of software-defined storage (SDS) and its objectives. Some pre-hyperconvergence implementations that still focus on enhancing traditional storage arrays are discussed. Chapter 6, "Converged Infrastructure," puts you on the path of hyperconvergence and examines the changes it will bring in moving away from storage arrays into a distributed storage approach that leverages clusters of servers with direct-attached storage.

References

[1] www.docker.com

[2] https://www.opencontainers.org/

[3] https://coreos.com/rkt/

Chapter 5

Software-Defined Storage

This chapter covers the following key topics:

- **SDS Objectives:** An introduction to software-defined storage (SDS) and its objectives in decoupling storage software from hardware, allowing software to run on standard x86 architectures, and offering easier management and automation.

- **Preserving the Legacy and Offering New Features:** Some early implementations of SDS focused on preserving the existing storage array implementations and enhancing them with an SDS layer that offers management for different hardware silos and new data services.

- **vSphere APIs for Storage Awareness (VASA) and Virtual Volumes (VVols):** An important architecture that is developed by VMware and based on integrating third-party storage arrays with vCenter through the use of application programming interfaces (APIs). VASA allows vCenter to have a better view of the storage and learn the storage array capabilities. The concept of VVols moves away from logical unit number (LUN) and offers the storage arrays better visibility to the application and finer granularity in applying storage data services.

As data continued to grow, it became obvious that legacy storage area network (SAN) deployments were not going to scale to meet the changing needs of storage. Managing arrays from different vendors is extremely difficult. It is even challenging if different products come from the same vendor. The main issue is that storage arrays are hardware-centric closed systems with software intelligence inside the storage controller and in lockstep with the hardware. As different applications are added to the data center, and each vendor builds its software around its preferred storage vendor, the data center can begin to look like islands of storage hardware working independent of one another. Each silo has its own set of management tools and its own hardware and software refresh cycles. Also, as new systems are added to the data center—for example, all-flash storage—it becomes harder and harder to integrate the new systems with the existing ones to have a unified pool of storage. Storage administrators have spent most of their time moving data from one storage array to another and trying to figure out how to manage backups.

A second paradigm shift is the changing data types and enormous data growth rates. Traditional data consisted of what was called "structured," and it was mainly used by databases such as Oracle or SAP Structured Query Language (SQL) databases. With the introduction of many Internet web applications, the data became "unstructured" and object oriented, such as data created by files, photos, videos, and so on. If you take a simplistic 80/20 rule, you can assume that 20% growth is in structured data, whereas 80% growth is unstructured data. Storage arrays were mainly targeted toward block storage and not for unstructured data.

A third factor to look at is that storage arrays do not have knowledge of the application and its requirements. Data services such as replication and snapshots are tied to the hardware and come in different flavors on different hardware. They do not react dynamically to the changing needs of the application. Legacy provisioning models are bottom up, where the data services are provisioned at the array level and enforced on the application level. Future applications require a top-down view, where the application dictates its needs that would translate into storage provisioning through policies and automation.

Last is the introduction of public clouds and the need to integrate storage policies between private and public data centers. This requires a higher layer of abstraction with a holistic view of application requirements and its storage needs within and outside the data center.

SDS Objectives

The industry started looking in the direction of what is called software-defined storage (SDS) and sometimes called software-based storage. To cut down on the confusion, let's stick with the SDS terminology. The definition of SDS varies because different vendors have tried to address and solve different problems, so all new initiatives were lumped under software-defined storage.

The common denominators for all SDS initiatives are as follows:

- Decouple the control software and storage data services from the hardware so it can be run from outside the storage array.

- Leverage standardized x86-based processing architectures and virtual machines running on servers to run the SDS layer, thereby eliminating the need for costly storage arrays. The fact that closed hardware systems are bundled with proprietary software allowed vendors to overcharge for their products.

- Create a pool of storage capacities and present it as one logical pool that the applications can manipulate.

- Deliver a set of advanced data services that are policy based and more in tune with the needs of the applications.

- Offer a single pane of glass management, eliminating manual configuration and offering a set of policies and automation tools to make provisioning and management automated and simpler.

- Address the huge growth of unstructured data by handling object file systems in addition to block and file systems.

The vendors disagreed on what problems to solve first. It was obvious that the existing storage array vendors were not going to dissent, and they would continue to push their closed architectures with enhancements in software and hardware. The whole notion of convergence (not hyperconvergence) was one way to simplify the provisioning and management by bundling different pieces under unified management. Products such as Vblock offered by VCE were a combination of virtualized servers, networking switches, and storage arrays bundled together. This did not address the major pain points.

SDS is a software play, and it needs established software vendors and new entrants to make a change. This is where established software companies such as VMware and a few startup companies played a big role because they were the most aggressive in introducing SDS functionality and therefore putting pressure on established storage vendors to react. However, re-creating storage functionality that took years to develop with the traditional storage vendors is not easy. No one could solve all the problems at once, so each addressed the problem from different angles. What is described next are some early stages of SDS, where vendors started on the path of decoupling software from the storage array themselves. Two approaches are described: one adopted by some leading storage vendors such as EMC and the other by leading virtualization vendors such as VMware (now part of Dell/EMC). SDS implementations continued to evolve to address hyperconverged environments where storage data services were delivered over clusters of servers with direct-attached storage. This is discussed in Part III of this book.

Preserving the Legacy and Offering New Features

The first school of thought promoted the idea that you cannot overhaul the existing network because companies have invested too much money in their existing storage arrays and will continue to enhance the existing architecture. So SDS must integrate with the current architecture and enhance it with new functionality. From a management perspective, the objective was to create a single management layer, or a single pane of glass, that discovers and manages the unified pool of storage and delivers easier provisioning via a set of policies and automation. Figure 5-1 shows some of the initially proposed SDS architectures.

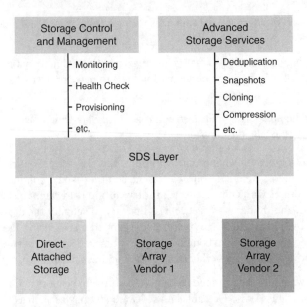

Figure 5-1 *SDS Addressing Legacy Installations*

In this architecture, the SDS layer offers the control function to manage the disparate silos of storage arrays and offers the data services functions in software. The abstraction layer can take over all the data services and protection functions that exist in the array or pick and choose what functionality to keep in the array and what functionality to deliver in the abstraction layer. For example, the SDS layer can perform the snapshots functions and let the array do the deduplication and RAID functions, or the SDS can pull all the disks and do its own RAID function. In this architecture, you can have a low-cost array with just a bunch of disks (JBOD) offering similar or advanced functionality to the most expensive storage arrays.

From a data migration perspective, SDS takes critical data from an older disk array and moves it to a newer flash array for higher performance. SDS takes data from a local data center and replicates it on a public data center for protection, and so on and so forth.

From a management perspective, the SDS offers a single pane of glass for the whole pool of storage that it pulls from the different systems. It monitors the performance and utilization across different storage platforms. This is normally hard to do between storage arrays from different vendors because each vendor has its own sets of tools. SDS works at a higher layer, so it has visibility into the different silos, providing a unified view of the storage.

This sounds great on the surface, but many challenges exist in this approach. So, let's look at the solution first from a control and management point of view and then from a data services point of view.

For control and management, what you are creating here is a manager of managers or a universal remote control. For those who have been in the networking and storage industry for so long, the first reaction would be, "Yeah, right." With everyone having closed systems, getting universal control over all available storage systems is still on the wish list. But as you became accustomed to vendors in the networking space telling you they integrate with other vendors via northbound interfaces, the storage vendors created the same story with southbound interfaces toward third-party storage arrays. In 2013, EMC introduced its SDS Vipr controller that manages third-party storage arrays. EMC announced that Vipr integrates its own storage products with NetApp. EMC later announced that it supported a southbound interface to OpenStack (OpenStack is discussed in Chapter 14, "Open Source—Compute and Storage"), and if other vendors were to support OpenStack, these products would presumably be managed by Vipr. The fact is that competing storage vendors do not really have a business incentive to be managed by each other even though all of them are riding the SDS bandwagon.

Looking at SDS from a data services perspective, there is also an issue. Although a pure software vendor wants to pull all the data services intelligence such as thin provisioning, replication, snapshots, and more into the software abstraction layer, an established vendor doesn't want to disrupt its essential products. In parallel to developing new products and new architecture in line with SDS, an established storage vendor, like an EMC, wants to keep selling and enhancing the existing products and augment them with new functionality. Going back to the EMC Vipr example, EMC kept all legacy block and storage data services inside its storage array and used Vipr as a vehicle to introduce object storage, automation, better data migration between its own products, and so on. EMC was just used as an example. Other leading vendors such as HP and IBM also introduced products supporting software-defined storage with their own version on how SDS adds value to the network.

vSphere APIs for Storage Awareness (VASA) and VVols

Another school of thought in SDS came from VMware, which introduced vSphere APIs for storage awareness (VASA) and the concept of Virtual Volumes (VVols). It is important to understand the VASA architecture and VVols terminology because many hyperconverged vendors still use VMware vSphere and vCenter for managing the virtualized environment and are working on the integration of hyperconverged systems with traditional data center environments based on SANs.

VASA allows, through the use of vCenter APIs, the integration with storage vendors and giving more visibility to vCenter for the different storage volumes on the storage arrays. Also, VASA allows the storage arrays to share their capabilities with vCenter. This allows vCenter to attach to the virtual machines (VMs) storage policies and data services that match the storage array capabilities.

All of this is in line with SDS in terms of easier management, automation, and decoupling the software from the hardware. However, at this stage, VMware did not try to take on the data services capabilities, but rather let the storage array perform the services while giving the application a better view of the storage so policies can be requested from the VM side. As you will see later, VMware implemented in parallel vSAN, which is a hyper-converged software that replaces the storage array proposition.

However, building the VASA architecture on top of LUNs is pointless. The coarse granularity of LUNs is not in line with the requirement to have policies delivered at the VM level. As such, VMware introduced other concepts different from those of LUNs and datastores, such as VVols.

Let's examine the concept of VVols and how they replace datastores and LUNs. Then we'll discuss the VASA mechanism through which VMs can attach storage policies that are in line with advertised capability of the storage array.

Creating More Granular Volumes with VVols

The concept of VVols was needed to allow the storage to apply its data services in line with the requirement of the VM and not the other way around. With LUNs/datastores, the VM inherited the data services of the LUN/datastore whether the VM wanted it or not. If, for example, ten VMs are in a datastore and one of the VMs requires hourly replication while the other nine VMs do not need replication, the nine VMs are replicated as well just because data replication is applied at the LUN/datastore level. Trying to match the requirement of the VM/application with what the storage array offers was a constant struggle between virtualization engineers and storage engineers to find the correct combination.

VVols per VMware's definition are virtual machine objects stored natively on array storage containers. The physical disks in an array are partitioned as "containers," and then the VVols are stored directly on the containers without the use of LUNs.

This is different from the traditional way where vSphere created the virtual machine disks (VMDKs) and put them on LUNs/datastores where the storage array had only physical visibility to the blocks but had absolutely no knowledge of VMs or VMDKs. The benefit of this new model is that the storage array is creating VVols, has visibility into the VVols, and can apply its data services directly on these VVols. The level of granularity is no longer at the LUN level but at the granular VVol level. So, if a storage array wanted to do a replication function, it does not have to do it for a LUN or a full datastore. It can do it at the VM VVol level, which is powerful. Figure 5-2 demonstrates the concept of VVols.

As the number of VVols increases, another level of aggregation is needed: a container. Containers aggregate the multitude of VVols in the same way a LUN used to do; however, there are big differences between LUNs and containers. While LUNs have fixed sizes and limited numbers, containers are flexible in size, and they can grow or shrink as needed up to the size of the storage array itself. There are also no set limits on the number of containers, as in LUNs. With the concept of containers, data services such as snapshots, cloning, and so on, are done on a group of VVols that share the same characteristics. This is powerful, because now storage arrays have visibility into the virtual machines and what is needed by the application. As the storage administrator configures the container, it adds data service capabilities to the container itself. Note that, to maintain continuity for functionality such as high availability, vMotion, automation, and so on, VMware made the datastore map one-to-one to the container. So, although a container is an abstract object recognized by the storage array, it is represented as a datastore at the vSphere or vCenter level.

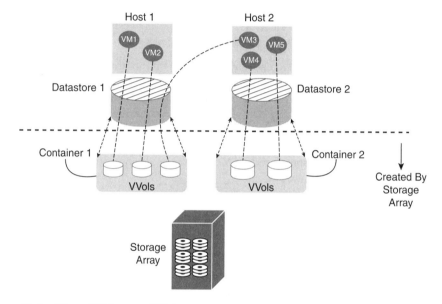

Figure 5-2   *Virtual Volumes - VVols*

Five different types of VVols are used:

1. **Config-VVol-Metadata:** These represent the information that describes a virtual machine, such as log files, NVRAM files that describe the hardware characteristics, and VMX configuration files.

2. **DATA-VVol-VMDK:** These constitute the bulk of the storage and represent the actual VMDK data files that used to be stored using the VMFS file system. They can no longer exist in the virtual volume architecture.

3. **MEM-VVol-Snapshots:** This is the memory dump that is saved whenever a snapshot of the VM is taken.

4. **SWAP-VVol-Swap:** These are the files used to run on disk whenever the VM exhausts physical memory.

5. **Other:** These are vendor-specific virtual volumes.

Learning Storage Array Capabilities Through VASA

To allow communication with storage arrays, a new mechanism was adopted. In the traditional architecture, the file systems such as the Virtual Machine File System (VMFS) and Network File System (NFS) communicate with the storage "in-band" through storage protocols such as Internet Small Computer System Interface (iSCSI) and NFS. With the new architecture, VMware moved to an "Out of Band" communication between ESXi and the storage array—that is, not through the input/output (I/O) protocols such as fibre channel (FC), NFS, or iSCSI, but through a set of application programming interfaces (APIs). ESXi will expose these APIs to the storage arrays, which will use them for communicating with ESXi. So, basically there is no longer a need for the VMFS because the communication between ESXi and the storage arrays is done via APIs.

However, this means that the storage vendor must write firmware upgrades to support the APIs. VMware calls these APIs, vSphere APIs for Storage Awareness (VASA). Both vCenter and the storage arrays connect and exchange the information through what is a VASA provider, which is normally part of the storage array firmware. Through the APIs, VMware bypasses the normal file system that is no longer needed and instructs the array to create the VVols' VMDKs on the storage array, without the use of LUNs. Because VVols are grouped inside containers, the VASA provider discovers the containers and advertises them to the VMware vCenter.

Figure 5-3 shows the different parts of the VASA architecture. Note the VASA provider, which is normally inside the storage array firmware and acts as an exchange point between ESXi/vCenter and the array. Also notice the protocol endpoints (PEs), which are described next.

For ESXi to send I/O to the storage array, it needs an access point. Traditionally, that access point was the LUN, which had two roles. One role is as a container for the VMDK files through datastores, and the other role is as an access point to reach the data. With the new VASA architecture, when the concept of LUNs goes away, a new access point to reach the VMDKs is needed to send I/Os. This access point is called by VMware a protocol endpoint (PE), which is created by storage administrators. Because the VMDKs are now grouped into containers that are flexible on sizes and numbers, the PE points to the newly created containers that can take any size of the array. The PEs support multiple protocols, such as FC, Fibre Channel over Ethernet (FCoE), iSCSI, and NFS. This takes the decision-making of whether to create blocks for FC and iSCSI or files for NFS out of the equation. Also, the PE inherits all the characteristics that used to be applied to LUNs, such as zoning, masking, and multipathing. So, visibility to the VMDKs or container from the host and which path to take to reach the container are decided at the PE level. A discovery process inside ESXi discovers all types of PEs, such as iSCSI, NFS, and so on, and maintains the PEs in a database to be used by the host. This way, ESXi discovers which arrays are VASA enabled and discovers all access points to the containers on these arrays.

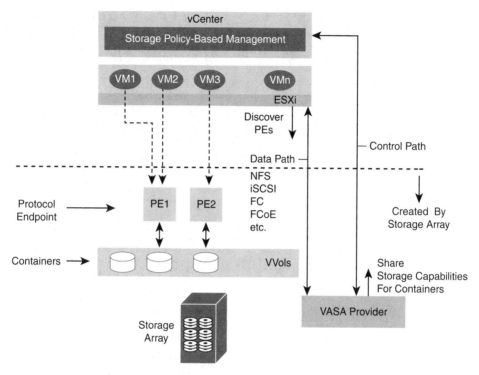

Figure 5-3 *VMware VASA*

Integration with Storage Policy–Based Management

Another important part for the VASA/VVol approach is in the presence of policy-based management. As briefly mentioned, containers can be labeled with a set of capabilities that they provide. These capabilities are set by the storage administrator at container creation, and they map into what the storage array hardware can provide. These capabilities include functionality such as snapshots, cloning, encryption, deduplication, replication, and so on. On the other hand, the VM administrator sets VM policies when creating the VM, and these policies are the set of data functionality required by the application. Examples of such policies are types of disks like solid-state drives (SSDs) or hard disk drives (HDD), whether deduplication is required, whether snapshots are required, and so on. Now you have a set of capabilities at the storage container level, as set by the storage administrator, that may or may not satisfy the requirements of the VM-required policies. Because storage policies are exchanged through the VASA provider, the storage can now apply its capabilities according to the VM requirement. So, let's say that 10 VMs are configured, and five of them require replication. The storage array can create two sets of containers with different replication policies that are applied to the VMs.

VMware implements a compatibility function part of its storage policy-based management. This function warns the virtualization administrator whether the VM requirement can be fulfilled or not at VM creation or when a VM is trying to move between servers. If, for example, a VM is defined to have replication and the underlying storage cannot support it, a flag shows that the VM is incompatible with the specified datastore. Another example is an array that has a disk failure and no longer provides data protection. The array relays the lack of such capability to vCenter, and the critical VMs are warned not to use that storage array.

What has been described so far, although in line with SDS, does not really rock the boat or move away from the traditional SAN or network-attached storage (NAS) architecture. It does in a way address some of the pain points with SANs and gives the SAN visibility into the virtual machine environment. It addresses storage array management issues and moves the focus from the storage and puts the application at the center. The model applies policies that are now viewed and executed at the storage array level. This model provides cost savings in disk space and efficiency as the storage becomes VM aware. Note that in the two examples that were shown, EMC Vipr and VMware VVol, the storage array is still king. As a matter of fact, the king is getting a better kingdom because you are pushing the data services functionality down to the hardware through management and APIs. Recall that one of the main issues that SDS was trying to solve was to decouple software from hardware at the storage array and move away from the closed systems and reduce costs. This definitely does not achieve the goal but rather gives the existing storage systems another lifetime while they continue building closed systems. This is kind of an API magic that puts you on the road to openness while still being closed.

Although it would be nice to expand more on the legacy or enhanced legacy, the topic of this book is hyperconvergence. Hyperconvergence was not created overnight, however. It is an evolution of all the functionality that has been discussed so far, but with a new line of thinking. And the thinking is that you can patch the legacy as much as possible and try to stretch it, but sooner or later it is going to break. What is needed is a new architecture that is built from the ground up to address the future storage needs.

Looking Ahead

This chapter discussed some of the pre-hyperconverged methods of SDS. As the data center designs started evolving, the early approaches were focused on preserving the installed base and trying to offer some level of integration between the storage silos. However, a new look at data center designs was needed, which prompted the efforts in hyperconverged infrastructure (HCI) designs.

Part III of this book defines and discusses the evolution from converged infrastructure (CI) to hyperconverged infrastructure (HCI). The HCI functionality, use cases, and benefits are introduced both from a technical angle as well as a business angle. Part IV of this book takes a deeper dive into the Cisco HyperFlex (HX) HCI implementation.

Hyperconverged Infrastructure

Chapter 6   Converged Infrastructure

Chapter 7   HCI Functionality

Chapter 8   HCI Business Benefits and Use Cases

Hyperconverged infrastructure (HCI) promises to revolutionize the data center design from both a hardware and software standpoint. HCI software will complement the advances seen in server virtualization with software-defined storage (SDS) and software-defined networking (SDN). HCI hardware will collapse the layers of compute, storage, and networking into hardware integrated systems that offer single vendor solutions compared to the traditional multi vendor silo designs.

On the path to hyperconvergence, however, you started with converged infrastructure (CI), which put the data center on the track of collapsing layers to simplify data center designs, speed up deployments, and offer one-stop support.

Chapter 6 offers an introduction to the converged infrastructure and how implementations such as Cisco Unified Computing System (UCS) changed the compute model of the data center.

Chapter 7 discusses the HCI functionality and its design elements.

Chapter 8 articulates the HCI benefits and use cases that are most important to chief information officers and IT managers, and discusses the HCI use cases and their different applications.

Chapter 6

Converged Infrastructure

This chapter covers the following key topics:

- **Cisco UCS—The First Step in Convergence:** An introduction to Cisco Unified Computing System (UCS) and how it has changed the server compute and networking landscape.

- **The Converged Systems:** A definition of converged infrastructure (CI) and its objectives in simplifying data center rollouts and management. Also covers the pros and cons of deploying CI.

Moving from a data center with physical servers to a data center with virtual machines created a whole new set of problems. In the traditional data center, the constraints were mainly physical. IT administrators' concerns revolved around how many racks they could fit in the data center, how many servers they needed, whether cooling would be adequate or not, whether there was enough power, and so on. The number of applications they could run and the services they could offer were limited to what they could fit in a room.

From a management perspective, administrators were really aligned around technology silos, and the technologies were aligned around product silos. The data center administrators were divided between networking experts, storage experts, compute experts, and management experts. Vendors also aligned around the same model and sold different products to different groups. When you look, as an example, at Network Management Systems (NMSs) that perform provisioning and monitoring, you see that these systems were built around the same silos and sold to the different groups. The networking team has its own NMS, the storage team has its NMS, and the same goes for the compute team. The life cycle and evolution of these management systems consider added functionality in deploying new services and applications but have always worked in the constraints of an anticipated growth curve for the physical environment. So, the operation cycles and procedures to manage a network have been well defined based on physical growth. If you were to manage 100 servers, 20 switches, and 2 TB of storage in the first year, you would anticipate, for example, 200 servers with 40 switches and 4 TB of storage the year after. As such, NMSs were upgraded to handle the anticipated growth.

When virtualization was introduced, it changed the whole operational cycle of a data center. Timelines were no longer based on physical constraints but rather on application needs and speed of delivery. If you had 100 physical servers in the first year, the year after could potentially grow to 1,000 virtual machines (VMs). Each VM would need its own operating system, networking requirement, and storage needs. The virtualization engineers might have to request from the storage engineers storage for 1,000 VMs. The virtualization engineers would also have to request from networking engineers connectivity for 1,000 VMs.

Managing this process between three different operational teams with three different management systems became problematic. The notion of convergence came about to facilitate the management of these systems by doing better integration between the different vendors and having one salesperson to chase and one technical support to call when things went wrong. Convergence boiled down to packaging multiple products and offering better integration and simplified management.

Cisco UCS—The First Step in Convergence

The emergence of virtualization in the data center really created a monster, even at the networking and compute levels. The adoption of blade servers translated into the use of a large number of servers in a smaller footprint and created a mess in how these servers were physically connected and configured. Each blade server had multiple physical network interface cards (NICs) for data connectivity and multiple host bus adapters (HBAs) for storage connectivity. Each blade server had to connect to two Ethernet switches to connect to the rest of the data network and two fibre channel switches to connect to the storage network. Basically, it was a combination of the three-tier networking architecture and the three-tier storage architecture that were discussed in Chapter 1, "Data Networks: Existing Designs," applied to hundreds of servers. The cabling on its own was a nightmare. In addition to this, each server at the hardware level had many parameters to be set over and over for hundreds of servers. Such parameters included server firmware, media access control (MAC) addresses, boot information, IP addresses, World Wide Node Name (WWNN) addresses, and more. This created another time-consuming task because many servers needed to be set up exactly the same way, and many of the configuration tasks were to be repeated.

The first step in convergence was the Cisco UCS architecture, which combined data networking, storage networking (not storage), and compute for the first time in a single architecture. It is important to mention UCS because it is still widespread in many data centers, and Cisco has extended this architecture in support of its HyperFlex (HX) hyperconverged product portfolio.

Cisco created a condensed architecture that allows many blade servers and rack servers to be presented to the rest of the data center as two main fabric interconnects (FIs). On top of the FIs runs a UCS manager that manages the many low-level parameters of each of the servers in the form of reusable templates. This is seen in Figure 6-1.

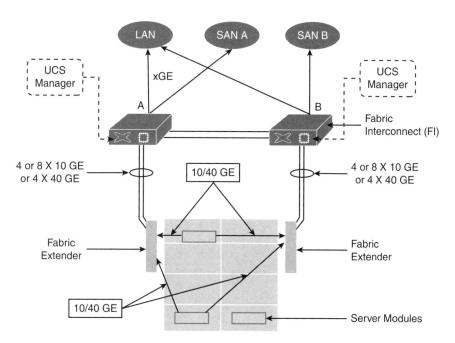

Figure 6-1 *UCS Basic Architecture*

As you see, the main components are the blade servers that connect via dual 10 GE ports or dual 40 GE ports to two FIs: A and B. Each chassis allows the housing of 8 midplane blades or 4 full blades, with each half blade having 2 × 10 GEs or 2 × 40 GE ports that directly connect to fabric extenders inside the chassis. Each fabric extender connects in turn to a unified FI with either 4 or 8 × 10 GE ports or 4 × 40 GE ports depending on the model of the fabric extender. The FIs in turn have xGE (1 GE, 10 GE, 40 GE) uplinks to the data network and fibre channel (FC) uplinks (4/8/16 Gbps) to the storage network. Each of the blade servers has converged NICs that support Transmission Control Protocol (TCP) and FC traffic. Fibre channel traffic is passed to the FI as Fibre Channel over Ethernet (FCoE) and from then on connects via FC uplinks to the rest of the storage network. To the outside world, access to the applications and data storage handling is concentrated in the FIs.

An important component of UCS is the converged cards on the server blades. These are the virtual interface cards (VICs) that allow data and storage connectivity between the server cards and the fabric extenders, which in turn connect to the FIs. The VICs have dual 10 GE or 40 GE uplinks and dual FC uplinks to the fabric extenders. The VICs themselves are a physical entity, but Cisco defines logical interface cards in the form of virtual NICs (vNICs) and virtual host bus adapters (vHBAs). Each physical VIC can support multiple vNICs and vHBAs. The VIC 1380, for example, supports up to 256 virtual interfaces.

The vNICs and vHBAs are mapped to the different VMs running on the server, practically giving each VM its own dual port data interfaces and dual port storage interfaces. Traffic from each VM is tagged according to the virtual interface, and the bulk of the traffic from all VMs is multiplexed over the physical VIC interfaces toward the fabric extenders and in turn toward the FI. The FI sees individual virtual Ethernet or FCoE ports coming from the VMs. This is seen in Figure 6-2. As you will see next, the configurations and policies applied to vNICs and vHBAs are defined using vNIC and vHBA templates that are applied to service profiles.

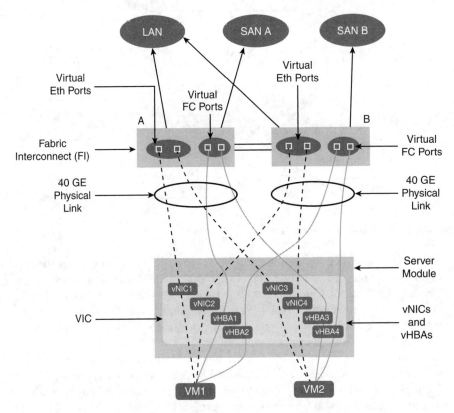

Figure 6-2   *vNICs and vHBAs*

The FIs run a daemon called the UCS manager that manages all the networking and server components and creates what is called UCS profiles and templates, described next.

With UCS service profiles, Cisco does to physical servers what virtualization does to VMs. In traditional server operation, if a bunch of servers needed to perform similar functions, such as boot from the network or have similar configurations such as attaching their NIC to a certain VLAN or having the basic input/output system (BIOS) information changed, the same functions and functionality had to be configured individually on each server. The service profiles capture a set of parameters associated with the servers, which can be duplicated on other servers, to allow a similar set of operations for all servers. Think of a UCS service profile as a "software definition" of the server itself, its storage, and its networking connectivity. The service profile is stored inside the UCS FI.

A powerful service profile is one that can override the server identity. This type of profile can, for example, override the MAC address and the server's Universal Unique Identifier (UUID), which allows physical hardware to be moved around without having to change the configuration.

Service profiles include four types of information:

1. **Server definition:** Defines the resources you are working with, such as a certain blade server that is inserted into a certain chassis.

2. **Identity information:** Includes the UUID of the server, the MAC addresses of the vNICs, and WWNs of the vHBAs.

3. **Firmware revision specifications:** Specifies the correct firmware revision that is needed for the proper operation of a hardware component.

4. **Connectivity definition:** Provides the configuration of network adapters, fabric extenders, and parent interconnects. However, the information is abstract because it does not specify how each component is configured.

Service profiles can be created manually, via cloning other service profiles, or from service templates. The service templates are used to create multiple service profile copies to associate with a group of servers instead of configuring the service profile manually on each server. There are two types of templates: initial and updating. When applying initial templates to a server profile, further changes to the template do not affect the running service profile. On the other hand, updating templates have a link between the parent template and the child objects. When the parent template is updated, the updates propagate to the link child objects. When starting a server, the template is applied as a starting point to a common configuration, and after that each server can get individual configurations such as MAC addresses. A representation of server profiles and templates is shown in Figure 6-3.

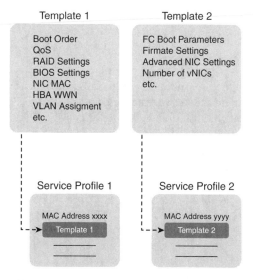

Figure 6-3 *Server Profiles*

The service profile points to a template and additional information needed to complete the profile, such as a MAC address. In Figure 6-3, service profile 1 points to template 1 and MAC address xxxx, whereas service profile 2 points to template 2 and MAC address yyyy. Service profiles allow you to define server policies, storage policies, and network policies. Examples of service profile parameters include the following:

- UUID
- NIC MACs
- HBA WWNs
- Number of vNICs
- VLAN tagging
- FC fabrics assignments
- BIOS firmware
- Adapter firmware
- QoS policies
- Storage policies

This dramatically simplifies any hardware configurations needed on a set of servers. For example, setting up the hardware of a database application such as SAP or Oracle requires a set of firmware to be deployed across all physical nodes, setting up the adapter firmware as part of a template, and assigning it to all hardware at the same time, greatly simplifies configuration.

The UCS service profiles and the integration between UCS and Cisco HX hyperconverged product give Cisco an edge in data centers, especially with the large UCS installed base.

The Converged Systems

The Cisco UCS architecture paved the way to fully converged systems where, in addition to the compute and networking for data and storage, actual storage arrays are added to provide a full solution. Examples of converged systems are the Cisco VxBlock, Cisco FlexPod, Cisco VesraStack, Cisco FlashStack, and others. The Cisco products integrated the Cisco Unified Computing System (UCS) platform, vSphere virtualization software from VMware, and storage arrays from a range of storage vendors including EMC, NetApp, IBM, and Pure Storage. Add to this multiple network management products from the different vendors. Figure 6-4 shows an example of a converged system.

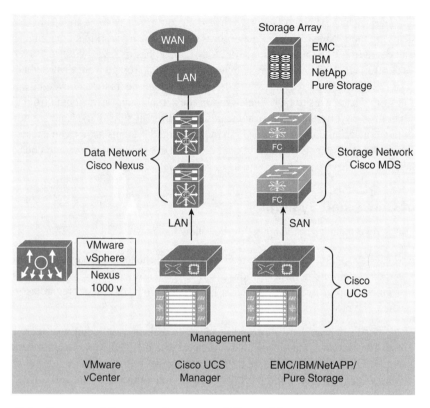

Figure 6-4 *Converged Compute, Storage, and Networking*

If you look at Figure 6-4, a converged system is basically Cisco UCS plus the actual storage arrays and additional network connectivity in the form of Ethernet and fibre channel switches to connect to the rest of the data center. This is mainly a packaging of UCS with storage area network (SAN) plus added integration on the management and a single point contact for customer support. Notice the different components from the vendors. On the software virtualization side, you see VMware's vSphere for the hypervisor. For the networking, you see the Cisco Nexus 1000 virtual switch running on the servers, Cisco UCS fabric interconnects, and the Cisco Nexus series of physical switches. For the compute, you can see the Cisco UCS Blade servers. For the storage networking, you see the Cisco MDS product line of fibre channel switches. For the storage array, you can see different products, such as hybrid storage arrays or all-flash arrays from different storage vendors. On the network management side, different management systems exist for the different technologies: vCenter from VMware for virtualization management, Cisco UCS manager to manage compute and networking, and specific network management products for the storage from EMC, IBM, NetApp, and Pure Storage.

Companies such as HPE and Dell have their own converged systems and claim that their systems are more "single vendor" than others because the networking, compute, and storage all come from the same vendor. HPE, for example, has its own switches, servers, and storage offerings. Dell has its own switches, servers, and storage from EMC, which is now part of Dell. However, irrespective of whether the components for a converged system are all from what seems to be a single vendor, the actual components come from different product groups, different engineering teams, and different subsidiaries and are not really built from the ground up as a single system. Converged systems are a clean packaging of the different components of existing data centers. Let's look at the pros and cons of converged systems.

Pros of Converged Systems

Converged systems have advantages in the following areas:

- Single salesperson and support team to call when things go wrong. Although a converged system might have a product from Cisco, another from VMware, and another from NetApp or EMC, the customer has a single point of contact regardless of where the problem is.

- Pretested software, hardware, and firmware to make sure all components are compatible. The system admin doesn't have to chase which NIC driver to use for which version of OS and which firmware to use for the disk controller. The vendor or vendor consortium that is selling the product makes sure all the firmware and drivers are tested and work together.

- Better integration on the management systems. Although there could be different management systems for the different components, some vendors implement a single pane of glass user interface (UI) that gives the user the feel of a unified system.

- Optimization around use cases. Converged systems can be optimized around the application they are used for. As an example, some databases, such as SAP HANA, perform processing in memory and need to be optimized for large amounts of it. Other applications, such as virtual desktop infrastructure (VDI), need to be optimized for CPUs. Vendors offer prepacked systems that are packaged around the use case.

Converged Systems Cons

If converged systems make it a lot easier for administrators to run compute, networking, and storage with ease of management and better integration, why is everyone looking at hyperconvergence as the next best thing for the data center? To answer this question, let's look at the cons of converged systems:

- Because converged systems are a packaging of different products, there are now too many interdependencies between the different products, especially in doing system upgrades. Traditionally, when administrators had different systems such as separate servers and separate storage arrays, making upgrades to the storage array, as an example, did not affect what happened to the NIC of the server. Also, changing the OS on a server might not affect what happens to a storage array. Because the different components now are managed as a bundle, vendors are upgrading in bulk. Therefore, a system upgrade might have a list of drivers for the NICs and a list of firmware for the servers and storage arrays. Once the upgrade is done, all of these components are upgraded at the same time because the vendors pretest and approve a set of components working together rather than individual components. The administrators of the different components don't welcome such upgrades that affect all components.

■ Individual components are not failproof. No matter how much a vendor guarantees it, a firmware or a driver will have a bug. Once that bug occurs, fixing it in one component might affect another component. So, vendors have to pretest the whole system again, and the cycle for problem resolution can become longer.

■ Convergence solves the problem of networking up to the top-of-rack (ToR) switch. Typical converged systems bundle a storage array with the servers and TOR switches. These systems also include fibre channel switches for storage networking. Beyond this, and except for Cisco, networking between the bundled systems is left as an exercise for both the data networking administrators and the storage networking administrators. So, although IP addressing, VLAN assignment, fibre channel zoning, and addressing are integrated up to the ToR, beyond that it is anybody's guess. If you want to expand from a single to multiple converged systems, integrating the data networking and storage networking with the rest of the data center is a full-time job.

■ Converged systems do not solve the issue of storage arrays being closed systems. The converged system still has the same old storage arrays with a closed software and hardware architecture. It might be easier now to integrate the storage array from EMC, IBM, NetApp, or Pure Storage with Cisco UCS and Nexus switches, but the storage architecture is still the same old SAN architecture that you had before purchasing a converged system. The upgrade cycles for storage still rely on the upgrade cycles of the storage array. The high costs related to closed systems remain the same. Because there is no way to decouple storage software and storage services from the storage hardware itself, the customer is always at the mercy of the storage array vendor release cycles and high prices.

■ Converged systems still need highly specialized resources in every area. Although the integration between the components is made easier, nothing really changed on the individual component level. Highly specialized people need to be hired for storage and storage networking, software virtualization, data networking, and network management. Any problem in each of these areas requires a special set of skills because the system remains closed and complex. With specialized resources comes a high cost of IT in addition to a high cost of hardware and software.

- Finally, and probably one of the main reasons data centers are moving toward hyperconverged systems, convergence does not solve the complexity of storage and storage networking. The demand for a variety of block storage, file storage, and object storage coupled with the need to simplify the deployment of storage services does not match well with converged systems. The complexity of having fibre channel for SANs coupled with a rigid architecture of logical unit numbers (LUNs) and the whole network complexity behind it demand a totally new architecture.

Looking Ahead

This chapter covered converged infrastructure—specifically, Cisco Unified Computing System (UCS). Cisco UCS revolutionized data center designs by dramatically simplifying the integration between compute and networking. Cisco UCS created a shift toward building converged systems, reducing deployment cycles, and simplifying data center management.

Although converged systems offered a one-stop shop for IT administrators and removed some of the headaches of managing silos, they did not address the main data center pain points.

A new architecture had to be built leveraging advances in software-defined storage and networking to transform the data center into what is now called the "private cloud."

Chapter 7, "HCI Functionality," defines the hyperconverged infrastructure (HCI) and details its functionality in simplifying data center deployments, reducing costs, and enhancing efficiencies. Chapter 8, "HCI Business Benefits and Use Cases," discusses HCI's technical and business benefits and use cases in preparation for a deeper dive into the Cisco HX product in Part IV of the book.

HCI Functionality

This chapter covers the following key topics:

- **Distributed DAS Architecture:** A description of HCIs physical and logical distributed architecture, including direct-attached storage (DAS) and the distributed data controllers. The chapter describes high-level HCI functionality such as scale-out architecture, performance, data protection, and hardware resiliency. You will see discussions about the file system, provisioning model, hardware assist, networking policies, and automation.

- **Advanced Data Storage Functionality:** A description of the different HCI data storage functionalities such as deduplication and compression, erasure coding, replication, backup, and disaster recovery. Security issues and the provisioning, management, and monitoring of HCI systems are also discussed.

Although this book attempts to be vendor agnostic, it becomes difficult to explain terminology that is created by marketing rather than engineering. If hyperconvergence came out of the Internet Engineering Task Force (IETF), it would have been a lot easier to explain how it works and where it is applied. *Hyperconvergence* and *hyperconverged infrastructure* are marketing terms that are being used as a catch-all. One thing is for sure: *hyper* comes from hypervisor, and *converged* comes from data center convergence. Therefore, the presence of the hypervisor is key to achieving hyperconvergence from a software level, but as you will see in the implementations, it might also become the bottleneck and a hindrance to performance. From a software perspective, software-defined storage (SDS) plays a main role in hyperconvergence because it defines distributed file systems capable of aggregating all storage under one pool.

From a hardware point of view, if you were to say that hyperconverged architecture means that storage and compute and networking are combined in a single system, you would be 80% accurate. Still, you will see architectures in which the networking is missing claim hyperconvergence, and others in which both networking and compute are missing and claim hyperconvergence.

Distributed DAS Architecture

Hyperconverged infrastructure (HCI) moves away from the traditional centralized storage area network (SAN) and network-attached storage (NAS) to a distributed direct-attached storage (DAS) architecture. It is interesting that the industry traveled full circle from DAS to SAN and back to DAS. The reasons that DAS is back are many:

- The compute power inside servers is now more powerful than any traditional storage array. It is true that storage arrays can now adopt faster central processing units (CPUs); but in a centralized storage model, the CPU still has to attend to hundreds of disks. In an HCI model, processing is distributed over many hosts, with each host having CPU power that could exceed the CPU power of a single storage array. HCI implementations use standard x86 CPU architectures that provide openness and cost savings compared to traditional closed systems.

- The price of disks, whether hard disk drive (HDD) or solid-state drive (SSD), also came down to the point where placing powerful Serial Attached Small Computer System Interface (SAS) or flash disks inside servers is not that expensive. One of the arguments of centralized architectures is that consolidating the functions in a central pool of flash disks is much less expensive than spreading disks over many servers. This argument holds true if each server works independently of the others and over-provisioning takes place on each server, but this is not true with HCI. Because HCI treats all storage as a single pool and uses policy-based storage that is application aware, the efficiency of using the storage even if it is distributed is extremely high.

- The Gigabit Networking speeds moving up to 40 GE and 100 GE are minimizing network latencies, making the convergence between storage networking and data networking viable. As such, combining compute, storage, and networking in the same system or cluster of nodes is the strong point for hyperconvergence.

Figure 7-1 shows how nodes are physically connected in an HCI cluster.

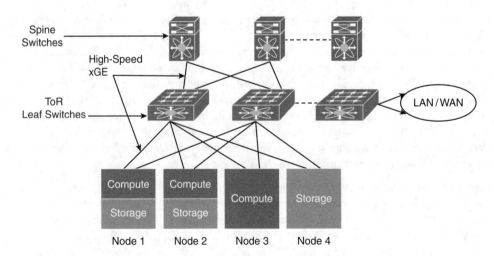

Figure 7-1 *Hyperconverged Infrastructure—Physical View*

Note that you moved into a distributed DAS and eliminated SAN and NAS. Nodes or hosts can be compute only, storage only, or compute + storage. This depends on the vendor implementation and whether the nodes/hosts are appliance-based or off-the-shelf servers. The connectivity between the nodes is done via high-speed Gigabit Ethernet interfaces. Smaller remote office implementations work well with 1 GE interconnect, whereas midsize and large implementations with lots of input/output (I/O) requirements are better served with 10 GE, 40 GE, and eventually 100 GE interconnects.

Normally, each node has two network interfaces that are dual homed to two top-of-rack (ToR) switches for redundancy. The ToR switches are called the leaf switches and are connected to each other via spine switches. The leaf and the spine switches grow as needed to accommodate more nodes in a cluster. The leaf switches form the edge of the network that connects to other data centers or the Internet over the campus or WAN connection.

Distributed Controllers

Hyperconverged architectures use a distributed controller model. Unlike storage arrays, where a pair of storage controllers controlled the I/O on disks, HCI has software controllers distributed across nodes. The naming of the software controllers differs between vendors. Some call it virtual storage appliance (VSA), others call it control VM (CVM), still others call it data platform controller (DPC), and so on. For consistency, let's call these software modules data platform controllers. The DPC is part of an SDS architecture that allows all nodes to participate in the I/O processing. The DPC runs as a virtual machine that communicates with the hypervisor or a container environment and makes all storage available on all nodes look like one central pool of resources that any virtual machine (VM) or container can use. Figure 7-2 shows the DPCs on each node. The DPCs communicate with one another to create the logical storage pool and work in parallel to perform the storage data service's functionality.

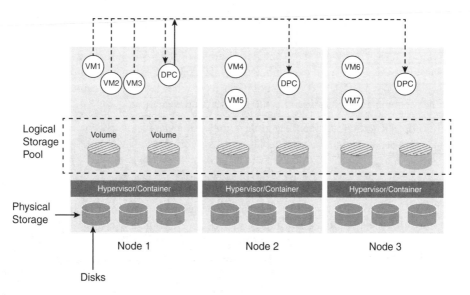

Figure 7-2 *HCI Logical View*

Scale-Out Architecture

The scaling of any architecture can be measured in its ability to scale out and scale up. Scaling up is when performance of a node is increased by boosting the compute and storage of the node itself. This is what you are used to with storage arrays; when an array runs out of steam, it is replaced with a bigger node that has more CPUs, memory, and storage.

In contrast, because HCI is a distributed architecture based on the concept of scaling by adding nodes, HCI is by design a scale-out architecture. The more nodes you add, the more CPU, memory, and storage I/O you get. The definition of node depends on the vendor implementation. Nodes can be individual off-the-shelf servers or custom-made hardware. Although from a software point of view both approaches deliver similar functionality, from a hardware point of view they are much different. Hardware that is appliance based with preconfigured nodes offers more peace of mind by being more uniform with the ability to apply service profiles on such nodes. Nodes are preconfigured for compute only, storage only, and a combination of compute and storage on the same nodes. All depends on what a particular vendor implements. As VMs or containers are deployed, and if more compute power is needed, more compute nodes can be added. The same goes for storage. If the system has enough compute power but not enough storage, more storage nodes can be added. And the same goes for combination compute plus storage nodes to grow both compute and storage at the same time. This type of granularity is powerful because it uses the hardware more efficiently without big jumps in unused compute or storage capacity. However, with added flavors of nodes comes added complexities. Therefore, some vendors, for example, decided not to build storage-only nodes, and some do not recommend adding compute-only nodes. In any case, because everything is built by the same vendor, there is one vendor to blame in case of any issues.

With implementations that rely on off-the-shelf servers for nodes, you have more flexibility to scale up by adding more storage or more memory to an individual node. However, with such flexibility comes the nightmare of balancing the different nodes in a cluster because most HCI vendors recommend that the nodes in a cluster are uniform, which means that the compute and the number of drives of the nodes in a cluster be somehow equivalent. Also, you need to do node customization, making sure that all components including server, HDD, SSD, network interface card (NIC), host bus adapter (HBA), and other components are certified for the HCI software vendor.

HCI implementations differentiate in their ability to make the process of adding storage and compute, as required by the application, as automated and as simple as possible.

HCI Performance

HCI promises increased performance in a higher number of input/output operations per second (IOPS) and lower latency in I/O operations. This is mainly attributed to HCI being a distributed system, in which multiple nodes work in parallel on reading and writing the I/O. In storage arrays, centralized controllers used to handle the I/O of the whole data center. Compare this to tens and hundreds of nodes, with each having powerful CPUs and memory sharing the I/O load. The bulk of the distributed systems reaches much higher performance than the handful of centralized arrays.

Another factor that affects performance is the proximity of data to the application. This is an area of debate in the industry because the distributed nature of hyperconvergence could result in having the data scattered over many nodes. Therefore, I/O has to cross the network as well. In traditional storage arrays, the application runs on the host, whereas the data is centralized somewhere in the network. This means that every I/O exchange between the VM and storage has to cross the network every time. With hyperconverged architectures, each node can utilize its cache to accelerate the I/O handling and could benefit from the fact that the data could be local. However, even if the data is distributed among many nodes, the fact that each node can participate in the I/O processing through the local controller greatly increases performance.

In principle, an HCI system centered on applications and their needs outperforms storage array systems that have no application visibility and are centered on disks.

All HCI vendors claim that they have the highest performance, but the reality is that some systems outperform others due to differences in software architectures and whether the software is designed from the ground up for HCI or is adapted for HCI. As HCI implementations were developed in the past few years, each emerged from different starting points. Some architectures were home grown as extensions of already built hypervisors. Some were built based on open source software for both hypervisor and SDS. And some were built from scratch and with distributed architectures and virtualization in mind. Although some implementations are 100% done in software, others try to leverage hardware acceleration to offload the CPU.

Measuring performance is tricky. To be fair to vendors, you should compare apples to apples. You should weigh performance with functionality. A cluster that is just doing compute and I/O reads/writes should not be compared to a cluster performing advanced functionality. Also, two HCI implementations that deliver similar performance should be benchmarked on whether they are using comparable compute and storage resources.

Resiliency Against Hardware Failures via Replication

Traditional storage arrays came in redundant configurations. Redundant storage controllers, redundant fabric switches, redundant HBAs, and multiple paths from any server to any storage are deployed. On the other hand, HCI is built on a distributed architecture and grows one node at a time. It is important that HCI offers the same level of resiliency as legacy storage. Protection needs to be done at the node level, at the network level, and at the virtual disk level. When a node fails, the disks attached to that node are no longer in the pool. HCI must ensure that the data is reconstructed and assigned back to the application. Some applications require high availability, where the application moves from a failed node to a working node with some level of disruption. Other applications require fault tolerance, where the application has zero downtime, so upon node failure, the application should continue working on other nodes with zero impact to the end user.

This is when replication becomes the cornerstone of HCI. Most HCI implementations use replication to distribute the data over multiple disks, whether in the same node or in different nodes inside a cluster as well as outside a cluster. Replication makes sure that the data is spread across many hardware entities such that if an entity fails, the data can be recovered. This is seen in Figure 7-3.

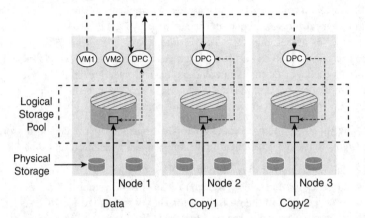

Figure 7-3   *Data Protection via Replication*

Notice that the data on Node 1 was replicated by the DPCs to Nodes 2 and 3. If Node 1 fails, for example, VMs 1 and 2 can be moved to Nodes 2 and 3, and the data will still be available. Note that the data is not necessarily a full virtual disk. The data could be a stripe of a virtual disk depending on the striping technique the vendor uses. The point is that a specific piece of data can be reconstructed upon a failure.

Protection via replication at some point becomes expensive and causes performance issues. IT administrators must decide whether to protect against a single failure or multiple failures. The good news is that such policies can be done at the granularity of a virtual machine or container. Some critical VMs and applications might need data protection against two failures, whereas other applications might need to be protected against a single failure. The more data is replicated, the more resources such as CPU, memory, and storage are used.

HCI systems differentiate in how they implement storage space reduction and protection via mechanisms such as deduplication, compression, and erasure coding and how well these functions are done without performance degradation.

File Systems

Chapter 2, "Storage Networks: Existing Designs," discussed the different types of storage, such as block-level, file-level, and object-based storage. Different HCI vendors use different file systems depending on the architecture. The choice of file system is important because it dramatically affects the performance upon doing I/O reads and writes. One file system that stands out as being one of the best used for HDDs and SSDs is a log-structured file system (LFS). LFS enhances the performance of reads and writes and minimizes the problems already discussed with flash, such as wear upon writes. LFS is used in some leading HCI architectures, such as with Cisco's HyperFlex. The next section provides a brief description of an LFS.

A log-structured file system (LFS) allows flexibility for the compute layer to access data as files, objects, or blocks. With traditional file systems, data is put anywhere on the disk. This creates disk fragmentation, causing performance issues for data reads and writes. The LFS solves performance issues for both HDDs and SSDs.

HDDs experience the best read and write performance when the data is sequential; the head of a magnetic disk does not have to jump around between random blocks to write or collect the data. For SSDs, erasing blocks dramatically shortens the life and performance of the drive because of flash wear. The log file structure solves these problems by always doing sequential writes and by not erasing stale or old blocks. This is explained next.

The log-structured file system is a "log" in the form of a circular buffer. When data is written, it is appended at the end of the log. Whenever a new block of data is added to the same object or file, the new data is appended to the log without modifying the older data. However, a new index is appended that references all blocks of the same object or file. This is illustrated in Figure 7-4.

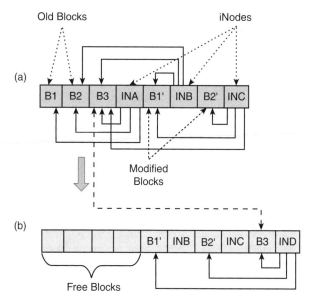

Figure 7-4   *Log-Structured File System*

Figure 7-4a shows that an object consists of a set of blocks: B1, B2, B3, and so on. These blocks are written sequentially, where each block is appended to the end of the log. An index called iNode is used as a set of pointers to the locations of the blocks in the same object. In this example, iNode A (INA) references the original blocks B1, B2, and B3.

Assume now that block B1 changed to B1'. Instead of erasing B1, a new block B1' is written at the end of the log, and a new iNode B (INB) is written. INB now references B1', B2, and B3.

Now assume that B2 is updated to B2'. The same process occurs because B2 is left untouched; the updated B2' is written sequentially to the log, and a new iNode C (INC) is written pointing to B1', B2', and B3.

As you see, you can get to the point that you have stale information that needs to be removed. Blocks B2 and B3 are not needed, and iNodes INA and INB are not needed. However, freeing these empty blocks causes disk fragmentation, which causes performance issues. Also, erasing these blocks is not good for flash SSDs.

In a typical file system, you must go into a big process of garbage collection and defragmentation. However, in a log-structured file system, there is more flexibility. The space can be divided into chunks of storage, and the cleanup of all data can be done within a chunk as needed. In this example, and as seen in Figure 7-4b, block B3 can be relocated to the end of the log, which frees up a series of continuous empty blocks from B1 to INA. The log-structured file system can keep relocating some blocks as needed to free up space without major performance hits. Once the end of the disk is reached, the process can continue at the beginning of the disk in a circular fashion.

Change in the Provisioning Model

HCI offers a different provisioning model than legacy storage arrays, a model that is top-down rather than bottom-up. With the legacy model, the storage administrator for a particular storage vendor starts by provisioning capacity logical unit numbers (LUNs). The LUNs are given a set of capabilities, such as whether the LUN needs to be replicated or not, protected or not. Zoning and masking are also configured per LUN.

Overprovisioning is the norm to ensure that an application always has enough capacity. Because storage has no knowledge of the application, when a virtualization administrator creates a VM, a request is sent to the storage administrator with the specific requirements. The storage administrator in turn tries to match the requirements with the available LUNs and capabilities or create entirely new LUNs. After that, the storage administrator specifies a datastore to be used. This provisioning model normally results in hundreds of datastores and islands of unallocated storage. Storage administrators spend most of their time migrating data and creating LUNs, while virtualization administrators wait until storage is provisioned. It could be a week or more of back-and-forth negotiation between the two departments before the storage is allocated.

The HCI model is top-down and is application centric when it comes to specifying storage policies. With HCI, the distributed file system creates a shared pool of storage resources from the different physical nodes. Upon creating a virtual machine, a user indicates the storage policies needed by the application. As such, the VM data is placed in the storage pool in a manner that satisfies the policies the application needs. The HCI model is extremely efficient and does not leave wasted resources because it can be implemented at the virtual machine level and instantaneously leverages resources from a dynamic pool, as data services are set per virtual machine.

Hardware Acceleration

Hardware acceleration will prove to be a key element in differentiating between HCI implementations moving forward. Although HCI is software defined, software on its own will run out of steam. Hardware assist becomes crucial when dealing with advanced functionality that is CPU intensive. Many HCI vendors are betting on host CPUs to deal with most of the storage I/O functions. This should remind you of the early stages of networking, where the control path that handles routing protocols, as well as the data path that handles traffic forwarding and policies such as access lists and firewalls, was all done in the CPU. You know how long that lasted until the routers started melting down and becoming bottlenecks. It seems that this is moving along the same path now, but with the added advantage that CPUs are much more powerful, and the distributed node architecture can divide the load between the CPUs.

However, HCI implementations that are architected to be 100% tied to CPUs will eventually struggle and take many iterations before moving toward hardware acceleration. To give an example, hypervisors such as VMware ESXi are becoming a catch-all for functionality. If you dig deeper, you will find that VMware's networking functionality such as NSX, which includes switching, tagging, encapsulation, routing, and tunneling, is part of the hypervisor. VMware's HCI implementation vSAN is also bundled with the hypervisor. Advanced functionality such as deduplication and compression are part of the hypervisor, too. Not to pick on VMware, because this book is intended to be vendor neutral, but such architectures will eventually break unless they are rearchitected to offload some of the software functions to hardware acceleration.

SDS allowed us to decouple the storage functionality from hardware in such a way that vendors now develop storage policies independent of the hardware and move away from hardware-closed systems. However, there is now a risk of moving in the direction of software-closed systems, where even if you run the software on commodity hardware, you cannot decouple functionality from the hypervisor to take advantage of the hardware. Cost savings is achieved, but it could be at the expense of performance.

Networking Integration

HCI is supposed to combine compute, storage, and networking in a single system. With HCI, the fibre channel storage networking disappears. As you recall, the SAN consisted of HBAs connected to fibre channel switches to form redundant fabrics. The redundant fabric in turn connected to redundant storage arrays. Masking and zoning were used to segment the network logically, and mechanisms such as multipath were used to access the storage. Links worked in active-active or active-passive modes to fully leverage the network capacity as much as possible while offering fault tolerance in case of network component failure.

HCI eliminates the SAN, as nodes individually connect to ToR switches. Instead of having one HBA for storage and one NIC for data connectivity, the servers now have one converged NIC that handles storage and data networking over a fast GE network. Compute/storage nodes talk to each other over a high-speed 10 GE, 25 GE, 40 GE, 50 GE, or eventually a 100 GE network.

Most HCI vendors downplay the networking part. First implementations of hyperconvergence focused mainly on the SDS and left out the storage-defined networking (SDN). Because the claim to fame of hyperconvergence is faster rollouts and ease of provisioning and automation, vendors who do not focus on the networking piece will be at a major disadvantage.

Two areas to watch out for when looking at HCI are networking policies and networking automation. These are discussed briefly in this section and examined in a lot more detail in Part VI of this book.

Networking Policies

One of the main differentiations of HCI from traditional SANs is that HCI is application centric rather than storage centric. You are now taking a top-down approach, and the starting points are the storage needs of the application and the access security rules for the application. HCI allows you to specify per-VM security rules. In a multitier web, app, database three-tier architecture, you can specify how the tiers are accessed among each other or from external entities. You can also decide whether to process security rules at the VM level or redirect these rules to other software or hardware appliances that deliver networking services such as firewalls or load balancers.

Networking Automation

Another essential component of HCI is the ability to automate the IP address assignment and reachability. You can also automate the network connectivity between the HCI nodes within the data center, between data centers, and with the public cloud. Traditionally, this exercise was done via L2 and L3 protocols such as spanning tree, Open Shortest Path First (OSPF), Intermediate System to Intermediate System (IS-IS), Multi-Protocol Border Gateway Protocol (MP-BGP), and other protocols. In addition, VM mobility within the data center to handle better traffic distribution or protection around failure necessitates IP-level mobility, where an application can move around without affecting its connectivity to other applications and the outside world. This requires the adoption of tunneling protocols such as the Virtual Extensible LAN (VXLAN), Network Virtualization using Generic Routing Encapsulation (NVGRE), Stateless Transport Tunneling (STT), Generic Network Virtualization Encapsulation (GENEVE), and others.

In addition, a major issue is that the network needs to handle flooding optimization techniques such as broadcast, unknown unicast, and multicast (BUM) traffic. Manual configurations to handle flooding are error prone and if done wrong can cause major networking issues. HCI implementations need to adopt techniques to minimize flooding and automate the configuration.

Networking can get nasty, and having virtualization administrators go back and forth with networking administrators to configure the data center defeats the purpose of the simplicity and faster rollouts promised by HCI. As such, networking automation is essential and must be present in every HCI implementation.

Part VI of this book discusses in detail networking implementations such as Cisco ACI, VMware NSX, open source Open vSwitch (OVS), and Open Virtual Network (OVN) as they relate to HCI deployments.

Advanced Data Storage Functionality

The challenge that HCI has from a technical point of view is that it must compete with traditional enterprise class storage. It is true that HCI is designed having cloud scalability in mind, but the bread and butter of storage is still in enterprise applications. Databases from Oracle, SAP, IBM, and others have been particular about what they need from enterprise storage and have validated with traditional storage arrays. HCI must live up to the challenge and not only match but exceed the enterprise class storage requirements at much lower capital expenditure (CAPEX) and operational expenditure (OPEX).

HCI offers advanced functionality such as space efficiency, protection, and security. It also implements mechanisms that are used with traditional storage arrays such as deduplication, compression, and encryption.

With traditional storage arrays, such functionality was initially delivered on external appliances because CPUs inside the storage array were barely keeping up with the basic I/O functionality. External appliances with specialized hardware offloaded these CPU-intensive functions.

Protection methods such as redundant array of independent disks (RAID) were good enough to protect against a few disk failures but did not give storage administrators a peace of mind that the data itself was actually protected. Therefore, a storage administrator ended up making multiple copies of the same data on different disk arrays. A combination of manual RAID 1 mirroring and mirroring the data on different disk arrays, in addition to monitoring and tracking the data, created a storage space explosion and a management nightmare.

In addition, backup and disaster recovery (DR) were yet another exercise that needed their own software and hardware systems. For some enterprises, backup and DR are more of a luxury than a necessity because they are costly exercises that require their own software and hardware parallel to the essential data storage needs.

HCI has the challenging task of delivering all such mentioned advanced functionality while adapting to the new distributed storage architecture. Add to this the need to scale to handle hundreds and thousands of virtual machines and containers. Successful HCI implementations deliver all such functionality, including the backup and DR as part of the architecture rather than an add-on. When an HCI system replicates the data locally or remotely, it is considering that other measures for backup and disaster recovery might not be needed. However, all this depends on whether the HCI functionality matches the backup mechanisms and functionality offered by traditional enterprise software backup.

The differentiation in the HCI implementations in advanced data functionality boils down to the following:

■ The level of automation and simplicity in provisioning advanced storage policies and services

■ The performance of the system while advanced functionality such as deduplication and compression are turned on

■ How well the system can take advantage and integrate with other utility services for storage and compute, such as the public cloud

The next section provides a high-level overview of what HCI offers in terms of advanced functionality and how that compares to traditional disk arrays.

Deduplication and Compression

Chapter 2 discussed the principles of deduplication and compression. However, unlike traditional storage architectures, where such functionality is done via appliances, HCI offers such functionality as part of its system architecture. Because HCI uses replication as the basis behind data protection and fault tolerance, causing the data to spread over multitudes of disks and nodes, space optimization is paramount. Deduplication and compression of the data before committing to persistent storage are a must. Having said that, many HCI vendors struggle with this functionality because it is a CPU hog, and some have resorted to adjunct hardware acceleration to offload the CPU. Also, because data is spread over many disks and nodes, vendors differ in how they perform these functions. Some perform deduplication on a node level, and others perform it globally on a cluster level.

HCI also uses replication for backup and DR between the local data center and other private data centers or the public cloud. The backup and DR data centers are usually remote to avoid putting the data in the same fault domains. As such, the data must cross WAN links that are slow and expensive. Deduplication and compression are a must to avoid sending unneeded data on the WAN links.

Erasure Coding

Erasure coding (EC) is a protection mechanism that offers the benefit of RAID protection, but with much more space savings. EC balances the benefit of having data protection while minimizing the overhead of doubling or tripling the size of the data caused by two-way or three-way replication. Similar to what is done in RAID 5 and 6, which was described earlier, EC uses the concept of parity bits to rebuild lost data upon data corruption. A corrupted piece of data is reconstructed by sampling other parts of the data that exist on other disks or nodes.

EC uses mathematical oversampling to reconstruct original data by using additional data. If you have "k" data stripes to be protected, EC creates "m" additional parity stripes to reconstruct the original data. So, the notation EC k/m means that "m" parity stripes protect "k" data stripes. If, for example, you have a total of four nodes and want to protect against a one-node failure (RAID 5), use EC 3/1 so one parity stripe is used for three data stripes. If you have six nodes and want to protect against a two-node failure (RAID 6), use EC 4/2.

The benefits of erasure coding in protecting data while optimizing storage become significant as storage increases and becomes geographically dispersed. Assume that you want to protect 10 TB worth of data that is spread over five nodes, where each node has 2 TB. You normally decide whether to protect against one node failure, two node failures, and so on. If you are protecting against a single node failure, with traditional data replication, each piece of data must exist somewhere else in the system to be recovered. So, with one-time replication, the 10 TB of storage has 5 TB of usable protected storage, and 50% overhead is lost on replication. If you use EC 3/1 as an example, the overhead is 1/3 = 33% instead of 50%, and the 10 TB storage has usable 7.7 TB. In general, with EC k/m, the overhead is (m/k) %, which is always smaller than the overhead of two-way or three-way replication.

Erasure coding provides great storage efficiency, but at the expense of added computation for parity. The more the parity stripes, the more computation is done to calculate the parity and to restore the original data. As a standard practice, the number of parities is either m = 1 protecting against one node failure (RAID 5) or m = 2 protecting against two node failures (RAID 6) to parallel the replication factors normally used in HCI implementations. HCI implementations must weigh the use of EC against performance degradation of the system.

Replication and Backup for Disaster Recovery

In hyperconverged environments, the lines between replication and disaster recovery are blurring. This is because replication by itself is creating multiple copies of the data to protect against data corruption or a node failure. However, local replication of the data does not constitute a backup because backup needs to be done on a remote site. With hyperconvergence, remote replication is also possible, not only to private remote data centers, but to public cloud data centers. Remote replication can leverage data optimization techniques such as sending delta changes and compressing and deduplicating the data. Also, replication managers can schedule such replicas to be done synchronously or asynchronously to meet a certain recovery point objective (RPO). In a way, this is what backup software does. The only difference is that software companies that perform backup have a lot more mileage in this area, and their software can be a lot more mature and scalable. Well-known companies in the enterprise software backup area are the likes of Veeam, Zerto, and EMC Avamar. Some of these companies are widely deployed in the enterprise and offer solutions that can scale to huge backups, with the ability to create backup domains, backup proxies, easy cloud backup, monitoring, and many advanced functionalities. Hyperconverged solutions are aiming to reach such an advanced stage to compete with traditional software backup solutions. Many hyperconverged solutions still integrate with third-party software vendors for backup and disaster recovery solutions.

Another topic worth mentioning is hyperconverged primary versus hyperconverged secondary storage. This terminology is now canned by some new secondary storage start-ups to differentiate between active storage and backup storage. In an enterprise environment, primary storage is data that is frequently accessed by applications where response time, high I/O performance, and near-zero RPO are essential. On the other hand, secondary storage is data that is not frequently accessed. The data is backed up in remote sites and available for data protection and DR, but with a more relaxed RPO. In reality, all HCI vendors are working from a similar base point, which is a distributed file system that creates a shared pool out of DAS. Secondary storage vendors focus more on backup in private and public clouds, DevOps, and analytics to make better use of the huge amounts of data that are not frequently accessed. Secondary backup implements advanced indexing, where files or objects can be individually restored. Primary storage vendors focus more on the application lifecycle in virtualized environments, near-zero RPO, hypervisor and containerized environment development, portability of applications between private and public clouds, and so on. Primary storage vendors also develop software for secondary storage and integrate with third-party software backup vendors. So, this becomes a software functionality game, and the end user needs to select an HCI vendor based on the problem the user is trying to solve.

HCI Security

Security is a huge topic by any means. HCI's distributed nature opens the door for more scrutiny than the traditional centralized SAN architectures. Because HCI relies on replication of information to many nodes and drives, it widens the circumference of possible attacks on the data. Traditionally, there was one main copy of the data and one backup somewhere else, and you usually knew where the data was. Now it's moving into a space in which there are two or three copies, and finding the data is not straightforward. Add to this the push for hybrid and multicloud environments, where some data is in your private data center, and its copies are on other systems in other data centers or on a public cloud. Things can get a little crazy. For HCI to succeed, it must address the security risks that bog down traditional SANs and backup and DR systems as well as its own security risks that result from its distributed architecture. If you try to oversimplify security, you divide it into two areas: physical security and cyberattacks.

Physical security can be mitigated by protecting your assets. Traditionally, administrators protect their assets in cabinets and locked-down data centers so that no one walks away with your server or storage array. With HCI, there is no central storage array. Information is on all the disks. Any node in an HCI cluster can have data that can be physically stolen. As such, many HCI vendors recommend the use of self-encrypting drives (SEDs) for their HDDs and SSDs. The merits of such drives and the fact that data is encrypted at rest with a security key management were discussed in Chapter 2. Even if the disk is stolen, the data is useless without access to the key. This type of encryption is good for data at rest but has the disadvantage of added costs to the hardware. SEDs provide security without performance impacts because the drives themselves encrypt and decrypt the data in hardware. If you want VIP service, you must pay for it. Some HCI vendors are implementing data-at-rest encryption without the use of SEDs but rather implementing encryption on regular SSDs and HDDs. This, of course, reduces the cost of the SSD and HDD hardware but loses some of the performance benefits of SED hardware-based encryption.

SEDs are good for data at rest, but most of the data is being constantly accessed and is moving around in and out of the data center. The risk of cyberattacks is not specific to HCI because any server or any SAN can be attacked; however, the combination of virtualization and SDS can be deadly. Each node now carries hundreds of VMs, and each VM can have its data spread over many nodes. Any time data is changed, it is replicated over multiple disks and nodes. Therefore, cyberattacks on hypervisors can affect hundreds of VMs.

HCI implementations started addressing the security threats. As a common denominator, most implementations support SEDs, software-based encryption, and enterprise Key Management Interoperability Protocol (KMIP). Also, implementations were hardened using the Security Technical Implementation Guide (STIG). However, much work remains to be done to provide security at the VM level. Some vendors are doing their own encryption software to secure the data exchanged between the VMs and the datastores and when VMs move between nodes. Other vendors are partnering with third-party security vendors such as Trend Micro to do the same. With such measures, data exchanged between the nodes can be optionally encrypted and secured to prevent attacks on data in transit.

Other security measures involve the implementation of strict security policies. Most HCI implementations implement "zero trust" security policies. This means that a user or an application gets just enough permissions to operate no more or no less. By default, no user or application can access another application unless it is specifically permitted. To better apply policies, it becomes important to have visibility into the applications and how they interact. Many running data centers have hundreds of policies and access control lists (ACLs) defined, but not a single administrator actually knows where these policies came from and what would be affected if they were removed. To have a better handle on application security, some HCI implementations, such as Cisco Tetration, track the exchange of the applications at the flow level to better understand the interdependencies between the different applications.

HCI Provisioning, Management, and Monitoring

This is another huge topic because it touches many areas, including automation for ease of provisioning and faster rollouts. Reacting against failures requires the monitoring of network performance and the health of the system. The differentiation between HCI implementations depends on who can provide more holistic solutions in approaching all of these areas. The functionality to watch out for in comparing different systems includes the following:

■ **Simplifying hardware deployment:** Because you are dealing with hundreds of compute and storage nodes, it is important to easily add, remove, or move nodes around without having to replicate configurations. Servers require firmware, basic input/output system (BIOS), boot information, NICs, media access control (MAC) addresses, and more. Duplicating such information on similar servers goes against simplicity. HCI implementations need to start with simplifying server hardware provisioning.

- **Simplifying networking connectivity and cabling:** The simple act of connecting NICs to Ethernet switches for hundreds of servers in a data center could become a nightmare. Add to this a major requirement that an HCI system cannot just create another silo. Therefore, an HCI cluster also has to connect to existing SAN networks and storage arrays via fibre channel. Managing Ethernet and fibre channel connectivity in an easy way is a huge differentiation.

- **Ability to size and optimize the system:** Deciding on the compute and storage resources needed to run an application and protect it against failure is not easy. A sound HCI implementation should provide the user tools to size the resources needed. The good news is that HCI is a scale-out system, so you can always add nodes to increase performance. However, sizing and optimizing the system to fit the changing needs of the workload are not a one-shot deal. This is an ongoing process that requires a certain level of automation so the system gives feedback when and where resources are needed.

- **Multiple access methods:** In principal, most HCI implementations allow access to their systems via a user interface, command-line interface (CLI), or application programming interface (API). The HTML5 GUI interface is the most adopted by HCI vendors due to its ease of use. Also, APIs are widely used to allow third-party software to interface with the HCI cluster for added functionality.

- **Simplified configuration:** This includes automating the configuration of compute storage and network.

- **Simplified management and monitoring:** HCI systems offer simple management via dashboards and menus that show the following:

  - Detailed system information, such as software and firmware versions

  - System status, such as number of nodes and number of VMs or containers

  - System health, such as status of nodes and VMs

  - Storage capacity with and without data optimization

  - The number of datastores and allocation of datastores per VM

  - Performance metrics such as I/O latency and IOPS

  - Set of configured storage policies per VM

  - Detailed alarms and the ability for the system to send notifications

  - Ability of the system to send telemetry information such as system inventory for component hardware and software

- **Application performance monitoring:** HCI systems should enable the user to monitor the performance of every application and evaluate the following:

  - Whether the application has enough resources

  - Whether the application has been allocated more resources than required

  - Whether the application is having performance issues

  - Whether performance has been impacted if the application moved between clusters

  - Root cause analysis for application performance issues

  - Response time for the different business services the application is providing

- **Management and policies:** Last is the concept of unified management and policies. With HCI systems being deployed in multiple data centers, remote offices, and public clouds, it becomes important to have a common blueprint for management and policies. Traditionally, this was done from an enterprise headquarters data center, which oversees all branch offices. However, with the scale of deployments reaching many data centers—private and public—and hundreds of branch and remote offices, IT administrators need a little help. As such, HCI implementations are adopting a strategy to deploy management systems in the cloud through virtual software appliances. This gives the administrators a global view of the network and a feedback mechanism for every point in the network.

Looking Ahead

This chapter covered the topic of hyperconvergence at the architectural level. The distributed DAS architecture with distributed controllers is a major shift from centralized storage arrays. The fibre channel storage area network disappeared and was replaced with high-speed 10/40 Gigabit Ethernet.

As the industry moves toward hyperconvergence, the focus shifts to the application and its needs. The application will drive the proper provisioning of storage services and networking services and not the other way around.

Although this chapter discussed the technical aspect of hyperconvergence, it also helps to understand the business aspect and the use cases for hyperconvergence. Chapter 8, "HCI Business Benefits and Use Cases," covers in detail the business benefits that will help CIOs and IT managers make the shift from the traditional SAN- and NAS-based architectures. It will also discuss some HCI use cases that range from enterprise applications to remote office applications. Part IV of this book takes a deep dive into the Cisco HyperFlex (HX) hyperconverged product line.

Chapter 8

HCI Business Benefits and Use Cases

This chapter covers the following key topics:

- **Hyperconverged Infrastructure (HCI) Business Benefits:** Covers HCI business benefits as seen by chief information officers (CIOs) and IT managers who want justification for moving from a legacy storage area network (SAN) and converged environment to hyperconverged. This includes faster deployment cycles, easier scalability with pay as you grow, a better operational model inside the IT organization, easier system management, cloud-like agility, better availability at lower costs, better entry point costs, and better total cost of ownership (TCO).

- **HCI Use Cases:** Discusses the multitude of HCI use cases ranging from simple server virtualization to more complex environments. It includes details about sample applications such as DevOps, virtual desktops, remote office branch office, edge computing, tier-1 enterprise class applications, backup, and disaster recovery.

So, what does hyperconvergence bring to the table? Hyperconvergence promises to bring simplicity, agility, and cost reduction in building future data centers. Hyperconvergence is coined as a "webscale" architecture, a term in the industry that means it brings the benefit and scale of provider cloud–based architectures to the enterprise. Although convergence was able to eliminate some of the headaches that IT professionals had in integrating multiple technologies from different vendors, it didn't simplify the data center setup or reduce its size, complexity, and time of deployment. And although software-defined storage (SDS) as applied to a legacy environment can enhance the storage experience and enhance efficiency, it still does not address the fact that traditional storage area networks (SANs) remain expensive and hard to scale to address the data explosion and the changing needs of storage. This chapter discusses the business benefits of hyperconvergence and its use cases.

HCI Business Benefits

Hyperconverged infrastructure (HCI) brings a wealth of business benefits that cannot be overlooked by CIOs and IT managers. As the focus shifts to the speed of application deployment for faster customer growth, IT managers do not want to be bogged down by the complexity of the infrastructure; rather, they want to focus on expanding the business. As such, HCI brings many business benefits in the areas of faster deployment, scalability, simplicity, and agility at much lower costs than traditional deployments. The HCI business benefits can be summarized as follows: fast deployment, easier-to-scale infrastructure, enhanced IT operational model, easier system management, public cloud agility in a private cloud, higher availability at lower costs, low-entry cost structure, and reduced total cost of ownership.

Fast Deployment

Compared to existing data centers that take weeks and months to be provisioned, HCI deployments are provisioned in minutes. When HCI systems are shipped to the customer, they come in preset configurations. Typical HCI systems come in a minimum configuration of three nodes to allow for a minimum level of hardware redundancy. Some vendors are customizing sets of two nodes or even one node for environments like remote offices. The system normally has all the virtualization software preinstalled, such as ESXi, Hyper-V, or kernel-based virtual machine (KVM) hypervisors. The distributed file system that delivers the SDS functionality is also preinstalled.

Once the hardware is installed and the system is initiated, it is automatically configured through centralized management software. The system discovers all its components and presents the user with a set of compute and storage resources to be used. The administrator can immediately allocate a chunk of storage to its application and increase or decrease the size of storage as needed.

The environment is highly flexible and agile because the starting point is the application. The networking and storage policies are assigned based on the application needs.

Enterprises highly benefit from the shorter deployment times by spending less time on the infrastructure and more time on customizing revenue-generating applications.

Easier-to-Scale Infrastructure

Scaling SANs to support a higher number of applications and storage requirements was traditionally painful. Storage arrays come in a preset configuration with a certain number of disks, memory, and central processing units (CPUs). Different systems are targeted to different markets, such as small and medium-sized businesses (SMBs) and large enterprises (LEs). Storage arrays were traditionally scale-up systems, meaning that the system can grow to a maximum configuration, at which point it runs out of storage capacity, memory, or CPU horsepower. At that point, enterprises must either get another storage array to handle the extra load or go through a painful refresh cycle of the existing system.

The storage arrays are not cheap. The smallest configuration can run hundreds of thousands of dollars. Enterprises must go through major planning before adding or replacing a storage array. A large storage array could waste a lot of idle resources, and a small array could mean a shorter upgrade cycle. Also, the fact that the storage array architecture is based on rigid logical unit numbers (LUNs), you always have the bin-packing problem: trying to match storage requirements with physical storage constraints. When a storage array capacity is exceeded, the data of a storage application might have to be split between storage arrays or move from the older to the newer, larger array.

HCI systems are scale-out because they leverage a multitude of nodes. The system starts with two or three nodes and can scale out to hundreds of nodes depending on the implementation. So, the capacity and processing power of the system scales linearly with the number of nodes. This benefits the enterprise by starting small and expanding as required. There are no rigid boundaries on where the data should be in the storage pool. Once more nodes are added to the system, the data can be automatically reallocated to evenly use the existing resources. This results in smoother scalability of the overall system.

Enhanced IT Operational Model

Another paradigm shift from an operational point of view is that HCI evolves the IT operation from single-function IT resources to a multifunctional, operational model. Today's IT operations have hard boundaries between storage engineers, networking engineers, virtualization engineers, and network management engineers. HCI can change this model due to the ease of operation and embedded automation in the system, which requires lesser skills for the individual functions.

With HCI, a virtualization administrator can take control of the storage required for his applications. That is something that storage administrators do not like to hear because they are supposed to be the masters of their storage domain. With HCI, the virtualization administrator can decide at virtual machine (VM) creation what storage policies to attach to the VM and request that those policies be delivered by the underlying storage pool. The storage pool itself and its capabilities are under the control of the same administrator. The beauty of this model is that virtualization administrators do not need the deep knowledge in storage that storage administrators had because policy-based management and automation hides many of the storage nuts and bolts settings that used to keep storage administrators busy.

In the same way, virtualization engineers can move their applications around without much disruption to the network. In traditional SAN setups, anytime an application is moved around, the virtualization administrator has to worry about both the storage networking and the data networking. Moving an application can disrupt how certain paths are set in the fibre channel network and how a VLAN is set in the data network. With HCI, the fibre channel storage network disappears altogether, and the setup of the data network can be automated to allow application mobility.

HCI promotes the notion of cross skills so that an enterprise can take better advantage of its resources across all functional areas. Instead of having storage engineers, virtualization engineers, and networking engineers, an enterprise can eventually have multifunctional engineers because many of the tasks are automated by the system itself. HCI implementations that will rise above the others are those that understand the delicate mix of IT talent and how to transition the operational model from a segmented and function-oriented model to an integrated and application-oriented model.

Easier System Management

HCI systems offer extremely simple management via graphical user interfaces (GUIs). Many implementations use an HTML5 interface to present the user with a single pane of glass dashboard across all functional areas. Converged systems tried to simplify management by integrating between components from different vendors. The beauty of HCI is that a single vendor builds the whole system. The integration between storage, compute, and networking is built into the architecture. The same network management system provides the ability to manage and monitor the system and summarizes information about VMs and capacity usage. Sample summary information shows the used and unused storage capacity of the whole cluster, how much savings are obtained by using functions such as deduplication and compression, the status of the software health and the hardware health, system input/output operations per second (IOPS), system latency, and more. The management software drills down to the details of every VM or container, looking at application performance and latency. The provisioning of storage is a point-and-click exercise, creating, mounting, and expanding volumes.

It is important to note here that not all HCI implementations are created equal. Some implementations' starting point is existing virtualization systems such as vCenter, so they try to blend it with already existing management systems. Examples are Cisco leveraging vCenter and using plug-ins to include management functionality for the HyperFlex (HX) product. This is a huge benefit for Cisco's Unified Computing System (UCS) installed base, which already uses vCenter. Other implementations start with new management GUIs, which is okay for greenfield deployments but creates management silos for already established data centers.

Public Cloud Agility in a Private Cloud

One of the main dilemmas for IT managers and CIOs is whether to move applications and storage to the public cloud or to keep them in house. There are many reasons for such decisions; cost is a major element, but not the only one. The agility and flexibility of the public cloud are attractive because an enterprise can launch applications or implement a DevOps model for a faster release of features and functionality. An enterprise can be bogged down in its own processes to purchase hardware and software and integrate all the components to get to the point where the applications are implemented. HCI gives the enterprises this type of agility in house. Because the installation and provisioning times are extremely fast, an enterprise can use its HCI setup as a dynamic pool of resources used by many departments. Each department can have its own resources to work with, and the resources can be released back into the main pool as soon as the project is done. This constitutes enormous cost savings by avoiding the hefty public cloud fees, which can be leveraged to invest in internal, multifunctional IT resources.

Higher Availability at Lower Costs

HCI systems are architected for high availability, meaning that the architecture anticipates that components will fail and, as such, data and applications must be protected. The HCI availability is a many-to-many rather than a one-to-one as in traditional storage arrays. With traditional arrays, an array has dual controllers; if one fails, the input/output (I/O) is moved to the other. Also, traditional RAID 5 or RAID 6 protects the disk. However, in traditional SANs, failures affect the paths that I/O takes from the host to the array, so protection must be done on that path as well. This means that high availability (HA) results in dual fibre channel fabrics and possible multipath I/O software on the hosts to leverage multiple paths. Also, when a controller fails, 100% of the I/O load goes to the other controller. During a failure, applications can take a major performance hit if individual controllers are running at more than 50% load. Basically, achieving high availability in storage array designs is expensive.

Because HCI is a distributed architecture, the data is protected by default by being replicated to multiple nodes and disks. The protection is many-to-many, meaning that upon a node failure, the rest of the nodes absorb the load and have access to the same data. HCI systems automatically rebalance themselves when a node or capacity is added or removed. Therefore, HCI systems are highly available and have a better cost structure.

Low-Entry Cost Structure

HCI systems start with two or three nodes and grow to hundreds of nodes. This eliminates the decision-making that IT managers and CIOs must do in choosing how big or small a storage array needs to be. The low-entry cost structure encourages enterprises to experiment with new applications and grow as they need. When converged architectures such as the Vblock were introduced to the market, the systems were marketed with small, medium, and large configurations with huge upward steps between the different configurations. Bear in mind that the prices ranged from expensive to very expensive to ridiculously expensive, with a big chunk of the cost going to the bundled storage arrays.

This is not to say that storage arrays cannot be upgraded, but the long upgrade cycles and the cost of the upgrade could sway CIOs to just get another bigger array. IT would overprovision the systems and invest in extra capacity that might remain idle for years just to avoid the upgrade cycles. With HCI, the systems are a lot more cost effective by nature because they are built on open x86 architectures. In addition, the system can start small and be smoothly upgraded by adding more nodes. When nodes are added, the system rebalances itself to take advantage of the added storage, memory, and CPUs.

Reduced Total Cost of Ownership

TCO is a measure of spending on capital expenditures (CAPEX) and operational expenditures (OPEX) over a period of time. Normally in the data center business, this calculation is based on a 3- to 5-year average period, which is the traditional period of hardware and software refresh cycles.

CAPEX in a data center for storage environment is calculated based on hardware purchases for servers, storage arrays, networking equipment, software licenses, spending on power, facilities, and so on. Some studies by analysts have shown that savings in CAPEX when using HCI versus traditional SAN storage arrays are in the range of 30%, considering savings in hardware, software, and power. Also, the reduced times, ease of deployment and operation, and reliance on a IT general knowledge in HCI could result in about 50% savings in IT OPEX. These numbers vary widely among research depending on what products are compared, so take analyst numbers lightly. However, the takeaway should be that HCI runs on x86-based systems that are more cost effective than closed hardware storage array solutions. The benefit in simpler IT, shorter deployment cycles, and added revenue from efficiently rolling out applications makes HCI a product offering that needs to be seriously considered.

HCI Use Cases

It helps to look at the different HCI use cases in comparison to traditional storage architectures. After all, HCI needs to deliver on the simplicity and agility of deploying multiple business applications and at the same time exceed the performance of traditional architectures. Some of the main business use cases for HCI are these:

- Server virtualization

- DevOps

- Virtual desktop infrastructure (VDI)

- Remote office business office (ROBO)

- Edge computing

- Tier-1 enterprise class applications

- Data protection and disaster recovery (DR)

Server Virtualization

Server virtualization is not specific to hyperconvergence because it mainly relies on hypervisors and container daemons to allow multiple VMs and containers on the same hardware. However, hyperconverged systems complement the virtualization layer with the SDS layer to make server virtualization simpler to adopt inside data centers. The adoption of server virtualization in the data center, whether in deploying VMs or containers, will see a major shift from traditional SAN environments and converged systems to hyper-converged infrastructures. Enterprises benefit from the fact that storage and backup are already integrated from day one without having to plan and design for a separate storage network.

DevOps

To explain DevOps in layman's terms, it is the lifecycle of an application from its planning and design stages to its engineering implementation, test, rollout, operation, and maintenance. This involves many departments working together to create, deploy, and operate. This lifecycle sees constant changes and refresh cycles because any changes in any part of the cycle affect the other. With the need to validate and roll out hundreds of applications, enterprises need to minimize the duration of this lifecycle as much as possible.

Performing DevOps with traditional compute and storage architectures is challenging. Every department needs its own servers, data network, storage network, and storage. Many duplications occur between the departments, and IT needs to create different silo networks. Some of these networks end up overutilized, whereas others are underutilized.

Hyperconverged infrastructure creates the perfect setup for DevOps environments. One pool of resources is deployed and divided into virtual networks. Each network has its own virtual compute, network, and storage sharing the same physical resources. Adding, deleting, or resizing storage volumes or initiating and shutting down VMs and containers is done via the click of a button. Once any resource is utilized and is no longer needed, it goes back to the same pool. The network can start with a few nodes and scale as needed.

For this environment to work efficiently, HCI implementations need to support multitenancy for compute storage and the network. Because each of the different departments needs its own storage policies and network policies, multitenancy support at all layers including the network is a must.

Virtual Desktop Infrastructure

Virtual desktop infrastructure (VDI) was one of the first business applications that resulted from the virtualization of the data center. VDI allows users to use their desktops, laptops, personal digital assistants (PDAs), and smartphones as basically dumb terminals, while the actual application and data run securely on servers in the data center. The terminal just receives the screen shots over the network, while all heavy lifting and processing are done on the server. Any types of end devices can be used as terminals because the end device is not doing any of the processing and does not need to have the application or data local on the device. Figure 8-1 shows a high-level description of VDI.

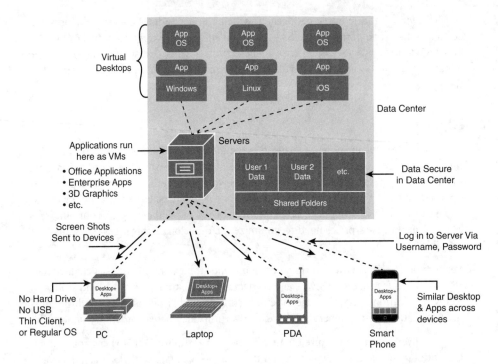

Figure 8-1 *VDI High-Level Description*

As you can see, the virtual desktops run on the servers as VMs. Each VM has its own OS and applications that are associated with the user plus the data associated with the VM. The terminals themselves could run thin clients that operate a simple browser or can operate a regular OS such as Microsoft Windows, Apple iOS, or Linux. The client accesses the server via a URL and, as such, is presented with a user ID and a password to log in. After login, each user receives his own desktop, which has the same look and feel of a regular desktop on a PC or laptop. The terminals also receive a preconfigured set of applications. The desktops have their CPU, memory, and storage resources tailored to the type of user. For example, light users can have one vCPU and 2 GB of RAM, whereas power users can have two or three vCPUs and 32 GB of RAM, and so on. There are normally two types of desktops:

1. **Persistent desktops:** These desktops maintain user-specific information when the user logs off from the terminal. Examples of user data that are maintained are screen savers, background and wallpaper, and desktop customization settings.

2. **Nonpersistent desktops:** These desktops lose user-specific information upon logout and start with a default desktop template. Such desktops are usually used for general-purpose applications, such as student labs or hospital terminals, where multiple users employ the same device for a short period of time.

There are many business cases behind VDI. Here are a few:

- VDI eliminates expensive PC and laptop refresh cycles. Enterprises spend a lot of money on purchasing PC and laptop hardware for running office and business applications. These desktops go through a three-year refresh cycle, where either the CPUs become too slow or the storage capacity becomes too small. Add to this that operating systems such as Microsoft Windows and Apple iOS go through major releases every year; the OS on its own cripples the system due to OS size and added functionality. By using VDI, the desktop hardware remains unchanged because the application and storage are not local to the desktop and reside on the server.

- Because the end user device acts as a dumb terminal, users can bring in their own personal devices for work purposes. The user logs in and has access to its desktop environment and folders.

- With VDI, access to USB devices, CD-ROMs, and other peripherals can be disabled on the end user device. When an application is launched on the server, the data is accessed inside the data center and is saved in the data center. Enterprises can relax knowing that their data is secure and will not end up in the wrong hands, whether on purpose or by accident.

- Any application can be accessed from any end user device. Microsoft Windows office applications are accessed from an iOS device, and iOS applications are accessed from a device running Android. Business-specific applications that usually required dedicated stations are now accessed from home or an Internet cafe.

Problems of VDI with Legacy Storage

Initially, vendors promoted converged systems as a vehicle to sell the VDI application. However, this failed miserably. Other than the huge price tag, converged systems failed to deliver on the performance, capacity, and availability needs of VDI.

With VDI, administrators must provision hundreds of virtual desktops on virtualized servers. Each virtual desktop contains an OS, the set of applications needed by the user, desktop customization data that is specific to the user for persistent desktops, and an allocated disk space per user. Each virtual desktop could consume a minimum of 30 GB just to house the OS and applications. Add to this the allocated storage capacity for the user folders. From a storage perspective, if you multiply 30 GB per user times 100 users, you end up with 10 TB just to store the OS and applications. Now imagine an enterprise having 3,000 to 5,000 users, and you want to change that environment to VDI. The centralized storage needed in that case is enormous. The storage that normally is distributed among thousands of physical desktop now has to be delivered by expensive storage arrays.

On the I/O performance side, things get a lot worse. As soon as thousands of users log in to access their desktops at the start of a business day, thousands of OSs and desktops are loaded, creating a boot storm with hundreds of thousands of I/O requests that cripple the storage controllers. Also, any storage array failures, even in redundant systems, would overload the storage controllers, affecting user experience in a negative way.

IT managers really struggled with how to tailor converged systems to their user base from a cost and performance perspective. They had to decide between small, medium, or large systems, with big-step functions in cost and performance.

How HCI Helps VDI

The HCI-distributed architecture, when used for VDI, helps eliminate many of the deficiencies of converged systems and legacy storage arrays. As a scale-out architecture, enterprises can scale the compute and storage requirement on a per-need basis. The more nodes that are added, the higher the CPU power of the system and the higher the I/O performance. The I/O processing that was done via two storage controllers is now distributed over many nodes, each having powerful CPUs and memory. Also, because the growth in storage capacity is linear, with the use of thin provisioning, enterprises can start with small storage and expand as needed. This transforms the cost structure of VDI and allows enterprises to start with a small number of users and expand.

Also, because VDI uses many duplicate components, data optimization techniques help minimize the number of duplicated operating systems and user applications. With HCI, the use of data optimization with inline deduplication and compression, erasure coding, and linked clones drastically reduces the amount of storage needed for the VDI environment.

Remote Office Business Office (ROBO)

Managing ROBO environments is challenging for enterprises. Remote offices and branch offices can grow to hundreds of locations, with each location having its own specific networking needs. The main challenges facing ROBO deployments follow:

- Deployments are not uniform. No two ROBOs are the same. Some require more compute power and less storage, and some require more storage than compute. Some need to run services such as Exchange servers, databases, and enterprise applications, and others just need a few terminals.

- There is no local IT. Most deployments are managed from headquarters (HQ), except for some large branch offices. Adding IT professionals to hundreds of offices is not practical or economical.

- Management tools are designed for different technologies, compute, storage, and networking. Keeping track of a variety of management tools for the different offices is extremely challenging.

- WAN bandwidth limitations to remote offices create challenges for data backup over slow links.

IT managers are challenged to find one solution that fits all. Converged compute and storage architectures used in the main data center are too complicated and too expensive for remote offices. HCI can handle them, though. The benefits that HCI brings to ROBO follow:

- Small configurations starting from two nodes, with a one-to-one redundancy.

- Ability to run a multitude of applications on the same platform with integrated storage.

■ Ability to remotely back up with data optimization. Data is deduplicated and compressed; only delta changes are sent over the WAN. This efficiently utilizes the WAN links because it minimizes the required bandwidth.

■ Centrally managed with one pane of glass management application that provides management as well as monitoring for the health of the system. It is worth noting here that with HCI, central management no longer refers to the network management systems sitting in the HQ data center. The public cloud plays a major role in the management and provisioning because management software is deployed as virtual software appliances in the cloud. This allows the administrators to have a uniform view of the whole network as if it is locally managed from every location.

■ Periodic snapshots of VMs, where applications can be restored to previous points in time.

■ Consistent architecture between the main data center and all remote offices that leverage the same upgrade and maintenance procedures.

■ Similar hardware between all remote office, but with different numbers of nodes depending on the use case.

Figure 8-2 shows a sample ROBO deployment.

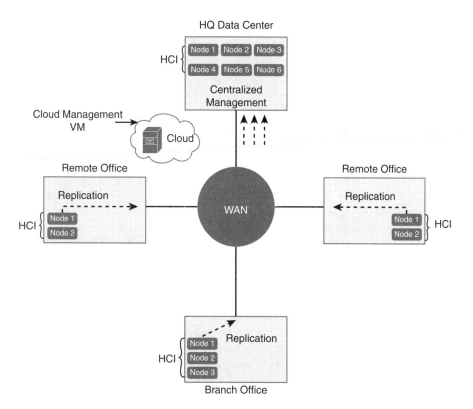

Figure 8-2 *HCI ROBO Application*

As you can see, the hardware configuration in all offices is uniform and varies only on number of nodes. Replication and data optimization ensure efficiency in backups over slow links. Notice also that management is not restricted to centralized management in HQ but can be extended to management servers in the cloud that run as virtual software appliances. The adoption of cloud management allows easy and fast configuration and management as well as a unified management across all locations.

Edge Computing

The trend of edge computing is growing due to the need of enterprises to put applications closer to end users. Some applications that require high performance and low latency, such as databases and video delivery, should be as close to the end user as possible. Other applications, such as the collection of telemetry data from the Internet of things (IoT), are driving the use of compute and storage in distributed locations rather than large centralized data centers.

Similar to the case of ROBO, edge computing requires the deployment of infrastructure in what is now called private edge clouds. These are mini data centers that are spread over different locations that act as collection points for processing the data. This greatly reduces latencies and bandwidth by avoiding constantly shipping raw data back and forth between endpoints and large centralized data centers.

As with ROBO, the mini data centers lack the presence of IT resources and require a unified architecture that is tailored to the size of the data centers. As such, HCI provides the perfect unified architecture that scales according to the deployment and is easily managed from centralized management systems located in main data centers or from virtual software appliances in the public cloud.

Tier-1 Enterprise Class Applications

Enterprise class applications such as enterprise resource management (ERM) and customer relationship management (CRM) from companies such as Oracle and SAP are essential for the operation of the enterprise. Such applications work with relational databases (RDBs), which have high-performance requirements for CPU processing and for memory. For such enterprise applications, although application servers run in a virtualized environment, the databases traditionally run on dedicated servers because they consume most of the resources on their own. Even with the introduction of virtualization, some of these databases still run on dedicated bare-metal servers. Enterprise applications and Structured Query Language (SQL) databases enjoy stability on traditional SANs. These applications are surrounded by a fleet of experts, such as application engineers, system software engineers, and storage administrators just because they are the sustaining income of the enterprise.

Some of these applications evolved dramatically over the years to handle real-time analytics, in which a user can access large amounts of historical data and perform data crunching in real time. An example is a sales manager wanting to base her sales projections in a geographical area based on the sales figures for the past 10 years in a particular region. Traditionally, such an exercise required loading large amounts of data from tape drives. Crunching the data required days to compile the required information. Today, the same exercise needs to happen in minutes. As such, the historical data must be available in easily accessible storage, and powerful processing and memory are needed to shorten the time.

Some implementations, such as Oracle Database In-Memory, require moving the data into fast flash disks or dynamic random-access memory (DRAM). Other implementations, such as SAP HANA, require the whole database to be moved into DRAM. Traditional storage arrays and converged systems are easily running out of processing power in supporting such large amounts of data and processing requirements. To handle such requirements, converged systems require millions of dollars to be spent on storage controllers and storage arrays.

HCI vendors have fast jumped on the bandwagon to certify such applications on the newly distributed data architecture. The modular nature of HCI allows the system to grow or shrink as the enterprise application requires. Also, regardless of whether HCI comes as hybrid or all-flash configurations, the use of flash solid-state drives (SSD) in every node accelerates the reads and writes of sequential data as the applications need.

However, the HCI implementations that stand out are the ones that can mix virtualized servers with bare-metal servers under the same management umbrella.

An HCI implementation must be able to scale the compute and memory regardless of the storage needs. Figure 8-3 shows an example of Cisco HX/UCS implementation, where application servers such as SAP Business Warehouse (BW) are running on an HX cluster. The SAP HANA in-memory database is running on a separate Cisco C460 rack server that offers expandable compute and memory. The virtualized servers and bare-metal servers are running under one Cisco UCS domain.

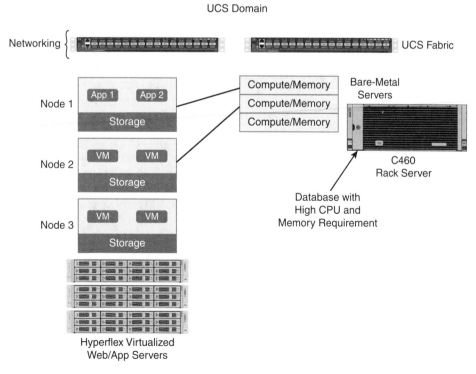

Figure 8-3 *Enterprise Class Applications—Virtualization and Bare-Metal*

Data Protection and Disaster Recovery

Data protection and DR are essential for the continuous nonstop operation of any enterprise application. However, the complexities and costs of building multiple data centers to protect the data and applications are cost prohibitive. Building SANs with traditional fibre channel switching and storage arrays in multiple data centers and backing up the data over WAN links is an expensive proposition. HCI presents a cost-effective solution by handling data protection and DR natively as part of the architecture. Let's look at the different aspects of data protection and DR that HCI offers:

- **Local data protection:** HCI allows data replication and striping in a distributed fashion on many nodes and many disks. Data is replicated either two times or three times, and even more depending on how many node failures or disk failures are tolerated. Data optimization techniques such as deduplication, compression, and erasure coding ensure space optimization.

- **Local snapshots:** HCI allows for periodic snapshots of VMs without affecting performance. Techniques such as redirect on write are used to eliminate performance hits when copying the data. Recovery time objective (RTO) and recovery point objective (RPO) can be customized depending on the frequency of the snapshots.

- **Active-active data centers:** DR is provided while making full use of the resources of a primary and backup data centers. A pair of data centers can run in different locations, with both being active. Data can be replicated locally or to the remote data center (DC). VMs are protected in the local DC as well as the remote DC in case of total DC failure. Data optimization such as deduplication and compression is used, and only the delta difference between data is replicated to the remote site.

- **Cloud replication:** HCI also allows data protection and replication to be done between an on-premise setup and a cloud provider. This could be built in the HCI offering so that an HCI cluster can interface using APIs with cloud providers such as AWS, Azure, and Google Cloud Platform. The level of interaction between the on-premise setup and the cloud depends on whether the customer wants data protection only or full disaster recovery. In the case of full DR, VMs are launched in the cloud as soon as a VM cannot be recovered on premise.

Figure 8-4 shows a high-level data protection and DR mechanism with HCI.

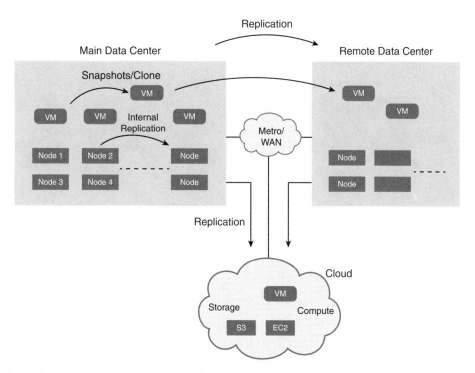

Figure 8-4 *HCI Data Protection and DR*

Looking Ahead

This chapter discussed the main architecture and functionality of HCI and the different storage services it offers. It also examined the business benefits of HCI and a sample of its many use cases.

Future chapters take a much deeper dive into HCI and the specific functionality of some HCI-leading implementations. Part IV of this book is dedicated to the Cisco HyperFlex HCI product line and its ecosystem. Part V discusses other implementations, such as VMware vSAN and Nutanix Enterprise cloud platform, and touches on some other HCI implementations.

PART IV

Cisco HyperFlex

Chapter 9   Cisco HyperFlex

Chapter 10   Deploying, Provisioning, and Managing HyperFlex

Chapter 11   HyperFlex Workload Optimization and Efficiency

Cisco Hyperflex is one of the leading platforms in building hyperconverged infrastructure (HCI). Part IV of this book discusses the Cisco HyperFlex product in detail, including the integration with Cisco Unified Computing System (UCS). The integration with UCS further enhances the virtualization and the simplicity of provisioning a data center. Tools and software products used for sizing the system, optimizing the workload, deploying, provisioning, and managing the platform are also discussed.

Chapter 9

Cisco HyperFlex

This chapter covers the following key topics:

- **Physical Components:** An overview of the Cisco HyperFlex and its physical components, which include Cisco Unified Computing System (UCS) nodes and HyperFlex specific appliances.

- **HyperFlex Performance Benchmarks:** A reference to a performance comparison report that compared the performance of the HX product with other undisclosed competing products. The report focused on different benchmarks for hybrid and all-flash configurations.

- **Integration with UCS:** Covers the integration between HyperFlex and the widely adopted Cisco UCS. The use of service profiles in defining servers in software and integration with legacy storage area networks (SANs) gives HyperFlex an edge over other vendors.

- **Cisco's HX Data Platform:** A detailed description of the HyperFlex data platform. This covers the data platform controller, support of VMware ESXi, Microsoft Hyper-V, and Docker containers. The chapter also covers data distribution in the cache and capacity layers, and the life of read and write input/output (I/O).

- **Advanced Data Services:** Covers HyperFlex advanced data services including deduplication and compression, snapshots, clones, synchronous replication for backup and disaster recovery, and integration with third-party backup software vendors. Also provides a discussion on HyperFlex security with the use of self-encrypting drives and the adoption of industry security standards.

As early as 2009, Cisco was one of the pioneers in unified computing with the introduction of its Unified Computing System (UCS) offering. UCS was one of the first platforms to integrate compute and networking in a single platform. Cisco worked on integrating UCS with leading storage vendors to create a suite of converged products such as VxBlock, FlexStack, VersaStack, and FlashStack. UCS is widely accepted in many enterprises because it offers ease of configuration and mobility for physical servers.

HyperFlex (HX) is Cisco's move into the hyperconvergence space with a new product line designed for hyperconverged environments. However, Cisco did not abandon its roots in UCS, and it is part of the HyperFlex system. HyperFlex uses the Cisco HX Series of x86 servers, Cisco UCS fabric interconnect (FI), UCS blade and rack servers, Cisco's built-in software-defined storage (SDS) software through the acquisition of Springpath, and direct-attached storage (DAS). Cisco HX can support multiple hypervisors, such as VMware ESXi, Microsoft Hyper-V, and KVM (roadmap); it also supports virtualization through containers.

For management, provisioning, and monitoring, Cisco does not move too far from its roots because it adopts the UCS Manager (UCSM) and UCS Director (UCSD) for managing the computing environment. For better integration with existing virtualization management and storage management systems, HX uses VMware's management plug-ins, Microsoft's System Central Virtual Machine Manager (SCVMM), and Microsoft Hyper-V Manager. HX also supports Kubernetes for container management in private and public clouds. Cisco designed its own Cisco HyperFlex Connect, a single pane of glass, easy-to-use HTML 5 GUI. Other management products include Cisco Intersight for cloud management as a service. For multicloud, Cisco introduced its CloudCenter product to migrate workloads between private and public clouds. This gives Cisco an edge in extending its already-large footprint in the data center market.

Cisco was one of the latecomers to hyperconvergence for one reason or another. If you think about it, though, Cisco's strength was always in networking because it had good success with UCS. However, Cisco did not have its own virtualization or software-defined storage software. Similarly, other vendors have their strengths and weaknesses. VMware was strong in software virtualization but weak in hardware. EMC was strong in storage and weak in virtualization and networking.

Cisco was able to enter the software-defined storage market via cooperation with Springpath, which it eventually acquired in September 2017. With Cisco's roots in networking and unified computing, and the addition of highly innovative software, the HX product line promises to leapfrog other established hyperconvergence solutions.

The following sections discuss the different elements of HX.

HyperFlex Physical Components

One of the highlights of Cisco HX that distinguishes it from other solutions is that it is an extension to its widely accepted UCS platform, which is already adopted into data centers. This ensures a continuity for data center deployments and leverages existing hardware and familiarity with management tools. This point is important because many products from HCI vendors create yet another silo that does not integrate with existing infrastructures.

A key distinction for HX is that it uses compute plus storage nodes, called *converged nodes*, and UCS compute-only nodes to tailor for the needs of different applications. In some situations, an application has high demand for compute but not much demand for storage, and in other situations an application is compute and storage hungry. In yet other situations the storage requirement is high and requires storage-only nodes. Most hyperconverged products do build combined compute and storage nodes. Some nodes are storage heavy, whereas others are compute heavy. However, finding the right mix that doesn't leave compute or storage oversubscribed or undersubscribed is difficult. HX offers combined compute and storage nodes and integrates storage-only nodes, but it also offers compute-only nodes via the UCS blade servers. The difference here is in the software's capability to allow compute nodes to access the pool of storage. With VMware's hyperconverged product vSAN, which relies on off-the-shelf servers, VMware allows users to add compute-only servers. However, VMware does not recommend building such imbalanced configurations. Although a vendor might physically allow storage and compute imbalances in the nodes, the software might not be able to handle such configurations properly, causing performance hits.

Another difference is in the fact that HX compute nodes do not need extra software licenses for hypervisors or software-defined storage. For compute-only nodes, Cisco offers the IOVisor software, which allows the compute-only node to access the storage pool for free. This capability is important because hypervisors such as VMware ESXi are licensed per central processing unit (CPU), and adding compute nodes with VMware vSAN means extra licenses.

As described in Chapter 8, "HCI Business Benefits and Use Cases," some high-end enterprise applications such as Oracle's Database In-Memory and SAP HANA require the databases to be on separate bare-metal servers. Cisco HX allows the integration of bare-metal servers such as the Cisco C460 rack server to gradually add compute and memory.

Cisco HX is packaged in different platforms. Each converged node comes with a solid-state drive (SSD) used as a caching tier. In a hybrid configuration, a node comes with a set of hard disk drives (HDDs) for a capacity tier. In an all-flash configuration, the capacity tier is all SSDs.

The fifth generation (M5) of the HX nodes comes with dual sockets to house one or two Intel Xeon processors with up to 28 cores each. These processors provide high memory channel performance and three Intel Ultra-Path Interconnect (UPI) links across the sockets for high-performance interconnection between the cores. The M5s also support up to 3 TB of memory per server. All HX series servers also have a modular LAN-on-motherboard (MLOM) adapter for Ethernet connectivity without consuming a PCIe slot.

The HX M5 hardware is designed to leverage high-speed interfaces and protocols, such as PCIe with NVMe. This design gives superior bandwidth for connecting NAND flash SSD drives that are used for caching. In addition, the M5 is designed to take advantage of Intel Optane technology with 3D Xpoint memory for SSD drives. This gives high-end applications extremely high performance because 3D Xpoint offers lower latencies and higher density than dynamic random access memory (DRAM) but can deliver multiples of the performance of traditional SSD drives.

Cisco HX also offers support for graphics processing units (GPUs) from leading vendors such as NVIDIA to enhance the performance of graphics-intensive applications, such as 3D graphics in a virtual desktop infrastructure (VDI) environment.

The HX platform continues to evolve to offer small form factor (SFF 2.5") drives and larger densities with large form factor (LFF) 3.5" drives.

It is important to note that currently Cisco does not support mixing different types of HX servers in the same cluster. This might result in different nodes having a different number of drives and different types of drives that might affect performance. However, Cisco allows the mixing of generations, so fourth-generation M4 and fifth-generation M5 of the same HX series can be mixed in a cluster to allow compatibility between generations. The user can build different smaller clusters with each having uniform types of systems and still have everything under the same umbrella management.

HX comes in different types of hybrid and all-flash configurations. All-flash systems are obviously more expensive but provide much higher levels of input/output operations per second (IOPS). Capacity also plays a factor in choosing a system because HDDs still come in higher capacities than SSDs. With LFF drives, users can pack a lot more capacity in a node. However, this comes at the expense of performance, especially in hybrid systems. A hybrid system with a large number of small-capacity drives performs much better than a hybrid system with a small number of large-capacity drives.

The different flavors of the HX nodes are described in the following sections.

Cisco HyperFlex Hybrid Nodes

The HX hybrid nodes use serial-attached SCSI (SAS), serial advanced technology attachment (SATA) drives, and SAS self-encrypting drives (SED) for capacity. The nodes use additional SSD drives for caching and an SSD drive for system/log.

- **The HX220c M4/M5:** Hybrid node targeted toward small-footprint and small-capacity clusters. This type of node supports up to eight HDD capacity drives for smaller implementations.

- **The HX240c M4/M5:** Hybrid node targeted toward larger-footprint and high-capacity clusters, such as enterprise business applications. This type of node supports up to 23 HDD drives for larger implementations.

Cisco HyperFlex All-Flash Nodes

The HX all-flash nodes use fast SSD drives and SSD SED drives for capacity. The nodes use additional SSD drives or NVMe drives for caching and an SSD drive for system/log.

- **The HX220c M4/M5 AF:** All-flash node targeted toward small-footprint high-performance clusters. This type of node supports up to eight SSD capacity drives for smaller high-performance implementations.

- **The HX240c M4/M5 AF:** All-flash node targeted toward a larger footprint with high-capacity and high-performance clusters. This type of node supports up to 23 SSD capacity drives for larger high-performance implementations.

Cisco HyperFlex Edge Nodes

The **HX220c M4/M5 Edge:** Hybrid node targeted toward remote office/branch office (ROBO) application.

Cisco HyperFlex Compute-Only Nodes

These nodes contribute memory and CPU but do not contribute to capacity.

- **UCS B200:** Blade server with the UCS 5108 chassis and UCS 2204 XP, 2208 XP, or 2304 fabric extender

- **UCS C220:** Rack server with small compute footprint

- **UCS C240:** Rack server for larger compute footprint

Cisco USC Fabric Interconnect

In the Cisco UCS 6200/6300 fabric interconnect (FI), all nodes in a cluster connect to each other and the rest of the customer network via the Cisco UCS 6200 and 6300 fabric interconnect.

Figure 9-1 shows a sample of the HX physical components. These components are by no means a complete list because more hardware and different configurations are constantly added. Refer to [1] for a complete and updated list.

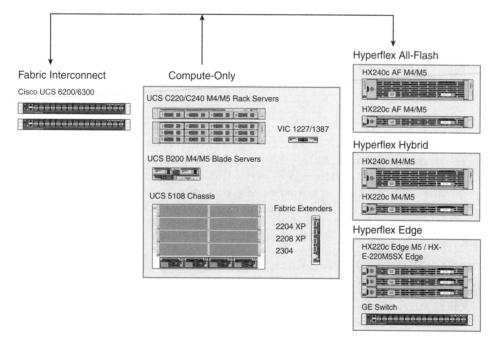

Figure 9-1   *The HyperFlex Physical Components*

Cisco UCS 6200 and 6300 Fabric Interconnect

Cisco integrates its UCS 6200 and 6300 series fabric interconnect [2] as part of the HX cluster. The switches come in pairs and are dual-homed to the HX series nodes as well as fabric extenders inside the compute-only chassis. The Cisco UCS 6200 series works with the Cisco UCS B-Series server platforms, whereas the Cisco UCS 6300 works with both UCS B-Series and C-Series server platforms. The FI ensures that any two points in the HX cluster are one hop away from each other.

Cisco UCS 6248UP 48-Port FI

The Cisco UCS 6248 FI is a 1 RU, 10 GE, Fibre Channel over Ethernet (FCoE), and fibre channel (FC) switch that offers up to 960 Gbps throughput and up to 48 ports. The switch has 32 fixed 1/10 GE fixed Ethernet, FCoE, and FC (4/2/1 and 8/4/2 Gbps) ports and one expansion slot for the remaining 16 ports.

Cisco UCS 6296UP 96-Port FI

The Cisco UCS 6296 FI is a 2 RU, 10 GE, FCoE, and FC switch that offers up to 1920 Gbps throughput and up to 96 ports. The switch has 48 fixed 1/10 GE fixed Ethernet, FCoE, and FC (4/2/1 and 8/4/2 Gbps) ports and three expansion slots for the remaining 48 ports.

Cisco UCS 6332 32-Port FI

The Cisco UCS 6332 32-port FI is a 1 RU, 40 GE switch that offers up to 2.56 Tbps full-duplex throughput. The switch has 32 × 40 Gbps Quad Small Form Factor Pluggable (QSFP+) ports. Depending on selective ports, the ports can be configured as either 40 Gbps QSFP+, or 4 × 10 Gbps SFP+ breakout ports or outfitted via Quad to SFP adapter (QSA) for 1 or 10 Gbps operation.

Cisco UCS 6332-16UP 40-Port FI

The Cisco UCS 6332-16UP 40-port FI is a 1 RU 10 GE, 40 GE, and native fibre channel switch offering up to 2.43 Tbps full-duplex throughput. The switch has 24 × 40 GE and FCoE ports and 16 1/10 GE/FCoE or 4, 8, 16 Gbps FC unified ports. Depending on selective ports, the ports can be configured as either 40 Gbps QSFP+, or 4 × 10 Gbps SFP+ breakout ports, or as SFP+ universal ports operating at 1/10 Gbps Fixed Ethernet or 4, 8, 16 Gbps FC.

Cisco C220/C240 M4/M5 Rack Servers

The Cisco C220 and C240 are rack servers [3] that integrate with UCS. These servers can be used as part of the HX cluster to offer compute-only systems. The M5 serves as an example offering two-socket Intel Xeon CPUs with up to 28 cores per socket and up to 24 DIMMs for up to 3 TB of memory. The C220/C440 can house the

MLOM adapter to connect virtual interface cards (VICs) for 10 Gbps or 40 Gbps Ethernet connectivity.

Cisco VIC MLOM Interface Card

The Cisco UCS VIC [4] is a PCIe MLOM adapter that connects to the UCS servers without consuming a PCIe slot. The Cisco VIC 1227 offers dual-port Enhanced Small Form-Factor Pluggable (SFP+) 10 Gbps Ethernet and Fibre Channel over Ethernet (FCoE). The VIC 1387 offers dual-port 40 Gbps QSFP Ethernet and FCoE ports. The VIC is a next-generation converged network adapter (CNA) that enables a policy-based, stateless, agile server infrastructure that presents up to 256 PCIe standards-compliant interfaces to the host that is dynamically configured as either network interface cards (NICs) or host bus adapters (HBAs). The Cisco UCS VIC supports Cisco's Data Center Virtual Machine fabric extender (VM-FEX) technology, which extends the Cisco UCS fabric interconnect ports to virtual machines, simplifying server virtualization deployment.

Cisco UCS 5108 Blade Chassis

The Cisco 5108 UCS blade chassis is used to house the compute-only modules B200 M4 and M5 nodes [5]. It comes in a 6 RU chassis that houses half-width or full-width nodes. The chassis houses up to eight half-width B200 M4/M5 compute-only nodes. The rear of the chassis contains two I/O bays for Cisco fabric extender. The chassis offers 40 Gbps of I/O bandwidth per server slot from each fabric extender.

Cisco UCS B200 Blade Server

The B200 comes in two versions: M4 and M5 server nodes. Each node is a half-width blade that fits inside one of the eight half slots of the 5108 blade chassis. The B200 M4/M5 nodes are used as compute-only nodes that do not add any storage capacity; they are used for environments that need only added compute and memory. The B200 M5, for example, offers one or two multicore Intel Xeon processors with up to 28 cores per CPU. The B200 M5 has up to 3 TB of memory and up to 80 Gbps of I/O throughput. The B200 connects via the backplane of the 5108 chassis and to the fabric extenders. The B200 nodes also have an MLOM adapter for optional Ethernet connectivity via VIC.

Cisco UCS XP Fabric Extender

Cisco UCS XP fabric extenders come in different flavors, such as the 2204 XP, 2208 XP, and 2304 models. The fabric extenders multiplex the traffic coming from the B200 M4/M5 nodes that are housed in the Cisco 5108 UCS chassis. The uplinks of the fabric extenders depend on the particular model. The 2204 XP has 4 × 10 GE interfaces that form upward links to the fabric interconnect. The 2208 XP has 8 × 10 GE, and the 2304 has 4 × 40 GE uplinks. Two fabric extenders are inserted in the 5108 chassis.

Figure 9-2 shows a sample cluster configuration that contains the HX240c servers and the B200 compute nodes housed in the 5108 blade chassis. The B200 compute nodes connect to the rest of the HX nodes via a fabric extender that multiplexes traffic and connects to the fabric interconnect switches via 10 Gbps or 40 Gbps links.

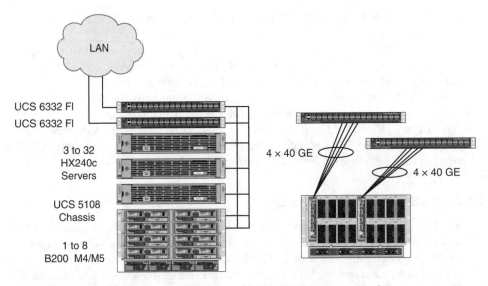

Figure 9-2   *Sample Cluster with HX Servers and B200 Compute Nodes*

In the current implementation of HX, a cluster can have a total of 64 nodes with 32 HX converged nodes and 32 compute-only nodes. The cluster requires 3 HX nodes as a minimum to ensure high availability (HA). The number of compute-only nodes cannot exceed two times the number of converged nodes. The maximum of compute-only nodes is 32. When the size of a cluster is reached, you can add additional clusters to the same UCS domain and manage them through the same vCenter server.

HX continues to scale the number of nodes in a cluster. However, it is important to note that although vendors try to differentiate the number of nodes they support in a cluster, the reality is that many enterprises rarely reach those upper limits and stay within the limits of 8 to 24 nodes in a cluster and opt to add more clusters.

For ROBO configurations, Cisco supports the HX220c Edge M5 nodes, which are targeted for small deployments. The Edge system comes with a minimum of three nodes for HA, either as a hybrid or all-flash configuration. However, because ROBO deployments are usually more lightweight than traditional enterprise deployments, the Cisco HX220c Edge M5 nodes can be interconnected with traditional 1 × GE switches normally deployed in a remote office environment.

HyperFlex Performance Benchmarks

Before we get into the details of the HX software architecture, it is worth mentioning that Cisco differentiates itself from other leading HCI implementations based on performance.

Cisco Systems released a performance comparison report that compared the performance of its HX product with other undisclosed competing products. The report focused on different benchmarks for hybrid and all-flash configurations as follows:

■ Number of virtual machines (VMs) supported at 5 ms latency

■ IOPS and latency for a number of VMs under a certain I/O block size and different read/write percentages

■ IOPs and latency for a number of VMs—Vdbench Structured Query Language (SQL) Server Curve Test

■ IOPS per VM in an all-flash—Vdbench SQL Server Curve Test

The results of the tests clearly showed the variation in performance between HX and other implementations. The test results, as shown in Figure 9-3, were obtained using workloads that simulate real-world applications. For example, they used 4 KB and 8 KB online transaction processing (OLTP) and SQL Server. The test was run with an OLTP I/O mix of 70 percent reads and 100 percent randomized traffic with the intention to find out how many VMs a system can run while the write latency remains below 5 milliseconds. The test clearly showed that HX maintains the 5 ms latency with up to 140 VM density, a 3× factor from other vendors that started exceeding the latency at around 48 VMs.

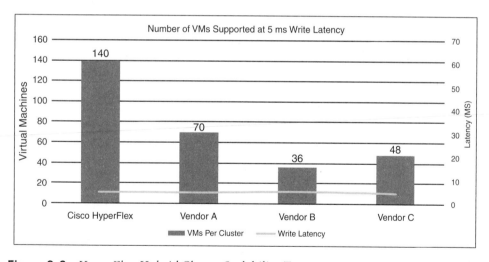

Figure 9-3   *HyperFlex Hybrid Cluster Scalability Test*

Other tests showed that for HX, the number of IOPS delivered per VM remained fairly constant irrespective of the number of VMs, whereas for other implementations the IOPS varied widely per VM depending on the number of VMs. This benchmark is important because scale-out architectures are supposed to deliver consistent performance results for every VM regardless of the number of VMs. This is shown in Figure 9-4.

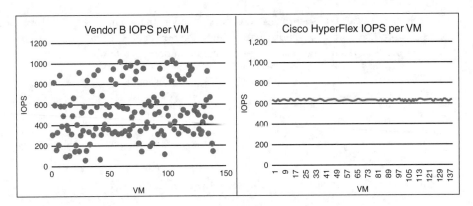

Figure 9-4   *All-Flash Cluster Performance—IOPS per VM*

You can access the full performance test by accessing the link in reference [6].

Cisco offers its customers an HX Bench performance tool based on the Vdbench tool. Vdbench is an open source I/O load simulation tool that was originally created by Oracle. Vdbench gives the user control over parameters such as I/O rate, logical unit number (LUN) size, file size, transfer size, and cache hit percentages. The HX Bench tool puts a simple-to-use HTML5 UI interface in front of this tool, further simplifying the user inter-action. You can access this tool with a CCO Login from reference [8].

With HX Bench, Cisco provides a set of profiles with different types of loads to be used to benchmark the performance of your actual enterprise deployment.

Integration with UCS

One of the main benefits of Cisco HX is that although it introduces a new hypercon-verged architecture, it blends in with existing data center deployments based on UCS. This capability is important for customers who have already invested in UCS because they do not have to introduce yet another management domain and create additional silos. The UCSM supports all management of the compute components of the relevant UCS series and HX. The Cisco UCSM is embedded in the Cisco 6200 and 6300 fabric interconnect in a clustered active-standby configuration for management traffic and active-active for data traffic. UCSM supports the B200 M4/M5 series blade servers and C220/C240 B4/M5 rack servers in addition to the HX nodes. The HX logical network design is described next.

Logical Network Design

As seen in Figure 9-5 [7], the HX network operates in different logical zones:

- Management zone

- VM VLAN zone

- vMotion zone

- Storage zone

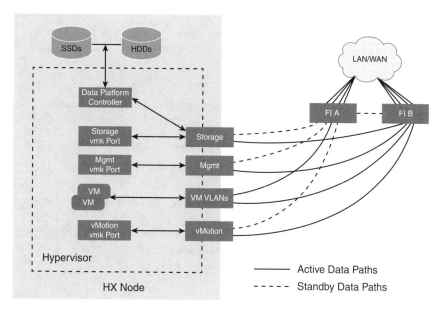

Figure 9-5 *HyperFlex Logical Zones*

The management zone has all the management connections to the physical components, the hypervisors, and the HX Data Platform controllers running on the hosts. This zone allows management reachability via IP addresses to all users who are managing the platform. It also provides access to services such as the Domain Name Server (DNS) and Network Time Protocol (NTP). The components of this zone include the following:

- Fabric interconnect (FI) management ports

- Management interfaces used by the UCS blades and servers

- HX data controller VM management interfaces

- Roaming HX cluster management interface

- Storage controller VM replication interfaces

- Roaming HX controller replication interface

The VM VLANs zone contains the connections needed to service network I/O to the guest VMs running inside HX. It contains the necessary IP addresses, interfaces, and VLANs so that users on the LAN/WAN can access the VMs. This zone contains a VMkernal (vmk) interface for the VM traffic.

The storage zone contains all connections via IP addresses and interfaces needed for the internal communication between the different elements of the HX distributed file system. The components of this zone include a vmk interface for storage traffic, HX Data Platform storage controller interfaces, and a roaming HX cluster storage interface.

The vMotion zone contains all the necessary connections to allow VMs to move from one host to another during vMotion. This zone contains a vmk interface for the vMotion traffic.

In Figure 9-5, notice the solid lines from the VM VLANs zone to the FIs. The reason is that for I/O data traffic, the FIs work in active-active mode, thus offering the full capacity for data traffic. For other zones such as management, for example, the UCSM runs on active (FI A) standby mode (FI B).

Service Templates and Profiles

As discussed in Chapter 6, "Converged Infrastructure," UCSM automates the installation of physical nodes by creating service templates and profiles that basically define every single aspect of the server. You use these templates to launch nodes with similar characteristics without having to configure every single parameter every time. Table 9-1 and Table 9-2 show a sample service profile of an HX node.

Table 9-1   *Service Profile hx-nodes*

Service Profile Template Name	hx-nodes
Setting	Value
UUID Pool	Hardware default
Associated Server Pool	None
Maintenance Policy	HyperFlex
Management IP Address Policy	hx-ext-mgmt
Local Disk Configuration Policy	hx-compute
LAN Connectivity Policy	HyperFlex
Boot Policy	hx-compute
BIOS Policy	HyperFlex
Firmware Policy	HyperFlex
Power Control Policy	HyperFlex
Scrub Policy	HyperFlex
Serial over LAN Policy	HyperFlex
vMedia Policy	Not defined

Table 9-2 *Service Profile compute-nodes*

Service Profile Template Name	compute-nodes
Setting	Value
UUID Pool	Hardware Default
Associated Server Pool	None
Maintenance Policy	HyperFlex
Management IP Address Policy	hx-ext-mgmt
Local Disk Configuration Policy	HyperFlex
LAN Connectivity Policy	HyperFlex
Boot Policy	HyperFlex
BIOS Policy	HyperFlex
Firmware Policy	HyperFlex
Power Control Policy	HyperFlex
Scrub Policy	HyperFlex
Serial over LAN Policy	HyperFlex
vMedia Policy	Not defined

Note that HX has two different service templates—one for the converged HX nodes (compute plus storage) and one for the HX compute-only nodes. The templates are practically the same except for some variations in specific areas, such as local disk configuration and boot policies.

It is worth noting some of the following policies:

- **Boot Policy:** UCS defines a Boot policy called HX that indicates where a certain node boots from, and this is applied to all the nodes in the cluster, simplifying server configuration. The HX converged nodes, for example, have their boot files on a pair of secure digital (SD) cards; and the HX compute nodes boot from SD cards, onboard disks, from the SAN, Internet Small Computer System Interface (iSCSI) boot, and so on.

- **Firmware Policy:** UCS allows the creation of host firmware packages that offer the capability to control the firmware revisions of all blade and rack servers in the cluster. The HX installer creates the firmware packages that contain all the updated firmware. When the HX firmware policy is applied through the service profiles, all components are updated according to the host firmware package.

- **LAN Connectivity Policy:** The LAN connectivity policy aggregates all the vNIC templates into a single policy to be applied via the service profile. This configures all the networking elements, such as where to obtain the IP and Media Access Control (MAC) addresses and quality of service (QoS) applied to the traffic. A detailed description of the vNIC templates that are aggregated by the LAN connectivity policy follows.

vNIC Templates

As shown in Chapter 6, "Converged Infrastructure," vNICs are the logical representations for VM LAN connectivity. Depending on the VIC, up to 256 vNICs can be created. Each VM running on the server is associated with at least two vNICs that connect the VM to the fabric interconnects. Because there are two fabric interconnects, notice the representations A and B, where A indicates the primary connection and B indicates the secondary connection. If the VM also requires external fibre channel storage, the VM can have two virtual host bus adapters (vHBAs).

vNIC templates are used to simplify the configuration of the vNICs, and they are referenced in service templates and service profiles. The vNIC templates contain all the configuration of a vNIC, including MAC address pool assignment, the VLANs the vNIC belongs to, quality of service (QoS) policies, network policies, fabric A or B assignment, maximum transmission unit (MTU) size, and so on. A feature called *vNIC redundancy* allows vNIC templates to be created in pairs. The vNIC template connected to fabric A is considered the primary template, and the vNIC template connected to fabric B is considered the secondary template.

The different types of vNIC templates correspond to the different logical zones that were described earlier: management, vMotion, storage, and VM VLANs. The vNICs templates are as follows:

- **hv-management-a and hv-management-b:** These are the vNIC templates relative to the vNIC connectivity to the management network.

- **hv-vmotion-a and hv-vmotion-b:** These are the vNIC templates relative to the vNIC connectivity to the hypervisor's vMotion network.

- **storage-data-a and storage-data-b:** These are the vNIC templates relative to the vNIC connectivity to the HX Data Platform distributed storage file system.

- **vm-network-a and vm-network-b:** These are the vNIC templates relative to the vNIC connectivity to the network that services the I/O to the guest VMs.

A sample vNIC template is shown in Table 9-3.

Table 9-3 *Sample vNIC Template*

vNIC Template Name	Storage-data-a
Setting	Value
Fabric ID	A
Fabric Failover	Disabled
Target	Adapter
Type	Updating Template
MTU	9000

vNIC Template Name	Storage-data-a	
MAC Pool	Storage-data-a	
QoS Policy	Platinum	
Network Control Policy	HyperFlex-infra	
VLANs	<<hx-storage-data>>	Native: No

Notice that the template is associated with FI A; it has a set of parameters that indicate the fabric failover policy, size of MTU, QoS and network control policies, the pool to obtain the MAC addresses and VLANs from, and so on.

Notice the QoS policy platinum and the network control policy HyperFlex-infra. The QoS policy indicates what QoS parameters to enforce on the traffic passing through the vNIC. A system class platinum policy, for example, is assigned to the storage-data-a and storage-data-b templates. It indicates that traffic should be allocated a certain class of service (number 5), no packet drops are allowed, the MTU size of the packet should be Jumbo 9000 bytes, and so on. Other possible policies are gold, which applies to the vm-network-x templates; silver, which applies to hv-management-x templates; and so on.

The network control policy specifies other aspects of the behavior of the vNIC, such as Cisco Discovery Protocol (CDP), MAC address registration, and the actions taken in case of an uplink failure. In this sample template, the network control policy is defined as HyperFlex-infra. The HyperFlex-infra indicates that CDP should be ON, the link should be set to DOWN in case of an uplink failure, and so on.

HyperFlex Integration with External Storage

One of the differentiators of HX is the use of UCS to easily integrate with external storage. HX integrates with existing storage infrastructures via the UCS connectivity to SANs and network-attached storage (NAS). Outside fibre channel storage connects to the fabric interconnect via fibre channel interfaces. Similarly, iSCSI storage connects via Ethernet. Storage devices also connect to the UCS VIC. Interfaces on the VICs are configured, via software, as either FCoE or Ethernet depending on the storage requirement. This enables the customer to work with both SANs and hyperconverged infrastructure and easily migrate traffic. Examples of some applications where HX integrates with legacy infrastructure include

- Boot and run VMs that are stored on the legacy SAN.

- Use the SAN for storage backup.

- Migrate VMs and storage to the newer hyperconverged infrastructure.

- Use raw device mapping (RDM) from the fibre channel array for Microsoft clustering.

By connecting HX to external storage arrays, administrators can connect fibre channel LUNs from an IBM VersaStack or connect to Network File System (NFS) volumes on a NetApp FlexPod. RDM, for example, allows a VM on HX to use the full LUN on a storage array that is used for Microsoft clustering services, thus allowing multiple Microsoft servers to share storage.

To connect to external storage, administrators need to configure additional vNICs (for iSCSI) or vHBAs (for fibre channel). They should be added preferably during the cluster creation or later. During the installation process and UCSM configuration, the user enables iSCSI or FC storage. This creates dual vNICs or dual vHBAs for the service profile templates named hx-nodes and compute-nodes. Also, for each HyperFlex node, dual vNICs and vHBAs are created for the service profiles of the respective nodes.

Cisco's HX Data Platform

The engine that runs Cisco's HyperFlex is its Cisco HX Data Platform (HXDP). It is a software-defined storage software that offers distributed storage capabilities over a cluster of converged nodes as well as compute-only nodes. It leverages the Cisco UCS fabric interconnect, the Cisco UCS servers for compute-only nodes, fabric extenders, and new HX converged nodes. Let's examine the HXDP architecture and software components.

The HXDP is designed to run in conjunction with a variety of virtualized operating systems such VMware's ESXi, Microsoft Hyper-V, Kernel-based virtual machine (KVM), and others. It also has a way of running the software stack as a Docker container or on bare-metal environments. Currently, Cisco supports ESXi, Microsoft Windows Server 2016 Hyper-V, and Docker containers.

Figure 9-6 shows a high-level view of the HX Data Platform.

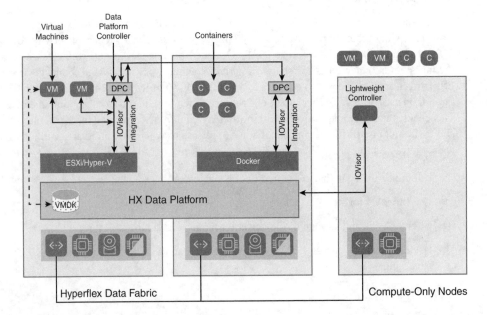

Figure 9-6 *HX Data Platform (HXDP)*

HX Data Platform Controller

The HX Data Platform (HXDP) has a controller that runs as a VM on top of the hypervisor or a container environment. Decoupling the controller from the hypervisor allows the HXDP to run on a variety of hypervisors and container environments. We refer to the Cisco controller in this book as the data platform controller (DPC).

The DPC runs in each node and implements a scale-out distributed file system using the cluster's shared pool of SSD cache and SSD/HDD capacity drives. The DPC runs on converged nodes and includes a lightweight software layer called the IOVisor. The compute-only nodes run the IOVisor by itself in a stripped-down control VM. The DPCs communicate with each other over the network fabric via high-speed links such as 10 GE or 40 GE, depending on the specific underlying fabric interconnect. Aside from creating the distributed file system, the DPC handles all of the data service's functions such as data distribution, replication, deduplication, compression, and so on. The DPC uses PCI/PCIe pass-through to have direct ownership of the storage disks. The DPC creates the logical datastores, which are the shared pool of storage resources. The hypervisor itself does not have knowledge of the physical drives; any visibility to storage that the hypervisor needs is presented to the hypervisor via the DPC itself.

The DPC runs as a VM that is allocated a specific amount of CPU and memory resources to ensure proper performance. As such, the DPC VM needs resources to operate as it is doing the heavy lifting for the I/O functions. The following are recommendations for the resources for the DPC on different HX nodes:

- **Compute:** The HX 220 and 240 nodes require at least eight vCPUs for good performance.

- **Memory:** The HX 220 requires 48 GB of memory, and the HX 240 requires 72 GB of memory.

The compute-only nodes have a lightweight controller VM to run the IOVisor that requires only one vCPU and 512 MB of memory.

As seen in Figure 9-6, the DPC integrates with the hypervisor using two preinstalled drivers: the IOVisor and an integration driver for specific integration with the particular hypervisor.

The IOVisor gives the HX Data Platform the flexibility to interact with the hypervisors for accessing and presenting I/O functions dynamically. Some of the general use cases of the IOVisor in HX Data Platform are

- The IOVisor is used to stripe the I/O across all nodes. All the I/O toward the file system—whether on the local node or remote node—goes through the IOVisor.

- The IOVisor allows compute-only nodes such as the B-Series and C-Series servers to have access to the storage pool to provide additional compute and memory resources. The I/O is sent through the IOVisor from the compute-only nodes to the storage nodes. This differentiates HX from other implementations that cannot leverage compute-only nodes to access existing storage. Some HCI implementations do offer compute-only nodes, but such implementations create a one-to-one mapping between a compute-only node and a storage node. This creates a hotspot because all VMs on the compute-only node use the one node in the cluster for storage. HX, in contrast, leverages the IOVisor to offer the compute-only nodes access to the full datastore that is created by all storage nodes.

HyperFlex in VMware ESXi Environment

When ESXi is run as a hypervisor, the DPC bypasses the hypervisor when accessing the physical resources. The DPC PCI/PCIe pass-through is done via the VMware VMDirectPath feature.

VMDirectPath allows the DPC to have PCI/PCIe pass-through control of the physical server disk controllers without any intervention from the hypervisor. This is done with hardware assistance from the CPUs with mechanisms such as Intel Virtual Technology for Directed I/O (VT-d). This ensures high performance in having the VM access the hardware resources directly. VMDirectPath gives the most savings in CPU cycles with high IOPS environment; it is powerful in the sense that it gives the HXDP the flexibility to implement features independent from the hypervisor and apply hardware assistance to these features when needed.

The DPC integrates with ESXi using three preinstalled vSphere Installation Bundles (VIBs). Think of them as drivers that are installed in the hypervisor to deliver specific functions:

- **IOVisor:** The VMware IOVisor VIB presents the storage to ESXi as a regular NFS mount datastore. However, at this point, the HX Data Platform does not use the NFS file system to deliver file-sharing services. This is just to give ESXi visibility into the storage. The IOVisor also intercepts I/O from the VMs and redirects all I/O to the data platform controllers for load sharing across all nodes.

- **VAAI:** The vStorage API for Array Integration (VAAI) is a set of application programming interfaces (APIs) that were originally defined by VMware to offload some of the advanced storage functionality, such as snapshots, cloning, and thin provisioning to the storage arrays. This allowed vendors to offer hardware assistance to I/O functions offloading the host CPU from spending cycles. This evolved to vSphere APIs for Storage Awareness (VASA) and the notion of virtual volumes (VVols) in later versions of ESXi to also give more transparency to executing such functionality outside ESXi.

  In the context of the HX Data Platform, VAAI allows vSphere to request advanced functionality, such as snapshots and cloning, through the HX data controller. In turn, the DPC performs such functionality through the manipulation of metadata without doing expensive data copying. Snapshots and cloning are discussed further in this chapter.

- **stHypervisorSvc:** This VIB offers enhancements and the needed features for the HX Data protection and VM replication. This module coordinates the snapshot process in the background and facilitates the replication of snapshots between clusters.

ESXi support is shown in Figure 9-7. Note that ESXi sees the storage as an NFS datastore.

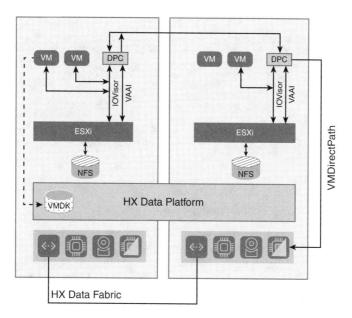

Figure 9-7 *ESXi Support*

HyperFlex in Hyper-V Environment

HX multi-hypervisor support includes support for Microsoft Hyper-V and support for the SMB3 file protocol. HX implements the Microsoft Windows 2016 Data Center Core and supports Hyper-V features. It also supports new Microsoft application stacks with native failover clustering, checkpoints, replica, and Active Directory (AD).

For added integration with existing environments, the Hyper-V hosts are managed via Microsoft's System Center Virtual Machine Manager (SCVMM), Microsoft Hyper-V Manager, and PowerShell. This allows integration with existing applications such as back-up software for Microsoft applications. Integration with the HX Data Platform is also delivered via a set of HX RESTful APIs and Cisco Connect HTML5 GUI. The high-level architecture is shown in Figure 9-8.

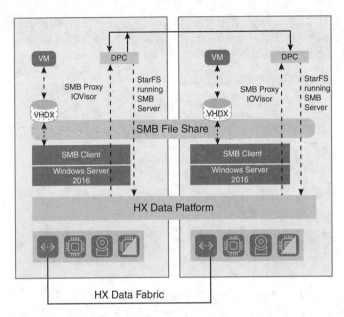

Figure 9-8 *Support for Hyper-V*

Notice that Windows Server 2016 is installed. The DPC forms the HX datastore that is presented to the VMs on Hyper-V as a Server Message Block (SMB) file share. Microsoft applications have the virtual hard disk X (VHDX) files running on the SMB file share. The VHDX files in Microsoft are similar to logical hard drives that contain all sorts of information such as operating system and data. Similar to the ESXi environment, the VMs use IOVisor to redirect the I/O to all the nodes on the HX datastore. However, for Hyper-V, there isn't a notion of VAAI as in ESXi; instead, Microsoft Server implements a layer called Offload Data Transfer (ODX), which is similar to VAAI in the sense that it offloads storage functionality to the underlying storage layer without involving the host. The ODX performs functions such as cloning, taking snapshots, and copying files directly between storage devices without going back to the host VMs.

Docker Containers Support and Volume Driver

Containers have found increased adoption among the developer community in the past few years mainly because they are lightweight, consume less memory and storage resources, and launch much faster than VMs. Containers bring to the table new levels of agility and speed in launching and modifying applications. In the containerized environment, Docker containers have found wider adoption, possibly because Docker was one of the early movers in licensing the technology.

Containers were first adopted in the cloud environment, where thousands of applications were deployed. However, container adoption in the enterprise is still struggling due to many challenges that administrators must overcome. The challenges fall in the area of container management and monitoring, ways to integrate containers in an existing environment, the engineering skill set needed to work with containers, and so on.

To that regard, Cisco started a partnership with Docker in 2017 to work on different areas to simplify and enhance the deployment of containers in enterprise environments. The Cisco and Docker partnership spans different areas including networking, security, orchestration, and data management.

HX supports a Docker container environment to run applications and enable developers to have an environment similar to cloud services. When running containers in the cloud, you normally request a certain amount of persistent storage to run applications. Such storage gets automatically configured on demand without your knowing what goes on behind the scenes. In an enterprise environment, things can become more complicated. Virtualization engineers need to request storage from storage engineers. In a containerized environment, allocating storage is a little more complex. Containers are normally transient in nature, and so is the storage associated with them. Normally, storage is associated with the container's *union file system*. The container union file system has multiple read-only layers and a read/write layer. When changes are made to a file, they go into the read/write layer. When a container is deleted, all the changes are gone, and you are left with the read-only layers.

Also, containers run on bare-metal servers in addition to VMs. When running on VMs, a container can move from one VM to another, and as such, it needs to keep its persistent storage. The complexity of keeping persistent storage for containers depends on the type of back-end storage. So, to save data to persistent storage and share data between containers, Docker implements container volumes.

Container volumes are files and directories that sit outside the union file system and can be saved on the host or on shared storage and can be accessed by multiple containers.

Cisco implements the Docker volumes using the FlexVolume Driver, as shown in Figure 9-9.

As you'll notice, the containers are run inside a VM. The FlexVolume driver allows the user to request storage on demand, and that storage is allocated outside the container union file system, so it can be saved and shared by multiple other containers. Data volumes are allocated via block storage. The FlexVolume allows storage to be requested from the HX Data pool by presenting the block storage as an iSCSI LUN.

The existence of the containers inside VMs and the use of FlexVolume give containers the same resiliency that HX applies on VMs. VMs and their data—and hence containers and their data—benefit from all the data services such as snapshots, replication, deduplication, compression, and so on.

The area of containerization continues to be a moving target as the technology continues to evolve. Cisco is continuously evolving the containerized architecture to allow containers to work inside VMs as well as directly on bare-metal servers. The Cisco container platform puts together a lot of open source tools to create effective ways to manage Kubernetes clusters, including the storage and networking components.

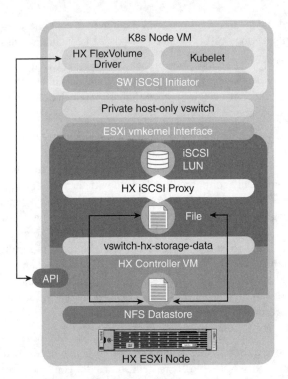

Figure 9-9 *Docker Container Environment*

HyperFlex Data Distribution

HX has a highly distributed architecture that leverages every single component in the cluster and treats resources as a shared pool. HX data distribution through the use of data platform controllers, data replication, cluster resiliency, and the life of reads and writes inside the system are discussed next.

The HXDP distributed file system, using the DPC VMs, creates a pool of storage that is shared by all nodes. The shared pool of resources can be divided into different datastores. There is no one-to-one relation between the datastores and the physical nodes because the data is distributed across multiple nodes. The VMs use the datastores to store their virtual machine disks (VMDKs). The only restriction is that a VM needs to keep its VMDKs in a single datastore. This is needed to do snapshots and clones on the VM level. HX creates an even distribution of data among all the physical nodes. When a VM requests a certain space for a VMDK, the space is allocated by leveraging disks from all nodes. This creates a high disk space utilization compared to implementations that lock the VMDK to the nodes where the VM exists. Such implementations normally create an uneven distribution of storage on disks and a low utilization.

Datastores are created via the vSphere web client or the HX Connect User Interface (UI). Datastores are automatically "thin provisioned." The size of the datastore is increased or decreased as needed based on the requirement of the application with no restriction on the size of the datastore because it is not tied to any specific physical disk. The HyperFlex system monitors the total thin-provisioned capacity of the cluster to ensure that it is less than the actual usable physical capacity. The system alerts the user when the actual storage consumption results in low amounts of free space. The alerts are sent to the user via emails from the vSphere plug-in on HX connect. Datastores are illustrated in Figure 9-10.

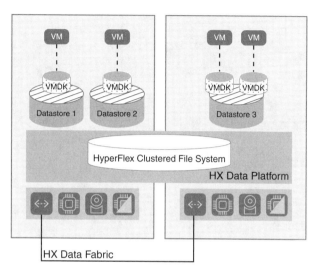

Figure 9-10   *HyperFlex Datastores*

The DPC handles all read and write operations from the VMs to their respective VMDKs that are stored in the distributed datastores in the cluster. Many of the DPCs participate in these operations at the same time. HX uses two tiers of data: a caching tier and a capacity tier. A hybrid HX node has one SSD drive used as a read/write log cache, and HDDs for capacity. An all-flash node has an SSD or NVMe drive for a write log and SSDs for capacity.

HX does dynamic distribution of the data leveraging storage and compute resources in the cluster. This is done by striping the data over multiple disks and nodes and using replication when needed and according to protection policies. A major difference for HX is that it uses a highly distributed approach leveraging all cache SSDs as one giant cache tier. All cache from all the nodes is leveraged for fast read/write. Similarly, HX uses all HDDs as one giant capacity tier.

The HX distributed approach uses HX DPCs from multiple nodes. The controllers run inside a VM on top of the existing hypervisor or Docker. The distributed approach where all nodes share the I/O for all VMs eliminates hotspots if multiple VMs in the same node put stress on the local controller. In this case the local controller engages other controllers from other nodes to share the load. This scenario is represented in Figure 9-11. Notice that the workloads and data services for VMs 1 to 4 are shared by the local DPC on node 1 and the remote DPCs on nodes 2 and 3, where nodes 2 and 3 are also used for I/O. The purpose is to eliminate any hotspots in any single node. Other HCI implementations on the market use what is called *strict data locality* or *partial data locality*. With such implementations, I/O basically follows the VM, and the preference is to do the writes on the node where the VM is located, which might create hotspots.

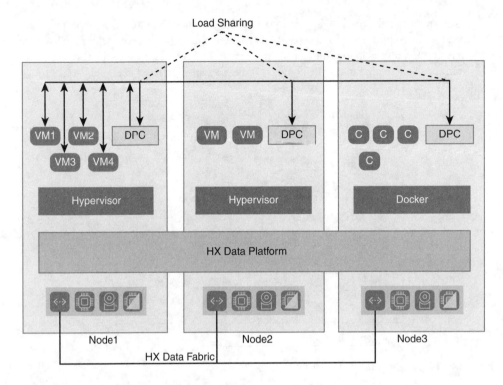

Figure 9-11   *HyperFlex Controller Sharing*

HyperFlex Data Striping

HX uses the caching layer as an L2 read cache in hybrid configurations and as a write cache for both hybrid and all-flash configurations. HX moves away from data locality, as in other hyperconverged implementations, and adopts a fully distributed system leveraging resources across the fabric. HX treats all caching devices from all nodes as one caching pool where a VM can leverage the cache from its own node and in other nodes in the cluster. This configuration is shown in Figure 9-12.

Note that for a hybrid node, the read and write are done using the SSD cache. In an all-flash configuration, the reads are done directly from the SSD capacity tier or the cache tier (if the data is still in the cache). Note also that any of the local or remote cache can be used in all nodes as one large pool.

The data is striped between all the SSDs in the caching tier of the cluster. A file or object such as a VMDK is broken in smaller chunks called a *stripe unit*, and these stripe units are put on all nodes in the cluster. A stripe unit could be 256 MB, for example, and the number of stripes could be 1, 2, 3, and so on. If the total number of converged nodes in a cluster is 32, the maximum number of stripes is 32. Stripe units are placed on the nodes using a hashing algorithm performed by the IOVisor, which determines where to place the primary blocks.

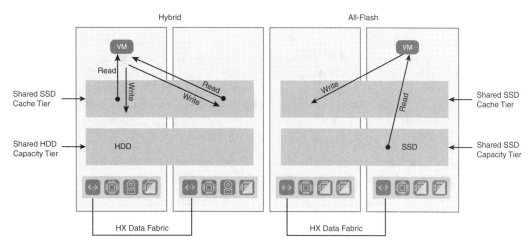

Figure 9-12   *Read/Write Operation Hybrid Versus All-Flash*

An example is illustrated in Figure 9-13. In this example, four stripes are selected, so an object VMDK whose data is represented by blocks A, B, C, D, and E, is striped over the four nodes. In this case, primary block A1 goes to node 1, primary block B1 goes to node 2, primary block C1 goes to node 3, primary block D1 goes to node 4, and primary block E1 loops back to node 1, and so on. The index 1 in A1, B1, C1, D1, and E1 indicates that these are the primary blocks.

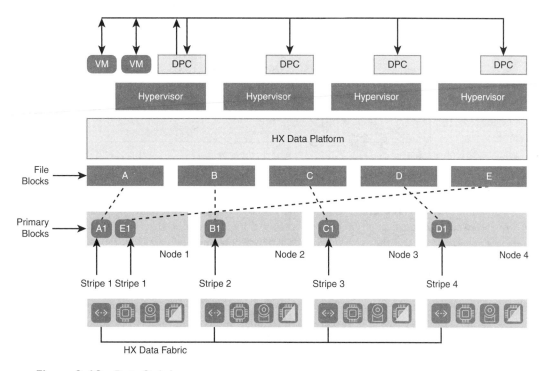

Figure 9-13   *Data Striping*

Data Protection with Replication Factor

In addition to data striping, a protection policy can be applied to protect the cluster from disk or node failure. This is done via replication of the data over multiple nodes. HX has a default replication factor (RF) of 3, which indicates that for every I/O write that is committed, two other replica copies exist in separate locations. With RF = 3, an HX cluster can withstand two simultaneous disk failures on different nodes or two node failures, where the data is recovered without resorting to any other backup and restore methods. If RF = 2, a total of two copies can withstand one failure.

In the example shown in Figure 9-14, if a replication factor of 3 is applied (RF = 3), the stripe units are replicated onto two more nodes in addition to the primary node.

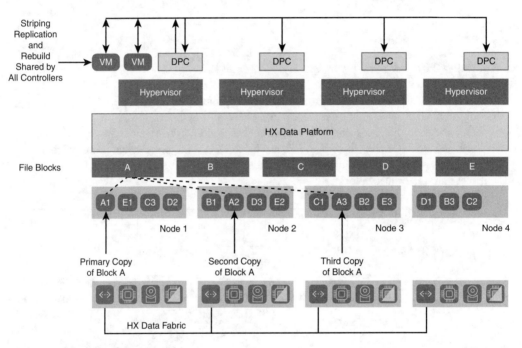

Figure 9-14 *Data Replication*

Note that block A is replicated on nodes 2 and 3 as A2 and A3 to indicate the second and third copies. The same is done for blocks B, C, D, and E. Also note that a stripe unit is always replicated on different nodes than the original node so that the original and the copy are not lost at the same time. In case of a disk failure, the data is recaptured from the remaining disks or nodes. In this example, if node 4 fails, the stripe units for D, B, and C are still available on nodes 1, 2, and 3. In such cases, the VMs that were running on node 4 are redistributed to other nodes using VM high availability, and the VM has access to their data. Upon the failure of node 4, you lose the replication policy RF = 3 because data now has only two copies. If for some reason node 4 does not come back online, the data blocks that were lost on node 4 will be replicated on the other nodes to maintain RF = 3. This happens automatically after two hours or sooner with user intervention.

After restoring the disks or node, the data on that disk or node is rebuilt according to the striping and replication policies, and the data is rebalanced between all nodes. One advantage of the distributed architecture is that all data platform controllers participate in the striping, replication, and rebuild. If a failed node does not come back online, the rest of the nodes participate in rebuilding the failed node so that any single node does not have any hotspots.

Disk failure does not affect the VMs at all because the VM continues to access its data from other nodes. The data that was influenced by the disk failure can be reconstructed on other disks in a matter of minutes, depending on the replication policy, to have the system back in a healthy and protected state.

The capability to move the data around and rebalance the system after failures makes one-click software updates viable because you can easily take a node offline, update the software and firmware, and then bring up the node again.

Cluster Resiliency

Rebalancing occurs in a cluster when it is self-healing and recovering from a failure. Failure occurs on a node when a disk fails or when the controller fails or when the node itself fails. As discussed previously, when a disk fails, there is no impact on the VMs and I/O because the data is already available on other disks in the cluster. However, the system needs to rebalance the data to put the lost data on other disks to maintain availability in case another failure occurs. Similarly, when a DPC fails, the I/O that was serviced by that controller is rebalanced by being sent to other controllers in the system. So also in this case, a DPC failure does not impact the VMs or the I/O on the particular node, but the I/O load gets rebalanced on other nodes. Rebalancing also occurs if a node recovers after failure and gets added to the cluster or in scale-out scenarios where more nodes are added to the cluster.

Failures in a node can be simultaneous when the node incurs a failure while still unhealthy and is still recovering from a failure. Failures are considered nonsimultaneous when a recovered and healthy node incurs another failure. HX is particular about how failures are handled to maintain data integrity. HX allows the user to set resiliency policies depending on the failure tolerance in the cluster. Because a node might take up to two hours to self-heal, it is important to ensure that the system has a level of fault tolerance while recovering. This is the reason HX starts with a minimum of three nodes; this way, when a node failure occurs, the system is still fault tolerant. The resiliency policies range from having a cluster allow full read/writes during node failure (Lenient), to allowing read-only (Strict), to taking the cluster offline. A sample of resiliency policies for node failures and HDD failures is shown in Tables 9-4 and 9-5. A sample cluster status is shown in Table 9-6.

Table 9-4   *Cluster Resiliency Policies for Node Failures*

Number of Simultaneous Node Failures	Cluster Size = 3	Cluster Size = 4	Cluster Size = 5+
1	Read/Write	Read/Write	Read/Write
2	(offline)	(offline)	Read-Only
3	(offline)	(offline)	(offline)

Table 9-5   *Cluster Resiliency Policies for HDD Failures*

Number of Simultaneous HDD Failures (Across Different Nodes)	Cluster Size = 3+
1	Read/Write
2	Read-Only
3	(offline)

Table 9-6   *Cluster Status*

Status	Online
Health State	Healthy
Policy Compliance	Compliant
Space Status	Normal
Replication Factor	2
Access Policy	Strict
Reason	Storage cluster is healthy

Note how the policies are set to show the behavior of the cluster depending on the number of node or disk failures. The access policies can be set to Strict, for example, to indicate that at least two instances of all data blocks must be available for the cluster to be read/write. A Lenient access policy indicates that the cluster remains read/write even if only one instance of the data blocks remains. The tables show an example where a cluster with three nodes automatically goes offline if more than one node failure occurs. A cluster of five or more nodes goes into read-only mode if two node failures occur and goes offline if three node failures occur. A cluster of three nodes goes offline if three simultaneous HDD failures occur across the cluster. These measures can be taken to ensure the cluster reacts if systematic failures start to occur, which means that a major issue is taking place. In those cases, it is better to put the cluster in read-only mode or offline rather than experiencing data corruption.

Logical Availability Zones

Cisco HX supports logical availability zones (LAZs) to separate the cluster into failure domains. The LAZ concept applies only to the HX series nodes and not the compute-only nodes. In its first iteration Cisco HX is configured to automatically divide a large cluster into multiple failure domains. Data is not replicated within the same LAZ. This ensures that if a failure occurs to multiple nodes in the same failure domain, data is still available or can be reconstructed. LAZs allow a cluster to sustain a larger number of nodes or disk failures because of the multiple fault domains. Further extensions to logical availability zones allow manual configuration so the user can define what set of nodes constitute a failure domain. This is done around different boundaries such as nodes in rack, nodes in a data center, or nodes that have the same power source.

LAZs create the foundation for building stretched clusters between different data centers. However, as you will see in more evolved implementations of failure domains, there is always the headache of having network segmentation if fault domains become isolated. In such cases, "witness" nodes must be created to avoid race conditions, where the same VM gets created in different fault domains. Failure domains are covered further in Chapter 12, "VMware vSAN."

Details of Read and Write Operations

Each HX node contains a caching tier and a capacity tier. HX uses a log structured file system for writing and reading data from both the cache and capacity tiers. In addition, the HX contains a data virtualization layer that decouples servicing the data from the actual physical location of the data on disk. The use of the log file system, the details of the virtualization layer, and the lifecycles of read and write for both cache and capacity tiers are discussed next.

Log-Structured File System

HX adopts a hardware-agnostic log-structured file system (LFS) that is written in the Portable Operating System Interface (POSIX) user space code. This LFS gives HX the flexibility to have the compute layer access data as files, objects, blocks, or via API plug-ins. The HX file system uses mainly objects to store information, but it presents an NFS datastore toward the ESXi hypervisor or an SMB3 datastore toward a Hyper-V hypervisor.

The log-structured approach gives HX many advantages in accessing both HDDs and SSDs compared to traditional write-in-place file systems. Unlike with write-in-place file systems where the data is written in different places, with LFS, information is always written sequentially, which improves seek times for reads and writes for HDDs. Also, because the same blocks are not modified and written in the same space as in traditional write-in-place file systems, LFS extends the life of flash devices and gives better write latency by avoiding the write cycle of writing into existing flash cells. To remove old data from the log, HX uses a cleaner that operates on a schedule or a free space threshold, depending on what is appropriate for the amount of capacity used in the system. The cleaner operates daily if not executed by the threshold.

Also, the index of a block, or metadata, is the result of a hash function that gives the block a unique identifier. By looking at the index of the block, you can tell whether the block changed or not. If the block did not change and there is a write operation for the same block, the block remains intact and does not have to be written again. The LFS also gives better advantages to write-in-place file systems when data is being compressed. With traditional write-in-place file systems, if the data is to be modified and it is already compressed, the system must do a read, decompress, modify, compress, and then write. In LFS, because the new data is appended to the log, it is just compressed and written. This gives huge performance advantages.

Data Virtualization

HX data platform contains a virtualization layer that decouples servicing the data from the actual physical location of the data. This ensures consistency in performance when VMs move around because the performance is consistent regardless of where the data resides. HX uses the concept of pNodes and vNodes. The pNode is the actual physical node. A vNode is an abstraction that decouples the data from the physical node. The three types of vNodes are as follows:

- **Cache vNode:** The cache vNode is the data that exists in the cache tier. The data is not deduplicated, but it is compressed. The more cache vNodes you have, the faster the data will be processed.

- **Data vNode:** The data vNode is the actual data such as files, objects, and database data. This data is in the capacity tier, and it gets deduplicated while moving from the cache to the capacity tier.

- **Metadata vNode:** The metadata vNode has all the metadata information about the data itself. The metadata also contains the hashing key of the data, which helps in determining whether to deduplicate or compress the data.

Figure 9-15 shows how stripe units from different VMDKs map into the cache vNodes.

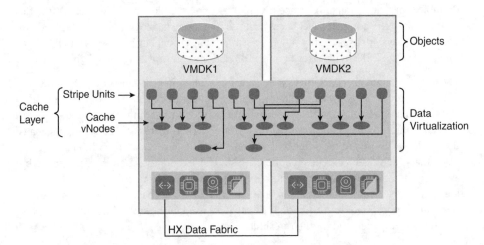

Figure 9-15 *Data Virtualization*

The stripe units from the VMDKs map into cache vNodes, which represent a virtual node that is used to address the data. The virtual node in turn maps into different physical nodes. This creates a mapping structure between stripe unit cache vNodes and pNodes and the mapping is tracked in the HX cluster resource manager. Having cache vNodes allows HX to rebalance the information in the cache to avoid hotspots, by moving the cache vNodes between different pNodes. This means that a VM running on node 1 could have its caching for a certain VMDK done on node 4, and the system has to deal with this.

Addressing a stripe unit into cache vNodes utilizes a combination of consistent hashing and a mapping service to map the stripe unit to the cache vNode. If multiple stripe units hash to the same location, the mapping service can move the stripe unit to a different location and track it. Also, as vNodes move around between caches, the mapping service needs to keep track of the location of the data.

The Lifecycle of a Write Operation

When an application performs a write, the VM sends the data to its VMDK. The IOVisor intercepts the write operation and sends it to the primary controller that is servicing the VMDK. The write operation in the caching tier is performed by doing an I/O write to the caching SSD of the local node in the *write log area* and striping the data between the cache SSDs of the different nodes in the cluster. This is done using an LFS.

Also, depending on the replication factor, a *fork* makes a simultaneous copy of the stripes to the write log SSDs of other nodes. HX leverages the IOVisor to do the initial write and the replication. The write operation is not acknowledged until all replicas are written to cache. This ensures data integrity in case of a node or disk failure that might occur during the write operation. At the same time, a copy of the data is also put in the memory cache (L1 cache). This is seen in Figure 9-16. The data remains in the cache tier and is not destaged—that is, moved into the capacity tier—as long as it is current, not updated, and not old. When it is writing the data into the write log, the data is compressed but is not deduplicated at this stage. Compression at this level allows more data to be placed in the cache and enhances performance. HX uses the Google Snappy compression algorithm, which is optimized for speed.

In a hybrid node, a portion of the caching SSD is allocated to the write log and the remaining portion is the L2 *read cache*. In the case of an all-flash node, the full SSD or NVMe is dedicated for the write log because the reads do not need their own L2 read cache. The write log for both hybrid and all-flash is also available in the memory area of the controller VM. The write log and read cache are all based on a log-structured file system (LFS).

The write log is divided into two partitions whose state changes between Active and Passive, depending on writing into the cache or destaging from the cache. Other than the primary partitions, two sets of partitions are available in the write log to accommodate two more copies of other mirrored stripe units. HX uses an 8 GB or 32 GB write log for hybrid nodes and a 60 GB write log for all-flash nodes. In the case of a hybrid node, the remainder of the cache SSD is used for the read cache.

Note that the size of the write log is not really a big issue as long as the data is destaged fast enough into the capacity tier, as shown in Figure 9-16. The faster the data is destaged, the faster the write log empties and goes back to active. Having very large write logs might affect performance because it takes a long time for the data to be flushed from the cache into the capacity tier.

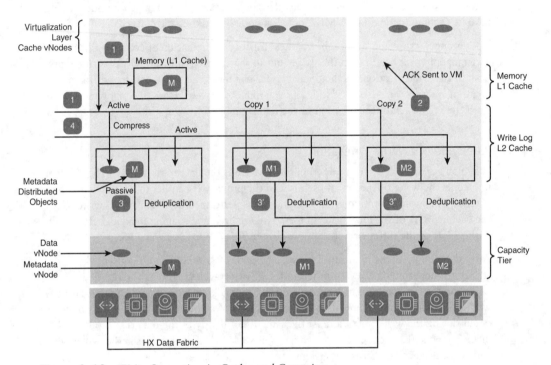

Figure 9-16   *Write Operation in Cache and Capacity*

When the VM is writing to a cache vNode, the data goes into the active partition of the primary unit and then is replicated into the active mirrored partitions. When the write into the partitions is complete, an acknowledgment is sent back to the VM. At this point the data is still not deduplicated inside the cache. The size of the write depends on the block size advertised by the NFS or SMB datastore. For example, if a 64 KB block is advertised, the guest OS inside the VM does the writes in 64 KB, and these 64 KB blocks are written in the active partition of the write log.

HX also keeps a layer that sits on top of the LFS and maintains *distributed objects*, which are the metadata. The metadata keeps track of the data itself and its location. The metadata is first kept in cache and then written to the capacity tier. The distributed objects layer also keeps track of the deduplication and compression ratios plus other information relevant to the objects.

Here are the steps when writing into the write log, as seen in Figure 9-16:

1. The status of both partitions is Active-Active. Data for cache vNode is written into the first active write log partition of the SSD cache and is written at the same time in the memory cache of the node. Depending on replication, data is copied into the active write log partitions of other nodes.

2. When the replicas are done, an acknowledgment is sent to the VM indicating that the write is done.

3. If the first active partition fills up or the memory cache fills up, the data must be destaged. The state of the first active partition is switched to passive, and the data starts getting destaged to the capacity tier. The destaging in all nodes does not have to happen at the same time. Each node destages whenever its own memory or active write log fills up. During destaging, data is deduplicated. For hybrid nodes, recently written data is copied into the L2 read cache.

4. New data coming into the cache gets written into the second active partition and replicated into other nodes. When the second active partition gets full or memory cache gets full, the state of the second partition is set to Passive, data gets destaged, and the first partition is set to Active to accept data, and the cycle continues.

Destaging and Data Optimization

Now that the active part of the write log is filled, or the memory consumption in the cache in relation to the write log hits its limit and gets full, the data is ready for active destaging and is moved into the capacity tier (step 3). During the destaging process, in hybrid nodes the recent writes are added to the read cache area (L2 cache) of the SSD cache. This speeds up processing read requests for data that was already written and is still being accessed.

The capacity tier is also based on an LFS. The log segments are called *data vNodes* and *metadata vNodes*. The metadata vNodes represent the distributed objects layer that keeps track of the object and help determine whether deduplication and compression must be applied.

The data vNodes can span one host or multiple hosts. This is done to make sure that capacity across the cluster is leveraged because storage in some nodes could be full while storage in other nodes is empty. This also enables the system to do faster rebuilds when a disk fails because the data vNodes can be collected from all over the cluster.

When data is written to the capacity tier, it is replicated into multiple mirrored copies depending on the policy, exactly as was done in the caching tier. The metadata itself is also written to both the caching and capacity tiers and maintains the information about the data and how it is indexed. When data is written to the capacity tier, it is also check-summed to maintain data integrity.

When data is moved into the capacity tier, it goes through inline deduplication. As already mentioned, deduplication is not done on the write log but only while data is moved into the capacity tier after an acknowledgment is received that the data and its copies were written to cache. Data is written to the capacity tier in blocks of 4 KB or 8 KB, depending on the configuration of the block size of the object, so deduplication and compression are always done on fixed blocks.

The deduplication is based on fingerprints of the data block, meaning each data block has a unique fingerprint that distinguishes it from other data blocks. If two blocks have the same fingerprint, the data is not written again. Not all data blocks are indexed because this process uses too much memory. HX does indexing based on frequency of hits, so the more the data is active and is being read or written, the better likelihood that it is indexed.

The Lifecycle of a Read Operation

Reading I/O is done differently for hybrid and all-flash nodes. Hybrid nodes read from the read cache area of the SSD cache (L2 cache), whereas for all-flash nodes there is no L2 cache. All-flash nodes read directly from the SSD capacity pool. When doing a read, the IOVisor knows which node has the primary copy of the block. In all-flash nodes, the read always tries to get the primary block. In hybrid nodes, it is possible to request the primary block or any of the copies, depending on which operation is faster. The lifecycle of a read is shown in Figure 9-17.

1. For data that was recently written and not destaged yet, the data may be found in the active write log of the SSD cache.

2. If the data is not in the active write log, check the metadata to see whether the data is in the active write log of remote nodes.

3. Check the L1 memory cache.

4. Check the L2 read cache of the local node (for hybrid).

   It is interesting to note that each node keeps an index cache not only for its own cache but also the full cache of all nodes. This enhances the performance in doing lookups for data blocks across the whole cluster.

5. If all of these searches cause a miss and still the data is not found, the last resort is the capacity tier. The data is then put in the L1 memory cache and the L2 read cache (in case of hybrid).

6. After that, the data is decompressed and sent to the VM.

Information about the data blocks, such as whether the data block is compressed, is found in the metadata, that is, the distributed objects. Also, because the identification of the data is done based on fingerprints, the fingerprints are kept in the SSD cache and memory cache. If a data block is already in the cache and another data block is read and found to have the same fingerprint, it is not moved into the cache because it already exists.

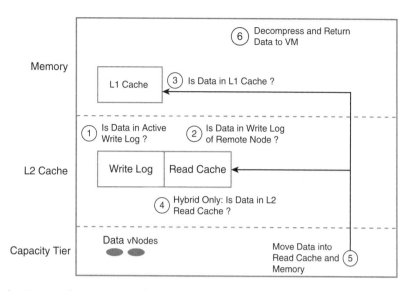

Figure 9-17 *Read Operation*

Advanced Data Services

HX supports inline deduplication and compression, native snapshots and clones, native replication for backup and disaster recovery (DR), as well as integration with third-party software backup vendors.

Deduplication and Compression

Previous sections that discussed the read and write operation inside the HX system examined how deduplication and compression are applied. It is worth noting here that inline deduplication and compression inside HX are always on and are part of the architecture. The advantage of HX compared to other vendors is that this functionality is done without any performance hits to the system. The fact that this functionality is inline ensures that storage efficiencies occur from the start and before the data goes into the capacity tier. Placing data into the capacity tier without deduplication and then doing this function offline increases storage need by two to three times depending on the replication factor. Even if the data is deduplicated later at rest, the storage requirement has already been increased.

Cisco did not implement erasure coding (EC) in the early HX releases because the embedded inline deduplication and compression minimize the need for such functionality. Bear in mind that the benefits of EC could be outweighed by the performance hit to the system in reconstructing the data using parity information. However, EC is on the HX roadmap.

Snapshots

As discussed previously in this book, snapshots are a way to take a point-in-time snapshot of a VM and its data. The snapshots are used for restoring the state of a VM at a particular point in time in case of a problem and are used to enhance backup and disaster recovery mechanisms. HX has multiple types of snapshots for different use cases:

- **Native Snapshots:** These snapshots capture the *states* of working VMs. In case of problems, the VMs can be reverted back to a known state.

- **Replication Snapshots:** These snapshots are used for data protection. At a scheduled point in time, a snapshot is taken from a running VM. The snapshot is then copied to a remote cluster that is used for disaster recovery. These types of snapshots are internal to the system and are not seen by the user; therefore, they cannot be used to recover the state of a VM in the local cluster.

- **Recovery Test Snapshots:** These temporary snapshots are used to verify that the recovery system is working.

- **Recovery VMs:** These restored VMs are created by restoring the most recent replication snapshot from the recovery cluster.

- **ReadyClones:** These are copies of existing VMs that created a separate guest VM.

In hyperconverged environments, creating snapshots and clones is a straightforward task, depending on the flexibility of the architecture. For VM recovery in the local cluster, HX uses native snapshots that are taken via the HX data distributed system rather than the VMware redo-log snapshots. If ESXi is used as a hypervisor, the first snapshot taken should be a "native" snapshot. This is done through the Cisco HX Data Platform menu inside the vSphere web client and *not* via the vSphere client snapshot menu. This first native snapshot is called Sentinel. It makes sure that the first snapshot is a native snapshot and not done via VMware redo-log. From then on, any further snapshots can be taken from any snapshot menu and are also native snapshots, which dramatically improves the performance of the snapshot process.

HX uses the Redirect on Write method of doing snapshots; this method was described in Chapter 2, "Storage Networks: Existing Designs," where its advantages were compared to traditional Copy on Write methods. HX uses a metadata approach to snapshots, by doing zero copying of the actual data. This approach facilitates backup operations and remote replication, which are crucial for enterprises that require always-on data availability. A snapshot is done by keeping pointers to the data. For fast snapshot updates, when modified data is contained in a snapshot, it is written to a new location, and the metadata is updated without the need for read-modify-write operations.

All of the information about pointers and locations of the snapshot is kept via metadata in the cache until the data is destaged. After that, simple metadata is kept in the capacity drive to reference changes in data. The snapshots can be done at the VM level or at the VMware folder level (VMware folders allow a task—restart, for example—to be done on a group of VMs) or for a group of VMs and are easy to add or delete. Deleting a snapshot only requires deleting the metadata in cache without having to do any disk consolidation because the data itself is not copied to start with. This eliminates the need for a long consolidation process as needed by solutions that use delta-disk techniques such as VMware vSAN, which is covered in Chapter 12, "VMware vSAN."

HX supports snapshot in the ESXi/VAAI environment as well as Hyper-V.

As new software and hardware storage products are introduced into the data center, it is crucial that these products integrate with existing management offerings so that they do not become yet another silo. The HX Data Platform took that aspect into consideration to offer management integration with existing tools such as vSphere vCenter Snapshot Manager. This allows support of a snapshot management functionality such as scheduling the frequency or number of snapshots and retention. This is a value-add for VMware customers who are already familiar with the platform. Any newer functionality such as performance metrics or cluster status is added via plug-ins to the vSphere web client.

Cloning

The HX clones are writeable snapshots. This means that if clones are specified to be created, the snapshot taken at that time is written into the capacity tier at the same time the data writes are taking place. HX uses metadata to create many clones at very high speeds without a CPU hit compared to methods that do full copies. As clones are being created, data is also deduplicated and compressed similar to any write to disk. Space savings are achieved only by keeping track of any changed data while all other data is handled via pointers and metadata to keep track of the pointers. Similar to snapshots, clones integrate with ESXi/VAAI and Hyper-V/ODX. Clones are done at the granularity of a VM, folder level, or a group of VMs. HX offers a tool called ReadyClones that allows fast clone provisioning with a wizard. Hundreds of clones are created by simply using a prefix name, a description of the clones, and the number of clones. The wizard automatically creates the clones starting with the prefix and appending a number that is incremented. Ready clones also provide customization via scripting to allow each clone to obtain its own IP address or other parameters on startup.

Asynchronous Native Replication for DR with Remote Clusters

The HX Data Platform data protection allows for the asynchronous native replication for DR (NRDR) for replicating and protecting VMs between remote clusters. Asynchronous replication can be done at scheduled times and can tolerate some latency on the WAN links because it is not done in real time and does not affect the input/output processing on a running application. To perform data protection, two clusters have to be paired with each other. After that, replication networking is set up by having HX Connect provide IP addresses to be used by the local cluster nodes to replicate to the remote nodes. HX Connect also creates VLANs through UCSM for dedicated replication network use.

After you set up the pairing and network connectivity that is specific for replication, VMs can be replicated at specific intervals that range from 5 minutes to 24 hours to match the selected recovery point objective (RPO). VMs are replicated to the remote cluster by making a copy of the replication snapshot to the remote cluster. In the event of a disaster at the local cluster, the most recent copy of the VM in the remote cluster can be used to recover the VM. VMs are optionally grouped inside protection groups, which assign similar attributes to the protected VMs. Configuration of the time intervals for scheduled replication and monitoring of the replication process in and out of a cluster are done via HX Connect.

Synchronous Native Replication for DR with Stretched Clusters

HX uses synchronous native replication for disaster recovery (NRDR) with stretched clusters. This is normally used for a tier-1 application that cannot afford any data loss and requires a zero recovery point objective. Stretched clusters allow the data center to be stretched between two data centers over a campus or metropolitan area network or WAN for active-active redundancy. Nodes replicate their data in the local and remote data centers. Unlike asynchronous replication, where replication can happen at scheduled times, with synchronous replication, when a write is done local and remote, it must be acknowledged for the I/O operation to be committed. This, of course, adds extra latency to the write operations. Cisco recommends the use of 10 GE links between the sites and that round-trip time (RTT) for a packet not exceed 5 milliseconds. For read operations, the reads are done from the local data center where the application exists and there is no performance impact. Stretched clusters result in zero recovery point objective because the data is always consistent between the two sites. Recovery time objectives (RTOs) could also get near zero with VM HA mechanisms where a VM is copied and synchronized to the second site but remains inactive until the primary VM fails. Figure 9-18 shows an example of a stretched cluster.

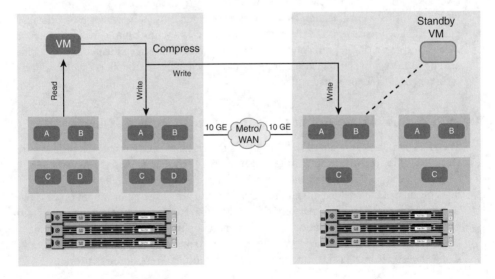

Figure 9-18 *Stretched Cluster*

In Figure 9-18, note that the reads are done locally while writes are local and remote. As data is sent over the WAN, it is compressed to efficiently use the WAN bandwidth.

Integration with Third-Party Backup Tools

In addition to synchronous and asynchronous native replication for disaster recovery, HX integrates with third-party backup and recovery tools. HX integrates with enterprise backup software vendors such as VMware, Veeam, Commvault, and Zerto. HX offers APIs to allow third-party vendors to offer their data protection solution through the HX Data Platform. With VMware, for example, HX is managed by vCenter and uses VMware's data protection and vSphere's replication with vCenter Site Recovery Manager.

Integrating with third-party vendors through APIs allows for better backup functionality while enhancing performance by utilizing the system's native replication capabilities. Keep in mind that many HCI vendors also compete in the backup space and secondary storage by enhancing the functionality of their own backup software in support of secondary storage.

Figure 9-19 shows a sample integration between HX and Veeam.

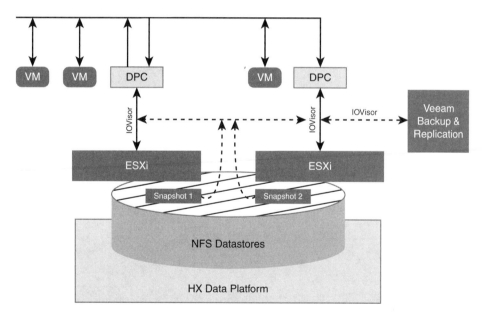

Figure 9-19   *HyperFlex Integration with Veeam*

A close integration with Veeam allows for better backup functionality and better performance by having Veeam rely on HX 's capabilities in creating and deleting snapshots. Without the integration, Veeam must rely on native VMware's snapshots. As writes are done, VMware redirects the writes to the Redo-Log snapshot, Veeam reads the data from the Redo-Log, and then snapshots are deleted. This extra layering is inefficient because deleting the snapshot takes a long time. By integrating with HX, Veeam relies on HX to create and delete the native snapshots for more efficiency. As seen in Figure 9-19, Veeam integrates with HX through the IOVisor. Because the IOVisor redirects all I/O from the VMs and does load distribution between all nodes, Veeam reads the native snapshot data from the IOVisor.

In the case of ESXi, the IOVisor presents the storage network to ESXi as NFS datastores. Veeam uses the IOVisor to read the data directly from the HX snapshot, using the NFS HX data network. In addition, Veeam uses the capabilities of VMware's Changed Block Tracking (CBT) to receive the delta difference between snapshots, so future backups on updated snapshots are done only on the changed data. This improves backup efficiency over WAN links by reducing the amount of data that must be exchanged during the backup.

It is worth noting that many advancements are taking place in backup and restoration for secondary storage. Secondary storage is longer-term storage that is not actively used by the applications. Also, with secondary storage nonzero RPOs and lower service-level agreements (SLAs) can be tolerated. Other than working with established software backup vendors, Cisco has done joint solutions with secondary storage startups, such as running Cohesity hyperconverged secondary storage software on Cisco UCS servers. This gives HX deployments added capabilities in historical tracking of the data, archiving, file versioning, file indexing, advanced file search engines, data analytics on backed-up data, and so on.

HyperFlex Security

HX adopts multiple security mechanisms for securing the data as well as securing access to the platform. These security mechanisms are grouped under the following categories:

- Securing data-at-rest
- Operational security
- Complying with security regulations and certifications
- Management security

Securing Data-at-Rest

HX uses self-encrypting drives (SEDs) to encrypt the data-at-rest inside the physical HDDs or SSDs. This ensures that if drives are taken from the system, data is protected. Because the encryption and decryption are done via the disk hardware itself, no additional load is added to the CPU. Only the key management is done via software. To use data-at-rest security, all disks in all nodes on the cluster must be SEDs.

Each drive comes with a factory-generated *data encryption key* (DEK). The internal disk circuitry uses this key to encrypt or decrypt the data. However, when the drives are initially installed, they are in an unlocked mode by default, so data can be read. To secure the data, the system must lock the SED and put it in an auto-lock mode. This is done via software, using another key called the *key encryption key* (KEK). The KEK is externally generated and is passed to the disk via the disk controller. The KEK is used to encrypt or decrypt the DEK (not the data). When the DEK is encrypted, the data cannot be accessed, and when the DEK is decrypted, the data can be accessed. As long as the disk is powered on, the KEK can be sent by the system to the controller to unlock the DEK. However, if the disk is removed from the system and loses power, the disk goes into automatic lock. Without the KEK, the DEK cannot be decrypted, and the data is secure.

The KEK in HX can be generated through three methods: locally generated, remotely generated using a trusted certificate authority, or remotely generated using self-signed certificates.

Locally generated KEK is the simplest method but the least secure. HX uses the Cisco UCSM to generate the KEK from an encryption passphrase. This creates a single KEK that is used by all disks on all nodes of the cluster. This type of key generation can be used in test or proof-of-concept setups but is not secure enough for production environments.

For remote key generation, HX complies with the Key Management Interoperability Protocol (KMIP) 1.1 and works with leading key management solutions such as Gemalto SafeNetKeySecure and Thales Vormetric Data Security Manager. Such products are offered via physical appliance or virtual appliances and offer, among other functionality, centralizing the administration of the encryption policies and keys. Such solutions also provide reporting, auditing, and compliance tracking.

When getting a key remotely, the UCSM uses KMIP to retrieve the key from a Key Management Server (KMS). The client/server communication between the UCSM and the KMS is secured using trusted certificate authority (CA) signed keys created from certificate signing requests (CSR). The second method is for client/server communication between the UCSM and KMS to be done via self-signed certificates. In both cases, remote key configurations create a separate KEK for each node and can be used for all disks in that node.

In support of key management, HX is managed by an HTML5 Cisco Connect interface that facilitates the configuration, enabling rekeying and erasing data on the SEDs inside the HX cluster. Cisco Connect controls the workflow and offers a certificate-based chain of trust between the HX Data Platform and the KMS.

Operational Security

Having a consistent operational model in delivering security is important. When dealing with policies and key management among hundreds of nodes and servers, it is crucial that a systematic and consistent approach be adopted that requires a level of automation across all nodes. The UCSM, which runs inside the fabric interconnect, adopts a set of service profiles and templates that define all the characteristics of the HX nodes in software. These profiles define all server characteristics such as network interface cards, adapters, and firmware; they allow a uniform configuration across the HX cluster. The Cisco UCSM specifies the HX Data Platform security policies and the key management software. By defining such interaction within service profiles, the operator is assured of consistent security behavior across the whole data center.

Complying with Security Regulations and Certifications

Cisco HX with the use of SEDs complies with a number of security regulations, such as the Health Insurance Portability and Accountability Act (HIPAA), Payment Card Industry Data Security Standard (PCI-DSS), Federal Information Security Management Act (FISMA), General Data Protection Regulation (GDPR), and Sarbanes-Oxley Act.

The key management solutions that HX works with are validated for Federal Information Processing Standard (FIPS) 140-2, which is a government publication by the National Institute of Standards and Technology (NIST) for "approving cryptographic modules" for transferring sensitive information.

Cisco HX has completed Common Criteria certification for Evaluation Assurance Level (EAL) 2 for Information Technology Security Evaluation Criteria (ITSEC). HX certification activities are ongoing for future releases. The ITSEC is an international standard certification that ensures that the security features of a product are properly implemented. EAL numbering is between 1 and 7. A product with higher-level EAL does not mean that the product is more secure than others; it just indicates the level of documentation and testing to certify the security functions.

Cisco HX also implements the Secure Technical Implementation Guide (STIG) for hardening the product against security attacks using best practices. An example is an implementation of the ESXi Server security recommendations, which is done via automation scripts for setting STIG parameters.

Management Security

HX uses many management tools to ensure the security of the product. The Cisco HX Connect HTML5 interface manages the whole cluster operation and the lifecycle of the data-at-rest encryption. The UCSM and the service profiles ensure consistent security policies across all nodes. In addition, Cisco HX uses authentication and authorization mechanisms integrated with vSphere single sign-on (SSO), Microsoft Active Directory, and Lightweight Directory Access Protocol (LDAP). The SSO, for example, deals with the identity management of the users and applications that interact with the vSphere platform. SSO is an authentication service in which clients send authentication messages to a Security Token Service (STS), which checks the user credentials and, if validated, generates a token. The user or application uses that token to access resources. vCenter uses the token to perform vSphere operations on behalf of the client. SSO is not a replacement for Active Directory or LDAP but rather complements them by doing single token authentication on the identity.

HyperFlex also uses role-based access control (RBAC) to specify the role of a user or administrator and their access privileges for doing configuration or for monitoring the system. All transactions to the system through the command-line interface (CLI), APIs, or Connect UI are monitored and tracked to identify the source of any operation.

Looking Ahead

This chapter covered the details of the HX HCI implementation. The integration of HX with UCS is a major differentiator between Cisco and other vendors. The adoption of the widely adopted UCS service profiles turns the whole compute system into reusable software modules. The integration with legacy SANs and converged systems via fibre channel and iSCSI will facilitate the migration of data from older systems to the new hyperconverged environment.

Also, the way Cisco differentiates from other vendors is a suite of tools and software products to allow better management, provisioning, monitoring, and automation for HCI deployments.

Chapter 10, "Deploying, Provisioning, and Managing HyperFlex," covers the deployment provisioning and management of the HX platform. This includes references to tools to help with sizing the platform depending on the workload. The tools also help in managing all aspects of deploying and monitoring the data services from inside the private data center. Other products such as Cisco Intersight help in the provisioning and management of the platform from the public cloud.

Chapter 11, "HyperFlex Workload Optimization and Efficiency," discusses methods for workload optimization via the Cisco Workload Optimization Manager and Cisco Tetration for traffic visibility at the flow level. Also, with the introduction of Cisco AppDynamics, Cisco delivers advanced workload optimization and troubleshooting by tracking the performance of each application, analyzing the root cause of any performance issues, and tracking the business impacts on end users.

References

[1] https://www.cisco.com/c/en/us/products/hyperconverged-infrastructure/
    hyperflex-hx-series/index.html

[2] https://www.cisco.com/c/en/us/products/servers-unified-computing/
    ucs-6300-series-fabric-interconnects/index.html

[3] https://www.cisco.com/c/en/us/products/servers-unified-computing/
    ucs-c-series-rack-servers/index.html

[4] https://www.cisco.com/c/en/us/products/interfaces-modules/
    unified-computing-system-adapters/index.html

[5] https://www.cisco.com/c/en/us/products/servers-unified-computing/
    ucs-b-series-blade-servers/index.html

[6] http://www.esg-global.com/cisco-hyperflex

[7] https://www.cisco.com/c/en/us/td/docs/unified_computing/ucs/
    UCS_CVDs/HX171_VSI_ESXi6U2.html

[8] https://hyperflexsizer.cloudapps.cisco.com

Deploying, Provisioning, and Managing HyperFlex

This chapter covers the following key topics:

- **Installation Phase:** Explains the different steps in the HyperFlex installer process.

- **HyperFlex Workload Profiler:** Covers the workload profiler to extract storage and user stats.

- **HyperFlex Sizer:** Describes some of the tools used for planning and sizing a HyperFlex cluster to provision resources accordingly.

- **Management, Provisioning, and Monitoring:** Describes the different management products for managing, provisioning, and monitoring the HyperFlex cluster and nodes, including Cisco HyperFlex Connect HTML5 GUI, VMware vSphere plug-in, and Cisco Intersight Cloud management platform.

The Cisco HyperFlex Data Platform (HXDP) has simple management interfaces that allow easy provisioning, deployment, and monitoring of the HyperFlex (HX) cluster [1], [2]. Let's start with an overview of the installation of the system and then move into the management, provisioning, and monitoring.

Installation Phase

The following gives you a simplified rundown of the steps needed to get up and running. This is by no means an installation guide, and you are better off looking at the latest releases of Cisco documents, such as the installation guide for the Cisco HXDP Installation Guide [3]. This is just to give you a high-level view of the process.

1. The first step, of course, is the actual physical installation and cabling of the system when you connect the servers to the fabric interconnects (FIs).

2. Unless you are a new user with the appropriate software stack on your hardware, the initial step is to upgrade to the appropriate firmware on the FIs. This includes the UCS Manager (UCSM) firmware and firmware on your HX nodes if they are being reused.

3. A direct connection to the FI allows you to access the setup mode. From there, you enter your admin password, IP address for the FI, IP address for the cluster, default gateway, domain name system (DNS), and other initial configuration parameters. A connection to the second FI allows you to add the FI to the same cluster.

4. In a new HX installation, your nodes have the hypervisor already installed from the factory. If you have wiped your nodes or need to reuse them for some reason, you can download the Cisco version of your specific hypervisor and install it on each node before proceeding. Only do this if necessary and if you have nodes that have HX product IDs (PIDS) from the factory.

That basically concludes the hardware setup. The next step is to run the HXDP installer [3]. Before you run the installer, download and complete the HX Preinstallation Checklist [3]. This is a document that helps you gather and record all of the appropriate information for a successful installation. It is a critical step in a successful build.

The installer installs and configures the HX cluster. It also adds a plug-in to vCenter for ESXi-based installs. The installer runs on any ESXi host that can access the cluster network, including VMware Workstation or Fusion. Once the HXDP Open Virtual Appliance (OVA) runs, and credentials are entered, the installer walks you through the configuration process. Enter all the values you collected in the preinstallation checklist. This includes virtual local area network (VLAN) names and IDs, IPs, passwords, and services (DNS, Network Time Protocol [NTP], and so on). The process normally takes about half an hour.

The process goes through different stages, from UCSM validation to USCM configuration, hypervisor configuration, deployment validation, deployment, creation validation, and cluster creation.

The validations phase ensures that your firmware is correct and that you have compatible hardware. The UCSM configuration builds an inventory of the available connected HX servers. The installer starts configuring the FI and builds an HX service profile for the nodes. This includes configuring the following:

■ Quality of service (QoS) policies

■ MAC address pools and VLANs

■ Boot policy

■ BIOS policy

The hypervisor configuration phase installs an appropriate plug-in for ESXi—set static IP addresses—and builds the required vSwitches. These settings are checked for availability in the deployment validation phase before proceeding. The deployment phase then installs the HX Control VMs on each node. Once this is complete, the configuration is checked again to make sure all IPs are available and responding and that name resolution is working.

Once the deployment phase is complete, a final check is conducted. If everything passes, the cluster is created, the storage pool built, and the distributed cluster services activated. You are presented with a cluster summary screen when all this is done. From here, launch directly into HX Connect and begin provisioning storage for your VMs from the HXDP storage pool.

HyperFlex Workload Profiler

The HX workload profiler extracts storage usage and performance statistics from an existing running cluster. The data collected from the workload profiler is used to size the needs of the cluster. The profiler is installed as an OVA on an ESXi host and connects to vCenter. A collection period, such as 30 days, can be set to obtain a good view of the stats. It shows what the output of the profiler looks like with detailed information about read and write percentages, throughput, input/output operations per second (IOPS), and latency that is collected for a period of time.

HyperFlex Sizer

The HX sizer helps the administrator properly size the compute and storage resources of a cluster according to the workload. The input data of the sizer is taken from user input about the needs of the workloads or taken from the workload profiler. Performance data is imported from the HX workload profiler using a comma-separated file. Depending on the workload, the sizer determines the number and the type of nodes needed in the cluster and the compute and storage needs per node. The sizer accommodates for replication inside the cluster (called the replication factor; it is used for data protection) and the availability of self-encrypting drives (SEDs) or Non-Volatile Memory Express (NVMe) storage. The sizer displays the different workloads running on the cluster and the estimates for what is needed as far as CPU, memory, storage, and IOPS. The sizer tool provides the user with guidelines, but the user is to apply best judgment when configuring the nodes on the cluster.

Management Provisioning and Monitoring

Cisco offers multiple platforms in support of the management, provisioning, and monitoring of the HXDP. This allows HX to be managed on-premise or from the cloud using software as a service (SaaS). The different platforms are as follows:

- Cisco HyperFlex Connect HTML5 Management
- VMware vSphere management plug-in
- Cisco Intersight

Cisco HyperFlex Connect HTML5 Management

Cisco developed an HTML5 Management web interface to manage, provision, and monitor all aspects of the HX cluster. The user can monitor the health of the cluster, manage resources, create datastores, and manage the scalability aspects of the cluster. HyperFlex Connect is accessible via the cluster IP address. Accessing the interface is done via a local username/password or preferably via the vCenter single sign-on (SSO) for enhanced security. The role-based access control (RBAC) aspect of HyperFlex Connect allows for administrative roles for full read and modify of the configuration or read-only roles for the purpose of monitoring.

Let's examine the main components of the interface.

Dashboard

The dashboard displays different information, such as the following:

- Operational status of the cluster

- Resiliency health in terms of failure tolerance

- Storage capacity

- Storage usage and free space

- Storage optimization stats

- Number of nodes and individual node health

- Cluster IOPS

- Throughput and latency

Figure 10-1 shows the Dashboard view of HyperFlex Connect.

Monitor

The Monitor view of Cisco HyperFlex Connect offers information about alarms, events, and activity logs. Cluster alarms are viewed, acknowledged, and reset. Event logs are viewed, filtered, and exported. Activity logs such as for ReadyClones are viewed and monitored.

Analyze

The Analyze view displays the cluster performance charts over a period of one hour or can be customized for different intervals. Information about IOPS, throughput, and latency is displayed per node or per datastore depending on the selected view. This is shown in Figure 10-2.

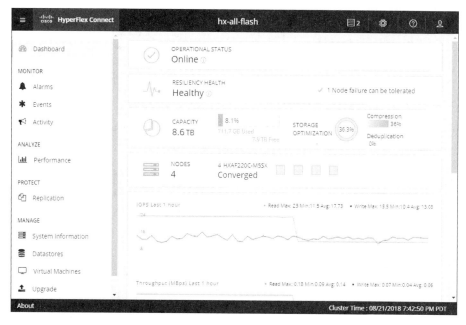

Figure 10-1   *Cisco HyperFlex Connect*

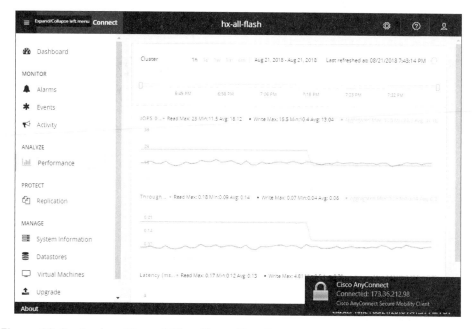

Figure 10-2   *Analyze View of Cisco HyperFlex Connect*

Protect

The Protect view is used to manage the data protection features such as VM replication and data-at-rest encryption. These functions were described in Chapter 9, "Cisco HyperFlex."

Manage

The Manage view contains multiple elements for managing the cluster, including these:

- **System Information:** This presents a view of the cluster configuration, including views of the individual nodes and disks. The view shows software revisions, hosts, uptime, and more. The nodes are placed in maintenance mode, and support bundles are created and shared with the Cisco Technical Assistance Center (TAC) for support.

  Placing an HX node into maintenance mode through the system information individual node view, or through the HX maintenance mode of the vSphere web client, allows a node's controller a graceful shutdown. During this process, any primary copies on the node in maintenance mode are assumed by promoted secondary copies on the other nodes.

- **Datastores:** Allows the management of datastores, including creating, resizing, mounting, unmounting, and deleting.

- **Virtual Machines:** This view shows the VMs that are present in the cluster and allows for cloning, snapshots, and VM protection via replication.

- **Upgrade:** Allows the upgrade of the HXDP software and Cisco Unified Computing System (UCS) firmware.

- **Web CLI:** A web-based interface that allows system configuration via the use of command-line interface (CLI) commands.

The Manage view is seen in Figure 10-3.

Figure 10-3 *Manage View of Cisco HyperFlex Connect*

VMware vSphere Management Plug-In

Administration of HX daily operation in a VMware environment is done via vCenter. This allows you to provision and monitor virtual machines and storage. The storage provisioning of the HX datastore is done via a vSphere management plug-in. The portal shows simple views to manage the HX storage, such as the Summary, Monitor, and Management tabs.

Summary Tab

This tab shows summary information of the system, including capacity, status, and performance. The Capacity view shows usable capacity, used capacity, and free capacity. It also shows provisioned and overprovisioned capacity along with storage optimization gains through always-on deduplication and compression. The Status view shows system health information such as online or offline cluster status, number of hosts and controllers and their status, the replication factor used for data protection, and so on. The Performance view gives information about IOPS, throughput, and latency.

The Summary tab is seen in Figure 10-4.

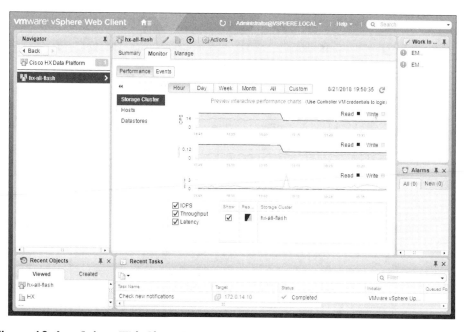

Figure 10-4 *vSphere Web Client Summary Tab*

Monitor Tab

The Monitor tab drills down into the details of every component. It shows information at the cluster level, host level, and datastore level. The Cluster Performance view, as an example, shows aggregate cluster IOPS, throughput, and latency numbers displayed side by side. The user can customize the intervals that give the history of these parameters over a certain time period, such as hour, day, week, or month. These parameters also show at the granularity of a host or a data store. The Events view in the Monitor tab displays the different cluster events and alerts and correlates with vCenter. Examples of such events are cluster health status and policy compliance status. vCenter notifies a user that a critical event or alarm occurred. The alerts are also seen from the Alerts view of vCenter.

Manage Tab

The Cluster view in the Manage tab displays system hardware at the individual node level and shows the individual hardware system components, including the physical disks. The Datastore view in the Manage tab allows the management of the individual datastores, such as creating, mounting, unmounting, and editing the datastore. Editing a datastore is as simple as clicking on the datastore and changing the name or the capacity of the datastore. Thin provisioning is built into the system, giving the ability to overprovision a datastore. For example, you may have only 10 TB available, but you can create a datastore that is 100 TB in size. Make sure you don't overprovision and then run out of usable capacity.

Cisco Intersight

Cisco Intersight [4] (originally called Starship) complements the existing Cisco management platforms such as UCSM and Cisco HyperFlex Connect by providing a cloud-based management platform with embedded analytics for UCS and HX. In other words, Cisco Intersight is a SaaS offering that runs in the cloud and is capable of overseeing the management, configuration, provisioning, inventory, and status of the whole network of UCS-based blade and rack servers, HX nodes, and HX Edge nodes. It gives a single pane of glass that administrators use to enforce a uniform set of policies and automation across the whole UCS and HX network.

Figure 10-5 shows the conceptual view of Cisco Intersight.

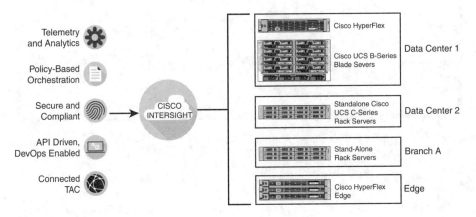

Figure 10-5 *Cisco Intersight*

As noted, Cisco Intersight puts under the same umbrella the management and analytics of a whole suite of platforms, including these:

- HX platforms in data centers

- HX Edge in remote offices

- Cisco UCS C-series rack servers

- Cisco UCS B-series blade servers

- Cisco UCS S-series server

The advantages of Cisco Intersight follow:

- **Unified management:** Cisco Intersight allows administrators to manage all of their UCS and HX platforms from the cloud and without the need to have direct local access into these systems. This is a major advantage for large enterprises with national and international data centers as well as many widespread small offices.

- **Unified policies:** One of the main advantages of UCS manager is the ability to create service templates and profiles to be applied to a multitude of servers in a cluster. Now the same concept can be extended beyond a single data center and be adopted enterprise wide. Because Cisco Intersight has visibility into the whole network, applying the same policies via the templates and profiles is done uniformly network wide.

- **Inventory information and status:** The status and health of every node is seen and collected network wide. The user can collect inventory about the servers, firmware revisions, FIs, and more. The user can employ a search engine to find any node based on node names or tags. All events and alarms are seen from a single location.

- **Telemetry and analytics:** Cisco Intersight collects telemetry data from the UCS and HX nodes. Examples of such data are node serial numbers, software versions, firmware, IP addresses, and other valuable data. This data is collected and fed to the Intersight recommendation engine, which identifies and notifies the user of any potential issues that might exist in the user information.

- **Integration with TAC:** As the telemetry information is collected, it can be fed directly to Cisco TAC, which quickly reacts to the data without much user intervention. Rather than the TAC asking the user to debug, collect, and send information, all of the information is already gathered and ready to be processed.

Claiming the Nodes

Cisco has the Intersight cloud portal deployed on www.intersight.com. Customers with a valid login can use the portal and start managing their HX and UCS nodes depending on the Intersight service they have.

To have a node managed under Cisco Intersight, you must claim it. This is done via device connectors, which are software modules that are embedded into the management controllers of the devices. For Intersight to claim a node, it needs the node's device ID and claim code. You can only obtain such information by accessing the actual device with administrator access. There are two steps in getting the device ID and claim code:

1. For the node to reach the Intersight portal, it needs IP connectivity. This is established by setting up default gateways on the node or optional https proxy server information, such as IP address and port.

2. From the Cisco HX Connect UI, the administrator accesses the cloud management menu, which provides the connection menu to Intersight. Upon connecting to the Intersight portal, and if the connection status is "claimed," the device displays its claim code.

Once the information is entered in the Intersight portal, the device is claimed and comes under the Intersight umbrella, where it is managed. Figure 10-6 shows a device connector, where a device was claimed and is showing its device ID.

Figure 10-6   *View of Device Connector from Cisco HyperFlex Connect*

Figure 10-7 shows the Cisco Intersight high-level view, with information about all devices that are claimed.

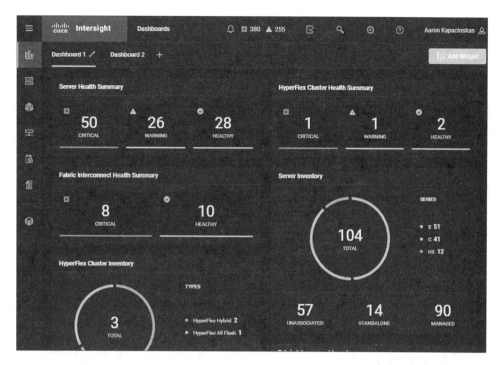

Figure 10-7 *Cisco Intersight Portal View*

The top-left menu allows drill-down access to the following:

- **Dashboard menu (displayed in the figure):** Notice information such as server health, HX cluster health, FI health and inventory, information about HX cluster storage, and so on.

- **Server menu:** Shows details of UCS-managed B and C series servers attached to FIs or standalone. The user can search for servers and see details such as server health, configuration, and tags. The user also can launch Cisco UCSM.

- **HyperFlex cluster menu:** Shows detailed information on all HX clusters, including cluster name, software revision, hypervisor revision, storage capacity, storage utilization, storage optimization, number of nodes, and so on. By accessing individual clusters, other management tools can be cross-launched. For example, Cisco HX Connect can be launched for a cluster, and it would show the same menus as if the administrator is running Cisco HX Connect locally on the cluster.

- **Fabric Interconnect menu:** Shows information about all FIs, including UCSMs that are running, IP address, FI model, expansion modules, ports used, ports available, firmware versions, and more.

- **Service profile:** This is similar to the UCSM profile, which allows the user to define the configuration of an HX cluster, define new profiles, or take the profiles of existing clusters and "clone" them to produce a copy of profiles. Those copies can then be modified to accommodate the required configuration of the new HX cluster setup. Hundreds of clones can be created, for example, to duplicate a profile for remote offices that have similar configurations. Figure 10-8 shows a service profile cluster configuration menu for HX.

Figure 10-8 *Intersight Service Profile for HX*

Different parameters can be configured, which include the following:

- Security
- DNS
- NTP and time zone
- vCenter
- Storage configuration
- Auto support
- IP and hostname
- Network configuration
- HX storage network

Each of the configurations is attached to a specific policy, so you can modify it easily. If, for example, you need to change the VLAN in the network configuration, detach the relative cluster-network-policy, change the VLAN information, and create a new policy with the new VLAN. Like UCSM, the profile and templates can be created offline even if the node is not available. Later, you can assign these templates to an active node.

- **Policy menu:** The policy menu allows Intersight to configure system policies.

- **Device menu:** This shows a consolidated view of all devices with connection status, device ID, type, IP, and the ability to add, delete, or launch specific devices. The Intersight portal allows the user to go to any device and launch UCSM, which allows the exact UCS capabilities that the administrator would have accessing UCSM locally. The administrator can access service templates and profiles and perform any other UCSM capability.

The top-right part of the Dashboard allows access to alarms, the search engine, settings, the user account, the Help menu, and more.

- **Alarms menu:** The Alarms menu shows a consolidated view of all alarms from UCS servers, standalone servers, HX clusters, and FIs.

- **Search engine:** Allows the search for any UCS or HX component by name or ID. It is a global index search across all menus. You can, for example, search for any alarm that a device generates.

- **Settings menu:** Manages users' access and permissions, information about performed actions, historical changes made to the system, active sessions, and view status.

- **Help menu:** Provides walkthrough assistance for any of the functionality in Intersight. It also allows the user to submit feedback that goes back to the development team.

- **User menu:** Shows specific details about the user account, such Cisco ID and Cisco Intersight account ID. It allows customization of theme colors, language settings, and other things. It also allows the user to log in and out of Intersight.

Looking Ahead

This chapter covered the tools and software products HX uses to easily install and manage the platform. Being able to configure and roll out applications in about 30 minutes is a big shift from the traditional SAN model, where similar tasks took weeks. The ability to perform configuration from the cloud via Cisco Intersight gives HX a clear advantage in creating uniform configuration, management, and monitoring for wide-scale deployments.

Chapter 11, "HyperFlex Workload Optimization and Efficiency," covers additional products that complement the HX platform in workload optimization. Software products include Cisco Tetration for traffic workflow visibility, Cisco Workload Optimization

Manager (CWOM) for optimizing the resources inside the cluster, and Cisco AppDynamics for monitoring application performance to meet business metrics and finding root cause analysis of performance issues down to the code level.

References

[1] https://www.cisco.com/c/en/us/td/docs/unified_computing/ucs/UCS_CVDs/hyperflex_25_vsi.html

[2] https://www.cisco.com/c/en/us/products/hyperconverged-infrastructure/hyperflex-management.html

[3] https://www.cisco.com/c/en/us/support/hyperconverged-systems/hyperflex-hx-data-platform-software/products-installation-guides-list.html

[4] https://www.cisco.com/c/en/us/products/collateral/servers-unified-computing/intersight/datasheet-c78-739433.html

HyperFlex Workload Optimization and Efficiency

This chapter covers the following key topics:

■ **Enterprise Workload Issues:** Describes the workload issues that enterprises face, including reactive mode to growth, lack of visibility into their applications, overprovisioning, and cloud creep.

■ **HyperFlex with Cisco Tetration:** Describes better visibility into the traffic flows and the service chain between the applications.

■ **Cisco Workload Optimizer:** Covers the automation software product that monitors the performance consumption of applications and matches the resources with the needs of the application.

■ **Cisco AppDynamics:** An application and business monitoring platform that allows enterprises to monitor their business applications and transactions and make sure they are delivering the best performance. The product gives root cause analysis of performance issues at the code level.

HyperFlex is surrounded by a suite of software products to optimize the workload and enhance application performance and efficiency in the data center while minimizing the cost of operation. In an environment where workloads are growing at almost 30% per year, the human factor in information technology (IT) organizations cannot keep up. Also, IT budgets are falling short in keeping up with the infrastructure growth. The combination of growing workloads and lower budgets is a recipe for disaster.

Enterprise Workload Issues

Enterprises are challenged today by rolling out applications as fast as possible to grow their business and capture new customers. With this comes the challenge of managing the rollout and provisioning cycles, using private or public clouds, and monitoring the application performance for customer satisfaction. The main issues facing enterprises in efficiently growing workloads follow:

- **IT reactive mode to growth:** As data center applications grow, the nature of any business requires fast turnaround time in deploying applications to meet revenue goals. IT administrators are in a reactive mode trying to fix a moving vehicle. More applications mean more resources. Add standalone servers or blades, purchase more hypervisor licenses, initiate more virtual machines or containers, and include more central processing units (CPUs), memory, storage, and network.

- **Overprovision everything:** As IT administrators launch their applications, they operate under the "just in case" model and overprovision everything. An application that needs 1 vCPU, 2 GB of RAM, and 500 GB of storage gets 2 vCPUs, 4 GB of RAM, and 1 TB of storage "just in case" the application needs more resources next year. The result is an imbalance between idle resources committed to lightweight applications while heavyweight applications are starved for resources.

- **Cloud creep:** As chief information officers are pressured to reduce budgets, their first safe haven is the cloud. Enterprises spending too much money running and growing their data centers want to offload the workload and the work to the cloud. IT administrators just take their applications and dump them on Amazon Web Services (AWS), Azure, or Google cloud "as is." This means that any inefficiencies they had in their data centers translate into a lot of resources and money spent in the cloud. And now instead of just having an inefficient data center model, the enterprise topped it with an inefficient cloud model.

- **Lack of visibility:** One of the main issues leading to workload inefficiencies and hence higher capital expenditures (CAPEX) and operational expenditures (OPEX) is the lack of visibility into the workload and the resources that it needs. Most of the time, IT does not know why an application is performing poorly, and its first reaction is to add more resources to it, which can cause lower performance. There is a lack of visibility in how the applications interact with each other and why performance sometimes suffers. Applications that have all the resources they need still perform poorly.

Also, as applications move around from private data centers to other geographical locations and into public clouds, the business does not really know whether the user experience remained the same, got better, or became worse.

Cisco HyperFlex addresses all of these issues via a suite of products, with the main focus on enhancing the application performance while minimizing the cost of resources. This chapter discusses three main products that work hand in hand with HyperFlex to reach that goal.

HyperFlex with Cisco Tetration

In plain terms, Tetration allows an IT administrator to monitor the Internet Protocol (IP) flows between the different applications of the data center. This allows you to monitor which application is talking to which application, what ports and services are being used, what users are accessing the application, what users can access the application, and what the service flow is between the applications.

In addition, as applications are moving between private and public clouds, Cisco Tetration allows the user to monitor traffic to and from the application regardless of the underlying infrastructure.

Based on such information, the IT administrator has a clear map of the applications and the flow of services that are actually running. Cisco Tetration falls under the umbrella of what Cisco calls intent-based networking, meaning that the product captures how the user "intends" the network to behave in the form of policies between the different endpoints. Tetration then checks the user policy versus what is happening in the network and alerts the user whether the network complies with the user intent.

Users might have conflicting policies. An example might be when the Applications team sets allow and deny rules that conflict with the Database team. Cisco Tetration resolves these conflicts. So, if two teams set conflicting policies between two endpoints—say one team allows port 80 and the other denies port 80—then conflict is flagged and resolved based on which team has a configured higher priority.

The information from Cisco Tetration is exported and leveraged toward enforcing additional functions either at the network layer or at the application layer.

On the network layer, information from the Tetration platform forms the basis of network profiles, allowing the users to define policies to be enforced inside the network switches. These policies define service flows between the applications. This is discussed in Chapter 17, "Application-Centric Infrastructure."

Alternatively, information from the Cisco Tetration platform can be leveraged to offer workload optimization services. Knowing where the application sits in the network and what other applications it interacts with helps move the workload around to optimize the use of resources. This is discussed in this chapter under "Cisco Workload Optimizer."

Let's start with the basic Tetration architecture, as seen in Figure 11-1.

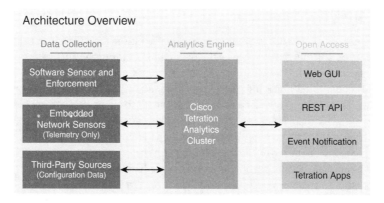

Figure 11-1 *Tetration Architecture Overview*

The three main components of the architecture are the data collection, the Tetration analytics cluster, and open access.

Data Collection

The data collection component defines the different methods to collect the data. Tetration captures only the headers of IP flows between two endpoints. Tetration does not capture the payload itself. When data is captured and sent to the analytics engine, it is encrypted for added security. Tetration relies on multiple methods for data collection:

- **Hardware sensors:** These are basically advanced application-specific integrated circuits (ASICs) inside the Nexus 9000 switches that collect IP flows at wire speed with no impact on the CPUs. The ASICs also annotate the data with switch-specific context information and provide the analytics engine with telemetry data.

- **Software sensors:** These are lightweight software binaries that are loaded inside the operating system where the application runs. The software runs in the user space of the operating system (OS), which could be running on bare-metal servers or as a guest OS inside the virtual machine (VM). The sensors stream data to the analytics engine, and they annotate the data with information gathered from the host, such as users and processes. Also, the software sensors enforce policy inside the host itself. The software sensors are based on Linux VMs, Windows Server VMs, the host OS, or other.

- **Third-party sources:** A third point of collection is from Encapsulated Remote Switched Port Analyzer (ERSPAN) agents. This is done by having collection points on the network, where a flow is copied and encapsulated inside a generic routing encapsulation (GRE) tunnel across L3 networks to reach the Tetration appliance. Data flows are augmented with information from third-party sources. Examples are configuration from network services such as load balancers, or IP addresses from an IP address management (IPAM) device, or possible asset tagging where the flow is tagged as a production flow, an operation flow, and so on. This allows filters to be applied on the flows to enforce policy.

Tetration Analytics Cluster

Another piece of the Tetration architecture is the Tetration analytics cluster. This is a Big Data–type appliance that receives the data collected from the software and hardware sensors and analyzes it. The cluster comes in different form factors. The hardware appliances come as a 39 rack unit (RU) large form factor platform (C1-Tetration) for data centers with more than 5,000 servers or an 8 RU small form factor platform for data centers with fewer than 5,000 servers. The analytics cluster also comes as a software-based virtual appliance Tetration-V that targets smaller installations that do not exceed 1,000 servers. The Tetration-V runs on-premises on the customers' own servers but manages and monitors workloads from public clouds such as Amazon Web Services (AWS) and Microsoft Azure. Cisco also launched Tetration as a software as a service (SaaS). The SaaS offering makes it easier for customers to use the service on per-license basis and to handle large and small environments without initial investment in hardware or software.

Open Access

This identifies the different methods where the user accesses information from the analytics engine. Data is accessed via different methods such as a web graphical user interface (GUI), which allows a user with limited Big Data knowledge easy access to the information. Other methods are event notification using Apache Kafka, which allows subscription and streaming of records. Access to the cluster is also done via Representational State Transfer application programming interfaces (REST APIs) and the Tetration apps. The Tetration apps allow the user to write Python or Scala programming language scripts that are executed in the Tetration platform with full access to the collected data.

Using the Data

Cisco Tetration displays an application map and shows the interaction between the different endpoints and all the flows within a cluster. Because agents are running inside the OS of the application, they collect information such as the processes running, the process IDs, usernames that are attached to the processes, and so on.

The Tetration appliance uses advanced algorithms to have a better and more accurate insight into the application and its components. Here are some examples of the output of the Tetration appliance:

- Grouping of endpoints into different tiers such as web tiers, app tiers, and so on.

- A whitelist policy recommendation for applications. A whitelist is a list of approved applications that are permitted to be present in the network. The appliance also monitors and enforces the whitelist.

- Forensic analysis of the data using search filters.

- Impact of applying a certain policy on the network and how it affects the existing applications.

In addition, Tetration offers a powerful filtering engine that instantly accesses any piece of information that the user requires. Different parameters can be applied to the filter to capture the flows. Examples of such parameters are duration of the flow, IP addresses, ports, host names, process IDs, application latency, and network latency.

Based on the output of the Tetration appliance, the IT administrator can now automate the creation of policies in the data center. The Tetration platform also allows the administrator to experiment with new policies and use what-if scenarios to understand whether the new chosen policy has adverse effects on the current operation of the network. The application map displays every flow in the network.

Finally, the data that is collected by Tetration is exported via different formats such as JavaScript Object Notation (JSON), Extensible Markup Language (XML), and YAML Ain't Markup Language (YAML) and imported by other engines such as Cisco ACI to enforce policies on the network [1].

Cisco Workload Optimizer

One of the software products that benefits enterprises as they run their applications on HyperFlex is the Cisco Workload Optimizer (CWOM). This product is based on the Turbonomic platform. CWOM is an automation tool that monitors the performance consumption of applications and matches the resources with the needs of the application. If applications are starving for resources, CWOM suggests manual adjustments to the user or does the adjustments automatically. In the same manner, if an application is oversubscribed, CWOM suggests or automates freeing up resources.

The CWOM is an agentless technology, meaning there are no software agents installed on hosts. CWOM detects all the elements in the network and draws an application map showing the interdependencies between the elements.

CWOM tracks, reports, and views the behavior of elements such as CPU, memory, storage, input/output operations per second (IOPS), latency, and database transaction unit (DTU) between regions. The DTU, for example, is a blended measure of CPU, memory, and input/output (I/O) reads and writes given to a database that benchmarks the level of performance of that database to decide whether it needs more or fewer resources.

CWOM works for private, hybrid, and multicloud workloads. It is more of a demand supply model for both performance and cost. An application, a VM, and a container demand a set of resources that the respective infrastructure supplies. CWOM first determines if the supply meets the demand, is below the demand, or exceeds the demand. CWOM then decides what to do with the resources. If a VM, for example, is experiencing low performance, CWOM evaluates whether this is because of lack of CPU, lack of memory, or lack of IOPS. Based on this evaluation, CWOM might suggest giving the VM more resources on the host it is running on or simply suggest moving the VM to another host with more resources.

Also, CWOM has a supply-demand-cost model based on where the application is running: in a private data center or on the cloud. Because each resource has a cost—whether a CAPEX/OPEX cost that you can enter or a resource cost published on AWS or Azure—CWOM calculates the different component costs and makes a recommendation to the user. Some applications have a better cost running on AWS, others on Azure, and others in your private data center. When calculating the cost of running an application on AWS, for example, multiple components come into play, such as the cost of compute, cost of storage, cost of IP addresses for a virtual private cloud, and cost of load balancers. CWOM gives a full view of the cost and compares the cost of running the same application on the cloud and on-premise so the user can make the best decision.

CWOM integrates with other tools from Cisco, such as the Cisco Tetration [2]. Feedback from Cisco Tetration is passed to CWOM via REST APIs. Based on this information, CWOM has an actual view of the interaction between different applications running in the network. If, for example, two VMs are chatty and possibly congesting the network, CWOM suggests that the user move the VMs to closer hosts or maybe to the same host to alleviate the network congestion and lower the latency of the east-west traffic inside the data center.

In principal, the CWOM (Turbonomic) platform allows you to define different physical or virtual entities. In this example, the entities are the physical servers inside a Unified Computing System (UCS) domain, virtual machines taken from vCenter, or flows between virtual machines taken from Cisco Tetration. CWOM creates an application map and interdependencies between all of these components. CWOM defines elements called dPods, which are hardware resources that are closely related inside the data center. As an example, the dPod groups all the UCS server blades or rack servers in a HyperFlex cluster in the same UCS domain. CWOM also defines vPods, which represent a collection of endpoints such as VMs with interdependencies as taken from Cisco Tetration.

CWOM also gives an exact view of how resources—such as CPU, memory, storage, and network utilization—are consumed between endpoints. CWOM detects, for example, that the network utilization for a particular flow has reached 100% between two endpoints, causing congestion.

As such, CWOM gives recommendations for better placements of the VMs, such as moving a VM from one host to another to drop down the utilization. If it is configured to do so, CWOM does the VM placement automatically, considering all of the other components and resource utilization in the application map.

CWOM works below the VM level to understand the infrastructure resources and optimize the supply-demand model of resources to lower the cost of usage.

Another product that digs deeper into the applications to monitor the transactions between the end user and the application and between applications is called Cisco AppDynamics, which is discussed next.

Cisco AppDynamics

AppDynamics [3] provides an application and business monitoring platform that allows enterprises to monitor their business applications and transactions and make sure they are delivering the best performance. In case of misbehaving applications or slow business processes, AppDynamics identifies the root cause of the problem down to the software code level. Cisco AppDynamics works in conjunction with the HyperFlex platform, Cisco Tetration, CWOM, and other cloud orchestration products such as Cisco CloudCenter to optimize the use of the applications and business transactions in private, hybrid, and cloud data centers.

As explained, CWOM optimizes the workload in a HyperFlex environment by monitoring and efficiently allocating resources to an application such as CPU, memory, storage, and network. AppDynamics takes the monitoring process even further and deeper into the application. AppDynamics looks at every transaction that is occurring in distributed applications and evaluates the health of not only the application but also the "transactions" in terms of different metrics such as response time. The transactions are monitored in the context of the business. Examples of business transactions are logging into a retail website, placing products into a shopping cart, researching a product from within the site, checking out, and making payment transactions. Each such transaction triggers a set of interactions between different endpoints. These endpoints could be the user talking to a web server or the web server talking to the app server that is talking to a Structured Query Language (SQL) database. Because problems can occur at any point in the transaction, AppDynamics gives the IT administrator the ability to dig deeper and identify the cause of any potential problem.

Cisco AppDynamics is a powerful tool to be used by IT operations, production support, developers, architects, and basically anyone who is accountable for enhancing the application performance from a technical standpoint as well as a business standpoint.

Cisco AppDynamics is divided into multiple components:

- Application performance management (APM)

- End user monitoring

- Infrastructure visibility

- Business monitoring

Delivering business applications is becoming complex. Business delivery through web applications involves many distributed applications working together, such as distributed web servers in different locations, distributed application servers, and databases. When users complain about a bad web experience, such as being unable to log in or to browse, purchase, or deposit, pinpointing the problem has surpassed the ability of any manual troubleshooting. The AppDynamics APM gives the user the following functionality:

- Automatically discover the application topology map from user to web, application, and database services.

- Discover all end-to-end transactions between the elements of the topology map.

- Visualize and prioritize the business transaction performance.

- Create a performance baseline for transactions and alert the administrator to deviations from the baseline.

- Monitor every transaction, but only capture data from misbehaving transactions to ensure scalability of the solution.

- Integrate with incidents and alerting systems such as ServiceNow, PagerDuty, and Jira.

- Isolate performance issues by digging deeper at the software code level.

- Cover popular programming languages and frameworks, including Java, .NET, Node.js, PHP, Python, C, and C++.

- Monitor applications inside private data centers as well as across multiple clouds.

- Create a war room where different entities can collaborate and troubleshoot while sharing the performance data.

- Solve issues such as uptime and availability, slow response time, memory leaks, thrash, stalls, deadlocks, slow database response, database connection pool areas, end user monitoring, mobile APM, and so on.

AppDynamics gives the user visibility into the different elements of a distributed application all the way from the user to the databases. Performance characteristics of the transactions are displayed, and issues are highlighted where they can be easily resolved.

AppDynamics collects information from the application and displays it using agents and controllers. Agents are plug-ins that monitor the performance and behavior of an application. The agents are deployed inside devices, applications, hosts, and more. The agents monitor the transactions down to the code level and tag the code requests and headers to be able to trace a transaction from beginning to end. The agents send the information to a controller, which helps monitor, troubleshoot, and analyze the transaction details.

In addition to APM, Cisco AppDynamics supports end user monitoring, infrastructure visibility, and business monitoring.

With end user monitoring, every user interaction is monitored. AppDynamics monitors all network requests and collects errors, crashes, and page load details, among other things. This allows the system to track the user experience such as response time and benchmark it against healthy user interactions. Infrastructure visibility is done by monitoring the health of servers, databases, network service devices such as load balancers, and so on. Last, AppDynamics provides business monitoring by correlating application performance and end user experience with business outcome. Business iQ tracks business transactions such as accessing a website home page and login, adding an item to a cart, and so on. It identifies the performance metrics of such transactions to understand how the performance of such transactions affects the business.

Looking Ahead

Part IV of this book covered the Cisco HyperFlex product line and the different tools and products that offer a high level of automation in deploying and managing the hyperconverged environment. Many HCI implementations are on the market today, and all claim high performance, advanced storage functionality, and cloud-like simplicity. However, when you dig through the details, you will discover that not all implementations are created equal.

Part V lists some of the known implementations on the market and covers in more detail implementations from VMware and Nutanix. Part V also discusses some aspects of OpenStack as they relate to compute and storage so the reader gets comfortable with the terminology when it's discussed in the context of hyperconvergence.

References

[1] https://www.cisco.com/c/en/us/td/docs/switches/datacenter/aci/apic/white_papers/Cisco_IT_Tetration_Deployment_Part_1_of_2.html

[2] https://www.cisco.com/c/en/us/products/data-center-analytics/tetration-analytics/index.html

[3] https://www.appdynamics.com

Alternative HCI Implementations

Chapter 12   VMware vSAN

Chapter 13   Nutanix Enterprise Cloud Platform

Chapter 14   Open Source—Compute and Storage

HCI vendors are plentiful, and it is hard to cover the full list of different implementations. If you search online for hyperconverged infrastructure vendors, you get a bucketload of HCI vendors. You see names such as Cisco HyperFlex, VMware vSAN, Nutanix Enterprise Cloud Platform, EMC DELL VxRail/VxRack, Dell EMC XC Series, HPE (Simplivity), Stratoscale, Scalecomputing, Pivot 3, and many more.

Part V covers two of the important vendors in this space, VMware and Nutanix, as well as efforts in OpenStack. This is not to say that other implementations are better or worse, and this in not an endorsement of these selected vendors. VMware is a pioneer in the virtualization space, and many of the implementations use VMware ESXi and vCenter as a baseline. The VMware installed base is very large, so it is important for you to understand how VMware is evolving into HCI. Nutanix, on the other hand, is a pioneer in hyperconvergence that has pushed the envelope in this space. Understanding Nutanix and its functionality gives you a baseline for comparing and contrasting when evaluating other HCI vendors.

Chapter 12

VMware vSAN

This chapter covers the following key topics:

- **vSAN Physical Components:** Describes vSAN's (formerly Virtual Storage Area Network) hardware implementations, including ready nodes and integrated systems.

- **vSAN Hyperconvergence Software:** Covers the vSAN hyperconvergence software, including the object file system and the input/output (I/O) operation within the cache and capacity layers.

- **vSAN Advanced Functionality:** Includes the vSAN advanced data services, such as deduplication and compression, erasure coding, snapshots and clones, disaster recovery (DR), and backup.

- **Integration with Legacy SAN and NAS:** Covers integration of vSAN with legacy storage area network (SAN) and network-attached storage (NAS).

- **Persistent Storage for Containers:** Describes support for persistent storage for containers.

- **vSAN Management:** Highlights some of the important management products and tools to look at when comparing vSAN with the HCI vendors.

- **Thoughts on vSAN Versus HyperFlex:** Offers a high-level comparison between HyperFlex and vSAN.

vSAN is VMware's hyperconverged "software" product. It is software that has gathered early acceptance because it is integrated with VMware's ESXi vSphere and vCenter, which are flagship products that customers are accustomed to. vSAN is software whose hardware comes in different flavors, such as off-the-shelf components that are vSAN certified, complete servers that are vSAN ready, and third-party appliances and converged systems such as EMC's VxRail or Cisco Unified Computing System (UCS).

One of the major advantages of vSAN is the familiarity that enterprises have with VMware, vSphere, and vCenter. Virtualization administrators who are accustomed to creating virtual machines (VMs) with vCenter will hit the ground running with vSAN. Although vSAN itself fits nicely within the software-defined storage (SDS) framework and allows for integrating compute, storage, and networking in single systems, vSAN as marketed now by VMware runs on third-party hardware vendors. VMware attempted to release a modular hyperconverged product called EVO:Rail and did not succeed. EVO:Rail was supposed to be a standalone modular hyperconverged appliance that comes in preset hardware configuration and software licenses. This product was announced by VMware in 2014 but soon after faded away and was cancelled. The same product re-emerged in 2016 under EMC as VxRail, with partnership with VMware.

vSAN Physical Components

Unlike other hyperconverged infrastructure (HCI) vendors who offer specific appliances to run the software, the physical components of vSAN range from integrated hardware appliances to ready-nodes servers that are approved by VMware to build-it-yourself models. VMware approves hardware from third-party vendors under multiple configurations:

- **Integrated systems:** These are hardware appliances from different vendors that are sold with vSAN already integrated. Examples are Dell EMC VxRail, Dell EMC VxRack, Fujitsu PRIMEFLEX for vSAN, and Lenovo ThinkAgile VX Series.

- **vSAN-ready nodes:** These include validated server configurations and hardware that is certified for use by vSAN. VMware maintains a list of server hardware vendors at its partner website.

- **User-defined vSAN cluster:** This is a build-it-yourself model in which VMware allows users to select individual software and hardware, such as servers, storage input/output (I/O) controllers, firmware, drivers, hard disk drives (HDDs), Flash, central processing unit (CPU) core, and memory from a list that is approved by VMware and shown on its vSAN Compatibility Guide (VCG) website. Although this approach offers the users flexibility in picking and choosing the hardware vendors and components to work with, it comes with a big list of dos and don'ts and lots of moving parts and finger-pointing. After all, hyperconvergence means simplicity and automation and putting systems in cruise control. This model definitely does not fit the bill; it creates added complexity and is not for the faint of heart.

The next section discusses the main highlights of the vSAN architecture. Many details about hyperconvergence and specifically HyperFlex were already discussed. However, some major fundamental architectural differences must be highlighted.

vSAN organizes the disks in a host in disk groups. Each host has from one to five disk groups. Each disk group has one flash device for caching and acceleration of the I/O reads and writes and one to seven HDDs or solid-state drives (SSDs) for capacity. The flash device is not considered part of the overall capacity but rather is used as a caching device. Figure 12-1 shows how disks inside a host are organized for hybrid configurations and all-flash configurations.

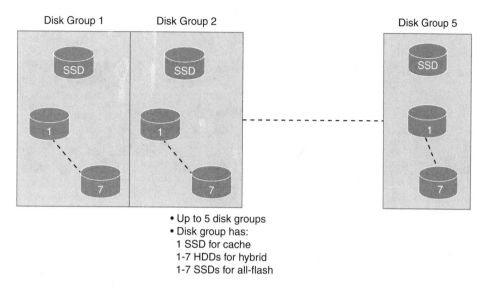

• Up to 5 disk groups
• Disk group has:
 1 SSD for cache
 1-7 HDDs for hybrid
 1-7 SSDs for all-flash

Figure 12-1 *vSAN Disk Groups*

Note that in both hybrid and all-flash, a single high-endurance flash SSD is used for caching. The capacity of the caching SSD is 10% of the overall capacity, and it serves only the disk group it is in. This flash SSD normally has a high Total Bytes Written (TBW) for high endurance. The rest of the disks in the disk group are lower cost magnetic disks in the case of hybrid, and low endurance with low TBW for all-flash configurations.

So far, from a high level, this looks like a superset of a HyperFlex node, in which each HyperFlex has an SSD for caching and either HDDs or SSDs for capacity. However, with vSAN, the added flexibility of adding more disk groups to a node creates further complications. For example, the failure of an SSD cache drive in a disk group translates into a failure in the whole disk group. If the cache in a disk group fails, the remaining seven disks in the disk group are unusable until the SSD is restored.

vSAN Hyperconvergence Software

Unlike other HCI implementations in which the storage file system and services are delivered via controller VMs, VMware has the vSAN hyperconvergence software integrated with vSphere. vSAN runs inside the ESXi kernel. The pros and cons of this approach are discussed later in this chapter. vSAN runs on any x86-based server, although, as already discussed, the user must go by the recommended VMware vSAN ready nodes such as VxRail from EMC or pick components from the VMware VCG.

The vSAN high-level software architecture is seen in Figure 12-2.

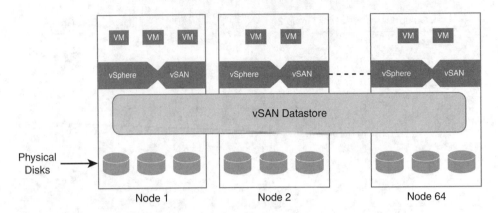

Figure 12-2 *vSAN vSphere Integration*

The vSAN cluster scales up to 64 nodes. Notice that many HCI implementations that use ESXi as a hypervisor try to reach this limit as a minimum requirement to keep up with VMware environments. For edge configurations, vSAN has a 2-node minimum limit for a cluster. And for stretched clusters, vSAN has a limit of 30 nodes, with 15 nodes in each of the stretched cluster sites.

vSAN works by pooling HDDs and SSDs from different hosts in a cluster and providing a shared datastore for all VMs to use. vSAN supports enterprise-class scale and performance and offers policies at the granularity of a VM and VMDK level. It supports hybrid as well as all-flash configurations. vSAN distributes data over multiple disks in the cluster per defined protection policies.

At the heart of vSAN is a scalable object-oriented file system that is described next.

The Object File System

vSAN introduces an object-oriented file system that offers more flexibility and scalability than the Virtual Machine File System (VMFS). As discussed earlier in this book, VMFS brings some deficiencies in scaling the number of VMs because of contention for metadata when sharing files. With the object-oriented file system, the granularity is at the object level, with no dependencies between the objects as you have in file dependencies in file systems. This makes moving data around, adding new services, and scaling a lot easier.

VMware stores data and metadata in object files. The object file is a logical volume that has its data and metadata distributed across a vSAN cluster. A single vSAN object has a maximum size of 255 GB. The object itself is divided into "components" that stripe the data across multiple disks in case vSAN is configured to do so. Some examples of the different types of objects follow:

- **VM home namespace:** This constitutes the home directory of the VM, and it contains all relevant configuration files, such as the .vmx file showing operating system and disk sizes and other information. Other files include log files, snapshot delta descriptor files, and VMDK descriptor files. The VM home object is formatted with a VMFS file system and mounted under the root directory vSANDatastore (for example: /vmfs/volumes/vSANDatastore/foo/).

- **VMDK:** A VM disk that stores the contents of the VM's disk drive.

- **VM swap object:** This object is created when a VM is powered on. If the VM does not have enough physical memory to run on, it uses the swap object from the disk drives. The size of the VM swap object is the difference between the configured memory of the VM and the physical memory the VM has access to.

- **Snapshot delta VMDKs:** These objects contain the delta—that is, the difference in data—when a snapshot is taken, such as snapshot delta memory objects.

- **Memory object:** This is a snapshot of the memory when creating or suspending a VM.

Each vSAN object is deployed as a Redundant Array of Independent Disks (RAID) tree. The "components" are the leaves of that tree. For example, if RAID 1 mirrors a VMDK, the two copies are considered the components of the original object. Also, if RAID 0 is used to stripe an object, the stripes at the end of the RAID tree are the components.

Figure 12-3 shows how objects and components are distributed across nodes and different disk groups.

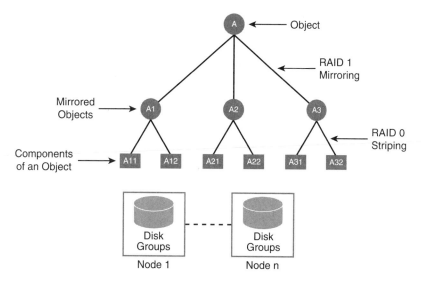

Figure 12-3 *Objects and Components*

The objects and components are distributed according to the applied policies. In Figure 12-3, RAID 1 mirrors object A between nodes. The RAID 0 policy stripes the mirrored objects between different capacity disks to enhance the I/O performance. The disks where the data is replicated are normally in different nodes, and the stripes could be within a disk group, between disk groups of a node, or between nodes. It all depends on the load-balancing measures vSAN takes to distribute the data for better performance. The leaves of the RAID tree—in this case, the stripes of the mirrored objects—are called components.

vSAN Datastore

The vSAN Datastore is a logical container (just a terminology, not to be confused with Docker containers) that contains all the vSAN objects. vSAN has only one datastore shared by all hosts in the same cluster and serves as one shared pool of storage. The vSAN datastore provides different service levels to VMs and virtual disks. Such storage characteristics are presented to vCenter as storage capabilities. Upon creating a VM, storage policies are defined based on the storage capabilities. When a VM is assigned a certain policy, it is placed in the datastore in a manner that satisfies the policy. For example, if a VM is created and set with a policy that protects the VM if a host fails, this policy translates into a mirroring capability in the datastore, where the appropriate VM object is mirrored on two different blocks of disks on different hosts. If one host fails, the other host takes over.

vSAN Storage Policies

Policies define the storage requirements of a VM. Such requirements relate to performance and protection and map into the capabilities of the underlying datastore. Upon the creation of a vSAN cluster, the datastore is created and assigned default policies. Each VM has to have at least one assigned storage policy. VMware storage policy–based management (SPBM) is done at the VM level or even at the virtual machine disk (VMDK) level. vSAN checks whether the system can fulfill the policy or not and hence indicates whether the VM is compliant or noncompliant with the policy. Examples of policies as offered by VMware follow:

- **Number of disk stripes per object:** This is the minimum number of capacity devices (HDDs or SSDs) used to stripe the objects of a VM and its replicas. This is a "performance use case" with a default of 1 and a maximum of 12. As you recall, the benefit of RAID 0 striping is improved read and write performance. This distributes the read and write functions over more disk groups. Take care when setting this policy because the higher number of disks used, the more system resources, and that can affect overall system performance.

- **Primary level of failures to tolerate (PFTT):** This is an "availability use case," and it protects the VM against multiple node failures. The PFTT ranges between 0 and 3, with the default being 1. Protecting against node and disk failures requires having replicas of the VM and data in multiple places. Different schemes such as RAID 0, RAID 1, RAID 0+1, RAID 5, and RAID 6 are used. The number of copies depends on the number of failures to tolerate and is equal to PFTT + 1. So, one failure to tolerate, PFTT =1, requires two copies of the data to be made, PFTT = 2 require three copies, and PFTT = 3 require four copies. The higher the number of failures to tolerate, the more expensive the protection becomes because more resources are being used. It is recommended that you have more hosts available than the number of copies to be made. This ensures that after failure, the new system is also protected. vSAN has the concept of a "Witness" component that acts as a tie breaker if a network is segmented. The witness ensures that a VM has more than 50% of its components before being started or restarted. Any time vSAN does replications, a witness can be used. This is discussed further in the next bullet, "Fault domains."

■ **Fault domains:** Fault domains are used as an extra measure of protection by spreading redundancy components across servers in multiple racks. In this case, vSAN does not protect components with other components that are in the same rack just in case the rack fails.

Each fault domain can contain one or multiple servers. The number of fault domains is dependent on the PFTT a VM is configured to tolerate. When fault domains are configured, vSAN places replicas and witnesses in different domains.

The minimum number of fault domains is twice the PFTT plus one (2* PFTT + 1), so if PFTT is 1, then a minimum of three fault domains must be configured. However, it is recommended that you have more fault domains than the minimum—for example, four fault domains if you are tolerating one failure—to make sure that the new configuration still has some protection after failure.

Figure 12-4 shows an example of PFTT and fault domains. This example shows a sample configuration of a 16-node cluster that is divided into four racks with four servers per rack. For this example, the primary level of failure to tolerate is set to 1 (PFTT=1), with each rack configured as a fault domain.

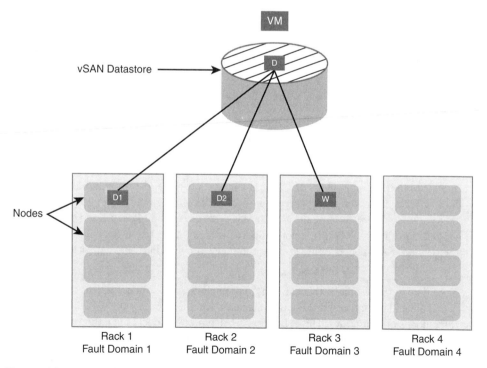

Figure 12-4 *Sample PFTT and Fault Domains*

Figure 12-4 shows that fault domains were configured per rack to protect against failure within the rack. The PFTT = 1 for a VM indicates that the VM will tolerate one node failure by having two different copies of object D. The components of object D are D1 and D2. D1 is copied to a node in Rack 1, and D2 is copied to a node in a different rack, Rack 2. A "witness" is also created on a separate node in Rack 3.

The concept of a witness is used to avoid situations where, for one reason or another, a network is partitioned and nodes in one partition are isolated from the nodes in the other. This causes what is called a split brain, in which the same VM can be launched in both partitions. This situation is detrimental to, for example, databases where the same database is launched in two places and data corruption starts to occur. To alleviate this situation, vSAN needs to make sure that a VM can be launched in only one partition at a time. To do so, a witness that has connectivity to at least one of the partitions is needed to tip the balance where the VM is created. The witness itself is a component of an object and is formed of metadata, so it does not consume much storage space.

Also, vSAN has introduced in its 6.0 release the concept of "voting." Each component of an object gets one or more votes. The witness is also a voting component. For a VM to be accessible and placed on a node, it needs its full data to be available and more than 50% of the "votes." A "quorum" is achieved if there are enough votes to make a decision. Normally, this means an "odd" number of votes needs to be available from all components. If there aren't enough votes, witnesses are created to form a quorum. In some cases, one or more witnesses are needed, and in other cases they are not.

If you are confused, you are not alone; many IT professionals struggle with understanding the witness. The good news is that vSAN does the witness election automatically. All you have to do is provide enough nodes to comply with the PFTT you chose; the rest is automatic.

Going back to the example in Figure 12-4, VM1 is protected with PFTT = 1. Because fault domains were configured, the object's components of VM1 are not replicated on any server on Rack 1 but are replicated on nodes on Rack 2. A witness, which is a third copy of the object's metadata, is also created on a server in Rack 3. If the network is partitioned and Racks 1 and 2 become isolated, vSAN goes through an election process and looks for the components of VM1 on all nodes. If vSAN detects that more than 50% of votes are available for a certain node, vSAN considers the object accessible and that node capable of running the VM. In this case, the node in Racks 1 and the node in Rack 3 both have 50% of the votes. So, the witness is created in Rack 3 to break the tie, and vSAN selects either node to run the VM depending on whether Rack 3 has connectivity to Rack 1, Rack 2, or both.

Note that, in this example, the addition of a fourth rack is not necessary or required but is recommended. You could make the same case whether a policy of PFTT = 1 requires three nodes or four nodes. This is because when a problem occurs in a three-node scenario, the remaining two nodes become unprotected unless there is yet another node. The same case can be made for fault domains, where protection can be made with three domains, but when a problem occurs, the remaining two domains become unprotected.

- **Flash Read Cache Reservation:** This is a performance use case that is specified as a percentage of the logical size of the VMDK object, with the default being 0 and maximum being 100% of the cache. This ensures that a certain portion of the cache is reserved for a critical VM, such that no other VM can use that portion of the cache. The Flash Read Cache Reservation is normally left as 0 because vSAN dynamically allocates cache for each VM object based on demand; however, the policy can be set for critical applications where read performance must be predictable and not affected by other noisy applications that will try to use the cache. This policy is supported only for hybrid configuration and not for all-flash configurations because for all-flash there isn't a read cache. Be careful with using such a policy because it is tied to the VM object even when it moves from host to host and can result in wasting cache resources.

- **Object Space Reservation:** This indicates the percentage of the logical size of the VMDK object that needs to be reserved or thick provisioned.

- **Failure Tolerance Method:** This indicates whether fault tolerance optimizes on performance or capacity. RAID 1 optimizes on performance but uses more capacity. RAID 5 and 6 with erasure coding (EC) use less capacity at the expense of lowered performance.

- **IOPS Limit for Object:** This defines the IOPS limit that an object can have. IOPS are the number of I/O operations per second calculated based on 32 KB size. So, a 64 KB I/O, for example, triggers two I/O operations.

- **Disable Object Checksum:** This value is set to either Yes or No, and it indicates whether a checksum must be calculated for an object to ensure data integrity. The checksums ensure that the object is not corrupted during transport and is repaired in case of data corruption.

- **Force Provisioning:** This value is set to either Yes or No and indicates whether an object can be provisioned even if the required storage policy cannot be met by the capabilities that can be provided by the datastore. For example, if the object policy is set, for example, to PFTT = 1, and you only have two hosts, protection cannot be provided, but the object can still be provisioned. This is normally used in outage scenarios when normal provisioning can no longer occur.

Two more policies are used with "Stretched Clusters": secondary level of failures to tolerate (SFTT) and Affinity. Stretched clusters refer to clusters that span data centers and are connected remotely, such as the case of data centers in metro areas or across an enterprise campus. These policies are designed to ensure better control where the VMs run.

- **Secondary level of failures to tolerate (SFTT):** In a stretched cluster, this rule indicates the number of node failures that an object can tolerate after the number of site failures as defined by PFTT is reached. The default is 1, and the maximum is 3.

- **Affinity:** In a stretched cluster, if PFTT is set to 0, then Affinity can be set to None, Preferred, or Secondary. This limits the creation of VM objects to a specific site in the stretched cluster. The default value is None.

Caching

vSAN uses a similar approach to HyperFlex in using a cache tier and a capacity tier in performing I/O reads and writes. The major difference, however, is in the highly distributed approach in HyperFlex, where all cache from all nodes and all controllers are leveraged to perform the I/O operations. vSAN mainly utilizes the cache of the specific disk group where the data is being destaged.

The presence of the flash device in a disk group is essential for "caching" the I/O reads and "buffering" the I/O writes. If you recall, one of the main performance metrics is latency, which reflects how long it takes to read or write a block on a disk. The other factor is "flash-wear," which was discussed in Chapter 3, "Host Hardware Evolution," and which affects the life and performance of a flash device. In performing reads and writes, vSAN has two main objectives. One is to use the caching device to speed up the reads and writes if the disks are magnetic. The other objective is to minimize the writes on SSD flash devices to avoid the flash-wear. To do so, vSAN needs at least one flash device for caching in the disk group whose size is about 10% of the remaining 1–7 disks in the group. For all-flash configurations, it is also recommended to use 10% for flash to minimize the flash-wear on writes.

vSAN uses the local dynamic random-access memory (DRAM) cache as much as possible as a first place to look for data. vSAN caches based on the frequency of the use of the object and based on spatial locality of the data being accessed.

It is important to note that vSAN does not attempt to perform data locality when VMs are moved around. This means that the data does not follow the VM, and it remains where it was originally created. vSAN assumes that the network latencies for 10 GE networks and beyond are in microseconds and are much smaller than NAND flash latencies that are measured in milliseconds; therefore, having the data follow the VM is unimportant and would provide inconsistencies in data access. This is contradictory to other lines of thought that believe that flash access latency will eventually be in the microseconds, and the network might cause congestions that affect the access of storage.

I/O Operation Details

In the case of hybrid configurations where all capacity drives are magnetic HDDs, the caching device allocates 30% of the cache for write-back buffers and 70% as a read cache. A 100 GB SSD that is used for cache in a disk group, for example, allocates 30 GB of its cache for the write operation and 70 GB for read. The write operation happens as follows:

Step 1.   The OS of the guest VM initiates a write operation to the virtual disk.

Step 2.   The host, which is the owner of the VM, initiates the cloning operation according to the PFTT policy. If, for example, PFTT = 1, two copies of the object must be made.

Step 3.   If Checksum is enabled, then a cyclic redundancy check (CRC) 32 operation takes place between the source and the destination to ensure that there is no data corruption during the process.

Step 4.   If a number of disk stripes per object were configured as higher than 1, the data is striped accordingly to different disks in the cluster.

Step 5.   The write is going to be done on the write cache buffer, and an acknowledgment is sent to the guest OS after the replicas are made.

Step 6.   In parallel, a "destaging" operation takes place asynchronously between the cache buffer and the capacity devices. The cache buffering before destaging helps in having the I/O written sequentially rather than randomly, which has huge latency savings.

As far as reading I/O, in the case of hybrid, 70% of the cache is allocated for reads.

The read operation happens as follows:

Step 1.   The OS of the guest VM initiates the read operation.

Step 2.   The host owner of the VM chooses a replica to read from. The replica does not have to be local to the host where the VM is; it can be on any host. vSAN load balances between replicas; however, the same block must be read from the same replica.

Step 3.   The local DRAM cache is checked for the data. If it exists, the data is taken locally from the DRAM; if not, then the flash cache (in the case of hybrid) must be checked. Check the write cache just in case the data is already available there if it was recently written.

Step 4.   If the data is not available in the flash cache, it must be brought from the capacity device. Every time a 4 KB block is brought into the read cache, an additional 1 MB of data is also brought into the cache. This increases the read performance with the assumption that if a block is read, most likely the blocks that come after it are read as well. Bringing 1 MB into the read cache saves on further read access to the HDDs.

Step 5.   The read is completed, and data is returned to the owner.

In the case of all-flash configurations in which all capacity drives are flash SSDs, the caching device is used only for write operations to minimize the flash-wear on write for the low-endurance capacity disks. vSAN delays the writes as much as possible, allowing multiple copies to be updated on the flash device before eventually writing to the capacity disks. In the case of reads, the first attempt is always from local DRAM; if not found, check the write cache just in case the data was not written to the capacity disks yet. If it is still not found, all reads are done directly from the SSD capacity devices because they are already flash devices, and read I/O has minimal latency.

vSAN Advanced Functionality

vSAN offers a set of advanced functionality in the following areas:

- Data integrity
- Data security

- Storage optimization

- Snapshots

- Cloning

- Data backup

- Disaster recovery

Although on the surface this sounds like most HCI implementations, there are some architectural differences worth discussing. The list of vSAN advanced functionality follows.

Data Integrity

As objects move around in a cluster due to protection and fault-tolerance mechanisms, it becomes extremely important to protect the data from being corrupted. Also, because data remains stale in hard disks, it might incur what is called *bit rot*. vSAN provides data integrity mechanisms for data both in flight and at rest.

vSAN uses a 32-bit cyclic redundancy check (CRC-32) for doing checksum on the data to detect data errors that might have occurred during transport. Checksum is initiated on the host that contains the VM because it is important to do the checksum at the start of the I/O operation. The checksum is verified at the destination host where the I/O is written. Checksum is performed for both writes and reads. Checksum is on by default but can be turned off. Checksum can cause some I/O amplification due to the added CRCs, but it does not cause major effects. Many of the recent CPUs do checksum offload functions, which prevent performance degradation.

vSAN also performs checksums for data at rest. Data at rest could incur bit rot, or silent corruption, due to the deterioration of data stored on media. vSAN performs disk scrubbing for data at rest to ensure data integrity.

Data Encryption

VMware has implemented data encryption for VM and vMotion in vSphere release 6.5. For vSAN, VMware introduced vSAN encryption as of vSphere release 6.5.

VMware implements VM encryption inside the hypervisor and beneath the VM. When I/O comes out from the virtual disk controller, it is encrypted before it is sent to the storage layer. Files that are encrypted are VM Home files and VMDK files. VMware encryption key management is based on Key Management Interoperability Protocol (KMIP) 1.1. The key management client resides within vCenter, which works with a range of key management servers. The VMware VM-level encryption gives flexibility to the use of guest OS and the type of datastore because it is done beneath the VM.

For vMotion encryption, VMware uses a vCenter randomly generated one-time use 256-bit key, in addition to a 64-bit nonce (an arbitrary number that is used once). The combination key and nonce are sent to the two end hosts, where the VM vMotion occurs and, from then on, the vMotion data is encrypted to prevent malicious attacks.

For vSAN, VMware introduced in vSphere 6.6 native data-at-rest encryption, called vSAN encryption. The vSAN encryption is enabled per cluster. It allows the encryption of data-at-rest without the use of specialized self-encrypting drives (SEDs). vSAN encryption is hardware agnostic and runs on any type of HDD or SSD. VMware uses the XTS AES 256 Cipher, with two factor authentication, part of a Defense Information Systems Agency (DISA)–approved Security Technical Implementation Guide (STIG) for HCI. The solution is compliant with KMIP 1.1 for key management. The VMware VMKernel cryptographic module has also achieved Federal Information Processing Standards (FIPS) 140-2 validation under the National Institute of Standards and Technology (NIST) Cryptographic Module Validation Program (CMVP).

vSAN encryption does not conflict with other data services such as deduplication, compression, or EC because encryption occurs above the device driver layer of the storage stack. Encryption can be turned on and off.

Deduplication and Compression

vSAN can be configured to perform block-level deduplication and compression, but *only* on all-flash configurations. Deduplication offers major disk space reduction by removing duplicate data. vSAN enables deduplication and compression on a per-cluster basis, but it is applied only per disk group and not between disk groups. Deduplication is based on 4 KB blocks; it reduces duplicate block copies in a disk group to a single copy. Compression is applied after deduplication to further reduce the size of the block using an LZ4 algorithm.

For clusters where deduplication and compression are already enabled, vSAN performs these functions inline. However, when data moves into the write SSD flash, it comes in hydrated, meaning as is. As data is destaged and moves from the SSD cache to the flash capacity drive, a Secure Hash Algorithm 1 (SHA-1) is performed on the block to ensure that the data is unique. If it is unique, further compression can be applied on the block. However, if the data already exists, there is no need to perform compression on the data or to have it written and a pointer pointing to it. Also, as far as compression, vSAN ensures that if a block can be compressed to 2 KB or below, it is compressed; if a block cannot be properly compressed or compressed at all, such as with an encrypted block, it is left hydrated, meaning as is. This is to reduce CPU cycles on attempting to decompress blocks that are poorly compressed to start with.

Take care when enabling deduplication and compression on existing vSAN clusters. Each disk group must be evacuated (meaning all data moved somewhere else), the disk group formatted to support deduplication and compression, and then the data moved back. This can cause major disruption and can conflict with protection policies because during the process of data evacuation, VMs in other disk groups can be unprotected. There are many restrictions that vSAN enforces with deduplication and compression. Examples of such restrictions are adding and removing disks from a disk group. One disk failure can cause the whole disk group to fail. Such restrictions make such functionality tricky to implement.

Erasure Coding

vSAN implements RAID 5 or 6 EC; however, like deduplication and compression, EC is supported on all-flash clusters only. EC was explained in Chapter 7, "HCI Functionality." With EC, vSAN supports a high level of protection on all-flash clusters by performing data mirroring, but with data optimization. EC protects against one (PFTT = 1) or two (PFTT = 2) capacity disk or node failures. It was already discussed that with RAID 5, for example, the storage overhead for achieving one disk or node protection is only 33% compared to 50% with RAID 1 mirroring.

Snapshots

Snapshots are a mechanism to preserve the state of a VM and its data at a certain point in time. There are different types of snapshots, such as physical, copy on write, redirect on write, and others. VMware uses the redirect on write snapshots, which is one of the preferred methods to optimize disk space. Performing snapshots involves the creation of different types of files, such as .vmdk to maintain the virtual disk data; -delta.vmdk to maintain the delta difference between a parent VM and its child; .vmsd, which is a database of the snapshot information that contains the parent/child relationship and is used primarily by the Snapshot Manager; and .vmsn, which captures the memory state of the snapshot.

VMware adopts the concept of snapshot chains. Whenever a snapshot is taken, the original or parent virtual disk is marked as read only, and a child is created. VMware uses the terminology of child disk and redo log interchangeably. Redo logs are known to have consolidations and chain issues. The child is linked to its parent, and it stores the differences from the parent when data is modified. The process continues as such when a child has its own child that points to it, and each child contains the delta differences from the parent. Although this method is great for saving storage, it creates scalability and performance issues if the parent/child chain becomes too long. Also, it creates latency issues on reads because the chain must be traversed to collect the data from the last child all the way to the original parent virtual disk. An alternative and more efficient method was discussed in Chapter 9, "Cisco HyperFlex," where metadata is used to create zero-copy snapshots, and changed data is written into new locations. This eliminates the need of snapshot chaining with higher performance.

Cloning

Cloning is a way to make a copy of a VM so the same VM can be reused and launched multiple times. This makes the installation and configuration of OSs and applications much simpler. In some use cases, such as virtual desktop infrastructure (VDI), you must launch many instances of the same OS and application for many users. An example is launching desktops for many students with the same Microsoft Office environment, or in a development environment where the same environment must be duplicated. Instead of having to install the OS and setting up the configuration every time, a VM is set up once and then duplicated.

Cloning, however, consumes storage as the whole data is being mirrored. As such, different techniques are used to optimize storage. VMware uses two types of clones: full clones and linked clones.

When doing a full clone, all the data, files, and disks related to that clone are mirrored, and an exact copy is made somewhere in the cluster. The clone does not share anything with the parent virtual machine. The clone has the full complete set of data and runs independently from the original parent VM. Bear in mind that cloning has nothing to do with the replication used in a hyperconverged environment to protect the data. If an RF factor of 2 is applied on every VM, the original VM has two copies and the clone has an additional two copies if it is disassociated from the parent VM. This dramatically increases the storage requirements if many clones must be created. To optimize the storage, VMware created the concept of linked clones.

Linked clones are made from a snapshot of the parent. As previously discussed, the snapshot is a point-in-time image of the VM. The linked clones share all the virtual disks of the parent VM at the time the snapshot was taken. This allows multiple VMs to be created instantly without having to duplicate all of the virtual disks of the original parent VM. Linked clones cannot exist without the parent VM, and they always must be linked to it. If any changes occur on the linked clone level, as in modifying the data of the virtual disks, the changes are kept in *delta disks*. This is to make sure that multiple virtual clones that are linked to the same parent can have their own set of files while still sharing the common set of unmodified files they inherited from the snapshot of the parent. On the other hand, when modifications are made to the parent VM, these changes are not reflected at the level of the linked clones. If, however, these changes need to be reflected at the linked clone level, VMware has the option to "recompose" the linked clones. Unfortunately, doing so wipes out all changes that were made in the delta disks and resets all link clones to the parent VM's updated state. Figure 12-5 shows linked clones. Notice the snapshot and replica (clone) created from the parent VM. For the replica, linked clones are created; all share the parent's virtual disks but maintain their own changes in delta disks.

Linked clones are very powerful in a VDI environment. In VDI, hundreds of similar desktops (for example, Windows 7, 8, 10) running on centralized servers are created and accessed by users remotely. In a traditional VDI, hundreds of VMs are initiated, each having its own OS and Microsoft Office files, among other data. This consumes enormous amounts of storage because data is duplicated all over the hyperconverged cluster. With the concept of linked clones, a snapshot of a parent image is taken, and then linked clones sharing the parent virtual disk are created instantly without having to rebuild the OS and data every time, which consumes processing and storage. VDI allows each desktop to be customized with different resolutions, backup screens, home screens, and more. The data modifications are kept on the delta disks of each of the linked clone's VMs, saving enormous amounts of storage.

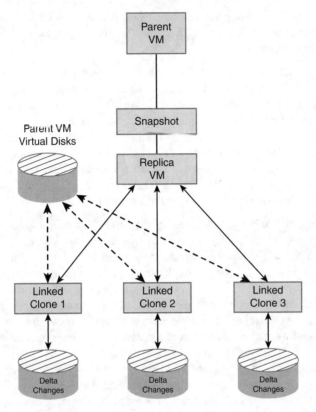

Figure 12-5 *Linked Clones*

vSAN Replication for Disaster Recovery via Stretched Clusters

vSAN inherits its replication techniques from VMware vSphere, where replication is done natively at the hypervisor level. Replication has multiple use cases, such as these:

■ Local replication to provide protection inside the cluster, and examples with PFTT 1 and PFTT 2 where duplicate copies of the data are distributed between nodes.

■ Synchronous replication between vSAN-stretched clusters for disaster recovery and zero recovery point objective (RPO).

■ Asynchronous replication between vSAN-stretched clusters for disaster recovery with VMware Site Recovery Manager. The RPO is between 5 minutes and 24 hours.

■ Disaster recovery to a public cloud data center using VMware Cloud Air Disaster Recovery service.

■ Data migration between vSAN clusters and existing storage area network (SAN) and network-attached storage (NAS) or direct-attached storage (DAS) deployments.

Designing for protection is always a matter of evaluating the cost of adding extra resources versus how much you can tolerate if an application goes down. vSAN uses remote replication across remote data centers to create what is called a *stretched cluster*, as seen in Figure 12-6.

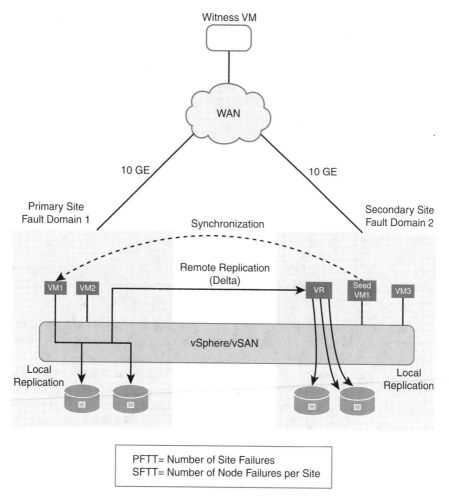

Figure 12-6 *Stretched Clusters*

The stretched clusters are extended across sites with near proximity, such as in metropolitan area networks or campus networks. Stretched clusters provide simple disaster recovery or maintenance windows where one site is down and the second remains active. Stretched clusters use active-active protection by having the VMs spread out between the two clusters. Protection of the VM is done locally, as in traditional protection within a cluster or on a site level. If the site fails, the VM is automatically restarted at the remote active site using high availability (HA). For zero RPO disaster recovery for tier-1 applications, vSAN uses synchronous replication between the stretched clusters. As such, the write operation must be performed locally and remotely and be committed before an acknowledgment is sent back to the application. This puts restrictions on the roundtrip time over the WAN, which should not exceed 5 milliseconds, and the need for high-speed 10 GE links between the sites.

In addition to synchronous replication, VMware uses an asynchronous replication method via the Site Recovery Manager (SRM). With asynchronous replication, as soon as the write is committed locally, an acknowledgment is sent to the application. After that, replication to remote sites can be scheduled based on set intervals to meet certain RPOs. The VMware SRM replication works at the individual VMDK level and allows setting of the RPO from 5 minutes to 24 hours. It also allows the creation of multiple points in time (MPIT) recovery points to revert to previous states. This relaxes the restrictions about the round-trip delay and distances between the sites because the replication is scheduled and not real time. A combination of vSAN synchronous replication and asynchronous replication via SRM can meet the needs of different applications. vSAN replication is also integrated with the policy manager, allowing replication based on VM set policies.

For remote replication, vSphere does an initial full synchronization between the source VM and its remote copy (replica). To speed up the process, a seed replica is placed remotely via different means such as manual configuration, FTP, an ISO image, a VM clone, and more. The seed copy is then synchronized with the source VM. This is shown in Figure 12-6, where VM1 has a seed replica in the secondary site and is synchronized with the replica. If VM1 fails or the whole primary site fails, the replica is immediately started.

After full synchronization is done between the local and the remote VM, only delta changes are sent to the remote site, which minimizes data that is sent over WAN links. Replication with SRM is done by having an agent inside vSphere. The vSphere kernel tracks the writes done to protected VMs and only replicates the data blocks that have changed. This ensures faster RPO because only changes are passed remotely. The changes are replicated to a vSphere replication (VR) appliance that sits remotely and adds the data to the remote replica. Advanced data optimization such as deduplication and compression can also be applied before replicating, with the restriction that vSAN supports deduplication only on all-flash configurations.

Note that each data center is put in a separate fault domain. One of the sites is considered primary, and the second site is considered secondary. The primary site is chosen if there is network disconnect between the two sites. A third site is needed to have the "witness" host. The witness host, which is none other than a VM running on a server, has a copy of the metadata of the VM objects. The witness acts as a tiebreaker when connection between the sites is lost. The witness host first attempts to form a cluster with the preferred site unless there is a network disconnect between the witness and the preferred site. In that case the witness forms a cluster with the secondary site. Whenever network connectivity is restored, the two sites are resynchronized.

Fault tolerance between the sites and within each site is affected by PFTT and SFTT. The PFTT as applicable to stretched clusters indicates the number of "site" failures a VM can tolerate. The stretched cluster's PFTT is either 0 or 1. As mentioned, in stretched clusters each site constitutes a fault domain. However, unlike the case of a regular cluster, vSAN allows host protection via replication of objects within the fault domain. This is done via SFTT, which indicates the number of host failures that an object can tolerate in the local cluster. SFTT has a default of 0 and a maximum of 3. For EC, the maximum SFTT is 2. If PFTT = 1 and SFTT = 2, for example, then the VM can tolerate one site failure and two host failures in the local cluster.

Another storage policy that is applicable to stretched clusters is Affinity, which allows you to restrict VM objects to a selected site in the stretched cluster. Affinity can be set to None, meaning that the objects can be in either site; Preferred, meaning the objects are restricted to the preferred site; or Secondary, meaning the objects are restricted to the secondary site. However, this only applies when PFTT is 0, meaning that the objects are not protected at the site level.

Stretched clusters have optimization to ensure that the bandwidth of the WAN link is not wasted. As discussed for zero RPO targets, VMware recommends at least 10 Gbps bandwidth between the sites and less than 5 ms latency round trip time (RTT). For the witness node, the connection to any of the sites should have at least 100 Mbps bandwidth and less than 200 ms latency RTT. WAN bandwidth is expensive, and data optimization is a must. For example, when I/O reads are complete, care is taken to have the objects read from within the site and not across sites. If object replication is made, only one copy is sent across the WAN link, and then that copy is replicated locally in the other site. When doing writes, however, I/O must still be sent across the WAN and acknowledgments received across the WAN to ensure synchronization.

vSAN Backup for Disaster Recovery

vSAN backup for disaster recovery is called vSphere Data Protection (VDP). It is based on VMware's parent company EMC Avamar backup, deduplication, and recovery software. vSphere uses the EMC software with certain limitations on functionality and backup capacity. For a full-fledged backup, vSAN replicates the data to the actual EMC Avamar backup appliances to take full advantage of the software functionality. vSphere uses the concept of a VDP appliance that is deployed as a VM on the local site as well as the remote. For special applications such as Microsoft Exchange Server, Microsoft Structured Query Language (SQL) Server, and Microsoft SharePoint, special agents are deployed inside these VMs for better granular and consistent database backups. For Microsoft SQL, as an example, the agent leverages the Virtual Backup Device Interface for backup and restore for databases in standalone configurations and clustered environments.

In general, the traffic is first backed up locally and then replicated to the remote VDP appliance, which updates the data in the remote location. Advanced data optimization techniques are applied at the replicated data, such as compression, deduplication, and encryption. It is worth noting that the EMC Avamar software uses variable-length deduplication, unlike the fixed-size block deduplication that is normally done in the native HCI software. Variable-length deduplication achieves better deduplication because it identifies more similar data patterns; however, this is done at the expense of added CPU overhead. This is illustrated in Figure 12-7.

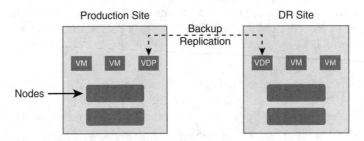

Figure 12-7 *vSAN Disaster Recovery*

A combination of data replication (synchronous and asynchronous) and data protection is used for the same vSAN cluster, where some applications have their data replicated to remote sites, whereas other applications have their data backed up locally and then to the remote site. Notice that the lines between remote replication and backup for disaster delivery are blurring on the high level. However, the devil is in the details. Software backup companies have invested a lot of time optimizing their software with added functionality and scale to meet rigorous data backup needs. HCI vendors are working to include such functionality natively. Some start-up companies in the HCI space have built a SDS file system and are just focusing on backup and data replication for secondary storage rather than virtualization and primary storage. These companies are including functionality such as versioning and indexing to be able to restore specific files rather than doing full-blown restores. Other functionality includes analytics on the backed-up data.

It is worth listing some of the functionality inside EMC Avamar to give you an idea of the maturity of the backup software. Companies such as Veeam, Zerto, and others also offer advanced solutions. Some of the functionality follows:

- Cloud data protection through integration with the EMC data domain to allow enterprises to copy local backups with Avamar to the public cloud, such as AWS.

- Failover to the cloud and failback in case of disaster recovery scenarios.

- Hashing on a file-segment level to ensure that the same data is backed up only once.

- Variable length deduplication working on variable block sizes to better capture duplicated data.

- Instant recoverability by backing up a VM on an EMC data domain and using vMotion to restore the VM into the production site.

- Encrypted replication for multisite data recovery.

- Integration with VMware to take advantage of Changed Block Tracking (CBT) for faster backup and recovery with intelligent load balancing across multiple proxy VMs. Integration with VMware vRealize Automation (vRA) and vCloud Director (vCD).

- Integration with Hyper-V/Microsoft Azure Cloud.

- Integration with KVM and OpenStack data protection extensions.

- Backup of NAS and SAN environments.

As you can see, the use for third-party applications for backup software opens a flood of functionality.

Integration with Legacy SAN and NAS

The integration between legacy SAN and NAS with the hyperconverged infrastructure is crucial. Many enterprises, while opting to deploy HCI, still want to leverage the legacy infrastructure. After all, a lot of money and effort were invested in the legacy, and although inefficient, it is already paid for. vSAN integrates well with legacy SANs using methods that are covered next.

vSAN iSCSI Target

The vSAN iSCSI target service allows hosts that are physical or virtual acting as iSCSI initiators to use vSAN as an iSCSI target. This allows devices to transport block-level data to the vSAN iSCSI target. One or more iSCSI targets that are identified by an iSCSI qualified name (IQN) are defined, offering the initiator one or more logical unit numbers (LUNs) per target. The size of the LUNs is defined, and storage policies are assigned for the LUNs. The vSAN targets are discovered by using the IP address of any of the hosts in the vSAN cluster. If multiple IP addresses are used to identify the target, multipathing is configured to allow multiple paths to reach the target. Also, target initiator groups (TIGs) are configured to allow specific initiators to reach the vSAN iSCSI targets.

The vSAN iSCSI target, as of vSphere 6.7, supports legacy clustering methods such as Windows Server Failover Cluster (WSFC). This legacy clustering allows physical or virtual WSFC iSCSI initiators to use the vSAN cluster as a target storage for failover services.

vSAN and VVols

The concept of VMware Virtual Volumes (VVols) was explained in Chapter 4, "Server Virtualization." It is worth noting that vSAN and VVols can coexist in the same vSAN cluster because they are both under vSphere. However, vSAN and VVols are two different things. vSAN is based on an object-oriented file system that builds its datastore from DAS, whereas VVols are object-oriented volumes that are built from legacy shared SAN storage. Although both can exist in the same cluster, vSAN cannot leverage SAN disks to augment the vSAN datastore. However, VMs in the cluster have visibility to both types of datastores, in the same way a VM in the cluster has visibility to LUNs built via tradi-tional NFS and iSCSI protocols. The common denominator between vSAN and VVols is that they both work under the same Storage Policy-Based Management (SPBM), where VMware assigns storage policies per VM. For example, if you define a set of policies for a VM such as availability or data optimization, VMware can apply these policies to a VM if a VM is moved from a VVol-based datastore to a vSAN-based datastore. This allows easy migration of VMs and their data from legacy SAN environments to vSAN.

SMB and NFS Support

vSAN uses a proprietary protocol to build the object-based datastore in the cluster. vSAN does not use any of the Network File System (NFS) and Server Message Block (SMB) protocols. So, unlike what you saw with HyperFlex, where through the Hyper-V and Microsoft Server 2016, an SMB datastore can be created and leveraged for shared folders, vSAN does not support such services natively.

Instead, vSAN relies on add-on virtual storage appliances (VSAs) such as Dell EMC Unity VSA [1]. Such a controller allows vSAN to be used as an SMB or NFS datastore to deliver NAS-type services.

Persistent Storage for Containers

As with other HCI vendors, VMware invested in delivering container-based services in vSphere and vSAN. As discussed with HyperFlex, solving the problem of persistent storage with containers is on everyone's agenda. VMware Project Hachway addresses the persistent storage issue for containers as of vSphere release 6.7. This release offers persistent storage for containers in a vSAN environment and provides integration between vSAN and container orchestrators such as Docker Swarm and Kubernetes.

vSAN Management

Provisioning management and monitoring is a huge topic. This book spent a couple of chapters on this topic with HyperFlex. This section does not go into the details but highlights some of the important packages to look at when comparing vSANs with the HCI vendors. vSAN offers access into the clusters via different methods, including user interface (UI), application programming interfaces (APIs), and PowerCLI as a command-line interface (CLI). It also offers tools for ease of installation, health and performance diagnostics, unified management, analytics, and root cause analysis. vSAN tools are offered from on-premises as well as cloud management software. Let's examine a few of these tools.

Graphical Interfaces

vSAN, as in vSphere in general, supports the vSphere Web Client for configuration and monitoring purposes. However, as of vSphere release 6.7, a new UI HTML5 interface was introduced. The HTML5 is a redesign of the user interface that gives the vSAN users a more intuitive and simple way to manage and display the different system functionality and status.

Ease of Installation

As of vSphere 6.6, VMware delivered to its customers a tool, Easy Install [2], that simplifies the installation of the vSAN cluster. It allows the installation on a single host, a vCenter Server Appliance (VCSA) and vSAN, allowing the user to bootstrap the deployment of a greenfield vSAN cluster.

Cloud-Connected Health Checks

vSAN uses the vSAN Support Insight [3] as a next-generation platform to analyze the health, configuration, and telemetry data of a vSAN cluster. Once it's enabled, the log information is automatically pushed to the VMware Analytics cloud for processing. This checks information such as hardware compatibility, network connectivity and settings, system device health checks, and more. The new checks are delivered through the vSphere web client and automatically updated without having to upgrade vSphere or vSAN.

Performance Diagnostics

vSAN offers performance diagnostics to analyze the performance of a vSAN cluster. The performance diagnostics compare the performance of an existing cluster against predefined benchmarks using tools such as HCIBench. The benchmark could be set to predefined metrics such as highest performance or lowest latency. The result of the analysis is shown through the UI and automatically uploaded to the VMware Analytics cloud to receive recommendations on how to improve the performance of the cluster.

VMware Update Manager

vSAN can take advantage of the VMware Update Manager (VUM) [4]. This allows the cluster to be updated to the latest vSAN releases. The user receives recommendations on software updates, patches, and drivers up to the latest VMware Hardware Compatibility List (HCL) database.

vSAN vRealize Operations and Log Insight

VMware enhanced its vRealize [5] automation software in support of vSAN. vSAN vRealize Operations (vROps) gives a holistic view of all vSAN clusters. This is the analytics part of vRealize that gives information about monitoring, events history, alerting, and trending. vROps helps the user monitor the health of vSAN, how the workload performs in a vSAN environment, whether vSAN is properly configured and healthy, and so on. It also gives a unified management view for the vSAN software-defined data center (SDDC). The user can manage vSAN from the premises or use the vRealize cloud management capabilities to manage all its vSAN clusters from the cloud.

vRealize Log Insight is the forensic part of vRealize. It allows the users to automatically sort through the logs to resolve and troubleshoot issues quickly via actionable dashboards. Log Insight allows the user to sort through machine data at scale to find root cause analysis of any performance issues across physical, virtual, and cloud environments.

Thoughts on vSAN Versus HyperFlex

Both vSAN and HyperFlex are SDS products in different wrappers. VMware and Cisco draw on their own strengths to differentiate their products. The fact that Cisco was a latecomer to the market with the acquisition of Springpath gives Cisco an advantage into a highly innovative and distributed software architecture with performance benefits. Add to this Cisco's strong foothold in networking and a successful UCS platform. On the other hand, VMware is a pioneer in software virtualization and has done several enhancements to vSphere ESXi to improve its performance. VMware is also making a big push into host-based networking, an area where VMware was traditionally weak. The fact that VMware is part of Dell EMC gives VMware a large channel for selling its software products.

It is worth noting that VMware vSAN faces competition from its own Dell EMC mother company as well. Dell EMC does not have an attachment to any of its products. It is sales and channel oriented, which creates some confusion at the customer level. If you look at the partnerships, merger, and acquisition history, in 2013 EMC acquired ScaleIO, a company building virtual SANs out of direct-attached servers. In 2014, Dell struck an OEM agreement with Nutanix to build the Dell XC product line based on Dell servers and Nutanix software. In October 2015, Dell struck a deal to acquire EMC. In December 2015, EMC struck a deal to acquire VMware.

Today Dell EMC is juggling between vSAN, ScaleIO, the Dell EMC XC series based on Nutanix, and its traditional converged products based on VxBlock. The positioning from Dell EMC is nothing short of theatrical, and it goes something like this at a high level. If you want a solution that is die-hard vSphere and ESXi and does not scale to a large number of nodes, vSAN is your choice. If you want a solution that scales to thousands of nodes and supports ESXi, Hyper-V, KVM, Linux, and containers, ScaleIO is your choice. If you want a solution that supports Hyper-V and other hypervisors than ESXi, the XC series with Nutanix is your choice. If you want a specialized solution for large enterprises that is custom made for specialized applications, convergence with VxBlock is your choice. Let's leave it at that.

This next section avoids vendor bashing per se and gives you some bullet points to think about when trying to evaluate your vSAN versus HyperFlex solution. Differentiation based on bullet-point functionality is a moving target. Whatever HyperFlex does not have today, it will have in a future release, and the same goes for vSAN. The highlight of this section is on some fundamental architecture differences that can affect a vendor positively or negatively. This is to help you ask the right questions from your favorite vendors and challenge them to get answers that are beyond the marketing jargon that you hear repeatedly.

Hardware Comparison

vSAN is a software solution that depends on third-party hardware. VMware attempted to build its own hardware appliance EVO and failed. Therefore, when speaking of vSAN, consider the following:

- Off-the-shelf components that are certified by VMware for vSAN

- Third-party systems from Cisco, Dell, EMC, HP, IBM, and others that are certified by VMware to run vSAN

- Integrated systems such as VxRail or VxRack, where VMware and EMC work closely to create highly integrated products

If you want to compare HyperFlex to vSAN, the closest apple-to-apple comparison is between HyperFlex and VxRail. Both products are appliance based and come integrated and ready to go. However, Cisco seems to be more aggressive on the hardware front in adopting and using the latest in CPU processing and memory from Intel. The fact that the Cisco HyperFlex hardware is homegrown gives Cisco headway in producing hardware appliances compared to VMware, which has to co-engineer VxRail with EMC.

When it comes to other vSAN hardware solutions such as those from approved off-the-shelf server vendors and off-the-shelf approved components, this is really asking for a big headache. The build-it-yourself model is not for the faint of heart, and other than the fact that it moves away from SAN, it still inherits all the complexities of multivendor integration and headaches.

Scaling Up

With HyperFlex, Cisco limited the choices that the user can make on the hardware: smaller systems with the HX220 and larger systems with the HX240. Also, Cisco allows the mixing of different generations in the same cluster, such as M4 and M5, but it does not allow the mixing of different series such as HX220 and HX240 in the same cluster. The reason behind this is that the more you give the user flexibility to have major variations in the number of disks between nodes, the more performance inconsistencies occur. Take, for example, a cluster where some nodes have eight HDD disks with 2 TB each, and other nodes have two HDD disks with 8 TB each. In principle, these nodes have the same storage capacity, but the nodes with two HDDs will perform much lower on reads and writes compared to the nodes with the eight HDDs. This is because with HDDs, input/output operations per second (IOPS) increase with the number of disks because you can leverage simultaneous reads and writes from all disks. Also, with even-load distribution, the 1 TB disks fill up much faster than the 8 TB disks. So, soon enough, the system will have the smaller disks full and will rely on a small number of large disks.

vSAN, on the other hand, supports the concept of disk groups, where each group is an SSD cache and seven capacity disks. With disk groups, vSAN can scale up the hardware up to 5 × 7 = 35 disks per node. More flexibility gives the users more chances to make mistakes. Also, VMware cautions against not having uniform systems in the cluster.

Although disk groups are supposed to increase the flash for performance and the number of capacity disks, the dos and don'ts list that comes with disk groups would make the user think twice before using them.

For example, the failure of the SSD cache disk in a disk group renders the disk group unusable. If the SSD cache fails, you automatically lose seven other capacity disks. If you loaded the disk group with high-capacity HDDs or high-capacity SSDs, the chances of losing and having to build a big chunk of your data all at once increase.

For storage engineers, this is kind of unheard of with traditional SANs. Normally with storage arrays, there is a tight hardware and software integration, whereby if a disk fails it is simply decommissioned and the data is backed up by other disks. However, in the vSAN architecture, the SSD cache device is the king of the disk group; everything hinges on it for the capacity disks in the group. This raises the question of whether the file system is really distributed or based on single system file systems. With HyperFlex, the controller considers the cache disks of all nodes as a single cache. If a cache disk fails, you just send your I/O to other cache disks in the cluster.

vSAN In-Kernel Versus Controller-Based Solutions

Having the storage file system and services as part of the hypervisor kernel as in vSAN versus controller based such as with Cisco, Nutanix, and others is an ongoing debate. VMware claims that embedding functionality in vSphere gives more performance to I/O handling. With an embedded approach, VMs exchange I/O directly through the kernel, whereas with controller VMs, the I/O must go from VM to hypervisor to controller and then to the hypervisor and back to controller and then the VM. This seems to be the headline slide in most vSAN presentations. Also, VMware claims that having dedicated controllers like Cisco data platform controller or Nutanix CVM consumes more CPU resources and memory that lowers the number of VMs to be serviced on a node. VMware gives the example that vSAN requires a minimum 32 GB of memory and consumes only 10% of the CPU resources. Cisco HyperFlex requires 48 GB of memory for HX220 and 72 GB of memory for HX240. For CPU, HyperFlex recommends dedicating 8 vCPUs for the controller.

In principle, the first point that I/O takes an extra step in and out of the hypervisor is true. However, saying that this extra step will affect the system performance is a major overstatement. I/O through the system takes many steps in and out of queues starting from the VM, through the hypervisor, and through the different disks and network interface card (NIC) controllers and into the network and back again. Any of the extra layers can be detrimental to the performance if done incorrectly. Cisco, for example, states that the distributed file system in HyperFlex is built from scratch for load distribution, whereas other file systems are single-node that just use mirroring on other nodes. So, the statement that in-kernel is better than controller based is simplistic. Many of the vSAN services run as VMs and are not in-kernel, and the same reasoning applies for such services.

The argument that controllers require more CPU and memory might be a valid point; controllers require some extra horsepower. However, unless you can get into an apple-to-apple comparison into what services the controller is offering versus what services the in-kernel is offering, it is unfair to label controllers as CPU and memory guzzlers. For example, a controller could be doing inline deduplication and compression all the time, but the hypervisor is not. As a matter of fact, VMware states that if deduplication and compression are on, up to 10 more percent of CPU could be needed. Also, a controller could be doing checksums all the time as it should, while this needs to be turned on with vSAN. The controller could be doing management functions, while with vSAN these could be additional VMs that are not part of the hypervisor. So, in general, a vSAN implementation could be consuming as much memory or CPU as HyperFlex or other HCI implementations and even more, depending on what features are turned on.

Another point worth discussing is the overall stability of the system for in-kernel versus controller based. When the SDS software is in-kernel, any bugs that affect the storage software can cause the hypervisor to fail. In that case, the whole node and its VMs fail. However, with the controller approach, any bugs in the controller software could cause the controller to shut down or reboot without affecting the VMs as the I/O is redirected to other controllers.

Also, when looking at in-kernel versus controller, keep in mind that not all users who deploy HCI want to be on the vSphere bandwagon. There are other hypervisors, such as Microsoft Hyper-V and open source KVM, that come with their own set of benefits. Microsoft's support for Hyper-V and Microsoft Server 2016 gives Microsoft applications a home field advantage when run in private or public Azure clouds. KVM, on the other hand, is open source and is finding a lot of acceptance even with cloud providers. So, having a storage system use data controllers, with the flexibility to decouple services from the virtualization software, is not to be understated. However, if all you have or will ever have is tied to VMware and vSphere, integrating vSAN with vSphere is a plus.

Chapter 9, "Cisco HyperFlex," discussed some performance benchmarks done by HyperFlex that showcased its ability to handle almost three times the VMs for certain levels of latency using VMware ESXi and separate controller VMs. Engineers and market-ers can debate the validity of these tests and whether they reflect real-time applications or are just benchmarks. However, the take-away is that statements of in-kernel versus con-troller being better or worse are not that straightforward to anchor your differentiation.

Distributed Versus Not-So-Distributed File System

One area that is worth discussing is the distributed nature of file systems. On the surface, it looks like all HCI vendors are doing practically the same thing: replicate the data in one or two places to ensure availability, and stripe the data across disks to enhance I/O performance. Use a cache layer for performance, and then destage to a capacity layer. However, if you look closely at vSAN versus HyperFlex, there is a big difference in the two approaches.

vSAN, PFTT, and the number of stripes per object were discussed. The PFTT mirrors the data over additional nodes, and the number of stripes stripe the data over different capacity disks that could be in the same disk group or different disk groups, or in the same node or different nodes. However, the preference per VMware is to leave the number of stripes per object to 1, meaning do not stripe. VMware recommends that data stripes not be increased unless the user determines that the application performs better with data stripes applied. Again, this goes against the fundamentals of HCI, where the system is supposed to make the administrator's life easier by automatically improving performance and not having the user make the tough decisions. If the number of stripes is 1, it means the VM is mostly serviced by the two or three nodes that have the mirrored data. This could create hot spots while other nodes in the cluster are idle. VMware argues that, in the case of hybrid clusters, if a VM is not I/O heavy, striping the data could cause more harm than good because it increases the likelihood of misses in the read cache, which would translate into an access to the HDDs in the capacity tier. So again, leaving such decisions to the end user to stripe or not to stripe and not addressing them automatically with software goes against the simplicity of HCI.

With HyperFlex, on the other hand, the basis of data distribution is to have all data striped across all cache of all nodes and all capacity drives, regardless of the replication factor. Such data distribution makes better use of all the available cache in the system to lower cache misses and eliminate hot spots. HyperFlex keeps an index via hashing of all data stripes within the cache and capacity disks, and that index is known by every node. For example, if there is a cache miss on a certain node, the node easily knows whether the data exists in the cache of any of the other nodes, again leveraging the cache of the full cluster, not just the mirrored nodes.

One-to-One Versus Many-to-Many Rebuild

When a node fails and the VM is moved to another node, most HCI systems wait for a certain period of time such as one or two hours to see if the failure persists. After that time, the HCI systems restart rebuilding the lost data. This rebuild process can be CPU intensive and might disrupt running applications depending on the implementation. With vSAN, the replication process is a one-to-one process from node to node. Normally, the node that still has copies of the components rebuilds them to another node. With the HyperFlex distributed architecture, where the data is spread to all nodes in the cluster, the replication is many-to-many, where all nodes participate in the replication, alleviating hot spots.

Implementations of Compute-Only Nodes

One major roadblock for vSAN is the adoption of compute-only nodes, both technically and commercially. From a technical point of view, because vSAN is integrated with the hypervisor kernel, compute-only nodes require the full vSAN stack to be part of the cluster. Although it is possible to deploy compute-only nodes with vSAN, it creates major imbalances between the nodes, where some nodes have lots of disks and others have none.

From a storage point of view, such an imbalanced storage configuration can cause performance side effects. In VMware's documentation, it is advised not to build imbalanced configurations.

In HyperFlex, on the other hand, the compute-only nodes are integrated using the IOVisor, which is a lightweight shim layer. As such, compute nodes do not create storage imbalances and blend in with the architecture.

From a commercial point of view, vSAN is licensed per CPU socket, regardless of whether the node is compute plus storage or compute only. HyperFlex has licensing per compute plus storage physical node and no licensing for compute-only nodes. So, deploying vSAN in a compute-heavy environment is not price efficient. Having said that, pricing is not permanently fixed, and VMware might or might not change its pricing structure. So, pricing remains a differentiation until it is changed.

Advanced Data Services

Both HyperFlex and vSAN support advanced data services, although their approach is much different. HyperFlex deduplication and compression are embedded into the architecture and are always on. Due to the highly distributed architecture, in which every node in the system is used to access the node, deduplication and compression are accomplished cluster wide. Cisco received some flack because some applications such as databases would rather have deduplication and compression off because of the adverse performance impacts for such services. However, Cisco's response is that in HyperFlex, deduplication and compression have no performance impacts because they are native to the architecture and not bolted on later. Also, Cisco believes that if a user is given a choice to turn deduplication and compression on or off, knowing that on means bad performance for the system, the user will keep these services off. Also, Cisco has not yet developed EC, claiming that deduplication and compression on the cluster level provide enough capacity savings that would outweigh performance impacts caused by EC and parity. Cisco needs to address the issue of EC and its performance because EC has major capacity reduction benefits. Cisco EC is slated for future releases.

vSAN, on the other hand, gives the user the option to turn deduplication and compression on or off. However, deduplication and compression might adversely affect the performance of some applications. Also, VMware decided to run such services only on all-flash clusters and not on hybrid clusters. In addition, the vSAN deduplication and compression are performed on the disk group level and not on the cluster level. This means that deduplication and compression are not global to the cluster but only done on the host level, which is inefficient. Another caveat is that with vSAN, when deduplication and compression are enabled, a failure of "any disk" inside a disk group will cause a total failure of the disk group because of how data is spread on the disks. With such restrictions, when deduplication and compression are turned on, any disk failure capacity or flash renders a whole disk group down. Add to this the reluctance of turning on the services due to potential performance impacts; this will deter the users from taking advantage of such functionality.

On the other hand, vSAN does support EC, another performance hog, which offers ample capacity savings. However, this does not make up for deficiencies in deduplication and compression because such services are needed for efficient backups and replication between clusters and the cloud.

Management Software

Both HyperFlex and vSAN have an advanced suite of software tools and packages to size, install, provision, monitor, and manage HCI clusters. The software packages can be deployed on-premise as well as from cloud environments. Cisco Connect and vSAN HTML5 offer an advanced HTML5 interface with dashboards for monitoring the status and health of the cluster. Cisco Intersight and vSAN vRealize allow the unified management of HCI clusters locally and from the cloud.

Cisco and VMware are pushing into the cloud management area to enhance application performance because they realize that application performance is key to any successful deployment. However, it is important to note some differentiation that gives Cisco an edge.

The Cisco UCS service profiles are unique to Cisco in offering a simple way to scale compute and networking. This gives a structured way to define servers and networking in software and to scale the deployments of large installations. VMware and most other vendors lack in that area and have been relying on Cisco UCS to offer their compute bundles. With Cisco Intersight, such capabilities are now offered from the cloud for large-scale deployments that are uniform and systematic.

Also, Cisco has made a large investment by purchasing AppDynamics, putting major emphasis on the business aspect of tracking the performance of applications. The variations in application performance affect the adoption of such applications. A website that experiences a slow shopping cart or a slow checkout heavily affects the user experience negatively and deters a user from coming back. With Cisco AppDynamics, the root cause analysis of any performance issue is determined down to the code level. The performance of the application is benchmarked to understand any deviations when an application is accessed from different locations in the network.

Networking

Finally, the battle between host-based networking and switch-based networking continues. VMware is placing all its eggs in the host-based networking basket via the network virtualization and security platform (NSX), where the networking control and forwarding planes are done in software, inside the hypervisor. Cisco puts a lot of emphasis on the application-centric infrastructure (ACI) by automating the deployment and enhancing services in the leaf/spine switch fabric that connects the HCI nodes. Both NSX and ACI come with elaborate ways for setting networking policies and automatic configuration.

Although Cisco has a lot of mileage in the networking space, VMware is playing catch-up. You would have to expect that when it comes to deploying advanced networking services, Cisco is ahead. However, on the flip side, VMware has a lot of mileage in virtualization and has direct touch into the host and the application. With Cisco's Tetration platform and AppDynamics, Cisco is getting closer to the application and the host, where VMware was always rooted.

Looking Ahead

This chapter briefly discussed the VMware vSAN HCI implementation and compared it to HyperFlex. Cisco and VMware are not the only HCI players out there as the HCI market continues to heat up. Other leading players such as Nutanix are challenging the incumbents in the software-defined storage area.

Chapter 13, "Nutanix Enterprise Cloud Platform," goes over the Nutanix Enterprise Cloud Platform implementation similar to what was done for vSAN. Nutanix is challenging the incumbents on multiple fronts, in the software-defined storage as well as with hypervisor virtualization.

Chapter 14, "Open Source—Compute and Storage," briefly covers OpenStack and the different initiatives that are developing in the software-defined storage area.

Part VI of this book goes into further detail of hyperconverged networking, discussing implementations such as Cisco ACI, VMware NSX, and open source OVS/OVN.

References

[1] https://www.emc.com/products-solutions/trial-software-download/unity-vsa.htm

[2] https://storagehub.vmware.com/t/vmware-vsan/vsan-support-insight/

[3] https://storagehub.vmware.com/t/vmware-vsan/vsan-6-6-proof-of-concept-guide/

[4] https://www.vmware.com/support/pubs/vum_pubs.html

[5] https://www.vmware.com/products/vrealize-suite.html

Chapter 13

Nutanix Enterprise Cloud Platform

This chapter covers the following key topics:

- **Nutanix Enterprise Cloud Platform:** Describes the Nutanix Enterprise Cloud Platform (ECP) software components.

- **ECP Hyperconvergence Software:** Describes the distributed storage fabric and its elements. This includes the different cluster components, details on how the physical drives are segmented, the I/O path, and data protection.

- **ECP Advanced Data Services:** Describes capacity optimization techniques, such as deduplication, compression, and erasure coding. You also see details about snapshots and clones, stretched clusters, and data at rest encryption. Also described are block and file service, support for Hyper-V, and containerized environment.

- **Provisioning, Managing, and Monitoring:** Describes briefly the Prism management system and a description of the different tools and packages used for management and orchestration.

- **The Nutanix Competitive Landscape:** Describes Nutanix's competitive position in the market as well as differentiation between ECP and the Cisco HyperFlex platform.

Nutanix was founded in 2009 and is one of the leading players in the hyperconvergence space. Nutanix started with a hardware and software solution that combined compute and storage in a modular 2 Rack Unit (RU) appliance and a distributed storage file system. Nutanix was one of the early comers in the hyperconvergence space, and it brought attention to this market as a viable alternative to the legacy storage area network (SAN) and network-attached storage (NAS) markets.

In November 2017, Nutanix announced that it would adopt a software-centric strategy and that open source code would be a major piece of the company's pure software play. In a way, Nutanix always focused on the software aspect of hyperconvergence and worked with many hardware original equipment manufacturer (OEM) vendors such as Lenovo and Dell EMC. One of the joint products that found success on the market was the Dell EMC XC Series, which runs the Nutanix software.

Nutanix is growing its software portfolio and competing on multiple fronts. Nutanix is competing with VMware ESXi with the Acropolis Hypervisor (AHV), which is based on kernel-based virtual machine (KVM). The Nutanix software-defined storage (SDS), Acropolis, competes with vSAN and the HyperFlex HX Data Platform software. On the networking front, Nutanix is working hard to improve its networking portfolio by using Open vSwitch (OVS) open source. This is not a small undertaking; even VMware had to acquire software companies to get the NSX network virtualization and security portfolio in shape. Nutanix uses OVS for the distributed virtual switch as a starting point for networking. In 2018, Nutanix announced Flow, a software-defined networking solution that allows policy setting and enforcement at the virtual machine (VM) level. As of the writing of this book, Flow is comparable to NSX's policy-based management portion, but it is still based on OVS and VLANs with basic L2 switching capabilities.

The following section discusses in detail the Nutanix components, the distributed file system, and the advanced data services. It does not cover Nutanix's hardware in solidarity with the Nutanix's decision to be more software focused.

Nutanix Enterprise Cloud Platform

The Nutanix Enterprise Cloud Platform (ECP) is divided into a suite of management, planning, and automation products called Prism and a suite of virtualization and software-defined storage products called Acropolis. The Nutanix high-level enterprise cloud portfolio is seen in Figure 13-1.

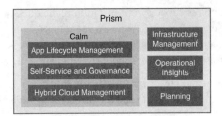
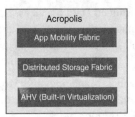

Figure 13-1 *Nutanix Enterprise Cloud*

Nutanix was one of the early vendors that released solutions that support multiple hypervisors: ESXi, Hyper-V, and XenServer. Nutanix also evolved the CentOS KVM hypervisor, hardened it for enterprise environment, and released it as its own AHV. Other than the technical advantage of having a home-grown hypervisor, there is a big commercial advantage because AHV is license free compared to the hefty prices enterprises pay for vSphere ESXi, which is licensed per CPU socket.

Also part of the software architecture, Nutanix built an abstraction layer called the Application Mobility Fabric that sits between managed objects such as VMs, containers, volumes, and the hypervisor itself. This gives the flexibility for applications that leverage such objects to move between the same hypervisor or different hypervisors in the same cluster or even a private cluster and the cloud. This chapter primarily focuses on the SDS architecture, and it briefly touches on the management and orchestration tools. Many of the technical details in this chapter are extracted from *The Nutanix Bible* [1], which goes into much more depth. Although this book does not cover the nuts and bolts of the architecture, it attempts to stay at the same level of details as HyperFlex and vSAN for comparison purposes. Also, it briefly scans through functionality that was already covered with Cisco and VMware so it does not become too repetitive.

ECP Hyperconvergence Software

Nutanix was one of the pioneers in building HCI software. The ECP hyperconvergence software is formed via multiple elements, including a distributed file system that creates the storage pool and a set of modules to handle I/O management, storing the metadata and handling replication and load distribution. Next, you see a detailed description of such elements, including the read and write I/O path and how data is replicated for protection within the cluster.

Distributed Storage Fabric

The distributed storage fabric (DSF) is the Nutanix distributed file system (originally called NDFS). Similar to other hyperconverged infrastructure (HCI) implementations that require a virtual storage appliance, Nutanix uses a controller VM (CVM) on every node to run the file system. Nutanix allows multiple hypervisors, including VMware ESXi, Microsoft Hyper-V, XenServer and the hardened CentOS KVM as its own Acropolis hypervisor AHV. The CVMs are clustered and work together to form the DSF, as shown in Figure 13-2.

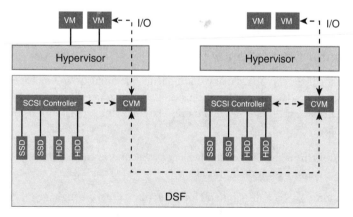

Figure 13-2 *Nutanix DSF*

The CVM allows Nutanix to implement the data services features such as deduplication, compression, replication, and more. The CVM also defines the I/O interfaces between the hypervisor and the DSF. Nutanix supports multiple interfaces; examples are Network File System (NFS), Internet Small Computer System Interface (iSCSI), and Server Message Block (SMB).

Unlike other vendors that have upper limits on the number of nodes in a cluster, Nutanix does not specify an upper limit when using its own KVM-based hypervisor AHV. However, when using vSphere ESXi, Nutanix specifies the VMware limit, which is 64 nodes per cluster. For edge nodes, Nutanix started with a 3-node limit as a minimum and then later introduced 2-node and 1-node edge implementations. Although Nutanix is getting out of hardware itself, its software supports OEM configurations for storage-heavy nodes, compute-heavy nodes, and compute plus storage nodes.

The DSF defines multiple high-level constructs such as these:

- **Storage pool:** Includes the physical drives such as the solid-state drives (SSDs) and hard disk drives (HDDs).

- **Container:** A logical pool of VMs and vDisks that are presented to the hypervisors as datastores (NFS, SMB, iSCSI).

- **vDisks:** Files larger than 512 KB that include the .vmdk files. vDisks are built using extents.

- **Extent:** 1 MB of "logical" contiguous data. An extent is formed with a number of contiguous blocks, depending on the size of the block of the guest operating system (OS). Typical sizes of blocks are somewhere between 4 KB and 8 KB. Extents are read, written, or modified using "slices." Slices are also somewhere between 4 KB and 8 KB. Extents are distributed over extent groups for data slicing over multiple physical disks.

- **Extent groups:** 1 MB or 4 MB of "physical" contiguous data. The extent groups represent contiguous chunks of data on the physical disks, and the extents are spread over multiple extent groups using slices. The hierarchy is better explained visually in Figure 13-3.

Nutanix Cluster Components

The Nutanix cluster comprises many components, including an I/O manager, a database that holds the metadata, a configuration store, a MapReduce framework, a replication manager, a management gateway, and more. The following are definitions of some of the components.

- **Stargate:** This is the I/O or data manager. It facilitates the NFS, iSCSI, or SMB3 requests coming from the hypervisor.

- **Cassandra:** This is a distributed Non Structured Query Language (NoSQL) metadata store for keeping all cluster metadata key-value pairs in a ring-like structure. It is based on a modified Apache Cassandra database.

- **Zookeeper:** This is the configuration store that keeps configuration information for hosts, disks, IP addresses, and so on.

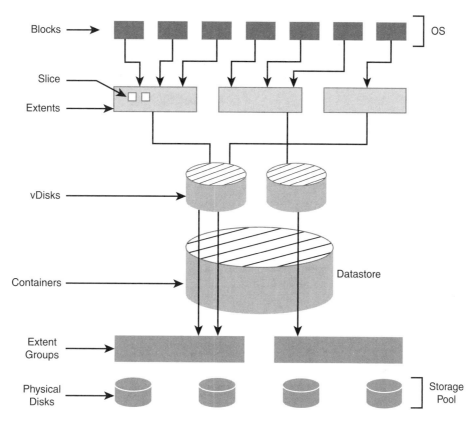

Figure 13-3 *The Nutanix Filesystem Breakdown*

■ **Curator:** This is a MapReduce Framework that is responsible for managing and distributing tasks throughout the cluster. Map Reduce is a framework that splits tasks into smaller chunks that are processed in parallel in a cluster. The curator also handles functions such as disk balancing, data scrubbing, data tiering, and data rebuilds in case of disk or node failure.

■ **Cerebro:** This is the replication/disaster recovery (DR) manager responsible for the scheduling of snapshots and the managing of replication and DR activities to remote sites, as well as data migration and failover. All nodes run the Cerebro engine and participate in the replication to remote sites.

■ **Prism:** This is the management gateway for administrators to configure, manage, and monitor the nodes. It provides interfaces via Nutanix command-line interface (NCLI), graphical user interface (GUI) via HTML5, as well as application programming interface (API) access.

A complete list of components is described in *The Nutanix Bible* [1].

Physical Drive Breakdown

The physical drives in a Nutanix cluster are segmented as follows to house the different components, such as CVM, cache, and persistent storage. All calculations are in gibibytes (GiB) rather than gigabytes, where 1 GiB = 1024 MB, as shown in Figure 13-4.

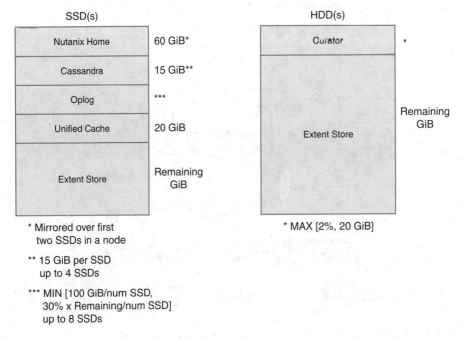

Figure 13-4   *SSD and HDD Breakdown*

The different segments that constitute the SSDs and HDDs include the home of the controller VM, the metadata store, a persistent write buffer, a dynamic read cache, persistent storage, and a MapReduce cluster management and cleanup. This is described next:

- **Nutanix Home:** This is where the CVM lives, and it is allocated 60 GiB out of the SSD storage. The Nutanix home is mirrored over the first two SSDs in a node.

- **Cassandra:** This is the metadata store that contains all relevant information about the data, such as its location on disk, a fingerprint that specifically identifies the data, and so on. Metadata is assigned 15 GiB per SSD. If there are two SSDs, Cassandra is mirrored and consumes 15 GiB per SSD. If there are four or more SSDs, Cassandra is shared by up to 4 SSDs for a total of 60 GiB.

- **Oplog:** This is the area of the SSD that is used as a persistent write buffer to coalesce the data before it is written to the extent store. The size of the Oplog per node is dynamic and is taken as 30% of the capacity of the formatted SSD after deducting the size of the Nutanix home and Cassandra, or a minimum of 100 GiB. The Oplog capacity is distributed over up to 8 SSDs in a node.

- **Unified Cache:** This is the portion of the SSD that is used as a dynamic read cache. It spans the memory allocated to the CVM and the SSD. The size of the content cache is 20 GiB.

- **Extent store:** This is the portion of the SSD or HDD that is used for the persistent storage. It is worth noting that the extent store in a Nutanix node could be a combination of SSDs and HDDs for hybrid nodes, or SSD only for all-flash nodes. This is different from what you saw with HyperFlex and vSAN, where a hybrid node uses only HDDs for capacity. As such, the Nutanix architecture for hybrid nodes has a touch of "storage tiering," which was discussed in Chapter 2, "Storage Networks: Existing Designs." In storage tiering, data moves between HDD and SSD tiers depending on frequency of access.

- **Curator:** This is the MapReduce cluster management and cleanup. For HDDs, a portion of the storage is reserved for curator storage and is allocated (depending on the Nutanix software release) the maximum of 2% of disk capacity or 20 GiB on a single HDD in a node. The curator runs on every node, and a master is elected. If failure occurs, other curators perform the task.

I/O Path

The I/O path in Figure 13-5 describes the path a write and read takes throughout the system. Notice that a Nutanix hybrid node uses both HDDs and SSDs for the capacity tier, which is different from what you saw with HyperFlex and vSAN.

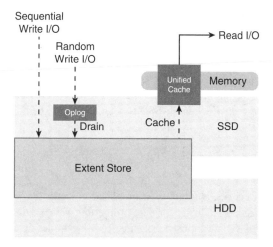

Figure 13-5   *I/O Path*

Write I/O

When the guest OS requests an I/O write, the path the write takes depends on whether the data is sequential or random. Data is deemed sequential if there is a certain outstanding amount of I/O to be written, such as 1.5 MB of data. If the data is sequential, then the write goes straight into the extent store. If the data is considered random, the write goes into the Oplog, where the data is coalesced before it is drained into the extent store. When the data is written into the Oplog, it is synchronously replicated to another node's Oplog for availability. The Oplog write buffer is allocated per vDisk, where an upper limit is set (such as 6 GB, depending on the Nutanix software release) per vDisk. The decision of whether the data goes into the SSD portion or the HDD portion of the extent store is based on a decision taken by the information lifecycle management (ILM), which decides whether the data is hot or cold depending on the frequency of access of the data.

To maintain data integrity, a checksum is applied on the data and then saved in the metadata. Whenever the data is read, the checksum is calculated to see if it matches what was saved in the metadata. If the checksum is the same, the data is valid and there is no corruption. If the checksum does not match, there is data corruption and the data needs to be brought from elsewhere in the cluster.

Deduplication and compression on write I/O is covered in the next sections.

Read I/O

The unified cache, which spans both the CVM memory and SSD, services all read I/O requests. Upon a read request, if the data is not already in the unified cache, it is decompressed and moved from the extent store into the unified cache. The data is moved into the cache at a 4 KB granularity. If data still exists in the write buffer (Oplog) and is not yet drained to the extent store, reads are serviced from Oplog.

The unified cache is divided into three tiers. The first tier, which Nutanix calls the single touch pool, is a small portion of the CVM memory. This pool is used for the hottest data that is most frequently accessed. The cache uses a least recently used (LRU) counter to decide whether the data needs to be evicted or kept inside the in-memory cache. For subsequent read requests, the data will be put into the multi-touch pool, which spans both the CVM memory and the SSD. Also, LRU is used to decide whether the data moves into the third tier, which is the SSD tier. So, in a way, the hottest data always moves to the highest cache tier, where it is serviced faster.

Data Protection

As with other HCI vendors, Nutanix uses a replication factor (RF = 2 or 3, and so on) to replicate the data inside the cluster for data protection. When data is written into the Oplog of a node, it is synchronously replicated to other nodes depending on the RF. If RF = 2, then in addition to the copy written on the local node, the data is replicated to another node. If RF = 3, the data is replicated to two other nodes, and so on. When replicating, the CVMs of the other nodes where the data is being replicated are involved in the replication process. After the data is replicated to the remote nodes, an acknowledgment is sent to the source to indicate that the write operation is complete.

Metadata

Nutanix puts emphasis on how it keeps track of the metadata, especially in a distributed file system. Metadata needs to be accurate, consistent, and scalable. Different scenarios must be handled, such as multiple sources trying to write the same data at the same time, data being modified in the middle of a read operation, and so on. So, it is paramount to properly synchronize the data and metadata access because multiple sources are constantly modifying data.

Nutanix DSF applies a lock at the vDisk level. Only the owner of the vDisk where the VM is running can remove the lock. This ensures that the data is being accessed by only one source at a time. In most cases, the vDisk is not shared between nodes, so the vDisk lock also ensures that the metadata is only accessed by one node at a time. However, in cases such as snapshots and deduplication or when the vDisk is moving between nodes, the metadata might be accessed simultaneously for read/write by multiple nodes. So, another mechanism must synchronize the metadata for multiple concurrent access and allow it to roll back to a previous state if a failure occurs in the middle of metadata modification.

Nutanix has built its metadata based on the Apache Cassandra NoSQL key-value store, with added modification for consistency, performance, and reliability to ensure the accuracy and proper handling of the metadata. The metadata is kept in a ring-like structure, and the metadata is replicated to multiple nodes for protection. The metadata is not kept on every node but rather an odd number of nodes (3, 5, and so on) based on what RF is used for protection. Upon a write or modification of the metadata, the metadata is written first to the local node and then replicated to other peer nodes in the ring depending on the number of replicas to be used. DSF assumes that any modification for the data itself results in a modification of the metadata key to ensure that the metadata is accurate. DSF uses atomic compare and swap (ACS) for synchronizing writes for the metadata keys. DSF also uses the Paxos distributed consensus protocol to ensure that one key is chosen at any time. DSF ensures high performance in applying the consensus protocol and consistency guarantees for write-after-write, read-after-write, and read-after-read scenarios. Some of these scenarios, such as read-after-read, prove to be extremely tricky. As an example, when doing a replication and the write I/O fails on one node but succeeds on another, this creates inconsistencies if the data is being read again. In summary, Nutanix considers metadata handling and its adoption for multiple services such as storing configuration for VMs as one of its differentiators.

Availability Domains

In the same way that you saw vSAN and HyperFlex adopt availability domains, Nutanix has the concept of availability domains in term of nodes, blocks, and eventually racks. A *block* is defined as a four-node chassis that is populated with at least three nodes. The data is replicated into nodes that are in different blocks, so if a full block fails, such as multiple nodes in the same chassis, the replicated data is available on other blocks. Nutanix uses the concept of availability domains to protect the data, metadata, and configuration files. If you take what was previously discussed about metadata being in a ring-like structure, when copies of the metadata are done, they are spread out in different blocks to ensure that no two consecutive metadata in the ring fail if one block fails.

Data Path Resiliency

Ensuring instant recovery after a component failure, with no data loss, is essential in any HCI implementation. The Nutanix DSF protects against different types of failures at the following levels:

- Disk level
- Node level
- CVM level

A disk is considered failed if it was proactively removed, has a dye failure, exhibits high latency and errors, and so on. Upon disk failure, the Curator or MapReduce framework looks at the metadata to identify the data that was affected based on the disk failure. Based on this information, the Curator redistributes the replication tasks to the nodes where the disk is to be replicated. It is important to note that all CVMs can be involved in the replication so a single node is not overloaded and the time for replication is reduced.

Upon a node failure, high availability (HA) is invoked to move the VMs running on the failed node to other nodes. Similarly, the Curator looks at the metadata to identify all disks and data that were affected and orchestrate what nodes need to be involved in the replication of the data to ensure the required resiliency factor.

Upon a CVM failure, the I/O that the failed CVM served is redistributed to other CVMs. The mechanism of redistribution is done according to the hypervisor. In the case of ESXi or Hyper-V, the I/O is rerouted to the IP addresses of the new CVMs. This is called *CVM Autopathing*. Once the CVM is back online and is stable, the I/O goes back to the original CVM. In the case of AHV/KVM, iSCSI multipathing is used. The primary path is the local CVM, and the remote paths are used as backup if the primary fails. When the original CVM is restored, the primary path is taken.

Nutanix Advanced Functionality

As with other HCI vendors, Nutanix implements a set of advanced data services that include capacity optimization with deduplication, compression, and erasure coding. Advanced functionality also includes disk balancing, storage tiering, snapshots and clones, backup, and disaster recovery.

Deduplication

Nutanix uses what is called a hybrid approach for deduplication, meaning a combination of post-process and inline deduplication depending on whether you are doing a write or a read. In summary, Nutanix does not do inline deduplication on writes; post-process deduplication is done on writes inside the capacity tier, and inline deduplication is done only on reads.

This is an area of controversy, especially the post-process versus inline deduplication on I/O writes. There are write-ups galore in this area from different vendors, and it is interesting that each vendor describes only selective knobs to make one approach better than the other.

With Nutanix, a write is done either to the write cache (Oplog) for random writes or directly to the extent store on sequential writes. A SHA-1 hash is done to create a fingerprint on the data. The hash is done when the data chunk is 64 KB or larger and the hash is done at 16 KB granularity. If hashing is not done on the data because it is in smaller chunks (less than 64 KB), hashing can be done post-process in the extent store. The resulting key is stored persistently in the metadata store. However, the data itself is not deduplicated on write; rather, it is drained as is from the cache to the capacity tier. If deduplication is turned on, the deduplication is done as post-process on the capacity tier by leveraging the keys that are stored in Cassandra, the metadata store. This process is done in the background and does not interfere with the writes happening in real time. Nutanix also tracks the frequency of a fingerprint key being used for deduplication. If the key is not used that often, it is removed from the metadata store to minimize the overhead. All nodes in a cluster participate in the deduplication process, which is done globally in the cluster.

This is much different from what you saw with HyperFlex. In HyperFlex, when doing a write, the metadata is calculated and the data is compressed in the write cache buffer but is not deduplicated. However, when the data is drained into the capacity tier, inline deduplication is applied, and the data is deduplicated right from the start.

Nutanix handles the read differently. When a read is requested, the data is deduplicated inline and put into the unified cache which, as explained before, is a multi-tier cache that spans memory and SSD. Any further reads get the deduplicated data from the unified cache. This is similar to HyperFlex except that HyperFlex structures its read cache differently.

Data Compression

Another area of data optimization is data compression. Nutanix does data compression inline and post-process via its Capacity Optimization Engine (COE). Compression can be turned on and off, while post-process compression is turned on by default. Let's look at the I/O path in both the write and the read scenarios for inline and post-process.

In the case of inline compression, large I/O is sent to the COE to be compressed in memory, and then it is moved to the extent store. For smaller I/O or random I/O, the data is sent to the Oplog, where it is coalesced and then sent to COE to be compressed in memory and then written to the extent store. If you compare this with Cisco HyperFlex, the process is kind of similar because HyperFlex also compresses the data inline while writing it in the write-log buffer.

With Nutanix, post-process compression is turned on by default. In the case of post-process compression, the data path is like what was described in the "Write I/O" section, where large writes go directly into the extent store and random or small writes go into the Oplog. After that, in hybrid nodes, the ILM migrates the data from SSD to HDD as it gets cold. Once in HDD, a configurable timer is checked to decide when to compress. Based on this time delay, the data is sent to the COE to be compressed and then sent back to the HDD portion of the extent store. During post-process compression, all nodes become involved in the compression process.

In the case of a read request, if the data is in the HDD, it is sent to the COE to be decompressed, and then it is directly read. If the data is hot, the ILM moves the data into the SSD portion and then sends it to the COE engine for decompression. From then on, the data is read based on what was described in the "Read I/O" section, where data moves between the different content cache tiers depending on the frequency at which the data is accessed.

Erasure Coding

Nutanix uses EC to offer protection for the data at the VM level while optimizing for disk storage. Similar to RAID 5 or 6, EC encodes a strip (a collection of stripes across the different nodes) and calculates parity. Each data block is an "extent group," and each data block must be on a different node and belong to a different vDisk. This ensures that the data is spread out between the different physical disks. Nutanix uses EC only on write-cold data, meaning data that was not written to for more than one hour and is already residing in the extent store. This ensures that EC is done post-process to lessen the computational impact on the running applications. The Curator (MapReduce Framework) scans the write-cold data in the extent store and looks for data where EC can be applied depending on the different k/m factors. Because this can be done per application/VM, one VM could have EC 3/1 to reflect an RF = 1 protection, and the other VM could have EC 4/2 to reflect an RF = 2 protection. It is recommended to have at least one extra node—that is, k + m +1—to allow the rebuilds of the other nodes upon a node failure. So, EC 3/1 requires 3 + 1 + 1 = 5+ nodes, and EC 4/2 requires 4 + 2 + 1 = 7+ nodes.

Disk Balancing

The Nutanix DSF allows mixing of heterogeneous nodes that offer compute-heavy or storage-heavy configurations. As data is spread out in the cluster, there is a need to rebalance the storage in the cluster to ensure that all resources are utilized efficiently. Such situations occur, for example, when scaling out a cluster and a storage heavy node is added. At that point, the storage of that node is empty while other storage is overutilized. This is illustrated in Figure 13-6.

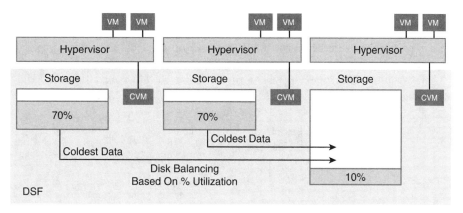

Figure 13-6 *DSF Disk Balancing*

Notice that the addition of a storage heavy node gives the opportunity to offload some of the nodes that already reached a certain level of storage utilization. If such a node reaches a level of utilization of configurable value then DSF identifies the coldest data (data that was not written to in a certain amount of time) and moves that data to the newly added storage to rebalance the system.

Disk balancing uses the Curator (MapReduce Framework) as a scheduled task or when a certain level of disk utilization is reached. In some cases, where some nodes are getting a very high write activity, the disk balancing is activated to offload the cold data and allow room for newly added data. In other cases, it is possible to add storage only nodes, and use such nodes to keep the cold data, offloading other systems that are having high storage utilization.

Storage Tiering

Nutanix DSF utilizes the storage pool for cache tiers, SSD tiers, and HDD tiers cluster wide. Any node in the cluster can leverage the full cache, full SSD, or full HDD across the cluster. In addition, DSF tries to utilize SSD as much as possible for hot data because it gives the best performance for I/O. In the case of SSD, if the utilization on a certain node exceeds a certain configurable utilization threshold, the data from the SSD is migrated to other SSDs using the disk balancing that was discussed earlier. In addition, as the data gets cold, the ILM starts migrating the data from the SSD tier to the HDD tier to free up SSD resources. Because the intent is to keep the data on SSDs as much as possible, the amount of data moved from SSD to HDD depends on the SSD's utilization level. For example, if the SSD is 95% utilized, 20% of the coldest data is moved to the HDD tier. However, if the SSD is 80% utilized, only 15% of the coldest data can be moved.

Snapshots and Clones

Nutanix uses the redirect on write (ROW) method for snapshots and clones, as explained in Chapter 2. The starting point for VM data is the base vDisk, which references via a block map the different extents that form the vDisk. The block map is the metadata mapping of the vDisks to its extents. This is illustrated in Figure 13-7.

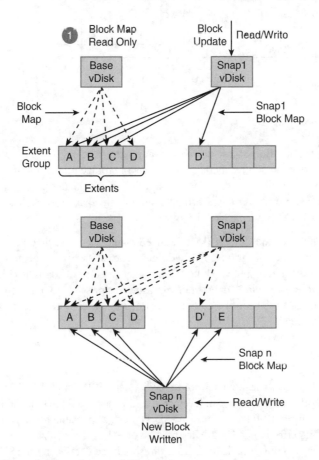

Figure 13-7   *Nutanix Snapshots and Clones*

Whenever the first snapshot Snap 1 is taken, the block map of the base vDisk is marked as read only so the blocks cannot be modified. Another vDisk that is specific to Snap 1 is created and inherits the block map of the base vDisk. As such, Snap 1 has its own vDisk—let's call it Snap1-vDisk—and has its own block map—let's call it Snap1-block-map. From then on, any read/write to the data is done in Snap1-vDisk, and the Snap1-block-map is modified to change the pointers from the original blocks to the changed blocks. It is worth noting that, unlike other implementations of snapshots such as VMware's replication where ROW is used, the concept of parent/child chains does not exist in the Nutanix implementation. As you noticed, each snapshot has its own vDisk and its own block map. As such, each snapshot is self-sufficient, and it has all the information that leads to the data without resorting to its parent. This allows the creation of a multitude of snapshots without the performance impact caused by chaining the snapshots. If more snapshots are created, the new vDisks are created, and a new snapshot inherits the block-map of the older snapshot, does new read/writes in its own area, and updates the pointers.

The process of making clones is like making snapshots. Unlike traditional clones where data is mirrored, the Nutanix clones are also done by using metadata and pointers without moving any actual data. Basically, when a VM is cloned, the block-map of the base vDisk is kept as read only, and the clone inherits the block-map of the base vDisk. Further clones of the original VM are created the same way, and each has its own vDisk that it reads and writes to, and its own block-map. When cloning a clone (not the original VM), two vDisks and block maps are created. One of the block-maps points to the original VM, and another block-map points to the clone that you want to clone.

Shadow Clones

The concept of shadow clones allows distributed caching of vDisks in a multi-reader scenario, when a large number of VMs is trying to access the same disk. A sample environment is the virtual desktop infrastructure (VDI) that was described in Chapter 12, "VMware vSAN" Cloning. In that situation, all VMs send read requests to the base vDisk, which constitutes the parent VM. Because Nutanix is high on data locality, the system monitors the local CVM, where the base vDisk exists, as well as remote CVMs. If the same vDisk is accessed by the local CVM and at least two remote CVMs, and all access is read request I/O, the base vDisk becomes a candidate for a shadow clone. In this case, the base vDisk is cached locally for any CVM that is sending it the read requests. This local caching of vDisk is called a shadow clone. The process continues as long as the base vDisk is not modified. If the base vDisk is modified, the shadow clones become inconsistent with the base vDisk, and all shadow clones are removed. The process restarts with the new updated vDisk.

Era Database Services

As an enhancement to its replication and cloning services, Nutanix introduced the Era software package to enhance provisioning and management of databases. The explosion in the number of database instances that IT must manage made the job of IT extremely challenging. Thousands of database instances with their associated files must be provisioned, managed, refreshed, restored, and more. Many of these databases live on disparate legacy systems, which makes the management task more difficult. The database data could be spread over multiple disks and storage systems depending on the type of information such as data files, logs, and backups. Add to this that the database administrator must create snapshots and clones of everything and back up the data, with the ability to restore any older information if problems occur.

As such, Nutanix introduced Era, which is a suite of software that automates database management. The package allows administrators to perform database provisioning, cloning, refreshing, and restoring databases to any point of time, thereby simplifying the database lifecycle management.

Backup and Restore, Replication, and Disaster Recovery

A *protection domain* (PD) in Nutanix is a grouping of VMs or files that must be protected (replicated) together, where a PD is assigned a replication schedule. The PD can be applied to a full container or to a select group of VMs and files. The replication schedule is flexible; hourly, daily, or weekly replication can be assigned. Also, variations can be done, in which an X number of snapshots can be taken and a Y number of these snapshots replicated to site 1, and a Z number replicated to site 2.

Multiple consistency groups (CGs) can also be configured per protection domain. The CGs contain VMs/files that are crash-consistent, which means that when these VMs/files are recovered, they come up in a consistent state. During failover, all VMs in a PD can fail over, or a select number of VMs. This type of application-aware DR is powerful compared to older techniques, where disaster recovery was done at the logical unit number (LUN) level. The PDs and CGs are illustrated in Figure 13-8.

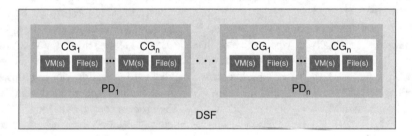

Figure 13-8 *Nutanix DR Construct*

The Nutanix DSF uses the Replication and Deduplication Manager (Cerebro) to perform snapshots, remote replication, and disaster recovery. Unlike other implementations that perform node-to-node replication, Nutanix can handle node-to-node, many-to-one as in hub and spoke, or many-to-many as in a mesh replication.

Cerebro runs inside every CVM, where every node participates in the remote replication process. A Cerebro master is elected, and the rest of the nodes in the cluster run a Cerebro slave in their CVMs. If the master fails, a slave is elected as the new master. The Cerebro master decides which data to replicate, such as data that was modified, and shares the task with all other CVMs in the cluster to perform the replication. The Cerebro engines in both master and slaves inform the I/O manager (Stargate) which data to replicate and where. The Cerebro master interacts with another Cerebro master that is elected in the remote site. The remote master shares the replication task with all the Cerebro slaves in its local site. This is illustrated in Figure 13-9.

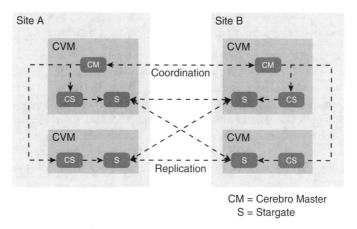

CM = Cerebro Master
S = Stargate

Figure 13-9 *Nutanix Replication Architecture*

Different replication configuration is adopted in case a full mesh of replication is not possible. A proxy can be elected on the remote site to perform the coordination with the local Cerebro master and the I/O managers of the local slaves. The proxy in turn coordinates with the remote Cerebro master and I/O managers to perform the replication. SSH tunneling is used between local and remote sites to allow similar coordination.

As far as knowing what data to send remotely and what not to send, the same concept of global deduplication is used. Before sending data to the remote site, DSF queries the data on the remote site to check whether a fingerprint exists. If so, the data is not sent because it already exists on the remote site. If there is no fingerprint, the data is compressed and sent to the remote site.

The Nutanix Replication and DR also leverage public clouds, such as Amazon Web Services (AWS) and Azure. Replication and DR to public clouds is revisited in Part VII of this book after AWS functionality is further explored.

Metro Availability: Stretch Clustering

Like HyperFlex and vSAN, Nutanix supports the concept of a stretched cluster, which allows compute and storage to be stretched between two sites. In this way, VM HA is across sites. Each site works independently, and the data containers are synchronously replicated between sites. This means that when a write is done, it is synchronously replicated to the remote site before the writes are acknowledged. In the case of a site failure, HA causes the VMs on one site to be restarted on the other site. With a link failure between the two sites, take care not to get into a split-brain scenario where each site restarts the VMs of the other site. You will end up with the same VMs running on both sides. In this case, either manual intervention is needed to disable the metro availability, or a third "witness" site must be available to select which site to run.

Replication does not come free; it takes its toll on the CPU as well as the wide area network (WAN) bandwidth if it's used between remote sites as in stretched clustering.

Different types of replications are adopted to minimize the impact while maintaining certain recovery time objectives (RTOs) and recovery point objectives (RPOs).

Asynchronous replication has a minimal effect on running read/write I/O but incurs a high RPO—near a one-hour period. With asynchronous replications, vDisk-based snapshots are taken. Replicating such snapshots to remote locations can take up to 60 minutes. Also, because the replication is done for a protection domain and consistency groups, you would see big spikes in CPU and bandwidth over WAN links. However, because the administrator is more relaxed about the criticality of the application, asynchronous replications are timed whenever the administrator sees fit, such as on off hours when the systems are not heavily used. Asynchronous replication is not sensitive to latency because it doesn't affect the real-time write I/O.

On the flip side, synchronous replication is normally used for critical applications that can require zero RPO and near zero RTO. For such applications, the replication is done in real time, and the write must be acknowledged from the remote site before the write is committed. This type of replication is sensitive to bandwidth and latency, and that is why vendors recommend no less than 10 GE bandwidth for WAN links and no more than 5 ms latencies over the WAN.

Nutanix also implemented what is called a *NearSync replication*, which uses lightweight snapshots (LWSs). NearSync gives an RPO between 1 minute and 15 minutes. This method is more of a compromise between asynchronous and synchronous replication. The LWSs are taken inside the write cache buffer (Oplog) of the SSDs and not inside the extent store as in normal vDisk-based snapshots. When an I/O write is taking place, the system keeps markers on the I/O so it can take intermediate snapshots. These snapshots can be replicated to other Oplogs of other nodes local or remote. When snapshots are configured with a frequency ≤15 minutes, the system enters the NearSync replication mode. The system first takes a vDisk snapshot. If the snapshot is done in less than 60 minutes, the system starts the NearSync process and takes another vDisk snapshot while taking intermediate LWSs. When the second snapshot is finished, the LWSs become valid and the system is in full NearSync mode. If the NearSync snapshots start exceeding 60 minutes, the system reverts back to vDisk-based snapshots.

Data At Rest Encryption

In addition to supporting self-encrypting drives (SEDs), Nutanix added support for data at rest encryption in software. This is like the vSAN encryption software implementation, so the details will not be repeated. The encryption is FIPS 140-2 certified and done via a third-party key management server (KMS) or local key generation.

Nutanix Acropolis Block Services

Nutanix has the flexibility to support bare-metal servers via its Acropolis Block Services (ABS). Via ABS, legacy applications that have a restriction of using physical servers use block-level iSCSI to access the Nutanix clusters. Storage on the cluster is presented in the form of LUNs. The legacy infrastructure can be on standalone physical servers or in a virtualized environment. Examples of such applications are Oracle Real Application Clusters (RAC), Microsoft Structured Query Language (SQL), and IBM DB2.

Nutanix ABS manages the storage allocation via volume groups (VGs). A VG is a collection of vDisks that is presented to VMs and bare-metal servers as LUNs. However, the Nutanix implementation avoids the need to use multipathing I/O (MPIO) software in clients. As explained in Chapter 2, MPIO is needed on clients because the initiator (client) can reach the iSCSI target via multiple paths, and MPIO helps in load-balancing the traffic over all the paths. Nutanix uses the concept of a data services IP, which is a virtual IP address for the whole cluster. The iSCSI initiator is configured with the data services IP as the target portal, where all the LUNs can be reached. This shields the host from the internals of the cluster (and which CVM and Stargate I/O manager are used to reach the target). The login from the initiator to the data services IP is redirected to a CVM/Stargate I/O manager. If, for example, the CVM and therefore the Stargate I/O manager that is being used fails, the next login from the initiator to the data services IP is redirected to a healthy CVM/Stargate.

In essence, the ability of Nutanix to deliver block services on its clusters allows an easy migration for legacy applications from a traditional storage array set up to a hyperconverged infrastructure.

Nutanix Acropolis File Services

The Nutanix cluster delivers file services similarly to NAS. Different file servers are deployed, where users store home directories and files. This allows the delivery of file services such as Windows directories, shares, user profiles, and so on. Multiple file servers are deployed on the same Nutanix cluster, with each file server having its namespace and with complete isolation between the different namespaces. This is seen in Figure 13-10.

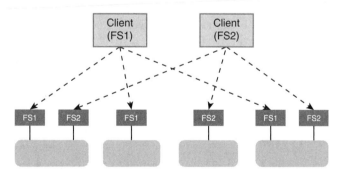

Figure 13-10 *Different File Servers on the Same Nutanix Cluster*

Each of the file servers is run using three different file server VMs (FSVMs) that are spread out over different nodes for redundancy. Each FSVM requires a minimum of four vCPUs and 12 GB RAM. It is possible to scale out a file server by adding more FSVMs or by adding more vCPU and memory to existing FSVMs. The file services are fully integrated with Microsoft Active Directory (AD) and DNS, which allows the leveraging of authentication and authorization capabilities of the AD. At the front end, the client can leverage the full file-sharing capabilities, such as namespace, shares, and folders. On the back end, the Nutanix Acropolis Block Services give the file system access to a distributed storage system with added redundancy. The interaction between the FSVMs and DSF is seen in Figure 13-11. Notice that the clients have access to three different IP addresses that represent the FSVMs. The client does not need to see all three IPs because the system redirects to the correct FSVM.

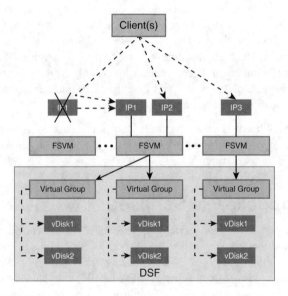

Figure 13-11   *FSVM Connectivity to DSF*

The FSVMs connect to the back end block services via the virtual groups that contain the vDisks. If FSVM failure occurs, the IP is redirected to different running FSVMs.

The file system inherits all the advanced data services capabilities of the Nutanix cluster, including native backup and disaster recovery, file-server cloning, file-level recovery, storage optimization such as deduplication, compression, EC, and so on.

Support for Hyper-V

Nutanix was one of the early vendors to support multiple hypervisors, including ESXi, Hyper-V, XenServer, and Nutanix's own AHV based on KVM. Nutanix offered early on support for Microsoft Windows Server 2012, whereas other vendors waited until the introduction of Microsoft Windows Server 2016 because it constitutes a major architecture overhaul. With the release of the Acropolis OS (AOS) version 5.5, Nutanix introduced support for Microsoft 2016 with the ability for its users to easily upgrade from 2012 to 2016.

Nutanix Windows Server 2016 implementation uses Discrete Device Assignment (DDA) to allow pass-through between the CVM and the PCI devices such as disks. This is like using VMDirectPath in the ESXi environment and allows the CVM to bypass the hypervisor for reaching the disks. DDA gives better storage performance improvements.

With Windows Server 2016, security is paramount. Because Nutanix presents storage to Hyper-V as an SMB3 share, authentication must be done via Kerberos, which Nutanix enables by default.

Windows Server 2016 presents a new configuration file format for VMs. The new configuration files are stored in binary files with a .vmcx format. Nutanix enhanced its data protection workflows to support the new format when doing snapshots as well as asynchronous and synchronous replication for disaster recovery between clusters supporting Microsoft Server 2012 and 2016.

With Window Server 2016, Nutanix supports Data Protection Manager (DPM) hypervisor-level backup for VMs. Also, Nutanix uses the resilient change tracking (RCT) feature, which is native to Windows Server 2016. RCT is like the changed block tracking (CBT) feature in ESXi that allows the tracking of delta changes when doing snapshots and backup. By adopting the Resilient File System (ReFS) block cloning technology to store incremental backups, you drastically improve the storage performance for backups.

Docker Containers

Nutanix supports docker containers and persistent storage. This is similar to what was discussed already for HyperFlex and vSAN. Nutanix also supports persistent storage for containers by implementing a docker volume plug-in, which creates a volume and attaches it to the container using the ABS feature. This allows the storage to persist, even if the container is terminated.

Provisioning, Managing, and Monitoring

Nutanix deviates from other HCI vendors by creating its own management system, called Prism. As seen, for example, with HyperFlex, Cisco adopted well-known virtualization management platforms such as VMware vCenter as a starting point and augmented it with different software packages. Nutanix, however, uses its own Prism management platform.

Prism is at the center of configuration, management, and monitoring of the Nutanix clusters. Prism Element is specific to a single cluster, whereas Prism Central is used to put multiple Nutanix clusters under single management. All function calls within Prism are implemented via RESTful APIs. This allows third-party software to manage and automate functions via APIs.

Prism has a distributed architecture that runs in each CVM. One of the CVMs is used as a leader and the first entry point into the cluster for HTTP requests; however, in case of a failure, another CVM is elected as a leader. Prism interacts with a distributed database to collect configuration information and with a distributed NoSQL key value store to collect statistics. Prism also interacts with the hypervisor to collect information about the VMs and their status, performance, and other related information.

Some of the high-level functionality Prism offers is discussed next.

Infrastructure Management

Prism presents via an HTML5 interface a summary of the hardware and software in the cluster, including performance reports and user alerts. This gives the user a simple overview of the cluster health and status of every component. Infrastructure management entails the following components:

- **Cluster management:** This includes information such as number of nodes, model numbers, total CPU capacity, and total available memory. This also gives a summary view on top-performing hosts in terms of CPU, memory, and I/O. If you want more details, enter table views that give full details of the resource consumption.

  An expand cluster feature allows the user to scale out the system by discovering new nodes that would be added to the cluster.

- **One-click upgrades:** The one-click upgrade is a nondisruptive workflow that allows a rolling upgrade inside the cluster on a node-by-node basis. You can use one-click upgrade for a variety of software packages, such as the AOS, the DSF, host firmware, and other.

- **Storage management:** As with cluster management, Nutanix offers a simple UI for storage management that shows storage performance charts, capacity summaries, alerts, warnings, and more. Detailed table view gives information about the volume groups, containers, and storage pools.

- **VM management:** Prism also provides a simplified view for managing the VMs in a cluster. The VM summary shows VM counts, power status, and usage stats of used amounts compared to provisioned amounts. Examples are views of CPU and memory utilization, input/output operations per second (IOPS), latency, and so on. A detailed view for each VM is also seen in a tabular form showing the difference between used and provisioned. Prism also manages the lifecycle of VMs in a mixed environment when multiple hypervisors are installed, such as ESXi and AVH. The interface allows the user to enable different processes such as taking snapshots, adding resources to a VM, vDisk operations, and more.

- **Networking:** With Prism, you can display networking stats relevant to the VMs. Such stats are taken from the virtual switches in the hypervisor or from physical switches through the Simple Network Management Protocol (SNMP). Such information includes IP addresses, media access control (MAC) addresses, sent and received packets, packet drops, and more. Prism also allows you to create new networks for the virtual machines and provide Dynamic Host Configuration Protocol (DHCP) address management for allocating IP addresses from an IP address pool.

■ **Data protection:** The data protection view offers a single point of management for asynchronous and synchronous replication as well as backups. It gives a view of pending and ongoing and successful replications. This view also summarizes the number of remote sites and failure domains. It shows the top remote sites for bandwidth consumption used for replication. This helps the user manage the amount of bandwidth being consumed for replication. The data protection view also gives tabular information about the configuration, performance, and status of the different protection domains (PDs) that provide backup and DR in the cluster. This includes information about the resources consumed by the PD, pending snapshots, time the successful snapshots were taken, and so on.

■ **User management and authentication:** Prism allows user authentication using two different methods: local authentication or directory service via Microsoft Active Directory or OpenLDAP.

Operational Insight

Nutanix also helps users manage their clusters via what is called operational insight, which offers the user gathering of alerts, metrics, and the ability to analyze data. The different elements of the operational insight include alerts, analytics, analysis, VM I/O metrics, and network virtualization, as described next:

■ **Alerts:** Prism provides different types of customizable alerts about the status of elements in the cluster. The alerts are color-coded depending on the severity of the alert, the different entities involved in the alert, the timestamp, and possible root cause analysis. Also, to help in resolution, the system gives you the most likely resolution.

■ **Analytics:** Prism keeps data based on hundreds of metrics relevant to different elements, including hosts, clusters, physical disks, vDisks, storage pools, containers, VMs, protection domain remote sites, replication links, and others. Prism draws charts for each of the elements and gathers data based on configurable intervals such as 3 hours, 6 hours, 1 day, 1 week, week to date, and 1 month.

■ **Analysis:** This gives a graphical view correlating all the data collected in one single view. This view stacks all the charts and lines them up synchronized in time. Alerts and events are shown for the different elements, and a vertical line stretched between charts correlates the alerts from the different elements. This gives you an easy way to find root cause analysis by identifying related elements that are at the root cause of the problem.

■ **VM I/O metrics:** Prism keeps track of the I/O metrics of all VMs, giving the user a historical view of the I/O behavior. These metrics include read and write performance distribution per I/O block size, average read/write I/O latency, percentage of sequential versus random read/write I/O, and so on.

■ **Network virtualization:** Prism gives a view of the interconnected components in the network. The display shows the connectivity of the VMs or groups of VMs or even hypervisors to the Nutanix nodes and through the network switches and ports. Network virtualization is currently supported only for the AHV hypervisor.

Nutanix Tools

Nutanix also developed a set of tools and technologies that help in assessing, planning, sizing, and migrating applications. To list a few:

■ **Sizing tool:** The sizing tool takes the workload as an input and recommends the configuration needed to run the workload. This helps in applications such as VDI, which are normally compute and storage intensive. The tool displays bar charts showing the capacity utilization. It gives a visual display of the nodes and racks and the ability to size multiple design scenarios.

■ **X-ray tool:** This tool provides a suite of tests for the hyperconverged environment that allows organizations to evaluate different key areas in the infrastructure lifecycle under real-world stress scenarios. After the tests are done, the tool offers easy and visual reporting of the test logs and summary reports that allow you to evaluate different hyperconverged platforms or different software versions of the same platform. Example of areas that the tool tests for are these:

  ■ Infrastructure performance

  ■ Application performance

  ■ Data protection

  ■ Infrastructure resiliency

  ■ Infrastructure scalability

■ **Xtract tool:** This tool helps in the migration of VM and database instances from an existing environment to a Nutanix enterprise cloud. The VM Xtract allows bulk migration of VMs with minimal disruption. The DB Xtract looks for different database instances and understands their configuration and performance characteristics and helps in the migration to a Nutanix cluster.

Calm Orchestration Tool

Calm offers application-level orchestration and automation to streamline the application development and delivery. Calm focuses on some key areas:

■ **Lifecycle management:** Automation of the provisioning, scaling, and deletion of applications using blueprints.

■ **Customizable blueprints:** Incorporating all elements of VM creation, configuration, and binaries into blueprints that the IT team manages. The blueprints can be reused for different development and delivery environments and by different private or public clouds.

■ **Nutanix marketplace:** The blueprints are published directly to end users via the Nutanix marketplace. This allows instant provisioning of applications upon request.

- **Governance:** Role-based governance limits user operations based on permissions. All user activities are logged, ensuring a secure environment.

- **Hybrid cloud management:** Management of applications across private clouds and public clouds such as AWS. Calm can show the utilization and cost of public cloud consumption.

Nutanix has also enhanced its multicloud portfolio through different packages, such as Beam, a multicloud optimization platform. Multicloud is discussed further in Part VII of this book.

The Nutanix Competitive Landscape

Nutanix is considered one of the leaders in the HCI space, but it faces competition on multiple fronts as it tries to establish its place among the incumbents. Nutanix is growing its software platform in multiple directions, and as such abandoned having its own hardware and decided to work with an original equipment manufacturer (OEM) such as Dell EMC, Lenovo, and others. Following is a list of some of the Nutanix software initiatives, with each being a major undertaking on its own that other vendors spent years building or resorted to acquisitions to fill the gap.

- **Virtualization:** Nutanix is trying to take VMware head on by building its own home-grown AHV that is based on KVM. Nutanix included AHV with its software free of charge. This is an attractive proposition compared to vSphere ESXi's hefty prices because it is licensed per CPU.

  As of AOS release 5.5, Nutanix has introduced AHV turbo with advanced functionality, such as parallel processing for the multitude of hardware queues presented by next-generation NVMe devices. AHV Turbo also takes advantage of newer technologies such as RDMA and 3D Xpoint in achieving faster CVM-to-CVM communication over the Ethernet fabric.

  Although Nutanix is catching up on hypervisor functionality and AHV being adopted by partners, VMware is not standing still and continues to improve functionality with vSphere. So, the hypervisor battle continues and requires a continued investment that Nutanix hopes to make up through incremental sales of the HCI software products.

- **SDS:** This is the second battle that Nutanix is fighting with its competitors as well as its partners. Because Nutanix transformed into a software vendor, it must work with channel partners in the compute and storage business. Most of these partners have their own HCI solutions. Dell EMC cooperates and competes with Nutanix on multiple fronts. The Dell EMC solutions such as VMware vSAN, ScaleIO, and converged solutions are stumbling blocks for Nutanix, which is counting on sales from the Dell EMC XC series. So, Nutanix finds fierce competition from a large Cisco UCS base and a large VMware base and cannot count on full loyalty from its OEM partners.

■ **Networking:** Although Nutanix has a lot of mileage with SDS, it is lagging in software-defined networking (SDN) and trying to catch up. VMware made an early investment in 2012 in Nicira, one of the early companies that helped develop the Open vSwitch (OVS). This translated into VMware's SDN portfolio with NSX. Cisco, on the other hand, has its roots in networking and developed its application-centric infrastructure (ACI) to automate policies and networking. To help build its networking portfolio, Nutanix is supporting OVS and open source initiatives. Nutanix introduced its Flow software, which handles microsegmentation with policy setting and enforcement at the VM level. However, Nutanix still relies on basic OVS functionality for L2 switching and has not reached an advanced stage of networking yet. With many years invested in networking, to date Cisco has the most advanced offering among all vendors. More on networking is covered in Part VII of this book.

■ **Cloud:** Another huge area in software development is hybrid cloud and multicloud. Both Cisco and VMware are investing in internal development and acquisitions in this area. This is also one of Nutanix's main initiatives. Nutanix is investing in platforms such as Calm for application-centric automation and management in a hybrid and multicloud environment. Other platforms such as Nutanix XI are targeting integration between private and public clouds, with onboarding services for backup and DR on the cloud.

Other development areas that Nutanix is working on are block, file, and object-level services. Developing NFS file sharing, for example, allows Nutanix to compete in the NAS market. Developing object storage allows Nutanix to offer object-level storage capabilities such as AWS S3. Add to this development in database lifecycle management.

The main challenge for Nutanix is to decide which areas to focus on. Investing in many initiatives at the same time requires a huge investment in engineering, sales, and support. Investments in networking alone are a major undertaking. Nutanix is fighting many battles trying to compete in networking, virtualization layers, SDS, NAS storage services, object storage services, block storage services, and more. Nutanix also announced its intension to build Nutanix XI, which allows Nutanix software to be consumed as a service by public clouds such as AWS, Microsoft Azure, and Google Cloud Platform (GCP).

The following section, like what was done for vSAN, focuses on differentiation between Nutanix Enterprise Cloud Platform and Cisco HyperFlex based on some fundamental architecture differences. Both Nutanix and Cisco are fearlessly adding more functionality in every release, so a bullet-by-bullet comparison is a moving target.

Hardware Comparison

Nutanix started with building hardware appliances in the form of a modular chassis that contains compute plus storage nodes, storage-only nodes, and compute-heavy nodes. However, soon after, Nutanix changed its strategy into a software-only approach. This puts Nutanix on par with VMware vSAN working with OEM hardware vendors and leaves Cisco HyperFlex differentiated by having a software and hardware solution.

However, when it comes to how Nutanix supports SSD, HDD, and cache, the architecture is much different from HyperFlex and vSAN.

The HyperFlex cluster is a lot more uniform. With Cisco, the cluster is either hybrid or all-flash. Within the same cluster, you can use either the HX220 series or the HX240 series, in addition to the compute nodes. With this approach, Cisco is making the nodes more uniform, avoiding variations in IOPS and latencies by mixing nodes with different numbers of disks, disk sizes, and disk performance.

Nutanix, on the other hand, offers too much flexibility in the sense that it mixes different types of nodes in the same cluster. So, hybrid nodes and all-flash nodes can be mixed. In addition, hybrid nodes have multiple SSDs that are used as a fast-performing capacity tier and HDDs as a lower performance capacity tier. The ILM software decides where to put the data.

Basically, such flexibility starts leading to non-uniform configurations and enough rope to hang yourself. A customer might add too much SSD on a single node or too little on another. In HyperFlex, for example, adding an additional hybrid node to the cluster just expands the total cache pool with the added cache SSD and increases the HDD capacity pool. While in a Nutanix setup, adding a hybrid node with a large SSD could shift much of the I/O to the SSD capacity tier of that node. If that node fails, the I/O takes a major performance hit. So Nutanix recommends adding nodes in pairs of similar capacities. In summary, flexibility is good, but it adds more restrictions that you have to manage to avoid affecting performance.

Distributed Architecture

Both HyperFlex and Nutanix have distributed architectures, but they do vary widely. HyperFlex's basic principle is uniform nodes, where data is striped across all nodes. The concept of a virtualization layer ensures that servicing the data is decoupled from where the data lives in the system. With HyperFlex, data is uniformly spread over all nodes and then replicated for availability. Writes are done on any cache buffer in the cluster.

With Nutanix, the VM data is basically in two or three locations depending on the replication factor. If the data is not found locally, the data is serviced from the other copies found in the system. Also, Nutanix checks the latencies in the system to decide whether to read locally or remotely. With different VMs running on different nodes and data replicated on multiple nodes, there is a sense of distribution and that every controller in the system is active and performing I/O. In a perfect world where all nodes are uniform and all VM workloads are the same, the behavior of a Nutanix might get close to a HyperFlex. However, the fact that Nutanix allows a mix and match of nodes with different disks and capabilities, with some VMs lightweight and others heavyweight and moving around in the system, the Nutanix and Cisco architecture will definitely diverge. With Nutanix, a heavy load consumes much of the resources of its local node and its replica, whereas with HyperFlex, the nodes are evenly loaded by design.

To get to the point where there are no hot spots, Nutanix needs to do work in the background to make sure that the data is evenly distributed, the disks are evenly used, and VMs are not creating CPU hot spots. The Nutanix Curator process, which is a MapReduce framework, rebalances the disks and makes sure that all disks are evenly utilized. However, you might still get a hot spot if the local node where the VM is running and the nodes that have the replicas are overloaded. So Nutanix has a dynamic scheduler that runs at certain intervals and checks the Stargate process utilization; if it discovers that a VM is overloading a CPU, it works on migrating the VM to other lightly used nodes. Again, with Nutanix you eventually get to an even distribution, but you have to believe that the distribution process comes at a cost in CPU resources, while in the HyperFlex model the distribution is more embedded in the architecture itself.

Log-Structured Versus Write-in-Place File System

Cisco HyperFlex highlights the fact that the log-structured file system inside the cache and the capacity tiers ensure that data is written sequentially, which increases the read/write performance in HDDs. The fact that modified data is not deleted but rather appended to the head of the log minimizes the wear leveling with SSDs.

Nutanix, on the other hand, sends large blocks of I/O directly to the capacity tier, while random I/O is coalesced first in the write buffer (Oplog) and then drained to the capacity tier. This helps in having writes being done sequentially. However, Nutanix does not elaborate much on how multiple writes are done in the capacity tier, as there is no mention of logs. So, one would assume that the model is still a write-in-place model that leads to disk fragmentation, where you would have a chunk of blocks that are written and a bunch of empty blocks in between, which is a hindrance for HDD magnetic drives. Also, for SSDs, Nutanix does not mention how data is modified, so one would assume a write-in-place model where blocks are overwritten, which can cause flash wear. Again, Nutanix deals with disk scrubbing and garbage collection using the Curator process, which is run on different intervals to do garbage collection and perform disk cleanup. In this case, one assumes that this also comes at a cost in CPU resources.

Data Tiering

HyperFlex's concept of data tiering is that hot data is in cache or in memory and cold data in the capacity tier, either HDD or SSD. With Nutanix, data tiering is more elaborate because data can be in cache/memory, in an SSD capacity tier, or in an HDD capacity tier. The ILM process monitors the frequency of data usage to decide when data moves from SSD to HDD. As mentioned already, Nutanix services the data from the local node or the remote node where the replicas exist; basically, a VM has access to its cache or its SSD capacity tier, or the cache and SSD tiers of its replicas. In HyperFlex, the VM has access to all cache in all the nodes.

Deduplication

With HyperFlex, on writes, deduplication is done inline while data is being destaged from the cache to the capacity tier. With Nutanix, deduplication on write is done post-process, based on metadata, and after the data is moved into the capacity tier. This merits a discussion on the usefulness of deduplication and which is better: inline or post-process.

Both inline and post-process, if not done correctly, cause performance issues on the system. However, vendors on either side of the aisle will argue that their side is better.

Deduplication in general causes anywhere between zero benefit to maybe 80% benefit on storage capacity. It is hard to benchmark exactly the benefits of deduplication because it depends on the data itself. Some applications, like virtual desktop infrastructure (VDI), have up to 80% storage benefit from deduplication, but if the data cannot be deduplicated to start with (for example, some small logs that are tagged with a timestamp), then applying deduplication does not help.

Also, the granularity of deduplication can have positive or negative effects on performance. Most deduplication engines today are done on fixed-size blocks in the ranges of 4 KB to maybe 16 KB. This is because working with variable-size blocks can cause major overhead on the CPU just to find the data that can be deduplicated. With fixed-size blocks, granularity matters. The smaller the block size, the more chances that common data will be found, but this is at the expense of more overhead. Each block must be hashed to find a key, and the key must be stored, so the overhead can be enormous on CPU, RAM, and disk. Couple that with data that cannot be deduplicated, and the system will slow down for no benefit. Most implementations, as shown with Cisco and Nutanix, keep an eye on the frequency of either the data or the metadata being accessed to decide whether to perform hashing. This is great for optimizing on resources.

Another issue of deduplication is whether it affects the performance on reads. Normally, best efforts are done by the file systems to make sure that the data is written sequentially. This makes the reads much faster, especially with spinning disks such as HDDs. However, with deduplication, when a block is written to disk, the next block is referenced by a "pointer" to a block that is not next to the first block. Deduplication relies on keeping pointers to existing similar blocks rather than writing the same data. So while saving on storage, the data might end up being fragmented, which hurts the read performance. Techniques such as log-structured file systems, when applied to capacity and caching tiers, do their best to keep the data written sequentially, but sometimes fragmentation cannot be avoided.

Arguments Against Post-Process Deduplication

The argument against post-process is that you lose the storage optimization from the get-go. This is because you already put all your data in the capacity storage. With inline, your initial requirement for storage is less because the data goes deduplicated into the capacity tier. This is a valid argument if you believe that deduplication on that particular data will cause major savings. Another argument is that if the capacity tier is SSD based as in all-flash storage, inline deduplication minimizes the number of writes on the flash and thus reduces flash wear. This is another valid argument, but deduplication should not be turned on as a flash wear management technique; deduplication should be turned on for storage efficiency and if the application really needs it.

The other argument against post-process is that the system will waste major cycles, reading the data once again from the capacity tier to search for duplicate patterns and remove them. This is a valid argument if the implementation is inefficient to adopt such techniques. However, as you see with Nutanix, the deduplication is not done by reading the data, but rather scanning the metadata; based on hash keys, duplicated data is removed. This is more efficient than reading the actual data and indexing it on the full cluster, but still there is overhead for accessing metadata in the capacity tier (versus cache) to perform the deduplication. Even if this process is done as a background, it still consumes CPU cycles.

Arguments Against Inline Deduplication

The argument against inline deduplication is twofold. The first argument regards whether inline deduplication is "always on," and the second argument is whether inline deduplication slows down the write process. Some databases do not get major benefits from deduplication because relational databases, for example, store data in tables with unique keys and checksums, making the data unique to start with. Other cases involve encrypted data that cannot be deduplicated. Applying always-on deduplication on systems that might not need it, although good for minimizing flash-wear, might have adverse effects. Now if the vendor, as in the case of Cisco HyperFlex, can show that always-on inline deduplication causes minimal performance hits and minimal use of resources, always-on inline is acceptable.

Another argument against inline deduplication is that it has a performance impact because it is done in real time while the data is being written. This is a valid argument if deduplication slows down the write process. However, as shown with the Cisco HyperFlex implementation, the data is written first into a write cache buffer, where in parallel it is replicated to the remote systems. Then when the data is ready to be destaged, it is deduplicated while moving it into the capacity tier. This hardly affects the running application performance in any shape because the system acknowledges the writes while the data is still in cache and moves on to another I/O operation. In this case, there is no issue with inline deduplication.

To conclude, Nutanix deduplication techniques on write are different from other approaches such as HyperFlex. Both inline and post-process techniques have their advantages and disadvantages. It all depends on whether the implementation of either one is good or bad. The main goal should always be a balance between storage optimization and performance optimization, with minimal use of CPU and RAM resources.

Data Locality

Data locality is one of the hot buttons with Nutanix that in one way differentiates it from many HCI implementations but also earns it criticism in the way data locality has negative performance effects. The notion of data locality is broad and can be taken in many directions; some negatively affect performance.

To explain the basics, data locality states that it is always better to have the data closer to the VM that needs it, meaning on the local host where the VM is running. Although this might be true, for that particular VM, and in case the local system is not already overloaded, many situations would arise that would cause a diverse effect.

Just make sure you don't make the wrong assumption. The way Nutanix describes its implementation of data locality should not cause the adverse effects that many of its competitors claim. The approach that Nutanix takes is that the first copy of any write is done on the local system and then replicated throughout the system. When doing reads, Nutanix prefers to have the "hot" data read locally. Any data that is hot is moved 1 MB at a time to the local system, and remote data that exists beyond the needs of the replication factor (RF) is deleted. Also, Nutanix has implemented some algorithms in which, if the delays in local reads exceed the delays in the remote reads, the data is read remotely. When a VM is moved in the system, Nutanix tries to place the VM on the system that has the most available local data. Basically, the attacks on Nutanix in this area are unwarranted as long as data locality is handled properly.

Data locality and its pros as explained by Nutanix are discussed next. The negative effects of data locality, if not implemented correctly, are covered also.

Pros of Data Locality

Because data locality promotes having the data closer to the VM, there are positive performance impacts in the following cases:

- Reducing round-trip delays
- Reducing I/O chat on the network

The round-trip delay in the data center is measured around 0.5 ms or less. Compared to retrieving a block of data from HDDs, which ranges in the tens of milliseconds, the overhead in the network is considered minimal. However, when you talk about SSDs, time to read 1 MB of data sequentially could be in the 1 ms or so range. With the advances in flash technology and access speeds getting smaller and smaller, the network must minimize the round-trip delays to keep up. With networks moving into 40 GE and 100 GE and the introduction of technologies such as Remote Direct Memory Access over Fabric (RDMAoF), the network remains a nonissue for a while. When NVMe SSDs are widely deployed, the performance of the host CPUs becomes the bottleneck way before the network does.

It is true that the more the data is read or written locally, the less I/O chatter is done on the network. This is true if you assume that a chunk of data that is hot and constantly read by a VM is brought locally once, eliminating further remote reads. However, there is no indication at this point that the added traffic on the network affects the performance of individual systems in a negative way; it does, however, alleviate the 10 GE/40 GE interfaces from added traffic. The performance issues related with individual systems having enough resources, such as CPU and memory to handle the I/O, far outweigh any issues with network congestion.

Cons of Data Locality

Data locality, if not implemented properly, could have some negative effects. It is not fair to address these issue in the Nutanix section because this does not relate to Nutanix; however, because Nutanix uses this topic to highlight its advantages, it is cursed with discussions about disadvantages even if they do not relate to Nutanix.

Some implementations in the industry require strict locality. This means that the data must be local to the system where the VM is running. This goes against the notion of distributed file systems while the data by design is spread over many nodes, and the controllers from many nodes share the load. Strict locality creates the following issues:

- If all data is moved to the local host where the VM is running and the host does not have enough storage for the VM, the VM does not run. In this case, the data spills over to other nodes. This requires some special storage management to know which nodes have enough storage to spill over to.

- When performing vMotion, if VMs are restricted to run only on the nodes that have replicas of the data, the mobility of the VMs becomes restricted and might create the same space availability problems.

- When data reduction techniques are used, such as in deduplication or cloning metadata on multiple systems, you end up with many VMs accessing the same data via pointers. This means that whether you like it or not, VMs are accessing the data remotely. Otherwise, you must put the same piece of data on every host, which goes against the idea of deduplication. So once again, data locality, when applied with stringent restrictions, goes against all the principles of data distribution and optimization that HCI promotes.

- In containerized environments, containers can be short lived. This means a container can be initiated on one host, deleted, and then reinitiated on another host. Data locality means that the data keeps moving around between the nodes trying to chase the container.

Many other examples can be used against data locality, but you have probably gotten the point by now.

Looking Ahead

This chapter discussed the details of the Nutanix Enterprise Cloud platform software architecture and how it compares with other leading vendors such as Cisco HyperFlex. There are multiple open source initiatives in the industry, such as OpenStack, that are tackling the same issue of hyperconvergence between compute, networking, and storage. Vendors are also offering an integration path between their implementation and open source via the use of application programming interfaces (APIs). Chapter 14, "Open Source—Compute and Storage," discusses open source implementations for compute and storage as they relate to HCI to familiarize the reader with the open source terminology and how it integrates with different vendor implementations.

Part VI of this book discusses the networking aspect of hyperconvergence and different software-defined networking (SDN) implementations.

Reference

[1] http://nutanixbible.com/

Chapter 14

Open Source—Compute and Storage

This chapter covers the following key topics:

- **OpenStack:** High-level description of OpenStack and its components, and the objective to automate and simplify the configuration and deployment of private and public clouds.

- **Nova:** A description of the OpenStack compute service module that allows OpenStack to initiate and remove the virtual machines and manage their lifecycle.

- **Cinder Block Storage:** A description of the OpenStack storage service module that provides virtual machines with block storage services used for structured data and performance-sensitive applications.

- **Swift:** A description of the OpenStack object storage service module that offers the ability to store massive amounts of data for scale and ease of accessibility.

- **Ceph:** A distributed storage system that is open source and supports object-, block-, and file-level file systems. Ceph is getting good traction in the industry due to its flexibility in offering multiple file systems under the same architecture.

With so many different hyperconverged infrastructure (HCI) implementations, it seems that the industry might be moving from storage array silos to hyperconverged silos. Each vendor has its own implementation of HCI, and no two implementations work together. Multiple open source initiatives were developed to create a suite of software modules in the different areas of compute, storage, networking, management, and orchestration, to put a common framework for collaboration and interoperability. It is hard to go over all the initiatives, so only some important initiatives that are getting good traction, such as OpenStack and Ceph, are mentioned here.

OpenStack is broad and covers the A to Z of storage, compute, networking, and management. Ceph is a distributed storage system that offers object, block, and file services.

This chapter covers the compute and storage aspects of OpenStack. Chapter 15, "Software-Defined Networking and Open Source," covers OpenStack networking through Neutron and Open vSwitch (OVS), as well as an open source initiative called Open Virtual Network (OVN).

OpenStack

OpenStack [1] started as a joint effort between Rackspace and NASA in 2010 to cooperate on scaling compute and storage systems. Initial efforts from Rackspace (via the acquisition of Slicehost) worked on server virtualizations and were able to scale virtualization to build a cluster of roughly 200 servers. In parallel, NASA was working on a Nova cloud compute project and had objectives of reaching clusters of 5,000 servers. The joint effort between Rackspace and NASA led to OpenStack, with a compute initiative called Nova and a data storage initiative called Swift. The objective was to make all code open source. Soon after, many companies wanted to get involved in the OpenStack project, which led to the creation of the OpenStack Foundation, where many leading companies joined to evolve the project.

OpenStack's objective is to automate and simplify the configuration and deployment of private and public clouds and alleviate the end user from the rocket science of stitching compute, storage, and networking equipment to deliver working platforms where applications run. In a way, this is what Amazon Web Services (AWS) did to the public cloud. Many other operators and enterprises want to follow suit, duplicate the model, and enhance it.

Several projects launched in OpenStack into different areas. These projects were loosely coupled and ran independent of one another. Figure 14-1 shows a high-level view of the OpenStack "early" main components. As OpenStack evolved, almost 50 projects were created, and more projects continue to be added. OpenStack promoted the use of northbound Representation State Transfer (RESTful) application programming interfaces (APIs) to tap into the system and easily provision, manage, and monitor compute, storage, and network. A RESTful API uses the Hypertext Transfer Protocol (HTTP) requests to GET, PUT, POST, and DELETE data.

As seen in the previous figure, OpenStack presents the user/applications with a common interface, where the application can request services such as compute, storage, and network, similar to how AWS presents cloud services. Many enterprises jumped on the OpenStack bandwagon to offer infrastructure as a service (IaaS) inside the private cloud and to create a model that highly resembles the public cloud. OpenStack offers a set of services on the front end and interface, with the physical or virtual infrastructure on the back end. The physical/virtual infrastructure can be none other than the hyperconverged infrastructure built by Cisco HyperFlex or other vendors. This way, the user can leverage both open source and best-of-breed vendors that deliver scalable software-defined storage (SDS) and storage-defined networking (SDN). An enterprise can then build a common set of interfaces and functionality without a vendor lock on the back end. Any vendor who is capable of interfacing with open source is a viable solution for the enterprise.

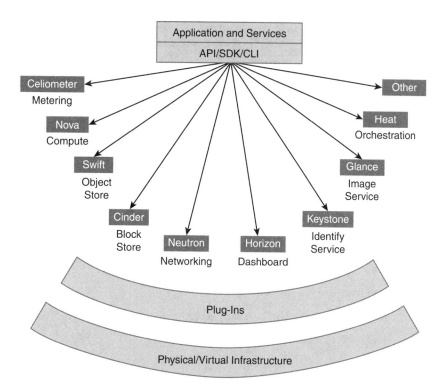

Figure 14-1 *The OpenStack Main Components*

For the reader to become familiar with the OpenStack terminology, following is a summary of current OpenStack projects:

- Compute

  - **Nova:** Compute services

  - **Glance:** Image service

  - **Ironic:** Bare-metal service

  - **Magnum:** Container orchestration engine provisioning

  - **Storlets:** Computable object store

  - **Zun:** Container management service

- Storage backup and recovery

  - **Swift:** Object store

  - **Cinder:** Block store

  - **Manila:** Shared file systems

- **Karbor:** Application data protection as a service
- **Freezer:** Backup restore and disaster recovery
- Networking and content delivery
  - **Neutron:** Networking
  - **Designate:** DNS service
  - **Dragonflow:** Neutron plug-in
  - **Kuryr:** Container plug-in
  - **Octavia:** Load balancer
  - **Tacker:** NFV orchestration
  - **Tricircle:** Networking automation for multiregion deployments
- Data analytics
  - **Trove:** Database as a service
  - **Sahara:** Big data processing framework provisioning
  - **Searchlight:** Indexing and search
- Security identity and compliance
  - **Keystone:** Identity service
  - **Barbican:** Key management
  - **Congress:** Governance
  - **Mistral:** Workflow service
- Management tools
  - **Horizon:** Dashboard
  - **OpenStack Client:** Command-line interface (CLI)
  - **Rally:** Benchmark service
  - **Senlin:** Clustering service
  - **Vitrage:** RCA (root cause analysis) service
  - **Watcher:** Optimization service
- Deployment tools
  - **Chef OpenStack:** Chef cookbooks for OpenStack
  - **Kolla:** Container deployment
  - **OpenStack Charms:** Juju charms for OpenStack

- **OpenStack-Ansible:** Ansible playbooks for OpenStack

- **Puppet OpenStack:** Puppet modules for OpenStack

- **Tripelo:** Deployment service

- Application services

  - **Heat:** Orchestration

  - **Zaqar:** Messaging service

  - **Murano:** Application catalog

  - **Solum:** Software development lifecycle

- Monitoring and metering

  - **Ceilometer:** Metering and data collection service

  - **Cloudkitty:** Billing and chargeback

  - **Monasca:** Monitoring

  - **Aodh:** Alarming service

  - **Panko:** Event, metadata indexing service

Someone can eventually write books about each of these components, but this book only discusses the details of specific components that relate to compute, storage, and networking.

OpenStack has some frequently used components that allow for functionality such as user authentication and component authentication, image management, user interface, cloud metering, and orchestration. This is described next:

- **Keystone:** At the basis of OpenStack, you have the Keystone component. Keystone offers authentication and authorization to users who are accessing OpenStack and to components that are trying to access other OpenStack components.

- **Glance:** Glance provides the image management to keep track, save, and deploy different software images. Once a virtual machine (VM) image is created, it can be saved as a golden image that can be reused to launch different VMs with the same configuration.

- **Horizon:** This is a user interface (UI) dashboard.

- **Ceilometer:** This provides the metering for the usage of the cloud.

- **Heat:** This is an orchestration layer deploying specific blueprints that allow specific applications to be deployed and then destroyed and reused.

The following section goes into detail about important services such as the compute service Nova and storage services such as Cinder and Swift. It also covers an open source project, Ceph, that is not under OpenStack, but is getting a high level of acceptance in the market.

Nova

This is the compute services module that allows OpenStack to initiate and remove the VMs and manage their lifecycle. Nova itself does not define a hypervisor, but rather supports any type of hypervisor the user wants to choose. Nova API acts as a translator between the specific hypervisor and the user. This is achieved by installing a small instance called "compute" inside the hypervisor that provides the API layer used for the translation. Any time a user wants to spin a VM, it sends the request to Nova, which in turn translates it into what the specific hypervisor understands. Also, any time changes happen on the VM side, the information is registered by the compute instance and can be accessed by the user. In addition, Nova implements support for Elastic Compute cloud (EC2) API, which is the API that AWS defines. This allows OpenStack clouds to interact with AWS clouds. (More about AWS and cloud support is discussed in Part VII of this book.)

Nova supports other virtualization technologies via containers (Magnum project) and bare-metal servers (Ironic project).

Let's look closer now at the sequence of events between the different Nova components as seen in Figure 14-2.

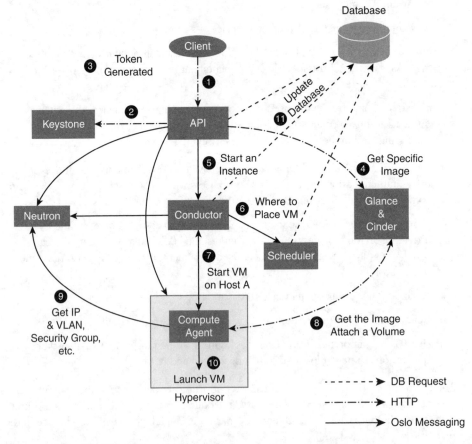

Figure 14-2 *The Nova Components*

The communication between processes in OpenStack is done via oslo.messaging, which is a framework for remote procedure calls (RPCs) that use different back-end messaging drivers; an example is RabbitMQ messaging. With RabbitMQ, messages are exchanged per service, and each service listens to its own messages. The network service listens to messages addressed to the network service, and the compute service listens to messages addressed to the compute service.

The sequence of events and the communication between the client and the Nova service and between the components of the Nova service are described next:

Step 1.   The first interaction with the Nova component is via APIs.

Step 2.   Any call to the API initiates a call to the Keystone identity service for authentication.

Step 3.   This generates a token that gives permission to the client to use the Nova service.

Step 4.   Once it's authenticated, a query is made to Glance to find out what size images (flavors) are available for the VMs to use. The flavor specifies the size of storage allocated, how many virtual CPUs (vCPUs), and how much random access memory (RAM) is allocated to the particular flavor. So, for example, flavor 1 would be 10 GB of disk space with two vCPUs and 32 GB of RAM, whereas flavor 2 could be 20 GB of disk space, three vCPUs, and 64 GB of RAM. Also, the query to Glance returns the specific images to boot from. These images could be already baked images that you get from a public cloud, such as Ubuntu or Windows. Or these could be images that an administrator of a private cloud custom built. After getting the flavors and the actual images, the next step is to boot the VM instance.

To boot the VM, you need to decide where it will reside.

Step 5.   The conductor comes in to take the request about starting an instance.

Step 6.   The conductor sends a request to the scheduler and coordinates with the database. The scheduler gets involved and applies filters and weights to find out the information. The filters find out which hosts are on, whether they have enough central processing units (CPUs) and RAM, and so on. The weights give more preference to hosts based on resources, such as a host that has more RAM. Based on that information, the scheduler decides which host runs the VM.

The database itself is an SQL database that contains built-time and run-time states for the cloud infrastructure, which includes the different instance types, instances in use, available networks, projects, and more.

Step 7.   Once the scheduler makes the selection and the instance state is updated in the database, the conductor places a message to the compute agent that resides on the hypervisor of the selected node.

Step 8.   The compute agent prepares for the instance launch by calling Glance/Cinder for retrieving the image to be launched.

Step 9.   The compute agent calls Neutron to get the networking information such as IP subnets, VLANs, and security groups to call Cinder for attaching a storage volume if needed.

Step 10.   The compute agent uses the hypervisor API to launch the VM.

Step 11.   The compute agent uses the conductor to update the state of the VM in the database.

To address cloud scalability to thousands of nodes, Nova divides the network into "cells," where each cell contains its own database and message queuing environment. The concept of cells keeps one compute environment but tries to scale the database and messaging by creating the cell structure. Normally, each cell should handle approximately 200 nodes. Efforts in OpenStack are ongoing to eliminate issues of cell-to-cell interaction, what to keep global, and what to keep local to a cell. Another approach to scale compute involves using segregation of compute resources by using logical grouping such as different geographical regions, data centers, racks, and more. Normally, sharing of services between the regions is limited, except for the Horizon and Keystone services, which offer shared configuration and authentication between all regions.

Other possible logical grouping could be on "metadata," which gives specific descriptions of the host capabilities. "Host Aggregates," for example, is a logical grouping based on host specifics such as having 40 GE network interface cards (NICs), solid-state drives (SSDs), Peripheral Component Interconnect express (PCIe) bus, Non-Volatile Memory Express (NVMe), and so on. Hosts can be in different host aggregates if one host, say, has 40 GE and an SSD.

Other grouping is done via availability zones, similar to what is seen with AWS. Availability zones define a fault domain based on different factors such as networking, power source, and flood areas. The objective is to spread compute, storage, and networking into separate zones, where disastrous events do not affect all nodes at the same time. Unlike host aggregates, hosts can only be in one availability zone, which constitutes a failure domain.

Cinder Block Storage

The OpenStack Cinder provides VMs with block storage services. As discussed earlier in this book, block-level storage is normally used for structured data and performance-sensitive applications such as Structured Query Language (SQL) databases. A VM has access to block storage in the form of a volume that the operating system accesses. Most production applications, databases, dev/test environments, and so on, use block storage, where the content is highly dynamic with a requirement for high input/output operations per second (IOPS).

Cinder offers an infrastructure for managing volumes and provides volumes for VM instances by interacting with Nova. Following is a list of high-level Cinder components as seen in Figure 14-3.

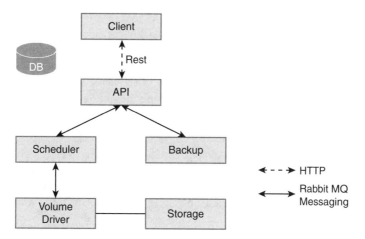

Figure 14-3   *Cinder Components*

A Cinder client uses RESTful APIs to access the cinder-api component. The client could be an OpenStack Horizon dashboard, a client for URL (cURL) call, or any other element that can send RESTful HTTP requests. The cinder-api in turn uses message queuing such as RabbitMQ to exchange messages with the rest of the components. This is in line with other OpenStack architectures, as with Nova that were just discussed. The cinder-api accepts API requests and routes them to the cinder-volume via the cinder-scheduler.

The cinder-volume service responds to read and write input/output (I/O) requests sent to the storage service and interacts with the scheduler. Storage vendors can use their own drivers to have their products interact with the cinder-volume. The drivers are placed in the cinder-volume and use different data-interchange formats such as JavaScript Object Notation (JSON) to send RPC to the back-end storage. Cinder also has its own built-in logical volume manager (LVM) driver to interact with outside storage with protocols such as iSCSI and iSER.

The cinder-scheduler decides which is the optimal storage node to put the volume on.

The cinder-backup service backs up the volumes over different types of storage. Also, storage vendors can have their own drivers to interact with this service.

Some of the Cinder functionality includes creating and deleting volumes, creating clones and snapshots, specifying certain volume types to indicate what back-end storage to go to, backing-up volumes to object storage (Swift) or other unified storage such as Ceph, copying images from Glance to a volume, and vice versa.

Swift

Swift [2] is the OpenStack object storage project that offers the ability to store massive amounts of data with a simple API. Unlike block storage, which is focused on structured data such as SQL databases that require high performance and high IOPS, object storage is more focused on scale and ease of accessibility. It allows a globally distributed and scalable storage without the hassle of maintaining tons of drives like in block storage or managing namespaces, file hierarchies, and file locking as in file-based storage. As already discussed in Chapter 2, "Storage Networks: Existing Designs," object storage is more suited for unstructured data such as video/audio files, photos, and data from social media such as Facebook and Twitter. It is experiencing phenomenal growth. One of the early providers of object storage is AWS with the Simple Storage Service (S3) that allows users to store massive amounts of storage on the cloud.

As described earlier, an object constitutes a file and the metadata that describes the file. The file could be an image, as an example, and the metadata is the information about where the image is taken, the image size, people who are tagged with the image, and so on. Swift, as any object store, uses APIs that are accessed via HTTP, which gives a lot of flexibility in how the data is accessed, how much of it is accessed, and where it can be stored. Swift is formed out of different components that are described next.

Proxy Server

Proxy servers redirect the HTTP API requests for read and write to the storage servers that are connected to the storage devices. There must be at least two proxy servers for redundancy. Proxy servers are front ended by load balancers that distribute the traffic between the servers. The proxy server abstracts the storage itself from the end user and allows for simple mechanisms such as PUT, GET, and DELETE to access the data. This is seen in Figure 14-4.

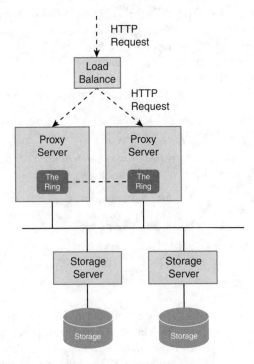

Figure 14-4 *Swift Proxy Servers*

Swift organizes data into accounts, containers, and objects. A sample URL to reach an object is https://swift.xyz.com/v1/Account/Container/object.

The proxy server has the task of finding the information on disks by looking up the information on a mapping table called the *ring*.

Swift has a special way of organizing data and mapping the name of an object with its location. The data is also replicated for protection into different failure domains and deployed into accounts, containers, objects, and partitions. The Swift data is organized using the following mechanisms:

- The ring

- Zones

- Accounts, containers, objects, and partitions

The ring is a table that has mappings between the name of an object and its location on the storage devices. The ring is formed of partitions that contain the data and are replicated—normally three times in the cluster for high data availability. The ring has a mapping of where these partitions are located on physical storage devices. The proxy servers use the ring to have access to the actual data. The ring uses an MD5 hashing algorithm on the object path (the URL of the object) to index the partition on a physical device. The ring keeps track of the partition and its replicas, and in case of disk failure, it has the location of the other devices that hold the rest of the partitions.

To avoid single-failure domains, Swift includes the concept of zones, like AWS availability zones. Each zone constitutes a failure domain, which could be a disk or a group of disks, a server, a rack of servers, multiple racks that have a similar power source, a fire zone, a flood zone, and so on. The replicas that are created for the different partitions must be placed in different zones for added protection. So, if three replicas are made in a three-server setup, the replicas cannot all be on a single disk of a server or on a single server. It is better to define each server as a zone and put each replica on a different server. Also, if zones are defined as racks, it is better not to have two servers that each carry a replica located in the same zone.

Swift includes the concept of accounts, containers, objects, and partitions. A user is allocated an account. In each account is a set of containers, and each container has a set of objects. Each container and each account are individual SQLite databases that are distributed in the cluster. An account can have multiple containers that are referenced by the account database. Each container can have multiple objects, which are the individual files. This is seen in Figure 14-5.

Because replication must be performed in a cluster, instead of at the level of individual objects, Swift does a coarser level grouping called *partitions*. A partition constitutes a group of account databases, container databases, and objects that are put in a larger group called a partition. When replication is done in the cluster, three copies of the partitions are maintained in the cluster. The partitions are put in different zones for protection. The partition itself is similar to a set of directories. Each directory has a hash value that results from the MD5 function. The list of all hashes represents a hash file for the partition.

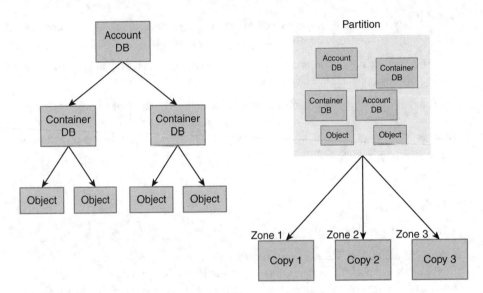

Figure 14-5   *Accounts, Containers, Objects, and Partitions*

The replicator function ensures that the exact copies of the partitions exist in the different zones. The replicator checks the hash table for a partition and checks the hash values of each directory in the different zones. If the hash value does not exist in a zone, the corresponding directory is replicated. When the replication is done, at least two of the three copies must be written before the client is notified that the write was successful. Swift tolerates having two out of three successful replications because the third copy is eventually recovered and made consistent with the rest of the copies. This is called an *eventually consistent system*, meaning that portions of the data (the third copy) at some point in time are not exactly similar to the other copies, but "eventually" becomes consistent.

Ceph

Ceph [3] is a distributed storage system that is open source and supports object-, block-, and file-level file systems. Ceph is getting good traction in the industry due to its flexibility in offering multiple file systems under the same architecture. Ceph is based on Reliable Autonomous Distributed Object Store (RADOS). RADOS offers a distributed object store system with no single point of failure that can scale horizontally using commodity standard hardware.

The flexibility in Ceph stems from its ability to offer different access methods to the storage system, as described in Figure 14-6. Access to the object store is done directly via the library (LIBRADOS) or via a web services RADOS Gateway (RGW). Access to block-level storage is done via RADOS block device (RBD), and access to file services is done via a distributed Ceph File System, CephFS. All of these services are built on top of the distributed object storage system, RADOS.

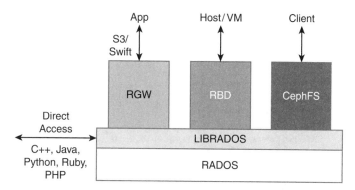

Figure 14-6 *Ceph Architecture Components*

Librados is the library that allows direct access to the storage system via multiple languages, including C++, Java, Python, Ruby, and Hypertext Preprocessor (PHP).

In addition to allowing direct access to the object store through Librados, Ceph offers a simpler interface that is compatible with the AWS S3 and Swift. The RADOS gateway (RGW) does the translation between S3 and Librados so that applications can use the S3 RESTful APIs to access the object storage functionality without having to know the intricacies of the Librados library.

The RADOS block device (RBD) allows block-level services to use RADOS. When a VM or a bare-metal host does a block I/O read or write request to the hypervisor or host kernel, the system uses the RBD library LIBRBD to stripe the blocks into the object store. The writes are done in chunks of 4 MB objects and are striped and distributed over multiple nodes in the storage system. RBD allows live migration so that VMs, with the support of the hypervisor, can easily move around in the cluster, especially since the VM is not tied to a specific host but sees the whole cluster.
RBD supports operations such as replication, snapshots, and copy-on-write clones.

The Ceph File System (CephFS) delivers file-level storage services on top of the RADOS Object store. CephFS keeps track of the data and its metadata. Tracking the metadata is done via metadata servers. There could be multiple metadata servers, and the system figures out a way to equally assign each metadata server to a set of nodes in the system to balance the load.

The metadata servers use the Librados interface to store the data inside the RADOS cluster. All I/O operations to the data are done directly through Librados into the cluster, with the support of the metadata servers to locate the data.

RADOS is a distributed object storage system that is based on the concept that many smaller elements composed of compute and disk have a peer-to-peer relationship with each other to create a highly fault tolerant system. Think of each of the elements as a disk plus file system plus an object store daemon (OSD). This is seen in Figure 14-7.

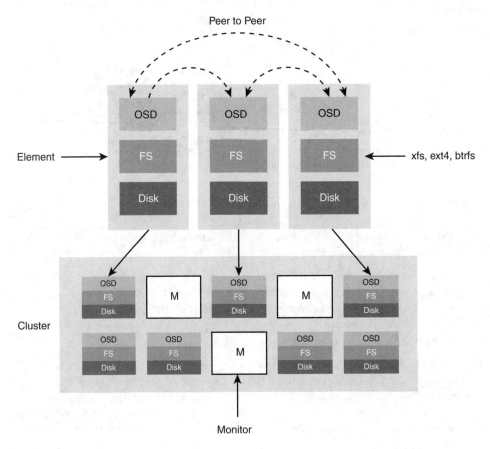

Figure 14-7   *RADOS*

The disk could be an individual disk or a RAID group. The file system (FS) is any file system that Ceph supports; the current list includes xfs, ext4, and btrfs file systems. The OSD is a software layer that takes the individual disks or RAID groups and makes them part of the object store system. Note that with Ceph, unlike what was seen with the hyperconverged file systems, there is no controller VM on each host but rather an OSD per disk or RAID group. This is because in Ceph, all disks/OSDs work in a peer-to-peer relationship at the granularity of a disk. When a client, an application, or a VM interacts with the system, it is not working with an individual host but rather with the full cluster of disks.

The cluster could have a handful of OSDs to thousands of OSDs depending on the configured granularity. The OSDs are responsible for getting the data to the clients and work in a peer-to-peer relationship to make sure the data is replicated, to work around disk failures, and to make sure the system is fault tolerant.

Ceph defines another set of RADOS members called the monitors (M). The monitors are not in the data path but rather keep track of the state of the OSDs/disk and "vote" to have consensus on which members are up or down and on the state of the cluster.

Ceph uses controlled replication under scalable hashing (CRUSH) as a hashing algorithm to figure out where the data is. Because Ceph works with many OSDs that could be in the tens of thousands, performing hashing and indexing at the granularity of an OSD becomes hard. As such, CRUSH has a sort of hierarchy that first hashes on the object name to create different placement groups. After that, the CRUSH algorithm takes as input the three-tuple (placement group, cluster state, rule set) to calculate which target OSDs to use. The CRUSH algorithm uses this input to distribute the data in the cluster in a pseudo-random fashion, taking into account the state of all members, weights, and a statically uniform distribution.

Looking Ahead

In this chapter, the main focus was on the open source compute and storage aspects as they relate to HCI. Policy setting and networking are important aspects of HCI as well. Because the mantra of HCI is simplicity, scale, and ease of provisioning, rollout, and management, any implementations that do not focus on the automation of networking and policy setting will fall short.

Networking constitutes a big piece in the HCI puzzle. The simplicity of HCI requires a high level of automation when it comes to automating the networking configuration and the setting of policies. This is covered in Part VII of this book, which focuses on hyperconverged networking.

References

[1] www.opensource.org

[2] http://docs.openstack.org/swift

[3] www.ceph.com/docs

Hyperconverged Networking

Chapter 15   Software-Defined Networking and Open Source

Chapter 16   VMware NSX

Chapter 17   Application-Centric Infrastructure

Networking is a very important piece of HCI deployments, but normally it gets downplayed by many of the storage vendors. This is not because it is not important but because many HCI vendors do not have the networking piece ready or at least in shape. When discussing networking, the first thing that comes to mind is switching and routing and companies like Cisco systems, Juniper, Arista, and others. However, within HCI, networking might start taking a different form starting in initiatives in the open source community. Host-based networking will start competing with switch-based networking, where the edge routing starts within the hypervisor rather than the physical edge switch. The two methods referred to in this part of the book as "Switch-Based Networking" versus "Host-Based Networking" will compete for years to come.

This part of the book discusses the state of software-defined networking (SDN) and how it is shaping HCI implementations.

Chapter 15 discusses SDN in general, the data center switching and routing model, and the Open vSwitch (OVS) and Open Virtual Network (OVN) initiatives in open source.

Chapter 16 discusses VMware's approach to networking with NSX.

Chapter 17 explores the details of the Cisco Application Centric Infrastructure (ACI).

Chapter 15

Software-Defined Networking and Open Source

This chapter covers the following key topics:

- **The SDN Background:** The software-defined network (SDN) background and its adoption in today's networking implementations.

- **The Overlay and Microsegmentation Edge:** Description of the two networking models focused on host-based versus switch-based networking.

- **The Switching Fabric:** Description of the switching fabric leaf/spine terminology.

- **The Underlay Network:** A description of the underlay network and how it offers L3 connectivity between the different L2 broadcast domains. You will see how routing and multicast are performed.

- **The Overlay Network:** A description of the overlay network through the use of the Virtual Extensible LAN (VXLAN) technology. You will see how switching routing and multicast are performed.

- **Microsegmentation in the Data Center:** A description of how microsegmentation is used to set policies at the virtual machine and container levels.

- **Networking Open Source Initiatives:** Multiple networking initiatives are described such as Neutron from OpenStack and the open source Open vSwitch (OVS).

- **OVN—The Open Source SDN:** Describes the Open Virtual Network (OVN) projects and how it enhances and extends the OVS functionality.

- **State of Vendors with Open Source:** A description of how vendors are integrating their own networking implementations within an open source framework.

The SDN Background

Software-defined networking (SDN) is another term that the marketing professionals use and abuse. SDN was intended to decouple control from the forwarding functions in networking equipment to allow software to centrally program the hardware to perform forwarding.

If you look at how traditional switching and routing were built, there are three different elements that allow such devices to function:

1. **The management plane:** This gives the ability to configure the different interfaces, assign virtual LANs (VLANs) and IP addresses, turn on protocols, and so on. This is done via a command-line interface (CLI) or via graphical user interfaces (GUI). Each switch and router vendor has its own naming convention and command set to configure the different elements of the networking device.

2. **The control plane:** This defines the set of protocols that build the L2 media access control (MAC) and VLAN tables or the L3 IP routing tables and the way switches and routers exchange reachability information for end nodes. The protocols themselves—such as Open Shortest Path First (OSPF), Intermediate System to Intermediate System (IS-IS), Border Gateway Protocol (BGP), Multi-Protocol BGP (MP-BGP)—are standardized. The routing protocols run in central processing units (CPUs) and build the switching and routing tables. Devices from different vendors can talk to each other, but the way these protocols are configured and how the information is displayed depend on the vendor implementation.

3. **The data plane:** This constitutes how data is forwarded inside the hardware from interface to interface. This is vendor specific and depends on the hardware; however, most vendors push the MAC, VLAN, and IP tables into hardware forwarding tables inside content-addressable memory (CAM) or ternary CAM (TCAM) that allow wire speed packet switching and forwarding.

So, control planes were always decoupled from data planes, but there is no central brain that controls the configuration and forwarding. Control in switches and routers is distributed, with each device having its own brain and exchanging information with the rest of the devices.

SDN brought to the table the notion that a centralized controller would have a global view of the network, using a management protocol to configure the switches and routers. The controller calculates reachability information on behalf of the individual devices and pushes a set of flows inside the switches. The flows are used by the hardware to do the forwarding—a move from a distributed brain approach to a central brain approach. One of the open source implementations of SDN controllers was done in the Open vSwitch (OVS) project using the OVS Database (OVSDB) management protocol and the OpenFlow protocol.

So, let's look at the contribution of SDN in the areas of management, control, and data planes. In the areas of control and data planes and how packets are routed and forwarded, SDN did not really change the model in physical switches. The concept of big hardware switches managed by a controller did not fly too well. With some exceptions to the rule, the bulk of switches and routers out there are running their own L2 and L3 protocols, calculating reachability and pushing it into hardware TCAMs. However SDN changed the control and data plane models in software-based switches with virtual switches inside the hypervisors. The launch of the Open vSwitch project was a turning point in the beginning of a battle between hosts and switches/routers on where the switching and routing edge starts.

In the area of management, SDN seems to be thriving in both physical switches and logical switches. SDN has slowly morphed into data centers as a means to automate setting networking policies and configurations in a way that makes the deployment of the network agile and flexible. In virtualized environments, the value of SDN is in the ability to have the administrator, through centralized controllers, automate the virtual machine (VM) and application policies and push networking information and policies to either hardware- or software-based switching and routing functions. SDN also provides mechanisms, through application programming interfaces (APIs), to allow network programmability to the point where you can define a data center full networking setup through software and duplicate that setup when needed. Because hyperconvergence is all about simplifying data center setups and offering automation, SDN plays a powerful role in hyperconverged networks, in the same way that software-defined storage (SDS) dramatically changes how to approach storage.

The Overlay and Microsegmentation Edge

The introduction of SDN controllers and virtual switches inside hypervisors started the first battle between hosts and switches/routers on where the overlay and microsegmentation edge lies.

Basically, an overlay deals with segmenting traffic into L2 broadcast domains and extending L2 domains over L3 routed networks. This involves the creation of IP tunnels and encapsulating L2 Ethernet traffic inside the L3 tunnels. Switching occurs in the overlay within the L2 broadcast domains, and routing occurs between the different L2 broadcast domains. The overlay network can also be built to support multitenancy and multiple virtual routing and forwarding (VRF) domains.

The underlay, on the other hand, delivers IP packets between the endpoints of the IP tunnels created by the overlay and provides some IP multicast functions in support of the overlay.

Microsegmentation mainly deals with virtual segmentation at the application level. This sets and enforces security policies that determine the interaction between clients and applications and between applications. Microsegmentation sets and enforces polices at the VM or container level, regardless of the physical location of the application and which VLAN or IP subnet it belongs to.

Traditionally, a host used to be a single server where the application ran. The server as an IP end node talked to other nodes via an L2-switched network or an L3-routed network. Both clients and servers were physically connected to the network via a physical network interface card (NIC), and the NIC connected to the switch or router. The switches also ensured logical separation via VLANs and connected to other appliances or offered integrated software/hardware for network services such as load balancing, firewalls, and security.

Fast forward to server virtualization. Now multiple VMs or containers run inside a server, and they need to be grouped logically and talk to each other within the server as well as to other VMs and containers in other physical nodes. This is where the concept of virtual switches was introduced. The open source community started the OVS project, and vendors such as VMware and Cisco launched their own versions of virtual switches.

This is the first battle between software and hardware. Next, the different approaches, mainly host-based networking and switch-based networking, are discussed.

Host-Based Networking

In this approach, the host becomes the edge for microsegmentation functionality and the overlay network. This model leaves the Ethernet switch fabric to perform basic IP routing functionality. VMware, for example, is on a software-only path, with most functions done by the CPUs inside the host. VMware expanded the functions of its distributed switch and expanded its networking portfolio through its network security software (NSX). NSX was widely adopted by most VMware customers because it provides an easy way of deploying the networking functions, with a point-and-click easy-to-use environment. So eventually this approach took away most of the networking functions from the top-of-rack (ToR) switches and embedded them into the ESXi hypervisor. Similar approaches are taken by other vendors, such as Nutanix, that are building their policy handling and networking solutions. So far Nutanix has implemented microsegmentation with its Flow product and still relies on the fabric switches for the overlay functionality. Open source seems to be the vehicle for implementing the overlay functionality with the use of OVS and Open Virtual Network (OVN).

In the host-based networking model, the interaction between the virtualized environment and the external switches is still needed. For hosts that perform only microsegmentation and do not perform overlay functions, the interaction between the host and the switch could be as simple as automatically setting the VLANs inside the switch based on VM configuration. This is good enough for basic operations and for small L2 broadcast domains.

For architectures that use the host mainly for setting both microsegmentation and overlay functions, the issue of maintaining adequate performance becomes important. As of the writing of this book, many of the HCI implementations offer basic acceleration by doing some Transmission Control Protocol (TCP) offload and tunneling in the NICs. This area will become a differentiator in the next few years as NVMe and 40 GE/100 GE NICs become more widely adopted.

There is an end in sight, but for server vendors, it's a work in progress. This warrants a brief discussion of what are called smart network interface cards, or smart NICs.

Setting and enforcing policies, switching, routing, tunneling, encrypting, and decrypting are tasks that normally perform better with hardware assist. With the introduction of faster multicore processors and ample memory, many of these tasks started being implemented inside the host. With the advancement in server bus technology such as Peripheral Component Interconnect express (PCIe), Non-Volatile Memory express (NVMe), and faster Ethernet speeds, even multicore CPUs are challenged.

Cloud-scale architectures from Microsoft and Google struggled with delivering advanced services in CPUs. Many initiatives were born to try to accelerate host services via hardware acceleration techniques. Microsoft's Cloud-Scale Acceleration Architecture [1] is being deployed in many of the new Microsoft servers in its many cloud data centers. The architecture uses field programmable gate arrays (FPGAs), which offer hardware acceleration for the data path of a wide range of networking functions and services. Think of FPGAs as processing units that offer the advantages of software programmability while offering hardware acceleration. FPGAs are usually bulkier than application-specific integrated circuits (ASICs), consume more heat, and are more expensive; however, they offer software programmability for introducing new functionality accelerated via hardware. This is seen in Figure 15-1. This architecture is supposed to enhance the host performance by offloading the CPU from networking functionality and even create a distributed approach in which a host leverages the FPGAs in other hosts to distribute loads between heavy-loaded hosts and idle hosts.

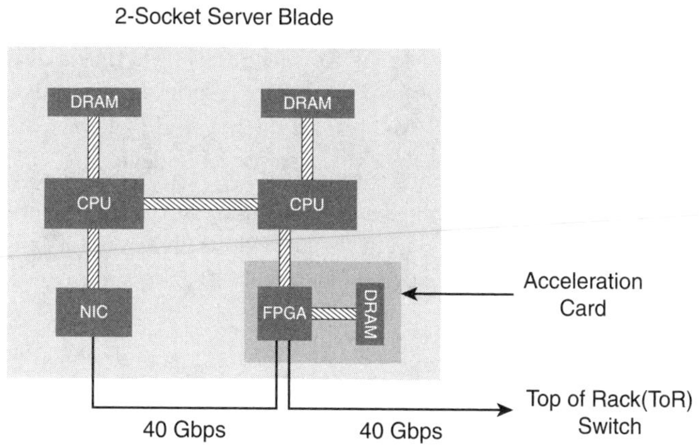

Figure 15-1 *Microsoft Cloud-Scale Acceleration*

The adoption of such architectures in cloud environments has not yet translated into adoption in the enterprise environment. As a matter of fact, most of the HCI architectures that are discussed still use regular NICs with some offload functionality for networking functions such as TCP offload engines, or offload for some network encapsulation functions.

This leads many vendors to start working on what is called a smart NIC. Examples of such vendors [2] are Accolade Technology Inc, Broadcom Ltd, Cavium Inc., Intel Corp, Mellanox Technologies Ltd., Solarflare Communications Inc., and many more.

The main intent of smart NICs is offloading the CPU from data path functions and performing such functions on the NIC hardware. Some of the smart NIC functionality includes the following:

- Inspecting packets at high speed

- Distributed network acceleration

- Policy setting and enforcement

- Data encryption and decryption

- Tunneling

- Monitoring

- Analytics

Smart NICs use a combination of FPGAs and Network Processors Units (NPUs) to accelerate the data path. However, the challenge of smart NICs is to provide hardware acceleration but still at prices that are close to regular NICs.

Smart NIC vendors are also taking advantage of what is called Universal Kernel Bypass (UKB), which are architectures where applications bypass the operating systems, kernels, and hypervisors for faster data processing. An example of UKB is Data Plane Development Kit (DPDK) [3], which is an open source Berkeley Software Distribution (BSD) project that defines a set of libraries and drivers for fast packet processing. An example of another initiative is NVMe-OF for carrying NVMe traffic directly over the fabric, such as Ethernet. Another initiative is the single root input/output virtualization (SR-IOV). SR-IOV allows different VMs to share the physical PCIe bus. SR-IOV allows the PCIe device to appear to virtual machines as separate PCIe devices.

So, the introduction of smart NICs helps enhance much of the HCI functionality that was discussed and take the heavy lifting from the CPU. Smart NIC vendors are also playing the SDN game by introducing APIs that allow software vendors to take advantage of their hardware capabilities.

Switch-Based Networking

The other approach in deploying networking functions and policies is the traditional method of offloading the CPU and the host by moving policy and networking functions into the external physical switches. In this case, the physical leaf switch becomes the edge for microsegmentation and the overlay network. This necessitates that information from within the host, such as the different VMs and the virtual NICs, be visible to the physical leaf switch. And because a cluster has multiple leaf switches, there must be a way to apply the networking policies at the cluster level to make networking a lot easier to deploy and manage. This is where Cisco introduced its application-centric infrastructure (ACI) architecture. Cisco ACI, for example, offers setting policies at the application and VM level through the ACI fabric and offers automation for the fabric itself. Cisco offloads the networking functions and services to the switches, which offer advanced networking functionality and hardware assist performance to most of the networking functions.

Having said that, a combination of hardware acceleration at the host as well as the switch could be optimal. For example, smart NICs accelerate functions such as indexing and hashing for storage, compression, and deduplication, whereas network switches take on functionality such as policy enforcement, fast switching, and routing between the VMs, load balancing in the fabric, and so on.

So, there is a struggle in the industry of where the microsegmentation and overlay edge should be: in the host or in the ToR switch. If you look at the vendors, Cisco approaches SDN from the perspective that software is a tool to provision and automate the networking functionality that sits in the switch hardware, whereas VMware's approach is to put everything in the software and dumb up the switching hardware. Both approaches have their own merits, and the difference is not so obvious as long as host CPUs can keep up. The minute CPUs start faltering due to NVMe and 100 GE, hosts will have a tough time maintaining performance. Also, host routing is still in its infancy compared to the advancements in switching and routing inside physical switches and routers. Vendors focusing on host routing are still playing catch-up.

To fully appreciate the two models, let's look at the data center switching fabric in detail and at the different network functionality that must be built, such as the underlay and overlay networks.

The Switching Fabric

Chapter 1, "Data Networks: Existing Designs," showed a brief description of the existing data center multitier design, which consisted of an access layer, a distribution layer, and a core layer. Such a design was optimized for North-South traffic between the enterprise and the Internet. Newer data center architectures adopt a leaf spine architecture, or "Clos" (in reference to Charles Clos who formalized a multistage switching system in 1952 [5]). The leaf spine architecture promotes an East-West architecture, where the majority of traffic is between tiers of applications such as web servers, application servers, database servers, media servers, and so on, inside the data center. The traffic crosses a switching fabric, which is now two tier.

The leaf layer consists of the ToR switches that connect directly to the server nodes. Some of these server nodes are bare-metal, whereas others are virtualized and run the virtual machines. Consider anything that connects to the leafs as being part of the "user space."

An important function of the leaf layer is that it now connects the physical networking services such as next-generation firewall (NGFW), load balancers (LBs), and WAN optimizers. As you recall, such networking services used to connect to the distribution layer in the three-tier design. Also, in a virtualized data center, the network services could be embedded into the servers as software appliances in the form of virtual machines. The leaf layer provides the capability of integrating such virtual appliances with the rest of the network.

Also, other connectivity to the intranet (campus network), or Internet which used to connect to core routers in the three-tier design, can connect to this layer via what is called border leaf nodes. The border leaf nodes exchange routing protocols with the external WAN router to inject external routes into the fabric. This is shown in Figure 15-2.

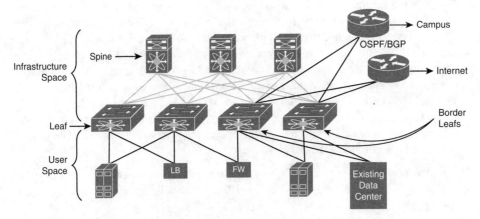

Figure 15-2   *Leaf Spine Two-Tier Design*

It is important to note that most data centers still operate as three tiers. Migration from a three-tier to a two-tier data center is an important step. Integrating the existing infrastructure and the new infrastructure is also done at the leaf layer, as seen in Figure 15-2, where you notice connectivity between leaf nodes and the existing data center.

The spine nodes are an important part of the fabric because they create a path between one node and any other node in the network with a maximum of two hops. The spine with the leaf nodes forms what is called the "infrastructure space" as it forms the fabric at the heart of the data center. Notice that every node has a connection to two leafs for redundancy, and every leaf has a connection to every spine; however, neither leaf connects to leafs or spine connects to spines. A connection between two nodes connected to the same leaf is switched within the leaf (one hop). A connection between two nodes that are connected to different leafs is switched from leaf to spine to leaf (two hops). The spine nodes allow for active load distribution because the traffic coming from the leafs is distributed between the spines. If the network has two spines, each spine potentially takes 50% of the load. If a network has four spines, each spine takes 25% of the load, and so on.

The leaf spine design allows a pay-as-you-grow approach. When the number of nodes grows, more leafs are added to provide the physical ports. Once you run out of physical ports, you add more leafs. Once leafs are added, more spines are added to share the load. Note that you always must accommodate for enough ports on the leafs and the spines because a leaf connects to all spines.

The Underlay Network

The underlay network is an L3 routed network inside the fabric that is preferably built using the leaf spine architecture. Network connectivity between the endpoints of the fabric is done via Layer 3 protocols such as OSPF, IS-IS, and MP-BGP. Other protocols for multidestination traffic include the Internet Group Management Protocol (IGMP) and the Protocol Independent Multicast (PIM).

Where the underlay network starts depends on the vendor implementation. As you will see shortly, Cisco ACI and VMware NSX approach the overlay and underlay from different angles. However, one common functionality of the underlay is to provide a robust fabric that delivers traffic from one point to the other using IP routing. Whether the underlay needs to support multicast routing and whether it uses unicast or multicast for handling unknown unicast and address resolution protocol (ARP) broadcasts depends on the vendor implementation. The fabric switches in the underlay should have enough redundancy to recover from hardware or software failures and have the capability to load balance the traffic between multiple paths using Equal Cost Multi-path (ECMP).

The Overlay Network

Data centers are moving toward L3 infrastructures because they offer capabilities such as L3 load balancing via ECMP, better scalability, and many other benefits in the areas of faster convergence and in limiting packet flooding. As the industry began to shift in the direction of building L3 data centers, a mechanism was needed to connect VMs and containers between servers without changing the networking attributes of a VM. This is achieved by adopting an overlay model over an L3 network. In other words, this new mechanism allows you to tunnel L2 Ethernet domains with different encapsulations over an L3 network.

The overlay network is a logical network that runs on top of the underlay L3 IP network. The overlay is formed of tunnels to carry the traffic across the L3 fabric. The underlay also needs to separate between different administrative domains (tenants), switch within the same L2 broadcast domain, route between L2 broadcast domains, and provide IP separation via VRFs.

Many IP tunneling mechanisms were introduced, including Virtual Extensible LAN (VXLAN), Network Virtualization using Generic Routing Encapsulation (NVGRE), Stateless Transport Tunneling (STT), Generic Network Virtualization Encapsulation (GENEVE), and others. All of these tunneling protocols are similar in the way they carry an Ethernet frame inside an IP frame; the difference is in the type of the IP frame used. VXLAN, for example, uses a standard User Datagram Protocol (UDP) packet, whereas STT uses a TCP packet. In the context of this book, VXLAN is used as the reference point due to its wider adoption. The overlay tunneling concept with VXLAN is shown in Figure 15-3a and 15-3b.

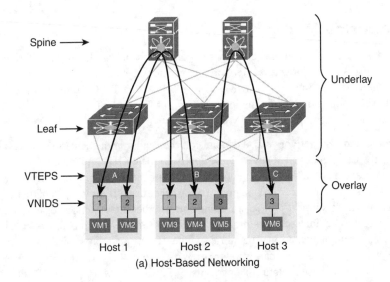

(a) Host-Based Networking

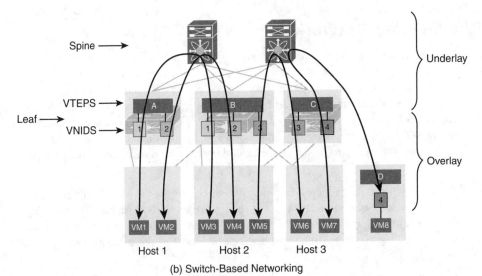

(b) Switch-Based Networking

Figure 15-3 *The Underlay and Overlay Network*

Notice in the figure the notion of an underlay and an overlay network. The edge of the overlay network—that is, the location of the endpoints of the IP tunnel called Virtual Tunnel End Point (VTEP), varies depending on whether host-based Figure 15-3a or switch-based networking Figure 15-3b is adopted. In a VMware NSX or OVN environment, for example, which adopts host-based networking, the VTEP resides inside the host at the hypervisor level. To the contrary, in a Cisco ACI environment, the VTEP mostly resides in the physical leaf switch, but it can accommodate VTEPs that reside inside the host at the hypervisor. In both cases, the VXLAN Network Identifier (VNID) is an identifier or a tag that represents a logical segment, which is an L2 broadcast domain that is tunneled over the VTEP tunnels. So, in this example, the logical L2 segments (VNID), tunnels, and endpoints (VTEP) are shown in Table 15-1.

Table 15-1 *Mapping Between VNID and VTEP*

	VNID (Segments)	VTEP
VM1, VM3	1	A, B
VM2, VM4	2	A, B
VM5, VM6	3	B, C
VM7, VM8	4	C, D

VM1 and VM3 belong inside the same L2 broadcast domain. As such, they are both attached to VNID 1, and the traffic is tunneled between VTEPs A and B.

Notice that in the host-based networking model (a), the switch fabric is doing a simple L3 routing function, and the host is doing the heavy lifting. In switch-based networking (b), the switch fabric does the heavy lifting, offloading the host CPUs.

VXLAN is a tunneling mechanism that originated to create L2 overlay networks on top of L3 networks. VXLAN encapsulates an Ethernet packet into an IP UDP packet from one end of the tunnel and delivers it to the other end of the tunnel over the L3 routed fabric. The use of UDP allows routers to apply hashing algorithms on the outer UDP header for load balancing the traffic. Because the tunnels leverage the L3 network, VM traffic that is riding the tunnels in the overlay is load balanced over multiple links using ECMP. This is a major advantage compared to the traditional three-tier designs, where access switches connect to distribution switches via L2, which causes redundant links to block due to spanning tree.

The VXLAN frame format is seen in Figure 15-4.

Looking at the VXLAN frame, you can identify the original Ethernet frame that is tunneled, the outer IP and UDP headers, and the addition of eight bytes in the VXLAN header.

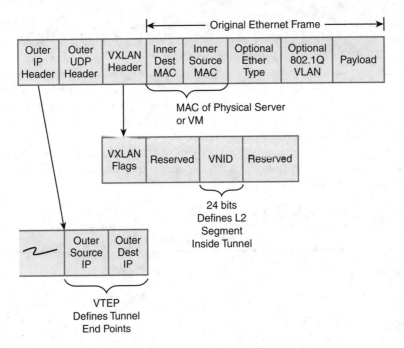

Figure 15-4 *The VXLAN Frame Format*

Inside the original Ethernet frame, notice the inner destination and source MAC addresses. These are the addresses of the end nodes whose traffic is being tunneled. These could be the addresses of physical servers or the virtual MAC (vMAC) address of the virtual NICs (vNICs) of the VMs.

You can also notice the 8-byte VXLAN header that contains the VXLAN segment identifier, called VXLAN Node ID (VNID). The VNID is the VXLAN segment identifier that is comparable to a VLAN number. However, unlike the VLAN, which uses 12 bits with a maximum of $2^{16} = 4096$ VLANs, a VNID is a 24-bit number with a maximum of $2^{24} = 16,777,216$ VNIDs, offering a much bigger scale. Inside the VXLAN header, there are flags and reserved bits to further segment the traffic (microsegmentation) so it can be identified based on other constructs within the same segment.

Inside the outer IP header, notice the outer source IP address and outer destination IP address of the devices that are performing the VXLAN encapsulation and decapsulation. These are called the VTEPs. The VTEPs are normally virtual or loopback IP addresses. A loopback IP address is one that is not associated with a physical port but rather is a logical entity that identifies a certain device. Depending on whether routing is done inside or outside a host, the VTEP could be the loopback IP address of the host or the loopback IP address of the leaf node in a leaf and spine topology.

Because VXLAN adds an additional header to the packet and the original Ethernet frame is encapsulated in a UDP packet, the maximum transmit unit (MTU) size of the IP packet changes. The original Ethernet payload is 1500 bytes. The inner Ethernet headers are 14 bytes without VLAN tags or 18 bytes with VLAN tags, the VXLAN header is 8 bytes, the outer UDP header is 8 bytes, and the outer IPv4 header is 20 bytes; therefore, the MTU size varies between 1550 bytes and 1554 bytes, depending on the implementation. Cisco, for example, strips the VLAN header (4 bytes) when doing the VXLAN encapsulation, which means the MTU size should be at least 1550 bytes. This necessitates the use of jumbo Ethernet frames, which extend the MTU size from the standard 1500 bytes to 9000 bytes.

Microsegmentation in the Data Center

Traditionally, networking in the data center was based on simple networking concepts that were on one hand straightforward but created a lot of overhead on the back end. As seen in Chapter 1, servers and applications were assigned subnets and VLANs. This was simple but created a lot of complexities because application segmentation and policies were physically restricted to the boundaries of the VLAN within the same data center. With the addition of virtualization and every physical server having multiple applications, the problem became harder. Now there is a requirement that applications be mobile and can move around between servers to balance loads for performance or high availability upon failures.

Another issue with the simple segmentation based on VLANs is that you offload all policies, such as which application needs to talk to which application and who can access an application, to centralized firewalls (FWs) that are normally connected to the distribution layer. This puts a huge burden on the firewall, especially because most traffic in data centers is now "East-West" between web server VMs, application server VMs, and database VMs. Traffic that must be inspected used to travel all the way to the firewall and back for every connection between servers and now between VMs.

A new model must be adopted in the data center, where policies applied to applications are independent from the location or the network tied to the application. The decision to have application A talk to application B or database C should not be bound by which VLAN or IP subnet the application belongs to and whether it is in the same rack or even in the same data center. Also, traffic should not make multiple trips back and forth between VMs and centralized firewalls to decide on whether a VM should talk to another VM. This is achieved via what is called *microsegmentation*, which is segmentation at the VM level regardless of a VLAN or a subnet. This type of segmentation is application aware and starts and ends with the application itself. With this new level of microsegmentation, most vendors are implementing a *zero-trust model*, in which users cannot talk to applications and applications cannot talk to other applications unless a defined set of policies permits them to do so. This brings a heightened level of security that is in line with today's application requirements.

Efforts in microsegmentation are ongoing on multiple fronts. Examples of such efforts are the OVS and the OVN. Other efforts are specific to containerized environments, such as project Contiv [4]. Contiv is an open source project that facilitates the deployment of microsegmentation services in a container environment.

Networking Open Source Initiatives

This section discusses different open source initiatives for networking. This includes Neutron from OpenStack, Open vSwitch (OVS), and OVN.

Neutron

This is the networking part of OpenStack, whose objective is to provide "networking as a service" between devices that are managed by other OpenStack services. Cloud tenants interact with Neutron with a set of APIs to configure the networking services. These entities could be end users using configuration tools, other open source services such as Horizon (Dashboard, Web UI), or Nova compute service. In addition, Neutron allows vendors to use plug-ins to deliver advanced networking capabilities. Neutron consists of the neutron server and a database that handles persistent storage and plug-ins to provide additional services. Figure 15-5 shows the high-level API and plug-ins constructs of Neutron.

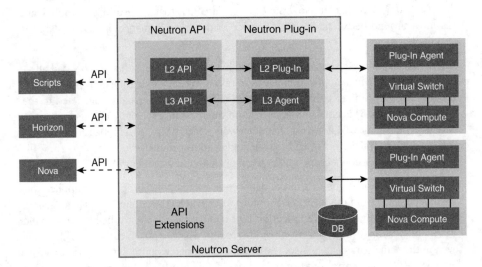

Figure 15-5 *Neutron Server*

Now let's define some of the Neutron terminology.

Neutron Server

The Neutron server acts as a "controller" that delivers a set of APIs that interact with outside tenants using scripts or other OpenStack services such as Horizon service for management and Nova service for compute. For each API, the server provides one plug-in. For example, for an L2 API, the server allows an L2 plug-in, and for an L3 API, the server allows an L3 plug-in, and so on. In addition, the Neutron server manages a database for persistent storage.

Neutron-APIs

The APIs allow tenants to use the Neutron service. For example, a tenant could use scripts to request a networking configuration of a three-tier web, app, and database application. The APIs request from Neutron the configuration of networking functions such as IP addresses, subnets, firewalls, load balancers, and more for the particular application. APIs can come from other OpenStack services such as Nova. A Nova compute service, for example, initiates multiple VMs and requests from the Neutron server to give IP addresses to these VMs and to connect these VMs to a virtual switch. The Neutron server instructs the compute nodes and networking nodes directly or by using plug-ins to implement these services. Other APIs allow networking services to be configured, such as Firewall as a Service (FWaaS) and VPN as a Service (VPNaaS).

Neutron Plug-Ins

For each of the APIs, Neutron has a plug-in. The plug-in allows different vendors to provide networking services for Neutron to use. The core plug-ins allow L2 connectivity and IP address assignment, whereas the service plug-ins allow additional services such as routing, firewalls, and load balancers. Examples of plug-ins are the Cisco/Unified Computing System (UCS) Nexus, Cisco Nexus 1000v, Modular Layer 2 (ML2), plus many more plug-ins from other vendors.

The ML2 plug-in has special importance because it allows OpenStack to simultaneously use different Layer 2 networking technologies. The ML2 plug-in obsoletes older plug-ins like the Open vSwitch plug-in and the Linux-bridge plug-in. The ML2 plug-in is composed of two drivers: the type driver and the mechanism driver.

1. **ML2 type drivers:** These define the different networking types that are used. For ML2, the type drivers are for VLANs, VXLAN, Generic Routing Encapsulation (GRE) tunnels, and more.

2. **ML2 mechanism drivers:** Mechanism drivers apply the ML2 type drivers to different networking mechanisms. Examples of vendor-specific mechanism drivers are the Cisco Nexus mechanism driver that supports the Nexus switches 3000–9000 for type driver VLAN and Nexus 3100 and 9000 mechanism drivers that support the type driver VXLAN, the Cisco APIC ML2 driver that supports API, and API extensions for networks, subnets, ports, external networks, routers, security groups, and more. Another important open source mechanism driver is the OVS that provides L2 switching capabilities.

The Neutron plug-ins on the Neutron server interact via remote procedure call (RPC) messaging with agents that sit on the compute or networking nodes.

Agents

Agents are the modules inside the hypervisors or host kernel that provide, among many things, the L2 and L3 connectivity to the VM instances and the translation between the virtual environment and the physical environment. The agents reside inside the compute nodes, such as on a hypervisor or kernel, initiate the configuration of virtual switches, and connect the VM to these switches. A Dynamic Host Configuration Protocol (DHCP) agent, for example, instructs the DHCP server to allocate the IP addresses for the VMs. The agents interact with the Neutron server plug-ins via the RPC messaging, as already discussed for other OpenStack components. Figure 15-6 shows the interaction between the driver and the agent.

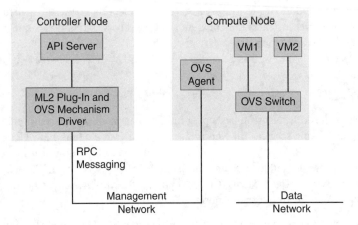

Figure 15-6 *Neutron Plug-Ins and Agents*

As you can see, inside the controller that has the Neutron server, the ML2 plug-in has an OVS mechanism driver. The driver interacts with the OVS agent inside the host via RPC messaging. The OVS agent, in turn, configures the OVS switch in the host. The VM initiation already occurred via the Nova engine on the host.

OVS Architecture

The OVS architecture as originally defined by OpenStack had many inefficiencies in virtual networking that resulted in performance overheads. As an oversimplification, think of the architecture as being based on provider networks and self-service networks.

The provider network, based on VLANs, basically gives L2 functionality and optional IP addressing and provides connectivity to the external physical network. Provider networks are provisioned by administrators who want to offer basic L2 functionality using the OVS.

Self-service networks expand the L2 provider network into a virtualized network that is self-provisioned and provides the concept of virtual routers to allow the provider network to connect to other provider networks and outside entities such as the Internet. In addition to L3 routing, self-service networks introduce the concept of tunneling via overlay protocols such as VXLAN, GRE, and others. Self-service networks also introduced floating IP addresses, which are public IP addresses that access hosts in the data center from the Internet. Floating IP addresses can be moved around between hosts and VMs and are an entry and exit point from and to the Internet. Private IP addresses can be used for local access and mapped via network address translation (NAT) to connect to public IP addresses.

The self-service network uses L3 agents to implement L3 routing, where one or multiple agents are deployed on networking nodes. L3 routing uses the concept of namespace, and each namespace has its set of IP tables. For those who are familiar with L3 routers, this is the same concept as VRF, where a VRF table has a set of IP addresses and subnets that overlap with other VRFs. This allows multiple projects or organizations to use the same overlapping IP addresses while they are perfectly shielded from one another.

L3 routing as done with Neutron in conjunction with the OVS plug-ins creates performance issues as routing is centralized. Whenever traffic crosses subnets, it must be directed to the centralized L3 engine. As you will see next, the OVN project introduced many enhancements to avoid such inefficiencies. Figure 15-7 shows an oversimplified view of Neutron and OVS routing.

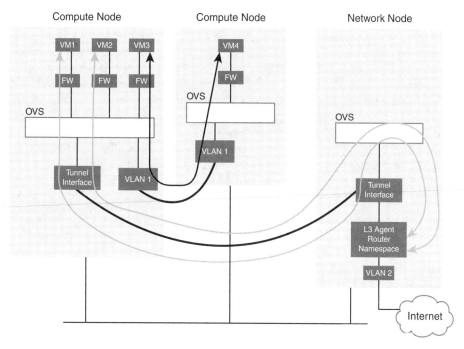

Figure 15-7   *L3 Routing with OVS and Neutron*

Notice that the VM instances created by Nova belong to different subnets. VM3 and VM4 belong to the same subnet (VLAN1), whereas VM1 and VM2 belong to different subnets. Each of the instances connects to a firewall before connecting to a port on the OVS switch. This creates microsegmentation where the FW is distributed and applied at the VM level. The L3 function is done in the networking node via the L3 agent that delivers the routing function. Traffic between VM1 and VM2 that lives on the same compute node must be sent over a tunnel interface (VXLAN, for example) and travel the physical network to reach the L3 function and then go back to the same OVS. This causes inefficiencies and performance overhead because inter-VLAN traffic must always travel to a centralized router in the cluster. This type of routing is referenced in the industry as the "routing on a stick" approach.

Multiple initiatives spawn out in the open source community to perform enhancements to the control and data planes of the initial Neutron/OVS architecture. One project called the OpenDaylight (ODL) [6] was founded in 2013 and is focused on the enhancement of SDN controllers to facilitate network services across multiple vendors. One of the specific projects of ODL interacts with Neutron and attempts to solve the existing inefficiencies. ODL interacts with Neutron via a northbound interface and manages multiple interfaces southbound, including OVSDB and OpenFlow. So, ODL, for networking, acts as a layer between Neutron and Open vSwitch and replaces inefficiencies that exist in RPC message queuing, centralized L3 agents, and so on. ODL uses a centralized controller model to push functionality down to the Open vSwitch via the use of OpenFlow.

However, as is typical in the open source community, engineers get together as a group and create their own alternative solutions to solve the same problem. Hence, the creation of the OVN project, which started as an extension of the OVS project with the objective of simplifying the Neutron/OVS control and data planes. Comparing ODL to OVN is not a fair comparison, as ODL is more focused on SDN controllers that solve a multitude of issues, and one of them overlaps with OVN. However, from a velocity point of view, focused projects usually go a lot faster than generalized projects, so OVN has more momentum in the specific areas of network virtualization. Also, ODL is community based, like OpenStack, which means that whoever contributes must give back to the community. In contrast, OVN can be licensed under the Apache license, and although vendors are encouraged to contribute with enhancements, they are not obliged to do so.

For the purposes of this book, which deals with hyperconvergence, OVN so far is seeing more adoption in hyperconverged architectures. So, you will see a lot of similarities between OVN and VMware NSX as an example, mainly because the roots of NSX were in OVS and evolved to OVN. Other vendors such as Nutanix are riding the same bandwagon.

The next part of this book goes into more detail about SDN and discusses different implementations, including open source OVN, VMware NSX, and Cisco ACI.

OVN—The Open Source SDN

The concept of SDN is broad, and every vendor takes it in a different direction.

Open source and OpenStack in the areas of compute, storage, and networking were already discussed. This section goes into more detail on OVS and OVN. This sets the stage for discussion on VMware NSX and Cisco ACI in the next two chapters.

First let's start with a brief introduction to OVS.

Open vSwitch

Open vSwitch (OVS) is an open source implementation of a multilayer virtual switch inside the hypervisor. It is licensed under the Apache 2.0 license. The virtual switch basically does what a physical switch does; however, all the switch components are defined in software. The virtual switch has interfaces and multiple interfaces form ports. Bridges are defined to forward traffic between ports, and VLANs are defined to separate traffic. Tunnel ports tunnel traffic between virtual switches, and so on. Open vSwitch introduced an architecture that comprises an SDN controller that configures and manages virtual switches via the OVSDB protocol and pushes flows inside the switches via the OpenFlow protocol. The architecture is described in Figure 15-8.

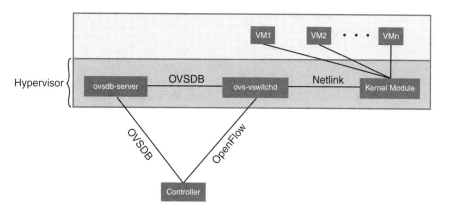

Figure 15-8   *Open vSwitch Architecture*

OVSDB, as in Open vSwitch Database, is a protocol written in the JavaScript Object Notation (JSON) that basically sends and receives commands via JSON RPCs. OpenFlow is a protocol that sends flow information into the virtual switch so the switch can forward the packets between the different ports. Flows are defined based on different criteria such as traffic between a source MAC address and a destination MAC address, source and destination IP addresses, TCP ports, VLANs, tunnels, and so on.

The components of the OVS are an ovsdb-server database, an ovsdb-vswitchd daemon, and a kernel module.

Ovsdb-server is a configuration database that controls and stores the switch-level configuration. It contains information on creating bridges, attaching interfaces, attaching tunnels, and so on. The database contains a set of tables that point to each other in a sequence. So, on the top level, for example, you would have an Open vSwitch table that points to a bridge table that in turn points to a port table that then points to an interface table. The database is stateful in the sense that information is maintained on disk and recaptured if the system is rebooted. The ovsdb-server database talks to the outside controller via the OVSDB protocol.

Ovsdb-vswitchd is a daemon that performs flow handling and is the core of Open vSwitch. It connects to the outside controller via the OpenFlow protocol and to the ovsdb-server via the OVSDB protocol. It connects to the kernel via a Netlink interface for Linux. ovsdb-vswitchd has all the different defined bridges and all the flow tables needed to forward packets. Ovsdb-vswitchd handles the forwarding of all sorts of flows that are communicated to it via the OpenFlow protocol.

Ovsdb-vswitchd pushes the flows to the kernel module for fast forwarding. When the first packet arrives, it goes through the kernel module, where the headers are hashed to find a flow entry. If the flow entry is not found, the packet goes to ovsdb-vswitchd for normal processing. Ovsdb-vswitchd then pushes the flow to be cached inside the module kernel. If a similar flow comes in, it is forwarded via the fast path inside the kernel module. The kernel module does not contain any of the OpenFlow tables that are known to ovsdb-vswitchd; rather, it contains the result of the different lookups in the flow tables. The kernel module also handles the tunneling of packets via protocols such as GRE, VXLAN, and others.

OVN

OVN [7] stands for Open Virtual Network. This project is an evolution of the Open vSwitch (OVS) project that focused on building a virtual switch. OVS focused mainly on building the basic elements of an L2 virtual switch. Advanced functionality such as L3 distributed routing, L4 policies, quality of service (QoS), network address translation (NAT), and so on, were not part of OVS itself.

The focus of OVN was to build upon the basics of OVS but expand into the area of virtual networking with ease of provisioning and better performance. OVN is open source, and it is vendor neutral with many leading vendors contributing to the project. It is sold under the Apache License, similar to OVS. Unlike OpenStack Neutron, which is a community-type project, vendors can license OVN and do their own developments without being obliged to share the development with the rest of the community.

Although the OVN project is progressing and functionality is being added, it is hard to work with open source projects while playing catch-up. A vendor has the option to wait for OVN releases to introduce the functionality or start with a certain release and build his own functionality at the expense of diverging from OVN, at least until the vendor can converge with OVN again. OVN is a good starting point for companies that want to develop virtual networking, but at the expense of always lagging behind nonstandard implementations.

OVN Functionality

The following is a list of functionalities under the OVN project. More functionality is added every release:

- L2 and L3 switching functionality

- Support for multiple tunnel overlays, such as GENEVE, STT, and VXLAN

- Support for policies through the use of security groups and access control lists (ACLs)

- Distributed L3 routing for IPv4 and IPv6

- Support for NAT

- Support for DHCP

- Support for load balancing

- Support for L2 and L3 gateways; gateways could be software or hardware based

- Ability to work with multiple Linux hypervisors, such as kernel-based virtual machine (KVM) and Xen

- Ability to work with Microsoft Hyper-V

- Support for containers

- Support for DPDK

- Ability to integrate with multiple cloud management systems (CMSs), such as OpenStack, Kubernetes, Docker, Mesos, and oVirt

OVN High-Level Architecture

OVN is based on a distributed database architecture that gives performance improvements over the original OVS architecture and the way it interacts with CMSs such as OpenStack Neutron, as shown in Figure 15-9.

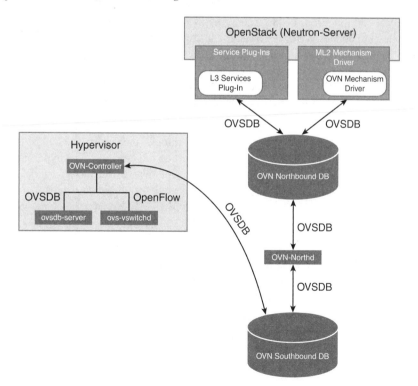

Figure 15-9 *OVN High-Level Architecture*

OVN is designed to work with multiple types of CMSs; however, the first implementation was done for OpenStack and specifically Neutron. The Neutron server acts as a CMS controller and interfaces with the rest of the OVN components via the different OVN plug-ins.

OVN has a northbound database that contains all the logical networking constructs that the controller requires. The northbound database contains the logical view of the network, such as logical switches and routers, ports, ACLs, and so on. The northbound database has absolutely no knowledge of the physical network or the existence of hypervisors. The northbound database has an upward link to the CMS controller and a downward link to an OVN module called ovn-northd.

ovn-northd takes the logical concepts that are kept in the northbound database and translates them into constructs that the hypervisors and Open vSwitch understand. So, a logical router, for example, is translated into logical flows that are like the flows the OpenFlow protocol defines. The main difference is that the flows are logical rather than physical. So instead of the flows referencing physical ports, they reference logical ports that the hypervisor uses. This logical flow information is then saved into another database called the southbound database.

The southbound database now contains all the logical information, such as logical ports, that the hypervisor understands. The southbound database has the hypervisors as clients. Inside each hypervisor, the southbound database interacts with an OVN controller.

The OVN controller runs inside each hypervisor. It sends to the southbound database the ports that are bound on the hypervisor. The controller also takes the logical flows that are in the southbound database and translates them to physical flows. So, for example, if a logical flow references a hypervisor that is on a different physical host, the logical flow is mapped to a tunnel interface that takes it to that hypervisor. The ovn-controller inside the hypervisor talks to the Open vSwitch via a regular OpenFlow protocol, and it talks to an ovsdb-server via the OVSDB protocol.

So, the communication for OVN is always done through databases. The logical view of the world as desired by a CMS is kept in the northbound database. The hypervisor view of the world is kept in the southbound database. The ovn-northd acts as a translator, and the ovn-controller is the vehicle to interact with the southbound database and the hypervisor. It performs the final configuration to the Open vSwitch to stitch together the virtual network.

Improvements over OVS and Neutron Integration

OVN is built to integrate with CMS controllers. The first solid implementation is with OpenStack—specifically with Neutron. However, OVN is replacing many of the OVS drivers and agents defined for Neutron, to the point where OVN is becoming self-sufficient for network virtualization and does not rely on Neutron for these functions. The objective of

OVN is to use Neutron only as a CMS controller, while leaving all the other networking functionality to be built inside OVN. Areas of differentiation between OVS and OVN fall into different areas.

Control Plane Improvements

There are major differences between OVS and OVN when integrating with Neutron. You already saw how OVS works based on having an ML2 plug-in and an OVS driver inside the Neutron server that talks via RPC messaging with an OVS agent inside the compute node. The agent is written in Python.

OVN, on the other hand, replaces all the agents and works based on a distributed database architecture. It is written in the C language. The control plane operates through databases and distributed controllers that reside inside the hypervisors. Some of the performance issues with OVS and Neutron, as an example, are related to the interaction between Nova and Neutron; through RPC messaging, Nova requests the networking parameters to the VMs before powering the VMs and waits on Neutron. Neutron, in turn, instructs Nova that these parameters were configured, which prompts Nova to power the VM. Through the adoption of a database architecture, OVN improves the synchronization and reporting between Neutron and Nova, thereby improving the performance.

Data Plane Improvements

OVN also makes many improvements in the data plane, including security groups (OVN ACLs) and L3 routing. For security groups, OVN clearly simplifies the number of stacks when traffic moves between one VM and another. In the traditional OVS architecture, when defining an OVS bridge, a Linux bridge is created. This is because security rules or ACLs are applied in the Linux bridge by checking iptables. Traffic from VM1 to VM2 had to go from VM1 to a Linux bridge, where the iptables are checked and ACL applied. Then traffic goes to an OVS bridge, to a Linux bridge, and then to VM2. This is seen in Figure 15-10.

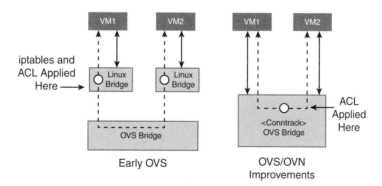

Figure 15-10 *OVN Simplifications in the Data Plane*

In the latest OVS releases, OVS relies on the Kernel Connection tracking (Conntrack) to perform stateful packet inspection. As such, OVN security groups now use OVS support of Conntrack to apply ACLs; they do not have to rely on checking iptables and namespaces. This dramatically improves the performance of security groups. Figure 15-10 shows how instances connect directly now to an OVS bridge where security rules are applied.

When it comes to L3 routing, notice with the OVS/Neutron integration that L3 routing and forwarding is done via centralized L3 agents and namespaces. Routed traffic must pass through these agents that reside in network nodes. OVN, in contrast, replaces the L3 agents with OVN controllers inside the compute nodes and creates a distributed router where L3 packet processing is done inside Open vSwitch. This decreases the multiple routing hops and IP classifications by using cached information about flows to modify the destination MAC address to the final target destination and modifying the time to live (TTL) of the packet. Also, OVN minimizes the ARP flooding on the network by suppressing ARP and replying to ARP requests on behalf of the destination node. Figure 15-11 shows the OVN integration with Neutron [7] and the simplification presented by using databases. As you can see, the L3 routing and networking services are performed inside the compute nodes and are controlled via each OVN controller.

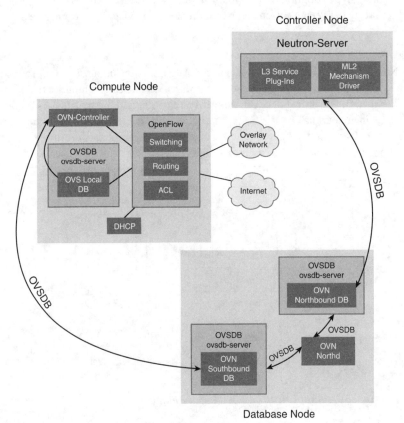

Figure 15-11 *OVN Integration with Neutron*

OVN is now being adopted by HCI vendors that are building their networking portfolio.

Nutanix announced in 2018 its SDN offering called Flow. However, the Nutanix implementation focused only on microsegmentation per the OVS implementation. As far as networking, Nutanix still relies on basic OVS L2 switching constructs and relies on external switch fabric for the heavy lifting.

State of Vendors with Open Source

What you saw so far is a brief and condensed view of some OpenStack and open source components as they relate to compute, storage, and networking. As you saw, OpenStack is not straightforward and has many moving parts. Enterprises need support from the vendors to facilitate and streamline the OpenStack deployments.

Vendors in the HCI space are involved with OpenStack in many forms. Cisco, for example, was a contributor to OpenStack since day one. Cisco's approach to OpenStack is mainly via integration with UCS and Nexus. From a UCS perspective, Cisco, Red Hat, and Intel have created a Cisco Validated Design (CVD) to facilitate the ease of deployment of OpenStack in enterprise networks.

The Cisco UCS Integrated Infrastructure for Red Hat Enterprise Linux OpenStack (UCSO) combines cloud orchestration with the ability to deliver compute, storage, networking, and management under a single platform. This gives enterprises the ability to easily deliver infrastructure as a service (IaaS), platform as a service (PaaS), and software as a service (SaaS) capabilities to the end user. This entails an integration between Red Hat Enterprise Linux OpenStack Platform with Cisco UCS Manager. Cisco offers OpenStack plug-ins for servers, switches, and virtual NICs (vNICs), which eliminate setup delays and the possibility of errors in repetitive configuration for the same tasks.

In general, the integration between OpenStack and vendor platforms is accomplished via APIs (see Figure 15-12).

Basically, an OpenStack controller is used as an entry point for the client requests to provision the OpenStack compute, storage, and networking cloud. The controller itself could be a third-party controller or something vendor developed. Vendors such as Cisco, VMware, and Nutanix wrote drivers for the specific services. These drivers can be an integrated part of a vendor-specific controller or an interface with external controllers via RPC messaging.

This allows enterprises to have a uniform infrastructure based on OpenStack, while still interfacing with one or multiple vendor HCI devices on the back end.

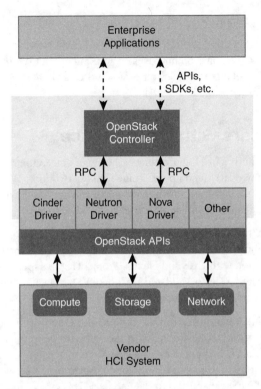

Figure 15-12 *Integration with OpenStack*

Looking Ahead

This chapter described the basics of software-defined networking and the different development tracks in the open source community. When it comes to networking, each of the hyperconverged vendors that is listed—VMware, Cisco, and Nutanix—is on a different track. Cisco implemented an ACI hardware fabric with an APIC controller, VMware implemented a software-only solution called NSX that has its roots in open source, and Nutanix announced solutions based on open source.

Chapter 16, "VMware NSX," discusses the VMware NSX implementation.

Chapter 17, "Application-Centric Infrastructure," discusses the Cisco ACI and APIC implementation.

References

[1] www.microsoft.com/en-us/research/wp-content/uploads/2016/10/Cloud-Scale-Acceleration-Architecture.pdf

[2] www.accoladetechnology.com; www.broadcom.com; www.cavium.com; www.intel.com; www.mellanox.com; www.solarflare.com

[3] www.dpdk.org

[4] http://contiv.github.io

[5] https://ieeexplore.ieee.org/document/6770468/ - Clos, Charles (Mar 1953). "A Study of Non-Blocking Switching Networks." *Bell System Technical Journal.*

[6] www.opendaylight.org

[7] http://openvswitch.org/support/dist-docs/ovn-architecture.7.html

[8] https://docs.openstack.org/networking-ovn/latest/admin/refarch/refarch.html

Chapter 16

VMware NSX

This chapter covers the following key topics:

- **Setting and Enforcing Policies in NSX:** An introduction to VMware NSX and how you use it to set and enforce policies at the virtual machine (VM) level.

- **The NSX Control Plane Components:** A description of the NSX control plane components that define security policies and networking functionality, including the NSX manager and NSX controllers cluster.

- **VXLAN Enhancements for vDS:** A description of the vSphere distributed switch (vDS) enhancements in support of VXLAN.

- **Flooding Avoidance:** A description of how NSX avoids flooding with the help of the NSX controller and via APR suppression.

- **NSX L2 Switching and IP Routing** A description of NSX L2 switching and details on IP routing and its components. This includes a description of the distributed logical router (DLR) and the edge services gateway (ESG).

- **Handling of Multidestination Traffic:** A description of the mechanisms used to handle broadcast, unknown unicast, and multicast (BUM) traffic.

VMware's network virtualization and security platform (NSX) is the solution for bringing automation, policy, and security into the networking environment. NSX attempts to simplify the deployment of the networking in the data center and to automate the configuration of policy and networking for the applications.

NSX falls under the host-based networking category. The overlay functions and microsegmentation are mainly performed inside the host at the ESXi hypervisor level, with some added support from the NSX controller. In this model, the Ethernet fabric itself plays a simple role of L3 routing of packets.

Let's look deeper at NSX, starting with how NSX applies policies and then how data control and forwarding are accomplished.

Setting and Enforcing Policies in NSX

NSX adopts microsegmentation in the data center by decoupling policy from the physical network. NSX sets policies at a fine granularity based on networking constructs, virtual machine (VM) attributes, service names, and so on. In NSX, policy enforcement is done at the VM virtual network interface card (vNIC) level, which limits the solution to virtual endpoints only. In data center environments where policies must be applied on VMs, as well as applications that run on bare-metal servers such as databases, NSX and host-based networking solutions in general cannot handle the full scope and require physical gateways.

NSX has a service composer to deploy security services in a data center. The service composer allows the setting of security groups, security policies, and integration with third-party vendors to apply networking services.

Security Groups

With NSX, a security group represents a set of virtual endpoints that have similar policies. The grouping is independent of networking constructs such as IP, virtual LANs (VLANs), and media access controls (MACs) and focuses more on grouping based on the requirements and the components of the application.

NSX grouping includes many criteria, such as VM properties, vCenter objects, and NSX objects. The classification is either dynamic or static. Dynamic classification relates to the VM properties, such as a VM name, an operating system name, or a tag assigned to the VM. Static classification relates more to networking constructs such as port groups, distributed switches, MACs, Internet protocol (IP), and vNIC.

An example of service grouping is illustrated in Figure 16-1.

Notice that VMs are spread out in the same host or across multiple physical hosts. The VMs could be on different IP subnets depending on the distributed switches and port groups they are connected to. A logical grouping of the VMs is a combination of what tier they belong to (WEB, App, DB) and what operational group they belong to, such as Finance (FIN) or Humane Resources (HR). The classification into such groups can be based on security tags applied to the VMs. Security tags provide contextual information about the VM. For example, a WEB VM in the finance department on an HP host number 1 could be named finance-webvm-hp-1. This VM would belong to security group SG-FIN-WEB and be assigned security tag FIN-TAG-WEB. A sample of the service groups is shown in Table 16-1.

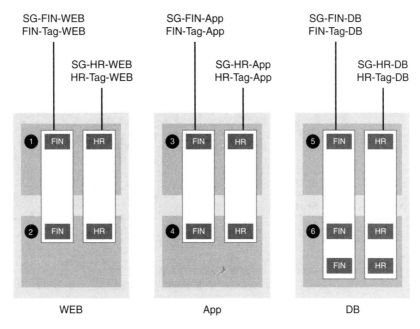

Figure 16-1 *NSX Service Groups*

Table 16-1 *Security Group Allocation*

Security Group	Selection Criteria: Security Tag	Included VMs
SG-FIN-WEB	FIN-Tag-WEB	finance-webvm-hp1, finance-webvm-hp2
SG-HR-WEB	HR-Tag-WEB	hr-webvm-hp1, hr-webvm-hp2
SG-FIN-App	FIN-Tag-App	finance-appvm-hp3, finance-appvm-hp3
SG-HR-App	HR-Tag-App	hr-appvm-hp3, hr-appvm-hp4
SG-FIN-DB	FIN-Tag-DB	finance-dbvm-hp5, finance-dbvm-hp6
SG-HR-DB	HR-Tag-DB	hr-dbvm-hp5, hr-dbvm-hp6

Security Policy

After defining security groups, a security policy needs to be defined. Security policies comprise security services, such as firewalls, load balancer, and intrusion prevention systems (IPSs). The security policy includes policies that are defined by NSX or published by third-party security vendors. Such policies are created as templates that are reusable and applied to security groups. Table 16-2 shows a template that can be applied to the security groups defined in Table 16-1.

Table 16-2   *Sample Policy Rules*

Rule Name	Source	Destination	Service	Action
FIN-Internet to Web	Any	SG-FIN-WEB	HTTP, HTTPS	Allow
HR-Internet to Web	Any	SG-HR- WEB	HTTP, HTTPS	Allow
FIN-Web to App	SG-FIN-WEB	SG-FIN-App	Tomcat (HTTP 8080), SSH (22)	Allow
HR-Web to App	SG-HR-WEB	SG-HR-App	Tomcat (HTTP 8080), SSH (22)	Allow
FIN-App to DB	SG-FIN-App	SG-FIN-DB	MySQL (3306)	Allow
HR-App to DB	SG-HR-App	SG-HR-DB	MySQL (3306)	Allow
Default	Any	Any	Any	Block

The rule table allows user traffic coming from the Internet (http, https) to access the Web tier. It allows Hypertext Transfer Protocol (HTTP) port 8080 and Secure Shell (SSH) port 22 traffic between the Web tier and the App tier, and it allows MySQL traffic port 3306 between the App tier and the DB tier. Notice that all other traffic is blocked, including traffic within the same tier. So, for example, any traffic between the FIN Web tier and the APP Web tier, other than what is listed in the rule table, is blocked. To allow some traffic to pass, such as "ping," for example, more rules should be added.

When multiple rules are applied to the same security group, NSX defines a "weight" to determine the rank of a policy compared to other policies. Also, NSX allows the creation of parent/child policies, where the child policy inherits the rules of the parent.

Policy Enforcement

NSX applies firewalls for policy enforcement either at the NSX Edge gateway for North-South traffic or inside the ESXi hypervisor for East-West traffic.

For East-West traffic, NSX inserts the distributed firewall at the vNIC level to create a "service pipeline." This is seen in Figure 16-2. Based on this pipeline, NSX chains the network services and decides what traffic should use the local distributed firewall and what traffic is redirected to third-party appliances. However, when redirecting the traffic, NSX sends only to virtual appliances that run as VMs in the cluster.

As shown in the figure, NSX uses the concept of slots to insert the service functionality. Slot 2, for example, is used to insert the distributed firewall (DFW), and slot 4 is used for third-party L4–L7 virtual appliances.

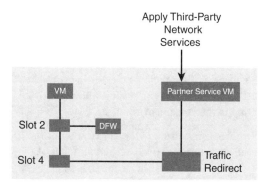

Figure 16-2   *Policy Enforcement at the vNIC*

The NSX Manager and Controller Cluster

Different NSX control plane components play a role in setting the security policies and networking functionality that dictate how applications interact with their environment. The NSX manager and the NSX controller cluster automate the configuration of policies and help implement the switching and routing in the cluster.

NSX Manager

The NSX manager is a virtual appliance that helps automate the configuration and deployment of the logical network. It has a one-to-one relationship with vCenter, and it provides the different networking and security plug-ins for the vCenter web UI that enable the administrators to configure the different NSX functionality. The NSX manager facilitates the deployment and configuration of the security policies as well as the elements to support the networking switching/routing functions. Figure 16-3 shows how the NSX manager interacts with the rest of the vCenter/vSphere environment.

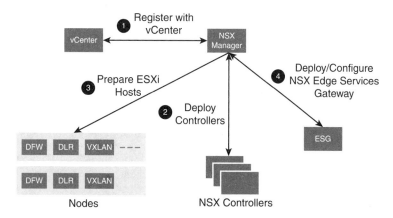

Figure 16-3   *NSX Manager Integration with vSphere and vCenter*

The process is shown in the following steps:

Step 1.   The NSX manager starts by registering with vCenter to give vCenter the different plug-ins that allow the operation of NSX.

Step 2.   The NSX manager then deploys the NSX controllers. The NSX controllers are discussed in the next section because they constitute the pillar of switching and routing in the virtual environment.

Step 3.   The NSX manager then starts the preparation of the ESXi hosts. The preparation of the ESXi hosts involves setting up most of the vSphere installation bundles (VIBs) for networking elements such as these:

- Enabling of VXLAN

- Distributed logical routing (DLR)

- Distributed firewall (DFW)

- Installation of agents inside ESXi for control plane communications

- Security of the control plane communication

Step 4.   The NSX manager deploys and configures the NSX edge services gateway (ESG) and configures the network services.

The NSX Controller Cluster

The controller cluster is the control plane element that is responsible for managing switching and routing with the logical switches. The NSX controller cluster is more in line with the traditional software-defined networking (SDN) approach of centralizing the control functions and pushing flows to be used in the data plane.

The NSX controller cluster is distributed over multiple controllers; usually a minimum of three controllers are spread out over separate physical hosts. The controllers are none other than virtual appliances running in the clusters that are protected via the traditional VMware high availability (HA) mechanism used to protect virtual machines. Each one of the controllers takes a piece of the control load and becomes a master for a set of logical switches, distributed routers, and other functions. Following are some of the main functions for the NSX controllers:

- Managing VXLAN for the logical switches.

- Exchanging with the different ESXi nodes information about MAC addresses, IPs, VXLAN Tunnel Endpoints (VTEPs), and more, and building different tables:

  - VXLAN Network Identifier/VXLAN Tunnel Endpoint (VNID/VTEP) table, which is sent to all ESX is on the same VXLAN segment.

  - VNID/MAC table, which is kept local to the controller and not sent.

  - IP to MAC ARP table, which is used for address resolution protocol (ARP) suppression.

- Supporting ARP suppression to reduce broadcast flooding in L2 domains.

- Each controller in the cluster shares the IP addresses of other controller nodes with the ESXi nodes that attach to it.

You will see down the line how the controller nodes eliminate the need for multicast in handling flooding. But first let's revisit the VMware vSphere distributed switch (vDS) and VXLAN.

Enhancements for vDS

The concept of vDS was briefly covered in Chapter 4, "Server Virtualization." As you might recall, the vDS extends across multiple ESXi hosts and offers L2 networking functionality similar to L2 switches. The distributed switch facilitates the configuration of networking functions by grouping multiple ports that VMs attach to. VMs connect to the vDS dv-ports via their vNICs. Multiple ports are grouped under dv-port groups that share the same characteristics. The vDS connects to the vmnics (physical NICs via dv-uplinks).

Traditional vDS supported the concept of VLANs only. With the introduction of NSX, the concept of VXLAN was introduced, so there is a minor change in terminology (see Figure 16-4).

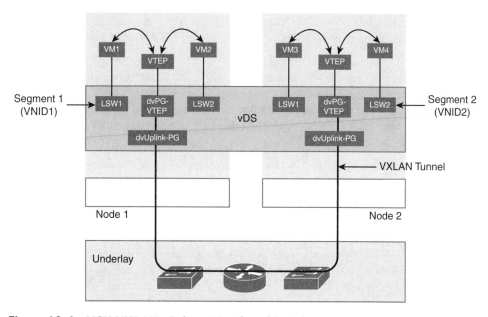

Figure 16-4 *NSX VXLAN vSphere Distributed Switch*

Notice the introduction of logical switch (LSW) terminology, which is simply a port group that supports VXLAN. Think of an LSW as an IP subnet. The LSW extends across the whole distributed switch and between different distributed switches if multiple departmental distributed switches are deployed. Every LSW is identified by a segment ID or VNID that is unique within an NSX manager.

LSWs are extended across the physical network via VXLAN tunnels that are identified with two endpoints: the VTEP. VTEP tunnels are referred to as VTEP segments. L2 frames associated with an LSW enter the tunnel via the VTEP and are given different VNIDs—one per logical switch. In this example, traffic from VM1 and VM3 enters the VTEP tunnel and is associated with VXLAN segment 1 (LSW1, VNID1). Traffic from VM2 and VM4 enters the VTEP tunnel and is associated with VXLAN segment 2 (LSW2, VNID2).

When VMs are communicating within the same logical switch (that is, on the same IP subnet), and the VMs are on different physical hosts, the traffic is encapsulated on one end of the tunnel inside an IP/User Datagram Protocol (UDP) packet and then is decapsulated on the other end. When VMs are within the same logical switch and are on the same physical host, the traffic is switched locally without the use of VXLAN.

When VMs belong to different LSWs—that is, in different IP subnets—an IP routing function is needed to route the traffic between tunnels or VTEP segments. The following section discusses IP routing within NSX and its different components.

Flooding Avoidance

NSX avoids flooding when doing L2 switching within a logical switch or L3 routing between logical switches. To do so, NSX relies on the NSX controller building VTEP/VNID/ARP tables.

Building the NSX controller tables is simple. Once a VM connects to an LSW, the corresponding ESXi host sends the VNID-to-VTEP mapping to the NSX controller. It also sends the VM MAC addresses and IP addresses. Based on this information, the NSX controllers build the VNID-to-VTEP table and the ARP table with IP-to-MAC address mapping of all VMs.

The NSX controllers send the VNID/VTEP information back to all hosts that use the information to replicate to the VTEPs, as described in the "Multidestination Traffic" section later in this chapter. However, for IP and MAC addresses, the NSX controllers use the information to build the ARP table for ARP suppression when handling ARP requests from the hosts.

The NSX controller performs what is called ARP suppression to prevent flooding of the ARP packets in an L2 domain. When a VM sends an ARP request to find the MAC address of another VM in the same LSW, the ESXi of the originating VM intercepts the request and generates a request to the NSX controller asking for the IP/MAC mapping for the destination VM. Based on such information, the originating ESXi generates an ARP reply on behalf of the destination with a source MAC address of the destination. If, however, the NSX controller does not already have the IP/MAC of the destination, it informs the originating ESXi host, which causes a regular ARP flooding to occur. The type of flooding depends on the method of handling multidestination traffic, as explained later in this chapter.

NSX L2 Switching and L3 Routing

NSX uses host-based networking in support of L2 switching and L3 routing. All switching functionality is done within the host and does not rely on fabric switches as with switch-based networking implementations. This is described next.

NSX L2 Switching

The NSX L2 switching between VMs is straightforward. Basically, if the VMs are in the same segment and inside the same physical node, local switching is done within the vDS. If the different VMs are on different physical nodes, VXLAN must be used to exchange traffic between the hosts over the L3 network. In either case, the source VM performs an ARP request to receive the MAC address of the destination. ARP handling, as stated before, is done through the support of the controllers. After receiving the IP-to-MAC mapping, the source VM already has in its tables a VNID/MAC/VTEP mapping received from the NSX controller. Assuming the destination MAC is on a separate host, the source VM encapsulates the L2 packet in the appropriate VTEP tunnel and sends it to the destination node. This is similar to the illustration described in Figure 16-4, where L2 switching is done within LSW1 and LSW2.

If the L2 exchange is between a VM and a physical server, NSX uses an L2 bridge part of the DLR function to bridge between a VXLAN and an outside VLAN. The L2 bridge runs part of a control VM. The node running the control VM performs the bridging function by mapping requests that come on a VXLAN to the VLAN ID of the external physical server.

NSX IP Routing

NSX IP routing has multiple components, including the controller cluster, a DLR control VM, a DLR kernel module, and an ESG. The ESG acts as the connection to external L3 routers for injecting external routes into the NSX domain. ESG handles North-South traffic between any VM and the physical world. The DLR handles routing East-West between the VMs. The next sections focus more on the DLR functionality.

Distributed Logical Router

This router stretches across the ESXi hosts. The DLR is created via the NSX manager or with application programming interfaces (APIs). The NSX controller pushes the DLR configuration into the ESXi hosts. The DLR has two components:

1. **The DLR Control VM** acts as a centralized router for all ESXi hosts and performs the control function with the help of the NSX controller. The DLR VM supports routing protocols such as Open Shortest Path First (OSPF) and Border Gateway Protocol (BGP) [1], exchanges routes with the ESG, and communicates with the NSX manager and the NSX controllers. HA of the DLR control VM is handled via an active/standby configuration.

2. **The DLR kernel module** is installed inside ESXi and handles the data plane forwarding functions. The DLR kernel module contains a routing information base (RIB) that is populated via the NSX controller. The DLR kernel module connects to the LSWs via logical interfaces (LIFs). Each LIF has an IP address that acts as a default gateway for the corresponding logical switch, plus a vMAC address. During vMotion, the default IP gateway and vMAC remain unchanged for a particular segment so they do not affect networking connectivity. Figure 16-5 shows the NSX routing components.

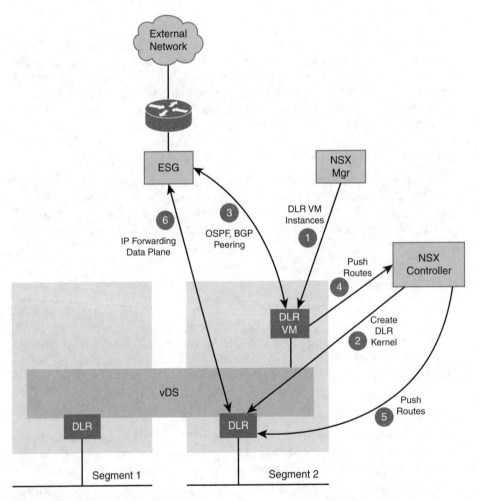

Figure 16-5 *NSX Routing Component*

The sequence of events shown in Figure 16-5 is described in the following steps:

Step 1.   The NSX manager installs the DLR control VM instance. The DLR control VM can also be created via APIs.

Step 2.   The NSX controller pushes into the ESXi hosts the DLR kernel module configuration, including LIF and IP addresses.

Step 3.   OSPF/BGP peering is enabled between the DLR control VM and the ESG for the purpose of exchanging wide area network (WAN) routes. The external routes are sent to the DLR control VM, with a default gateway being the ESG because it is the only exit point into the WAN. The DLR control VM also redistributes connected networks via OSPF, with the next hop for the connected networks being the corresponding DLR kernel. This way traffic goes directly in and out of the DLR kernel without doing one-arm routing at the DLR control VM.

Step 4.   The DLR control VM pushes all the routes it learns into the controller cluster.

Step 5.   The controller cluster pushes the RIB into the DLR kernel modules.

Step 6.   The DLR kernel modules handle the data plane IP forwarding function.

What was shown so far is basic switching and routing, but in an SDN flavor, where the NSX controller acts as the control brain. Instead of having a full-fledge routing control module on each host, the control is done via the NSX controller, and the flows are pushed into the ESXi kernels, where forwarding is done. Also, the presence of a DLR control VM module presents the NSX cluster as one router to the outside world rather than many routers in each ESXi host. The presence of VXLAN allows L2 over L3 segmentation without having to stretch VLANs across the whole NSX domain. Figure 16-6 is an example of routing within a VMware cluster.

As shown in this example, VM1 belongs to segment 1 (LSW1) with VXLAN ID (VNID) of 1000. VM2 belongs to segment 2 (LSW2) with VXLAN ID (VNID) of 2000. ESXi 1 has a DLR with two logical interfaces: LIF1 and LIF2. From VM1's perspective, the default gateway to reach other segments is the IP address of LIF1 on its local DLR, and the destination MAC address is the local DLR vMAC. The same goes for VM2, where the default gateway is the IP address of LIF2 of its local DLR, and the destination MAC address is its own DLR vMAC. Note that when a VM moves around in the cluster within its own segment, the default gateway and vMAC for the particular segment are kept unchanged.

VM1 sends the packet to its default gateway. The local DLR of ESXi 1 does a routing lookup and finds out that the IP address of VM2 is directly attached to VXLAN 2000. As such, the DLR of ESXi 1 performs an ARP for the destination IP of VM2 and gets its MAC address. The DLR then encapsulates the packet into VXLAN 2000 and sends it to the VTEP of ESXi 2. Note that when VM2 replies to VM1, it performs local routing via its own DLR of ESXi 2, as the DLR of the host that the VM belongs to performs the routing for each VM.

With NSX routing, it is possible to do multiple virtual routing and forwarding (VRF) by launching different control VMs, with each having different DLR kernel instances. This allows overlapping IP addresses because each DLR instance has its own IP addresses.

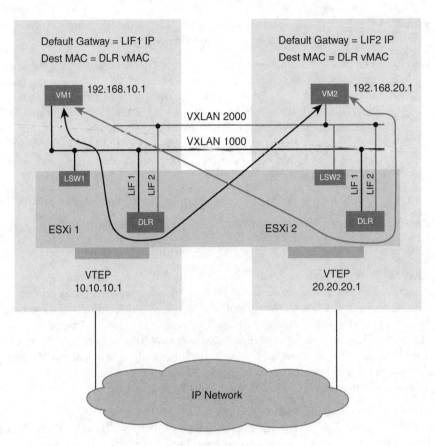

Figure 16-6 *NSX Routing Between Segments*

Handling of Multidestination Traffic

Multidestination traffic is the BUM traffic that arises due to end nodes not knowing the MAC destination of the other end nodes and needing to use ARP. Multidestination traffic can also occur when the destination MAC address is known by the end node but unknown inside the transit nodes or simply because you need to reach multiple destinations at the same time via multicast.

Things get trickier in the NSX environment because the switching and routing are moved into the hosts. In the NSX model, each host is an endpoint for the VTEP tunnels. With hundreds of hosts in a multicluster environment, you will end up with an explosion of tunnels to deal with. This is why NSX picks a designated host with a UTEP to act on behalf of other hosts for replicating traffic across the physical network.

In all cases, if a VM is sending BUM traffic inside a logical switch (that is, its own IP subnet), the traffic must be replicated to all other VMs in the same logical switch. The VMs could be spread out in the NSX domain over multiple physical hosts, and the physical hosts themselves could have their VTEPs in different IP subnets (VTEP segments). There are different ways of dealing with the replication and optimization to limit the flooding in the network.

Let's start with the basic multicast model that would occur in a network, without the support of optimization or flood optimization techniques.

Basic Multicast Model with No Optimization

In this model, no optimization is done to limit the flood of packets, and basic IP multicast with Internet Group Management Protocol (IGMP) and Protocol Independent Multicast (PIM) must be used in the underlay network physical infrastructure. The drawback of this method is that replication can occur from every VTEP endpoint to every other VTEP endpoint. This adds CPU overhead on the physical hosts. Also, as multicast traverses the physical network, the physical switches and routers in the network need to support IP multicast, which adds extra overhead and functionality. Let's see how this is dealt with in Figure 16-7.

Assume there are three VMs—VM1, VM2, and VM3—that belong to the same logical switch (that is, the same IP subnet and same VXLAN ID segment), but they are on physical hosts that belong to two different IP subnets (that is, VTEP segments). Hosts 1 and 2 have their VTEPs in subnet 10.10.10.0/24, whereas hosts 3 and 4 have their VTEPs in subnets 20.20.20.0/24. To replicate BUM traffic over the logical switch (VXLAN 1000), you assign a multicast address (239.1.1.1) to the VXLAN segment 1000. When the first VM is connected to a logical switch, the ESXi in the physical host sends an IGMP join indicating that it wants to receive traffic belonging to the multicast group. In this case, ESXi 1, 2, and 3 joined the multicast group, but ESXi 4 did not because it does not have an VM in VXLAN segment 1000.

If VM1 sends a BUM packet, it is flooded in the local physical host to other VMs in the same multicast group, and it is encapsulated via VXLAN 1000 to be sent over the physical network. The outer source IP is the IP of VM1s VTEP, 10.10.10.1, and the outer destination IP is the IP multicast address 239.1.1.1. When the physical switches see the packet, they use L2 multicast to send it to all ports that joined the multicast group via IGMP, including the L3 router. When the router receives the packet, it uses PIM to send the packet to the different subnets that also joined the multicast group. On the receiving end, the L2 switches use L2 multicast to send the packet to all ports that joined the multicast group. When ESXi 3 receives the packet, it removes the VXLAN 1000 header and replicates the packet to VM3.

Notice that this approach produces major overhead on the physical network, especially if there is a 1:1 mapping where every logical switch (IP subnet) is associated with a multicast group. Other methods with 1:n mapping configure one multicast group for all logical switches, but all VMs start seeing the BUM traffic from all other logical switches in the network, not just their own logical switch. Potentially, m:n mapping can be used, where groups of logical segments are mapped to different multicast addresses. This is a compromise where less multicast traffic is sent, but not all VMs receive unwanted multicast.

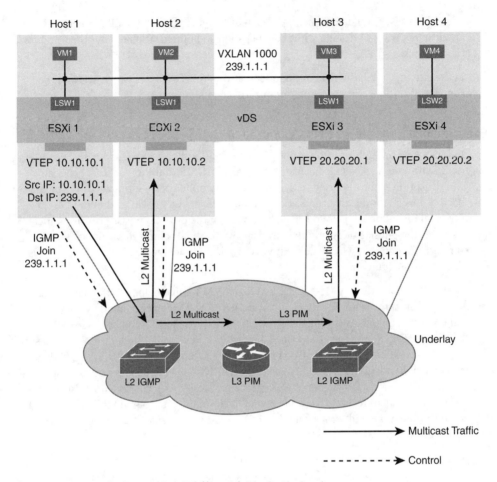

Figure 16-7   *Multidestination Traffic with No Optimization*

Unicast Method of Replication

In this method, IP multicast is not used in the underlay network. Switches and routers must support basic L2 switching or L3 routing, with no need to support L2 multicast with IGMP or L3 multicast with PIM. Hosts are grouped according to the VTEP subnets (VTEP segments). Within each VTEP segment, a host plays the role of a UTEP. The UTEP performs the replication on behalf of all other hosts that are in the same VTEP segment. The selection of the UTEP varies so the same host is not used every time. The replication is done only to hosts with VMs that attach to the logical switch where the replication must happen. Hosts rely on information they receive from the NSX controller to know the VTEPs-to-VNI (VXLAN ID) mapping of all other hosts. This information shows which logical segments are attached to which VTEPs. This information is used to select the VTEPs the traffic needs to be replicated to (see Figure 16-8). Let's take the same scenario as before and add VM4 on host ESXi-4 to the same segment VXLAN 1000 as VM1, VM2, and VM3. The two VTEP segments are 10.10.10.0/24 and 20.20.20.0/24.

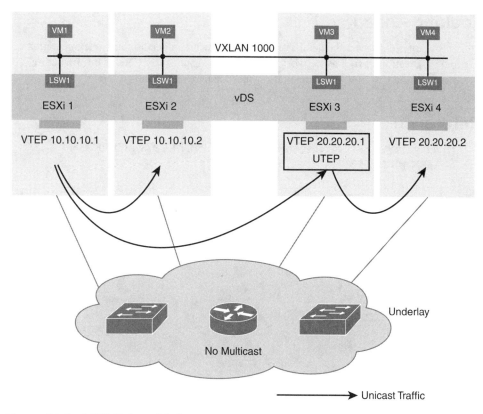

Figure 16-8 *NSX Unicast Mode*

When VM1 sends a BUM packet, ESXi 1 checks its VTEP table that has information it received from the NSX controllers. According to the VTEP table, ESXi 1 decides that it needs to send the packet to ESXi 2 in its local VTEP segment, and to ESXi 3, which is the UTEP of the second VTEP segment. Notice here that the overhead was minimized by having ESXi 1 performing replication only within its own VTEP segment and offloading the rest of the replication to the other UTEPs. Information in the local VTEP table ensures that hosts that do not have VMs attached to VXLAN 1000 do not get BUM packets. Because ESXi 3 receives the BUM packet, it also checks its local VTEP table and replicates to the other hosts within its VTEP segment, such as ESXi 4, which is now on VXLAN 1000.

A hybrid method can be used as a combination between multicast and unicast. A multicast TEP (MTEP) performs local multicast within the local VTEP segment, and a Unicast packet is sent to the remote MTEP. This approach uses the L2 multicast functionality to send the BUM traffic within the local VTEP segment and uses unicast to send the BUM traffic to the remote VTEP segments. This method allows scaling for large designs by leveraging L2 multicast in top-of-rack (ToR) switches but eliminates the need for PIM in the L3 routers.

Looking Ahead

This chapter discussed the details of NSX and how it can perform microsegmentation and the creation of overlay networks. Chapter 17, "Application-Centric Infrastructure," discusses the Cisco ACI implementation and compares NSX and ACI.

Reference

[1]   *Internet Routing Architectures*. Sam Halabi. ISBN-13: 978-1578702336, ISBN-10: 157870233X.

Chapter 17

Application-Centric Infrastructure

This chapter covers the following key topics:

- **Cisco Application Centric Infrastructure:** A definition of the Cisco application centric infrastructure (ACI) and its purpose.

- **ACI Microsegmentation Constructs:** Microsegmentation constructs including endpoint groups (EPGs), application network profiles (ANPs), and service graphs.

- **Cisco Application Policy Infrastructure Controller:** High-level description of the Cisco application policy infrastructure controller (APIC) and its role in pushing the policies, automating, and monitoring the fabric.

- **ACI Domains:** A description of the different virtual, physical, and external ACI domains and how they are used to integrate policies in virtual and physical environments.

- **The ACI Fabric Switching and Routing Constructs:** ACI switching and routing constructs, including tenants, virtual routing and forwarding (VRF), and Bridge Domains.

- **Virtual and Physical Connectivity to the ACI Fabric:** Connectivity into the fabric from both virtual environments such as ACI Virtual Switch (AVS) and physical environments.

- **The ACI Switching and Routing Terminology:** Description of the different switching and routing terminology such as leaf and spine loopback and anycast Internet Protocol (IP) addresses, mapping database, global and local station tables.

- **The ACI Underlay Network:** A description of the protocols that run inside the underlay network and the handling of external routes and load balancing inside the fabric.

■ **The ACI Overlay and VXLAN:** A description of the use of VXLAN to normalize the different encapsulations in and out of the fabric; L2 switching and L3 routing are also described in the overlay network.

■ **Multicast in the Overlay Versus Multicast in the Underlay:** Describes how multicast traffic is handled in the overlay and underlay networks.

■ **ACI Multi-PoD:** Describes the use of ACI for automating connectivity and policies between two different data centers while having routing isolation but still under a single APIC controller cluster.

■ **ACI Multi-Site:** The use of ACI for automating connectivity and policies between different sites with different APIC controller clusters but still under a single policy manager.

■ **ACI Anywhere:** How policies and automation can be managed across private and public clouds.

■ **High-Level Comparison Between ACI and NSX:** High-level comparison between ACI and VMware's networking and security software product (NSX).

Cisco Application-Centric Infrastructure

Application-centric infrastructure (ACI) is a measure to introduce a level of automation into setting and enforcing policies at the application level as well as configuring the switch fabric to support the connectivity requirements of the applications in the data center. ACI uses information related to the applications, such as which tier the applications belong to (web, app, database [DB], or the application environment [development, test, operation, and so on]), to configure the policies appropriately in support of such requirements. Automation of the fabric configuration makes building the fabric plug and play. ACI also aims to have the network offer feedback information such as network health check to understand whether the network is affecting the performance of the application.

ACI puts emphasis on the application for defining policies, regardless of whether the application is virtualized or running on bare-metal servers. This is independent of the physical location of the application and which virtual local area network (VLAN) or Internet Protocol (IP) subnet it belongs to. Applying policies to an application and defining which other application can access it and vice versa is easy on greenfield applications. While setting up the application, you can define polices to define how the application interacts with the rest of the network. However, not all networks are greenfield, and many applications already exist in the network and have a complex interaction with other applications. In this regard, Cisco was a pioneer in the industry in implementing the Cisco Tetration platform, which monitors the packet flows in the network at a fine granularity to identify how an existing application interacts with its environment and how it interconnects with other applications. Cisco Tetration in support of HyperFlex was already discussed in Chapter 11, "HyperFlex Workload Optimization and Efficiency." Based on Tetration, ACI policies can be intelligently set and monitoring can be done to alarm the end user if there is a deviation from the policy.

ACI focuses on multiple areas such as these:

- **Policy setting:** This involves automating the configuration of security policies or quality of service (QoS) that are applied on each application. Defining the endpoints for setting these policies is extremely granular. The policies can be set based on a virtual machine (VM), physical or logical ports, names, tags, and more.

- **Policy enforcement:** ACI enforces the policies inside the fabric at every endpoint. This creates a distributed firewall approach that eliminates centralized firewall overload. For services that need specialized handling, traffic can be redirected to virtual or physical network service appliances for processing.

- **Network configuration:** This involves automating the configuration of both the overlay and the underlay network. The overlay and underlay were described in Chapter 15, "Software-Defined Networking and Open Source." This is unique to ACI in the sense that ACI automates both the virtual as well as the physical switching and routing environment.

- **Monitoring and feedback:** By automating policies and networking for the virtual and physical environments, ACI monitors the network via "atomic counters" and gives feedback on problems that can affect the performance of the application.

ACI is working closely with open source initiatives such as OpenStack and the Contiv project. With OpenStack, ACI integrates with Neutron via application programming interfaces (APIs). In the Contiv project, Cisco ACI is looking to create a uniform environment for implementing microservices in a mixed environment of containers, VMs, and bare-metal servers.

ACI Microsegmentation Constructs

The following is a list of the main ACI microsegmentation constructs in setting and enforcing policies at the application level.

The Endpoint Groups

A base point for ACI is defining the endpoint groups (EPGs). The EPG is a group of applications or components of an application that have a common set of policies. The endpoint could be practically anything you can identify, including a virtual component such as a VM, a docker container, or a physical component such as a server or a network services appliance. The policies are applied to such endpoints regardless of the IP address or the VLAN the endpoint belongs to. An EPG, for example, can be a tier of applications or different components of the same tier. An EPG can represent the web tier (Web-tier), another EPG can represent the application tier (App-tier), and a third EPG can represent the database tier (DB-tier). Different application endpoints are grouped in an EPG, which becomes the instantiation point for the policies and forwarding for the endpoints. An Oracle application, for example, could be tagged as test, development, or production application. Identifying the components of such an application at such granularity and assigning the components to EPGs to apply policy is powerful.

EPGs offer the flexibility to place endpoints into a group based on many attributes—some traditional and some more advanced. For example, at its simplistic level, the endpoints can be defined based on VLANs, IP subnets, L4–L7 ports, or physical ports. However, there is flexibility even at this level, where applications in different VLANs or IP subnets can be in the same EPG undergoing the same policies, or applications within the same VLAN and IP subnets could be in different EPGs undergoing different policies. At a more advanced level, the endpoints can be defined based on VM attributes, an application DNS name, or other.

To further explain with an example, a set of applications is identified via the Transmission Control Protocol (TCP) ports they use. An application such as a web server has access to it and from it identified via TCP port 80. If you group such applications that use port 80 into one group, call that an EPG. When you apply policy to the group, decide whether to allow or deny traffic going to port 80 and that policy is applied to the group. Bear in mind that Web 1 could be on VLAN 100 and IP 20.20.14.0/24, whereas Web 2 could be on VLAN 200 and IP 20.20.15.0/24, which are completely different subnets. This is illustrated in Figure 17-1.

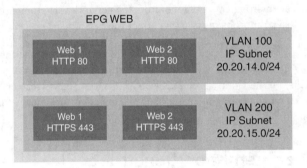

Figure 17-1   *Endpoint Groups*

Figure 17-1 shows that the EPG contains web applications belonging to different subnets, but all belonging to the same EPG where policy is applied at the EPG level, which could be allowing access to web applications that use the Hypertext Transfer Protocol (HTTP) (TCP port 80) or HTTP Secure (HTTPS) (TCP port 443) services.

Traffic from endpoints is classified and grouped under EPGs based on criteria to be configured. The main methods of classification are based on physical endpoints, virtual endpoints, and external endpoints. External endpoints connect from outside the ACI fabric, such as those behind an L3 wide area network (WAN) router.

The classification of traffic from endpoints and grouping into EPGs depends on the ACI hardware itself and how the connection is made to the endpoint. An ACI fabric could be connected directly to a bare-metal server; be connected to a server running the Cisco AVS switch; be connected to a server running VMware ESXi and the vSphere Distributed Switch (vDS) switch, kernel-based virtual machine (KVM), and Open vSwitch (OVS);

be connected to a traditional L2 switch; or be connected to an L3 WAN router. So, the actual classification depends mainly on hardware capabilities and software capabilities of the ACI fabric and what it connects to.

In general, different methods of classification are based on the following:

- VLAN encapsulation.

- Port and VLAN encapsulation.

- Network/mask or IP address for external traffic such as coming in from L3 WAN routers.

- Virtual network interface card (vNIC) assignments to a port group that ACI negotiates with third-party hypervisors such as ESXi, Hyper-V, and KVM.

- Source IP and subnets or media access control (MAC) address, from traffic coming in from a virtual environment like Cisco AVS or from a physical environment like bare-metal servers.

- VM attributes such as the name of a VM, a group naming of VMs, or the guest operating system running on the machine. The classification based on VM attributes depends on whether the information is coming from a host that has software that supports OpFlex (to be described next) such as Cisco AVS or from hosts that do not support OpFlex, such as VMware vDS or other. With AVS, for example, ACI relies on OpFlex to extract the information and does the classification in hardware based on VLAN or VXLAN ID. If, however, the host does not support OpFlex, classification based on VM attributes translates into the MAC addresses of the VMs.

- Based on containerized environments.

Application Network Profile

Now that the endpoints of different applications have been identified and grouped under EPGs and you know how to classify traffic coming into an EPG, you need to define a set of policies between these EPGs. These are called policy "contracts" because they define the interaction between the EPGs based on the set policy. These contracts look like access control lists (ACLs) but are actually very different. Traditional ACLs used to consume lots of entries in the memory of the switches and routers because they are not reusable. Thousands of similar policy entries were written to memory if the source IP, source MAC address, or destination IP or MAC changed. With the ACI contracts, the contract itself is an object that is reusable. Traffic from source endpoints to destination endpoints can reuse the same object contract regardless of IPs and VLANs, which provides much more scalability and consumes much fewer resources in the switch/router memory. The total set of contracts between the EPGs is what is called an application network profile (ANP), as seen in Figure 17-2.

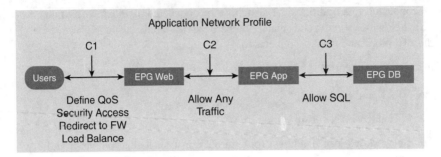

Figure 17-2 *Application Network Profile*

The level of complexity of the policy contract depends on where it is applied. This could be a complex or simple contract. So, Contract 1 (C1) could define quality of service (QoS) parameters, security access parameters, redirection to firewalls and load balancers, or configuration of the actual firewalls. A simple contract such as C2 could be to allow all traffic between the web servers and the app server. C3 could be to allow all Structured Query Language (SQL) traffic from the application server to go to the database server, and vice versa. The policy contract defines both inbound and outbound rules.

The contracts between EPGs have the notion of a consumer and a provider of a contract. This is shown in Figure 17-3. The consumer EPG is the one that initiates the request for a service. For example, when a Web-tier EPG initiates a connection to an App-tier EPG, the Web-tier is the consumer of the contract, and the App-tier is the provider of the contract because it must deliver the service in conformance to the contract.

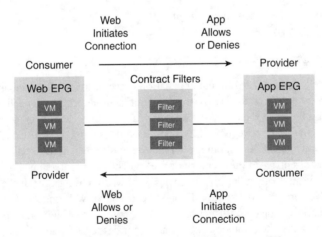

Figure 17-3 *EPG Consumers Versus Providers*

Contracts between consumers and providers are unidirectional. If a Web-tier (consumer) initiates a connection to an App-tier (provider) and the provider allows it, the reverse might not be true. To allow the reverse, the App-tier must become a consumer and the Web-tier must become a provider, and another rule must be defined referencing filters that allow or deny the traffic. In general, connections between endpoints in the same EPG are permitted by default, and connections between endpoints in different EPGs are denied by default unless a contract exists to allow such connections.

The contract is associated with entries in the content-addressable memory (CAM) that define RuleID, SrcEPG, DstEPG, Scope, FilterID, Action, and more.

A rule references a set of filters and has an action that is applied on the filters. Each of the rules in the CAM is identified by a rule ID, and the rules apply between a source EPG defined by an SrcEPG number and destination EPG defined by a DstEPG number. Also, a contract has a certain **scope**, where it can be global and used by everyone or belong to a certain administrative domain (tenant) or certain IP forwarding domain virtual routing and forwarding (VRF). The rules that you define are associated with filters, and each filter has a FilterID. Each filter has one or more entries, and these entries are similar to an ACL. The rule has an **action**. The action taken varies depending on what the consumer requires. For example, an action could allow or deny a certain filter. The action could also mark the traffic to apply QoS, it could redirect the traffic to L4–L7 network services devices like firewalls or next-generation firewalls (NGFWs) or load balancers, it could copy the traffic, log the traffic, and so on. Figure 17-4 is a sample of rules related to a contract as seen inside the memory of an ACI switch. Notice that Rule ID 1 identifies the SrcEPG—in this case, the Web-EPG with a SrcID of 32772 and destination EPG 49156—that is associated with a filter, with the scope being a specific VRF, and the action of the rule to permit the filter. Notice that Rule ID 2 is also needed to define the action in the reverse direction. Rule ID 3 indicates that all other traffic is implicitly denied.

Rule ID	SrcEPG	DstEPG	FilterID	Scope	Action
1	32772	49156	reference to the filter	VRF-number	permit
2	49156	32772	reference to the filter	VRF-number	permit
3	any	any	implicit	VRF-number	deny

Figure 17-4 *Rules Entries of a Contract as Seen in CAM*

The filter in this case could classify the traffic based on L2–L4 attributes such as Ethernet type, protocol type, and TCP ports. Figure 17-5 shows a partial screen capture of a filter. Notice that the FilterID is icmp. There is one filter entry called icmp, and there could be more entries in the same filter. The filter identifies the traffic with Ethertype IP. It defines the TCP source port or range and the TCP destination port or range. The rule entry defined in the contract and associated with this filter sets the action on the filter to permit or deny traffic as classified by the filter.

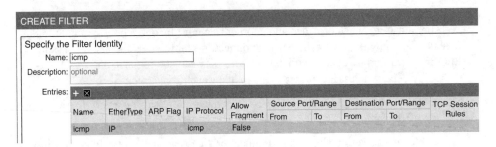

Figure 17-5 *Filter Example*

The reason for the hierarchy of having application profiles, contracts, rules, and filters is that Cisco ACI defines everything as objects that can be reused. A filter can be entered once in the CAM and reused by many rules, the rules can be used by many contracts, and the contracts can be used by many application profiles that can in turn be used by many EPGs.

Service Graphs

An important policy in the contracts is the service graph. A *service graph* identifies the set of network or service functions, such as firewall, load balancer, Secure Sockets Layer (SSL) offload, and more, and the sequence of such services as needed by an application. So, for example, say the application is a Web-tier, and the application needs a firewall, SSL offload, and load balancer. Assume that the sequence of actions is such:

Step 1. The firewall needs to permit all HTTP traffic (port 80) and deny User Datagram Protocol (UDP) traffic.

Step 2. SSL offload needs to be applied to all HTTP traffic.

Step 3. Traffic needs to be sent to a load balancer that applies a round robin algorithm to balance the traffic between web servers.

The graph is shown in Figure 17-6.

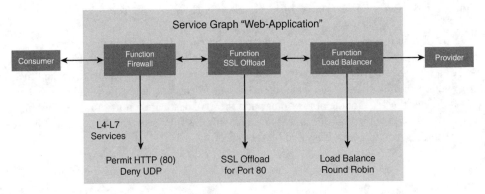

Figure 17-6 *Service Graph*

You define a service trajectory with a service graph. Different EPGs can reuse the same service graph, and the service can follow an endpoint if the endpoint moves around in the network. So, if you apply the service graph to a web application inside a Web-EPG and then decide to move the application from one EPG to another, the service profile applies to that endpoint, regardless of whether it lands on a different VLAN or a different subnet. Also, whenever an application is decommissioned, the rules that were pushed into the network service devices are removed from those devices, freeing up resources. If rules are pushed into a firewall, those same rules are removed from the firewall when the application that needs them is terminated.

Cisco has a few ways to allow third-party network services vendors to execute the policies requested by the application and instantiated through a service profile:

- **Redirection:** The traffic is just redirected to network service appliances. These are either physical devices or software devices. In this mode, ACI does not interfere with what the appliances need to do and just sends them the traffic as was traditionally done in most legacy data centers.

- **Device packages:** ACI uses the Cisco Application Policy Infrastructure Controller (APIC) to automate the insertion and provisioning of network services rendered by network services devices. To do so, the APIC requires a device package that consists of a device definition and a device script. The device definition describes the device functions, the parameters that are required by the device to configure each function and the interfaces, and network connectivity information for each function. The device script manages the communication between the APIC and the device. The device script is a Python file that defines the APIs between the APIC and the device. It defines the mapping between APIC events and device function calls. The device package is written by third-party vendors and end users, and it is uploaded into the APIC. So, an APIC can map, using the device packages, a set of policies that are defined in a service graph to a set of functions that are implemented by the network devices.

- **OpFlex:** OpFlex is a Cisco-initiated protocol that allows a controller to talk to a device and give the device instructions to implement a set of functionality. Cisco uses OpFlex as a way for the APIC to talk to the switches and configure the ACI fabric. OpFlex is also being pushed in the standard bodies to have it as an open protocol. OpFlex is different from the Open vSwitch Database (OVSDB) protocol from open source. Unlike OVSDB, which is designed as a management protocol for the configuration of Open vSwitch (OVS) implementations, OpFlex is more of an abstraction layer that does not get into the management or the configuration of the network device. Rather, OpFlex instructs the device to configure certain policies without getting involved in how the device performs the configuration. In the context of ACI, EPGs, and ANPs, OpFlex instructs the network service device like the firewall or the load balancer to implement the contracts between the EPGs. Each network services device must implement OpFlex and map the OpFlex requirements to its own configuration.

ACI Tetration Model

One of the main issues that face IT administrators is knowing the required policies needed for a safe and secure operation of the applications in the data center. Any data center contains newly deployed applications that may or may not interact with existing applications, and existing applications where policies can be enhanced but at the risk of disrupting the existing operation.

As seen so far, the pillars of deploying policies with the ACI fabric are knowing the EPGs and the contracts to be enforced between the EPGs part of an ANP. This is easy to do on newly deployed applications where, at the time of setting the application, the IT administrator knows exactly what the application is, what users need to access it, and what other applications it needs to talk to. Based on that, the IT administrator defines the EPGs and the required interaction.

This might not be so simple if you move into an existing data center that has existing tiers of applications. Some of these applications run on bare-metal servers, others on virtualized environments. A set of policies are already enforced, but whoever set those policies might be long gone and you, the IT administrator, doesn't even know the exact interaction between the applications. This makes it difficult to identify EPGs, what ports to allow or to deny, and whether applying a new policy to serve a new application could break an existing application. This is where the Cisco Tetration platform plays a big role in giving you insight into the traffic flows and interaction between applications.

Now let's take a closer look at the Cisco APIC and how it interacts with the rest of the network in the data center.

Cisco Application Policy Infrastructure Controller

The Cisco APIC is the centralized policy manager for ACI and the unified point for automation and management of the ACI fabric. APIC also has open API interfaces to allow integration with third-party L4–L7 network service devices and other platforms such as vCenter from VMware, Hyper-V and System Center Virtual Machine Manager (SCVMM) from Microsoft, OVS, OpenStack, and others. A brief functionality of the APIC controller follows:

- Pushing the security policies into the ACI fabric.

- Automation of the ACI fabric configuration and inventory. Most of the ACI configurations, such as routing protocols and IP addressing, are hidden from the end user. You just need to install the fabric in a leaf spine topology and select an IP subnet to apply for the fabric; the rest of the configuration to allow traffic in and out of the fabric is automatic. The APIC also handles the software image management of the leaf and spine switches.

- Monitoring and troubleshooting for applications and infrastructure to ensure a healthy and operational fabric.

- Fault events and performance management within the logical and physical domains.

- The management of the Cisco Application Virtual Switch (AVS).

- Integration with third-party vendors in the areas of L4–L7 network services, vCenter, vShield, Microsoft SCVMM, OpenStack, Kubernetes, and more.

The APIC connects to the leaf switches in the ACI fabric, and it comes in a cluster fashion, with a minimum of three controllers recommended for redundancy. Each of the APICs connects to a separate leaf switch or has dual connectivity to two leaf switches to protect against a single-point failure. The APIC takes the ANP that was discussed earlier and pushes it to the leaf switches. This is done either as a push model upon ANP configuration or based on endpoint attachments. In the endpoint attachment model, the APIC detects which endpoints (such as VMs in a host) were added and whether they belong to a certain EPG. As such, the APIC pushes the ANP to those endpoints. A policy agent that lives on the leaf switches then takes the ANP policies and translates them into actual configuration on the switches that conform to such policies.

The APIC interacts with the leaf switches via the OpFlex protocol; in turn, the leaf switches interact with the end hosts via OpFlex (in the case of AVS or any endpoint that supports OpFlex). This ensures scalability because you can scale the number of hosts and nodes by scaling the number of leaf switches. The APIC pushes a virtual switch into the server nodes connected to the fabric. The virtual switch could be Cisco's AVS or VMware's vSphere distributed switch (vDS). The open source Open vSwitch (OVS) also supports OpFlex, which allows a Cisco APIC to interact with an OVS switch. This is important for implementations that support the open source hypervisor KVM because it adopts OVS as a virtual switch.

Having a Cisco AVS as a distributed switch has more advantages in the ACI architecture because AVS also acts as a leaf switch and is managed by OpFlex. APIC interacts with the VMs, as well as bare-metal servers, to push the ANPs into the physical or virtual leaf switches (virtual switches) according to the needs of the applications. A high-level view of the APIC interaction with the rest of the network is seen in Figure 17-7. Note how APIC uses OpFlex to interact with the leaf switches. In turn, each leaf talks OpFlex with the virtual environment on the hosts, such as with the Cisco AVS distributed switch.

APIC can create an AVS, a vDS switch, or an OVS. One component of AVS is created inside vCenter and another component is created within a kernel module in the hypervisor. An OpFlex agent is also created in the AVS kernel module, and OpFlex is used to interact with the leaf switches. This is an advantage over creating a virtual switch that does not support OpFlex. In the example in Figure 17-6, the hypervisor is ESXi, Hyper-V, or KVM.

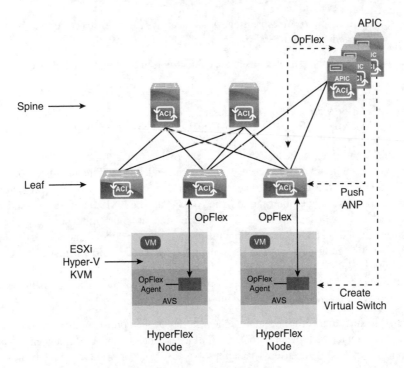

Figure 17-7 *APIC Use of OpFlex*

ACI Domains

ACI allows the creation of different domains and assigning different entities to these domains to allow the integration of policies for virtualized as well as physical environments. Let's examine some of the domains that ACI defines.

Virtual Machine Manager Domain

An ACI Virtual Machine Manager (VMM) domain enables you to configure connectivity policies for VM controllers and integrate with different hypervisors. Some of the controllers/hypervisors that ACI integrates with through the APIC are VMware vCenter/ESXi, Microsoft System Center Virtual Machine Manager (SCVMM)/Hyper-V, OVSDB/KVM, and OpenStack. A VMM domain profile groups controllers with similar policy requirements. So, controllers within the same VMM domain can share common elements such as VLAN/VXLAN pools and EPGs. Figure 17-8 is an example of the integration of APIC with a vCenter VMM domain. Because vCenter allows the creation of a data center and puts ESXi hosts inside the data center, ACI allows one VMM domain per data center. So, if vCenter creates a data center east (DC-East) and a data center west (DC-West), you allocate a VMM domain east and a VMM domain west. Each domain shares a separate VLAN/VXLAN pool and separate EPG groups. The following example, as shown in Figure 17-8, is a vCenter VMM domain that interacts with APIC.

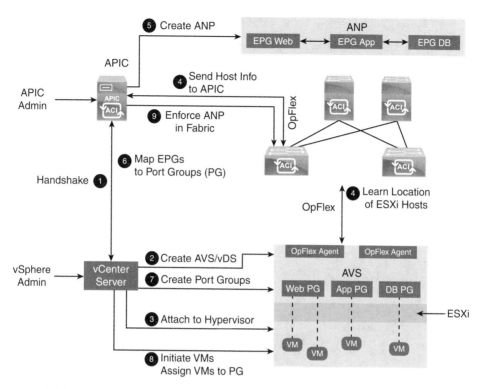

Figure 17-8 *vCenter VMM Domain*

If you take a closer look at how APIC applies the ANP inside the VMM domain, the flow of events proceeds as follows (see Figure 17-8).

Step 1. The APIC performs an original handshake with vCenter.

Step 2. An AVS or vDS virtual switch is created. If AVS is created, an OpFlex agent is created inside the AVS kernel module.

step 3. If an AVS is created, it is attached to the hypervisor. In this example, it is attached to ESXi.

Step 4. All the locations of the ESXi hosts are learned through OpFlex on the leaf switches and are sent to the APIC.

Step 5. The APIC creates the ANP.

Step 6. The APIC maps the EPGs to port groups (PG) that are sent to vCenter.

Step 7. vCenter creates the port groups on the different hosts and allocates a VLAN/VXLAN to each port from a pool of VLANs/VXLANs. As shown in the figure, EPG Web is mapped to port group Web, EPG App is mapped to port group App, and EPG DB is mapped to port group DB. The hosts use the VLANs to allow the port groups to communicate with the leaf switches.

Step 8.   vCenter instantiates the VMs and assigns them to the port groups.

Step 9.   The policy that is part of the ANP is enforced inside the ACI fabric.

In the previous example, all of the assigned VLAN/VXLANs, EPGs, and ANP profile are associated with the particular VMM domain. This creates separation between the different domains. In addition to vCenter, ACI creates VMM domains for Hyper-V and KVM environments.

Physical and External Domains

Other than the third-party controller VMM domain, ACI allows the creation of physical domains, L2 external VMM domains, and L3 external VMM domains, as shown in Figure 17-9.

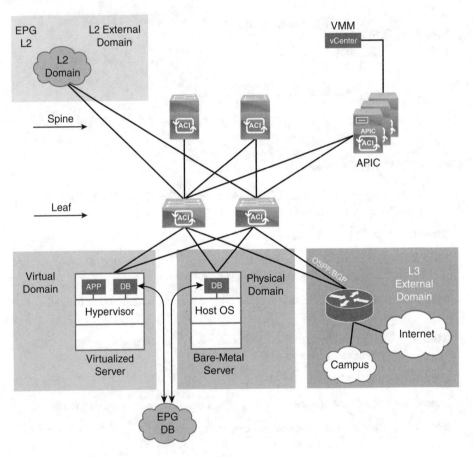

Figure 17-9 *Integrating Multiple VMM Domains*

Physical Domains

A physical domain allows the integration of physical, bare-metal servers with the rest of the virtualized environment. Assume there is an existing database that runs only on a bare-metal server. Now assume that you already created an EPG called EPG-DB that you assigned to a vCenter VMM domain containing database VMs. By assigning the physical server to the same EPG-DB, you can have the bare-metal server as another endpoint in EPG-DB. All of the policies applied to the EPG-DB apply to the physical server. This is done simply by having traffic coming from a specific VLAN on the physical port added to a particular EPG. So, if the physical server is on a specific VLAN and is connected to a leaf switch on a specific port, the traffic coming into that port is put in EPG-DB. Other VLANs on the same physical port are put in EPG-App or EPG-Web accordingly.

External Domains

You can integrate external domains such as L2 or L3 domains with the rest of the ACI fabric, so the newly designed data center based on the ACI fabric integrates with existing L2 networks or campus networks and WAN routers. Such L2/L3 networks form their own domains and have their own EPGs. The whole external network becomes a single EPG by adding all the VLANs in one EPG or is broken into multiple EPGs.

An L3 router forms an external L3 domain peer with leaf switches using traditional L3 protocols such as Open Shortest Path First (OSPF), Enhanced Interior Gateway Routing Protocol (EIGRP), static routing, and internal Border Gateway Protocol (iBGP) [1]. The whole ACI fabric acts as one big switch to the L3 routers. All the protocols running inside the fabric are abstracted from the L3 routers, which see the fabric as one neighbor. This is shown in Figure 17-9, where you see the L3 router peering with the ACI fabric via two leaf switches for added redundancy.

As Cisco tries to simplify the configuration of the L3 protocols running inside the fabric and how information is exchanged, ACI automates the configuration of the fabric so that the end user does not have to know the details. However, it is useful to understand what goes inside the fabric to appreciate the level of complexity. Let's get into a bit more detail on how the fabric works and how it integrates with the virtual and physical environment.

The ACI Fabric Switching and Routing Constructs

One of the major advantages of the APIC is that it automates the configuration of the fabric. You just add leafs and spines, and the IP address configuration and connectivity are automatically done in the fabric. This is a huge step into the road to hyperconvergence because the whole objective behind hyperconvergence is simplicity and automation. Still, you should not work with a black box; you need visibility into the networking ins and outs if problems occur. The next section gives some details about the ACI fabric, but bear in mind that most of the configuration inside the ACI fabric is automated and hidden from the end user.

Tenant

The ACI fabric is designed for multitenancy, where a tenant acts as an independent management domain or administrative domain. In an enterprise environment, tenants could be Payroll, Engineering, Operations departments, and more. In a service provider environment, a tenant could be a different customer. ACI supports the concept of a common tenant, which is one that has information that is shared with all other tenants.

VRF

ACI defines a virtual routing and forwarding (VRF) domain. A VRF is a private network that is a separate L3 routing and forwarding domain. So, think of tenants as separation at the management level and VRF as separation at the L3 routing and data plane forwarding level. Different VRFs have overlapping IP subnets and addresses and routing and forwarding policies. So, in an enterprise, if you wanted to reuse the IP addresses and separate IP forwarding policies within the Sales tenant, for example, a Local-Sales department could become one VRF and an International-Sales department could become a separate VRF. A VRF that contains DNSs and email servers or L3 WAN routers, or L4–L7 network services devices that must be shared with all other tenants, is normally placed inside a common tenant.

Bridge Domain

Inside a VRF, ACI defines bridge domains (BDs). Think of a BD as an L2 switched network that acts as one broadcast domain and that stretches across multiple switches. Although it's an L2 domain, the BD could have in it multiple subnets. For readers who are familiar with the concept of private VLANs, think of the BD as a variation of having a private VLAN inside an L2/L3 switch. The primary VLAN is assigned a primary IP subnet and what is called a switch virtual interface (SVI). Beneath the primary subnet, there could be multiple secondary subnets. When routing is enabled on the SVI, it acts as an L3 router between the different secondary subnets. These are the fun tricks in L2 switches that allow them to perform L3 IP switching similar to a router. Private VLANs and SVI were covered in Chapter 1, "Data Networks: Existing Designs."

The BD is more of a mechanism to control flooding of traffic when traffic is exchanged within the BD. Normally in an L2 domain when a packet arrives with an unknown unicast address or with a broadcast address, it is flooded over all interfaces. In this case the BD controls flooding within itself. A VRF could contain one or multiple BDs.

EPG

Inside a BD, ACI defines the EPGs. The EPG is referenced by an EPG identifier that allows the grouping of many subnets and VLANs within the same EPG. Basically, an EPG is not tied to a physical location, but rather represents a tier of applications. As discussed earlier, all endpoints inside an EPG share a common policy, like a Web-EPG or an App-EPG. A BD has one or multiple EPGs. The insertion of endpoints inside an EPG could be based on physical ports, virtual switch ports, VLAN IDs or VXLAN IDs, tags, subnets, and so on. Also, as explained, the EPGs themselves could be on different IP subnets, so there is a separation between the traditional VLANs and subnets. By default, there is no communication between the EPGs unless the user defines an ANP and defines contracts between the EPGs. Figure 17-10 shows the separation between tenants, VRFs, and BDs inside the ACI fabric.

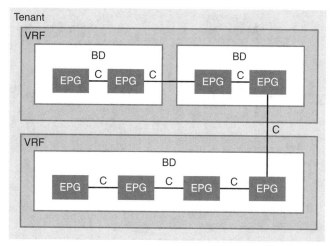

C = Contract

Figure 17-10   *Tenants, VRFs, BDs*

Note how ACI defines private networks or VRFs under the tenant. BDs are inside VRFs, and EPGs are inside bridge domains. ACI also allows information leaking, or route leaking, between the different VRFs, so an EPG inside one VRF could have a contract with another EPG in another VRF.

Virtual and Physical Connectivity to the ACI Fabric

Before looking at networking inside the ACI fabric itself, let's look at how virtual and physical connectivity are done to the fabric.

Virtual Connectivity to the Fabric

Switching is done between the Cisco AVS and the leaf switches. The AVS itself is a Layer 2 distributed virtual switch that is similar in concept to the VMware vDS. However, AVS integrates via OpFlex with the APICs, allowing better integration between the virtual and physical switches. The AVS works in two different switching modes: Local Switching, and No Local Switching, as seen in Figure 17-11.

■ **No Local Switching (NS) Mode:** In this mode, all traffic from the VMs destined to other VMs in the same EPG or other EPGs that reside in the same physical host is sent to the external leaf switches. This mode is useful if the external switch is analyzing traffic and you need the traffic to be visible to the switch.

■ **Local Switching (LS) Mode:** In this mode, all traffic between VMs in the same EPG in the same physical switch is switched locally. Traffic between EPGs in the same physical switch is sent to the external leaf switches. As shown in Figure 17-11, traffic within EPG-Web is switched inside the AVS, whereas traffic between EPG-Web and EPG-App is sent to the leaf switch.

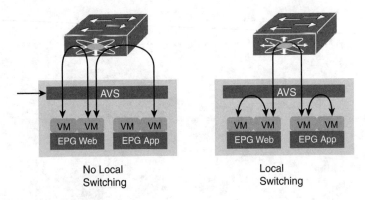

No Local
Switching

Local
Switching

Figure 17-11 *AVS Switching Modes*

Cisco does not yet support a full switching mode in which traffic between different EPGs in the same host is switched locally. This is a major area of difference between ACI and VMware NSX (networking and security software product), where ACI relies on the leaf/spine nodes to do the heavy lifting for switching and routing and policy setting, whereas NSX relies on the hypervisor ESXi to do the switching, routing, and policies. It is not straightforward to assume that the ACI way is better than the NSX way or vice versa just based on whether traffic within a physical server should leave the server. Most traffic in a data center is East-West and goes out the physical network interface cards (NICs) and across switches anyway. The main question to ask is whether the whole concept of switching and routing within software will scale to thousands of VMs, hundreds of nodes, and processing at data rates of 100 Gbps.

Physical Connectivity to the Fabric

Connectivity between the user space and the fabric is done directly to the leafs or by connecting existing L2 switches to the leafs. ACI offers such flexibility because it is obvious that not all installations are greenfield, and there should be a migration path between legacy setups and new setups. This section discusses the different alternatives.

When hosts connect directly to leaf nodes, the hosts normally use different (nowadays 10 GE) NICs for added redundancy. Connect the NICs to a pair of leafs for added redundancy.

Figure 17-12 shows a setup in which a host is connected to two leaf switches. To leverage the capacity of both links, the hosts should run what is called a *virtual port channel* (vPC). A vPC allows an end device, switch, or host to have a redundant connection to two other switches while still making the two connections look like one. This allows redundancy of the links and full use of the bandwidth of both links to transmit traffic. Other similar implementations in the industry go by the name multichassis link aggregation group (MLAG).

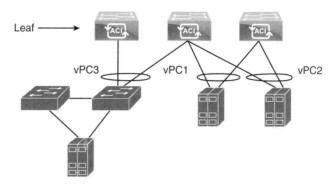

Figure 17-12 *vPC Groups with Leaf Switches*

vPC within an ACI fabric does not require the leaf switches to be connected via peer links or peer keepalive links. As a matter of fact, ACI does not allow you to connect leaf to leaf, as the leafs connect to all spines. Different methods can be used to allow the uplinks from the host to share the traffic. Some of these methods are Link Aggregation Control Protocol (LACP) and MAC pinning. LACP allows better use of the uplink bandwidth by distributing flows over the multiple links. MAC pinning involves pinning the MAC addresses of the VMs to one path or the other.

It is worth noting that hosts do not have to be directly connected to leafs because hosts are sometimes already connected to a legacy switching fabric. In that case, the legacy switching fabric itself connects to the leaf nodes.

The ACI Switching and Routing Terminology

Now let's examine most of the elements needed to understand reachability within the ACI fabric.

■ **User space:** This constitutes all physical or virtual end stations that connect to the fabric.

■ **Fabric space:** This constitutes all elements related to the fabric itself, including the leafs, spines, any physical interfaces on the leafs and spines, any IP addresses inside the fabric, any tunnel endpoints inside the fabric, routing protocols inside the fabric, and so on.

■ **VTEP:** A Virtual Tunnel Endpoint (VTEP) is a network device that terminates a VXLAN tunnel. The network device can be physical or virtual, it maps end devices to VXLAN segments, and it performs encapsulation and de-capsulation. A hardware

VTEP could be a physical leaf node or a spine node switch, whereas a software VTEP is the virtual switch inside the hypervisor. In Cisco's terminology, the IP address of a physical VTEP is called physical TEP (PTEP).

- **Leaf node loopback IP addresses:** The leaf nodes can have multiple loopback IP addresses as follows:

  - **Infrastructure loopback IP address (PTEP):** The APIC uses this loopback IP address to address a leaf. Multi-Protocol BGP (MP-BGP) uses PTEP for peering. It is also used for troubleshooting purposes, such as with Ping or Traceroute.

  - **Fabric loopback TEP (FTEP):** This is a virtual IP address to represent the fabric itself. Consider the fabric as one big switch and the FTEP as the IP address of that switch. The FTEP is used to create an entry point into the fabric from virtual leafs. The virtual leafs are the virtual distributed switches inside a host. The FTEP encapsulates traffic in VXLAN to a vSwitch VTEP if present. The FTEP is also an anycast IP address because the same FTEP IP address exists on all leaf nodes and is used to allow mobility of the downstream VTEPs that exist on the virtual distributed switches inside the hosts.

  - **vPC Loopback TEP:** This loopback IP address is used when two leaf nodes forward traffic that enters via a vPC. Traffic is forwarded by the leaf using the VXLAN encapsulation. The vPC loopback is shared with the vPC peer.

  - **Bridge domain SVI IP address/MAC address:** When IP routing is enabled for a bridge domain, the bridge domain is assigned a router IP address, also called a switch virtual interface (SVI). This IP address is also an anycast address that is the same IP across all leafs for the same bridge domain. End stations that are in the bridge domain use this anycast IP address as a default gateway to reach other bridge domains attached to the same leaf or across the ACI fabric. The bridge domain SVI also has a MAC address, and the MAC address is an anycast address in the sense that it is the same MAC address on all leaf switches. So, if an end station moves between one leaf and another, it does not have to change its default gateway because the SVI IP address and MAC address are pervasive and remain the same.

  - **Spine-proxy IP or spine-proxy TEP:** The spine-proxy IP is a virtual "anycast" IP address assigned to the spine switches. An anycast IP is an IP address that any of the spines use. When a leaf directs the traffic to the spine-proxy IP, the traffic can go to any of the spine switches depending on how the traffic is balanced inside the fabric. Leaf switches use spine-proxy IP or proxy TEP to access the mapping database, where the spine redirects the packets based on the destination MAC or IP address. There are separate spine-proxy TEP IP addresses in the spine. One is used for MAC-address-to-VTEP mappings, one for IPv4, and one for IPv6.

  - **Uplink subinterface IP address:** A leaf connects to the spines via uplinks. ACI routing inside the fabric is done via L3 protocols such as the Intermediate System to Intermediate System (IS-IS) protocol. ACI does not use routed interfaces inside the fabric but rather routed subinterfaces to exchange IP reachability within the fabric. Subinterfaces give more flexibility in the way a physical interface can be segmented and separated into multiple virtual interfaces that can be used differently inside the fabric. ACI uses the subinterfaces to pass the infrastructure VXLAN (iVXLAN) traffic inside the L3 routed fabric.

■ **Mapping database:** This is a database that exists inside the spine. It contains the mapping of IP host address (IPv4 and IPv6) and MAC address of every physical or virtual node in the user space to the VTEP of the leaf it connects to. It also contains the bridge domains, the VRFs and the EPGs with which they are associated. The spine uses this database to direct traffic such as unicast packets with unknown MAC address or address resolution protocol (ARP) request packets to the leaf (VTEP) that connects to the destination node (represented by the end node destination IP or MAC address). The mapping database is populated using different methods, including processing unknown unicast, ARP broadcast, gratuitous ARP (GARP), and reverse ARP (RARP). It also is populated from information it receives via the Council of Oracle Protocol (COOP) from the leaf switches that gather mapping information from active connections.

■ **Global station table (GST):** Each leaf maintains a table that maps IP host address (IPv4 and IPv6) and MAC addresses to remote VTEPs, based on active conversations. The GST contains the bridge domains, the VRFs, and the EPGs with which they are associated. This table is a subset of the mapping database that exists on the spine. This way the leaf easily finds which leaf it needs to send the traffic to based on a conversation that took place between two end nodes through this leaf.

■ **Local station table (LST):** The leaf maintains a table that maps IP host address (IPv4 and IPv6) and MAC addresses to "local" VTEPs, based on active conversations. The GST contains the bridge domains, the VRFs, and the EPGs with which they are associated. This allows fast forwarding between all end nodes connected to the same leaf.

The ACI Underlay Network

ACI uses a two-tier spine/leaf architecture that guarantees there are only two hops between any two end stations connected to the leafs. Layer 3 routing is used inside the fabric to provide reachability between all the fabric VTEPs and to allow the fabric to learn external routes. The fact that L3 is used ensures the ability to do load balancing between the links and eliminates the inefficiencies of L2 mechanisms such as spanning tree.

Different control plane protocols run inside the fabric, including these:

■ **COOP:** Runs on the PTEP loopback IP address to keep consistency of the mapping database. When new nodes are learned locally by the leaf switches, the IP and MAC-to-VTEP mappings are sent to the mapping database via COOP.

■ **IS-IS:** Runs on the uplink subinterfaces between leaf and spine to maintain infrastructure reachability. IS-IS is mainly used to allow reachability between the VTEPs.

■ **MP-BGP:** Runs on the PTEP loopback IP and is used to exchange external routes within the fabric. MP-BGP, via the use of route reflectors, redistributes external routes that are learned by the leafs.

Handling External Routes

The ACI fabric can connect to an external router such as a campus core router, a WAN router, or a Multiprotocol Label Switching (MPLS) VPN cloud. The external router connection is called L3Out and is done via different methods. The first method is done by connecting the external routers to leaf nodes via VRF-Lite and exchanging routes via different routing protocols such as OSPF, EIGRP, iBGP, and static routing. VRF-Lite allows VRF to be built but normally does not scale beyond 400 VRFs. For better scalability, peering with external routers can be done using MP-BGP or Ethernet VPN (EVPN) with VXLAN. This normally scales to more than 1000 VPNs if needed. The external routes are distributed inside the ACI fabric using MP-BGP. Usually a pair of spines are designated as route reflectors (RRs) and redistribute the external routes learned via OSPF/BGP/EIGRP into the leaf nodes. Figure 17-13 shows an example of L3 connectivity to WAN routers via a pair of boarder leafs. The external routes are learned via the leafs and redistributed inside the fabric via MP-BGP. Notice that two spine switches are configured as route reflectors and inject the external routes inside the leafs.

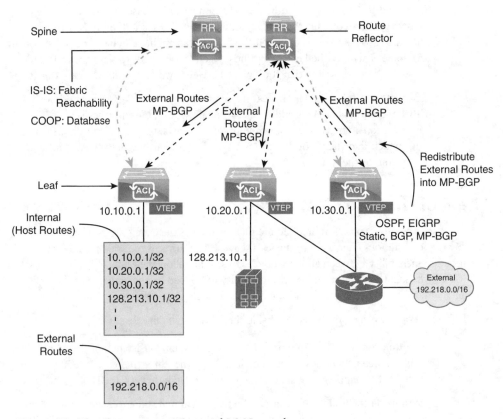

Figure 17-13 *Connecting to External L3 Networks*

The leafs distinguish internal routes from external routes by the fact that all internal routes in the fabric are host routes, the routes are /32 IPv4 or /128 IPv6 host routes. The terminology /32 indicates a subnet with a 32-bit mask for IPv4 or a 128-bit mask for IPv6, which means the endpoint IP addresses. External IP subnets are recognized by their longest prefix match (LPM). Because the external routes are redistributed via MP-BGP to the leafs, the spines do not see the LPM external routes, but only share host routes with the leafs. The ACI fabric can connect to multiple WAN routers and can pass external routes between WAN routers and as such becomes a "transit" fabric.

ACI Fabric Load Balancing

ACI uses different methods to load balance the traffic between the leafs and the spines. Traditional static hash load balancing can be used. This method does hashing on IP flow 5-tuple (source IP, source port, destination IP, destination port, protocol). The hash allows an even distribution of flows over the multiple links. However, because each flow is dedicated to a path, some flows might consume more of the bandwidth than others. With enough flows passing through the system, you might get close to an even distribution of bandwidth. Load balancing uses the path according to Equal Cost Multi-path (ECMP), where the load is distributed over the paths that have equal cost. In a leaf spine topology, and without adjusting path metrics, all paths between one leaf and every other leaf are equal cost, so all paths are used.

The ACI dynamic load balancing (DLB) measures the congestion levels on each path and adjusts the traffic allocation by placing the flows on the least congested paths. This enhances the load distribution to become very close to even.

The ACI DLB can be based on full IP flows or IP flowlets. When using IP flows, the full flow is assigned to a single path, as already described. However, when using the flowlet option, the same flow can be broken into smaller flowlets, and each flowlet sent on a different path. The flowlets are bursts of packets separated by enough time that allows the packets to arrive at the destination and still in order. If the idle time between the flowlets is higher than the maximum latency of any of the paths, a second burst of packets that belongs to the same flow can be sent on a different path than the first burst and still arrive without packet reordering. The flowlets use a timer with a timeout value. When the timeout value is reached, the second burst of packets is sent on a different path. The aggressive flowlet mode uses a smaller timer, where bursts are sent more frequently, resulting in a fine-grained load distribution, but at the expense of some packet reordering. A conservative flowlet timeout value uses larger timers with less chance of packet reordering, but there is a lesser chance of sending flowlets.

In general, DLB offers better load distribution than static load balancing. And within DLB, aggressive flowlets offer better load distribution than conservative flowlets.

The ACI Overlay and VXLAN

ACI uses VXLAN to carry the overlay network over an L3 routed network. Unlike traditional routing, where the IP address identifies the location of a node, ACI creates an addressing hierarchy by separating the location of an endpoint from its identity. The VTEP IP address indicates the location of the endpoint, whereas the IP address of the end node itself is the identifier. When a VM moves between leaf nodes, all the VM information remains the same, including the IP address. What changes is the VTEP, which is the location of the VM. Note in Figure 17-13, for example, that a VM inside a host is identified with its location (VTEP 10.20.0.1) and its identifier (128.213.10.1).

The Cisco ACI VXLAN implementation deviates from the simple VXLAN use of carrying L2 Ethernet packets over an L3 routed domain. Cisco ACI attempts to normalize the encapsulation inside the fabric by using a different VXLAN header inside the fabric. Cisco uses what is called an infrastructure VXLAN (iVXLAN). For the rest of this chapter, the Cisco iVXLAN is referred to as "VXLAN," but keep in mind that this VXLAN frame is seen only inside the fabric. Whenever a packet gets in and out of the fabric, it has its own encapsulation coming from physical hosts or virtual instances that could have their own VXLAN headers.

Any ingress encapsulation is mapped into the VXLAN. As shown in Figure 17-14, different encapsulations are accepted on the ingress, including traditional VLAN tagged or untagged Ethernet frames, VLAN tagged or untagged IP frames, other encapsulations such as Network Virtualization using Generic Routing Encapsulation (NVGRE), and the standard IEEE VXLAN encapsulation. Upon receiving the frame, the ACI fabric strips the ingress encapsulation, includes its own VXLAN header, transports the frame over the L3 fabric, and adds the appropriate encapsulation on the egress. The egress encapsulation could be any of the encapsulations that the egress endpoint supports.

The format of an ACI VXLAN packet is seen in Figure 17-15.

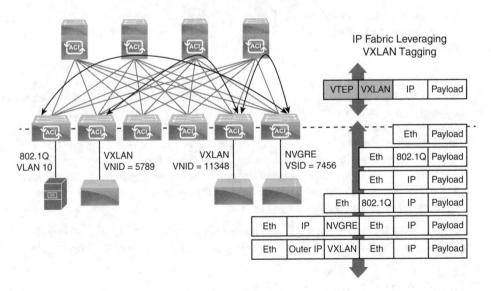

Figure 17-14 *VXLAN in the ACI Fabric*

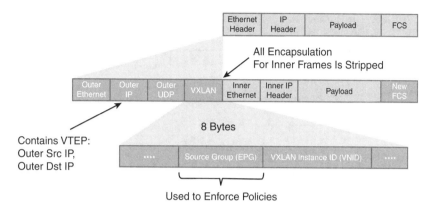

Figure 17-15 *ACI VXLAN Packet Format*

Notice that the VXLAN packet contains a source group identifier that indicates the EPG that the packet belongs to. The source group EPG is used to enforce the policies that are defined in the ANP. The EPGs in the user space map to either VLANs or VXLANs when entering the fabric. As discussed earlier, the leaf node classifies the traffic based on different parameters such as VLAN, VXLAN, IP address, physical port, VM attributes, and more. This classification puts the traffic in a certain EPG, and the EPG is identified in the VXLAN packet via the source group identifier.

Figure 17-16 shows an example of the association between an EPG and leaf nodes based on VLANs and a physical port on the leaf.

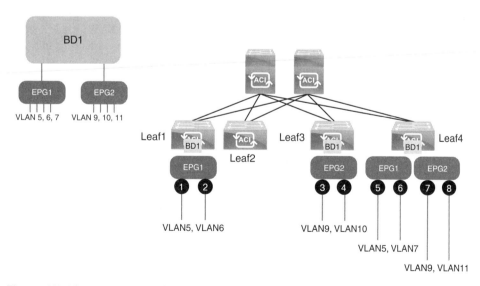

Figure 17-16 *Association Between EPGs and Bridge Domains*

Notice that bridge domain BD1 is spread across leaf switches 1, 3, and 4. BD1 has in it two EPGs: EPG1 and EPG2. The association between EPGs and BD is per Table 17-1.

Table 17-1 *BD1 EPG Port/VLAN Mapping*

BD1	Leaf 1		Leaf 2		Leaf 3		Leaf 4	
	Port	VLAN	Port	VLAN	Port	VLAN	Port	VLAN
EPG1	1	5					5	5
	2	6					6	7
EPG2					3	9	7	9
					4	10	8	11

The VXLAN Instance ID

Inside the ACI VXLAN frame, also notice a VXLAN Instance ID (VNID) that associates the traffic with a certain segment. The VNID allows the proper forwarding of the packet, and it differs whether the packet is L2 switched or L3 routed. In the case of routing, the VNID indicates the VRF that the IP address belongs to, and in the case of L2 switching, the VNID indicates the bridge domain that the MAC address belongs to.

Let's first look from a high level at an example of a packet that travels into the fabric. Then we'll go into more detail about L2 switching and L3 routing as shown in Figure 17-17.

As shown in Figure 17-17, a multitude of physical and virtual devices are supported through the fabric. Virtual switches, such as from VMware and Microsoft, can connect to the fabric. The virtual switches have different encapsulations, such as VXLAN for VMware and NVGRE for Microsoft. As such, the ACI fabric "normalizes" the encapsulation by stripping all encapsulation on the input, including its own VXLAN header, and then including the appropriate header on the output. So, if you trace a packet from a VM running on an ESXi hypervisor, it would occur in the following steps:

Step 1. The packet contains an IP header and payload entering the virtual switch or coming from a physical server.

Step 2. With a virtual switch, for example, the switch encapsulates the frame with a VXLAN header and then sends it to the leaf node using the leaf's VTEP IP address.

Step 3. The leaf node removes the VXLAN header received from the virtual switch and swaps it with the internal fabric VXLAN header. The leaf performs any required policy functions, such as allowing the packet or denying it depending on the set policies. The leaf checks the internal IP address of the frame and verifies its location. In other words, it checks the IP-to-VTEP mapping to locate which leaf it needs to send the packet to. If the egress VTEP is found, it is appended to the frame as the destination VTEP.

If the leaf does not find mapping, it changes the outer destination IP address (the VTEP) to the IP anycast address of the spines. This way all the spines see the frame.

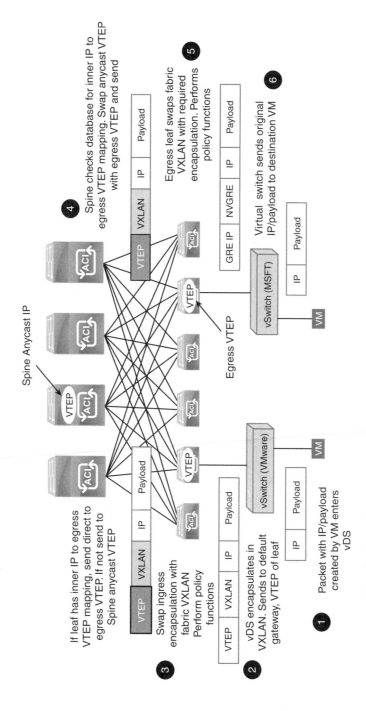

Figure 17-17 *Sample Life of a Packet Through the Fabric*

Step 4.   The spine that has the mapping changes the egress VTEP to the correct one and forwards the packet to the egress VTEP. All of these steps are done in hardware, with no added latency to the packet.

Step 5.   The egress leaf receives the packet. It removes the fabric VXLAN header and encapsulates the packet with the appropriate encapsulation. So, if the packet is going to a Microsoft virtual switch, it is encapsulated with an NVGRE header and sent to the GRE IP address of the virtual switch.

Step 6.   Upon receiving the packet, the Microsoft virtual switch strips the NVGRE and sends the IP packet with payload to the destination VM.

L2 Switching in the Overlay

When a source node needs to talk to another destination node, it normally identifies it with its destination IP address. The following are the steps taken when you perform Layer 2 switching in the overlay network. There are generally two cases. The first case is when the destination MAC address in known, and the other is when the destination MAC address is unknown.

If the node that is sending traffic knows the MAC address of the destination, it just sends traffic to that destination MAC address. When a BD receives a packet from an EPG and that packet has a MAC address different from the BD SVI MAC address, the BD knows that this packet is to be L2 switched, not routed, and performs L2 switching. When performing L2 switching, ACI sends the L2 packets over the fabric VXLAN. The L2-switched traffic carries a VNID to identify the bridge domain.

In some cases, the BD receives packets with a destination MAC address that the leaf node does not recognize. This could happen when the leaf node has flushed its ARP table, whereas the server still maintains mapping between an IP address and a MAC address, so the server already knows the destination MAC and does not ARP for it. In normal L2 switching, the switch takes the unknown unicast packet and floods it all over the L2 domain, until the node with that destination MAC address responds. The L2 switch then learns the MAC address through the response packet and includes it in its ARP table so it doesn't have to perform flooding the next time around.

Because a bridge domain is an L2 broadcast domain, any packet flooding, like ARP flooding or unknown unicast flooding, happens in the whole domain regardless of the VLANs. So, if a packet is flooded in BD1, every EPG and every VLAN associated with the EPG sees that packet. This is done by associating the BD with a VLAN called BD_VLAN, which is a software construct used to send all multidestination packets over the whole BD.

L2 switching is done in two modes: the traditional flood and learn mode and the proxy-spine mode.

In proxy-spine mode, when a leaf node receives an unknown unicast packet, it first checks its cache tables to see if there is a destination MAC-to-VTEP mapping. If there is, the leaf sends the packet to its destination leaf to be switched on that leaf. If the cache tables do not have the destination MAC-to-VTEP mapping, the leaf sends the packet to the proxy-spine, which checks the mapping database. If the destination MAC-VTEP is available, the spine sends the packet to the destination leaf. It is worth noting that the mapping database is always in learning mode for MAC-to-VTEP mapping regardless of whether L2 switching or L3 routing is enabled on the BD. The mapping database looks at active flows coming from the leafs and caches the information or learns the information from the APIC when node attachments take place on the hypervisor virtual switch. Figure 17-18 illustrates the proxy-spine mode.

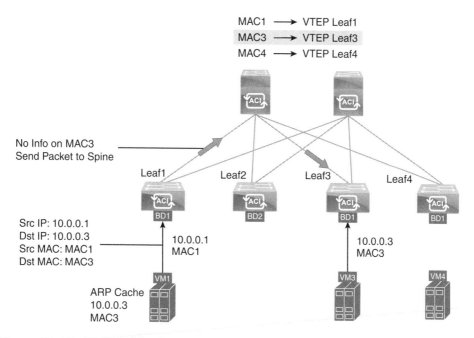

Figure 17-18 *L2 Switching Proxy-Spine Mode*

Note that VM1 is sending a packet to VM3, but Leaf1 does not know the MAC destination of VM3; therefore, it sends the packet to the spine. The spine checks its mapping database and finds a MAC-to-VTEP mapping for MAC3 address on Leaf3 and forwards the packet to Leaf3.

Flood mode is not the preferred method of learning MAC destinations, but sometimes it is required. In this mode, ACI floods the unknown multicast packets over VXLAN using a multicast tree. The multicast tree is built using IS-IS, and each leaf advertises the BDs that it has. When flooding is done, the unknown unicast packet goes only to those leafs that contain the particular bridge domain.

ARP handling in the flood mode is similar. When a node needs to send to another node that is in the same subnet, it needs to find the IP-to-MAC mapping for the destination node. This is done by having the source node send an ARP request using a broadcast MAC destination. Nodes that see the broadcast recognize their own IP and respond.

Because in an L2-switched mode (routing on the BD is disabled) the mapping is only between MAC addresses and VTEPs, the ARP request must be flooded. The flooding uses the multicast tree similar to the unknown unicast case. This is seen in Figure 17-19.

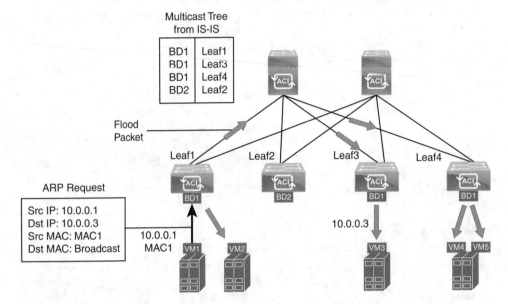

Figure 17-19 *L2 Switching—Unknown Unicast and ARP Flooding in the Bridge Domain*

Whenever a packet arrives to Leaf1 from VM1 and the MAC address of the destination is either unknown unicast or ARP broadcast packet, the packet is flooded to all leafs and ports that belong to BD. In this case, the multicast tree that is built using IS-IS indicates that BD1 exists on Leaf1, Leaf3, and Leaf4. Therefore, the packet is flooded to those leafs, and the individual leafs send the packet to all EPGs that are part of that BD. As in regular ARP, once a leaf node learns the local MAC addresses of the nodes that are connected to it, it keeps the MAC-to-VTEP mapping in its local cache table. This prevents further flooding on future packets because the destination MAC-to-VTEP mappings are present in all leafs until they are aged out at some point in time.

L3 Switching/Routing in the Overlay

L3 switching/routing can be enabled or disabled on bridge domains. A bridge domain realizes that a packet needs to be routed when the destination MAC address of the packet matches the bridge domain SVI MAC address. This is like any IP routed environment because the nodes use the router IP default gateway to send packets to subnets that are different from their own IP subnet. The end nodes send traffic to the leaf anycast IP gateway address, which is similar across all leafs for the same tenant. The packet is encapsulated in the fabric VXLAN using the VTEP as the outer source IP and is sent to the destination VTEP IP address to be decapsulated.

In the L3 mode, the inner IP destination (the IP of destination end node) is used to find the IP-to-VTEP mapping. Note that there are two types of routes in the fabric. The routes pointing to IP destinations inside the fabric are represented by /32 host routes or a bridge domain LPM route. External routes are always represented by LPM routes. The leafs first check an IP destination against /32 internal routes and, if not found, the leafs check in the LPM table if the IP destination is within the IP address range of the bridge domain subnets and if found, the leaf tries to find the destination from the spine. If the IP destination is not within the bridge domain subnets, the leaf checks the external LPM routes.

Figure 17-20 shows an example of L3 switching/routing between different subnets across the ACI. Traffic between VM1 10.1.1.1 and VM3 10.3.1.1 is L3 routed. VM1 sends the traffic to the SVI IP gateway, which is the same on all leafs for the same tenant. The MAC address is the MAC of the SVI IP gateway. The leaf checks the inner IP destination of the packet and realizes that it is connected to leaf3 via VTEP 3. The packet is encapsulated in VXLAN with a VNID of 10, which is the identifier of VRF 10, with a source IP as VTEP 1 and a destination as VTEP 3. After the traffic is decapsulated, it is sent to VM3 and IP 10.3.1.1. The IP-to-VTEP mapping as well as VRF information resides in cache tables of the leaf switches.

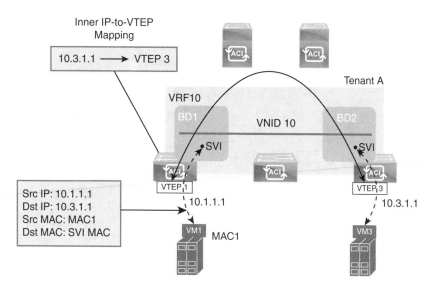

Figure 17-20 *L3 Routing in a Bridge Domain*

The VTEP information is exchanged using the IS-IS routing protocol, which is initiated on the subinterface IP address of the uplink between the leaf and the spine. The routing control information is carried across the fabric on what is called an infrastructure VLAN. The L3-switched traffic carries a VNID of 10 to identify the VRF that contains the bridge domains.

In addition to the MAC-to-VTEP mapping, which is always on, the leafs and spines learn the IP-to-VTEP mapping and keep that information in the cache tables and the mapping database.

In L3 routing mode, most of the IP-to-VTEP mappings and MAC-to-VTEP mappings are learned via the source MAC address of the ARP packet or the destination IP address inside the ARP packets. ARP packet handling differs whether ARP flooding is enabled or disabled. If ARP flooding is enabled, the ARP packets are flooded on the multicast tree to all relevant BDs, similar to the ARP flooding in the L2 switching mode. The only difference here is that the leafs and spines populate both their MAC-to-VTEP and IP-to-VTEP mappings because you are in a routed mode.

If ARP flooding is disabled, multiple situations could occur, as illustrated in Figure 17-21.

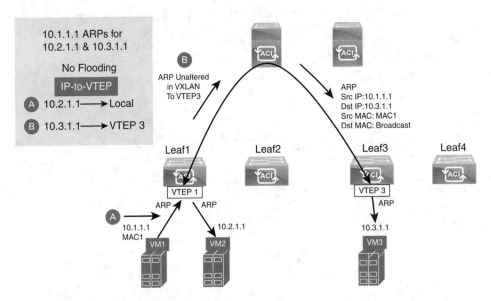

Figure 17-21 *L3 Routing—No ARP Handling*

The leaf receives an ARP request, and it knows the IP-to-VTEP destination of the packet. If the destination is local to the leaf, it switches the packet locally to the appropriate local port. If the destination IP-to-VTEP is remote, the leaf sends the ARP unaltered inside VXLAN as a unicast packet destined to the remote leaf. In both cases, if the node is a virtual node on a vSwitch, the ARP is flooded on the appropriate port group on the vSwitch.

If the source leaf receives an ARP request and it does not have an IP-to-VTEP mapping, enter proxy-spine mode. The leaf sends the ARP to the proxy-spine. If the proxy-spine has a mapping, it sends the ARP request unaltered to the destination leaf. If the spine does not have the IP-to-VTEP mapping, it drops the ARP and goes into what is called "APR Gleaning." In ARP Gleaning, the spine creates its own ARP with a source of the Cisco ACI bridge domain subnet address. The new ARP is sent to all leaf nodes in the bridge domain. In turn, the SVI of each leaf node sends the ARP in the bridge domain. In this case, the bridge domain must have a subnet address.

Multicast in the Overlay Versus Multicast in the Underlay

This is yet another topic that is a bit confusing. You saw how ACI handles flooding inside bridge groups. Multicast is used to allow the fabric to discover which bridge groups belong to which VTEPs. This multicast tree is built using IS-IS, and the multicast addresses that are assigned to bridge groups are called Group IP outer (GIPo), to indicate that this multicast is happening in the underlay network. This type of multicast is called underlay multicast because it is native to the underlay network inside the ACI fabric. Similarly, when using VXLAN between the virtual switches and the leaf nodes, EPGs are segmented using multicast. Each EPG is given a multicast address using an EPG GIPo. When the virtual switch (AVS) sends traffic via VXLAN, it encapsulates the traffic and sends it to the EPG multicast address. The ingress leaf removes the EPG GIPo and inserts the bridge domain GIPo to replicate the traffic to all bridge groups. At the egress leaf, the bridge group GIPo is removed, and the EPG GIPo is inserted to replicate the traffic to all EPGs on the egress side. So far, all of this refers to multicast in the underlay because multicast is native to the ACI fabric.

You also know that the overlay networks are the ones in the user space, or external networks that use the ACI fabric to go from one point to other. In the overlay network itself, there might be a need to run multicast. Hosts, for example, could be running the Internet Group Management Protocol (IGMP), which is a protocol that end nodes and routers use to create a multicast group. If such hosts need to communicate with each other via IGMP, the ACI fabric must find a way to carry such multicast traffic. Such multicast traffic initiated by IGMP is called the overlay multicast. The overlay multicast addresses are referred to as Group IP inner (GIPi) or multicast inside the overlay network.

To carry such traffic, the overlay multicast is carried inside the underlay multicast. Traffic destined for GIPi (overlay) is forwarded in the fabric encapsulated inside the GIPo (underlay) of the bridge domain. Only the leafs that have the particular bridge domain receive the packets using the GIPo address, and those leafs send the traffic to all hosts that are part of the GIPi multicast address.

ACI Multi-PoD

What has been discussed so far applies to a single ACI point of delivery (PoD); you have one leaf/spine network where you run an underlay via IS-IS and MP-BGP, and exchange information between leafs and spines via COOP. Eventually, the single PoD will need to be extended between different locations such as a campus network with two data centers extended over a metropolitan area network. Early implementations of ACI allowed leaf switches called transit leafs to connect between separate locations, creating what is called a *stretched fabric*. The problem with this approach was that the routing protocols were stretched between clusters creating a single failure domain on the network level.

As such, Cisco added functionality to allow what is called ACI Multi-PoD. With the Multi-PoD architecture, each PoD has its own routing instances, so IS-IS and COOP, for example, do not have to stretch across the data centers, but PoDs still have a single APIC cluster. This is shown in Figure 17-22.

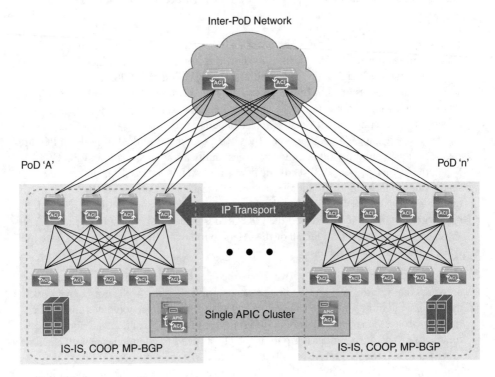

Figure 17-22 *ACI Multi-PoD Solution*

The exchange of information between PODs is done over an L3 IP Network (IPN) but both PoDs are still managed with a single APIC cluster. The two locations act in an active-active mode because, practically, this is still the same fabric running the same APIC cluster controller. Because this is still a single domain, the same policies that the APIC defines are spread across the two sites. The advantage of this design is that it is simple and straightforward; however, the disadvantage is that it represents a single tenant change domain in which policies that are applied at the tenant level are distributed across all sites. So, the concern is about the dissemination of misconfiguration, where a misconfiguration error hits all sites at the same time, which is not good for disaster recovery. In a sense, consider ACI Multi-PoD sites as being part of one availability zone (AZ) because they constitute a single fabric.

ACI Multi-Site

ACI Multi-Site addresses the issue of having a single APIC domain covering multiple sites with a single change tenant with no flexibility to apply policies per data center.

ACI Multi-Site solves this issue with the introduction of an ACI Multi-Site Policy Manager. The ACI Multi-Site Policy Manager is a cluster of three VMs that connect to the individual APICs via an out-of-band connection. The VMs are deployed on separate hosts to ensure high availability of the policy manager.

The ACI Multi-Site Policy Manager defines the inter-site policies and pushes these policies down to the individual APICs in each of the data centers, where these policies are rendered on the local fabric. This gives the flexibility of defining similar policies or different policies per data center depending on the requirement. For example, when defining ACI tenants, you can decide to which data center the tenants will stretch and extend the scope of the tenant into multiple sites. ACI Multi-Site creates a separate fabric or separate AZ. This is illustrated in Figure 17-23.

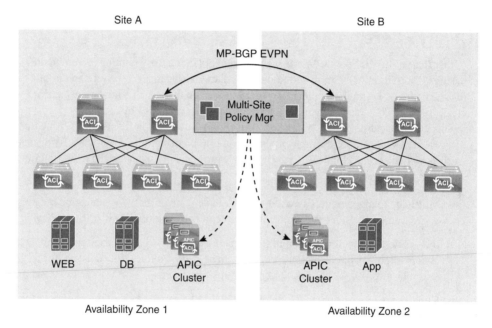

Figure 17-23 *ACI Multi-Site*

Multi-Protocol BGP (MP-BGP) Ethernet VPN (EVPN) is used to exchange end node reachability, such as IP and MAC addresses. MP-BGP EVPN runs between the spine nodes of the different data centers.

As far as the data plane, L2 and L3 traffic are exchanged via VXLAN across an L3 network that connects the multiple data centers. As discussed earlier, Cisco VXLAN carries segment information inside VNID, such as VRF or BDs depending on whether L2 forwarding or L3 routing is performed. Also, VXLAN carries the source EPG information to exchange the policies. However, because each data center has its own APIC domain, the values of bridge domain, VRF, EPG, and so on, are local to the site. Therefore, a translation function must take place at the spine nodes to translate between the namespace of one data center to the other. This translation function needs enhanced hardware such as the Cisco Nexus EX platform or newer.

ACI Multi-Site can define a schema, which is where you define and manage the ANPs. The schema consists of templates where the actual ANP is defined. For a specific three-tier application, you can define a template whereby you create a VRF and which bridge domains belong to the VRF. Assign the IP gateways and subnets, and define the EPGs that belong to the bridge group. Then define the actual filters and contracts and which EPG talks to which EPG. If the same policies must be applied to a multitier application, the same template can be applied in multiple sites.

In addition to the described functionality, the Policy Manager uses a health dashboard to monitor the health, logs, and faults for inter-site policies.

ACI Multi-PoD and Multi-Site work hand in hand, where Multi-PoD extends an APIC across the same AZ, whereas Multi-Site creates inter-site policies between different AZs.

ACI Anywhere

Other than using ACI Policy Manager to manage policies across multiple private data centers, Cisco uses ACI Anywhere to deliver policy management to private and public data centers. ACI Anywhere allows key attributes of ACI, such as policy management, single pane of glass management, and visibility into the fabric, to be available on public clouds including AWS, Microsoft Azure, and Google Cloud Platform. With Cisco Anywhere, Cisco can, for example, integrate ACI on premise policies with AWS policies such as virtual private cloud (VPC) and security groups. Following are the main functionalities of ACI Anywhere:

- **Multi-site management:** Gives the users a single pane of glass for managing policies across geographies between multiple data centers for a global view of the policy.

- **Integration between private and public clouds:** Policies that are used in private clouds can be mapped to public clouds such as AWS. Policies can translate, for example, into AWS VPC and security groups constructs.

- **Kubernetes integration:** Customers can deploy their workloads as micro-services in containers and define policies through Kubernetes.

- **Unified networking constructs for virtual and physical:** Unified policies and networking constructs can be defined for virtual environments such as VMs and containers, as well as physical machines such as bare-metal servers.

High-Level Comparison Between ACI and NSX

It is worth doing a high-level comparison between ACI and NSX. Each has its place in the network, and this depends on the use case.

As far as which approach is better, it is hard to make the comparison just based on setting and applying policies. The comparison must be done at a data center level, answering questions about whether you are deploying a VMware cluster that starts and ends with VMware or whether you are deploying a fabric architecture that supports virtual and physical environments. Such environments consolidate legacy and new data centers and multivendor solutions including Hyper-V and KVM. Also, when you discuss the data plane and packet forwarding, the difference becomes obvious between software-only solutions and hybrid software/hardware solutions.

Both ACI and NSX address policy setting and the L2/L3 networking. This is essential for simplifying the deployment of security and networking in hyperconverged environments. Implementations that do not address such automation fall short in fulfilling the promises of simplicity in deploying hyperconverged data centers.

From a high level, both ACI and NSX look similar. They both address the automation in setting policies and simplifying the configuration of the network. A virtualization engineer who is familiar with VMware will probably use NSX for setting policies, while a networking engineer would be more familiar with using ACI. From a commercial point of view, nothing comes for free. The investment with NSX is in NSX licenses, whereas the investment with ACI is in hardware that supports ACI and the APIC appliance with an optional Tetration appliance. So, the decision of which to choose goes beyond policy settings. Make your decision based on the following:

■ Policy setting

■ Policy enforcement

■ Performance requirements for VXLAN

■ Stability of the control plane

■ Performance of the data plane

■ Automation and visibility in the fabric

■ Networking learning curve

Policy Setting

For policy setting, the NSX starting point is the hypervisor with closer visibility to the VMs and the ability to perform networking services at the vNIC level. The starting point for Cisco ACI is the fabric. Instead of applying policies inside the host, ACI uses different ways to classify the traffic coming from the VMs into EPGs, and it applies policies at the EPG level.

The main difference between the two approaches is that ACI is a superset of NSX. The flexibility of setting the endpoints in the fabric allows the endpoints to be virtual or physical. It allows the user to break out from the vCenter construct where everything revolves around VMs. An EPG can have physical endpoints such as bare-metal servers, virtual endpoints such as VMs and containers, and physical or virtual network service appliances. In an NSX environment, everything is done at the virtual endpoint level only. Also, because the ACI VXLAN carries the srcEPG information, policy setting is achieved on a single site or multi-site basis for both virtual and physical.

Policy Enforcement

As far as implementing the policies, NSX and ACI have major differences. NSX does the enforcement in software at the vNIC level with the use of the distributed firewall (DFW), whereas ACI does the enforcement at every leaf switch level and in hardware. Anyone who has been in the networking industry for a while knows that the original firewalls were done in software in routers but slowly moved into hardware, either in adjunct cards or external appliances. So, you cannot ignore that software solutions will challenge the central processing units (CPUs). One might argue that because you are distributing the policy enforcement over multiple hosts rather than centralizing it, the performance impact is minimal because the load on each host is smaller. This might be true, but if you start loading the hosts with hundreds of VMs and eventually containers, connect NVMe drives, and pump up I/O to millions of input/output operations per second (IOPS) and the networking connectivity to 40 GE and 100 GE, you will need hardware assist at the host level. So, deciding whether policy enforcement is done in the host or the switch really depends on whether you believe that the host can scale in performance to handle current and future performance needs. Comparing an NSX DFW to ACI's policy enforcement is like comparing a software-based L4–L7 firewall with a hardware-based L4–L7. Both firewalls are distributed because even with ACI, the firewall function is distributed between all the leaf nodes.

Notice that the DFW and ACI were referred to as L4–L7, not next-generation firewalls (NGFWs). This is because DFW and ACI do not do policy enforcement at the application level. Such functionality is still suited for hardware-based NGFW application firewalls that get inside a session and do filtering based on application constructs. The issue of having NSX working only on the VM level is that NSX enforces policies and redirects traffic within the virtual environment. Although VM-based NGFWs and hardware-based NGFWs offer similar functionality, VM-based NGFWs have a fraction of the performance of the hardware version.

For NSX to tap into the physical environment, NSX must use centralized L2 software gateways such as the Edge Services Gateway (ESG) or centralized third-party hardware gateways. These gateways must stitch the VXLANs inside NSX with VLANs in the physical environment on a one-to-one basis. Added control mechanisms such as OVSDB must be used between NSX and third-party hardware gateway vendors to relay information between the virtual world and the physical world. So, getting the virtual and physical environments integrated in an NSX world is a bit complicated and might cause performance issues due to centralization. In an ACI environment and with classification at the leaf switch level, integration between physical and virtual is more built in.

Performance Requirement for VXLAN

In NSX, the VXLAN processing is done in the hypervisor. In ACI, the VXLAN processing is done in the switch. It is well recognized that VXLAN encapsulation and decapsulation—doing checksum for received packets, packet queuing, packet segmentation, and so on—are better with hardware assist. Even VMware recognizes that fact [2] and recommends using NICs that support VXLAN offload functions. Some examples of offload include TCP segmentation offload (TSO), which allows ESXi to send large packets to the NIC, and then the NIC splits the packets into smaller MTU size frames to be sent on the physical wire. Because VXLAN is a UDP packet, some NICs do not support it, which adds major overhead on the CPU. Other examples are in receive-side checksum offload where, if the receive-side NIC cannot do the checksum, it must be done by the CPU with big overhead. Other areas of NIC performance enhancements are in NetQueue and Receive Side Scaling (RSS), which distributes traffic based on MAC addresses or flows based on hashing. Such techniques bring major performance enhancements in dealing with VMs having to access the NIC and how the traffic is equally distributed between queues and processed in a parallel fashion inside the kernel.

Having VXLAN inside the host rather than the leaf switch can bring major overhead on the CPU if it is not dealt with in hardware. Advanced leaf switches with ASIC technology on the line cards can improve performance in this area. In this particular area, using NSX or ACI depends on how you envision accelerating the VXLAN-related processing at the host level or at the switch level.

Control Plane

Another area of difference between NSX and ACI is where the networking control plane lives. In ACI, the control plane still runs on the fabric. The leafs and spines run protocols like IS-IS, OSPF, EIGRP, and MP-BGP. Although an APIC automates the policies and configuration, the brain of the control is still within the fabric. In the NSX model, the control plane is spread out between the distributed logical router (DLR) VM modules, the NSX controllers, and the ESG. This is perfectly fine because control planes run in CPUs anyway, whether the CPU is on a switch or inside a host. As long as there is enough CPU power not to choke the control, the control plane runs fine. The issues that might arise must deal with the stability of the system itself. With hyperconvergence, you move from an environment where physical servers did the compute while fiber channel switches and storage arrays handled the storage to an environment where the host is running tens of VMs and supporting a distributed storage system with terabits of attached storage. Because hyperconvergence also adds networking to the mix, you have to step back and wonder whether networking is best suited inside the host or in the network fabric where it always was.

A node failure in a hyperconverged vSAN cluster now results in a possible failure of the DLR controller VM, which means another DLR controller VM must take its place. The active peering between the failed DLR and the NSX edge has to be established. The failed node also could have been running the Unicast Tunnel End Point (UTEP) that is carrying the multicast to other nodes.

The bottom line is that a failed host can affect the routing control plane, and the system must stabilize. Depending on the software implementation, the transition period until the system stabilizes and converges will affect networking and storage. So, trusting in one implementation versus another has to deal with your confidence in the stability of the networking control plane in hosts and how fast it converges because it took quite a while for switch vendors to reach the level of maturity you tend to take for granted now.

Performance of Data Forwarding

Another area to consider is the pros and cons of having data forwarding inside the kernel versus data forwarding in leaf and spine nodes. Let's divide this into two parts:

- **Switching within a host:** When switching or routing data within a host, NSX uses the vDS inside the kernel to switch and route the traffic. Cisco ACI can choose to do L2 switching inside the Cisco AVS or send the traffic to the physical leaf switch. One might argue that switching inside the kernel introduces less latency because you do not have to go to the NIC card, then to the switch, and back to the kernel. This is true if enough vCPUs are allocated to the switching function, which includes parsing of multiple headers inside the packet. However, if you need to do traffic monitoring and analysis, you are better off sending the traffic to the leaf switch, where traffic analysis is done in fast hardware ASICs.

- **Switching between hosts:** Most of the East-West traffic between the Web-tier, App-tier, and DB-tier is normally exchanged between VMs that exist in different physical servers. This is done to ensure high availability so you do not lose multiple tiers in the event of hardware failure. In a way, most of the traffic in the data center must travel across the VXLAN tunnels and the fabric from one physical host to another physical host. This is where hardware assist makes a difference because traffic must be encapsulated and decapsulated in VXLANs tunnels, and the host must deal with packet parsing, checksums, security enforcement, and more. As NICs move to 40 Gbps and 100 Gbps and you deploy Peripheral Component Interconnect express (PCIe) buses with NVMe, the CPUs fall short on performance. Hosts need to use Smart NICs that practically offload most of the tasks from the CPU.

On the other hand, in an ACI model, all data forwarding functionality, such as VXLAN encapsulation and decapsulation, switching between VXLAN tunnels, fine-grained policy enforcement, and switching and routing at 40 Gbps or 100 Gbps per port, are offloaded to the leaf switches. These switches exist today and keep getting commoditized and dropping in prices. Having next-generation NICs capable of offloading the CPUs for a wide range of advanced functionality is still under development and might turn out to be costly.

Automation and Visibility in the Fabric

In both ACI and NSX models, everyone agrees that there must be a fabric, and the fabric needs to move from the traditional three-tier access, distribution core to a leaf and spine design. So, the decision here is not whether to use NSX or ACI. The question is how intelligent you want your fabric to be. The Cisco ACI fabric brings a level of automation, where you just add leafs and spines and the system configures itself. ACI also brings a level of visibility in both the virtual space and the physical space. By using telemetry and atomic counters for checking on the health of the fabric, the end user can easily pinpoint whether any performance issues in an application are caused by the network.

One can argue whether this level of sophistication in the fabric is needed or not. The whole mantra of hyperconvergence is simplicity and getting to a level where clusters of compute, storage, and networking are built in minutes rather than weeks. For achieving such goals, introducing fabric automation via ACI becomes a must.

Networking Learning Curve

For environments that are 100% virtualized and VMware heavy, VMware virtualization engineers are probably more comfortable with NSX. It is unlikely that virtualization engineers will handle NSX routing because networking engineers who are involved in building the underlay network will have to get involved for the overlay. Networking engineers will have to go through a learning curve adopting the NSX switching and routing model that is still in the infancy stages. Networking engineers might still decide to go the ACI route for networking and network automation, leaving the policy setting and enforcement to the virtualization engineers.

On the flip side, if the fabric requires a mix of virtualized and physical environments, then networking engineers will have the task of building an ACI overlay and underlay. For setting policies, choosing NSX is more challenging in combining virtualized and physical environments. Cisco is facilitating the jobs of network engineers with the Cisco Tetration to become more familiar with the policy requirements of the applications. This will help the network engineer take control of the policy setting and enforcement within the ACI framework.

To conclude, in a VMware virtualized environment, virtualization engineers might find it more straightforward to play with policies. However, when it comes to switching and routing and integration between virtual and physical, NSX is challenging to networking engineers. A networking engineer who is used to advanced functionality in switches and routers and specifically with ACI will be constrained with what NSX does and will have to go through a steep learning curve.

ACI, on the other hand, is challenging to virtualization engineers and will probably need a networking engineer to launch it. Cisco is doing its best to enhance fabric automation and to bring application visibility to networking, to the point where all networking engineers will be very familiar with virtualization.

As far as investments, it is unrealistic to assume that with NSX, the user would not have to invest in advanced fabric functionality. With or without ACI, network switches will continue to evolve and enhance functionality to offer higher speed interfaces and hardware assist for specialized services such as firewalls, encryption, telemetry, encapsulation, and indexing. So, whether you like it or not, the fabric is evolving, and investment in newer and advanced switches must be done.

Looking Ahead

Part VI covered the networking aspect of hyperconvergence. Automation in networking is essential to the plug-and-play aspect of HCI.

One area of importance that wasn't covered yet is the concept of hybrid clouds and multicloud. As the adoption of cloud services skyrockets, it is important to understand how HCI fits in the multicloud model.

Part VII of this book discusses cloud services in general, with a special focus on Amazon Web Services (AWS). It then discusses how HCI integrates with one or more clouds and how vendors are helping users find the right cloud model to run their applications.

References

[1] *Internet Routing Architectures*. Sam Halabi. ISBN-13: 978-1578702336, ISBN-10: 157870233X.

[2] https://www.vmware.com/content/dam/digitalmarketing/vmware/en/pdf/whitepaper/vmware-vsphere-pnics-performance-white-paper.pdf

Public, Private, Hybrid, and Multicloud

Chapter 18   The Public Cloud

Chapter 19   The Private Cloud

Chapter 20   Hybrid Cloud and Multicloud

The topic of multicloud seems like the theme of 2018 and beyond. The definition of *cloud* also seems to have taken a life on its own. A few years back cloud was considered as a set of IT services that are outsourced to a public provider like AWS, Azure, Google Cloud, and many others. Also, vendors seemed to start building their own public cloud offerings such as Dell Cloud, VMware cloud, and others. Many such vendors closed their own clouds and resorted to selling their products and services on the traditionally established large cloud vendors. After all, building clouds with a national and international footprint is not for the faint of heart and requires a huge investment.

The initial shift from private data centers to public clouds was highly motivated by cost savings in building on-demand infrastructures and services that can be released when the task is done. Many in the development community jumped on this model due to the pains and costs of building their own setups just to run a task, and then were stuck with hardware and software they did not need.

The beauty of the cloud offering is in the ease of use and deployment: launching servers in minutes, attaching storage on demand, scaling up and down and out, and all done without chasing oversubscribed and underbudgeted IT departments. At some point, enterprises got so excited to the point where they thought they could offload everything to the cloud and run without an IT department. That did not work out as planned!

Fast-forward to when the hefty cloud bills started piling up. Enterprises ended up with, shall we say, a cluster-mess where they did not even know what project was running on the cloud, and who was paying for what. Add to it that the IT resources remained the same, and they all had to go through a huge and expensive cloud learning curve.

With the emergence of convergence and hyperconvergence, chief information officers (CIOs) realized that with better integrated products and better automation tools, they could duplicate the cloud model on-premise. After all, why pay all that money to cloud providers if the IT department could initiate virtual machines in minutes, allocate storage on demand, share the infrastructure with multiple departments, pay as you grow, and automate the tasks and duplicate the model in different regions. Thus, this created the notion of a "private cloud," which is basically your same old datacenter or datacenters with much better integration, software-defined networking, software-defined storage, and a new consumption model. Why let the public providers coin the term "cloud," when "private cloud" sounds more edgy.

Businesses pulled all the way to the right into the public cloud direction and then pulled all the way to the left into the private cloud direction. IT managers and CIOs realized that there are some cost models in the public cloud that are unattainable in a private cloud. When cloud providers build infrastructure at a very large scale— both national and international—certain services can be highly commoditized with very low cost points. If you take the analogy of figuring out where to store your extra furniture as an example, you can fill up your garage, fill up the attic, or waste an empty bedroom. Or you can rent public storage at $9.99 per month and dump it all in there. And assume here that you cannot live without the extra furniture, so you have to keep it. The same concept applies for data storage where the cost per gigabyte (GB) for AWS Simple Storage Service (S3) is a fraction of a cent per GB, and enterprises can leverage that service to dump in it terabytes of data rather than racking and stacking internal storage.

The point here is that there is room for both public cloud and private cloud services. Hence the notion of "hybrid clouds," meaning that some of the services you need are running inside your private cloud and some other services you need are running in a public cloud. So, while your application is running inside your data center, your backup storage could be at AWS.

Now that it is established that you need private, public, and hybrid, the next decision is whether to use AWS, Azure, Google, Rackspace, or many other providers that are popping up. This decision depends on which cloud can provide what service, whether the service is in your geographical area, whether the price performance is competitive, and so on.

The notion of multicloud will be the way to go moving forward as enterprises will have to decide a global IT strategy that involves their own IT resources and facilities and the resources and facilities of many cloud providers across the world.

To fully understand how hyperconverged products fit into this model, we will go into details of the public cloud and then look at the private, hybrid, and multicloud. Let's start with the public cloud, as this is where the concept of simplicity and automation started—and so far, private clouds are playing catch-up trying to mimic the services of public providers.

Chapter 18

The Public Cloud

This chapter covers the following key topics:

- **The Cloud Services:** A definition of the cloud model, including infrastructure as a service (IaaS), platform as a service (PaaS), and software as a service (SaaS).

- **Amazon Web Services:** An introduction to Amazon Web Service (AWS) and a highlight of networking, storage, compute, and monitoring capabilities.

- **Launching Multitier Applications in AWS:** How to launch multitier applications in AWS, including initiating compute instances, identity access management, security groups, storage, and monitoring.

- **Cloud Automation:** Cloud automation and the notion of infrastructure as a code.

The Cloud Services

Although many are familiar with the concept of public clouds, unless you are heavily involved in building a cloud service, you will feel like an outsider. It is an acronym wonderland: SaaS, PaaS, IaaS, S3, EC2, Cloudfront, CloudWatch, CloudFormation, and more. This section examines some of the main terminology and goes a bit deeper into examples of cloud services and automation drawn from AWS. This is a base point to compare with the same levels of automation that are happening inside the private cloud.

The main three cloud service models follow:

1. Infrastructure as a service (IaaS)

2. Platform as a service (PaaS)

3. Software as a service (SaaS)

The differences between these models are what components you as the customer must build and manage versus what components you want to outsource to a provider. There are many other acronyms in the industry, such as storage as a service, backup as a service, and xyz as a service, but they all fall under the categories just mentioned where you are outsourcing some type of service to the provider so you don't build it yourself.

Infrastructure as a Service

With IaaS, you the customer are getting the infrastructure from the provider. This includes the physical network, the hardware servers to run the application, the storage needed for the application, and network services such as load balancers, security, and more. For virtualized applications, the service provider also manages the virtualized environment such as the hypervisor or the container daemon, and you will get a virtual machine (VM) or a container on which to run the application.

The IaaS model was generally based only on virtualized services. In November 2017, AWS announced a bare-metal server model where the customer purchases the actual hardware services without virtualization. This is required for workloads that do not perform well inside VMs and require direct access to the hardware.

In other cases, some applications can use Intel VT-x, which is Intel's virtualization technology where the hardware itself—such as processor, memory, and input/output (I/O)—are shared while minimizing the overhead of doing virtualization in software.

An illustration of IaaS is seen in Figure 18-1.

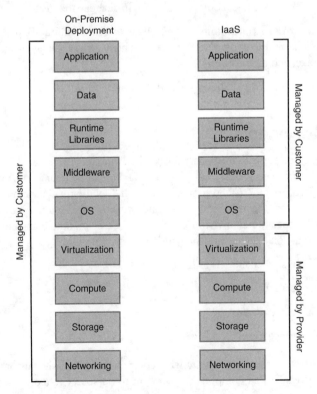

Figure 18-1   *Infrastructure as a Service (IaaS)*

As shown, you, the customer is responsible for providing most of the software components that are related to the application, including the application itself, the operating system, any runtime libraries, Hypertext Transfer Protocol (HTTP) servers, databases, and so on. The provider, on the other hand, delivers anything related to the infrastructure, including the servers, virtualization, storage, and networking. With virtualization, the customer operating system (OS) is the guest OS inside the VM. With a containerized environment, the provider must supply the container daemon, and you just deploy the container with the application. For bare-metal servers, the customer provides the host OS, libraries, application, and databases.

IaaS gives you full control of the software stack but eliminates any hassles in building the underlying infrastructure.

Examples of providers offering IaaS are AWS, Azure, Google Cloud Platform (GCP), Rackspace OpenCloud, HP Enterprise Converged Infrastructure, Digital Ocean, and IBM Smartcloud Enterprise.

Platform as a Service

With PaaS, the provider grabs a bigger chunk of the operation by also taking the management of the software components needed for the application to run. Such components include the OS, runtime libraries and tools, application server software, and HTTP server. In the IaaS scenario, you would have had to install all such components every time the application was deployed in the cloud. The software components had to be maintained and refreshed to stay up to date.

In the PaaS model, you get a "platform" that contains infrastructure components for both hardware and software and can focus on the application. You will spend most of your time developing and scaling the application itself, rather than focusing on how to deploy it. Examples of vendors that offer the PaaS model are Engine Yard, Red Hat OpenShift, Google App Engine, Heroku, Appfog, Azure, and AWS.

Software as a Service

The SaaS model offers you a fully outsourced model. In this model, the provider practically takes control of the full stack, from hardware resources, to software needed to run the application, to the application itself. In this case you get the application on a per-user subscription basis. You normally access the application via a web browser, and all the back end is done by the provider. Figure 18-2 shows a representation of the PaaS and the SaaS cloud models.

Many vendors are offering their product in the SaaS model for added simplicity and agility in having you use their applications. Examples of SaaS in the enterprise world are enterprise resource planning (ERP) software for accounting, human resources, supply chain, and more. Such services are offered as SaaS on a subscription basis, where you have access to the application and data without deploying a single hardware or software component.

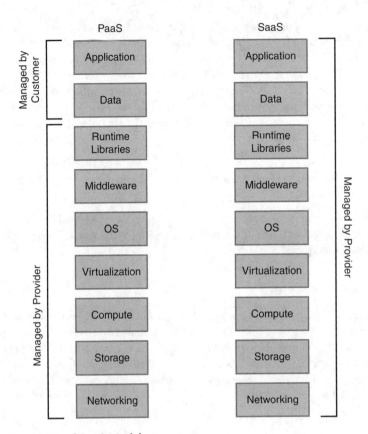

Figure 18-2 *PaaS and SaaS Models*

Amazon Web Services

The claim to fame of cloud services is the ease of deployment, simplicity, agility, and scalability. This is exactly what private clouds are aiming to achieve with hyperconverged products. As already discussed, hyperconvergence is drastically simplifying the deployment of infrastructure. However, for private data centers to fall under the category of "cloud," they must offer the simplicity and ease of deployment of public clouds. There are many clouds out there, and the numbers are increasing. Examples of cloud providers are AWS, Microsoft Azure Cloud, Google Cloud Platform, IBM Cloud, Rackspace, VMware Cloud, and Oracle Cloud.

This section delves into some of the services of public clouds, taking AWS as an example.

AWS [1] started offering IT services to enterprises as early as 2006. The model created a paradigm shift in how enterprises deploy and consume services. Instead of having the enterprise build its own IT infrastructure, AWS offered to build these services inside its public data centers on a rental model.

Soon enough, the capital expenditure (CAPEX) model that enterprises had in buying and owning servers, networking and storage equipment, and software transformed into an operational expenditure (OPEX) model of renting services. For chief information officers (CIOs) and IT managers, this represented a huge shift in operation, expenditure, and planning. Instead of spending weeks and months planning, purchasing, and installing equipment, IT can instantly spin up tens and hundreds of servers and storage in minutes and start applications a lot faster.

AWS offers a suite of cloud services targeted at different use cases such as business applications, the likes of SAP and Oracle databases, backup and recovery services, websites, DevOps, serverless computing, high-performance computing (HPC), content delivery, and Internet of Things (IoT).

To deliver such services with ease and simplicity, AWS offers a suite of products that enable you to launch the following:

- Servers

- Applications and databases

- Storage allocation

- Networking connectivity

- Networking services such as these:

  - Load balancers

  - Firewalls

  - Network address translation (NAT)

What is interesting about the services is the ease, simplicity, speed, agility, and scale of how these services are deployed. This type of service delivery is what private clouds aim to achieve and vendors are working hard to deliver inside the enterprise. The AWS products are extensive, but this chapter focuses on the topics that are in line with those in this book: compute, storage, networking, and orchestration of the service. This will help to compare and contrast with the orchestration of such services inside the private, hybrid, and multicloud.

AWS Global Infrastructure with Regions and Availability Zones

AWS offers a global infrastructure that spans more than 12 geographical regions, each having multiple availability zones (AZs). The regions are separate AWS clouds that are located in different geographical locations. The resources of the regions are independent from resources in other regions. This allows you as a business to launch services in national and international locations that are closer to your customers. Once you look at the resources in a region, you do not see resources in any of the other regions. By default, any resources you create in a region are not replicated in other regions unless you copy them manually. A sample of AWS regions is seen in Table 18-1.

Table 18-1 *AWS Sample Regions*

Code	Name
us-east-1	US East (N. Virginia)
us-east-2	US East (Ohio)
us-west-1	US West (N. California)
us-west-2	US West (Oregon)
ca-central-1	Canada (Central)
eu-central-1	EU (Frankfurt)
eu-west-1	EU (Ireland)
eu-west-2	EU (London)
eu-west-3	EU (Paris)
ap-northeast-1	Asia Pacific (Tokyo)
ap-northeast-2	Asia Pacific (Seoul)
ap-northeast-3	Asia Pacific (Osaka-Local)
ap-southeast-1	Asia Pacific (Singapore)
ap-southeast-2	Asia Pacific (Sydney)
ap-south-1	Asia Pacific (Mumbai)
sa-east-1	South America (São Paulo)

Notice the terminology of us-east-1 and us-east-2, as an example, showing two different regions on the U.S. east cost: one in Virginia and one in Ohio. The same applies for other geographical locations.

Within a single region, AWS has AZs. Think of an AZ as a fault domain, where faults in an AZ do not impact resources in other AZs. An AZ could be a set of data centers that share a power grid, are affected by a flood, or are in an earthquake zone. This ensures that a customer can optionally spread resources in physical locations that are not impacted by similar mishaps.

The AZs connect with one another via low-latency links, as seen in Figure 18-3. When you start the configuration of a server instance in a region, you must specify an AZ, or one is automatically assigned. AZs ensure that resources are not replicated within the same zone. If an instance fails within an AZ, another similar instance can be launched in another AZ. AZs are identified by a letter identifier at the end of the name of a region, so us-east-1a and us-east-1b, for example, represent AZs a and b inside region us-east-1.

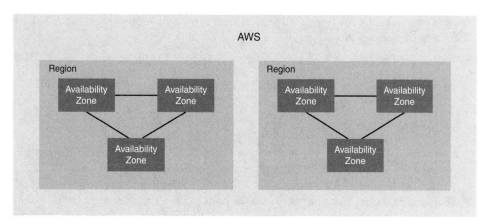

Figure 18-3 *Availability Zones*

Many hyperconverged architectures adopted the concept of AZs in some shape or form inside a private data center and for disaster recovery. You saw how HyperFlex, VMware vSAN, and Nutanix divide their nodes into different fault domains for added availability.

Networking

AWS networking allows you to create a virtual private cloud (VPC). A VPC allows you to create your own logical private network inside the AWS cloud. VPCs can span multiple AZs, and the VPCs can peer with one another to create larger networks. However, AZs and VPCs and the resources associated with them are associated to one particular region.

Inside a VPC, you can allocate a set of private IP addresses, subnets, and route tables. For connectivity to the Internet, AWS assigns static IP addresses, called elastic IPs. These IPs are public IPs that are reached by users and hosts on the Internet. The elastic IP addresses are transferred between compute instances, so if an instance fails, you can reach a similar running instance with the same elastic IP address. Inside your network, you can allocate an Elastic Load Balancer (ELB), which allows the Internet traffic to be distributed over multiple instances of your application.

A VPC allows you to do the following:

- Connect your network on AWS to the Internet so you can launch instances that are accessible from public IP addresses.

- Assign private subnets and IP addresses inside the network and request public IP addresses to connect to the Internet.

- Use NAT to translate between private and public IP addresses.

- Connect privately between different VPCs that are in your account or other accounts.

- Connect to any AWS-provided service, such as the Simple Storage Service (S3), without the use of gateways.

- Connect to any SaaS functions that AWS provides.

- Connect to your private data center with encrypted Internet Protocol Security (IPSec) tunnels.

- Connect to your private data center via AWS Direct Connect.

An illustration of the VPC is shown in Figure 18-4. Notice that inside the VPC, you are allocated the 10.0.0.0/16 private subnet; you can segment this subnet any way you please and allocate IP addresses from this range. Each host can belong to a private IP subnet or a public IP subnet. Connectivity between the hosts in the VPC is seamless and does not need router setup. Notice in the example that the databases are inside a private IP subnet 10.0.2.0/24, and web servers are inside a public IP subnet 10.0.0.0/24.

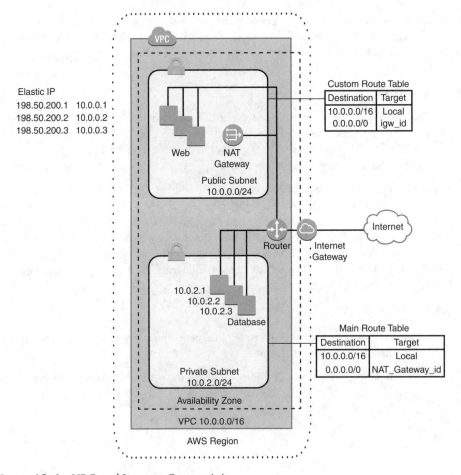

Figure 18-4 *VPC and Internet Connectivity*

Connectivity to the Internet requires a NAT gateway that AWS supplies for an extra charge. You specify a public IP subnet where the NAT gateway resides. You also associate the NAT gateway with an elastic IP. Hosts are also assigned elastic IP addresses. Notice hosts 10.0.0.1, 10.0.0.2, and 10.0.0.3 are assigned elastic IP addresses 198.50.200.1, 198.50.200.2, and 198.50.200.3, respectively.

Inside the Main route table, any connectivity for 10.0.0.0/16, which is the range assigned to the VPC, is considered local. Connectivity to any other IP addresses, such as public IP address, is sent to the NAT gateway (nat-gateway-id). Furthermore, when the NAT gateway receives packets sent to the IP address, it sends the traffic to the Internet gateway (igw-id), as seen in the Custom Route Table.

Note that, so far with such a setup, you can deploy applications that end users access on the Internet. You have not had to deploy any servers, routers, switches, NAT devices, or load balancers, and the whole network can be set up in minutes.

For connectivity between the corporate data center and the VPC, you can use different methods, such as IPSec or Direct Connect. With IPSec, you configure a physical router (customer gateway) on your end and initiate IPSec tunnels that connect to a virtual private gateway on the AWS side. You just need to configure an IP address for the virtual private gateway, and the trusted tunnels are initiated. This is illustrated in Figure 18-5.

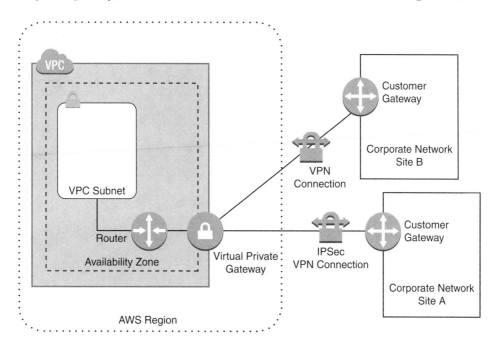

Figure 18-5 *IPSec VPN Connections to Corporate Network*

Another way for corporate networks to connect to AWS is via Direct Connect. AWS Direct Connect allows enterprises to have a dedicated direct connection between their private data center and their AWS VPC. AWS provides 1 GE or 10 GE connectivity. The private data center becomes an extension to the VPC, allowing resources to be moved back and forth between AWS and the enterprise with a fast connection and without relying on the Internet or Internet service providers (ISPs). Also, the connection itself can be logically segmented via VLANs, so the customer private data center can access your private resources in the VPC or connect to any other public resources inside AWS, such as S3 or Glacier storage. This is seen in Figure 18-6. Notice in this case that the connection has separate VLANs—one for all connectivity to resources inside the VPC, and the other for connectivity to public resources inside AWS. For public resources, you can leverage services such as S3 to back up your own data over a fast and secure connection. For more advanced setups, the connection can be used for synchronous replication of resources such as replicating VMs between the private and public data center.

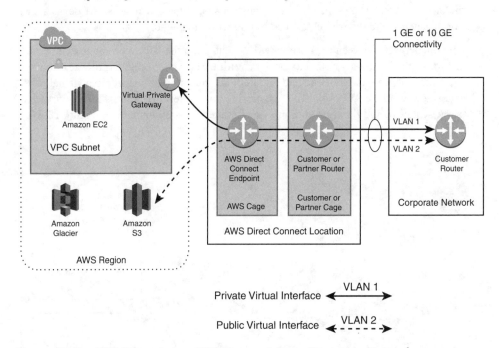

Figure 18-6 *AWS Direct Access VPC Connectivity to Corporate Network*

Storage

AWS offers different storage services in support of enterprise applications. Elastic Block Storage (EBS) is a low-latency, block-level persistent storage offered for enterprise workloads, including relational and Non-Structured Query Language (NoSQL) databases, Microsoft SQL Server, MySQL, mongoDB, Cassandra, and others. EBS is also used for Big Data analytics engines such as Hadoop, stream and log processing applications such as Kafka and Splunk, and data warehousing applications such as Vertica and Teradata.

Other types of storage are Elastic File Storage (EFS), which offers file-level storage that easily scales or shrinks and targets a wide range of applications that require low latency, and high availability, such as content management, container storage, and home directories.

Amazon S3 is an object-level storage with high durability; it is used for backup and recovery, archiving, and user-created content such as photos, audio, and video. Because S3 is object oriented, it offers the benefits of object-oriented storage, such as the ability to store massive amounts of data. It can be spread and easily tracked with the object identifiers over different geographical locations.

AWS S3 Storage

AWS S3 is a massive object store that offers eleven-nines durability and four-nines availability. AWS distributes its storage into at least three different physical locations within a region to ensure availability. There are many use cases for the S3 storage, including backup and recovery, data archiving, Big Data analytics, and disaster recovery. S3 offers tiered levels of storage with lifecycle management, allowing storage to be transferred between tiers depending on criteria such as how frequently the storage is accessed.

S3 Standard storage is used for frequently accessed data that requires low latency, high performance, high durability, and availability. This is typical for applications such as dynamic websites, content distribution, mobile and gaming, and Big Data analytics.

The S3 Standard Infrequent Access (IA) has similar performance, low latency, durability, and availability characteristics to S3 standard; however, it targets data that is not frequently used. AWS offers that service at a lower per GB price, but AWS charges a retrieval fee when you request the data. This makes S3 IA ideal for long-term storage.

AWS Glacier is the lowest cost storage, targeting data archiving. It has the same durability characteristics as S3 standard and IA; however, it is not immediately available for access. The time for data retrieval from Glacier ranges between minutes to hours depending on the service.

In addition to the already mentioned offerings, AWS offers Reduced Redundancy Storage (RRS), with four-nines durability and four-nines availability. This allows you to store, at a low cost, noncritical data such as thumbnails or transcoded media that are easily reproduced.

Storage lifecycle management allows data to be transferred between the different classes, such as from S3 Standard to IA to Glacier and back depending on the frequency of data access.

The S3 storage comprises buckets and objects. A bucket is a storage container that holds an unlimited number of objects. When creating a bucket, you must specify the region it is created in. The naming of S3 buckets is globally unique regardless of the region it is created in. Each bucket can contain an unlimited number of objects.

Objects can be up to 5 TB in size, and they contain the following components:

- **KEY:** This represents the name of the object.

- **Version ID:** AWS allows you to add a version ID to an object to uniquely identify the different versions of an object.

- **Value:** This represents the content that you are storing. An object value could be a sequence of bytes up to 5 TB per object.

- **Metadata:** This represents information that is relative to the object. Each object has a name-value pair that provides metadata about the object. There are two types of metadata: system and user defined. System-defined metadata includes information about the object, such as object size, date of creation, last modified, version ID, and storage class. User-defined metadata allows the user to customize information that is specific to an object, such as a tag or a description.

- **Sub-resources:** These are resources that are attached to the object and cannot exist without the object. An example of a sub-resource is an access control list (ACL), which contains a list of grants identifying the grantees and the permissions granted. This identifies, for example, who has access to the object other than the object owner.

- **Access-Control:** This identifies access permissions to the object.

Amazon Elastic Block Storage

The EBS service is a block storage service that allows you to attach block-level volumes to its instances. Block storage is normally used for applications that require access to raw unformatted persistent storage, such as databases and applications requiring file systems. EBS can persist even if the instance that uses the storage is stopped, terminated, or deleted. Many EBS volumes are attached to the same instance for higher throughput.

AWS EBS offers a flexible service for block storage, including:

- **High Performance and Throughput:** EBS provides different types of drives [2] depending on the application needs:

  - **SSD-backed volumes:** These are used for applications requiring high performance and high input/output operations per second (IOPS). This includes transactional databases and boot volumes. The user can choose between different types of drives, such as general-purpose solid-state drives (SSDs) for price-sensitive transactional data and provisioned IOPS SSDs that are targeted at latency-sensitive high IOPS transactional data.

  - **HDD-backed volumes:** These are used for applications requiring high throughput in MBps with a balance between throughput and price. Table 18-2 shows a sample of the AWS volume types.

Table 18-2 *EBS Volume Types*

	Solid-State Drives (SSDs)		Hard Disk Drives (HDDs) Solid-State Drives (SSDs)	
Volume Type	EBS Provisioned IOPS SSD (io1)	EBS General-Purpose SSD (gp2)	Throughput-Optimized Hard Disk Drive (HDD) (st1)	Cold HDD (scl)
Short Description	Highest performance SSD volume designed for latency-sensitive transactional workloads	Gencral-purpose SSD volume that balances price and performance for a variety of transactional workloads	Low-cost HDD volume designed for frequently accessed, throughput-intensive workloads	Lowest-cost HDD volume designed for less frequently accessed workloads
Use Cases	I/O-intensive NoSQL and relational databases	Boot volumes, low-latency interactive apps, development and test	Big Data, data warehouses, log processing	Colder data requiring fewer scans per day
API Name	io1	gp2	st1	sc1
Volume Size	4 GB–16 TB	1 GB–16 TB	500 GB–16 TB	500 GB–16 TB
Max IOPS/ Volume	32,000	10,000	500	250
Max Throughput/ Volume	500 MBps	160 MBps	500 MBps	250 MBps
Max IOPS/ Instance	80,000	80,000	80,000	80,000
Max Throughput/ Instance	1,750 MBps	1,750 MBps	1,750 MBps	1,750 MBps
Price	$0.125/ GB-month $0.065/provisioned IOPS	$0.10/GB-month	$0.045/ GB-month	$0.025/ GB-month
Dominant Performance Attribute	IOPS	IOPS	MBps	MBps

- **Data Encryption:** EBS can be created as encrypted volumes. In this case, AWS offers data encryption with the option of managing the encryption keys or letting you manage your own encryption keys for added control. Encryption is applied for data at rest inside the EBS volume as well as the data in transit between the volume and the instance where the volume is attached. If snapshots of the volumes are taken, the snapshots are encrypted. If volumes are created from the encrypted snapshots, these volumes are encrypted as well.

- **Snapshots:** Snapshots of EBS volumes can be taken to create a point-in-time backup of the data. The snapshot can be used to create other volumes in the same AZ or move the volumes between AZs. When moving data between AZs, a snapshot is taken, the snapshot is copied to a new AZ, and then a volume is created from the snapshot.

When a snapshot is taken, the data is backed up into S3 storage. When the first snapshot is taken, the full data is copied into S3. When further snapshots are taken, data optimization is applied by saving only the new changed data while keeping pointers to the unchanged data. This results in tremendous savings in storage. When a snapshot is deleted, only the data that is relevant to that snapshot is deleted; therefore, each snapshot has access to the full data at the time the snapshot is taken. To move EBS volumes to other AZs, a snapshot is taken of the volume and then restored to a volume in a separate AZ in the same region. AWS snapshots are illustrated in Figure 18-7.

Notice that when Snapshot 1 is taken, the full 5 GiB of storage is copied into an S3 bucket. However, when Snapshot 2 is taken, only the 2 GiB changed data is saved, and a pointer is kept to the unchanged 3 GiB of data.

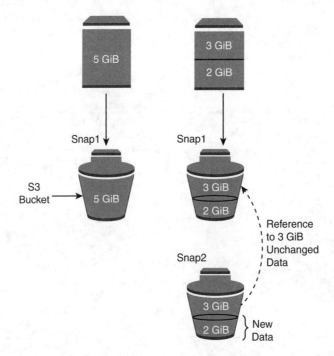

Figure 18-7 *EBS Snapshots*

- **Availability:** EBS offers 99.999% (five-nines) availability. Storage is automatically replicated within its own AZ to multiple physical nodes to offer added protection. This is similar to what was shown with hyperconvergence, where the data is replicated between nodes to protect it against single-node or multiple-node failures. The difference with a cloud offering like AWS is that you as the user do not have visibility to how the protection is done. All you care about is that your data is always available; it is the job of AWS to make sure that your EBS volume is available.

- **Elasticity:** The EBS volumes are elastic in the sense that after creating a volume with certain performance metrics such as capacity and throughput, EBS allows you to change the volume characteristics on the fly. You can increase the volume capacity, change the volume performance, and even change the type of volume without downtime. When changing volume types, AWS moves the data on the fly in the background without downtime to the application.

Launching Multitier Applications in AWS

Launching multitier applications in AWS is done without your investing in a single piece of hardware. AWS is elaborate, but let's stay within the context of what was discussed so far in hyperconverged infrastructure. The focus is on the ease of creating VMs and container instances and assigning the correct CPU, memory, OS, and storage. Now let's discuss the ability to perform snapshots and cloning of the VMs for added protection and how to monitor the health of the application.

Compute Instances

Launching a server—physical or virtual—inside AWS is referred to as an *instance*. An instance, for example, could be a VM or a container that you start. When a VM is started, as an example, you can control the compute requirements such as virtual central processing units (vCPUs) and memory, what guest OS runs on the VM, and what application services are started. You launch the instance inside a VPC, and you attach to it resources such as network devices and storage.

The compute service allows scaling the number of compute instances up and down depending on the load, server utilization, and so on. Some of the products under the Compute category are the Elastic Compute Cloud (EC2) for launching virtual servers, Elastic Container services for container and Kubernetes, ELB for deploying load balancers, and so on. One of the innovative compute services at AWS is the "Lambda" service, which is a "serverless" option that allows you to run applications and be billed based on processing time.

When launching an instance, you must specify the OS and software running on the image by selecting Amazon Machine Image (AMI). You also need to specify the permissions and security policies that define which users and resources can access the instance and what they can do with it. This is described next.

Amazon Machine Images

The AMI provides the information needed to launch an instance of a virtual server in the cloud. The AMI contains information such as what OS to use, application servers or applications that need to be launched on top of the OS, launch permissions that control which account can launch the instance, and a block device mapping that specifies which volumes should be attached when the instance is launched. The AMI also contains the type of storage for the boot device where the AMI will boot. If an AMI is backed by an Amazon instance-store, this means that the AMI boots from a template that is stored in S3, and the root volume is deleted when the instance terminates. However, if the AMI is backed by Amazon EBS, it means that the boot device is created from a snapshot that sits inside the EBS storage, and the data persists even after the instance is terminated.

Different types of AMIs are specified by AWS. AWS uses Quick Start AMIs, for example, to specify a prepackaged list of AMIs that you can use. Examples are AMIs for Linux OS and associated tools as well as AMIs for Microsoft Server OS and associated tools. An AMI for Linux, as an example, lets the user install the OS with a set of software applications such as Python, Ruby, Tomcat MySQL, and many other preinstalled packages. The AMI also includes packages that allow easy integration with AWS services, such as EBS. Some of these AMIs are under "free-tier," so you can use them without being charged.

You can use existing AMIs or build your own AMIs, purchase AMIs from the AWS Marketplace, or get and share AMIs with the community. Such AMIs can be leveraged to launch many other instances with similar software OS and toolkit without building the software packages every time you want to launch an instance.

Security Groups

A security group acts as a virtual firewall to control inbound and outbound traffic to the server instance. This is like the policies that were already discussed with HyperFlex and VMware. You access the instance via different methods such as Secure Shell (SSH), Remote Desktop Protocol (RDP), HTTP, and HTTP Secure (HTTPS). The security group allows you to access the instances by defining what protocols are permitted. The rules can be applied to inbound and outbound traffic. By default, anything that is not allowed is denied. AWS follows the rule of least privilege, meaning that you are given just the needed permission to perform the tasks and no more. Whether you are talking to instances or in the case of instances talking to other instances, security groups must be applied to allow communication.

An example of security group rules is seen in Table 18-3.

Table 18-3 *Sample Security Group Rules*

Inbound

Source	Protocol	Port Range	Comments
sg-111	ALL	ALL	Allows all inbound traffic from instances assigned to security group sg-111
0.0.0.0/0	HTTP	80	Allows all inbound HTTP traffic from any IPv4 address
201.13.1.1	SSH	22	Allows SSH traffic from the specific IP address 201.13.1.1

Outbound

Source	Protocol	Port Range	Comments
0.0.0.0/0	ALL	ALL	Allows all outbound IPv4 traffic

Identity and Access Management

Identity and access management (IAM) allows central management of security credentials such as access keys, and permissions that control who can access the resources inside an AWS account. IAM authenticates the user for signing in and controls who is authorized to use the service. AWS manages key pairs for the user, using private keys and public keys, or offers a separate key management server (KMS) for added security. Note that IAM is different from security groups. An IAM controls who can access a resource and what that person can do with a resource. For example, some users can create and delete EC2 instances, and some users can create an EC2 instance but cannot delete it. The same goes for other resources, such as storage. However, once an EC2 instance is initiated, the security group controls, for example, which IP address can access the instance and over which port.

A *principal* is an entity that takes an action on an AWS resource. An administrative IAM user is a principal. The administrative user defines roles that other users or services can assume, where the privileges for such users and resources are defined. A user of the service can also be a programmatic call or an application. All such entities are considered principals.

A principal accesses the AWS services via different methods such as a management console, a command-line interface (CLI), or the AWS application programming interface (API). In any such methods, the principal sends a request that specifies the actions and operations it wants to take; the environment in which such actions are requested, such as IP address of the requester; the permissions given to the requester; and so on. The request also specifies the resources that are requested and details about them, such as an EC2 instance name or tag.

After the request is made, AWS goes through an authentication process depending on how the principal made the request. If, for example, the request was made through the management console, the user has to enter a username password. However, if the access was done via an API or CLI, then the principal has to authenticate using an access key and a secret key.

Once the authentication is done, the authorization process begins to allow or deny the principal from using the resources. Such authorization is based on a set of defined policies that are stored in IAM as a set of JavaScript Object Notation (JSON) files. These policies are either identity based or resource based depending on the type of principal requesting the resource.

Launching an EC2 Instance

Having gone through the basics of AWS, let's look at a sample scenario in which an EC2 instance is being launched from the EC2 console. Before launching the instance, you need to do some preliminary steps, such as these:

Step 1.   Sign into AWS and get an account.

Step 2.   Create an IAM user.

Step 3.   Create a key pair so AWS secures the login into the instance.

Step 4.   Create a VPC to define the networking information, such as IP addresses and default gateway.

Step 5.   Create a security group to define the rules that classify access to the EC2 instance, such as IP addresses and Transmission Control Protocol (TCP) ports.

Some of the functions mentioned, if not defined in advance, are defined as defaults inside AWS. If, for example, a VPC is not defined, AWS assigns a default VPC that specifies what private IP subnet is used, a default gateway to reach the Internet, and an Elastic IP address to give the instance access from the Internet. Also, if a security group is not defined, a default security group is assigned but basically with one rule that says that anyone in this security group can access the instance, and traffic from the instance is allowed. So, without adding rules to the security group, you cannot access your instance via HTTP, SSH, or other login methods. After doing the initial prerequisite setup, the steps to launch the EC2 instance are as follows:

Step 1.   Select the region where the instance is to be launched. Examples are US-East (N. Virginia), US-East (Ohio), and other.

Step 2.   From the Console dashboard, choose Launch Instance.

Step 3.   Choose an AMI. In this step, you choose an AMI from a quick start menu, the marketplace, the community, or somewhere else. AWS lets you choose the root device type as the instance store or Amazon EBS. Also, in current Amazon AMIs, the Hardware Virtual Machine (HVM) virtualization technology is supported to offer the VMs higher performance. HVM uses hardware assist technology such as Intel VT.

Step 4.   Choose the instance type. In this step, choose the hardware configuration you need. Each instance type defines the number of vCPUs, the memory size, and storage and is grouped in the instance family. The list of instance types is extensive. Here are some examples:

- **General purpose:** Examples are T2 instances for general-purpose workloads such as low-latency interactive applications, small and medium databases, and virtual desktops. T2 instances provide a base-level CPU and can burst above the baseline. The CPU is allocated per CPU credit/hour. The T2 instances accumulate CPU credits when they are idle, and they consume credits when being used. An example is the instance t2.small, which is allocated 1 vCPU, 12 CPU credits/hour, and 2 GiB of memory (1GiB = 1024 MB).

- **Compute optimized:** These are instances targeted at compute-heavy applications. An example is c5.18xlarge, which offers 72 vCPUs, 144 GiB of memory, and 14000 Mbps dedicated EBS storage bandwidth.

- **Memory optimized:** These are instances targeted at databases with large memory requirements or in memory processing such as SAP HANA or Oracle in-memory database. An example on the high end is x1e.32xlarge, which offers 128 vCPU, 3904 GiB of RAM, 2 X 1920 GB SSD storage, and 14000 Mbps dedicated EBS bandwidth.

- **Accelerated processing:** These are instances targeted at applications requiring graphical processing units (GPUs) for enhanced analytics and engineering applications. An example is the P3.16xlarge, which offers 8 GPUs, 64 vCPUs, 488 GiB of memory, 128 GiB of GPU memory, and supports the Nvidia NVLink for peer-to-peer communication.

- **Storage optimized:** These are instances targeted at applications requiring large-capacity storage and high bandwidth. An example is the h1.16xlarge that comes with 64 vCPUs, 256 GiB of memory, 25 Gigabit of networking performance, and 8 X 2000 GB HDDs.

A full list of AWS instance is seen in [3].

The next step after choosing the instance type is to configure many of the parameters that relate to the instance. Some of these parameters are given defaults for commonly used values. Samples of such parameters are as follows:

- **Number of instances** to be launched. This is where you specify how many of the defined instances you need to launch at the same time.

- Launching an instance into an **auto scaling group** to scale the number of instances up and down based on specific metrics.

- **Purchasing option:** AWS allows you to choose the pricing for the instances. Choosing Spot Instances, for example, lets you bid on a price rather than using the AWS list price. You might get the lower price if offered by the marketplace at that point.

■ **Configuring the VPC:** You can keep the default VPC chosen for you or pick a VPC that you have already defined.

■ **Assign an IAM role** to the instance. AWS allows instances to assume a role that defines what resources or services an instance can use. For example, an instance can be allowed or denied access to S3 storage depending on the role it assumes.

■ **Add new volumes** to the instance by selecting the type and capacity of the storage device.

Many other parameters are used by the instance that define what the instance should do upon shutdown, prevent the instance from being accidentally terminated, enable monitoring via AWS CloudWatch, or assign user data to pass on to the instance upon launching security groups.

Let's discuss some of the preceding parameters, such as adding volumes for the instance and auto scaling.

Adding Volumes

The AMI selected for the instance already contains some default storage volumes that are attached to the instance. One of these volumes is the device root volume, where the image boots. If additional storage is needed, you can add further EBS storage volumes to the instance.

The volume type indicates whether it is an instance-store, meaning that the volume is deleted when the instance terminates, or EBS volumes where the data persists even if the instance is terminated. The volume type determines which type of device to choose from and the capacity of the device. For EBS volumes, as an example, you can choose general-purpose SSDs that are optimized for price performance or provisioned IOPS SSDs that offer high IOPs and are targeted for critical applications. When provisioned IOPs SSDs are chosen, you can select the number of IOPs that are needed, such as 10,000 or 32,000. For lower price capacity tiers, you can choose lower cost magnetic HDDs that are optimized for price per gigabyte.

By default, the volumes attached to the instance are not encrypted, but AWS gives you the option to encrypt the data and can manage the encryption keys within AWS or let you manage them.

Auto Scaling

It is worth discussing an auto scaling group in more detail because it is an important service that can either save you a lot of money or cost you a lot of money if not properly configured.

When launching instances inside an auto scaling group, the EC2 service allows you to set a desired number of instances to launch with, a minimum number, and a maximum number. Incrementing or decreasing the number of instances beyond the initial limit is based on different performance criteria such as CPU utilization. You can specify, for example, a desired number of instances of 2, a minimum of 1, and a maximum of 4. You can also specify that additional instances are to be created if the CPU utilization reaches or exceeds 80%, as an example, for a specific amount of time and to be removed when the CPU utilization of the instance goes below 20% for a specific amount of time.

The minute the CPU utilization reaches the upper limit and time duration that are specified, EC2 automatically launches another instance, and all running instances share the load. Similarly, when the CPU reaches the lower limit and duration, the instances are removed. Auto scaling is illustrated in Figure 18-8.

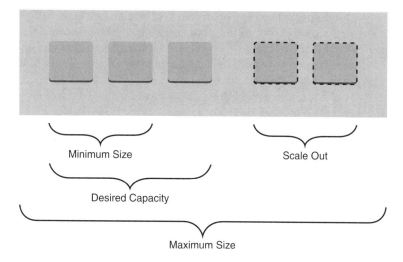

Figure 18-8 *EC2 Auto Scaling*

Auto Scaling is a great service for allocating resources on demand and according to the need of the application. It can save the enterprise a lot of money by not allocating more resources than needed. However, it can be a money sinkhole if it is misconfigured. To understand why, you need to go deeper into the details of AWS pricing. Every time you launch an instance, you are being charged. You are charged for the time the instance is running, additional elastic IP addresses you request, whether the instance is attached to flash storage, whether you are using the NAT function, and so on. Some of these charges are based on hourly rates, and some have a minimum of one day. So, if an instance is added and removed within one minute, as an example, you might be charged for one hour for the instance and for 24 hours for some other services such as NAT or other resources attached to the instance.

Assume, for example, that Bob wants to impress his boss by configuring auto scaling. Bob specifies a desired number of five instances, a minimum of three, and a maximum of ten instances. Bob also specifies that an instance is to be created if the CPU utilization of the desired instances exceeds 80% for a period of one minute and to remove the instances if the CPU utilization goes below 40% for one minute. Each instance has an elastic IP address, expensive SSD flash drives, and NAT gateways. Bob computes that total costs per day for his running instances is about $10 per instance, with an average of seven hosts running per day, so a total of $70 per day or roughly $2100 per month.

What Bob does not realize is that every time an instance is stopped and relaunched, his company is being charged a full hour for the instance and a full day for other services, regardless of whether the instance runs for 5 minutes or 30 minutes. Also, Bob does not realize that the load on his application is bouncing between 100% CPU and 30% every five minutes. The five initial instances constantly jump to ten instances and drop to three instances every five minutes. So, Bob's company is being charged more than ten times the regular fee. At the end of the month, the company receives a hefty bill. To cut the story short, Bob does not work there anymore.

This example highlights the importance of monitoring, which is crucial for efficiently using the AWS services and understanding the commercial impact. AWS offers several tools for allowing IT administrators to monitor the service usage, to monitor the state of any resource, to receive alarms, and even to track the billing associated with every resource. If Bob had configured alarms for monitoring the instances or even billing notifications, he could have easily discovered the problem early in the cycle. Cloud monitoring is explained next.

Cloud Monitoring

After launching the services, AWS allows the users to monitor the services and application using the CloudWatch. The CloudWatch service allows you to collect and track metrics, create and track logs, set alarms, and react to changes in the AWS services. It allows system-wide visibility into the resource utilization and the performance of the applications. Some of the CloudWatch features include these:

- Monitoring EC2 instances such as tracking CPU utilization, data transfer, and disk usage.

- Monitoring AWS resources such as relational databases (RDSs), EBS volumes, and ELBs.

- Monitoring custom metrics that the application generates.

- Monitoring and storing logs.

- Setting alarms.

- Viewing graphs and statistics.

- Reacting to changes in the application. Metrics or changes in metrics are used to create workflows in support of cloud automation.

- Monitoring charges with alerts and notifications.

Cloud Automation

Automation is a big topic when discussing AWS. Let's focus only on the following two aspects:

- Infrastructure as a code

- Setup through a software development kit (SDK)

Infrastructure as a Code

Infrastructure as a code refers to the ability to translate cloud configuration into reusable code. This means that a multitier configuration, as an example, where a web, app, and DB are set up through Console, CLI, or API could be translated into templates that can be reused to deploy similar setups over and over without manual configuration. All AWS resources and how they interact with one another can be modeled and put in code and easily be redeployed.

AWS allows infrastructure as a code through the CloudFormation service. This service allows you to code your infrastructure from scratch with the CloudFormation template language, which is either Java Script Object Notation (JSON) or YAML (Yaml Ain't Markup Language). Both JSON and YAML are data-exchange formats that humans can easily read and write to. They exchange data between clients and servers or between servers, and the format indicates how the actual infrastructure looks.

After CloudFormation transforms the configuration into a template, the code is uploaded into the S3 storage. After that, CloudFormation reads the JSON or YAML templates and uses the console, the CLI, or the API to form a "stack." The stack is used to create the AWS resources accordingly.

An AWS CloudFormation template written in JSON in shown in Example 18-1.

Example 18-1   *AWS CloudFormation Template Written in JSON*

```
{
  "AWSTemplateFormatVersion" : "2010-09-09",
  "Description" : "An example of a JSON template",

  "Parameters": {
    "InstanceType": {
      "Type" : "String",
      "Default" : "t2.micro",
      "AllowedValues" : ["t2.micro", "m1.small", "m1,large"],  <------ Properties
      "Description": " User can input any of the values t2.micro, m1.small, or
  m1.large - Default is t2.micro."
    }
  },


"Resources" : {
  "MyServer" : {
    "Type" : "AWS::EC2::Instance",
    "Properties" : {
    "InstanceType": { "Ref" :    "InstanceType" },
```

```
        "ImageId" : "ami-12345678",
        "BlockDeviceMappings" : [
          {
            "DeviceName" : "/dev/sdm",
            "Ebs" : {
               "VolumeType" : "io1",
               "Iops" : "200",
               "DeleteOnTermination" : "false",
               "VolumeSize" : "20"
             }
          }
        ]
      }
    }
  }
}
```

Format Version: Identifies the capabilities of the template. Example:

"AWSTemplateFormatVersion" : "2010-09-09"

Description: Allows you to include comments about the template. Example:

"Description:" : "This template describes the following …"

Parameters: Allow you to enter custom values to the template in the form of names and types and properties that you can reference from inside the template using the "Ref" function.

AWS defines different types for the parameter, such as String, Number, List, AWS-specific parameter types such as AWS::EC2::Instance:Id, AWS::EC2::Image:Id, and so on.

Optional properties are added to the parameter, such as Default, AllowedValues, MinLength, MaxLength, MinValue, and MaxValue, as shown in Example 18-2.

Example 18-2 *Parameters*

```
"Parameters": {
  "InstanceType": {                            <------- Name that you call via "Ref"
    "Type" : "String",                         <------- Parameter Type
    "Default" : "t2.micro",                    <------- Properties
    "AllowedValues" : ["t2.micro", "m1.small", "m1,large"],  <------ Properties
    "Description": " User can input any of the values t2.micro, m1.small, or
  m1.large - Default is t2.micro."
  }
}
```

Resources: The Resources section declares the AWS resources that you want to include in the stack, such as an Amazon EC2 instance or an S3 bucket. The resource has a name, type, and optional properties. The name is a unique identifier for the resources inside the template. The type indicates the AWS-defined resource types you are declaring. The properties are additional options you specify for the resources, such as the Amazon Machine Image (AMI), as shown in Example 18-3.

Example 18-3 *Resources*

```
"Resources": {
  "MyServer": {                                  <------ Name of the Resource
    "Type" : "AWS::EC2::Instance",               <------ Defines an EC2 Server
    "Properties" : {                             <------ List of Properties
      "InstanceType": { "Ref" :  "InstanceType" }, <---- Reference to "InstanceType"
  parameter.
      "ImageId" : "ami-12345678",                <------ AMI
      "BlockDeviceMappings" : [                  <------ Allocated storage devices
      {
        "DeviceName" : "/dev/sdm",
        "Ebs" : {                                <------ EBS
          "VolumeType" : "io1",          <------ EBS provisioned IOPS, SSD, io1
          "Iops" : "200",
          "DeleteOnTermination" : "false",
          "VolumeSize" : "20"


        }
      }
    ]
  }
 }
}
```

Notice in Example 18-3 how "Ref" is used to reference the template "InstanceType" parameter, which was defined earlier. "Ref" basically means replace with the parameter.

Outputs: The "Outputs" section declares the outputs you can import into other stacks or that you can return in response to a call or view inside the CloudFormation console. Outputs define a name and a type. You will see in the following example a reference to an "fn," which is an intrinsic function. AWS uses the intrinsic functions to return values of properties at runtime. For example, if you want to return an instance ID for use in a different template, the value of the instance ID is not normally known until the instance is defined and running. An example of an intrinsic function is Fn::GetAtt, which returns the value of an attribute from a resource in a template. Example 18-4 shows a sample of "Outputs."

Example 18-4 *Outputs*

```
"Outputs": {
  "PublicIP" : {
    "Description : "The public IP of an Instance",
    "Value" : { "Fn" :: GetAtt" : ["EC2Instance", "PublicIP"] }  <---- Return public
  IP at runtime
  }
}
```

This was just a brief introduction to CloudFormation. For a full description, please refer to the AWS CloudFormation user guide [4].

You can also check functional sample templates of CloudFormation at [5].

With CloudFormation, any configuration that is created via the console, CLI, or APIs can be saved as a template and the template reused to create a stack. Alternative methods for creating configuration is via the use of SDKs, as described next.

Software Development Kits

AWS allows you to access resources such as EC2, S3, and others through API calls from different programmatic languages. This is done via SDKs for the specific programming language. AWS provides SDKs for Java, JavaScript, Python, Ruby, .NET, PHP, iOS, and Android.

Think of an API as an interface between two software programs, where the interface allows one program to make certain requests and the other program responds using a certain format. The API is the vehicle (interface) that takes the request from a client and comes back with a response from the server. Because the server basically knows what it can do and can offer, it is the one that defines that API. The server shares the API with you, describing what information you can get from the server and which functions to use to request it. The server can also give you this information in different formats if you specify how you want it.

The formats of the response depend on what you request. You can request the response to be formatted as JSON. Assume you are a client and the function you want is sitting on the server. Say, for example, the server has information on the weather in a certain location and can give you such information if you specify the location and the range of dates. You, as the client, do not really know how the server gets such information. All you need to know is how to request the information and how to read the response.

There are different ways to make an API request and to get a response. If the request is done via HTTP, as an example, the API is referred to as REST or RESTful API. This basically refers to HTTP being the vehicle to embed these API requests and responses. If you (the client) want to send an API request to a web server, embed the request within an HTTP URL and send it. If, on the other hand, a software program wants to send the API request, the request is sent via the programmatic language of the software program. APIs are covered a bit further in Chapter 19, "The Private Cloud."

Think of AWS as the engine that gives you services such as EC2 and S3. You can request such services via specific APIs that are defined by AWS. If, for example, your application requires more instances, the application can request through the API to have AWS spin up more instances. If the client is a software program written in Java, Python, Ruby, or any other language, AWS provides SDKs to facilitate for such software programs to access the AWS resources via APIs.

So, to be specific, to access the AWS EC2 APIs via Java or Python, you can use an AWS-provided EC2 Java SDK or an EC2 Python SDK. The SDK makes it easier for you to embed the specific API requests and interpret the API responses from within the Java or Python program.

Looking Ahead

This chapter discussed the public cloud's services and its benefits. AWS was taken as an example because of its widespread usage and adoption. Other important cloud providers, such as Google Cloud Platform (GCP) and Microsoft Azure, are making their mark in delivering pubic services. As a matter of fact, Cisco Systems made a partnership with GCP in the area of containerized environments and in the creation of hybrid clouds. This becomes important for enterprises as they move in the direction of building private clouds, hybrid clouds, and multiclouds.

Chapter 19 describes, using automation and orchestration, how to transform hyperconverged data centers into private clouds. Some examples are taken from Cisco Systems and show how they apply to HyperFlex.

Chapter 20, "Hybrid Cloud and Multicloud," concludes the book with a brief description of the use cases and benefits of hybrid clouds and multicloud. It also draws on tools from Cisco Systems to allow the ease of migration of applications and services between the different clouds.

References

[1] https://docs.aws.amazon.com

[2] https://aws.amazon.com/ebs/details/#VolumeTypes

[3] https://aws.amazon.com/ec2/instance-types/

[4] https://docs.aws.amazon.com/AWSCloudFormation/latest/UserGuide/Welcome.html

[5] https://docs.aws.amazon.com/AWSCloudFormation/latest/UserGuide/cfn-sample-templates.html

Chapter 19

The Private Cloud

This chapter covers the following key topics:

- **What Is a Private Cloud?:** The characteristics and the different models of a private cloud and a description of the new consumption model that includes automation and orchestration.

- **Cisco UCS Director:** The Cisco UCS Director (UCSD) and the definitions of storage, compute, and networking policies. Also describes the virtual data center (vDC) and orchestration concepts.

- **Integration Between UCSD and HyperFlex:** Integration between UCSD and Cisco HyperFlex HX Data Platform including automation, orchestration, and creating infrastructure as a code.

Having explored the public cloud—specifically AWS—in Chapter 18, it is easy to see that its agility and ease of use come with its own baggage in terms of learning curve and costs. That has pushed IT administrators to evaluate what we call the private cloud. Let's first try to define the private cloud and then look at the reasoning behind the move toward this model.

What Is a Private Cloud?

The *private cloud* is simply a pool of physical and virtual resources that are owned and controlled by an entity and that can be assigned to users on demand with an agile and easy consumption model. The private cloud can be provided to its users as an infrastructure as a service (IaaS), platform as a service (PaaS), or software as a service (SaaS). To generalize, the private cloud can be consumed by its users as IT as a service (ITaaS).

This sounds a lot like the public cloud, with the only difference being that the cloud is private and is owned by the enterprise. The private cloud can be built and managed by the enterprise's own resources or outsourced to service providers that help manage or operate the cloud. The most important part is that the private cloud is under the full control of the enterprise and offers the security and peace of mind for many organizations who are protective of their data. Many enterprises opt to build their own private cloud even when public offerings for some applications are less expensive, as the importance of security outweighs any other cost benefits. Figure 19-1 shows the private cloud consumption models, fully self-managed or outsourced.

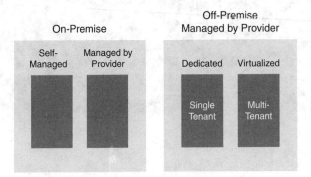

Figure 19-1 *Private Cloud Models*

Notice in the outsourced model that the cloud service provider offers to have your private cloud managed on your own premises or managed at the providers' data centers, where you still have full control over what equipment to get and what packages to install. The provider also offers a virtual private cloud where the physical equipment is shared between a few customers. Although this latter model alleviates the enterprise from carrying the full cost of equipment, it might not be acceptable by some enterprises who want full autonomy over their hardware and software and emphasize security.

You might wonder how the private cloud is different from the same old enterprise data center or hosting models that you were doing for years. The answer to that question is basically in the consumption model of a data center versus the consumption model of the private cloud.

Think of the traditional data centers as resources that different engineering groups manage. The data center consists of facilities, racks, power systems, heating and cooling, servers, switches, network appliances, storage arrays, and so on. Each of the storage, compute, networking, virtualization, and application engineers perform their own independent tasks. The end user at the receiving end gets the services allocated to him by the IT team. The user gets his email, WiFi, VPN, shared folders, IP Phone, WebEx account, and so on. Any requests for compute or storage resources or new applications must go through a huge manual chain reaction between the different departments, and it takes weeks or months to be implemented.

When you think of the private cloud, you shift your thinking into the public cloud consumption model. You start thinking about service portals, placing service requests online, launching web servers, application servers, and database servers on demand. You can think of turnaround times in minutes and hours and days rather than weeks and months. You also have full visibility into every resource you use and guidance as to whether the resources are efficiently used by the applications you are running. This gives a level of accountability for your consumption of the resources because you, and others, see the dollars and cents that are attached to them.

What turns data centers into private clouds, and what makes the consumption model possible, are two main things:

- Convergence and hyperconvergence
- Automation and orchestration

Convergence and Hyperconvergence

You should be an expert in this area by now. The fact that data centers have moved into converged and now hyperconverged infrastructure is a major facilitator for the private cloud. Administrators are turning into multifunctional engineers who perform network, compute, and storage administration tasks in a fraction of the time than before. The fact that hyperconverged systems are making advanced data functionality such as replication, backup, and disaster recovery native to scale-out architectures is dramatically simplifying the traditional data center.

Having said that, hyperconverged data centers on their own cannot transform the data center into private clouds and hybrid clouds without automation and orchestration. This is why many hyperconverged infrastructure (HCI) vendors, including Cisco Systems, are working fearlessly on augmenting HCI platforms with tools and software platforms to make the user consumption model is simple and flexible.

Automation and Orchestration

Sometimes automation and orchestration are confused as being the same, but they are actually different.

Automation simplifies the creation of certain tasks. A task could be the creation of a virtual machine (VM), the creation of one or multiple clones, shutting down a virtual machine, creating or resizing a datastore, and so on. Chapter 18, "The Public Cloud," discussed different techniques used by AWS, such as auto scaling. With auto scaling, as an example, automation makes adding and removing VMs based on central processing unit (CPU) utilization or other metrics a simple task. In this case, automation alleviates you from constantly checking that the application is consuming too much CPU and then manually adding more VMs and then balancing the workloads with the added VMs. Doing such tasks manually is tedious and inefficient and cannot scale. With automation, the vendor and service provider write functions dedicated to each task that simplify launching and executing the task.

Orchestration is a higher-level abstraction that aims to stitch the multiple smaller tasks into a workflow. The workflow puts the different tasks in a certain sequence to perform a higher-level business process. An example of an orchestrator is AWS CloudFormation, which defines higher level operations such as "deploy an auto scaled data center with backup," and "deploy a remote office" as code that can be reused and replicated. The code itself is none other than an interpretation of a sequence of tasks that lead to the final business process. So, the function "deploy an auto scaled data center with backup" orchestrates a set of tasks such as creating identity and access management (IAM) and security groups that define permissions of who can use the data center, what app servers talk to what databases, and so on. The orchestration function then creates auto scaled groups and sets the required resources, the minimum and maximum VMs to run, and the CPU utilization criteria. The orchestration function also assigns Elastic Block Storage (EBS) or Simple Storage Service (S3) to the VMs and creates replicas and backups based on a certain schedule.

So, automation and orchestration are both needed, with orchestration being the result and the final touch point for a user trying to launch a business process. The functions that an orchestrator creates are normally kept in application stores, service portals, cloud portals, catalogs, or whatever the name might be. The service layer contains the different business processes that launch a set of workflows and automated tasks that duplicate similar setups over and over. Orchestration hides all the smaller tasks and ensures you get the end result.

The private cloud environment, like the public cloud, is heading in that same direction of adopting orchestration. An application developer might want to launch a web portal that allows the users to browse the different display items, add them to a shopping cart, pay for the items, and schedule shipment. The application developer could care less about which server the application runs on, what VLAN is allocated, whether auto scaling is enabled, and so on. The application developer just wants to make sure that the service is always on, the customer information is always available, and the user shopping experience is excellent. This is where orchestration plays a major role in defining the tasks and the sequences and ensuring that the function can be repeated for different types of applications.

Look at Figure 19-2 to get a clearer picture of automation and orchestration in a private cloud environment. Notice that the self-service portal mainly targets the business process required, such as launching a retail portal. Depending on the vendor, the service portal could target lower level catalog items, such as creating a remote data center or creating a cluster. The orchestration in turn runs the workflow such as deploying databases, app services, and web services in the correct order. Automation works at the task level to initiate VMs, datastores, snapshots, and so on.

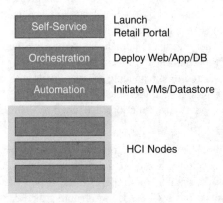

Figure 19-2 *Orchestration and Automation*

To fully understand the concepts of automation and orchestration in a private cloud, some important software platforms developed by Cisco Systems and targeted at the private cloud environment will be discussed. An example is Unified Computing System Director (UCSD). UCSD is currently standalone but is being integrated as part of Cisco Intersight to allow management, automation, and orchestration from the cloud.

Cisco UCS Director

UCSD is an orchestration and automation platform that allows the administrator to transform a data center into a private cloud. In plain terms, it enables you to use the data center as an IaaS, where applications are launched on demand and resources are assigned, tracked, and returned to the pool when done. UCSD allows for a set of compute, storage, networking, and service policies that define a virtual data center and a set of workflows that are published to create catalogs. UCSD can orchestrate and automate tasks in virtual and physical environments on Cisco as well as third-party equipment. So, for example, a data center that comprises the new HyperFlex hyperconverged infrastructure, traditional storage area network (SAN) storage, physical network appliances from Citrix, F5, and others is orchestrated under UCSD.

Usually IT administrators use scripts such as PowerShell to automate tasks. However, as tasks become more complex with many moving parts, scripting becomes inefficient especially in the areas of change control and rollback. With many people modifying scripts, it becomes hard to keep track of the different changes. Another area of importance is rolling back configuration in case of errors or bad output to a script. With UCSD, you have a controlled environment where it is easy to track who is doing what, and you can rollback to any step in the process if things go wrong.

UCS Director Policies

The policies created by UCSD are as follows:

UCSD Compute Policy is where you define a policy to set compute resources and a set of conditions to be met to let a VM be initiated on a host. Examples of policy parameters follow:

- Cloud name of where to launch a VM. This could be a specific vCenter VMware instance.

- Host Node/Cluster scope. This is where you specify whether to include or exclude selected hosts or clusters where the VM runs. If specific hosts are selected, every time a host is added to a cluster, the specification must be updated. However, if a cluster is used, then when adding a host to the cluster, that host automatically becomes a candidate for running the VM.

- Resource Pool. This resource is normally learned from the environment. UCSD, for example, learns all the vCenter resource pools and gives you the option to pick what resources to include or exclude.

- Hypervisor type, such as ESXi version in case of VMware or Hyper-V in case of Microsoft.

- Filter conditions indicating minimum conditions to be met for the host, such as these:

  - Total number of VMs in a host

  - Active VMs

  - Number of CPU cores in the host

  - CPU speed per core

  - Total memory per host

- Deployment options. An example is modifying parameters such as virtual CPU (vCPU).

- Resizing options, such as these:

  - VM resizing before provisioning or for an existing VM

  - Permitted values for vCPUs to indicate the range of vCPUs to be used

  - Permitted values of memory in MB to indicate range of memory to be used

UCSD storage policy is where you define a policy to set storage resources and a set of conditions to be met to let storage be assigned to a VM. Examples of policy parameters are these:

- Datastore's scope, indicating what datastores should be included or excluded.

- Storage options such as Network File System (NFS), SAN, or local.

- Filter conditions to indicate minimum datastore conditions to be met, such as these:

  - Datastore capacity

  - Datastore free space

  - Disk usage in KBps during a week or the past 24 hours

  - Disk latency

- Resizing options for VM lifecycle to allow disk resizing.

The *UCSD networking policy* is where you define a policy to set networking resources and a set of conditions to be met to let networking resources be assigned to a VM. Examples of policy parameters follow:

- Cloud name

- Port group types, in reference to the virtual switch that is used

- Port group name

- Adapter type and policies

- Allocation of IP addresses via static or Dynamic Host Configuration Protocol (DHCP)

The *UCS Services delivery policy* is where system-specific information is defined, including these items:

- VM name template, where a VM name is customized using variables the application provides

- Host name template, where a host name is customized using variables the application provides

- Domain name system (DNS) username and password

- Time zone

- VM image type (Linux, Windows, and so on)

UCSD can discover the environment it is connected to. Once a UCS domain account is defined, such as HyperFlex, UCSD discovers the infrastructure it connects to in the areas of compute, networking, storage, and virtualization.

Virtual Data Center

This is a logical construct that combines all the compute, storage, and networking policies that were discussed and defines who has access to such policies. Once a virtual data center (vDC) is defined, it can be published to form a service catalog. Users who have access to the vDC use the catalog to launch VMs that acquire the policies of the vDC. vDCs are assigned to groups, where a set of actions such as resource limits can be assigned. The constructs of a vDC follow:

- vDC name and description
- Group
- Cloud name
- Business approvers and contacts (group level)
- System policy
- Computing policy
- Network policy
- Storage policy
- End user self-service options, which define the actions that you can apply to a VM:
  - VM power management
  - VM resizing
  - VM snapshot management
  - VM disk management
  - Cloning
  - VM migration

In addition, the vDC allows you to define a cost model based on VM usage that gives an idea, dollar wise, of the level of consumption of VM resources. This gives IT departments some reference points on which users or departments are consuming resources. This also acts as a base point when comparing the costs of running an application on the private cloud versus the public cloud.

Orchestration Concepts

The orchestration in UCSD is done via tasks, inputs and outputs, workflows, and service requests. The tasks are the smallest units of work. UCSD defines many simple tasks that you can use, such as creating a VM and creating a user. If the tasks are not already defined, you can customize your own tasks.

Workflows are tasks that are arranged to automate a complex operation. A workflow can have one or multiple tasks and is arranged using a workflow designer. In the workflow designer, tasks are assigned and arranged in sequence.

Tasks and workflows have inputs and outputs that can be optional or mandatory. The output from one task might become the input to another task. Examples of inputs are simple text, an IP address, an OS type, and a memory size. Inputs and outputs can be connected to create a sequence of tasks. For example, a "create a user input" results in a user ID as an output. The user ID could become the input of an "add user to group" task, and so on.

When you run a workflow, a service request is created. The workflow can be scheduled to run immediately or at a later hour. The service request has one or several states, such as scheduled, running, completed, and failed.

Workflows are rolled back by simply reversing the sequence of states. For example, if a workflow creates a user and adds the user to the group, a rollback removes the user from the group and deletes the user. Figure 19-3 is a high-level representation of tasks and workflows:

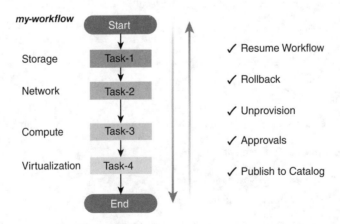

Figure 19-3 *Orchestration and Workflows*

Catalogs

A service catalog is the portal that contains all the catalogs that are standard or customized by the administrator. Catalogs are collections of predefined tasks and workflows. This is basically what allows you to place a service request.

Workflows are copied and modified to suit the actual installation. There are two types of catalogs: standard and advanced. Standard catalogs are prebuilt images. An example is a standard Redhat catalog that deploys a Linux VM or a standard Windows Server catalog to deploy a Windows-based VM. An advanced catalog is one that is built through a customized workflow and published to be used.

You, as an administrator, can create a set of tasks or use exiting tasks. From these tasks, a workflow is created, and the workflow or multiple simultaneous workflows are saved in a catalog, which is published for easy consumption. Many workflows were created by the UCSD community and have been published online for anyone to use. A sample repository of workflows is seen on [1].

Integration Between UCSD and HyperFlex

It is important to understand the integration between UCSD and HyperFlex [2] to get a feel for automation and orchestration in an HCI environment. A word of caution is that whatever is discussed here is a sample of the functionality. Because the private cloud is aiming to have functionality like the public cloud, functionality is being added in each release.

After a HyperFlex cluster is created, integration between UCSD and HyperFlex allows UCSD to communicate with different HyperFlex components, including these:

- VMware vCenter
- HX Data Platform
- Any supported UCS servers that UCS Manager manages

The UCSD manages different elements for HyperFlex, including inventory collection, discovery of clusters, disks, datastores, and data controllers. However, the main function to focus on is automation and orchestration of VM provisioning.

UCSD allows the creation of VMs via different methods. The vDC-based VM method allows users with administrator privileges to create one VM at a time. The ReadyClone VM method allows a user with administrative privileges rapid creation of many VMs in one shot.

UCSD has a set of predefined single-task workflows for HyperFlex. These workflows can be customized and augmented with more tasks to fit the requirement. Examples of predefined workflows follow:

- Creating ReadyClones
- Creating specific size datastores

- Mounting datastores

- Unmounting datastores

- Deleting datastores

- Creating virtual data centers and UCSD policies

UCSD offers HyperFlex an HTML5 self-service portal that allows you to self-request any workload catalog item and predefine any custom workflows for HyperFlex. Here is a list of the different catalogs:

- **HX VDI VMs:** For easy deployment of virtual machines for virtual desktop infra-structure (VDI) use cases

- **HX VMs and Applications:** For launching different applications such as Tomcat applications server, or VMs running different versions of operating systems (OSs) such as CentOS, Ubuntu, and Windows

- **HX—Virtual Storage Services:** For creating and manipulating HyperFlex datastores

A drill-down into the HX-VMs and Applications catalogs shows the tasks and workflows that are automated. Some of the tasks are already standard and predefined by the system for easy user consumption, and others are workflows customized by administrators to suit the deployment needs.

Many of the tasks used by users are automated with a one-click approach. When a user sends a request for a specific workload, UCSD checks different criteria before launching the workload. Criteria include checking budget allocations, resource limits, available resources, and workload approvals. After the VMs are launched, UCSD automates the rest of the configuration, such as IP addresses or application configuration.

A display of the virtual resources includes a summary of all workload request IDs, including the VM names, host names, IP address, associated vDC, and status of the tasks, whether running or scheduled. A drill-down into "More Actions" shows all the tasks that can be done on the VM, as defined by the administrator when set-ting the UCSD policies. Such actions include powering the VM on and off, shutting down the guest OS, and configuring virtual network computing (VNC) for remote connections.

Automation and orchestration for the private cloud through UCSD bring you closer to the level of automation in the public cloud that was discussed in Chapter 18. Launching VM instances through the self-service portal is like launching EC2 instances in AWS. Similarly, defining UCSD storage policies with type of disk and manipulating the size of the datastores allows administrators to define workflows and catalogs like assigning EBS in AWS.

UCSD Interfaces

UCSD offers different ways to allow multiple entities to interface with it. Interfacing with UCSD is done in several ways:

- **Self-service portal:** where end users select standard or advanced catalogs for running different types of workflows.

- **An administrator console:** giving administrators the ability to configure the different pods as in configuring a HyperFlex cluster. You can define compute, storage, networking, and virtualization policies. The administrator defines and sets user roles and permissions and creates workflows and catalogs.

- **Dashboard:** for easy access to reports.

- **System integration:** UCSD allows administrators to define integration setting with different functions such as:

    - Lightweight Directory Access Protocol (LDAP) for authentication

    - Single sign-on (SSO)

    - Role-based access control (RBAC)

    - IT ticketing systems

    - Configuration management database (CMDB)

    - Metering and chargeback

- **Application programming interfaces (APIs):** Third-party orchestration tools can use APIs to interface with UCSD.

An illustration of the UCSD interfaces is seen in Figure 19-4.

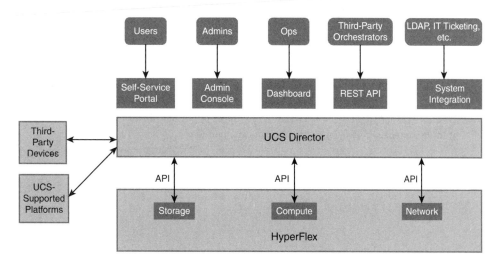

Figure 19-4 *Interfaces to UCSD*

Notice that UCSD allows integration with upstream and downstream APIs. Upstream APIs offer an open interface for third-party orchestrators. Downstream APIs allow orchestration to HyperFlex, any UCS-supported platforms, as well as third-party devices.

APIs and Infrastructure as a Code

APIs are probably the most important tool for allowing ease of configuration, automation, and orchestration. They offer a level of openness and prevent vendor lock-in. Any device that supports APIs can interface with any third-party application that offers automation and orchestration, as if you are sitting on the device command-line interface (CLI) or graphical user interface (GUI). The set of APIs, data exchange languages, and programming languages that surrounds them allows you to transform infrastructure into code that you can reuse. Infrastructure as a code and APIs were discussed in the context of the AWS and CloudFormation. APIs are also adopted to define a private cloud and the integration with the public cloud.

The challenge in infrastructure as a code is in the learning curve. In the past, IT administrators usually worked with CLI, GUI, and different network management tools to perform their tasks. Working with APIs requires programming skills and the knowledge of different programming languages, such as Java or Python. It requires the knowledge of operating systems such as Linux, Ubuntu, CentOS, and Windows. It requires the knowledge of different object-oriented, markup, and data-exchange languages such as JavaScript Object Notation (JSON), Extensible Markup Language (XML), and others. Moving forward, networking engineers, storage engineers, and virtualization engineers must become programmers or risk falling behind.

To further understand this new shift, let's look again at APIs and how they will be used with UCSD. You probably employed APIs with multiple applications without even paying attention. The CLI is a type of API because it is an interface between a client and a device with a set format. The Simple Network Management Protocol (SNMP) is a type of API that allows users to send configuration commands to a device or receive updates. A Representational State Transfer, known as REST or RESTful, API is an interface that uses Hypertext Transfer Protocol (HTTP) to exchange information between a client and a server or a device. The fact that RESTful APIs use HTTP, the language of the Internet, dramatically simplifies sending requests and receiving responses because any client with a web-based application can send API requests to a server over the Internet or an IP connection. Figure 19-5 is a representation of a RESTful API.

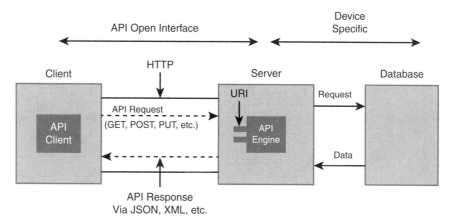

Figure 19-5 *RESTful API*

Notice that the API requests between the API client and the device running the API engine are done via the HTTP protocol on the front end. The vendors develop and publish their APIs for the specific functions. The way the server performs the function on the back end is device specific and hidden from the user. The API engine inside the server formulates a response to the API and sends it back to the client with specific data-exchange languages that are supported by the API engine and requested by the API client.

With REST APIs, different HTTP methods are part of the protocol that represent the action that is taking place.

The different HTTP methods are as follows:

■ **GET:** A GET request is used to retrieve data from the server. In the context of UCSD, as an example, a GET request asks for all workflows that are already defined.

■ **POST:** A POST request is used to submit data and create some new entry, such as a workflow.

■ **PUT:** A PUT request is used to update data that is already created on a server, such as an existing workflow.

■ **DELETE:** A DELETE request is used to delete an entry from the server.

There are other HTTP methods as well, but the ones listed are used the most.

When a client sends a request to a server via HTTP, it sends to a particular resource on that server. This resource is identified by a uniform resource identifier (URI). A URI is a compact sequence of characters that identify an abstract or physical resource. Also, as the client makes the request, it indicates to the server what language format it needs the server to respond with. The response is formatted in different languages. In the case of

UCSD, the response is formatted in either JSON or XML. Such data exchange languages are needed to have a standard and structured response that can be parsed by programs that understand the specific data exchange format.

When messages are exchanged between client and server, authentication is used for security purposes. With REST APIs, authentication comes in the form of cookies and headers that are sent inside the request. A header, for example, is formed with a string of characters that are interpreted as a username/password combination to authenticate the user. With UCSD, authentication comes in the form of an access key formed with a name:value header that is passed after the HTTP request. The access key authenticates a specific UCSD user account.

A sample GET REST API request to UCS Director looks like the following:

```
curl -v --header "X-Cloupia-Request-Key:  156D9F334532AB781111CC34D765
234F" http://myserver/app/api/rest?formatType=json\&opName=userAPIGetM
yLoginProfile&opData={}
```

The example just mentioned uses a "curl" command, which is a simple Linux utility to send a request. Other methods can send API requests, such as the Advanced REST client in Google Chrome.

Authentication is done using a header with key=X-Cloupia-Request-Key and name=156 D9F334532AB781111CC34D765234F. The request is sent to server "myserver," which indicates the UCS Director instance that is being targeted. The resource you are going after is placed at URI /app/api/rest, which indicates the access point inside myserver.

The question mark (?) after the URI indicates that what follows are the parameters you are sending within the request. In this example, the client requests via "formatType=json" that the server replies using the JSON data exchange language. The operation that you are requesting is specified via opName=userAPIGetMyLoginProfile, which indicates that you want to GET the profile of the logged-in user.

When the server receives the request, it replies using JSON format as follows:

```
{ "serviceResult":{"userId":"jsmith","firstName":"John","lastName":"Sm
ith","email": "jsmith@example.com","groupName":"EngGroup","role":"Regu
lar"}, "serviceError":null, "serviceName":"InfraMgr", "opName":"userAP
IGetMyLoginProfile" }
```

There are different ways to access APIs. UCSD, for example, offers a GUI developer menu that allows a developer to access APIs via a REST API browser. Other methods include a simple REST client to send REST API HTTP requests. Other clients can also be used, including Mozilla Firefox REST client and Google Chrome Advanced REST client.

Forming REST APIs manually and sending them one by one can become cumbersome and inefficient. Most developers resort to programming languages such as Python or Java for defining object classes and creating code that automates the process. A Python program can create hundreds of VMs and define vDC storage, networking, and compute policies.

As shown with AWS, providers and vendors define and create APIs and help simplify the task of developers by creating software development kits (SDKs) for different programming languages. UCSD, for example, defines a set of Java SDKs. The Cisco UCSD Java SDK bundle can be imported into the Java Eclipse integrated development environment (IDE), which gives the developer access to already predefined Java classes for the different APIs. An example of an SDK predefined bundle allows the developer to accomplish the following:

- Retrieve the profile of the logged-in user via userAPIGetMyLoginProfile. As shown in the previous API example, this gives the "groupName" that the user belongs to.

- Retrieve the list of vDCs that are available for the specific group via userAPIGetAllVDCs.

- Create a request to choose the vDC on which the VM is provisioned via userAPICreateVDC.

The creation of such SDKs by vendors facilitates transforming the infrastructure into reusable code and facilitates the interaction between the private cloud and the public cloud. Chapter 20, "Hybrid Cloud and Multicloud," addresses the topic of hybrid clouds and how enterprises are leveraging their own cloud as well as many public clouds to reduce their costs while increasing the velocity of deploying applications.

Looking Ahead

This chapter described the basics of automation and orchestration and how they offer a simple consumption model for the private cloud. The claim to fame for HCI products is to reach a level of simplicity and a consumption model that is comparable with today's public cloud.

With the attractiveness of both private and public clouds comes the need to use both clouds in a manner that promotes cost efficiency, a faster deployment strategy, and an easy deployment model. Chapter 20 discusses the topic of hybrid clouds and multiclouds and the orchestration tools that shift applications between private and public.

References

[1] https://community.cisco.com/t5/ucs-director-documents/tkb-p/5668j-docs-dc-ucs-director

[2] https://www.cisco.com/c/en/us/support/servers-unified-computing/ucs-director/products-installation-and-configuration-guides-list.html

Chapter 20

Hybrid Cloud and Multicloud

This chapter covers the following key topics:

- **Why Hybrid Cloud?:** A definition of the hybrid cloud. Also covers the advantages and use cases of the hybrid cloud in the areas of optimization of IT resources, leveraging public resources, backup, and disaster recovery.

- **Why Multicloud?:** A definition of multicloud and a discussion of the top reasons for taking the multicloud route.

- **Cisco CloudCenter:** A brief description of Cisco CloudCenter and its ability to decouple the application from the underlying cloud and orchestrating applications over private as well as public clouds. Also covers the HyperFlex ecosystem and how it integrates with CloudCenter.

So far, this book has examined the private cloud and how it presents a new consumption model based on simplicity and automation that is similar to the public cloud. It also has discussed the public cloud, drawing on functionality from AWS, and how it presents a highly automated on-demand model that shields administrators and users from performing tedious tasks.

A third area of importance is the hybrid cloud and its ability to give you the best of both worlds. The privacy, security, control, and automation that exist in the private cloud are complemented with the on-demand public model that leverages mass-scale to offer lower costs for the consumption of resources.

With the advantages of hybrid deployments and the fact that more than one cloud vendor offers different services, the enterprise is using multiple public clouds at the same time. The combination of private cloud, hybrid cloud, and multiple public clouds is referred to as *multicloud*. The rest of this chapter discusses the merits of the hybrid cloud and multicloud and presents a high-level introduction to Cisco CloudCenter, which facilitates the automation and orchestration of services for the enterprise in a multicloud environment.

Why Hybrid Cloud?

A *hybrid cloud* leverages resources and services from multiple environments. The private cloud leverages resources from its own private environment as well as resources that exist in a public cloud environment. An enterprise can have its own hyperconverged infrastructure (HCI) set up, for example, running compute, networking, and storage services and still leveraging resources from Amazon Web Services (AWS), Azure, and Google Cloud Platform.

The way the hybrid cloud will eventually look depends on whether you approach it from an enterprise angle or from a cloud provider angle.

If you examine a hybrid cloud from an enterprise angle, the starting point is a private cloud built with a mix of converged and hyperconverged environments with management, automation, and orchestration tools that the HCI vendors offer. The private cloud then leverages such tools to extend the reach into the public cloud. Most hybrid clouds in medium and large enterprises originate from this model because networking, compute, and storage vendors were aggressive in selling and deploying solutions in the enterprise long before the existence of cloud providers.

The other model to emerge for the hybrid cloud starts from cloud providers who target the enterprise. In this case, the cloud provider markets its management, automation, and orchestration tools to be the first touch point for the enterprise. Such tools monitor the state of the network inside the enterprise and offer compute, storage, and backup services on demand to extend the reach of the private cloud to leverage the resources of the public cloud. Figure 20-1 shows an illustration of a hybrid cloud.

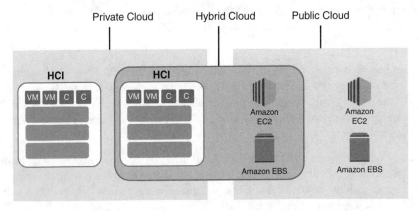

Figure 20-1 *The Hybrid Cloud*

Notice that the private cloud can deploy its own set of services and applications by converging storage, compute, and network, while still using the public cloud resources. The public cloud becomes an extension to the private cloud, where compute instances are launched on demand and lower cost storage services become an extension to the on-premise storage.

The hybrid cloud has many advantages and use cases, such as these:

- Optimization of IT resources

- Execution across clouds

- Cloud bursting

- Data backup

- Disaster recovery

In a fast-paced environment, the need for faster deployment cycles for new applications is outgrowing the capabilities of IT resources. Leveraging services from the public cloud and extending such resources to the private cloud gives IT resources some breathing room. For tasks that are on demand or transient, IT prefers leveraging the public resources and solving the problem immediately rather than staffing, learning, building, and then dismantling. A smart IT organization is one that leverages any resources available at hand to finish a task the fastest way possible.

Because applications are mostly composed of multiple tiers, load balancers, web, app, DB, and other, this opens the door for leveraging the private and public clouds for multiple tiers. If, for example, there is a restriction to have the database on-premise, but there is no restriction on web and app servers, then web and app servers can be leveraged from the public cloud. This gives easier access to the application because the public provider can leverage international presence and load balancing among multiple servers to scale the service. If the enterprise has its web and app servers already up and running and deployed in multiple private data centers and need a high-performance database with the ability to do constant backup on the cloud, a cloud provider can be used to run the database.

Another example is leveraging services that do not exist in the private cloud at the time they are needed. Deploying such services could be costly and unjustified for the duration. Examples of such services are analytics or machine learning for some data at hand. In this case, the enterprise could outsource the services to the public cloud at a fraction of the cost of building them in house.

This flexibility in leveraging private and public resources to run the application gives the enterprise faster deployment velocity and extreme flexibility.

Another use case for the hybrid cloud is cloud bursting. Enterprises might invest in ample compute resources. However, sometimes a period of increased traffic hits the enterprise. This can occur for an online retailer during holiday periods, special promotions, or Black Friday. Most enterprises cannot justify doubling up the compute resources just to handle the burst of traffic once or twice a year. A hybrid cloud easily adopts a scale-out architecture that extends beyond the boundaries of the private cloud. The cost savings in adopting such a strategy is enormous.

One of the main use cases for the hybrid cloud is the ability to leverage lower costs in storage backup on the cloud. The economies of scale make cloud backup pricing unbeatable, especially for data that is not frequently used. The AWS Glacier service in 2018 was as low as $0.004 per GB/month for storage and $0.0025 per GB for bulk retrieval

(5–12 hours access time). HCI deployments now support native backup strategies by asynchronously moving data to remote data centers or to the cloud.

A hybrid cloud can make a cloud provider part of the disaster recovery strategy. It was already discussed at length how HCI uses remote data centers for synchronous replication and launching standby virtual machines (VMs). The public cloud can easily become one of the remote data centers by stretching the HCI cluster between private and public.

Why Multicloud?

With the ability of enterprises to make the public cloud an extension of the private cloud, many enterprises are adopting multiple public cloud providers. Multicloud refers to the fact that enterprises can now pick and choose different resources from different cloud providers to complement the services they have in the private cloud. Multicloud is illustrated in Figure 20-2.

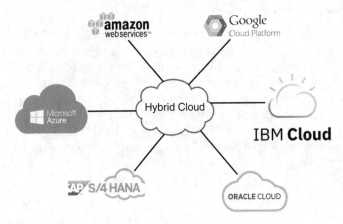

Figure 20-2 *From Hybrid Cloud to Multicloud*

Notice with the plethora of clouds and cloud services that adopting a multicloud strategy can become challenging for IT managers and chief information officers (CIOs). But first let's look at some of the main reasons for enterprises to adopt multicloud.

- Software as a service (SaaS)
- Speed of execution on a strategy
- Data locality and multinational decision
- Regulatory
- Provider lock-in and leverage
- Availability of a service
- Cloud tiering
- Cost

Many enterprises are already on the multicloud train just by using SaaS for some of their applications. Solutions such as Office 365, Cisco WebEx, Google Apps, Salesforce, and others already put enterprises on a multicloud strategy.

Making IT faster and application deployment faster is key to the success of the digital enterprise. By leveraging the capabilities of a specific cloud, enterprises can leverage existing code and innovations to launch their applications to market much faster. Most vendors are augmenting their products with cloud offering to facilitate the deployment of new services. Any functionality that does not exist in the vendor's on-premise products can be augmented with software and services deployed from the cloud.

A multinational corporation might decide that provider A in Asia is better suited to run its application than provider B in Europe or the United States. This could have valid technical merits based on the strength of a cloud provider in a certain geography or maybe because of time zones and the ability of the provider to offer 24-hour support.

In other cases, a decision to use one provider or multiple is simply based on conflicting business unit decisions and policies. In large multinational corporations, different regions might end up enforcing local decisions when choosing a provider.

The adoption of multicloud is heavily influenced by regulatory decisions. This relates to regulations dictated by different verticals such as healthcare, government, and oil and gas. An example is the Health Insurance Portability and Accountability Act (HIPAA), which sets special standards for protecting personal medical records and how information is stored or transferred. A healthcare provider must decide whether keeping the records in its private data centers is best or whether it should find a cloud provider that delivers the service at better cost with the required security and compliances. Other regulation could come from government mandates, such as enforcing that government data never leaves the country or is put on a public cloud.

Furthermore, enterprises are afraid to be locked into a single cloud provider. Giving too much business to one cloud provider might cause loss of control and lessen the ability to bargain for lower costs. Enterprises could choose to diversify to keep some leverage.

In some cases, one cloud provider might have a set of services not available with other providers, and those are the services you need. This results in a group of applications going to one provider and others going to another.

In the same way that tiers of an application can be split between a private cloud and a public cloud, the tiers can be spread over different public clouds. Application servers could be on one cloud, a database on-premise, and analytics on the second cloud.

Finally, cost plays a major role in choosing where to run the workload regardless of whether you are talking about a private cloud, a hybrid, or a public cloud. Evaluating costs is not easy because private clouds and public clouds have many hidden costs. The cost of running an application varies widely when run privately or with different public cloud providers. Costs might also vary within the same cloud provider depending on list prices or market prices. Also, there is no apple-to-apple comparison because the compute instances vary widely among providers, so you cannot make comparisons based on exact amounts of virtual central processing units (vCPUs), memory, and storage.

Calculating total cost of ownership (TCO) is difficult. It includes many factors depending on whether you are doing the calculation for private or for public. For instance, factors for a private cloud include these:

- Cost of the facility
- Cost of building the data center
- Power and cooling
- Hardware and software
- IT costs
- Percentage of usage of the equipment
- Cost of refresh cycles
- Opportunity cost

Factors that affect calculations for using the public cloud encompass these:

- Cost of running compute instances
- Cost of databases
- Cost of storage
- Cost of networking services
- Cost of network connectivity
- Cost of bandwidth
- Cost of advanced monitoring capabilities
- IT costs allocated by the enterprise to run the cloud
- Inefficiency costs

Notice that when considering costs for evaluating private versus public and which cloud provider is best, many factors come into play. When using public clouds, consider IT costs for training your staff on the specific cloud. Also, consider the cost of managing cloud deployments so you do not end up paying for resources that are sitting idle, paying for overlapping similar projects, or paying costs due to misconfiguration. For public clouds, the cost of running a workload might vary widely between one provider and the other; sometimes you end up comparing apples with oranges because public cloud resources are different for different providers. Add to this the cost of loss of control over resources and the costs to monitor whether the resources will be available when you need them.

Similarly, when using a private cloud, consider the costs of unused resources and inefficiencies. Whether the equipment is sitting idle or is efficiently used by multiple departments, consider the cost of hardware and software overhaul and maintenance, refresh cycles, and so on. But mainly, when using a private cloud, consider the opportunity cost, as in the cost of lost business if an application is not deployed on time or is delayed. It is better to evaluate costs in the context of an enterprise strategy for deploying a certain application and not just the cost of hardware and software.

There are many TCO and return on investment (ROI) calculators out there. The interesting part is that TCO calculators that cloud providers offer always show that using the public cloud gives a better cost than on-premise. Some enterprises are actually getting overwhelmed by public cloud costs and out-of-control projects and are pushing for building their own infrastructure. To give an example, you can spend some time on the AWS TCO calculator [1]. Major credit goes to AWS for the TCO calculator; there isn't a comparable TCO calculator from vendors.

Having said that, it is practically impossible to plug in a scenario that shows an AWS deployment that is more expensive than one that is on-premise. If this was the case, no enterprise would consider building a private cloud ever again, but you know that is not likely. The reality is that while the public cloud gives cost savings, the calculations do not take into effect that the resources on the enterprise side needed to manage a cloud environment for a midsize to a large enterprise are not that much different from those needed for an on-premise deployment. And the sunk costs are in the hundreds of public cloud accounts that consume resources on idle or out-of-control projects.

So TCOs must be taken lightly because you can easily change the assumptions to sway the results one way or another. The fact that private clouds with HCI deployments and automation leverage internal infrastructure 100% of the time and grow it as needed sways the balance toward using private clouds.

In conclusion, the reasons for enterprises choosing to spread their data and applications between their private data centers and different cloud providers are many. The tasks that become the most important are these:

- How to move data in a secure way between the private cloud and the public cloud and between public clouds.

- How to maintain the same application blueprint and policy when moving between clouds.

- How to monitor and enhance the level of customer experience and how it is affected when moving the application between clouds.

- How to interface with the different clouds given that each cloud has its own set of interfaces, different naming for the same service, and different services. Do you need to learn every cloud API out there?

- How to manage the application lifecycle once it moves to the cloud.

- How to wrap your arms around the expenditure to know where the money is going.

- How to know that you are making the best decision for your enterprise technically and financially.

As enterprises venture into the area of multicloud, IT managers and CIOs look for guidance from their vendors to make the best use of the different clouds.

To help support this initiative, vendors such as Cisco Systems are investing heavily in the multicloud strategy with many products in the areas of private to public cloud connectivity, security, application monitoring, cloud configuration, automation, and orchestration.

As already discussed, products such as AppDynamics, Intersight, and UCS Director offer support in the areas of application monitoring, configuration, and orchestration in the context of HyperFlex and on-premise. To further extend the reach into hybrid and multicloud, Cisco introduced the CloudCenter (formerly CliQr) product to facilitate the orchestration of services in a multicloud environment. Cisco is also working with multiple partners and application vendors such as SAP, cloud providers such as Google Cloud Platform (GCP), and others to facilitate the transition of workloads between the private and public cloud.

Cisco CloudCenter

Cisco CloudCenter [2] is a software product that allows you to model the application you want to run and its environment and then apply that model to any cloud you choose. This alleviates the user from writing infrastructure scripts that are tailored to every cloud.

This book already discussed private setups in a data center using Cisco HyperFlex, and public setups in public clouds using AWS. In each of these setups, the application needs to request compute resources, networking, and storage. In a private setup, for example, the different tools such as UCS Director and Cisco Intersight help you deploy and manage VMs and containers, assign security policies and networking parameters, add storage, and more. In the public AWS cloud, EC2 for deploying instances and S3 for storage were addressed.

Each cloud, private or public, offers its own set of application programming interfaces (APIs). These APIs allow the application to request services from the cloud. Also, each application has its own set of binary files and repository that form the environment of the application. For the application to run on a specific cloud, the application must have its environment on the specific cloud and request the resources using the set of APIs that are specific to that cloud. This puts an enormous burden on the user to write a set of infrastructure scripts that are tailored for each specific cloud.

The Cisco CloudCenter acts as the mediator between the application and the different clouds. It adopts a model, deploy, and manage strategy. CloudCenter allows you to model the application and its environment as an abstract, independent of the underlying cloud infrastructure. After that, the application can be deployed on any cloud environment and interacts with that cloud without the user intervention. This is seen in Figure 20-3.

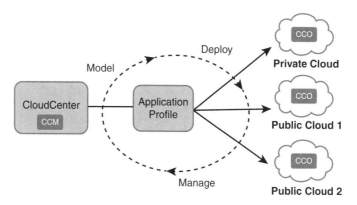

Figure 20-3 *Cisco CloudCenter*

In addition, once an application is deployed in a certain environment, CloudCenter allows you to manage and move the application or its components from one environment to another. So, an application can move from a HyperFlex cloud to an AWS cloud to an Azure cloud.

The cloud environments have different terminology and constructs but aim to perform the same functions. If you look at Table 20-1, you can easily see why porting applications manually from one cloud to the other can become a major hassle. If you look at the virtualization level, an application running on ESXi on-premise could end up on a cloud running Hyper-V. A Cisco application-centric infrastructure (ACI) networking environment with endpoint groups (EPGs) needs to be mapped to an AWS VPC environment, as an example, with security groups, and so on.

Table 20-1 *Sample Mapping Between Clouds*

	HyperFlex	**AWS**	**Azure**
Hypervisor	ESXi/Hyper-V	XEN, VMware, Hyper-V	Hyper-V
Networking	ACI	VPC	Virtual Network
Security	EPG	Security Groups	Network Security Groups
Storage	HyperFlex Datastore	S3/EBS	Azure Storage/Disk
Compute	VM creation	EC2	Azure Virtual Machines
Auto Scaling	Horizontal Scaling	Auto Scaling	Virtual Machine Scale Sets

To summarize, the functionality that Cisco CloudCenter delivers follows:

■ Application provisioning in a hybrid and multicloud environment

■ Virtual machine and container provisioning

■ Metering and quota enforcement

- Cost comparison between clouds

- Image management

- User onboarding

- Integration with ServiceNow for IT service management (ITSM)

CloudCenter uses a CloudCenter manager (CCM) to create an application profile. The application profile models each tier of the application, such as load balancers, application servers, web servers, and databases, independent from the underlying cloud. The application profile indicates that all the tiers would run on the same cloud or could segment the tiers over multiple clouds. For example, the CCM could indicate that an F5 load balancer and a web server would run on cloud 1 while the application server runs on cloud 2 and the database remains in house.

CloudCenter allows you to create a workflow for different services, such as including a load balancer, an Apache Web server, and an Oracle database. This creates a model of an interaction between the different tiers of the application regardless of where the application is deployed. From then on, CloudCenter allows the user to deploy the profile on any chosen cloud. CloudCenter uses a CloudCenter orchestrator (CCO) for each cloud. The orchestrator's function is to take the application profile that is specific to a particular cloud and use the cloud-specific API to deploy and manage the service.

You might ask how a system like HyperFlex integrates with all the automation and orchestration platforms, workload optimization platforms, networking and monitoring platforms that have already been discussed. Figure 20-4 shows a simplistic illustration of the HyperFlex ecosystem for an HCI deployment in a multicloud environment.

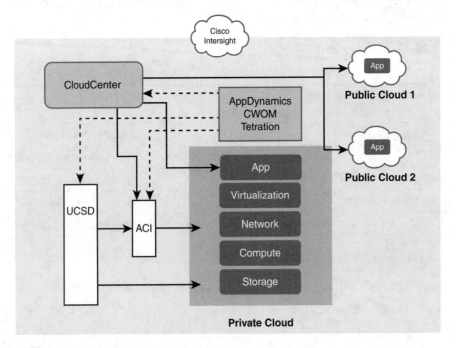

Figure 20-4 *HyperFlex Multicloud Ecosystem*

CloudCenter deals mainly with abstracting applications for different cloud deployments. It takes its input from other products, such as Cisco Tetration for network flows, Cisco ACI for policy, AppDynamics for application performance monitoring, and Cisco Workload Optimizer (CWOM) for workload monitoring. Based on this feedback, the CloudCenter manager updates the application profile and feeds it into the CloudCenter orchestrator for deployment. Think of CloudCenter as an orchestration tool for day-2 management. It is more focused on application deployment in a multicloud environment. CloudCenter interfaces with different products that are part of the HyperFlex ecosystem, including:

- **Infrastructure automation and orchestration:** UCSD is an automation and orchestration tool for day-1 infrastructure management. The UCS Director takes feedback from AppDynamics, CWOM, and Tetration. It offers a self-service portal that allows you to self-request any workload catalog and predefine any custom workflows for HyperFlex.

- **Fabric automation and microsegmentation:** The Cisco ACI forms the nucleus of network automation and practically ties into all other automation and orchestration tools. ACI allows automation at the fabric level and microsegmentation with policy setting and enforcement.

- **Cloud configuration and management:** Intersight is focused on global management from the cloud with consistent configurations and policies across all HyperFlex nodes and clusters. It also offers a reporting tool so that incidents are automatically fed into Cisco Technical Assistance Center (TAC) for fast resolution.

- **Workload optimization:** CWOM is a workload optimization platform that monitors the performance consumption of applications and matches the resources with the needs of the application.

- **Application and business monitoring:** AppDynamics provides an application and business monitoring platform that allows enterprises to monitor their business applications and transactions and make sure they are delivering the best performance and customer experience.

- **Network visibility:** Cisco Tetration allows network visibility at the flow level between the different applications. It maps user intent against actual flows between the different applications to flag any differences in intended behavior.

The enterprise is getting closer to a public cloud consumption model. You might say that this looks a lot more complex than the public cloud. That is probably because in the private cloud, you get to see the inner workings; in the public cloud, the details are hidden, but the underlying complexity is there.

Enterprise networks are now in the middle of the storm where all the tools and applications are evolving. You might see some overlap and some different tools performing similar tasks, but eventually you will see more consolidation where tools such as Cisco Intersight become the center of all action and the first touch point for users and developers.

Looking Ahead

This book has provided details on the data center landscape specifically in the areas of compute, storage, and networking. Hyperconverged infrastructure data centers are the launch point for private and hybrid clouds, promising an easy consumption model with a high velocity in deploying applications. This is much needed for what is now called the digital enterprise, whose survival depends on its ability to attract business and customers by launching and scaling applications at high velocity.

With such emphasis on the speed and agility in building applications, vendors cannot afford the six-month cycles to develop and add new functionality. That is why vendors in the private and hybrid cloud space are now targeting two different types of customers. The first customer is the consumer of the application, and the second customer is the developer of the application.

For the consumer of the application, the focus of the vendors is to augment the functionality that exists inside the private datacenter with functionality to be accessed from the cloud. This gives the end user immediate access to functionality from the cloud, as if it is an extension to the on-premise products. Cisco Systems for example is using the Cisco Intersight to allow faster access to products and functionality from the cloud with a smooth integration with the on-premise products. From the applications side, vendors such as SAP, and with cooperation with Cisco, are also deploying applications that work seamlessly between the private and public clouds.

For the developer of the application, the focus of the vendors is on shortening the DevOps cycles, so applications are easily developed, tested, and released for general consumption in the shortest amount of time. For a developer, the perfect outcome is to be able to develop the application in a desktop environment, such as on a laptop, and to have the application run in any other environment, regardless of the underlying infrastructure. This requires decoupling the application and its environment from the underlying infrastructure.

To achieve these goals for both the consumer and the developer, the industry is moving fast into the area of containerized environments and Kubernetes. Cisco Systems, for example, is partnering with Google Cloud Platform, on developing open source architecture allowing easy portability of the applications between on-premise private environment and a public cloud environment. This way, applications that are developed on top of the HyperFlex containerized environment can easily move into a Google Cloud Platform environment and vice versa.

The growth in the adoption of containers for running applications and the use of Kubernetes for container management is one of the fastest for the enterprise. It will pave the way for a feature-rich hybrid cloud environment and easier portability into multicloud. This area will be dissected in a future book, the same as it was done for HCI in this book, so stay tuned.

References

[1] https://awstcocalculator.com

[2] https://www.cisco.com/c/en/us/products/cloud-systems-management/cloudcenter/index.html

Glossary

3D-Xpoint A new type of flash memory that uses multiple layers of memory cells to produce higher densities in a smaller form factor.

A

Access Control List (ACL) A set of rules applying to network traffic that allows or denies the traffic based on a set of networking attributes such as IP address and TCP port numbers.

Access Layer Lowest layer in a multitier networking model. It constitutes the first entry point for a network device connectivity to a local area network (LAN).

Access Time of Storage The overall measure, normally in milliseconds, of the time it takes to start the data transfer operation.

Address Resolution Protocol (ARP) A protocol used to discover a media access control (MAC) address given an Internet protocol (IP) address.

Advanced Host Controller Interface (AHCI) A hardware mechanism that allows the software to talk to serial advanced technology attachment (SATA) devices.

Advanced Message Queuing Protocol (AMQP) An open standard messaging protocol used by OpenStack to exchange messages between different OpenStack components.

Advanced Technology Attachment (ATA) An interface standard for connecting storage devices.

Advanced Technology Attachment over Ethernet (ATAoE) A block-level storage protocol over an Ethernet network, based on serial advanced technology attachment (SATA), to exchange commands with disk drives.

Aggregation Layer The second layer in a multitier networking model. It aggregates the traffic coming from the access switches.

Alias of a Fibre Channel Node The simple naming representation of a fibre channel node or port that is mapped to the actual 8-byte World Wide Name (WWN).

Apache Kafka A distributed streaming software platform that allows high-throughput and low-latency data streaming.

Application-Centric Infrastructure (ACI) The Cisco approach for automating configuration of the switching fabric and setting and applying policies.

Application Network Profile (ANP)   Defines the total set of contracts between the EPGs.

Application Policy Infrastructure Controller (APIC)   A controller part of Cisco's software-defined networking (SDN). The controller facilitates the dissemination and enforcement of policies and the automation of the switch fabric.

Application Programming Interface (API)   An interface between two software applications—normally client and server. It allows the client simpler access to server functionality in a certain standardized format that humans or programmatic languages can understand.

Application Server (App Server)   A server that runs a certain application such as Apache Tomcat.

Application-Specific Integrated Circuit (ASIC)   Hardware chipset that offers hardware acceleration for specific functions; however, it is not programmable and comes with fixed functions set in hardware.

Application Virtual Switch (AVS)   Cisco Systems' implementation of a distributed virtual switch that is part of the application-centric infrastructure (ACI) architecture.

Asymmetrical Logical Unit Access (ALUA)   A protocol that allows the storage system to tell the clients which paths are optimized and which are not.

Authentication Key (AK)   A key that a cipher algorithm uses to encrypt or decrypt data. In the context of storage, the AK is exchanged between key management systems and disks to encrypt and decrypt data or other keys.

Automation   A process that helps in simplifying the creation of certain tasks. A task could be the creation of a virtual machine (VM), the creation of one or multiple clones, the shutting down of a VM, the creation or resizing of a datastore, and so on.

Availability Zone (AZ)   Also called logical availability zone, determines the fault domain for data protection. Better protection is achieved when data is spread over different AZs.

AWS Direct Connect   Allows enterprises to have a dedicated direct connection between their private data center and their AWS virtual private cloud via 1 GE and 10 GE connectivity.

B

Backup   In the context of storage, backup creates copies of data, normally in a different location, where it can be restored in case of failure of the main data.

Bare-Metal Server   A reference to a server whose software applications run directly on top of the server's physical resources without the use of virtualization software.

Big Data   The terminology that refers to the collection and storing of huge amounts of data to get deeper insight into a certain subject of study. Big Data analytics describes the mechanisms used to process and analyze such large amounts of data.

Border Gateway Protocol (BGP)   A protocol used to exchange reachability information between different autonomous systems. Normally used between service providers for traffic steering or between an enterprise and service providers.

Bridge Domain (BD)   An L2-switched network that acts as one broadcast domain stretching across multiple switches.

Broadcast Domain   Defines the boundaries where broadcast packets can be flooded.

Broadcast Packet A packet whose destination MAC address is all ones, in binary. The packet specifies all destinations, and it is processed by all networking devices on the same segment.

Broadcast, Unknown Unicast, and Multicast (BUM) All broadcast packets or Unicast packets that MAC addresses are unknown by the switches, or multicast packets.

C

Cache Write Log Area An area in storage cache where write I/O is written.

Caching The process of temporarily storing data in flash drives to allow faster writes and reads.

Capacity Tier A reference to permanent storage on HDDs or SSDs.

Capital Expenditure (CAPEX) The dollar amount spent by an organization for the procurement of hardware and software.

Catalogs Collections of predefined tasks and workflows. This is basically what allows the user to place a service request.

Central Processing Unit (CPU) The processing unit chip that contains the bus interfaces and L2 cache. The following items are related to CPU:

CPU Core The processing unit that receives instructions and performs mathematical and logical operations. The core contains the register file and L1/L2 cache and the arithmetic logic unit (ALU). A CPU can have one or more cores.

CPU Socket The connector on the motherboard that forms the contact between the motherboard and the CPU.

Logical Cores The total of physical cores and virtual cores.

Physical Core The actual physical core on a CPU chip.

Physical CPU (pCPU) Refers to the number of logical cores in a CPU.

Virtual Core A core obtained via hyperthreading.

Virtual CPU (vCPU) Refers to a slice of a CPU core.

Changed Block Tracking (CBT) A method VMware uses for incremental snapshots and backup. It tracks only the delta changes in blocks.

Checksum The result of a hashing algorithm that is applied on a piece of data. The checksum determines if the data is still the same or has been corrupted during transfer from source to destination.

Cipher Text Stealing Advanced Encryption Standard (XTS AES) A specific encryption mode that is used with the AES encryption standard.

Cisco Workload Optimization Manager (CWOM) An automation platform that monitors the performance consumption of applications and matches the resources with the needs of the application.

Classless Interdomain Routing (CIDR) An IP addressing method that divides the IP address into a network portion and host portion based on the mask. The mask is variable length between 0 and 32, which does not comply with the standard definitions of the Class A, B, and C IP addresses—hence, the naming Classless.

Cloning Creating a mirrored copy of data. Clones are snapshots that are written in the capacity tier and are used to create other virtual machines (VMs).

Clos Architecture A leaf spine architecture in reference to Charles Clos, who formalized a multistage switching system in 1952.

Cloud Management System (CMS) A system that manages cloud computing products and services. Examples are Kubernetes for containers and Neutron Server in OpenStack.

Cluster A grouping of servers (most of the time called nodes) that work together as a single unit to perform a set of functionality to clients.

Command-Line Interface (CLI) A set of commands that a client can use to perform specific functions on a device. CLIs are normally vendor specific.

Common Internet File System (CIFS) A set of message packets that define a particular version of the Microsoft Server Message Block (SMB) protocol.

Community VLAN A secondary VLAN that falls under a primary VLAN. Community VLANs can talk to other VLANs in the same community but need to go through an L3 switch/router to talk to VLANs in other communities.

Compression The process of eliminating duplicate data. Compression works at the file level or at the block level to eliminate repeating patterns, or unnecessary data.

Container Union File System Has multiple read-only layers and a read/write layer. When changes are made to a file, they go into the read/write layer, and when a container is deleted, all the changes disappear but the read-only layers remain.

Container Volumes Files and directories that sit outside the union file system and can be saved on the host or on shared storage and accessed by multiple containers.

Contiv An open source project that defines infrastructure operation policy specifications for containerized environments. It creates a uniform environment for implementing microservices in a mixed environment of containers, virtual machines (VMs), and bare-metal servers.

Contract Defines a set of policies between two Endpoint Groups (EPGs). Contracts are unidirectional, and they occur between a provider that initiates the request for service and a provider that delivers the requested service.

Converged Network Adapter (CNA) A network adapter card that combines Ethernet capabilities and storage capabilities.

Converged System A system that converges different networking, compute, and storage products with more integration on the management and support fronts.

Core Layer The networking layer that connects the LAN to the WAN or to the Campus Network via L3 switches or routers.

Council of Oracle Protocol (COOP) A protocol that keeps consistency of the Mapping Database in a Cisco application-centric infrastructure (ACI) environment. When the leaf switches learn new nodes locally, the IP and MAC-to-VTEP mappings are sent to the mapping database via COOP.

Cryptographic Module Validation Program (CMVP) A joint effort between National Institute of Standards and Technology (NIST) and Communication Security Establishment (CSE) of the government of Canada. It specifies compliances for the security and protection of data exchange.

Cyclic Redundancy Check (CRC) A mechanism done in networking to detect if there is data corruption when data is sent from a source to a destination.

D

Database A collection of data that is organized and stored on disk and can be accessed by a database management system.

Database Management System (DBMS)   Software that manages databases and enables users to store, search, and retrieve data.

Database Transaction Unit (DTU)   A blended measure of central processing unit (CPU), memory, and input/output (I/O) reads and writes given to a database that will benchmark the level of performance of that database to decide whether it needs more or fewer resources.

Data Center Bridging (DCB)   A set of standards defined in the Institute of Electrical and Electronics Engineers (IEEE) for enhancing Ethernet networks in the data center. DCB supports Converged Enhanced Ethernet (CEE) used for converging data traffic and storage traffic over the same network.

Data Encryption Key (DEK)   A factory-generated key that comes with a self-encrypting drive (SED). The internal disk circuitry uses the key to encrypt or decrypt the data.

Data Plane Development Kit (DPDK)   An open source project that defines a kit consisting of libraries to accelerate packet processing of workloads running on a variety of central processing unit (CPU) architectures.

Datastore   Logical volumes that virtualization software creates. The datastore contains information about virtual machines (VMs) and the data they use.

Deduplication   The technique of removing duplicate data in a data set. It can occur at the file level, object level, or block level. There are several types of deduplication:

Fixed-Based Deduplication   Deduplication is performed on fixed-size blocks.

Global   Deduplication is done across multiple nodes.

Inline   Deduplication is done in real time while being stored.

Local   Deduplication is done at the node level.

Post Process   Deduplication is done after being stored onto disk.

Source Based   Deduplication is done at the source.

Target Based   Deduplication is done at the target system.

Variable Length Deduplication   Deduplication is performed on variable-size blocks for better efficiency but at the cost of increased central processing unit (CPU) cycles.

Defense Information Systems Agency (DISA)   A US government agency part of the Department of Defense (DoD).

Delta Disks   Virtual disks that contain only the changed information.

Destaging   Moving the data from the cache tier into the capacity tier.

DevOps   The lifecycle of an application from its planning and design stages to its engineering implementation, test, rollout, operation, and maintenance.

Direct-Attached Storage (DAS)   The storage device, such as a hard disk drive (HDD) or solid-state drive (SSD), being directly attached to the server.

Disaster Recovery (DR)   A mechanism for backing up the data remotely to recover from a disaster by still having access to the original data.

Distributed Controller   In hyperconverged systems, storage controllers run as virtual machines (VMs) on different nodes. The controller function is distributed between all nodes and scales out with the addition of nodes. The distributed controller runs the storage distributed file system.

Note   Virtual storage appliance (VSA), data platform controller (DPC), and controller VM (CVM) are different names from different vendors for the same distributed controller function.

Distributed File System   A file system that is built from the ground up to handle an environment in which processing of data is spread and performed in parallel between multiple nodes.

Distributed Firewall (FW)   A firewall function that is done at the granularity of a virtual port and distributed among all virtual machines in a cluster.

Distributed Logical Router (DLR)   A software-based distributed router that stretches across the ESXi hosts.

Distributed Resource Scheduler (DRS)   A VMware functionality that monitors the server's utilization inside the cluster to evaluate where a virtual machine (VM) should run.

Distributed Virtual Port (dvPort)   A port on distributed virtual switches where a virtual machine (VM) attaches.

Distributed Virtual Port Group (dvPortGroup)   A grouping of dvPorts that have similar policies. It is a mechanism to automate in one shot the configuration of many ports with similar characteristics.

Distributed Virtual Uplink (dvUplink)   The connection between the virtual switch and the physical network interface card (NIC).

Distribution Layer   Also called the aggregation layer in a networking hierarchy. This is the layer that traditionally aggregated all the access switches before sending traffic to the core. It is also the layer where network services such as firewalls have traditionally been applied.

Docker Container   A lightweight, standalone, executable package of a piece of software that includes everything needed to run it: code, runtime, system tools, system libraries, and settings.

Domain Name System (DNS)   A service that translates domain names such as website names to Internet protocol (IP) addresses.

Dynamic Load Balancing (DLB)   In the context of Cisco application-centric infrastructure (ACI), DLB allows traffic to be load balanced between the different fabric links by considering the congesting level of each link.

E

East-West Traffic   Traffic that flows between the different application tiers within the same data center.

Edge Services Gateway (ESG)   A virtual machine (VM) in the VMware NSX architecture that provides gateway functions between the virtualized environment and the physical environment. The ESG acts as the connection to external L3 routers for injecting external routes into the NSX domain.

Elastic Block Storage (EBS)   A storage service Amazon Web Services (AWS) offers that attaches block storage to instances and allows the user to specify the type of disks according to performance requirements.

Encapsulated Remote Switch Port Analyzer (ERSPAN)   Collection points that sit on the network and that relay monitoring data through an Internet protocol (IP) tunnel.

Endpoint Group (EPG)   A functionality in the Cisco application-centric infrastructure (ACI) for putting endpoints such as virtual machines (VMs) or physical devices in a group where all endpoints share common policies.

Enhanced Interior Gateway Routing Protocol (EIGRP)   Cisco-developed protocol for exchanging IP subnet and IP address reachability within an IP routing domain.

E-Port   Expansion port that represents an interconnection port between two fibre channel switches.

Equal Cost Multipath (ECMP)   A traffic load-balancing technique that distributes IP traffic over multiple links according to specific hashing algorithms.

Erasure Coding (EC)   A data optimization technique that offers better space optimization than mirroring for storage data backup. EC uses parity data to restore original data in case of failure.

ESXi   A type-1 hypervisor that VMware developed.

Ethernet VPN (EVPN)   A mechanism that allows different networks to be connected as a Layer 2 private domain.

Eventually Consistent System   A system that is inconsistent for a certain period of time but eventually becomes consistent. An example is a system that makes multiple copies for protection where at some point one copy could not be accurate but eventually it will become so.

Extended Unique Identifier (EUI)   A format for representing iSCSI node addresses. It is formed with the prefix eui. and a 16-character name, which includes 24 bits of a company name assigned by the Institute of Electrical and Electronics Engineers (IEEE) and a 40-bit unique identifier.

F

Fabric   A reference to networking switches that interconnect the servers in a data center. Examples of fabric switches are Ethernet and fibre channel.

Fabric Interconnect (FI)   The Cisco Unified Computing System (UCS) architecture that includes two Ethernet FIs: A and B. Theses FIs run the UCS Manager software that is responsible for creating a virtual networking and compute environment.

Fabric Login (FLOGI)   A process whereby a fibre channel switch assigns fibre channel IDs (FCIDs) to each World Wide Port Name (WWPN).

Failure Domain   Defines physical or logical boundaries where faults might occur. Better protection occurs when data is spread over multiple failure domains.

Federal Information Processing Standard (FIPS) 140-2   A government publication by the National Institute of Standards and Technology (NIST) for "approving cryptographic modules" for transferring sensitive information.

Federal Information Security Management Act (FISMA)   A United States legislation for protecting government information against natural or manmade threats.

Fibre Channel (FC)   A high-speed network technology that runs at speeds of 1 Gbps, 2 Gbps, 4 Gbps, 8 Gbps, 16 Gbps, 32 Gbps, and 128 Gbps. FC is applicable for storage connectivity and for building storage area networks (SANs).

Fibre Channel Drives   Storage drives that connect via fibre channel (FC) interfaces.

Fibre Channel ID (FCID)   A 24-bit address that contains the fibre channel (FC) switch Domain ID, the switch F_port the FC node is attached to, and the N_port of the end node.

Fibre Channel Network Service (FCNS)   A protocol used to maintain a World Wide Node Name (WWPN)-to-fibre channel ID (FCID) mapping between fibre channel switches.

Fibre Channel over Ethernet (FCoE)   Works by encapsulating the Fibre Channel Protocol (FCP) over an Ethernet network. Unlike Internet Small Computer System Interface (iSCSI), which carries SCSI commands over Transfer Control Protocol/Internet Protocol (TCP/IP), FCoE still uses the FCP protocol to carry the SCSI commands directly over the Ethernet.

Fibre Channel Protocol (FCP)   The protocol that works on top of a fibre channel (FC) interconnect to carry the Small Computer System Interface (SCSI) commands over fibre channel (FC) packets.

Field-Programmable Gate Array (FPGA)   FPGAs offer hardware acceleration for the data path of a wide range of networking functions and services. They offer hardware acceleration with the ability to be software programmable.

Firewall   A network service provided via software or hardware that enforces security policies to allow or deny networking traffic.

Flash Memory   Non-volatile memory that can be used for storage and electronically written and erased. Traditional flash is called Planar NAND (as in NAND gate) and is built on a single layer of memory cells.

Flash Wear   Refers to the fact that NAND flash memory has the problem of cells deteriorating the more frequently writes are performed.

Flash Wear Leveling   Spreading the data across many blocks to avoid repetitive writing to the same block and thus cell failure.

F-Port   As in Fabric port. Represents a port on a fibre channel switch.

G

General Data Protection Regulation (GDPR)   A guideline for collecting and processing information and protecting data for European Union citizens.

Generic Network Virtualization Encapsulation (GENEVE)   A protocol that allows the tunneling of packets over an IP network. GENEVE provides a superset of the other tunneling protocols such as Generic Routing Encapsulation (GRE) and Virtual Extensible LAN (VXLAN) and offers variable-length options headers for more extensibility.

Global File System (GFS)   A file system that works on a cluster of nodes. If multiple network-attached storage (NAS) nodes are used, a GFS is needed to create a unified file system.

Guest OS   A reference to an operating system running inside a virtual machine (VM).

H

Hard Disk Drive (HDD)   A magnetic drive that offers high storage capacity. Has less performance than a solid-state drive (SSD). The following are sections of the HDD:

> **Head**   The part of the HDD that moves back and forth to access the magnetic fields on the rotating disk.
>
> **Platter**   A disk that spins around a spindle and contains the data in the form of magnetic fields.
>
> **Sector**   A track on a hard disk platter.
>
> **Seek Time**   The time it takes the read/write head to move from one track to another.
>
> **Spindle**   The central rod that the hard disks rotate around.
>
> **Track**   A data storage ring on a disk platter.

Hashing   The process of applying an algorithm on a piece of data that transforms the data into a shorter key or index that is representative of the original data. If the hashing results in the same key, the data is still the same.

Health Insurance Portability and Accountability Act (HIPAA) A set of security standards for protecting medical information.

Host-Based Cashing Hosts that use a cache layer to enhance input/output (I/O) performance.

Host Bus Adapter (HBA) A hardware adapter that connects to the server Peripheral Component Interconnect (PCI) bus or PCI express (PCIe) on the front end and to the storage devices on the back end via serial advanced technology attachment (SATA), serial attached small computer serial interface (SAS), or fibre channel (FC) interconnect.

Host OS A reference to the main operating system that runs on a physical host.

Hybrid Arrays Storage arrays that contain both hard disk drive (HDD) and solid-state drive (SSD) capacity drives.

Hybrid Cloud A cloud that leverages resources and services from multiple environments. The hybrid cloud can leverage resources from its own private environment as well as resources that exist in a public cloud environment.

Hyperconvergence Integrated systems that combine compute, storage, and networking in the same node. The nodes grow in a scale-out architecture and run a distributed file system that pools storage resources from direct-attached disks that are connected to the nodes.

Hypertext Markup Language 5 (HTML5) A language used to present information on the web. Most vendors have standardized on HTML5 for delivering their user interfaces (UIs) because of its simplicity.

Hypertext Transfer Protocol (HTTP) The protocol used for sending and receiving messages over the World Wide Web. Defines the interaction between clients and servers running web applications.

Hyperthreading A technology that allows the same central processing unit (CPU) core to process multiple threads at the same time.

Hyper-V A Type-1 hypervisor that Microsoft developed.

Hypervisor The software that makes virtualization happen by creating a shared pool of compute resources out of the server's physical resources. The following are types of hypervisors:

> **Type 1 Hypervisor** Also known as a bare-metal hypervisor. It replaces the host operating system (OS) and has direct interaction with the hardware.

> **Type 2 Hypervisor** Also known as a hosted hypervisor. It does not replace the host operating system (OS), but rather sits on top of the existing OS.

I

Information Technology Security Evaluation Criteria (ITSEC) An international standard certification ensuring that the security features of a product are properly implemented.

Infrastructure as a Service (IaaS) A cloud service where the enterprise outsources the infrastructure to the provider. This includes the physical network, the hardware servers, the storage and data, network services, as well as hypervisors and containerized environments.

Infrastructure VXLAN (iVXLAN) The Cisco implementation of VXLAN, which strips the encapsulation from all packets entering the fabric and adds a fabric-specific VXLAN called infrastructure VXLAN.

Initiator   Reference to the server that initiates a connection to a target port on a storage array.

In-Kernel   A reference to software functionality that is performed inside the kernel of the hypervisor rather than being done using a controller virtual machine.

iNode   A set of pointers to the locations of the blocks in the same object.

Input/Output Operations per Second (IOPS)   A performance measure for storage. It indicates the maximum number of reads and writes to noncontiguous storage locations. It is measured as an integer.

Intermediate System to Intermediate System (IS-IS)   An interior gateway protocol (IGP) used to exchange Internet Protocol (IP) reachability information within a routing domain.

Internal BGP (iBGP)   BGP peering is done between routers within the autonomous system to relay routes learned via external BGP (eBGP) from other autonomous systems.

Internet Group Management Protocol (IGMP)   A protocol that end nodes and routers use to establish membership in an Internet Protocol (IP) multicast group.

Internet Protocol Address Management (IPAM)   The administration of assigning IP addresses to end nodes in the network through domain name system (DNS) and Dynamic Host Configuration Protocol (DHCP).

Internet Small Computer System Interface (iSCSI)   An Internet Protocol (IP)–based storage standard that provides block-level access to storage devices. It carries the SCSI commands over a Transmission Control Protocol/Internet Protocol (TCP/IP) network.

Inter-VLAN Traffic   Traffic that crosses virtual local area network (VLAN) boundaries and passes from one VLAN to another.

Intra-VLAN Traffic   Traffic that stays within the boundaries of the same virtual local area network (VLAN).

IOVisor   A software implemented by Cisco System that allows the data controller to share the processing of input/output (I/O) traffic. It also allows compute-only nodes and third-party nodes to have access to the shared datastore.

iSCSI Qualified Name (iQN)   An addressing representation of iSCSI nodes. It consists of 255 characters in the format iqn.yyyy-mm.naming-authority:unique name.

ISO   Images that are a sector-by-sector copy of a disk stored in binary.

J

JavaScript Object Notation (JSON)   A data exchange language between a client and a server. JSON formats the data in a way that humans as well as programming languages can read.

Jumbo Ethernet   Large Ethernet frames that extend the maximum transmission unit (MTU) size from the standard 1500 bytes to up to 9000 bytes.

Just a Bunch of Disks (JBOD)   A group of smaller disks that work together to offer a larger array of storage.

K

Kernel-Based Virtual Machine (KVM)   An open source hypervisor based on Linux that allows the creation of virtual machines (VMs).

Key Management Interoperability Protocol (KMIP)   A protocol used for having a client request an encryption key from a server that handles key management.

Kubernetes   A platform for automating the deployment and management of containerized workloads and services.

L

Latency   The time it takes the head of the disk to reach the correct sector on the rotating platters.

Layer 2 Flat Domain   A domain where end stations use their media access control (MAC) addresses to exchange information. It is segmented via virtual local area networks (VLANs) that are segmented via L2 switches.

Layer 2 Switch   A switch that relays packets based on their media access control (MAC) addresses and the virtual local area networks (VLANs) they belong to.

Layer 3 Switch   A switch that relays packets based on Internet protocol (IP) subnet information.

Leaf   An access switch, normally known as a top-of-rack switch, that connects the server nodes in the data center.

Lightweight Directory Access Protocol (LDAP)   A protocol defined in the Internet Engineering Task Force (IETF) for accessing directory services such as files, folders, users, groups, and devices.

Linked Clones   Clones that are linked in a tree where the child shares the virtual disks of the parent.

Load Balancer   A software or hardware networking function that balances the traffic that hits the server based on networking information such as IP addresses, TCP port numbers, and types of application.

Logical Server Grouping   A group of servers that form a tier in a multitier application architecture.

Logical Unit Number (LUN)   A logical representation or a logical reference point to a physical disk, or partitions of a disk in redundant array of independent disks (RAID) arrays.

Logical Unit Number Masking   Allows a server to see certain logical unit numbers (LUNs) while hiding other LUNs.

Logical Volume Manager (LVM)   A storage management function that takes physical partitions and presents them as logical volumes to the operating system.

Log-Structured File System (LSF)   A "log," in the form of a circular buffer. When data is written, it is appended at the end of the log. LSF increases the performance of read and write input/output (I/O) operations.

Longest Prefix Match (LPM)   A search in the Internet Protocol (IP) routing or forwarding tables that matches an IP address with a subnet that has the longest mask. This allows traffic to be directed to more specific routes if multiple subnets exist that match the IP address.

LZ4   A data compression algorithm that provides a fast way of performing lossless compression.

M

Mapping Database   A database in a Cisco application-centric infrastructure (ACI) environment that exists inside the spine. It contains the mapping of Internet Protocol (IP) host addresses (IPv4 and IPv6) and media access control (MAC) addresses of every physical or virtual node in the user space to the Virtual Tunnel Endpoint (VTEP) of the leaf it connects to.

MapReduce   A software model that allows parallel processing of massive data on clusters of servers.

Maximum Transmit Unit (MTU)   The largest size packet in bytes that can be transmitted over the network.

Media Access Control (MAC)   An address at Layer 2 of the Open Systems Interconnection (OSI) layer that is usually burned into a network interface card (NIC) and used by nodes to recognize each other on an Ethernet network.

Metadata   Information about the specific data. If the data is a picture object, as an example, metadata would be the tag on the picture or the date the picture was taken.

Metropolitan Area Network (MAN)   An interconnect via high-speed optical fibre within a metropolitan area. Normally, the enterprise campus can stretch over a MAN for building-to-building connectivity.

Microsegmentation   A mechanism that allows policies to be applied at a fine granularity, such as at the virtual machine (VM) level. Such policies can be applied to the applications regardless of where the applications are physically running and to which Internet Protocol (IP) subnet they are attached.

Microsoft System Center 2016 Data Protection Manager (DPM) Update Rollup 1 (UR1)   Microsoft introduced new features to support Modern DPM Storage. System Center 2016 improves the storage usage and performance.

MLC Flash—Multilevel Cell   A less expensive type of flash memory that has lower endurance, less reliability, and lower write performance than SLC flash memory.

Modular LAN On Motherboard (MLOM)   A Cisco hardware architecture that provides a LAN module on the server's motherboard.

MongoDB   An open source NoSQL database that is used for storing documents.

Multichassis Link Aggregation (MLAG)   A protocol that makes links that are connected between a device and multiple chassis look like one large aggregated link.

Multicloud   The freedom of enterprises being able to pick and choose resources from different cloud providers to complement the services they have in the private cloud.

Multi-Core CPU   A central processing unit (CPU) that has multiple cores, such as 2-core CPU or 4-core CPU.

Multipathing   In a fibre channel network, a mechanism that provides multiple paths between an initiator fibre channel node and a storage target. The path could be formed via different HBA cards, different fabric switches, and different storage controllers.

Multipath IO (MPIO)   Software that usually runs on an initiator node, fibre channel, or iSCSI that allows the node to load-balance the traffic between multiple available paths.

Multi-Protocol BGP (MP-BGP)   An extension to Border Gateway Protocol (BGP) that allows the protocol to carry different networking layers, such as unicast and multicast reachability information.

Multitier Application Architecture   An architecture that segments different components of an application, such as web server, application server, and databases, into different tiers. This is used for scalability and fault tolerance.

N

National Institute of Standards and Technology (NIST) A nonregulatory agency of the US Department of Commerce focused on the advancement of measurement science, standards, and technology.

Native Command Queuing (NCQ) A mechanism that optimizes how read/write commands are executed to reduce the head movement of a hard disk drive (HDD).

Network Address Translation A networking function that maps private Internet Protocol (IP) addresses inside an organization or networking domain to public IP addresses that are accessible via the Internet.

Network-Attached Storage (NAS) A file-level storage system allowing clients to share and store files over the network.

Network File System (NFS) A file-sharing protocol developed by Sun Microsystems (now Oracle) that is mainly associated with the UNIX/Linux operating system. NFS allows clients to access files and folders in a server over the network.

Network Interface Card (NIC) An interface card (1 GE, 10 GE, or higher) that connects a server to the network top-of-rack (ToR) switches.

> **pNIC** A physical network interface card (NIC) in a server.
>
> **vmnic** A VMware terminology that also refers to the physical network interface card (NIC).
>
> **vNIC** A virtual representation of a network interface card (NIC) in software. A physical NIC could be split into multiple vNICs.

Network Virtualization Using Generic Routing Encapsulation (NVGRE) A network virtualization mechanism that tunnels L2 traffic over an L3 routed network.

Neutron The networking part of OpenStack whose objective is to provide "networking as a service" between devices that other OpenStack services manage.

New Technology File System (NTFS) File system that Windows NT uses.

Next-Generation Firewall (NGFW) An advanced network security service that can deny or allow traffic based on the state of a Transmission Control Protocol/Internet Protocol (TCP/IP) session (Stateful Firewall) and application information, in addition to the traditional firewall L3–L4 parameters.

Non-Volatile Memory Express (NVMe) A high-performance storage protocol that supports the PCIe technology.

Non-Volatile Memory Express over Fabric (NVMe-oF) A specification to allow the NVMe protocol to run over fabric such as Ethernet.

North-South Traffic Traffic that goes back and forth between the Internet (north) and the data center (south) of an organization.

NoSQL Database A database that is used for storing and retrieving information in formats that are different from the traditional relational database model with tables, rows, and columns. Such databases can be used, for example, to store and retrieve object-oriented storage.

N-Port Represents a port on a fibre channel node.

NSX VMware's virtual network virtualization and security platform.

NX-OS The Cisco Systems extensible, open, and programmable network operating system. It enables network automation and allows customers to programmatically provision and configure switches through comprehensive application programming interfaces (APIs), utilizing tools provided by Cisco and open source third-party solutions.

O

Offload Data Transfer (ODX)   A method that Microsoft Hyper-V uses to transfer data directly between storage devices without the involvement of the host.

Online Transactional Processing (OLTP)   Software applications that perform processing on transactional data normally found in Structured Query Language (SQL) databases.

OpenDaylight   A project founded in 2013 and focused on the enhancement of software-defined networking (SDN) controllers to facilitate network services across multiple vendors.

OpenFlow   A protocol that is part of a software-defined networking (SDN) architecture. It operates in an environment where software controllers direct traffic flows inside networking devices.

Open Shortest Path First (OSPF)   An interior gateway protocol (IGP) used to exchange internal reachability of Internet Protocol (IP) subnets inside a routing domain.

OpenStack   An open source cloud operating system with the objective of automating and simplifying the configuration and deployment of private and public clouds.

Open Virtual Appliance (OVA)   A set of files that describe a virtual machine (VM). An OVA is used to install a VM.

Open Virtual Network (OVN)   An open source project that is an extension of the OVS project. The focus of OVN is to build upon the basics of OVS but expand into the area of virtual networking with ease of provisioning and better performance.

Open vSwitch (OVS)   An open source implementation of a multilayer virtual switch inside the hypervisor. It is licensed under the Apache 2.0 license. The virtual switch basically does what a physical switch does, but all the switch components are defined in software.

Open vSwitch Database (OVSDB)   A protocol that sets the configuration of the Open vSwitch (OVS) and performs the flow handling inside the virtual switch.

Operational Expenditure (OPEX)   The dollar amount spent by an organization for the operation and management of the network. It normally relates to expenditure on IT resources and support.

OpFlex   A protocol initiated by Cisco that allows a controller to talk to a device and give the device instructions to implement a set of functionality.

Orchestration   A higher-level abstraction that aims to stitch the multiple smaller tasks into a workflow. The workflow puts the different tasks in a certain sequence to perform a higher-level business process.

Overlay Network   A network formed by tunneling L2 traffic on top of an L3 IP network.

P–Q

Parity   Data used as input to an algorithm to reconstruct missing data in case of disk failure.

Payment Card Industry Data Security Standard (PCI-DSS)   A security standard that credit card companies should abide by to ensure data protection.

PCI Root Complex   Allows connectivity to PCIe endpoints or a PCIe switch that can provide connectivity to many more PCIe endpoints, such as storage devices or high-speed Ethernet network interface cards (NICs).

Peripheral Computer Interconnect Express (PCIe)   A high-speed serial computer bus standard that offers a high-speed interconnect between the server motherboard and other peripherals such as Ethernet and storage devices.

Persistent Storage   Storage that is kept after a compute instance has been terminated.

Platform as a Service (PaaS)   A cloud service in which the enterprise outsources to a service provider the infrastructure as well as the management of the software components needed for the application to run. Such components include the operating system, runtime libraries and tools, application server software, and Hypertext Transfer Protocol (HTTP) server.

Plug-In   A software program that adds functionality to an existing program. For example, if we say vendor X implemented a plug-in into the vSphere web client, it means the vendor added its own set of commands and functionality into the existing web client software.

Point of Delivery (PoD)   A terminology used in networking to indicate a grouping of networking devices that deliver a certain service. The grouping of such devices represents a module that can be repeated to expand the capacity of the service.

Port Login (PLOGI)   An initiator fibre channel node performs a PLOGI process through a Simple Name Server (SNS) function running in the switch. During the process, each node sends to the switch its

mapping between its fibre channel ID (FCID) and its World Wide Port Name (WWPN).

Primary VLAN   A virtual local area network (VLAN) that can be split into multiple secondary VLANs. Secondary VLANs are split into communities. VLANs in different communities can only talk to each other via a routed interface assigned to the primary VLAN.

Private Cloud   A cloud that the enterprise fully manages and controls.

Private VLAN   A mechanism that allows a primary virtual local area network (VLAN) to be segmented into secondary VLANs for saving Internet Protocol (IP) space.

Process Login (PRLI)   A process by which an initiator fibre channel node connects to a target storage.

Protocol Endpoints (PE)   An access point for input/output (I/O) to access the vSphere APIs for storage awareness (VASA) containers on the storage array.

Protocol Independent Multicast (PIM)   A set of protocols allowing the transport of multicast traffic over an IP network.

Public Cloud   A cloud that is fully managed by a cloud provider and offers enterprises infrastructure, platform, and application services on a rental basis.

R

Rabbit Message Queuing (RabbitMQ)   A messaging mechanism that runs between processes, such as the different components within an OpenStack service.

RAID Controller or Storage Processor   A processing unit that performs the redundant array of independent disks (RAID) functions inside a storage array.

Raw Device Mapping (RDM)   A mapping mechanism between VMware's Virtual Machine File System (VMFS) and a physical device that allows a virtual machine (VM) to have direct access to the physical device's raw data.

ReadyClones   A method that Cisco HyperFlex uses for batch creation of clones with the use of a wizard.

Recovery Point Objective (RPO)   The maximum data loss that can be tolerated when a failure occurs.

Recovery Time Objective (RTO)   The maximum time that can be tolerated for a recovery process after failure occurs.

Redundant Array of Independent Disks (RAID)   Multiple disks that have been grouped to allow read and write operations to be done in parallel, offering faster input/output (I/O) processing. Different terminology such as RAID 0, 1, 5, 6, and so on indicates the level of data protection offered in the disk array.

Relational Database   A set of data that is organized in tables, rows, and columns. The data can be manipulated to find useful relationships between the different fields in the tables.

Remote Direct Memory Access (RDMA) Technology over Converged Ethernet (RoCE)   A technology that allows network interface cards (NICs) to bypass the central processing unit (CPU) in processing memory requests over an Ethernet network that supports data and storage.

Remote Office Business Office (ROBO)   Remote offices or satellite smaller business offices that usually get connected to the main enterprise via a wide area network (WAN).

Remote Procedure Call (RPC)   When a software program sends messages to other programs for performing a certain function.

Replication   Distributing the data over multiple disks, whether in the same node or in different nodes inside a cluster as well as outside a cluster. Replication ensures that the data is spread across many hardware entities, such that if an entity fails, the data can be recovered. The following are types of replication:

Asynchronous Replication   Replication of data after it has been moved into the capacity tier. Replication can be scheduled at any time.

Native Replication   Having the hyperconverged node perform the replication natively without the use of third-party software.

Synchronous Replication   Replication being done in real time, at the same time data is written. Written data must be acknowledged for the write to take place.

Replication Factor (RF)   A number that indicates the total number of data copies made in the cluster to protect the data.

Representation State Transfer Application Programming Interfaces (REST or RESTful API)   An interface between a client and a server, where the client requests certain functionality from the server using the Hypertext Transfer Protocol (HTTP).

Resilient Change Tracking (RCT)   A method Microsoft uses for incremental backup and snapshots. It tracks the delta changes in blocks.

Resilient File System (ReFS)   A block cloning technology Microsoft created to store incremental backups.

Role-Based Access Control (RBAC)   An access control mechanism that specifies the role of a user or administrator and the access privileges for performing configuration or for monitoring the system.

Round Trip Time (RTT)   Time for a packet to travel from a source to a destination and back to the source.

S

S3   An Amazon object-level storage with high durability that is used for backup and recovery, archiving, and user-created content such as photos, audio, and video.

Sarbanes-Oxley Act   An act Congress passed to reform corporate reporting and auditing accountability.

SAS Drives   Drives that connect to computers and the server via the serial attached SCSI (SAS) interface. SAS drives are high-performance drives that are more suited for servers.

SATA Drives   Drives that connect to computers and servers via the serial attached small computer serial interface (SATA). SATA drives are usually lower performance than serial attached small computer serial interface (SAS) drives.

Scale Out Architecture   An architecture whose system performance increases when you increase the number of nodes that work in parallel.

Scale Up Architecture   An architecture whose node performance increases when you increase the compute and storage of the node itself.

Secure Shell (SSH)   A client software used to achieve secure remote connectivity between a client and a server.

Secure Technical Implementation Guide (STIG)   A framework for standardizing security protocols for computers, servers, and other networking devices and for hardening the product against security attacks using best practices.

Self-Encrypting Drives (SED)   A type of hard disk drive (HDD) or solid-state drive (SSD) that allows data-at-rest encryption inside the drive using hardware support.

Serial Advanced Technology Attachment (SATA)   An integrated drive electronics standard for connecting drives to backplanes and personal computers.

Serial Attached SCSI (SAS)   A standard for connecting drives to backplanes and personal computers. It is an enhancement to the traditional parallel SCSI interface, and it carries the SCSI commands.

Serverless Computing   A service offered by Amazon Web Services (AWS) in which a customer requests to run an application and is charged only based on processing time. The customer does not have to launch server instances.

Server Message Block (SMB)   The SMB is a file-sharing protocol Microsoft developed for its Windows-based operating systems. SMB is a client server protocol that allows clients to share files on servers over the network.

Service Graph   Identifies the set of network or service functions (firewall, load balancer, SSL offload, and so on) and the sequence of such services as needed by an application.

Single Root Input/Output Virtualization (SR-IOV)   An architecture that allows different virtual machines (VMs) to share the physical PCIe bus. SR-IOV allows the PCIe device to appear to VMs as separate PCIe devices.

Single Sign-On (SSO)   An authentication mechanism that allows the user to use one username and password for multiple applications.

SLC Flash-Single Level Cell   Flash memory based on Single-Level Cells NAND Memory that has high performance.

Small Computer System Interface (SCSI)   A set of American National Standards Institute (ANSI) standards for connecting peripherals such as hard drives and CD-ROMs to the motherboard of a computer.

SmartNIC   A network interface card (NIC) that supports hardware acceleration via field-programmable gate arrays (FPGAs) or application-specific integrated circuits (ASICs). The hardware mainly offloads the central processing unit (CPU) from data path functions that overload the CPU.

Snapshots   A mechanism that allows data to be captured at any given point in time so it can be restored if there is corruption or damage to the data. The following are types of snapshots:

> **Continuous Data Protection (CDP)**   Snapshots are taken whenever there is a data update.
>
> **Copy on Write**   Whenever an original block needs to be updated, the block is copied to a different location in the snapshot volume and then written to the original block.
>
> **Logical Snapshots**   Snapshots are created instantaneously and disk space is minimized by keeping "pointers" to the original blocks instead of making full copies of the data.
>
> **Physical Snapshot**   A duplicate copy is created somewhere else in the disk.
>
> **Redirect on Write**   When a block on the original volume needs to be updated, the block in the original volume is left intact, and the new data is redirected and written to a different block area that the snapshot owns.

Software as a Service (SaaS)   A cloud service model where the enterprise outsources everything such as infrastructure, platform and application, to the service provider. In this case, the enterprise can get the application on a per-user subscription basis.

Software-Defined Networking   A software-defined architecture that decouples the control of networking devices from the underlying hardware forwarding. It allows a software controller to configure and set the forwarding path of network switches.

Software-Defined Storage (SDS)   A software-defined architecture that decouples storage management and policies from the underlying hardware.

Software Developer Kit   A set of software tools provided by vendors and operators to facilitate access to their application programming interfaces (APIs) via different programmatic languages such as Java and Python.

Solid-State Drive (SSD)   A storage device that contains flash memory. Used for caching or high-performance capacity storage.

Spanning Tree   A protocol implemented in L2-switched networks that prevents traffic loops from occurring by blocking certain traffic paths.

Spine   The second switching layer in a 2-tier networking architecture. It aggregates the traffic coming from the leaf switches, where each leaf connects to two spines.

Storage Area Network (SAN)   A block-level storage where data is accessed in blocks, appears as volumes to servers, and can be formatted to support any file system.

Storage Controller   Hardware logic that runs software performing storage management functions. Storage controllers could come in host bus adapter (HBA) form or processing units inside a storage array.

Storage Load Balancing   A function that evaluates where to place the VM "files" in the different available datastores. It makes decisions based on available capacity in the datastore and the input/output (I/O) latency in accessing files.

Storage Migration   Allows the mobility of the virtual machine (VM) files and virtual disks from one datastore to another without disruption to the operation of the virtual machine.

Storage Policy–Based Management (SPBM)   A set of policy management tools developed by VMware for applying storage polices to the virtualized environment.

Storage Tiering   The ability to store data on different types of media, such as hard disk drive (HDD), solid-state drive (SSD), and so on depending on parameters such as application performance needs and frequency of data access.

Stretched Cluster   A cluster that stretches beyond the local data center into a remote data center.

Stretched VLANs   A reference to VLANs that are configured across the whole Layer 2 switched network and touch all servers to allow the movement of applications between servers in the L2 network.

Striping   Dividing the data into small blocks and spreading it on multiple disks to allow read and write operations to be done faster and in parallel.

Structured Query Language (SQL)   A language used to manage data in relational databases. The data is normally structured in the form of tables, rows, and columns.

Sub-VLAN   A segmentation of a primary virtual local area network (VLAN) into subset VLANs, where each sub-VLAN becomes

its own L2 broadcast domain but is still under the primary VLAN.

Switched Virtual Interface (SVI)   A logical interface within an L3 switch that doesn't belong to any physical port. It acts as an interface for a logical router inside the L3 switch. SVIs are used to route traffic between different VLANs.

T

Target Portal Group (TPG)   A set of target ports on storage controllers that servers can use to reach a specific logical unit number (LUN).

TCP Offload Engine (ToE)   An engine that offloads the CPU from TCP functions such as encapsulation and decapsulation that are better done in hardware.

Telemetry   The process of collecting information from remote devices via software or hardware sensors. The data is collected and sent to a server for analysis.

Tenant   A separate administrative domain that can be managed independently of other tenants. A service provider can, for example, divide the same data center between different customers (tenants) that are managed independently.

Ternary Content Addressable Memory (TCAM)   A special type of memory used in networking switches to store IP tables, media access control (MAC), and virtual local area network (VLAN) tables. The TCAM allows fast access to the information, which dramatically increases switching performance.

Tetration   A Cisco technology that allows an IT administrator to monitor the IP flows between the different applications of the data center.

Thick Provisioning   A storage allocation technique that only allows allocation of actual physical storage without over provisioning.

Thin Provisioning   A storage allocation technique that allows a system to allocate virtual storage that exceeds the actual physical storage.

Throughput or Transfer Speed of Storage   The rate, measured in MBps, at which data is transferred to and from the disk media (the platter) in a certain period of time.

Top-of-Rack (ToR)   Access switches that are normally placed at the top of the rack and that connect all server nodes in a data center.

Total Bytes Written (TBW)   An endurance measure for flash solid-state drives (SSDs) that specifies the total terabytes that can be written per day on an SSD, during its warranty period, before the SSD starts failing.

Total Cost of Ownership (TCO)   A measure of spending on capital expenditures (CAPEX) and operational expenditures (OPEX) over a period of time. Normally in the data center business, this calculation is based on a 3- to 5-year average period.

Transit Fabric   In the context of Cisco ACI fabric. The fabric is transit if it allows external routes learned via one external network to be propagated to another connected external network. In this case, the fabric acts as transit for traffic between two external networks.

Transmission Control Protocol (TCP)   A network communication protocol used to establish sessions between end nodes to exchange traffic on an IP network.

U

Ultra Path Interconnect (ULI)   A high-speed interconnect that runs between the CPU sockets to provide high performance interconnection between the different cores.

Underlay Network   An L3 network that delivers Internet Protocol (IP) packets between the endpoints of the IP tunnels created by the overlay network and can provide some IP multicast functions in support of the overlay.

Unified Computing System (UCS)   A Cisco Systems approach that combines data networking, storage networking (not storage), and compute in a single architecture. The architecture virtualizes all elements of compute and networking and presents them as templates that can be reused.

Unified Computing System Manager (UCSM)   Software that runs on the Cisco UCS Fabric Interconnects. It manages all the networking and server components and creates UCS profiles and templates.

Unified Computing System (UCS) Service Profile   A UCS service profile is a "software definition" of the server itself and its storage and network connectivity. The service profile is built using templates that describe network and storage connectivity parameters and policies relevant to the networking and compute environment.

Universal Kernel Bypass (UKB)   An architecture where applications can bypass the operating systems, kernels, and hypervisors for faster data processing.

Unknown Unicast   Traffic to a unicast address that is not learned by the Ethernet switch. This causes the switch to flood the traffic to all ports in the same VLAN.

V

Vdbench   A software utility for generating storage input/output (I/O) workload that helps benchmarking the I/O performance of applications.

vHBA   A virtual host bus adapter in which a physical HBA can have multiple virtual

HBAs, with each vHBA connecting to a port on the software virtual switch.

Virtual Core   A CPU core obtained via hyperthreading.

Virtual Data Center (vDC)   A Cisco logical construct that combines all the compute, storage, and networking policies and defines who has access to such policies. Once a vDC is defined, it can be published to form a service catalog.

Virtual Desktop Infrastructure (VDI)   An architecture that allows users to use their desktops, laptops, and iPads as dumb terminals, while the actual application and data run securely on servers in the data center.

Virtual Extensible LAN (VXLAN)   A tunneling mechanism used to create L2 overlay networks on top of L3 networks. VXLAN encapsulates an Ethernet packet into an IP User Datagram Protocol (UDP) packet, from one end of the tunnel, and delivers it to the other end of the tunnel, over the L3 routed fabric.

Virtual Hard Disk (VHDX)   A file format Microsoft developed to represent a virtual hard disk in a Hyper-V virtual environment.

Virtual Interface Card (VIC)   Part of the Cisco UCS architecture, this allows data and storage connectivity between the server cards and the fabric extenders, which in turn connect to the fabric interconnects (FIs).

Virtual LAN (VLAN)   Represents a virtual segment on the physical switched network. End stations exchange traffic over the logical segment and are isolated from other virtual networks on the same physical switched network.

Virtual MAC (vMAC)   Media access control (MAC) addresses of a virtual network interface card (vNIC), where one physical NIC can be represented as multiple vNICs and each vNIC has its own vMAC.

Virtual Machine (VM)   Software that runs in a virtualized environment and contains a guest operating system (OS) and an application and its runtime.

Virtual Machine Disk (VMDK)   A logical representation of a virtual disk that contains the data of a virtual machine (VM).

Virtual Machine File System (VMFS)   VMware's clustered file system used for block storage in a virtualized environment.

Virtual Network Computing (VNC)   A client protocol that allows a client computer to access the screen and control of a remote computer.

Virtual Network Identifier (VNID)   Defines a specific segment inside an L3 Internet Protocol (IP) tunnel. In the case of Cisco, the VNID indicates the virtual routing and forwarding (VRF) for routed traffic and the bridge domain (BD) in case of L2-switched traffic.

Virtual Port Channel (vPC)   A mechanism that allows an end device, switch, or host to have a redundant connection to two other switches while still making the two connections look like one.

Virtual Private Cloud (VPC)   A service that Amazon Web Services (AWS) offers. The VPC allows the user to create his own logical private network inside the AWS cloud.

Virtual Private Network (VPN)   A private network between end nodes that is logically independent from other private networks on the same physical infrastructure.

Virtual Routing and Forwarding (VRF)   A construct in L3 routing that segments the Internet Protocol (IP) routing space into virtual domains that are independent of each other. Routing processes and IP addressing in one VRF run independently of other VRFs so that IP addresses can be reused.

Virtual Routing Forwarding Lite (VRF-Lite)   A lightweight implementation of VRFs that normally does not scale beyond 400 VRFs.

Virtual Switching   The networking function of the virtualization layer that delivers the basic functionality of a physical Ethernet switch but is done in software. Here are types of virtual switching:

>   **Distributed Virtual Switch**   Virtual switching being distributed between multiple nodes in a cluster.

>   **Standard Virtual Switch**   Virtual switching done within the same node in a cluster.

Virtual Technology for Directed I/O (VT-d)   A technology created by Intel that provides hardware acceleration and high performance by having the virtual machine (VM) access the hardware resources directly.

Virtual Tunnel Endpoint (VTEP)   A network device, represented via a VTEP IP address, that terminates a VXLAN tunnel. The network device can be physical or virtual. It maps end devices to VXLAN segments and performs VXLAN encapsulation and decapsulation.

Virtual Volumes (VVols)   Virtual machine (VM) objects stored natively on array storage containers. The physical disks in an array are partitioned as "containers," and then the VVols are stored directly on the containers without the use of logical unit numbers (LUNs).

Virtualization Layer   Software that runs on physical servers and provides an abstraction layer to processor, memory, storage, video, and networking.

VM Fault Tolerance   Ensures zero downtime for the virtual machine (VM) in case of node failure by making shadow copies of the VM at a different server in the cluster and keeping all information in lockstep and up to date.

VM High Availability   High availability (HA) ensures that if a server failure occurs, the virtual machines (VMs) can restart on different servers that are healthy.

VMDirectPath   Allows the data controller to have Peripheral Component Interconnect/Peripheral Component Interconnect express (PCI/PCIe) pass-through control of the physical server disk controllers without intervention from the hypervisor.

VMK (VM Kernel) Port Groups   Special distributed virtual port groups that contain ports with specific functions done in the kernel, such as dvPG-vMotion or dvPG-HA for moving virtual machines (VMs) and providing high availability.

vMotion   Having virtual machines (VMs) migrate from one node to another for different purposes, such as workload balancing or in case of node failure.

vSAN   The hyperconvergence software that VMware developed.

vSphere   VMware's suite of software for server virtualization. It includes the hypervisor ESXi, the web client, vCenter for virtualization management, as well as other tools for virtual machine (VM) storage migration and resource scheduling.

vSphere APIs for Storage Awareness (VASA)   An architecture developed by VMware that allows third-party storage arrays to share their capabilities with vCenter. This allows vCenter to attach to the virtual machines (VMs) storage policies and data services that match the storage array capabilities.

vSphere Installation Bundle (VIB)   A mechanism created by VMware to package a collection of files that can be distributed.

VXLAN Network Identifier (VNID) An identifier or a tag that represents a logical segment that is an L2 broadcast domain tunneled over the IP network.

W

Webscale Architecture A term in the industry indicating that the architecture brings the benefit and scale of provider cloud–based architectures to the enterprise.

Whitelist A list of approved applications that are permitted to be present in the network.

Wide Area Network (WAN) Remote connectivity of an enterprise to a service provider. The link could be low speed or as high as multiples of 10 Gbps.

Wide Area Network (WAN) Optimizer A networking device or software that optimizes WAN traffic via techniques such as rate limiting, compressing, and deduplication of traffic.

Windows Server Failover Cluster (WSFC) A Microsoft architecture that allows a group of servers to work together in a cluster to increase the availability of applications.

Witness A lightweight virtual machine (VM) that is used to break the tie during an election process of nodes so they do not get into a split-brain scenario.

Workflow A series of tasks that are arranged to automate a complex operation.

World Wide Name (WWN) The global addressing representation of a fibre channel node or port. It is an 8-byte address with 16 hexadecimal characters.

World Wide Node Name (WWNN) The global address name of a fibre channel node.

World Wide Port Name (WWPN) The global address name of a specific port number on the fibre channel node.

X–Y

x86 Architecture An architecture based on the Intel 8086 CPUs that were introduced in 1978. x86 is a family of instruction set architectures that have evolved over the years from 8-bit to 16-bit and 32-bit processors.

Z

Zero Trust Security Policy Represents a model where a user or an application will get just enough permissions to operate, no more or no less.

Zone In the context of fibre channel, a zone restricts the traffic exchange between fibre channel nodes to a specific zone.

Index

A

ABS (Acropolis Block Services),
272–273

acceleration, hardware, 125

access time, 24

Accolade Technology Inc., 311

ACI (application-centric
infrastructure), 252, 312–313

   ACI Anywhere, 386

   APIC (Application Policy
Infrastructure Controller),
360–361

   domains

      external, 364–365

      fabric connectivity, 367–369

      physical, 364–365

      *switching and routing,
365–367, 369–371*

      *VMM (Virtual Machine
Manager), 362–364*

   microsegmentation constructs

      *ANPs (application network
profiles), 355–358*

      *EPGs (endpoint groups),
353–355*

      service graphs, 358–359

      tetration model, 360

   multicast, 383

   Multi-PoD (point of delivery),
383–384

   Multi-Site, 384–386

   NSX (network virtualization and
security) compared to

      *automation and visibility,
390–391*

      control plane, 389

      data forwarding, 390

      networking learning curve, 391

      overview of, 386–387

      *policy setting and enforcement,
387–388*

      VXLAN performance, 388–389

   overlay network

      L2 switching in, 378–380

      L3 switching/routing, 380–383

      overview of, 373–376

      *VNIDs (VXLAN Instance IDs),
376–378*

overview of, 352–353

underlay network, 371–373

Acropolis Block Services, 272–273

Acropolis File Services, 273–274

Acropolis Hypervisor (AHV), 256

Acropolis OS (AOS), 274

ACS (atomic compare and swap), 263

active-active data centers, 148

address resolution protocol (ARP), 15, 315

addressing

FC (fibre channel), 42

IP (Internet Protocol), 12–13

iSCSI (Internet Small Computer Interface), 47–48

MAC (media access control), 108

WWNN (World Wide Node Name), 108

advanced catalogs, 431

Advanced Host Controller Interface (AHCI), 71–72

Advanced Technology Attachment over Ethernet (AoE), 40, 50

agents, Neutron, 321–322

aggregation switches, 7

AHCI (Advanced Host Controller Interface), 71–72

AHV (Acropolis Hypervisor), 256

Alarms menu (Cisco Intersight), 209

all-flash arrays, 73–75

all-flash nodes, 156

allocation, memory, 85

alternative HCI implementations. See Nutanix ECP (Enterprise Cloud Platform); OpenStack; vSAN

ALU (arithmetic logic unit), 66–67

Amazon Machine Images (AMI), 410

Amazon Web Services. See AWS (Amazon Web Services)

AMI (Amazon Machine Images), 410

ANPs (application network profiles), 355–358

Aodh, 293

AoE (Advanced Technology Attachment over Ethernet), 40, 50

AOS (Acropolis OS), 274

APIC (Application Policy Infrastructure Controller), 93, 360–361

APIs (application programming interfaces)

Cisco CloudCenter, 446

Cisco UCSD (USC Director) integration, 434–437

Neutron, 321

RESTful, 36, 215, 295, 297, 434–436

VMware vSAN, 244

AppDynamics, 217–219, 446

Appfog, 397

Application Mobility Fabric, 256–257

application network profiles (ANPs), 355–358

Application Policy Infrastructure Controller (APIC), 93, 360–361

application programming interfaces. See APIs (application programming interfaces)

Application Virtual Switch (AVS), 93

application-centric infrastructure (ACI), 252, 312–313

application-specific integrated circuits (ASICs), 311

arithmetic logic unit (ALU), 66–67

ARP (Address Resolution Protocol), 15, 315

arrays

caching storage, 60–61

flash, 73–75

storage, 102

ASICs (application-specific integrated circuits), 311

asynchronous native replication for DR (NRDR), 189–190

atomic compare and swap (ACS), 263

automation

ACI (application-centric infrastructure), 390–391

AWS (Amazon Web Services), 416

infrastructure as a code, 417–420

SDKs (software development kits), 420–421

networking, 126–127

NSX (network virtualization and security platform), 390–391

private cloud, 425–427, 431–432

availability. *See also* HA (high availability)

AWS (Amazon Web Services), 399–401

EBS (Elastic Block Storage), 409

Nutanix ECP (Enterprise Cloud Platform), 263–264

Avamar, 241–243

AVS (Application Virtual Switch), 93

AWS (Amazon Web Services)

AMI (Amazon Machine Images), 410

availability zones, 399–401

cloud automation, 416

infrastructure as a code, 417–420

SDKs (software development kits), 420–421

cloud monitoring, 416

CloudFormation, 417–420

compute instances, 409

EC2 instances

auto scaling, 414–416

launching, 411–412

volumes, adding, 414

Glacier, 441–442

global infrastructure, 399–401

IAM (identity and access management), 411–412

networking, 401–404

overview of, 398–399

regions, 399–401

S3 (Simple Storage Service), 36

security groups, 410–411

storage

EBS (Elastic Block Storage), 406–409

Glacier, 405

overview of, 404–405

RRS (Reduced Redundancy Storage), 405

S3 (Simple Storage Service), 405–406

Azure, 397

B

B200 blade server, 159

backup, 129–130

Nutanix ECP (Enterprise Cloud Platform), 270–271

third-party backup tools, 191–192

VMware vSAN, 241–243

balancing. *See* load balancing

Barbican, 292

bare-metal servers, 78–79, 396

BDs (bridge domains), 366

Berkeley Software Distribution (BSD), 312

BGP (Border Gateway Protocol), 8, 308

block-level deduplication, 56–57

block-level storage, 35

blocks (Nutanix), 263–264

boot policy, 165

Border Gateway Protocol (BGP), 8, 308

bridge domains (BDs), 366

Broadcom Ltd, 311

BSD (Berkeley Software Distribution), 312

buckets (S3), 405–406

BUM (broadcast, unknown unicast, and multicast) traffic, 15–16

business benefits

   deployment speed, 136

   HA (high availability), 139

   infrastructure scaling, 136–137

   IT operational model, 137–138

   low-entry cost structure, 139

   overview of, 135–136

   private cloud agility/flexibility, 138–139

   system management, 138

   TCO (total cost of ownership), 140

BW (Business Warehouse), 147

C

cache vNode, 182

caching

   caching storage arrays, 60–61

   host-based, 75

   VMware vSAN, 232

Calm, 278–279

CAM (content-addressable memory), 308

Capacity Optimization Engine (COE), 265

CAPEX (capital expenditures), 127, 140, 212, 216, 399

Cassandra, 258, 260

catalogs (UCSD), 431, 432

Cavium Inc., 311

CBT (changed block tracking), 192, 275

CCM (CloudCenter Manager), 448

CCO (CloudCenter orchestrator), 448

CEE (Converged Enhanced Ethernet), 49

Ceilometer, 293

CentOS KVM hypervisor, 256

central processing units. See CPUs (central processing units)

centralized firewalls, 319

Ceph, 300–303

Cerebro, 259, 270

certifications, security, 194

CGs (consistency groups), 270

changed block tracking (CBT), 192, 275

Chef OpenStack, 292

CI (converged infrastructure), 108–116

Cinder Block Storage, 296–297

CIOs (chief information officers), 399, 442

Cisco 5108 UCS blade chassis, 159–160

Cisco ACI (application-centric infrastructure), 312–313

Cisco AppDynamics, 217–219

Cisco application-centric infrastructure. See ACI (application-centric infrastructure)

Cisco AVS (Application Virtual Switch), 93

Cisco C220/C240 M4/M5 rack servers, 158–159

Cisco CloudCenter, 446–449

Cisco FlashStack, 112

Cisco FlexPod, 112

Cisco HyperFlex. *See* HyperFlex (HX)

Cisco HyperFlex Connect HTML5 Management, 200–202

Cisco HyperFlex Data Platform. *See* HXDP (HX Data Platform)

Cisco Intersight. *See* Intersight

Cisco Nexus 1000v, 93, 321

Cisco TAC, Cisco Intersight integration with, 205

Cisco Tetration. *See* Tetration

Cisco UCS (Unified Computing System). *See* UCS (Unified Computing System)

Cisco Unified Computing System (UCS), 223

Cisco Validated Design (CVD), 331

Cisco VesraStack, 112

Cisco VIC MLOM interface cards, 159

Cisco VxBlock, 112

Cisco WebEx, 443

Cisco Workload Optimizer (CWOM), 216–217, 449

Cisco/Unified Computing System (UCS) Nexus, 321

classless interdomain routing (CIDR). *See* SVI (switch virtual interface)

CLI (command-line interface), 244, 308

CliQr. *See* CloudCenter

cloning, 55

   HyperFlex (HX), 189

   Nutanix ECP (Enterprise Cloud Platform), 268–269

   VMware vSAN, 236–237

cloud bursting, 441

cloud creep, 212

cloud service providers (CSPs), 4

cloud technology. *See* multicloud; private cloud; public cloud

CloudCenter, 446–449

CloudCenter Manager (CCM), 448

CloudCenter orchestrator (CCO), 448

CloudFormation, 417–420

Cloudkitty, 293

Cloud-Scale Acceleration Architecture, 311

CloudWatch, 416

clusters

   definition of, 86–87

   Nutanix ECP (Enterprise Cloud Platform), 258–259, 271–272

   resiliency, 179–180

   VMware vSAN, 238–241

CMVP (Cryptographic Module Validation Program), 235

CNA (converged network adapter), 49

COE (Capacity Optimization Engine), 265

command-line interface (CLI), 244, 308

community switch ports, 14

compression, 58–59, 128

   HyperFlex (HX), 187

   Nutanix ECP (Enterprise Cloud Platform), 265–266

   VMware vSAN, 235

compute-only nodes, 154–155, 157, 250–251

Config-VVol-Metadata, 101

Congress, 292

consistency groups (CGs), 270

containers
  Docker, 80–82
    HyperFlex support for, 172–173
    Nutanix support for, 275
  Open Virtuozzo, 80–81
  persistent storage, 244
  Swift, 299
content-addressable memory (CAM), 308
Contiv project, 353
control plane, 308, 389
control VM (CVM), 119, 257, 264
Converged Enhanced Ethernet (CEE), 49
converged infrastructure. *See* CI (converged infrastructure)
converged network adapter (CNA), 49
converged nodes. *See* nodes
converged systems, 112–116
COOP, 371
copy on write (COW) logical snapshots, 52–54
core switches/routers, 7
CoreOS rkt, 80–81
COW (copy on write) logical snapshots, 52–54
CPUs (central processing units)
  dual-core, 66–67
  logical cores, 67–68
  Moore's Law, 65–66
  multi-core, 66–67
  pCPUs (physical CPUs), 67
  physical cores, 67–68
  single-core, 66–67
  vCPUs (virtual CPUs), 68–70
  virtual cores, 67–68
  x86 standard architecture, 66

CRC-32 (32-bit cyclic redundancy check), 234
CRE (generic routing encapsulation), 214
CRM (customer relationship management), 4, 146
CRUSH algorithm, 303
Cryptographic Module Validation Program (CMVP), 235
CSPs (cloud service providers), 4
Curator, 259, 261
CVD (Cisco Validated Design), 331
CVM (control VM), 119, 257, 264
CWOM (Cisco Workload Optimizer), 216–217, 449

D

daemons, Ovsdb-vswitchd, 325–326
DAS (direct-attached storage), 38–39, 118–127
Dashboard view
  Cisco Intersight, 207
  HyperFlex Connect HTML5 Management, 200–201
Data Center Bridging (DCB), 49
data compression. *See* compression
data distribution
  cluster resiliency, 179–180
  data protection via replication, 178–179
  data striping, 176–177
  overview of, 174–176
data encryption. *See* encryption
data encryption keys (DEKs), 192–193
data forwarding, 390
data locality, 175, 285–286
data networks, 4

design challenges

    BUM traffic flooding, 15–16

    firewall overload, 17–18

    flat L2 networks with stretched VLANs, 10–11

    interVLAN routing via SVI, 12

    IP4 address scarcity, 12–13

    loop prevention via spanning tree, 16

    oversubscription between tiers, 9–10

    private VLANs, 13–15

    traffic hopping between tiers, 11–12

  logical server grouping, 8–9

  multitier architecture, 6–8

  network equipment, 4

  security, 5–6

  traffic redirection and optimization, 5

  types of, 4

data optimization, 185–186

data plane, 308

Data Plane Development Kit (DPDK), 312

data platform. *See* HXDP (HX Data Platform)

data platform controller (DPC), 119, 169–170

Data Protection Manager (DPM), 275

data storage

  backup, 129–130

  deduplication and compression, 128

  EC (erasure coding), 128–129

  overview of, 127–128

  replication, 129–130

data striping, 176–177

data tiering, 282

data virtualization, 182–183

data vNode, 182, 185

database transaction units (DTUs), 216

databases, 4, 146

datastores, 82–83, 84, 228

DATA-VVol-VMDK, 101

DCB (Data Center Bridging), 49

DDA (Discrete Device Assignment), 274

deduplication, 128

  block-level, 56–57

  definition of, 55–56

  file-level, 56

  global, 58

  HyperFlex (HX), 187

  inline, 58

  local, 58

  Nutanix ECP (Enterprise Cloud Platform), 264–265

  Nutanix ECP versus HyperFlex, 283–284

  object-level, 56

  post-process, 58

  source-based, 57–58

  target-based, 57–58

  VMware vSAN, 235

Defense Information Systems Agency (DISA), 235

DEKs (data encryption keys), 192–193

DELETE method, 435

Dell EMC, 246, 255

delta disks, 237

denial of service (DoS) attacks, 6

deployment

  HyperFlex (HX)

    Cisco HyperFlex Connect HTML5 Management, 200–202

Cisco Intersight, 204

installation phase, 197–199

sizer, 199

*VMware vSphere management
plug-in, 203–204*

workload profiler, 199

iSCSI (Internet Small Computer
Interface) SANs, 46–47

speed of, 136

Designate, 292

desktops, VDI (virtual desktop
infrastructure), 141–144

destaging, 185–186

Device menu (Cisco Intersight), 209

DevOps, 141

DHCP (Dynamic Host Configuration
Protocol), 321

dies, 66–67

Digital Ocean, 397

direct-attached storage. *See* DAS
(direct-attached storage)

DISA (Defense Information Systems
Agency), 235

Disable Object Checksum, 231

disaster recovery, 148–149

   backup, 129–130

   HCI use case, 148–149

   Nutanix ECP (Enterprise Cloud
   Platform), 270–271

   replication, 129–130

   VMware vSAN, 238–243

Discrete Device Assignment (DDA),
274

distributed architecture

   DAS (direct-attached storage),
   118–127

   HyperFlex (HX), 281–282

   Nutanix ECP (Enterprise Cloud
   Platform), 281–282

distributed controllers, 119

distributed file systems, 249–250

distributed logical router (DLR),
343–345

distributed objects, 183

distributed resource scheduling
(DRS), 82

distributed storage fabric (DSF),
257–259

distributed virtual port groups
(dvPG), 92

distributed virtual ports (dvPorts), 92

distributed virtual uplinks (dvUplink),
92

distribution switches, 7

DLR (distributed logical router),
343–345

Docker containers, 80–82

   HyperFlex support for, 172–173

   Nutanix support for, 275

domains

   external, 364–365

   fault, 229–230

   identifiers, 44

   physical, 364–365

   VMM (Virtual Machine Manager),
   362–364

DoS (denial of service) attacks, 6

DPC (data platform controller),
119, 169–170

DPDK (Data Plane Development Kit),
312

DPM (Data Protection Manager), 275

DR. *See* disaster recovery

Dragonflow, 292

DRAM (dynamic random-access
memory), 147, 232

drives

   delta disks, 237

HDDs (hard disk drives), 22–23, 155, 406–408

Nutanix ECP (Enterprise Cloud Platform), 260–261

performance

access time, 24

IOPS (input/output operations per second), 24–25

latency, 24–25

throughput, 21–24

RAID (Redundant Array of Independent Disks), 26–30

SEDs (self-encrypting drives), 192–193

SSDs (solid-state drives), 23, 155

DRS (distributed resource scheduling), 82

DSF (distributed storage fabric), 257–259

DTUs (database transaction units), 216

dual-core CPUs (central processing units), 66–67

dvPG (distributed virtual port groups), 92

dvPorts (distributed virtual ports), 92

dvUplink (distributed virtual uplinks), 92

Dynamic Host Configuration Protocol (DHCP), 321

dynamic random-access memory (DRAM), 147, 232

E

EBS (Elastic Block Storage), 406–409, 425–426

EC. *See* erasure coding

EC2 instances, 411–416

ECMP (Equal Cost Multi-path), 315

ECP (Enterprise Cloud Platform). *See* **Nutanix ECP (Enterprise Cloud Platform)**

edge computing, 146

edge nodes, 157

Elastic Block Storage (EBS), 406–409, 425–426

email servers, 4

EMC

Avamar, 129–130, 241–243

Vipr controller, 99

VxRail, 223

Encapsulated Remote Switched Port Analyzer (ERSPAN) agents, 214

encryption, 59

disk, 59

EBS (Elastic Block Storage), 408

Nutanix ECP (Enterprise Cloud Platform), 272

SEDs (self-encrypting drives), 23, 59, 129–130, 192–193, 199, 235

VMware vSAN, 234–235

endpoint groups. *See* EPGs (endpoint groups)

Engine Yard, 397

enterprise class applications, 146–147

Enterprise Cloud Platform. *See* ECP (Enterprise Cloud Platform)

enterprise resource management (ERM), 146

enterprise resource planning (ERP), 4

enterprise workload issues, 211–212

EPGs (endpoint groups), 353–355, 366

Equal Cost Multi-path (ECMP), 315

equipment, network, 4

Era database services, 269–270

erasure coding, 128–129

  Nutanix ECP (Enterprise Cloud
    Platform), 266

  VMware vSAN, 236

ERM (enterprise resource
  management), 146

ERP (enterprise resource planning), 4

ERSPAN (Encapsulated Remote
  Switched Port Analyzer) agents,
  214

ESXi, 79, 136, 170–171

Ethernet, Fibre Channel over, 49–50,
  82, 109

EUI (Extended Unique Identifier), 47

Extended Unique Identifier (EUI), 47

Extensible Markup Language (XML),
  215, 434

Extent store (Nutanix), 261

F

fabric, 369

  ACI (application-centric infrastructure)
    connectivity, 367–369
    switching and routing,
      365–367, 369–371

  definition of, 44

  DSF (distributed storage fabric),
    257–259

  FIs (fabric interconnects), 108

  Nutanix Application Mobility
    Fabric, 256–257

  NVMe-oF (NVMe over fabrics), 72

  switching fabric, 313–315

Fabric Interconnect menu (Cisco
  Intersight), 207

Fabric Login process (FLOGI), 44

Fabric loopback TEP (FTEP), 370

failure tolerance (vSAN), 231

Fast Ethernet, 4

fault domains, 229–230

fault tolerance, 89

FC (fibre channel)

  addressing, 42

  drives, 23

  FCNS (fibre channel network
    service), 44

  FCoE (Fibre Channel over Ethernet),
    49–50, 82, 109

  interfaces, 4, 82, 109

  LUN masking, 43

  multipathing, 44–46

  overview of, 41–42

  switching, 44–45

  zoning, 43

Federal Information Processing
  Standards (FIPS), 235

field programmable gate arrays
  (FPGAs), 311

file server VMs (FSVMs), 273–274

file systems

  CephFS (Ceph File System), 301

  LFS (log-structured file system),
    122–124, 181–182

  NFS (Network File System), 36,
    82, 244

  Nutanix ECP (Enterprise Cloud
    Platform), 282

  object file system, 226–227

  overview of, 122–124

  union file system, 173

  VMFS (Virtual Machine File
    System), 82, 226

  vSAN, 228, 249–250

File Transfer Protocol. *See* FTP (File
  Transfer Protocol)

File Transfer Protocol (FTP), 5

file-level deduplication, 56

file-level storage, 35–36

FIPS (Federal Information Processing Standards), 235

firewalls, 6

  centralized, 319

  NGFWs (next generation firewalls), 314

  overload, 17–18

firmware policy, 165

FIs (fabric interconnects), 108

flash arrays, 73–75

Flash Read Cache Reservation (vSAN), 231

flash wear, 73

flash-based products, 72–75

FlashStack, 112

flat L2 networks, 10–11

FlexPod, 112

FLOGI (Fabric Login process), 44

flooding, 15–16, 342

Flow, 331

force provisioning, 231

forks, 183

FPGAs (field programmable gate arrays), 311

Freezer, 292

FSVMs (file server VMs), 273–274

FTEP (Fabric loopback TEP), 370

FTP (File Transfer Protocol), 5

fully converged systems, 112–116

G

GCP (Google Cloud Platform), 397, 446

GE (Gigabit Ethernet), 4, 20

generic routing encapsulation (GRE), 214

GENEVE (Generic Network Virtualization Encapsulation), 126, 315–316

GET method, 435

GFS (global file system), 40

GIPo (Group IP outer), 383

Glacier, 405, 441–442

Glance, 291, 293

global deduplication, 58

Google App Platform, 397

Google Apps, 443

Google Cloud Platform (GCP), 397, 446

GPUs (graphics processing units), 155

granular volumes, 100–101

Group IP outer (GIPo), 383

groups

  endpoint, 353–355, 366

  security, 410–411

  VMware NSX, 336–337

GST (global station table), 371

guest OS assignment, 85

GUIs (graphical user interfaces), 138, 244, 308

H

HA (high availability)

  datastores, 82

  HCI business benefits to, 139

  Nutanix ECP (Enterprise Cloud Platform), 264

  VMware vSAN, 239–240

hard disk drives. See HDDs (hard disk drives)

hardware. See host hardware

Hardware Compatibility List (HCL), 245

hashing
  CRUSH algorithm, 303
  MD5 algorithm, 57, 299
  SHA-1 algorithm, 57

HBAs (host bus adapters)
  Cisco UCS (Unified Computing System), 108
  overview of, 30–31
  vHBAs (virtual host bus adapters), 109, 166

HCL (Hardware Compatibility List), 245

HDDs (hard disk drives), 22–23, 155, 406–408

Heat, 293

Help menu (Cisco Intersight), 209

Heroku, 397

high availability. *See* HA (high availability)

Horizon, 292, 293

host bus adapters. *See* HBAs (host bus adapters)

host bus interconnect, 70–72

host hardware, 65
  CPUs (central processing units)
    dual-core, 66–67
    logical cores, 67–68
    Moore's Law, 65–66
    multi-core, 66–67
    pCPUs (physical CPUs), 67
    physical cores, 67–68
    single-core, 66–67
    vCPUs (virtual CPUs), 68–70
    virtual cores, 67–68
    x86 standard architecture, 66
  flash-based products, 72–75

hardware acceleration, 125

host bus interconnect, 70–72

host-based caching, 75

host-based networking, 310–312

HP Enterprise Converged Infrastructure, 397

HT (hyperthreading), 67

HTTP (Hypertext Transfer Protocol), 5, 338, 434–435

HX. *See* HyperFlex (HX)

HXDP (HX Data Platform)
  data distribution
    cluster resiliency, 179–180
    data protection via replication, 178–179
    data striping, 176–177
    overview of, 174–176
  Docker containers support, 172–173
  DPC (data platform controller), 169–170
  Hyper-V environment, 171–172
  installation, 197–199
  management platforms
    Cisco HyperFlex Connect HTML5 Management, 200–202
    Cisco Intersight, 204
    VMware vSphere management plug-in, 203–204
  overview of, 168
  read/write operations, 181–187
    data virtualization, 182–183
    destaging and data optimization, 185–186
    LFS (log-structured file system), 181–182
    read operation lifecycle, 186–187
    write operation lifecycle, 183–185

sizer, 199

VMware ESXi environment, 170–171

workload profiler, 199

hybrid arrays, 74

hybrid cloud, 439–442

hybrid nodes, 156

hyperconverged networking

SDN (software-defined networking)

host-based networking, 310–312

microsegmentation, 309–310, 319

open source initiatives, 320–324

overlay network, 309–310, 315–319

overview of, 308–309

OVN (Open Virtual Network), 326–331

switch-based networking, 312–313

switching fabric, 313–315

underlay network, 315

vendors, 331

VMware NSX (network virtualization and security platform)

flooding avoidance, 342

IP routing, 343–345

L2 switching, 343

multidestination traffic, 347–349

NSX controller cluster, 340–341

NSX manager, 339–340

overview of, 335–336

policies, 336–338

vDS (virtual Distributed Switch) enhancements, 341–342

hyperconvergence software

Nutanix ECP (Enterprise Cloud Platform)

availability domains, 263–264

cluster components, 258–259

data path resiliency, 264

data protection, 262

DSF (distributed storage fabric), 257–259

I/O path, 261

metadata, 263

physical drives, 260–261

read I/O, 262

write I/O, 261–262

VMware vSAN

caching, 232

datastore, 228

high-level software architecture, 225–226

I/O operation details, 232–233

object file system, 226–227

storage policies, 228–231

HyperFlex (HX), 138, 164–165. *See also* **HXDP (HX Data Platform)**

Cisco UCSD (USC Director) integration

APIs (application programming interfaces), 434–437

automation and orchestration, 431–432

infrastructure as a code, 434–437

UCSD interfaces, 433–434

cloning, 189

compression, 187

deduplication, 187

deployment
    Cisco HyperFlex Connect HTML5 Management, 200–202
    Cisco Intersight, 204
    installation phase, 197–199
    sizer, 199
    VMware vSphere management plug-in, 203–204
    workload profiler, 199
HXDP (HX Data Platform)
    data distribution, 174–182
    Docker containers support, 172–173
    DPC (data platform controller), 169–170
    Hyper-V environment, 171–172
    overview of, 168
    read/write operations, 181–187
    VMware ESXi environment, 170–171
hyperconverged product portfolio, 108
NRDR (native replication for DR), 189–191
Nutanix ECP versus
    data locality, 285–286
    data tiering, 282
    deduplication, 283–284
    distributed architecture, 281–282
    file systems, 282
    hardware comparison, 280–281
    overview of, 279–280
overview of, 153–154
performance benchmarks, 160–162
physical components, 154–156
    all-flash nodes, 156
    Cisco 5108 UCS blade chassis, 159–160
    Cisco C220/C240 M4/M5 rack servers, 158–159
    Cisco VIC MLOM interface cards, 159
    compute-only nodes, 157
    edge nodes, 157
    hybrid nodes, 156
    UCS 6200 and 6300 fabric interconnect, 158
security, 192
    data at rest, 192–193
    management security, 194
    operational security, 193–194
    regulation and certification compliance, 194
snapshots, 188–189
third-party backup tool integration, 191–192
UCS (Unified Computing System) integration, 162
    external storage, 167–168
    logical network design, 162–164
    service templates and profiles, 164–165
    vNIC templates, 166–167
VMware vSAN versus, 246
    advanced data services, 251–252
    compute-only nodes, 250–251
    file systems, 249–250
    hardware comparison, 247
    management software, 252
    networking, 252–253
    one-to-one versus many-to-many rebuild, 250

scaling up, 247–248

vSAN in-kernel versus controller-based solutions, 248–249

workload optimization and efficiency

Cisco AppDynamics, 217–219

CWOM (Cisco Workload Optimizer), 216–217

enterprise workload issues, 211–212

HyperFlex with Cisco Tetration, 212–215

overview of, 211

HyperFlex cluster menu (Cisco Intersight), 207

HyperFlex Connect HTML5 Management, 200–202

Hypertext Transfer Protocol (HTTP), 5, 338, 434–435

hyperthreading (HT), 67

Hyper-V, 136

HyperFlex in, 171–172

Nutanix support for, 274–275

hypervisors, 79–80

I

IA (Infrequent Access) S3 storage, 405

IaaS (infrastructure as a service), 396–397, 423

IAM (identity and access management), 411–412, 425–426

IANA (Internet Assigned Numbers Authority), 13

IB (InfiniBand), 40

IBM DB2, 272–273

IBM Smartcloud Enterprise, 397

identity and access management (IAM), 411–412, 425–426

IDSs (intrusion detection systems), 6

IEEE (Institute of Electrical and Electronics Engineers), 49

IETF (Internet Engineering Task Force), 117

IGMP (Internet Group Management Protocol), 315, 347

InfiniBand (IB), 40

infrastructure as a code, 417–420, 434–437

infrastructure as a service (IaaS), 396–397, 423

infrastructure loopback IP addresses, 370

Infrequent Access (IA) S3 storage, 405

inline deduplication, 58

input/output operations per second (IOPS), 24–25, 73, 138, 156, 199, 216, 247, 296

Institute of Electrical and Electronics Engineers (IEEE), 49

Intel, 155, 311

Intermediate System to Intermediate System (IS-IS), 8, 126, 308, 371

Internet Assigned Numbers Authority (IANA), 13

Internet Engineering Task Force (IETF), 117

Internet Group Management Protocol (IGMP), 315, 347

Internet Protocol. See IP (Internet Protocol)

Internet Small Computer System Interface. See iSCSI (Internet Small Computer Interface)

Intersight, 204, 446

advantages of, 205

claiming nodes in, 205–209

conceptual view of, 204–205

menus, 207–209

interVLAN routing, 12

intrusion detection systems (IDSs), 6

intrusion prevention systems (IPSs), 6

IOPS (input/output operations per second), 24–25, 73, 138, 156, 199, 216, 247, 296

IOVisor, 170

IP (Internet Protocol)

addressing, 12–13, 370–371

routing, 343–345

IP address management (IPAM), 214

IPAM (IP address management), 214

IPSs (intrusion prevention systems), 6

IQN (iSCSI Qualified Name), 47

Ironic, 291

iSCSI (Internet Small Computer Interface), 82

addressing, 47–48

deployments, 46–47

IQN (iSCSI Qualified Name), 47

iSER (iSCSI extensions for Remote Direct Memory Access), 40

LUN masking, 48

multipathing, 48–49

network segmentation, 48

vSAN iSCSI target service, 243

iSER (iSCSI extensions for Remote Direct Memory Access), 40

IS-IS (Intermediate System to Intermediate System), 8, 126, 308, 371

IT as a service (ITaaS), 423

J

Java Eclipse, 437

JavaScript Object Notation. *See* JSON (JavaScript Object Notation)

JBOD (just a bunch of disks), 98

JSON (JavaScript Object Notation), 434

CloudFormation templates, 417–420

exporting Tetration data to, 215

IAM (identity and access management), 412

K

Karbor, 292

KEKs (key encryption keys), 59, 192–193

Kerberos, 275

Keystone, 292, 293

KMIP (Key Management Interoperability Protocol), 131, 234

KMSs (key management servers), 411

Kolla, 292

Kuryr, 292

KVMs (kernel-based virtual machines), 136, 256

L

LAN connectivity policy, 165

large enterprises (LEs), 136–137

latency, 11–12, 24–25

Layer 2 (L2), 4, 343, 378–380

Layer 3 (L3), 4, 380–383

LAZ (logical availability zones), 181

leaf layer, 313

leaf node loopback IP addresses, 370

least recently used (LRU) counters, 262

legacy installations

SDS (software-defined storage), 97–99

VDI (virtual desktop infrastructure) with, 143–144

Lenovo, 255

LEs (large enterprises), 136–137

LFS (log-structured file system), 122–124, 181–182

LIBRADOS, 300–301

lightweight snapshots (LWSs), 272

linked clones, 237

Linux containers (LXC), 80–81

load balancing, 5, 266–267, 314

ACI (application-centric infrastructure), 373

computing, 89

storage, 90

local data protection, 148

local deduplication, 58

local snapshots, 148

local station tables (LSTs), 371

Log Insight, vRealize, 246

logical availability zones (LAZ), 181

logical cores, 67–68

logical network design, 162–164

logical server grouping, 8–9

logical snapshots, 52–54

logical switches (LSWs), 341–342

logical unit numbers. *See* LUNs (logical unit numbers)

logical volume manager (LVM), 33–35

log-structured file system (LFS), 122–124, 181–182

LPM (longest prefix match), 373

LRU (least recently used) counters, 262

LSTs (local station tables), 371

LSWs (logical switches), 341–342

LUNs (logical unit numbers), 31–33, 82, 124, 136–137

configuration, 84

masking, 43, 48

LVM (logical volume manager), 33–35

LWSs (lightweight snapshots), 272

LXC (Linux container), 80–81

LZ4 algorithm, 235

M

MAC (media access control) addresses, 108

Magnum, 291

management. *See also* monitoring

HXDP (HX Data Platform), 200–204

management plane, 308

NSX manager, 339–340

Nutanix ECP (Enterprise Cloud Platform), 275–279

overview of, 131–133

security, 194

server virtualization, 90

VMware vSAN, 244–246

vSAN versus HyperFlex, 252

Manila, 291

many-to-many rebuild, 250

mapping

between clouds, 447

databases, 371

MapReduce, 258

masking LUNs, 43, 48

MD5 hashing algorithm, 57, 299

media access control (MAC) addresses, 108

MEKs (media encryption keys), 59

Mellanox Technologies Ltd., 311

memory. *See also* caching

allocation of, 85

CAM (content-addressable memory), 308

DRAM (dynamic random-access memory), 147

NVMe (Non-Volatile Memory Express), 71–72, 199, 311

objects, 227

MEM-VVol-Snapshots, 101

Message Digest 5 (MD5) algorithm, 57

metadata, 182, 263

metadata vNode, 185

methods (HTTP), 435

MG-BGP (Multi-Protocol Border Gateway Protocol), 126, 371

microsegmentation constructs, 309–310, 319

ANPs (application network profiles), 355–358

EPGs (endpoint groups), 353–355

service graphs, 358–359

tetration model, 360

Microsoft Cloud-Scale Acceleration Architecture, 311

migration

storage, 90

VMs (virtual machines), 87

Mistral, 292

ML2 (Modular Layer 2), 321

MLAG (multichassis link aggregation), 18

MLC (multilevel cell) NAND, 73

MLOM (modular LAN-on-motherboard), 159

Monasca, 293

monitoring

AWS (Amazon Web Services), 416

HXDP (HX Data Platform), 200–204

Nutanix ECP (Enterprise Cloud Platform), 275–279

overview of, 131–133

Moore's Law, 65–66

MP-BGP (Multi-Protocol BGP), 126, 308, 371

MPIO (multipathing I/O), 273

MPIT (multiple points in time), 240

multicast, 383

multichassis link aggregation (MLAG), 18

multicloud, 442–446. *See also* hybrid cloud

multi-core CPUs (central processing units), 66–67

multidestination traffic

multicast model with no optimization, 347

overview of, 346–347

unicast mode, 348–349

multilevel cell (MLC) NAND, 73

multipathing, 44–46, 48–49

multipathing I/O (MPIO), 273

multiple points in time (MPIT), 240

Multi-PoD (point of delivery), 383–384

Multi-Protocol Border Gateway Protocol (MP-BGP), 126, 308, 371

Multi-Site, 384–386

multitier applications, launching in AWS (Amazon Web Services)

AMI (Amazon Machine Images), 410

compute instances, 409

EC2 instances, 412–416

IAM (identity and access management), 411–412

security groups, 410–411

multitier design, 6–8, 20–21, 41

BUM traffic flooding, 15–16

firewall overload, 17–18

flat L2 networks with stretched VLANs, 10–11

interVLAN routing via SVI, 12

IP4 address scarcity, 12–13

loop prevention via spanning tree, 16

oversubscription between tiers, 9–10

private VLANs, 13–15

traffic hopping between tiers, 11–12

Murano, 293

N

NAND flash, 73

NAS (network-attached storage), 39–40, 118, 243–244

NAT (Network Address Translation), 6, 13, 322–323

National Institute of Standards and Technology (NIST), 194, 235

native command queueing (NCQ), 71–72

native replication for DR (NRDR), 189–191

NCQ (native command queueing), 71–72

NearSync replication, 272

Network Address Translation (NAT), 6, 13, 322–323

network equipment, 4

Network File System. See NFS (Network File System)

network interface cards (NICs), 7, 85

Network Management Systems (NMSs), 107–108

Network Processors Units (NPUs), 312

network virtualization and security platform. See NSX (network virtualization and security platform)

Network Virtualization using Generic Routing Encapsulation (NVGRE), 126, 315–316

network-attached storage (NAS), 39–40, 118

networking and security software product. See NSX (network virtualization and security platform)

networks. See data networks; storage networks

Neutron, 292

agents, 321–322

APIs (application programming interfaces), 321

overview of, 320

plug-ins, 321

server, 320

Nexus 1000v, 93, 321

NFS (Network File System), 36, 82, 102, 244

NGFWs (next generation firewalls), 6, 314

NICs (network interface cards), 7, 85

Cisco UCS (Unified Computing System), 108

smart NICs, 310–312

vNICs (virtual NICs), 109

NIST (National Institute of Standards and Technology), 194, 235

NMSs (Network Management Systems), 107–108

No Structured Query Language
(NoSQL), 258

nodes, 154–155

all-flash, 156

claiming, 205–209

clusters, 86 87

compute-only, 157, 250–251

edge, 157

hybrid, 156

vNodes, 182, 185

nonpersistent desktops, 142

Non-Volatile Memory Express
(NVMe), 71–72, 199, 311

NoSQL (No Structured Query
Language), 258

Nova, 294–296

NPUs (Network Processors Units),
312

NRDR (native replication for DR),
189–191

NSX (network virtualization and
security platform)

ACI (application-centric
infrastructure) compared to

*automation and visibility,
390–391*

control plane, 389

data forwarding, 390

networking learning curve, 391

overview of, 386–387

*policy setting and enforcement,
387–388*

*VXLAN performance,
388–389*

controller clusters, 340–341

flooding avoidance, 342

IP routing, 343–345

L2 switching, 343

multidestination traffic

*multicast model with no
optimization, 347*

overview of, 346–347

unicast mode, 348–349

NSX manager, 339–340

overview of, 15, 252, 335–336

policies

enforcement of, 338

overview of, 335–336

sample policy rules, 337–338

security groups, 336–337

vDS (virtual Distributed Switch)
enhancements, 341–342

NSX (networking and security
software), 310

Nutanix ECP (Enterprise Cloud
Platform)

Acropolis Block Services, 272–273

Acropolis File Services, 273–274

availability domains, 263–264

backup and restore, 270–271

clones, 268–269

cluster components, 258–259

data at rest encryption, 272

data compression, 265–266

data path resiliency, 264

data protection, 262

deduplication, 264–265

disk balancing, 266–267

Docker containers, 275

DSF (distributed storage fabric),
257–259

Era database services, 269–270

erasure coding, 266

HyperFlex versus

data locality, 285–286

data tiering, 282

deduplication, *283–284*

distributed architecture,
    281–282

file systems, *282*

hardware comparison, *280–281*

overview of, *279–280*

Hyper-V support, 274–275

I/O path, 261

metadata, 263

overview of, 255–257

persistent storage, 275

physical drives, 260–261

Prism management system, 275–277

read I/O, 262

replication, 270–271

snapshots, 268–269

storage tiering, 267

stretched clusters, 271–272

write I/O, 261–262

Nutanix Flow, 331

NVGRE (Network Virtualization
    using Generic Routing
    Encapsulation), 126, 315–316

NVMe (Non-Volatile Memory
    Express), 71–72, 199, 311

NVMe-oF (NVMe over fabrics), 72

O

object file system, 226–227

Object Space Reservation, 231

object store daemons (OSDs), 301

objects

distributed, 183

object-based storage, 36–37

object-level deduplication, 56

S3 (Simple Storage Service), 405–406

Swift, 299

OCP (Open Container Project),
    80–81

Octavia, 292

ODL (OpenDaylight), 324

ODX (Offload Data Transfer), 172

Office 365, 443

Offload Data Transfer (ODX), 172

one-to-one rebuild, 250

Open Container Project (OCP),
    80–81

Open Shortest Path First (OSPF),
    8, 126, 308

open source, 289–290

Ceph, 300–303

networking initiatives

Neutron, *320–322*

OVS (Open vSwitch)
    architecture, *322–324*

OpenStack, 99, 331, 353

Cinder Block Storage, *296–297*

current projects, *290–293*

Nova, *294–296*

OpenStack Foundation, *290*

Swift, *296–297*

vendors, 331

Open Virtual Appliance (OVA), 198

Open Virtual Network. See OVN
    (Open Virtual Network)

Open Virtuozzo containers, 80–81

Open vSwitch Database (OVSDB),
    359

Open vSwitch (OVS). See OVS
    (Open vSwitch)

OpenCloud, 397

OpenDaylight (ODL), 324

OpenStack, 99, 331, 353

Charms, 292

Cinder Block Storage, 296–297

client, 292

current projects, 290–293

Nova, 294–296

OpenStack Foundation, 290

OpenStack-Ansible, 293

Swift, 290–293, 297–300

OpenVZ, 80–81

operating systems, 85–86

operational security, 193–194

OPEX (operational expenditures),
    127, 140, 212, 216, 399

OpFlex, 359

Oplog, 260–262, 265, 272, 282

optimization

    data, 185–186

    multidestination traffic without, 347

    traffic, 5

    workload, 211–219

Oracle Real Application Clusters
    (RAC), 272–273

orchestration

    Cisco UCSD (USC Director), 430

    installation, 431–432

    overview of, 425–427

OSDs (object store daemons), 301

OSPF (Open Shortest Path First), 8,
    126, 308

OSs (operating systems), 85–86

Other VVols, 101

OVA (Open Virtual Appliance), 198

overlay network, 309–310,
    315–319. *See also* ACI
    (application-centric infrastructure)

oversubscription between tiers, 9–10

OVN (Open Virtual Network), 127

    control plane improvements,
        328–331

    data plane improvements, 329–331

functionalities, 326–327

high-level architecture, 327–328

overview of, 326

OVS (Open vSwitch), 93, 127

    architecture, 322–324

    Nutanix's use of, 256

    OVN (Open Virtual Network)
        compared to, 328–331

OVSDB (Open vSwitch Database),
    359

Ovsdb-server, 325

Ovsdb-vswitchd, 325–326

P

PaaS (platform as a service), 397, 423

packet-based firewalls, 6

Panko, 293

partial data locality, 175

partitions, Swift, 299

PCI (Peripheral Component
    Interconnect), 30–31

PCIe (Peripheral Computer
    Interconnect express), 30–31,
    70–71, 311

PCIX (PCI eXtended), 70

pCPUs (physical CPUs), 67

PDs (protection domains), 270

performance

    disk

        access time, 24

        *IOPS (input/output operations
            per second), 24–25*

        latency, 24–25

        throughput, 21–24

    HCI (hyperconverged infrastructure),
        120–121

    HyperFlex (HX), 160–162

VXLAN (Virtual Extensible LAN), 388–389

persistent desktops, **142**

persistent storage, **244, 275**

PFTT (primary level of failures to tolerate), **228–230, 241**

physical cores, **67–68**

physical CPUs (pCPUs), **67**

physical domains, **364–365**

physical NICs (pNICs), **92–93**

physical snapshots, **52**

PIM (Protocol Independent Multicast), **315, 347**

Planar NAND, **73**

platform as a service (PaaS), **397, 423**

PLOGI (port login) process, **44**

pNICs (physical NICs), **92–93**

policies

　ACI (application-centric infrastructure), 387–388

　boot, 165

　firmware, 165

　LAN connectivity, 165

　networking, 126

　NSX (network virtualization and security platform), 387–388

　storage, 228–231

　VMware NSX (network virtualization and security platform)

　　enforcement of, 338

　　overview of, 335–336

　　sample policy rules, 337–338

　　security groups, 336–337

Policy menu (Cisco Intersight), **209**

Portable Operating System Interface (POSIX), **181**

ports

　community switch, 14

PLOGI (port login) process, **44**

promiscuous, 14

virtual switching, 90–93

POSIX (Portable Operating System Interface), **181**

POST method, **435**

post-process deduplication, **58**

Primar, **241**

primary level of failures to tolerate (PFTT), **228–230, 241**

principals, **411**

Prism management system, **257, 275–277**

private cloud. *See also* hybrid cloud; public cloud

　automation, 425–427

　Cisco UCSD (USC Director), 425–427

　　catalogs, 431

　　HyperFlex integration, 431–437

　　orchestration, 425–427, 430

　　overview of, 427

　　policies, 427–429

　　vDCs (virtual data centers), 429–430

　consumption models, 423–425

　convergence and hyperconvergence, 425

　HCI business benefits to, 138–139

　orchestration, 425–427

private VLANs, **13–15**

PRLI (process login), **44**

profiles

　ANPs (application network profiles), 355–358

　Cisco UCS (Unified Computing System), 111–112

　service, 111–112, 164–165, 207–209

promiscuous ports, 14

protection domains (PDs), 270

Protocol Independent Multicast (PIM), 315, 347

provisioning

  force, 231

  HXDP (HX Data Platform)

    Cisco HyperFlex Connect HTML5 Management, 200–202

    Cisco Intersight, 204

    VMware vSphere management plug-in, 203–204

  Nutanix ECP (Enterprise Cloud Platform)

    Calm, 278–279

    infrastructure management, 276–277

    operational insight, 277

    overview of, 275–276

    tools, 278

  overprovisioning, 212

  overview of, 124–125, 131–133

  server virtualization, 90

  thick, 50–51

  thin, 50–51

proxy servers, Swift, 298–300

public cloud, 406–409. *See also* hybrid cloud; private cloud

  AWS (Amazon Web Services)

    AMI (Amazon Machine Images), 410

    availability zones, 399–401

    cloud automation, 416–421

    cloud monitoring, 416

    CloudFormation, 417–420

    compute instances, 409

    EC2 instances, 412–416

    global infrastructure, 399–401

    IAM (identity and access management), 411–412

    networking, 401–404

    overview of, 398–399

    regions, 399–401

    S3 (Simple Storage Service), 36

    security groups, 410–411

    storage, 404–409

  IaaS (infrastructure as a service), 396–397

  overview of, 395–396

  PaaS (platform as a service), 397

  SaaS (software as a service), 397

Puppet OpenStack, 293

PUT method, 435

Q-R

question mark (?), 436

RabbitMQ, 295

RAC (Real Application Clusters), 272–273

Rackspace, 290, 397. *See also* OpenStack

RADOS (Reliable Autonomous Distributed Object Store), 300–301

RAID (Redundant Array of Independent Disks), 26–30, 98, 127

Rally, 292

RAM (random access memory), 65

Raw Device Mapping (RDM), 82

RBAC (role-based access control), 200

RBD (RADOS block device), 300–301

RCT (resilient change tracking), 275

RDBs (relational databases), 4, 146

RDM (Raw Device Mapping), 82

RDMA (Remote Direct Memory Access), 72

read/write operations, 181–187

data virtualization, 182–183

destaging and data optimization, 185–186

LFS (log-structured file system), 181–182

Nutanix ECP (Enterprise Cloud Platform), 261–262

read operation lifecycle, 186–187

write operation lifecycle, 183–185

ReadyClones, 188

Real Application Clusters (RAC), 272–273

recovery. *See* disaster recovery

recovery point objectives (RPOs), 51, 129–130, 148, 271–272

recovery time objectives (RTOs), 51, 148, 271–272

Red Hat Enterprise Linux OpenStack Platform, 331

Red Hat OpenShift, 397

redirect on write (ROW) logical snapshots, 52–54

redirection of traffic, 5

Reduced Redundancy Storage (RRS), 405

Redundant Array of Independent Disks (RAID), 26–30, 98, 127

redundant array of independent disks (RAID), 127

ReFS (Resilient File System), 275

regions (AWS), 399–401

regulations

multicloud adoption and, 443

security, 194

relational databases (RDBs), 4, 146

Reliable Autonomous Distributed Object Store (RADOS), 300–301

Remote Direct Memory Access (RDMA), 72

remote procedure calls (RPCs), 295, 321

replication, 55, 129–130

data protection via, 121–122, 178–179

Nutanix ECP (Enterprise Cloud Platform), 270–271

unicast mode, 348–349

VMware vSAN, 238–241

replication, cloud, 148

Representation State Transfer. *See* RESTful (Representation State Transfer) APIs

resilient change tracking (RCT), 275

Resilient File System (ReFS), 275

RESTful (Representation State Transfer) APIs, 36, 215, 295, 297, 434–436

return on investment (ROI), 445

RGW (RADOS Gateway), 300

rings, Swift, 299

ROBO (remote office business office), 144–146

RoCE (RDMA over Converged Ethernet), 72

ROI (return on investment), 445

role-based access control (RBAC), 200

routing equipment, 4

ROW (redirect on write) logical snapshots, 52–54

RPCs (remote procedure calls), 295, 321

RPOs (recovery point objectives), 51, 129–130, 148, 271–272

RRS (Reduced Redundancy Storage), 405

RTOs (recovery time objectives), 51, 148, 271–272

S

S3 (Simple Storage Service), 36, 405–406, 425–426

SaaS (software as a service), 214, 397, 423

Sahara, 292

Salesforce, 443

SANs (storage area networks), 4, 78, 118, 135. *See also* vSAN

converged systems, 113

FC (fibre channel)

  addressing, 42

  LUN masking, 43

  multipathing, 44–46

  overview of, 41–42

  switching, 44–45

  zoning, 43

FCoE (Fibre Channel over Ethernet), 49–50, 82, 109

iSCSI (Internet Small Computer Interface)

  addressing, 47–48

  deployments, 46–47

  LUN masking, 48

  multipathing, 48–49

  network segmentation, 48

overview of, 40

SAP Business Warehouse (BW), 147

SAP HANA, 114, 147

SAS (serial attached SCSI), 23, 70

SATA (serial advanced technology attachment), 22, 70

scaling

distributed DAS architecture, 120

EC2 auto scaling, 414–416

HCI business benefits, 136–137

scalable hashing, 303

vSAN versus HyperFlex, 247–248

SCSI controllers, 85

SDDC (vSAN software-defined data center), 245–246

SDKs (software development kits), 420–421, 437

SDN (software-defined networking)

host-based networking, 310–312

microsegmentation, 309–310, 319

open source initiatives, 320–324

overlay network, 309–310, 315–319

overview of, 308–309

OVN (Open Virtual Network)

  control plane improvements, 329

  data plane improvements, 329–331

  functionalities, 326–327

  high-level architecture, 327–328

  overview of, 326

switch-based networking, 312–313

switching fabric, 313–315

underlay network, 315

SDS (software-defined storage), 135

legacy installations, 97–99

objectives, 96–97

open source vendors, 331

overview of, 95–96, 135

VASA (vSphere APIs for Storage Awareness), 99–104

Vipr controller, 99

VVols (Virtual Volumes), 99–104

search engine, Intersight, 209

Searchlight, 292

secondary level of failures to tolerate (SFTT), 231, 241

Secure Hash Algorithm 1 (SHA-1), 57

Secure Shell (SSH), 338

Secure Sockets Layer (SSL), 5

security. *See also* policies

    data networks, 5–6

    data protection, 121–122, 148–149, 262

    HyperFlex, 192–194

    overview of, 130–131

security groups

    AWS (Amazon Web Services), 410–411

    VMware NSX (network virtualization and security platform), 336–337

Security Technical Implementation Guide (STIG), 131, 235

SEDs (self-encrypting drives), 23, 59, 129–130, 192–193, 199, 235

segmentation, 48, 342, 346–347

self-encrypting drives (SEDs), 23, 59, 129–130, 192–193, 199, 235

Senlin, 292

serial advanced technology attachment (SATA), 22, 70

serial attached SCSI (SAS), 23, 70

server load balancing (SLB), 5

Server menu (Cisco Intersight), 207

Server Message Block (SMB), 36, 244

servers. *See also* virtualization, server

    Cisco C220/C240 M4/M5 rack servers, 158–159

    Cisco USC B200, 159

    clusters, 86–87

    logical, 8–9

    Neutron, 320

    Ovsdb-server, 325

    storage-to-server connectivity, 38–40

    Swift proxy servers, 298–300

service catalogs (UCSD), 431, 432

service graphs, 358–359

service profiles, 111–112, 164–165, 207–209

ServiceNow, 448

services, virtualization. *See* virtualization, server

services delivery policy (UCSD), 429

Settings menu (Cisco Intersight), 209

SFTT (secondary level of failures to tolerate), 231, 241

SHA-1 algorithm, 57

shadow clones, 269

Simple Network Management Protocol (SNMP), 434

Simple Storage Service. *See* S3 (Simple Storage Service)

single root input/output virtualization (SR-IOV), 312

single sign-on (SSO), 200

single-core CPUs, 66–67

Site Recovery Manager (SRM), 240

sizer (HX), 199

Sizing tool (Nutanix), 278

SLB (server load balancing), 5

Slicehost, 290

smart NICs (network interface cards), 310–312

SMB (Server Message Block), 36, 244

SMBs (small and medium-sized businesses), 136–137

snapshots

    EBS (Elastic Block Storage), 408

HyperFlex (HX), 188–189

local, 148

logical, 52–54

Nutanix ECP (Enterprise Cloud Platform), 268–269, 272

overview of, 51–52

traditional or physical, 52

VMware vSAN, 236

SNMP (Simple Network Management Protocol), 434

software as a service (SaaS), 214, 397, 423

software development kits (SDKs), 420–421, 437

software-defined networking. *See* SDN (software-defined networking)

software-defined storage. *See* SDS (software-defined storage)

Solarflare Communications Inc., 311

solid-state drives. *See* SSDs (solid-state drives)

Solum, 293

source-based deduplication, 57–58

spanning trees, 16

spine nodes, 314

spine-proxy IP, 370

SQL (Structured Query Language), 146, 272–273

SR-IOV (single root input/output virtualization), 312

SRM (Site Recovery Manager), 240

SSDs (solid-state drives), 23, 66–67, 70, 82–83, 118, 147, 155, 406–408

SSH (Secure Shell), 338

SSL (Secure Sockets Layer), 5

SSO (single sign-on), 200

standard catalogs, 431

Stargate, 258, 270

Stateless Transport Tunneling (STT), 126, 315–316

stHypervisorSvc, 171

STIG (Security Technical Implementation Guide), 131, 235

storage area networks. *See* SANs (storage area networks)

storage arrays, 102

storage controllers, 30–31

storage efficiency technologies

caching storage arrays, 60–61

cloning, 55

data compression, 58–59

deduplication

block-level, 56–57

definition of, 55–56

file-level, 56

global, 58

inline, 58

local, 58

object-level, 56

post-process, 58

source-based, 57–58

target-based, 57–58

disk encryption, 59

replication, 55

snapshots

logical, 52–54

overview of, 51–52

traditional or physical, 52

storage tiering, 59–60

thin provisioning, 50–51

storage load balancing, 90

storage networks. *See also* SANs (storage area networks)

block-level storage, 35

caching storage arrays, 60–61

cloning, 55

DAS (direct-attached storage), 38–39

data compression, 58–59

deduplication

    block-level, 56–57

    definition of, 55–56

    file-level, 56

    global, 58

    inline, 58

    local, 58

    object-level, 56

    post-process, 58

    source-based, 57–58

    target-based, 57–58

disk encryption, 59

disk performance

    access time, 24

    IOPS (input/output operations per second), 24–25

    latency, 24–25

    throughput, 21–24

file-level storage, 35–36

HDDs (hard disk drives), 22–23

LUNs (logical unit numbers), 31–33, 82, 124, 136–137

    configuration, 84

    masking, 43, 48

LVM (logical volume manager), 33–35

multitier design, 20–21

NAS (network-attached storage), 39–40

object-based storage, 36–37

RAID (Redundant Array of Independent Disks), 26–30

replication, 55

snapshots

    logical, 52–54

    overview of, 51–52

    traditional or physical, 52

SSDs (solid-state drives), 23, 66–67, 70, 82–83, 118, 147, 155, 406–408

storage controllers, 30–31

storage tiering, 59–60

thin provisioning, 50–51

storage policies, 228–231, 428

storage tiering, 59–60, 267

storage-defined networking (SDN), 126

Storlets, 291

stretched clusters

    Nutanix ECP (Enterprise Cloud Platform), 271–272

    VMware vSAN, 238–241

stretched VLANs, 10–11

strict data locality, 175

striping, 176–177

Structured Query Language (SQL), 146, 272–273

STT (Stateless Transport Tunneling), 126, 315–316

subnetting, 12–13

Support Insight, 245

SVI (switch virtual interface), 12

swap objects, 227

SWAP-VVol-Swap, 101

Swift, 297–300

switch virtual interface. *See* **SVI (switch virtual interface)**

switches, 4

    logical, 341–342

    NSX L2 switching, 343

    OVS (Open vSwitch), 322–324, 328–331

    switch-based networking, 312–313

    ToR (top-of-rack), 7, 92–93, 115, 310, 313

    virtual, 90–93

switching fabric, 313–315, 367–371

    ACI (application-centric infrastructure), 365–367

    FC (fibre channel), 44–45

    multitier architecture, 6–8

    SDN (software-defined networking), 313–315

synchronous native replication for DR (NRDR), 190–191

T

Tacker, 292

target initiator groups (TIGs), 243

target-based deduplication, 57–58

TBW (Total Bytes Written), 73

TCAM (ternary CAM), 308

TCO (total cost of ownership), 140, 444–445

TCP (Transmission Control Protocol), 5, 46–47, 109

telemetry, Cisco Intersight, 205

templates

    CloudFormation, 417–420

    service, 164–165

    vNIC, 166–167

tenants, 366

ternary CAM (TCAM), 308

Tetration

    HyperFlex with

        data collection, 214

        data output, 215

        open access, 215

        overview of, 212–214

        Tetration analytics cluster, 214

    model for, 360

    Tetration-V, 214

thick provisioning, 50–51

thin provisioning, 50–51

third-party backup tools, 191–192

three-tier architecture. *See* multitier design

throughput, 21–24

tier-1 enterprise class applications, 146–147

tiers, storage, 59–60, 267

TIGs (target initiator groups), 243

time to live (TTL), 330

TOE (TCP Offload Engine), 46–47

ToR (top-of-rack) switches, 7, 92–93, 115, 310, 313

Total Bytes Written (TBW), 73

total cost of ownership (TCO), 140, 444–445

transfer speed, 21–24

Transmission Control Protocol (TCP), 5, 46–47, 109

Tricircle, 292

Tripelo, 293

Trove, 292

TTL (time to live), 330

U

UCS (Unified Computing System), 108–112, 138, 223

    HyperFlex integration, 162

        external storage, 167–168

        logical network design, 162–164

        service templates and profiles, 164–165

        vNIC templates, 166–167

UCS 6200 and 6300 fabric interconnect, 158

UCS Integrated Infrastructure for Red Hat Enterprise Linux OpenStack, 331

UCSD (USC Director)

catalogs, 431

HyperFlex integration, 431–437

orchestration, 430

overview of, 427

policies, 427–429

vDCs (virtual data centers), 429–430

UCSM (UCS Manager), 198

UDP (User Datagram Protocol), 5, 342

UKB (Universal Kernel Bypass), 312

underlay network, 315, 371–373

unicast mode, 348–349

Unified Cache, 261

Unified Computing System. *See* UCS (Unified Computing System)

unified threat management (UTM), 6

uniform resource identifiers (URIs), 435–436

union file system, 173

Universal Kernel Bypass (UKB), 312

Universal Unique Identifiers (UUIDs), 111

Uplink Subinterface IP addresses, 370–371

URIs (uniform resource identifiers), 435–436

use cases

data protection and disaster recovery, 148–149

DevOps, 141

edge computing, 146

overview of, 140

ROBO (remote office business office), 144–146

server virtualization, 140–141

tier-1 enterprise class applications, 146–147

VDI (virtual desktop infrastructure), 141–144

User Datagram Protocol. *See* UDP (User Datagram Protocol)

User Datagram Protocol (UDP), 5, 342

User menu (Cisco Intersight), 209

UTM (unified threat management), 6

UUIDs (Universal Unique Identifiers), 111

V

VAAI (vStorage API for Array Integration), 170

VASA (vSphere APIs for Storage Awareness), 99–104

vCenter Server Appliance (VCSA), 245

vCPUs (virtual CPUs), 68–70

VCSA (vCenter Server Appliance), 245

vDCs (virtual data centers), 341–342, 429–430

VDI (virtual desktop infrastructure), 55–56, 114, 141–144, 236, 269

VDP (vSphere Data Protection), 241–243

vDS (virtual Distributed Switch), 93

Veeam, 129–130

vendors, open source, 331

VesraStac, 112

VGs (volume groups), 273

vHBAs (virtual host bus adapters),
    109, 166

VICs (virtual interface cards), 109, 159

Vipr, 99

virtual cores, 67–68

virtual CPUs (vCPUs), 68–70

virtual data centers (vDC), 429–430

virtual desktop infrastructure (VDI),
    55–56, 114, 141–144, 236, 269

virtual Distributed Switch (vDS), 93

Virtual Extensible LANs. *See*
    VXLANs (Virtual Extensible LANs)

virtual host bus adapters (vHBAs),
    109, 166

virtual interface cards (VICs),
    109, 159

virtual local area networks (VLANs),
    10–11, 13–15

virtual MAC addresses (vMACs), 92

virtual machine disks (VMDKs), 82,
    100

Virtual Machine File System (VMFS),
    82, 102, 226

Virtual Machine Manager (VMM)
    domain, 362–364

virtual machines. *See* VMs (virtual
    machines)

virtual NICs (vNICs), 79, 92–93,
    109, 166–167

virtual port channels (vPCs), 18,
    368–369

virtual private cloud (VPC), 401–404

virtual routing and forwarding (VRF),
    323, 366

virtual storage appliance (VSA), 119

virtual switching, 90–93

Virtual Tunnel Endpoint (VTEP),
    369–370

Virtual Volumes. *See* VVols (Virtual
    Volumes)

Virtual Volumes (VVols), 83,
    99–104, 243–244

virtualization, server

    datastores, 82–83

    HCI use case, 140–141

    overview of, 77–78

    virtual switching, 90–93

    virtualization layer

        *bare-metal versus virtualized
            servers, 78–79, 396*

        Docker containers, 80–82

        type 1 hypervisors, 79

        type 2 hypervisors, 80

    virtualization services

        clusters, 86–87

        computing load balancing, 89

        fault tolerance, 89

        overview of, 86

        *provisioning and management,
            90*

        storage load balancing, 90

        storage migration, 90

        VM migration, 87

    VM (virtual machine) creation,
        84–86

        datastore configuration, 84

        guest OS assignment, 85

        LUN configuration, 84

        memory allocation, 85

        new VM creation, 84

        *NICs (network interface
            cards), 85*

        OS installation, 86

        SCSI controllers, 85

        virtual disk assignment, 85

Vitrage, 292

VLANs (virtual local area networks),
    10–11, 13–15

vMACs (virtual MAC addresses), 92

VMDKs (virtual machine disks), 82, 100, 226–227

VMFS (Virtual Machine File System), 82, 102, 226

VMK (vmkernel) port groups, 92

VMM (Virtual Machine Manager) domain, 362–364

vmnics, 92–93

vMotion, 87

VMs (virtual machines). *See also* vSAN

    creation of, 84–86

        datastore configuration, 84

        guest OS assignment, 85

        LUN configuration, 84

        memory allocation, 85

        new VM creation, 84

        NICs (network interface cards), 85

        OS installation, 86

        SCSI controllers, 85

    migration, 87

    vCPUs (virtual CPUs), 68–70

VMware. *See also* NSX (network virtualization and security platform); vSAN

    ESXi, 79, 170–171

    HCL (Hardware Compatibility List), 245

    VASA (vSphere APIs for Storage Awareness), 99–104

    vSphere DRS, 89

    vSphere management plug-in, 203–204

    vSphere Storage vMotion, 90

    VSS (vNetwork Standard Switch), 93

    VUM (VMware Update Manager), 245

VVols (Virtual Volumes), 99–104, 243–244

vNetwork Standard Switch (VSS), 93

vNICs (virtual NICs), 79, 92–93, 109, 166–167

VNIDs (VXLAN Instance IDs), 376–378

vNodes, 182, 185

volumes

    adding to EC2 instances, 414

    EBS (Elastic Block Storage), 407–409

    granular, 100–101

    groups, 273

    VVols (Virtual Volumes), 83, 99–104, 243–244

voting, 230

VPC (virtual private cloud), 401–404

vPCs (virtual port channels), 18, 368–369

vRealize, 245–246

VRF (virtual routing and forwarding), 323, 366

vROps (vSAN vRealize Operations), 245–246

VSA (virtual storage appliance), 119

vSAN

    backup, 241–243

    caching, 232

    cloning, 236–237

    Compatibility Guide, 224

    compression, 235

    data encryption, 234–235

    data integrity, 234

    datastore, 228

    deduplication, 235

    erasure coding, 236

    high-level software architecture, 225–226

HyperFlex versus, 246

    advanced data services, 251–252

    compute-only nodes, 250–251

    file systems, 249–250

    hardware comparison, 247

    management software, 252

    networking, 252–253

    one-to-one versus many-to-many rebuild, 250

    scaling up, 247–248

    vSAN in-kernel versus controller-based solutions, 248–249

integration with legacy SAN and NAS, 243–244

I/O operation details, 232–233

management, 244–246

object file system, 226–227

overview of, 223–224

persistent storage for containers, 244

physical components, 224–225

replication, 238–241

SDDC (vSAN software-defined data center), 245–246

snapshots, 236

storage policies, 228–231

Support Insight, 245

vROps (vSAN vRealize Operations), 245–246

vSphere APIs for Storage Awareness (VASA), 99–104

vSphere Data Protection (VDP), 241–243

vSphere DRS, 89

vSphere management plug-in, 203–204

vSphere Storage vMotion, 90

VSS (vNetwork Standard Switch), 93

vStorage API for Array Integration (VAAI), 170

VTEP (VXLAN Tunnel Endpoint), 342, 346–347, 369–370

VUM (VMware Update Manager), 245

VVols (Virtual Volumes), 83, 99–104, 243–244

VxBlock, 112, 246

VXLANs (Virtual Extensible LANs), 93, 126, 315–319

control plane, 389

overview of, 373–376

performance, 388–389

VNIDs (VXLAN Instance IDs), 376–378

VTEP (VXLAN Tunnel Endpoint), 342, 346–347

VxRail, 223

W

wafers, 66–67

WAN optimizers, 5, 314

Watcher, 292

WebEx, 443

Windows Server 2016, 275

Windows Server Failover Cluster (WSFC), 243

workload optimization

Cisco AppDynamics, 217–219

CWOM (Cisco Workload Optimizer), 216–217

enterprise workload issues, 211–212

HyperFlex with Cisco Tetration, 212–215

overview of, 211

workload profiler, 199

write operations. *See* read/write operations

WSFC (Windows Server Failover Cluster), 243

WWNN (World Wide Node Name) addresses, 108

WWNs (World Wide Names), 42–43

WWPNs (World Wide Port Names), 42–43

X

x86 standard architecture, 66

XenServer, 256

XML (Extensible Markup Language), 215, 434

XP fabric extenders, 159–160

X-ray tool (Nutanix), 278

Xtract tool (Nutanix), 278

Y-Z

YAML Ain't Markup Language, 215

Zaqar, 293

zero-trust model, 319

Zerto, 129–130

zones
  AWS (Amazon Web Services), 299
  FC (fibre channel), 43
  LAZ (logical availability zones), 299
  Swift, 299

Zookeeper, 258

Zun, 291

REGISTER YOUR PRODUCT at CiscoPress.com/register
Access Additional Benefits and SAVE 35% on Your Next Purchase

- Download available product updates.

- Access bonus material when applicable.

- Receive exclusive offers on new editions and related products.
  (Just check the box to hear from us when setting up your account.)

- Get a coupon for 35% for your next purchase, valid for 30 days.
  Your code will be available in your Cisco Press cart. (You will also find
  it in the Manage Codes section of your account page.)

Registration benefits vary by product. Benefits will be listed on your account page
under Registered Products.

CiscoPress.com – Learning Solutions for Self-Paced Study, Enterprise, and the Classroom
Cisco Press is the Cisco Systems authorized book publisher of Cisco networking technology,
Cisco certification self-study, and Cisco Networking Academy Program materials.

At **CiscoPress.com** you can
- Shop our books, eBooks, software, and video training.
- Take advantage of our special offers and promotions (ciscopress.com/promotions).
- Sign up for special offers and content newsletters (ciscopress.com/newsletters).
- Read free articles, exam profiles, and blogs by information technology experts.
- Access thousands of free chapters and video lessons.

Connect with Cisco Press – Visit CiscoPress.com/community
Learn about Cisco Press community events and programs.

Cisco Press